Elio Petri

Elio Petri

Investigation of a Filmmaker

ROBERTO CURTI

McFarland & Company, Inc., Publishers

Jefferson, North Carolina

All images come from the author's private collection.

ISBN (print) 978-1-4766-8034-7
ISBN (ebook) 978-1-4766-4283-3

LIBRARY OF CONGRESS AND BRITISH LIBRARY
CATALOGUING DATA ARE AVAILABLE

Library of Congress Control Number 2021029319

Front cover image is from the Hungarian poster
for *Investigation of a Citizen Above Suspicion.*

Printed in the United States of America

*McFarland & Company, Inc., Publishers
Box 611, Jefferson, North Carolina 28640
www.mcfarlandpub.com*

To my beloved wife, Cristina.
And to our love.

Table of Contents

Introduction

Between the late 1960s and mid–1970s, Elio Petri was one of Italy's most successful filmmakers, and possibly the most talked-about. *Indagine su un cittadino al di sopra di ogni sospetto* (aka *Investigation of a Citizen Above Suspicion*, 1970), starring Gian Maria Volonté, was a stunning box-office hit and the most controversial film of the year, and its international resonance culminated with the 1971 Academy Award for Best Foreign Film. Petri's following work *La classe operaia va in paradiso* (aka *Lulu the Tool*, 1971), also starring Volonté, was awarded the Grand Prix of the Jury at the 1972 Cannes Film Festival.

A politically committed filmmaker, often challenging in his stances, Petri told, in his own words, "stories of individuals—and the overall conditioning they find inside themselves—without losing sight of the social and historical events and their class essence as exterior conditioning factors,"[1] and his films touched social, religious and political themes in a thought-provoking way. *A ciascuno il suo* (aka *We Still Kill the Old Way*, 1967) dealt with the Mafia, a taboo subject at the time. *Indagine* was an apologue on the repressive nature of Power at a time the country was going through a paroxysmal climate of social tension. *La classe operaia* referred to the harsh worker struggles that took place throughout the 1960s in Italy and led to the "Hot Autumn" of 1969.

Despite its cultural and political relevance, Petri's work had mixed success among the critics. To quote French film historian Jean A. Gili, who curated the first volume on the director in 1974, "where others reassure, Petri challenges."[2] Indeed, his cinema was as ambitious as it was daring, and sometimes it was a disturbing forerunner of things to come. Together with Pier Paolo Pasolini, Petri was the Italian author who dared the most and who paid the most for it. Reviewers attacked his films violently, and someone even claimed they must be burned.

His most controversial work was *Todo Modo* (1976), a grotesque conspiracy tale in which the leaders of the country's ruling party, the Democrazia Cristiana—including a character, played by Volonté, who is a dead ringer for then-prime minister Aldo Moro—are killed one by one during a three-day stay at a secluded hermitage. Upon its release the film left many outraged and was quickly withdrawn from circulation. A couple of years later, Moro was kidnapped and killed by the terrorist group Brigate Rosse, a shocking event that changed Italy's history. *Todo modo* became a film *maudit*, and Petri found himself ostracized, reviled, relegated to oblivion in the critical debate and increasingly unable to make the movies he wanted, also because of the ongoing economic crisis of Italian cinema.

Elio Petri was a man of the Left, an ex-affiliate of the PCI (the Italian Communist Party) who at a certain point left the party when he felt it no longer reflected his own convictions. A free spirit and a free thinker, he was often vocal against his own side and was never afraid to be sincere, even when it hurt. "Courage is the ability to face reality; not a military virtue but a civic one, not exceptional but daily."[3]

This is why his works, though openly political, are far from being propaganda manifestos, and express the director's own doubts and questions on the state of the individual in the contemporary mass society, and sometimes his own personal issues. His feature film debut *L'assassino* (aka *The Lady Killer of Rome*, 1961) examines psychological alienation, whereas *I giorni contati* (aka *Days Are Numbered*, 1962) delves into the notion of work-related alienation. In the following films alienation gives way to schizophrenia, and the stories revolve around the relationship between rule and transgression, normality and madness. "Inside all of us there are mental processes, a debate, a continuing dialogue between sane and ill parts," Petri once stated. "It's the existential choices that merge all these incandescent details in our personality."[4] Hence, in Petri's cinema man becomes a split entity, and three of the director's best-known works—*Indagine*, *La classe operaia*, and *La proprietà non è più un furto* (aka *Property Is No Longer a Theft*, 1973)—are commonly identified as a so-called "trilogy of neurosis."

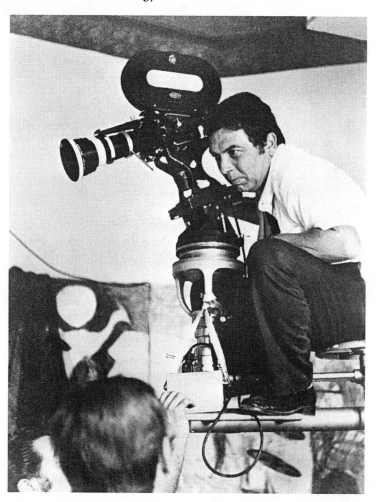

Elio Petri on the set.

Petri's view on society, especially in his final works, was downright gloomy, even apocalyptic. "I believe that the only way to understand the future is to watch the present with a certain pessimism," he claimed, adding that "pessimism is a weapon of research."[5] In fact, despite his own disenchantment, Petri firmly believed that cinema must first and foremost be useful, and therefore there must be a dialectical relationship between the film and its audience, for "pessimism generates utopia as a revolutionary ferment."[6]

The challenging essence of Petri's cinema emerges also in its exploration of film genres in a thought-provoking, formally invigorating way. *La decima vittima* (aka *The 10th Victim*, 1965) was a biting science fiction satire on the battle of the sexes, with visual nods to Pop Art and comics. *Un tranquillo posto di campagna* (aka *A Quiet Place in the Country*, 1968) was a ghost story told in experimental style about an artist's place in a society where art has become a commodity. Several of his films—most notably *L'assassino*, *A ciascuno il suo*, *Indagine*, and *Todo modo*—relate to the mystery genre, albeit in an inventive way, overturning its rules and structure to better serve the director's purposes. The stories are structured as investigations, for, as he once claimed, "our entire life is a form of private investigation—a detective story—on all sorts of matters. As children we begin to investigate about sex, then about culture, then economic and social structures. Society by and large is built upon mystery; it is as if they wanted to keep secret what is really happening."[7]

Petri's body of work, albeit relatively small, is among the most unique and dense in Italian post-war cinema, marking "the impossible encounter of abstract thought and the concrete materiality of the images of a film."[8] Therefore, it deserves an in-depth analysis encompassing not just the finished works, but also the director's shelved or aborted projects. These form a sort of parallel filmography, with such ambitious and thought-provoking works as *Zoo* (to be shot in the United States and starring Jack Nicholson) and *Chi illumina la grande notte*, the allegorical spy thriller Petri was about to start filming in 1982, just before his untimely death at the age of 53.

Writing about Petri's "atrociously premature" demise, and comparing it with those of scriptwriter Franco Solinas and director Valerio Zurlini, which took place in the same period, critic Lino Miccichè commented: "these deaths are becoming the terrible symbol of a cinema that is in danger of dying together with its makers."[9] By the end of his career, when it was becoming harder and harder for him to mount his projects, Petri was just as pessimistic, but stuck to his own romantic view of filmmaking:

> I must confess I stick up for cinema not just because it is the only thing I can do, but I stick up for it because it is an obsolete activity, as one must stick up for artisanship and artisans, agriculture and peasants, used bookstores, dialect, coffee, Neapolitan songs, folk festivals, Latin mass, peddlers, vaudeville, the parliament, the art of great painters and that of honest pickpockets. To me, everything fits, and cinema is part of this outdated, petty and vulgar culture, but a dreaming and anarchic one: sly and manipulative, but romantic. In short, human.[10]

The 2000s saw a renaissance of critical attention on Elio Petri in Italy, with the release of a documentary in 2005, the publication of some books and the restoration of his films.[11] Oscar-winning filmmaker Paolo Sorrentino openly acknowledged Petri's influence on his works, most notably *Il divo* (2008). Some of the director's more overlooked films—such as his 1979 swan song *Buone notizie*—finally got the consideration they deserved, and several titles found their way onto home video abroad. However, most of Petri's cinema remains sadly under the radar outside his home country.

Still, it must be pointed out that despite their complexity and cultural density—with references ranging from Antonio Gramsci to Sigmund Freud, from Jean-Paul Sartre to Wilhelm Reich—Petri's films were directed not to elites but to the masses. He worked with Italian cinema's finest actors and technicians, and pushed them to give their very best. Gian Maria Volonté, who starred in four of his films, said that Petri's style "oscillates between expressionism and the attempt of making cinema come out of the swamp of realism and head toward the imaginary."[12] To writer Tonino Guerra, "Petri was *inside* the images"[13] and his works feature outstanding and stylish visuals, resulting in engrossing viewing experiences. Franco Nero called him "the Italian Stanley Kubrick … he was a genius…. The most complete Italian director. He had a way of shooting that was already ahead of his time."[14] Ennio Morricone, who wrote the music for all of his films starting with *Un tranquillo posto di campagna*, stressed how

> Elio was able to transform his sharp and critical interpretation of reality into great cinema. He accomplished this in such an effective and proficient way, describing the complex relations between man and society. He was truly an extraordinary director, far ahead of his times.[15]

Today, a book on Elio Petri seems to me more timely than ever. With its rigorous dialectical approach, Petri's cinema can teach us many things about ourselves and the world we live in, a world we are gradually losing grasp of, adrift as we are in our own private Internet, losing memory of history and its teachings. A film must be studied in the context from which it emerges, and Petri's body of work is a challenging instrument to revise and understand Italian post-war history, its political, economic, sociological and cultural transformations, and its effects on individuals. His films were able to portray their times and urge viewers to reflect on them. They were the kind of movies that, once the lights turn on again, make people look at the outside world with different, and more conscious eyes. And this is something we desperately need today.

Author's Note

This volume examines Elio Petri's life and work, with a detailed production history and critical analysis of his films, placing his *oeuvre* within the social and political context of post-war Italy culture, politics and cinema. Sources include original film scripts, production papers with plenty of never-before-seen data and bits of information recovered from the Italian ministerial archives, comparison with original scripts, interviews, and excerpts from reviews of the period. Given the lengthy titles, some films are referred to in the text in abbreviated form: for instance, *Indagine su un cittadino al di sopra di ogni sospetto* becomes *Indagine*.

To put together the amount of material for the book I consulted the archives of some of Italy's major newspapers (*Corriere della Sera*, *La Stampa*, *L'Unità*, *Repubblica*), the original scripts retained at Rome's Centro Sperimentale di Cinematografia and the ministerial data at Rome's State Archive. I also had access to the Elio Petri fund at the Archivio Nazionale del Museo del Cinema in Turin (hereon, ANMC) which collects Petri's private correspondence and his unfilmed projects. Accession numbers are provided for reference in the footnotes.

Very special thanks to Paolo Mereghetti, Alberto Pezzotta, and Davide Vincenti, who helped me collect archive material, and old reviews and interviews. Their assistance has been invaluable, and so was that of Mario and Roderick Gauci, and David C. Tucker, who read the manuscript and helped with polishing it.

My most sincere thanks to the following, who in one way or another helped me during my research: Enrico Bettinello, Davide Cavaciocchi, Carla Ceresa (at ANMC), Alessio Di Rocco, Steve Fenton, Julian Grainger, Frank Lafond, Ivano Landi, Stefano Lecchini, Tom Lisanti, Domenico Monetti, Antonio José Navarro, Paola Pegoraro Petri, Pete Tombs, Stefano Zenni. Last but not least, thanks to Michael Blanton for his enthusiastic support.

ONE

Open City, Open Mind
The Early Years

Prologue: A Manifesto

At three in the morning of November 4, 1956, the Red Army entered Budapest. The Soviet government had sent 200,000 troops and 4,000 armed tanks to Hungary. Despite the rebels' desperate resistance, the disparity of force between the two factions was overwhelming. A few days later, on November 10, the Hungarian uprising that began on October 23 was over.

The failed revolution against the dictatorship of Mátyás Rákosi and the Soviet presence in the nation had a huge resonance worldwide. *Time* magazine even named the "Hungarian Freedom Fighter" its Man of the Year, while some nations (Spain, the Netherlands, and Switzerland) boycotted the Melbourne Olympics as a protest against the USSR. In his appearance on the *Ed Sullivan Show*, Elvis Presley requested that viewers donate money to the Hungarian refugees. In France, such illustrious intellectuals as Marguerite Duras, Albert Camus, Edgar Morin and Jean-Paul Sartre expressed an open condemnation of the Soviet intervention. Sartre, a longtime admirer of Communism, declared:

> I condemn the Soviet invasion wholeheartedly and without any reservation. Without putting any responsibility onto the Russian people, I nevertheless insist that its current government has committed a crime.... And the crime, to me, is not just the invasion of Budapest by army tanks, but the fact that this was made possible by twelve years of terror and imbecility.... It is and will be impossible to reestablish any sort of contact with the men who are currently at the head of the [French Communist Party]. Each sentence they utter, each action they take is the culmination of thirty years of lies and sclerosis.[1]

Although under American influence after World War II, Italy had the most deep-rooted Communist presence in Western Europe. The PCI (Partito Comunista Italiano) was Italy's second biggest party after the Catholic–inspired Democrazia Cristiana (DC), and its share was growing constantly under the guide of secretary Palmiro Togliatti. The Hungarian uprising and its abrupt and violent end affected the Italian left-wing deeply, not least because an Italian reporter, Luigi Fossati of the newspaper *Avanti!*, the house organ of the Italian Socialist Party (PSI), was the only Western journalist to witness the revolts, and his articles—published without any tampering—were openly critical of the Soviets. It was a strong blow against the myth of Communist Russia as the country of Real Socialism and it caused the PSI to detach itself from the Soviet regime. The secretary of the PSI, Pietro Nenni, wrote:

> The Hungarians ask for democracy and freedom…. The workers' movement had never lived a tragedy comparable to the Hungarian one, a tragedy which in different forms is hatching in all the Eastern European countries, even with the silences, which are no less anguishing than the outbursts of popular revolt…. We will make every effort to help the Hungarian people so they can achieve Socialism in democracy, freedom, and independence.[2]

The chain of events caused a deep crisis within the PCI. Togliatti and the leadership supported the Soviet intervention, whereas other prominent figures in the party expressed themselves against it. In Rome, on October 29, a group of 101 intellectuals—all of them belonging to the PCI or openly communist sympathizers—signed an open letter, the "Manifesto dei 101" (The 101 Manifesto), expressing a critical stance against the Soviet intervention. Its aim was to solicit a debate in the party, urging the heads of the PCI not just to condemn explicitly Stalinism and the Hungarian repression, but also to renovate the party's leadership. The petitioners were politicians, philosophers (Natalino Sapegno), literary critics (Alberto Asor Rosa, Enzo Siciliano), writers, and artists (painter Renzo Vespignani), among the most important and noted ones in the country. Among them there was a 27-year-old scriptwriter and aspiring filmmaker named Elio Petri.

The Son of the Coppersmith

Born in Rome on January 29, 1929, the only son of Mario Petri and Anna Papitto, Eraclio Petri bore a ponderous first name, which evoked no less than two Byzantine emperors (Heraclius I and Heraclius II), a Latin patriarch of Jerusalem of the 12th century, and, last but not least, the philosopher Heraclius the Cynic. No wonder that, with such a burden on his shoulders, Eraclio would soon be known to everybody as Elio.

Despite the cultural weight that his name bore, Elio came from a working-class family. His father Mario was originally from the Marche region. He had learned the craft of working copper from his father and had started his own workshop, making cauldrons for convents and barracks. After his father died, the workshop closed down and Mario found employment at the Nardi workshop. He was blond, meek, sturdy and short, with green eyes, rather gruff but ultimately cheerful. His friends called him "Callarella" (small boiler, in Roman dialect) and Elio thought he looked a bit like Leslie Howard.[3] Anna, on the other hand, looked like an Indian: "Dark, with olive complexion, and very long black hair, black eyes. A bit taller than my father. When she was young, she was beautiful, strong, very thin … she worked in a café, actually in a creamery run by her relatives. She served coffee. I think she and my father met there."[4]

Elio was born on the third floor of an 18th century house on via de' Giubbonari, number 23, in the Roman Jewish ghetto. He once described the house as "over-populated, swarming with people, full of pungent odors."[5] Nine people lived in three rooms: Mario, Anna, Elio, Mario's mother, her youngest son aged eighteen, and another of Mario's six brothers with his wife and two kids. The flat was less than thirty meters from the Nardi workshop.

One night—it was 1931, Elio was just two—Mario was arrested while on his way home. He used to work overtime and had finished in the middle of the night. He was halted by a night patrol but didn't have his ID card on him. He tried to explain to the guards that he lived just a few steps away, but to no avail. They wouldn't listen to reason. They wouldn't go upstairs to the third floor of number 23 and check whether he was telling the truth, nor would they go back to the Nardi workshop and find out if he was one of the employees. This is what living in Rome under Fascism was for an ordinary man like Mario Petri.

The Petris stayed in via de' Giubbonari for three years, before moving to Vicolo del Giglio, then to via del Conservatorio (actually in two different buildings) and eventually, in 1940, to the other end of the city, on Via Trionfale. Meanwhile, Italy had entered the war alongside Germany.

Mario's family was not rich, and the houses where little Elio spent his early years were small and lacking most commodities. The apartment on via del Conservatorio was actually a basement, a tiny cellar with a toilet and a gas stove for cooking, under a small shop that Anna kept during the day. As Elio recalled,

> At night I slept on the kitchen table. After supper, a mattress was spread out on it, and I slept there. My parents, for their part, slept on a folding camp-bed…. In the morning I went out into another world, to school. I do not think that after such a night one can go to school full of hope. Still, I did not feel this poverty to be degradation, since for me it was everyday reality, normalcy. It was devoid of hope, devoid of light.[6]

This is partly why Elio spent very little time at home. "There was no room for playing. I always went out in the streets."[7] Back then, there were very few cars in Rome, and the streets belonged to the kids. Little Elio was a shy one, sociable and vivacious but rather solitary. Being an only child, he was often overwhelmed by anguish and scared by loneliness. Being short and plump, he was frequently bullied by the other kids, but he was ready to fight when someone went too far. He soon learned how to gain respect. On Sundays, in the summer, Mario used to take his little son to the sea, only the two of them, sunbathing and swimming.

Elio was what the Latins would call a *homo novus*, someone who struggled to rise above his social status and build a brighter future for himself. His parents made sacrifices in order to give him the best education they could. Mario Petri never talked about politics at home (he talked very little indeed), but he was a staunch antifascist, and he was annoyed when at primary school his son was given the typical Fascist education. "At school I had learned to be a fascist, I dressed as a *balilla*[8] and believed in the national revolution," Elio recalled. "Back then kids were thoroughly indoctrinated."[9] Mario tried to give him some basic and clear moral principles: You must work and make sacrifices for a better future, you must be honest and laborious, you must respect others. His hope was that his son's life would be different from his.

From the public school in via de' Giubbonari, Elio moved to San Giuseppe de Merode, in the central Piazza di Spagna, a Catholic institute run by priests. It was the best in Rome. It was a tough decision for Mario Petri, and not just because its fees were extremely high and would result in further economic sacrifices for the family. Mario was an atheist, and it was Anna, who on the contrary was devout, who pushed her husband to give their son a Catholic education. But the effects were not those she envisioned. At the institute, Elio learned "to know authoritarianism. And all my doubts about religion started right there."[10]

At school he also quickly learned to understand the bourgeoisie. He was the only proletarian among rich kids and, as he put it, "in a short time I completely lost every illusion about the ruling class. Then I was expelled … for bad behavior."[11] Too vivacious, too disrespectful of the rules to suffer the many limitations and impositions of the Catholic education, Elio enrolled briefly at another Catholic institute, the Pio IX, before going back to the San Giuseppe de Merode.

In the meantime, war had started, and Elio was undergoing what he called his own "de-fascistization." He was paying attention to the political discussions around him, started reading regularly, and finally began to look at the world with different eyes. A passionate, omnivorous bookworm, he was impressed by the works of Stendhal, Kafka, Dumas' *The Three Musketeers*, and then Pirandello, Balzac, Tolstoy, Dostoevsky, Proust, Gide, Moravia…. But he also devoured political and philosophical works and was struck deeply by Karl Marx's *Economic and Philosophic Manuscripts of 1844* and *The Class Struggles in France, 1848–1850*. "I recall the years of adolescence and youth with great nostalgia, because in addition to the real world I was discovering—as if they were real too—all those other worlds that helped me understand life and people. It was like living many lives."[12]

It was his grandmother's passing that pushed Elio away from religion for good. "After grandma's death I had the certainty that God doesn't exist and that our body is destroyed for good. Religion didn't give me any consolation…."[13] A deep fear of death pushed him to escape daily life by taking refuge in the darkness of film venues. There, he could soothe his anguish by feeding his eyes and mind with the stories told on the silver screen and forget the horrible happenings in the real world. One such was a harrowing event that the 15-year-old Elio had witnessed a few months after the Liberation of Rome, and which marked his memory forever.

On September 18, 1944, the trial began against Pietro Caruso, appointed Quaestor of Rome during the Republic of Salò, and his secretary Roberto Occhetto. Both were responsible as accomplices in dozens of killings perpetrated by the Fascists and had helped compile the list of the 335 people killed by the Nazis in the Fosse Ardeatine Massacre of March 24, 1944. An angry crowd swarmed into the building and some recognized Donato Carretta, the ex-warden of the Regina Coeli penitentiary, who was to appear as witness for the prosecution. Carretta was considered responsible for the death of many convicts, even though before the Liberation he had released all the prisoners to avoid further retaliation on the part of the Fascists and Nazis. Carretta was assaulted and the attempt to have him transferred out of the tribunal failed as a crowd surrounded the car in which the police were carrying him away. The ex-warden was beaten to unconsciousness and the lynch mob attempted to have his body run over by a streetcar, but the conductor refused, exhibiting the card of the PCI. This didn't stop the lynching: Carretta was thrown in the river Tiber, where he tried to hold on to a boat. He was bludgeoned to death with an oar and his body was hanged outside the bars of a window at Regina Coeli, all this before the eyes of a large crowd. Elio Petri was among the bystanders, and the shock was such that he got high fever for days on end.[14]

As soon as Rome was an open city, after the liberation from the Nazis, the cultural life was reborn from the ashes of the war years and the German occupation, and Italian cinema with it. The main symbol of such a rebirth was Roberto Rossellini's *Roma città aperta* (1945): shot with odds and ends of raw stock, often assembled fortuitously due to the scarcity of film, it was like a cry of freedom and a call to arms. Elio saw it at the Quirino theater, at a festival which gathered the great films of the period: "I came and watched all the films of the festival, and the one that marked me was *Roma città aperta*," he recalled.[15]

Cinema and politics were the explosive mixture that would mold Petri's future. He watched three movies a day and absorbed film language, its grammar and syntax, like a sponge. In 1944 he had enrolled in the PCI, and in 1946 he was expelled from school again, this time for political motives: he was campaigning for the Communist Party for the forthcoming elections, definitely not the most appropriate thing to do in a priests' institute.[16] June 2, 1946, marked an historic date for Italy. On that day, the first political elections after the Fascist regime took place, to elect the Constituent Assembly. Citizens were called to decide via an institutional referendum whether Italy was to be a monarchy or a Republic. The second option won, with over 54 percent of votes.

Elio's political enthusiasm was infused with what he would later call "the myth of hope." It was something he had inherited from his family and developed from his own life conditions. It was the expectation that something was bound to happen. Not a revolution in the ordinary sense of the term, but "something more, I might even call it religious, but religious in quotes. Not religion in the sense of Catholic or Buddhist, but a bond between men, the impetus of a new solidarity for mankind."[17] That was what Communism was about, for him as well as for thousands upon thousands of young men like him. On the other hand, there was the frustration for what post-war Italy had become under the government of the Democrazia Cristiana. The country was in ruins, working conditions were poor, and very few things seemed to have changed after the fall of Fascism. One day in 1950, for instance, Mario Petri was arrested again, for the second time in his life. He happened to be walking near a large demonstration against the Atlantic Pact, in Piazza Colonna. Elio was among the protesters. "Naturally my father was arrested for the same reasons [as the first time], dressed in his worker's clothes as he was, by the police of a democratic state."[18]

In 1947, the 18-year-old Petri moved to the provincial FGCI (the Italian Federation of Young Communists) as a militant member: "What a joy it was to wake up on Sunday mornings, to climb into rickety carts, to set out for those cold, hostile villages, on the lookout for any blows we might be the butt of, blows dealt by the carabinieri, by the fascists or even the ordinary enemy of democracy…. We tried to bring progress to a set of conditions that had been the same for centuries, written in stone, like an immutable destiny."[19] He and his comrades were bringing hope.

The FGCI corridors were like a port by the sea, full of young men brimming with ideas and energy. The vice-secretary Aldo Natoli took a liking to that teen who was so intellectually curious, unlike most other members. "We would talk about cinema, music, books, just casually, as we walked along the corridors," Petri recalled. "I was one of the very few members of the Federation who were neither students nor workers."[20]

The PCI was the first Italian party to set up a small film division as part of the Press and Propaganda Department. Among other activities, it also ran the production and distribution company Libertas Film, which had the exclusive distribution of Soviet movies in Italy. The USSR comrades urged Libertas to open a distribution agency in the Veneto area, and Natoli asked Elio if he wanted the job. So, at the end of May 1947, Elio Petri became the head of Libertas Film's agency in Venice, for a salary of 30,000 *lire* a month, expenses included.

Elio set out to Venice with an older friend, who insisted on bringing a revolver with him, for Venice was considered a risky area. Their job was to go around the region, get in touch with venue owners and try to persuade them to take those Soviet films.

As soon as cinema-owners heard the word "Soviet" they would explode. They were scared, more than anything else. In that part of the world, there were communists galore—drunken, Venetian communists. They would stop at nothing…. Venice and its hinterland were seething with unrest. The owners would show *Il compagno P.*[21] and the like one night only, two at most, and then stop…. At bottom, the less they heard about such films, the better…. No such market existed…. But our bosses moaned because they had failed to set up a capitalist business, in Metro-Goldwyn-Mayer or 20th Century–Fox style. And they blamed us and our incompetence.[22]

By the end of the summer, the whole business of Libertas Film in Veneto ground to a halt. Still, as an official sales representative, Petri stayed in Venice for the Film Festival. There he met some students and graduates from the film school in Rome, the Centro Sperimentale di Cinematografia (CSC), namely future film director Lucio Fulci and stage actor Carlo Romano, with whom he later collaborated on some early unproduced scripts.[23] Painter Renzo Vespignani came as well. Elio made his acquaintance and the two struck up a friendship that would last a lifetime.

Then Summer came to an end, Elio was called back to Rome and became the only scapegoat for the disaster of the Venetian enterprise. The Soviets would not understand that their films were poles apart from the American ones that moviegoers ran in flocks to watch. The flood of Hollywood movies would lead to a breaking point when the 1949 cinema law conceived by the then-undersecretary to the presidency Giulio Andreotti attempted to put limits to the distribution of foreign films and help the national products.

As Petri would put it,

American cinema at that time also involved an invasion, an army of films through which America was already occupying Italy and Europe. Before the Americans landed in Salerno and Anzio during the war, they had already arrived through their films…. This was the real bridgehead of the Americans in Italy, the real victory.[24]

Following the debacle of his first job at Libertas, Elio didn't give up. He realized that Venice was the place where he would try and sell the prints of Soviet films he still had. He began to work with the Venice branch of the FGCI as agitprop, organizing free open-air screenings, little events in various Venetian locations. The party didn't like it one bit and Petri was called back to Rome for good. There he was appointed head of the Roman agency. Over the following years Libertas would be one of the main targets of film censorship in the post-war years, with Eastern films being regularly blocked or banned because of their political content. Eventually it closed down in 1957.

In March 1948 Elio felt he was ready for a new adventure. He attempted to enroll at the CSC and study filmmaking. He was rejected and hence was allowed only to audit the courses. Years later, he would frame and hang the rejection letter in his study, as a small act of retaliation: Elio Petri was not just stubborn but also very susceptible, and he could carry a chip on his shoulder for years. The years 1947 and 1948 marked another defeat, this time not merely individual, for the PCI was ousted from the government of national unity led by Alcide De Gasperi, who held office from June 1, 1947, to May 23, 1948.

Parallel to his political activism, which made him one of Rome's most enthusiastic agitprops for the Communist Party, Petri took his first steps in the world of journalism. He started writing for *Gioventù nuova*, the monthly magazine published by the FGCI, and founded and directed a weekly periodical, *Il Partito*. It was characterized by a groundbreaking approach, both in its design and content, with vignettes, posters designed by Petri's painter friends, and a modern language aimed at making the political message as clear as possible.[25]

It was through his activity in the FGCI that Elio became acquainted with Tommaso Chiaretti, film critic for the PCI's house organ, the newspaper *L'Unità*. Chiaretti managed to get him a job there as his aide. Petri would write reviews for the less important releases, the ones the titular critic wouldn't bother to watch, and signed them simply as "Vice," as was the rule in newspapers. "To Elio, it meant sheer happiness," his wife Paola explained. "He could watch movies for free and write about them."[26]

Elio would show up at the first screening of the day, early afternoon, when the venue was almost empty. He often came across novelist and film critic Alberto Moravia and his wife Elsa Morante. Petri recalled those occasions with amusement: "Moravia and Morante spoke in a loud voice all the time. 'What did he say?' 'He *who*?' Her sight was bad, and he was hard of hearing. A show within the show!"[27]

During his stint as vice critic, Petri got to watch many American movies. As a young communist, he was well aware of the Hollywood propaganda system, but nevertheless he was endlessly fascinated by American cinema. As he explained in a 1972 interview,

> It was not a matter of imperialism. America was using Hollywood films as propaganda in favor of the American system, presenting the American consumer society as a model.... And this is why I think American capitalism should be very grateful to Hollywood and its productions. Nevertheless, it must also be said that the healthy part of our youth, those with democratic tendencies, saw instead in the American cinema a democratic point of reference and an anti-fascist model. This ties in as well with the literary production in those years, from Hemingway to Steinbeck.[28]

On the other hand, he was not so enamored of Soviet cinema. "I remember that in my heart I wanted to write bad things about some Soviet films, but I just couldn't. There was no rule against it. I mean, no one prevented me from being severe with Russian films. But there was a Stalin-like 'super-ego' stopping me. Or rather, it made seem 'beautiful' what actually wasn't beautiful."[29]

Roma ore 11

On Sunday, 14 January 1951, a job advertisement appeared in the classifieds page of the Roman newspaper *Il Messaggero*:

> "Wanted: young intelligent lady, very willing to work and with modest pretenses on her first job, active knowledge of typewriting required. Call on Monday between 10–11 a.m. and 4–5 p.m. at 31, Flat 5, Savoia Street."

On the next day, two hundred girls showed up for that one job. Even though the "modest pretenses" hinted at small pay, the chance of a job was too tempting at a time when the country was still recovering from the wounds of war. But the two hundred girls amassed on the stairs of the building on Via Savoia 31 that day were in for a terrible experience, as four flights of stairs collapsed under the weight of that crowd. Seventy-seven were injured, many severely so, and 26-year-old Anna Maria Baraldi eventually died. It was a horrible, absurd tragedy. As *L'Unità* stressed, it was "directly linked to the increasingly distressing economic circumstances, unemployment and poverty in which a huge part of the population is struggling, not just in the working classes, but also among the white collars and the small bourgeoisie."[30] Among other things, the concierge had alerted the girls of the danger, but no one desisted for fear of losing the job opportunity. She then had called the local police, but the armed forces did not show up. They were too busy with the arrival in Rome of the American president, Dwight D. Eisenhower.

The story struck director Giuseppe De Santis deeply. After collaborating with the likes of Visconti and Rossellini, respectively on *Ossessione* (1943) and *Desiderio* (1946), De Santis had proved himself as one of the most talented filmmakers to emerge in post-war Italy with *Caccia tragica* (1947), *Riso amaro* (1949) and *Non c'è pace tra gli ulivi* (1950). He developed his own version of Neorealism, blending the observation of reality with diverse suggestions and influences, such as *film noir* for *Riso amaro*.

To make the movie about the Via Savoia tragedy, De Santis needed a detailed report on what had happened on that fatal day in the building, on the people involved, their life stories, their dreams and hopes. It had been Cesare Zavattini who suggested the necessity of having an investigation as a starting point to write the script for the tentatively called *Roma, un giorno di settembre*. In fact, at first De Santis and his collaborators (Gianni Puccini, Basilio Franchina, and Rodolfo Sonego) had devised a basic scheme centered on four or five individual stories, which took place on the day of the tragedy, from dusk till dawn. But as he joined the scriptwriting team, Zavattini pointed out that the investigation would shed light not only on the fates of the individuals involved, but also "on a cutaway of Roman life, both of the middle class and the common folk."[31]

For the job, De Santis needed somebody from Rome, who knew the places and the people, and who would be able to trace the witnesses and collect their stories. Puccini—who had co-scripted *Ossessione* and had been the editor for the prestigious journal *Cinema*—suggested to him that 22-year-old lad who worked as vice film critic at *L'Unità*, wore plus-fours as a teenager, had a big head and an even bigger enthusiasm. Four months after the tragedy, Elio Petri started his investigation, a word which would become central in his cinema.

To Zavattini, the mastermind behind Vittorio De Sica's *I bambini ci guardano* (1943), *Sciuscià* (1946), *Ladri di biciclette* (1948) and *Miracolo a Milano* (1950), cinema had to be a "stalking" of reality. Moreover, the observational method was one of the pillars of Marxist thought. Petri took the task seriously, and his proletarian roots helped him. He not only sought out the girls who had lived that tragedy, but also widened the scope to gather the largest possible number of testimonies, interviewing the firemen who had intervened on that day, the victims' neighbors, and the inhabitants of Via Savoia, including the concierge. With the help of Giovannella Otuori and *L'Unità*'s caricaturist Adolfo Cagnacci, he collected a total of about 90 interviews. He made a long list of questions for each and every one of them, about the working condition of women, their interests in life, their daily problems, their view on the tragedy of Via Savoia. No stone was left unturned.

The result was extremely valuable to De Santis, even though he didn't follow Zavattini's suggestion that the movie be an almost documentary-like adaptation of Petri's investigation, without any alteration nor plot to tie the stories together. The director gathered an impressive number of young starlets and "name" actors (Lucia Bosè, Carla Del Poggio, Delia Scala, Massimo Girotti, Raf Vallone, Paolo Stoppa…) and embellished the realistic premise with his consummate mastery, shooting entirely in studio and devising elaborate, outstanding long takes in which the various characters would interact. Even though Petri doesn't have any screenwriting credit, many excerpts from his interviews became lines of dialogue, many interviewees inspired supporting and main characters, and the spirit and tone of the film emerged directly from his inquiry. Moreover, De Santis called him on the set as assistant director together with Franchina and employed him during post-production as well.

To Elio, working on a De Santis film was like a dream come true: "I knew you were the scriptwriter for *Ossessione*, you had been Visconti's assistant on *Ossessione* and for me that film amounted to a discovery of Italy itself,"[32] he would later tell his mentor. And at that memorable 1947 Venice Film Festival he had seen *Caccia tragica*, which left a lasting impression on him. Short, sturdy, square-chested, with a big cranium which soon earned him the nickname "*Capoccione*" (Big head), Elio was moody but always ready with a joke, generous and sincere, highly intelligent and incredibly curious, always hungry for intellectual stimulation. De Santis immediately took a liking to him.

Released in 1952, *Roma ore 11* was a commercial success, but its grim view of contemporary Italy led to violent criticism. The Roman newspaper *Il Tempo* published a vicious attack against it, blaming the government for having allowed the making of such a film. This led to its boycotting on the part of the authorities, namely the General Director of Cinematography Nicola De Pirro, one of the many fascists who had survived the fall of the regime and kept their position in the corridors of power after the war. Despite its strong box-office grosses *Roma ore 11* was taken away rather abruptly from the "prima visione" (first run) circuit and basically disappeared. It was also deliberately omitted from the selection of Italian films for the Cannes Film Festival. Its fate is a testimony of the political censorship on the part of the DC toward those films that strayed from the "official narration" of the country as promoted by the ruling party.

Roma ore 11 represents Petri's very first screen credit. And it is fitting indeed that the director's body of work is inaugurated by an investigation, an *indagine*, echoing the title of his most famous film. Moreover, the story's tragic core reflects Petri and De Santis's view of post-war society and the psychological and human damage that was emerging:

> Those years in Italy after the war meant a defeat of the forces that had organized the resistance to fascism, not only to overthrow fascism, but to change also the social structure that had led to fascism. This was a period of strong capitalist restoration and a setback to the antifascist and popular parties. The new social relationships that were being established during this new phase of capitalist restoration immediately produced in society the phenomenon of alienation.[33]

Petri's research finally saw the light as a book only four years later, in 1956, published by Edizioni Avanti!, the PSI's publishing house, a sign perhaps that the author was already a troublesome presence inside the PCI even before the facts of Hungary. As De Santis himself pointed out in the foreword: "No acknowledgment has ever been given to Elio Petri's investigation, except our own.... I hope that its reading will make everyone realize how much the film and its authors owe to it and how much the act of inquiry can be useful to the realist tendency."[34]

The book is a fascinating, emotional and often harrowing read, with its collection of human types, first-hand recollections of the tragedy and tales of human misery. Petri interviewed typists, and one confessed to him that she was forced into prostitution to make ends meet. Another interviewee emphasized her employer's abuses: "Employers think they have the right to do what they want with the girls. They say that girls work to buy dresses. Going to bed with them is another way to allow them to dress better. They know nothing about female sensitivity. They are stupid and vulgar."[35] Other tales convey an almost unbearable despair, with poor families forced to sell their goods to pay hospital bills. Petri even spent some time at the public hospital where the injured had been taken after the collapse, and described its squalor, its dirt, and the almost inhuman treatment of the hospitalized. Finally, the investigation highlighted a discourse on the city's outskirts, the poor neighborhoods, the ongoing building speculation—akin to *Appunti su un fatto di cronaca*, the 1951 short film directed by Luchino Visconti and inspired by the killing of an eleven-year-old girl in the township of Primavalle—which De Santis's film bypassed altogether.

The investigation marked Petri deeply, and its effects would turn up two decades later, when scripting *La classe operaia va in paradiso* and *La proprietà non è più un furto*. Overall, the book painted a stark picture of contemporary Italy, exposing unemployment and exploitation and showing a squalid reality of a nation undergoing a slow process of moral and civic crumbling. Cesare Zavattini loved it:

> Blessed are you, dear Petri, who, despite being slightly over twenty years old, have dived into these things with such naturalness. I realized that inquiry is moral requirement number one very late, at about fifty, almost as an old man. Because my generation had a kind of fear to establish these contacts, feeling that in the end they might find the need to change many things, maybe everything.[36]

Salad Days

While working on the post-production for *Roma ore 11*, Petri met a young film critic who had just arrived in Rome from Trieste, Franco Giraldi. He introduced him to Chiaretti, and Giraldi took Elio's place as the "vice" critic for *L'Unità*. Later, Petri helped him take his first steps in the movie business and find work on De Santis's sets as production secretary and assistant director. Franco Giraldi eventually became a filmmaker himself, and never forgot Petri's help: "In my early days in Rome he had been like a brother to me, a person capable of extraordinary friendship and solidarity."[37]

Another filmmaker who was struck by "Capoccione" was Carlo Lizzani. They first met in Genoa, on the set of Lizzani's feature film debut, *Achtung! Banditi!* (1951), a World War II tale of partisans financed by communist cooperatives and ex-partisans. But the production stalled for lack of money and the crew was eagerly awaiting the arrival of a delegate from Rome's FGCI branch with the necessary funds to keep shooting. Carrying the money (stuffed in a shoebox!) from Rome to Genoa was a delicate effort that Petri volunteered to do. "One fine day," Lizzani recalled, "a young smiling man turned up, and I realized he was my guardian angel."[38] Elio stayed on the set to watch the filming, very attentive and interested. The film bug was eating him inside, and soon it would need to be fed.

It was again Giuseppe De Santis who helped Petri rise through ranks, hiring him as scriptwriter on his following five films, *Un marito per Anna Zaccheo* (1953), *Giorni d'amore* (1954), *Uomini e lupi* (1957), *La strada lunga un anno* (1958) and *La garçonnière* (1960). Another script dating from 1954, *Prima che vai soldato*, co-written by De Santis, Petri and Puccini and centered on the lives of some young men in a Southern village before their departure for military service, was left unfilmed. As Petri later acknowledged, De Santis taught him not just the love for directing, but also the need to be stubborn whenever he wanted to achieve something. "And he taught me to respect all the characters in a story, even the negative ones, because even though they are simulacra, they are human beings."[39]

On *Un marito per Anna Zaccheo* and *Giorni d'amore* Elio was also assistant director, learning the craft day by day from his mentor. De Santis was the only Neorealist filmmaker to depict the rural world, and he asked Petri to make a preliminary investigation for *Giorni d'amore*, the story of two poor peasants who have to postpone their marriage over and over because they can't afford the wedding expenses, and eventually decide for a romantic getaway (*fuitina*) instead, so that the ensuing shotgun wedding will not need a ceremony. As with *Roma ore 11*, the result was very thorough and with "an incredible amount of information on Italian rural society in the beginning of the 1950s, and it even offers a detailed calculation of the money necessary to wed."[40] Heavily tampered by the producer and censors, *Giorni d'amore* was a misstep for De Santis but an important experience for Petri. It marked the beginning of his bond with Marcello Mastroianni, who would become not only one of the key presences in Petri's *oeuvre* but also one of his best friends, almost like a brother, as Mastroianni himself would acknowledge.[41]

Even more important, in retrospect, was the experience on *Uomini e lupi*, starring Yves Montand, Silvana Mangano and Pedro Armendáriz, about two professional wolf hunters who arrive in a small mountain village in the Abruzzi region, where wolves prey on the livestock. On that occasion, Petri worked for the first time with the man who would become his most precious collaborator: Ugo Pirro.

Born in 1920, Pirro (real name Ugo Mattone) was nine years older than Elio. He, too, was a proletarian: the son of a railway man, he had moved to Rome from the village of Battipaglia, near Salerno, and like Petri he had become entangled with the political and artistic world of the Capital in the years immediately following World War II. The two had met for the first time in 1948, at sculptor Piero Consagra's workshop. One of the founders of the abstractionist group "Gruppo Forma 1" which also included future film director Mino Guerrini, Consagra was one of the key artistic figures in Rome, and his workshop was a meeting point for young leftist intellectuals. Here is how Pirro recalled the first time he saw him: "Elio Petri sat on the carpenter's bench, with an offended and incredulous look for what was happening in front of him. He judged his fellow artist companions with the typical severity of every young communist militant."[42]

The date was September 20, 1948, the 78th anniversary of the 1870 "Breach of Porta Pia" which marked the unification of Italy with the Capture of Rome and the end of the Papal States. The happening at Consagra's workshop was a mocking protest against the PCI, which had voted for the recognition of Mussolini's Lateran Pacts of 1929 (highly favorable to the Church) in the Constitution. Petri was not a habitué of Consagra's group, but he was a familiar face. Being a close friend of Vespignani, he spent plenty of time with the latter's circle of friends, such as Marcello Muccini, Graziella Urbinati, and Giovanni Checchi, the so-called "Banda del Portonaccio" who used to meet at the Caffè Rosati in Piazza del Popolo.[43] Those were figurative painters, and the dispute between figuratives and abstractionists had polarized the artistic world in post-war Rome, even though both sides were self-proclaimed leftists. PCI secretary Palmiro Togliatti stood for the figuratives, in what was first and foremost a political stance rather than an artistic one. In October 1948, on the pages of the party's monthly magazine *Rinascita*, under the transparent alias "Roderigo di Castiglia," he panned an abstractionist exposition in Bologna as "monstrous things," "horrors and rubbish" and "doodling."[44]

On that night of September 1948, Elio Petri did not take part in the alcoholic celebrations. "He was an outsider who had turned up among us, but no one made distinctions between the usual guests and the party crashers," Pirro wrote. "I don't think Elio ever got drunk, and that night he was certainly sober. He stayed vigil and looked at us with proletarian severity."[45] By then, Petri was still a disciplined communist, judicious and still living with his parents. He looked like an alien among those reckless drunken artists, and certainly worlds apart from the 28-year-old Pirro. But, as the latter would discover, they had more things in common that he thought.

Ugo Pirro too had been in the film business for several years, with various fortunes. De Santis had liked his first story written for the cinema, *Ti scrivo una lettera*, and Lux Film had optioned it, but the project was shelved. He made his debut as scriptwriter on *Achtung! Banditi!*, followed by uncredited work (as was the custom) for other scriptwriters in tandem with Franco Solinas, before his name turned up again in the credits on Antonio Pietrangeli's debut, *Il sole negli occhi* (1953).

The scripting sessions for *Uomini e lupi* took place at De Santis' place, each day for a couple of months. Petri, Pirro, Tonino Guerra, Mario Socrate and Gianni Puccini, the director's closest friend, were sitting at a huge table, discussing a scene for hours, sometimes with childish stubbornness, and with De Santis often acting as *provocateur*, encouraging the dispute to squeeze the best out of those brains. Petri, as Pirro recalled, was in turn provocative and paradoxical, and he often halted the development of a sequence to ask his friend Tonino Guerra embarrassing or jocular questions, which the latter took very seriously. "'Tonino, how much money would you want to have your finger cut off?' ... 'Tonino, how much money would you want to give Luchino Visconti a blowjob?' Petri had often these bursts of commoner jokes, which contradicted, almost in spite of himself, his proletarian moralism."[46]

Arbitrarily edited against De Santis's wishes, *Uomini e lupi* had a cinematic destiny akin to that of the director's previous films. Met coldly if not dismissively by the critics upon its release in February 1957, it even underwent an accusation of plagiarism.[47] But it marked the beginning of a strong friendship between Petri and Pirro, at a time when the Hungarian revolt and its effects, including the 101 Manifesto, were having shattering effects among Elio's circle of communist friends, overturning convictions and destroying bonds.

Counter-Current: Città Aperta

The Hungarian revolt marked a political and professional turn for Elio Petri. In the previous years, his name had appeared in *L'Unità*, together with those of other communist filmmakers, siding with the party's orthodox point of view. In June 1953 he had signed a petition to ask for the pardon of communist activists Julius and Ethel Rosenberg, who were executed in Sing Sing on June 19.[48] In March 1955 he had spoken against the recrudescence of films intent on "exalting the ends and conduct of the Fascist war"[49] which were being produced in that period. After the Budapest events, Elio came face to face with the ideological conflict between the party's official position and his own.

The 101 Manifesto was delivered to *L'Unità* and to the party's central committee. While some of the petitioners were having a heated discussion with the newspaper's editor in chief Giancarlo Pajetta, news came that the letter had just been made public by the agency ANSA. The next day, 14 petitioners, including Petri, wrote to *L'Unità*, complaining that their good faith had been betrayed, and that the document should have been confidential.[50]

Petri and others sought another way to express their views, by founding a literary review which would host the debate the party was denying them. Thus, *Città aperta* was born. Financed by the industrialist Gian Fabrizio Sacripante, it was directed by Tommaso Chiaretti and bore a significant cinephile title. "Open City" was not just a reference to Rossellini's film and to the liberation of Rome that had taken place a decade earlier. It was also a declaration of principles, as an open city is the natural place for open ideas to circulate, without any censorship nor imposition. The magazine hosted articles on literature, art, cinema, architecture and philosophy, penned by prestigious collaborators: novelist Italo Calvino, painter Ugo Attardi, literary critic Dario Puccini, poet Mario Socrate, philosopher Luca Canali, architect Piero Moroni, and more. Renzo Vespignani drew the cover image for the first issue, which came out on July 25, 1957: a prostitute raising her skirt and exposing three figures (a priest, a general, a politician) stuffed in her panties. More than just a satiric stab, it was a defiant act, the open rejection of the Italian reality in all its forms (religious, military and politic) and the expression of "the desire to discuss everything, among Communists, without hesitations."[51]

The first four issues of *Città aperta* were bi-weekly and looked like half-newspapers. Then, after an eight-month interval, three more issues came out monthly, with a different format, akin to literary reviews. The content was openly critical of the party, as in Calvino's short story *La gran bonaccia delle Antille*, a satirical seafaring tale about a corsair ship (standing for the PCI) which stands still for several months facing the Papist galleons (the DC) in a stretch with no wind. The rigid rules by Admiral Drake (Stalin), followed to the letter by the Captain (Togliatti), prevent any action to come out of the dead calm and even hinder from attacking the papists. Calvino's story meant to satirize the PCI's inaction, but its effect was only to provoke another satirical story in response published in *Rinascita*, *La grande caccia delle Antille*, which told the Old Man's (Togliatti) victory against the rebels, including one named Italo. The story was penned by Maurizio Ferrara and signed "Little Bald," a literal translation of the surname Calvino.

Among Petri's contribution to *Città aperta* were a long essay on Elia Kazan and McCarthyism, as well as a provocative piece titled *Morte di uno scrittore, appunti per un film in economia*. It was the outline for an imaginary film, satirical in tone, and inspired by the death of Curzio Malaparte, the controversial novelist and ex-Fascist intellectual, author of such successful and scandalous novels as *La pelle*. Upon his death in July 1957, Malaparte had been celebrated by the PCI, to which he had become close after the war, and he had even converted to Catholicism in the last months of his life. Petri's story sarcastically commented on that by having various left-wing intellectuals and priests gather at their ex-adversary's deathbed, mourning him as if he had always been "one of them." With its emphasis on dark humor and openly vivid tones, the short story predates Petri's work in the 1970s.

The Communist Party opposed *Città aperta* right from the start through some of its main exponents, namely Mario Alicata, in charge of the party's cultural line, and militant art critic Antonello Trombadori. As Vespignani recalled,

> With that magazine, we wanted to measure the fever within the party, its ability to resist our opposition. We were *provocateurs*.... After each issue there was the trial. We were summoned by Alicata at the Botteghe Oscure [Author's note: the PCI headquarters in Rome, located on

Via delle Botteghe Oscure], in a monastic, Spartan room, and there we found the magazine with notes, line by line ... each note was a question to us and required an answer, a correction, which would go unheeded.... Once, in the middle of an argument, I went out of the room to go to the toilet, and there I met Togliatti.... He didn't say anything, and just came out without even saying hello, but in a rage. Then Antonello [Trombadori] came in. He threw his arms around my neck and cried, I felt his tears on my skin. He said, "But what are you doing, what are you doing...?" I told him: "A magazine, Antonello, just a magazine."[52]

Eventually, Tommaso Chiaretti was expelled from the PCI. Petri, Vespignani, Canali, Socrate, Puccini and Attardi didn't renew their party cards for the year 1958. From that moment on, they were out. "And I found myself alone again," Petri commented, "for being in the party is like being in a family, with all the benefits that come with it."[53]

The Birth of a Champion

By the mid–1950s, Elio Petri had the chance to debut behind the camera. The format of the short film, mostly documentary, was very popular in Italy, not least because of economic reasons. The Andreotti law (#958, 29 December 1949), which redesigned the State's economic contributions to the film industry, encompassed State financings for short films. It was also a mandatory step for aspiring directors who would learn the trade.

Petri's first short film, *Nasce un campione*, submitted to the Board of Censors in October 1953, was about Italians' passion for cycling. The widespread poverty meant that very few people could afford a car, and most used the bicycle for their daily routine, including going to work (as shown in *Ladri di biciclette*). Moreover, cycling was as popular a sport as soccer, thanks to such internationally known champions as Fausto Coppi, Gino Bartali and Fiorenzo Magni. Bartali's triumph at the 1948 Tour de France was an epic event that somehow helped soothe the souls in a country very close to civil war, after Palmiro Togliatti had been shot in the back of the neck and severely injured by an anti-communist assailant in the morning of July 14, resulting in political and social tension throughout the nation.

Petri wrote the script for *Nasce un campione* with Tonino Guerra and produced it with the help of Arturo Zavattini (Cesare's son) and Pasqualino De Santis (Giuseppe's brother). The project took form in Guerra's hometown of Santarcangelo di Romagna, in the Romagna region, a vital cultural niche in post–World War II Italy. A teacher at an agricultural school in the nearby village of Savignano di Romagna, Antonio "Tonino" Guerra was one of the most vital personalities in the area. During the war he had been interned in a German concentration camp, and to "cheat the hard life," as he used to say, he had written a poetry book in dialect, *I scarabócc* (Scribbles), which received enthusiastic reviews. He and others formed the so-called *"circal de' giudéizi"* (Circle of Judgment), a group of locals who discussed literature, poetry, cinema, sport. Struck by one of Vespignani's drawings, Guerra had gone to Rome and convinced the artist to move to Santarcangelo. Vespignani's arrival brought a wind of novelty in the area. One day Petri came to visit his painter friend and became part of the circle himself.[54]

Nasce un campione was an eleven-minute-long recreated documentary with non-professional actors, patently influenced by Neorealism. It told the story of a young man from the Romagna region, nicknamed "Stampa" (Press) because every day he distributes newspapers in the various villages on his bicycle. He daydreams of becoming a cycling champion like many of his countrymen. The film describes his typical day and follows him during his first amateur race: Stampa wins and the trophy is a shining new bike which he has long dreamed of. Reviewing the film for the bi-weekly *Cinema*, Claudio Bertieri criticized its overt sentimental and pathetic tones, dismissing the color photography by Angelo Baistrocchi as "too vivid," and praising only "some images of provincial life, captured with adequate sincerity."[55]

And yet, *Nasce un campione* is much more uplifting than one would expect. It reeks with irony, and the narration (by Corrado Mantoni, later to become one of Italy's most popular TV hosts) is littered with quips. Commenting footage of people of all ages cycling through country roads, the narrator notes that in Romagna the bicycle accompanies man in "the longest tour ever known, from 3 to 80 years of age"; and as we see a rack filled with dozens of bikes, he underlines that "you can leave your bike unguarded here, and no one will ever steal it," an amusing nod to De Sica's film. The pacing is fast, with the camera often placed on a car to follow the protagonist's rides, such as when Stampa attempts an impromptu race with a train passing by.

The luminous photography conveys a climate of peace and beauty, and Petri's depiction of the country life is felicitous, with images of stonecutters resting in the shade by the river during the midday break and women doing their laundry in canals. The story gives ample room to suitably humorous vignettes, such as in the brief episode of Stampa taking his girlfriend Marisa atop his bike to the beach. Their romantic idyll amid the dunes is interrupted by a bicycle race in the streets nearby, and the young man runs to help the cyclists quench their thirst at a road fountain. Then he stands watching them ride away, oblivious of his girlfriend. Another bit has some local boys attempting to stand motionless on their bikes (*souplesse*, a typical move in track cycling) in the middle of a square, eliciting the other kids' amused reaction. Only the narrator's final words break the enchantment, as the bright future he envisions for the aspiring champion is reduced to the prospect of gaining enough money to open a bicycle shop in the nearby town. A realistic and down-to-earth coda to the protagonist's dreams of glory.

Petri's second short film was *I sette contadini*. Written by Cesare Zavattini, Luigi Chiarini and Renato Niccolai (with the latter providing the commentary read by Renato Cominetti), with color photography by Roberto Gerardi, it was produced and dedicated to the memory of the seven Cervi brothers, members of a family of peasants in the region of Emilia Romagna who took active part in the Resistance. Their farmhouse was a secure shelter for antifascists and partisans, as well as for the foreign prisoners fleeing from the Nazi-fascist army. They were captured on the night of November 25, 1943, tortured and eventually killed by the fascists on December 28, 1943, in Reggio Emilia.

The ten-minute long *I sette contadini* is divided into three parts. The first introduces the countryside where the brothers lived. It is an idyllic vision, with people dancing on a boat on the river Po, while the voice-over describes the post-war reconstruction in the region. The second part evokes the daily life of the Cervi brothers. Their father, Alcide Cervi (1875–1970), a longtime socialist and antifascist, recalls his sons' tragic end. The film ends with epic images of a crowd of peasants who gather outside the Reggio Emilia shooting range where the seven Cervi brothers were executed.

Petri's intent was not just to celebrate the brothers' heroic sacrifice, but to underline their efforts to achieve a modern agriculture, based on technical research and innovations. In the 1930s, despite their neighbors' initial disbelief, the Cervi farmhouse had become a model in the region, the result of intelligent and independent thinking. The title itself, "The Seven Farmers," stresses their strong bond with the land and the relevance of their example.

The commentary is impersonal and rhetoric, and sometimes it sounds forced and overly didactic, but the depiction of rural life is touching. The early scenes of the ball near the river convey a sense of community that evokes one of Petri's celluloid heroes, John Ford, and the depiction of everyday life shows a society "in which the individual lives in touch with the others and each one finds in the next man—in the 'comrades'—a human and social reference point."[56] It is as if Petri was trying to shake off the rhetoric of the PCI and find a more profound and sincere truth in the images, in the everyday gestures, in the faces and eyes of ordinary people. The most poignant moments are those when the octogenarian Alcide explains in simple words his sons' sacrifice: "You know, we are born and then we die. When one dies because of destiny, that's a natural thing. When one is killed, he is stolen from life."

Years later, Petri dismissed the result as "very bad … I made that movie at a very obscure political moment, immediately after the facts of Hungary, as if to prove that my dissidence from the PCI hadn't slowed down my political commitment."[57] According to critic Oreste Del Buono, *I sette contadini* can be considered "a farewell to the simplicity of clarity," at a time when Petri was drowning in "the darkness of doubt and discomfort, contrasts and fears."[58] Although made in 1957, it was submitted to the board of censors in June 1958, when Petri was already out of the party. Ten years later, Gianni Puccini would direct a feature film based on the same story, *I sette fratelli Cervi* (1968), starring Gian Maria Volonté.

In the late 1950s, Giuseppe De Santis was finding it harder and harder to make the films he wanted, so much so that he had to shoot *La strada lunga un anno*, a typical Italian story, in Yugoslavia. The Yugoslavian stay allowed Petri to get in touch with screenwriter Rodoljub Andric. The two discussed adapting a novel by Serbian novelist Oskar Davičo[59] but the project eventually fell through in early 1959. It was during location scouting in Yugoslavia that Petri and Pirro met again, and their friendship cemented. The pair collaborated on two more projects with De Santis, which sadly remained unfilmed.

L'uomo senza domenica (The Man Without Sunday), also known as *Furore d'autunno—Chi muore e chi vive*, was dated 1957, shortly after *Uomini e lupi*, and was based on the true case of a suicidal worker. Petri did preparatory research as he had done for *Roma ore 11* and worked on the script with Guerra, De Santis and Pirro. It was to be an Italian-French co-production between Giovanni Addessi's company and the Parisian Cinétel.

The intriguingly titled *Pettotondo* (Roundchest) was based on a ballad by folksinger Matteo Salvatore about a peasant prostitute who sold herself in exchange for grain, eggs, or flour. According to Pirro, the story (subtitled *Ti sei fatta la veste rossa*, "You Made Your Own Red Dress") was "the first attempt in Italy to make a movie about the female condition by way of an extreme character."[60] In typical Neorealist style, Pirro, Petri and De Santis took a trip to the southern region of Puglia, where the story would be set, to meet the local people and study the peasant world, the consequences of the 1950 agrarian reform, the depopulation of the countryside, the emigration to the North.

Initially to be financed by Neapolitan producer Roberto Amoroso with his company Sud Film Produzione Cinematografica, to whom De Santis, Petri and Pirro sold the rights to the story on July 9, 1959,[61] *Pettotondo* ended up shelved. Its subject matter was too critical toward the State and too frank about the working conditions in Southern Italy, and its main character was too risky and controversial. De Santis' cinema had woman at its center, and everything moved around and in function of her, even politics and the rise of class consciousness. It was something the common morals could not accept.

De Santis went on to make *La garçonnière* for Amoroso instead. Co-written by Petri, Guerra, Giraldi and Roberto Gerardi, from a story (by De Santis, Petri, Giraldi and Pirro) titled *Amore nel pomeriggio*, it centered on a husband (Raf Vallone) who betrays his wife (Eleonora Rossi Drago) with various women whom he takes to an apartment he rented in a popular neighborhood. The film was a critical and commercial flop, and the result was so unsatisfying to Petri that he, Guerra and Giraldi asked that their names be removed from the credits.[62] Amoroso didn't oblige. It would take five years before De Santis could make another movie, *Italiani brava gente* (1965).

Besides his work with De Santis, Petri kept busy during the 1950s on a variety of collaborations, usually collective. Signed by no less than eight scriptwriters, including De Santis, Puccini, and Zavattini, *Donne proibite* (1954, Giuseppe Amato) was the choral tale of several prostitutes based on a novel by Bruno Paolinelli. Then came *Quando tramonta il sole* (1955, Guido Brignone), also co-written with Puccini, and *Un ettaro di cielo* (1958) directed by Aglauco Casadio, with Franco Giraldi as assistant director and starring Marcello Mastroianni. For the film, Petri and Casadio made once again the trip to Santarcangelo to persuade Tonino Guerra to give up his job and come to Rome to pen the script with them and Ennio Flaiano (uncredited in the film). As Guerra recalled, they were "looking for someone familiar with the way the people of Romagna spoke. It was, in a sense, a technical choice on their part. That was my first job. Then I decided to go to Rome for a 300,000 *lire* contract. I was a teacher, making just 39,000 *lire*, so I felt I could buy the Coliseum."[63]

Between 1959 and 1960, Petri's name appeared in the credits of several pictures. The little-seen *Le notti dei teddy boys* (1959, Leopoldo Savona), a juvenile delinquency drama co-written with Chiaretti, Giraldi and Savona himself, saw the participation of Pier Paolo Pasolini.[64] Then came the Yugoslavian film *Vlak bez voznog reda* (1959, Veljko Bulajić), unreleased in Italy, and a melodramatic Mafia tale, *Vento del sud* (1960, Enzo Provenzale), about a young man who refuses to commit a murder commissioned by the Mafia and flees to Palermo with his girlfriend (the victim's daughter). The girl is killed, and he exacts his revenge.

The most interesting of Petri's scripts of the period is the one he co-wrote for Puccini's *L'impiegato* (1960), an amiable comedy about a clerk (Nino Manfredi) who is unsatisfied with his boring job and evades his daily routine by reading the popular *Giallo Mondadori* paperbacks and dreaming he is a mystery writer in love with a seductive dancer on the run from her ex-lover, a ferocious Las Vegas gangster. Besides the nods to *The Secret Life of Walter Mitty* (1947, Norman Z. McLeod), the film featured one of the themes that would become staples in Petri's work, namely the main character suffering an inner split as the result of an alienating job. Moreover, the oneiric inserts were ingeniously integrated into the story, often by way of elaborate takes that move from reality to dream without cuts. Petri would reuse this gimmick in his films as director. *L'impiegato* is also noteworthy for its depiction of the role of popular culture in everyday life. Himself an avid reader of the Mondadori detective novels, Petri would often have them turn up in his own movies.

Petri co-authored also the original stories for Puccini's next film, *Il carro armato dell'8 settembre* and for Lizzani's *Il gobbo* (both 1960). The former counted among the scriptwriters such noted names as Pier Paolo Pasolini and novelist Goffredo Parise. Set in the chaotic days following the armistice of September 8, 1943, between Italy and the Allies, which led to the Nazi army occupying the country in retaliation, it was the picaresque tale of a corporal who decides to bring a tank back from the Tirrenian coast to his barracks. *Il gobbo* was based on a real-life figure, ex-partisan Giuseppe Albano, nicknamed "Il gobbo del Quarticciolo" (the Hunchback of Quarticciolo), who became a bandit after the end of the war. Petri wrote the story with Luciano Vincenzoni and Tommaso Chiaretti, while Pirro and Mario Socrate were among the scriptwriters. Lizzani's film featured a cameo by Pasolini.

But it was the commercial success of *L'impiegato* that made Elio Petri a reliable name among producers. "Well, it's not that I wanted to become a director at all costs, but if the chance came, I would be quite happy to accept,"[65] he would quip. Soon, very soon, such a chance would come.

Two

The Burden of Guilt
L'assassino *(1961)*

Presumed Guilty

In the last couple of years, Petri had been working steadily and had some scripts on his desk. One such was the intriguingly titled *L'uomo nero* (The Man in Black), co-written with Tommaso Chiaretti. Inspired by real-life events, it was the story of a spy during the Fascist regime. Petri and Chiaretti possibly took inspiration from *Una spia del regime*, the memoir-cum-novel of the anti–Fascist intellectual Ernesto Rossi. Published in 1955, it was centered on the figure of Carlo Del Re, a Milanese lawyer who in 1930 denounced to the OVRA (the secret Fascist police) all the members of an anti–Fascist clandestine organization in which he himself was involved. Del Re's role was fully uncovered only after the war, when the names of OVRA agents were made public. The release of Rossi's book caused Del Re's definitive expulsion for unworthiness from the register of lawyers, from which he had already been expelled in 1946 and later re-admitted.

"*L'uomo nero* is, in its own way, a 'giallo,'" Petri later explained. "I wanted to depict the damage that dictatorships do to individuals … without losing the taste to tell stories and draw interesting characters."[1] *L'uomo nero* was to star Marcello Mastroianni, who would also produce it. But it all came to nothing.[2] Petri tried to resume the project a few years later, but to no avail.

However, Nino Manfredi was interested in doing another story that Petri had penned with Tonino Guerra, *L'assassino* (The Murderer). A sort of existential murder mystery influenced by Antonioni's cinema and with nods to Franz Kafka's *The Trial* and to Albert Camus' *The Stranger*, it further displayed Petri's love for the genre. It was the story of a young and successful antique dealer who one morning is arrested by the police with no explanation whatsoever. At the police station he finds out that his mistress Adalgisa, an older woman with whom he had a financial debt, has been murdered the night before, just after he paid her a visit at the resort she was renovating. A fatherly commissioner interrogates him, and through a series of flashbacks we learn about the man's past and present and his many skeletons in the closet. He is a ruthless and dishonest businessman, is about to marry a rich girl for her money, lives above his means and is ashamed of his proletarian roots. Forced to spend a night in jail, he is joined in his cell by a pair of creepy informants who try to push him to confess. But the protagonist is innocent, and the next morning he is released, while the commissioner announces to the press that the real murderer has been arrested. Still, the experience has struck him deeply.

The original story—dated 24 February 1960 and carrying the mark of Lorenzo Pego-raro's PEG Produzione Films[3]—showcases the authors' literary influences and ambitions. It is told in the first person by the protagonist and is envisaged as a short story, with an uncommon attention to style. The initial idea was that Petri and Manfredi would pro-duce it (most likely through Pegoraro's company) together with a mutual friend, lawyer Umberto Cortina. But Dino De Laurentiis offered Manfredi an exclusive deal as he had done with Alberto Sordi. It was an offer one could not refuse, given the amount De Lau-rentiis could (and would) pay. Petri then handed the script to Marcello Mastroianni, who accepted on the spot. Cortina proposed the deal to Goffredo Lombardo, the head of Tita-nus. Lombardo, who had an old contract pending with Mastroianni, was willing to make the movie but with another director. Cortina and Mastroianni replied that either Petri would direct L'assassino or they wouldn't do the film. By the end of April, Petri signed the deal with Titanus.

The scripting phase involved Tonino Guerra, Pasquale Festa Campanile and Mas-simo Franciosa, while Giuseppe Patroni Griffi appears in official papers as co-scriptwriter but not in the credits. Petri surrounded himself with friends for the crew: Giuliano Mon-taldo would be his assistant, Renzo Vespignani and his wife Graziella Urbinati would take care of the art direction and design the costumes, respectively. Lombardo provided him with top-notch collaborators, such as director of photography Carlo Di Palma, composer Piero Piccioni (who provided a jazzy score in tune with the director's musical tastes) and editor Ruggero Mastroianni, Marcello's brother.

L'assassino was an Italian-French coproduction, with Titanus covering 70 percent of the budget (estimated at 227 million *lire*) through its associate, Franco Cristaldi's Vides, and the Societé Generale de Cinematographie providing the other 30 percent. Originally the co-production was to be split between 80 percent (Titanus) and 20 percent (Societé Generale de Cinematographie). As compensation for selling the rights to the scenario, Pegoraro was paid the notable sum of 4,120,000 *lire*. Petri was paid 51,500 *lire* for the sce-nario (Guerra got 515,000 *lire*), 257,000 *lire* for the script (Festa Campanile and Franci-osa got 2,781,000 *lire* each, Patroni Griffi 257,000 *lire*, Guerra 154,500) and 5,781,000 for directing. Overall, his fee was four times less than Mastroianni's 28 million. The news of L'assassino being in production urged Dino De Laurentiis to change the title of Mario Camerini's whodunit comedy *Gli assassini*, to be released just before Christmas with an all-star cast including Alberto Sordi, Vittorio Gassman, Silvana Mangano and Nino Man-fredi, into *Crimen*, to avoid confusion.[4]

The coproduction deal required the presence of a couple of French actors, namely Micheline Presle and Mac Ronay.[5] One of the divas of 1940s French cinema, Presle had been the unforgettable protagonist (alongside Gérard Philipe) of Claude Autant-Lara's scandal-ous *Le diable au corps* (1947), a film with a long history of censorship issues in Italy. After a brief stint in Hollywood, most notably in Fritz Lang's *American Guerrilla in the Philippines* (1950), Presle had returned to Europe. Over the following years she had appeared in some important Italian films such as *Casa Ricordi* (1954, Carmine Gallone) and *Beatrice Cenci* (1956, Riccardo Freda), and had recently played in Joseph Losey's crime drama *Blind Date* (1959), a story that had some points in common with Petri's film. The 39-year-old actress had what Petri sought in the character of Adalgisa, a woman with a strong personality and a beauty on the verge of fading who nevertheless retains an alluring sensuality.

Mac Ronay (real name Germain Sauvard) was an ex-acrobat who had turned into an illusionist after the war and became a sensation in French nightclubs with his surreal act.

Alfredo Martelli (Marcello Mastroianni) and his lover Adalgisa (Micheline Presle) in *L'assassino.*

Aided by his angular, slender features and effective mimicry, he created the character of a goofy, clumsy mime-magician, who is unable to perform his own tricks and comes up accidentally with other, amusing ones instead. He was noticed by Maurice Chevalier, who helped him cut a deal with the Casino de Paris, leading to a popularity that went beyond the French borders. Sauvard found his way to the big screen in Italy thanks to Mario Monicelli, who cast him in a bit role as an illusionist in *Risate di gioia* (1960), and Luigi Comencini, who wanted him in a dramatic role in his World War II masterpiece *Tutti a casa* (1960). His brief, silent cameo in *L'assassino* made the most of his wide-eyed stare and off-the-wall appearance.

For the role of Commissioner Palumbo, Petri had thought of Jean Gabin, but the French actor would be too expensive. So, he opted for Salvo Randone, one of Italy's most noted stage thespians, and one of the great interpreters of Luigi Pirandello's work. Born in Syracuse, Sicily, in 1906, the 55-year-old Randone was an unmistakable presence: hooked nose, high forehead, protruding cheekbones, sagging cheeks, liquid eyes with a perennial inquiring look. On top of that, he had what Vittorio Gassman would call "the most beautiful voice in Italian theater."[6] Randone struck up a friendship with the director and would turn up in most of his subsequent films. Here, his presence underlined the affinities with one of Pirandello's main themes, the search for one's identity. Randone was paid little more than 4 million.

The rest of the cast featured reliable supporting actors: Cristina Gaioni, Andrea Checchi (whose brother Giovanni Checchi took care of production design together with

Vespignani), Franco Ressel, Enrico Maria Salerno, Marco Mariani. The naïve hotel maid Rosetta was played by Giovanna Gagliardo, in her only screen role. She would become a scriptwriter (with several works written for Miklós Jancsó, including *Vizi privati, pubbliche virtù*) and director.

Shooting started on December 12, 1960, and was scheduled to last 48 days. For the occasion, Cristaldi sent Petri a telegram wishing him success. "Dear Elio, I am sure that you will make a great movie and will confirm the irrational trust that we all have in you," the producer wrote. Petri's witty reply: "Dear Franco, I poorly feign self-confidence, confirming my own irrational distrust in myself."[7]

The presence of Mastroianni and Presle granted *L'assassino* suitable coverage in newspapers, and rumors from the set described it as a *giallo* with a twist ending.[8] The previous year, Pietro Germi's *Un maledetto imbroglio* (1959), an adaptation of Carlo Emilio Gadda's novel *Quer pasticciaccio brutto de via Merulana*, had been labeled by some as Italy's first *giallo* (which it wasn't). It was a clever move, given the high popularity of the *Giallo Mondadori* paperbacks, which in a few years would result in such widely influential works as Mario Bava's *La ragazza che sapeva troppo* (1963) and *6 donne per l'assassino* (1964). Still, as with Germi's film, the term *giallo* was used to pinpoint a work with mystery elements which nevertheless did not belong to genre production but on the contrary had definite *auteur* ambitions. The label, no doubt suggested by Lombardo's press office, implied that Titanus believed *L'assassino* had commercial potential and could perform well with mainstream audiences.

The crew celebrated the new year on the set, while shooting the scenes set in the holding cell at the Titanus Appia studios. The *Corriere della Sera* underlined the friendly atmosphere of the shoot: "All in the family, because this is a strange crew composed of brothers, spouses, various relatives. There were the two Mastroianni…; Renzo Vespignani and his costume designer wife, Carlo Di Palma and his brother Dario; Giovanna De Santis, the daughter of poet Diego Valeri and wife of director Giuseppe De Santis, who's the script supervisor, Andrea Checchi and his brother Giovanni…"[9]

Near the end of January, however, the apparently pleasant shooting was upset by the news that Enrico Maria Salerno (cast as one of the two informants) had left the film. According to a news article, "after rehearsing the scene for a whole day, Salerno suddenly noticed that his role was secondary compared to Mastroianni's. And he threw a tantrum. In his place, director Elio Petri immediately cast Paolo Panelli, who had accompanied Salerno on the set and was watching the shooting out of curiosity."[10] It is unlikely that things went as described, as Salerno was cast for only four days (January 12–16) and was well aware that his was a bit role. His desertion must be attributed to other motives, possibly an argument with the director. Curiously, his name is still featured in the credits. The other confidant was originally to be played by Andrea Checchi, but eventually Petri switched him to the role of Adalgisa's ex-husband and cast Toni Ucci as the second informant.

Shooting went on till February 4, four days less than expected, and Petri managed to save on the budget: *L'assassino* cost only 177 million *lire* instead of the estimated 227.

Cops Never Yawn

At the time *L'assassino* was made, Italian film censorship was still regulated by a fascist law dating back to 1923. The set of rules had survived the fall of the regime and had been retained in its entirety in post-war Italy. It would be only the next year that a new law (#161, 21 April 1962) was promulgated.

Among other things, the ongoing law provided that the script for the film be deposited in advance and submitted to preventive review on the part of the Direzione Generale della Cinematografia (General Direction of Cinematography). The board would then produce a detailed synopsis based on the script, followed by a "judgment" which consisted of a brief review of the story, its meaning and (if any) political implications. This would sometimes be accompanied by "suggestions" to the makers (with scripts being tampered or partially rewritten accordingly) or "warnings" to the rating board when dealing with the screen adaptation of the scripts' most controversial parts. Reviewing the script for *L'assassino* on December 2, 1960, the 7th division (headed by the Maltese-born Annibale Scicluna Sorge, another ex-fascist dignitary) highlighted the story's existential essence, calling it

> a psychological study of the inner turmoil which torments a man's conscience…. The protagonist's mood turns into the heartfelt necessity to undergo a deep examination of conscience which … ends up even projecting on episodes and actions totally extraneous to the murder.[11]

Overall, the General Director of Cinematography De Pirro underlined fourteen remarks about the script. Some concerned mild erotic moments, such as a scene in which the protagonist—called Nello Polletti in the original story, Marcello in the script, and Alfredo Martelli in the film—is in a solitary spot with one of his lovers, Rina. Marcello's hand raises her skirt and exposes her stocking, supported by a rubber band. He asks her: "Are you still wearing these?" (The scene disappeared overall in the film). Other observations concerned some veiled references to male homosexuality, still a taboo theme at the time. A case in point was Marcello's line: "In the field of interior furnishing they [homosexuals] rule. There's nothing to do, they do have taste." Later, a cop asks Marcello: "Say, are you sexually normal?" Both lines would disappear in the film.

The most controversial passages dealt with the depiction of the armed forces. Sometimes it was a matter of an allusive line, such as Marcello's reply to the commissioner: "With anyone else, I would have complained. I would have rebelled. But with them, no. Because they were the police. Because we Italians *are scared of the police*" (the underlining is in the official paper).

Other bits showed inappropriate behavior on the part of the armed forces, such as a cop replying brusquely "Ma che mi frega" (What do I care) when the protagonist tells his name, or another one (off-screen) making a raspberry when Marcello, having to spend the night in the security room, asks for pajamas (the latter remains in the film). Ditto for references to police brutality, such as the following:

> p. 170: The two inmates who are in the holding cell with Marcello are discussing police methods. First inmate: "They'll kill him. I'm going to talk … they can make you impotent, you know?" Marcello: "Impotent?" First inmate: "Sure, sure. Because they hit you in the weak spots. Hit, hit, hit!"

Another warning concerned a scene depicting an inmate who has been severely beaten by the cops until he is almost unrecognizable: "A stream of blood drops down the forehead and, passing over his semi-closed swollen eye, completely covers half of his face." The scene disappeared.

Finally, De Pirro was uncomfortable with the characters of the two prisoners who turn out to be police informants, and who try to persuade Marcello to confess. "The tone of their dialogue and the tricks they come up with surely don't bode well for the systems adopted by the Police in the exercise of their functions," a final note pointed out. Even though the final judgment on the script was overall positive, this mild warning nevertheless hinted that there might be issues with the finished film.

By March 14, 1961, *L'assassino* was ready to be submitted to the rating board. First, however, Lombardo organized a private confidential screening for the committee members. This was not a required step, but an informal practice on the part of the most powerful producers, in order to learn beforehand what would be the response to the film and adjust whatever issues there might be before submitting it officially to the board. This would save time and money and avoid the risk of the film being rejected.

In this case the result was no less than tragicomic, as Tommaso Chiaretti labeled it in a controversial article that shed light on the tortuous "labyrinths of censorship."[12] At the end of the screening, lights turned on again, and Lombardo was all ears. One member suggested that the producer might want to "lighten" the film. Lombardo asked what exactly needed to be "lightened." The response was, first of all, the policemen's Southern Italian accents. Then, the tone of their voice, too menacing. And it would be preferable that the commissioner not address Martelli with the informal personal pronoun "*tu*" but with the more formal "*lei*," to avoid suggesting an arrogant behavior on the part of the law. In the redubbed version, although Alfredo immediately recognizes their accent ("Sicilians? Agrigento, Taormina … beautiful, very beautiful…"), this is hardly noticeable in the voice of actor Marco Mariani, who plays Dr. Margiotta; and Salvo Randone's character always uses the respectful "lei."

But there was more. Another member suggested that the protagonist's line when he enters the cell, "Che schifo!" (How disgusting!) be suppressed. Italian cells are not disgusting, stinking, dirty, he objected. When Martelli meets the two informants, the line "We have seen your face next to Tambroni's" must be altered, for it was better not to mention the Democrazia Cristiana politician Fernando Tambroni, who had fallen from grace after his stint as prime minister, from March to July 1960. Lombardo asked what name could be used as replacement in the dialogue and was told that Congo president Joseph Kasa-Vubu was just fine: nobody would ever see the movie in Congo anyway.

Eventually the committee members agreed that, after such alterations, it was likely that the film would be given a screening certificate, *but* it was preferable that another informal screening be arranged for the armed forces, given their prominent role in the story. Lombardo duly obliged and screened *L'assassino* for the secretary of the Chief of Police, who pointed out that there were many more things he didn't like one bit. For instance, when they enter the building where the antique dealer lives, the cops walk on the floor which the concierge is washing and carelessly leave their footprints all over. This must be eliminated, as cops are not ill-mannered. All that is left of the scene is the concierge complaining: "Where are you going? You're making a mess!"

A scene where a cop blows his nose noisily was cut for the same reason. Ditto for a shot in which the commissioner yawns. A line in which Palumbo tells Martelli, "We know you were listed in the Communist party" was changed to "We know your name often honors the promissory notes of protest," because it implied that the police had a bias against communists. Another line had the expression "family of subversives" changed into "family of anarchists." Similarly, other lines of dialogue were altered in order to make the commissioner more humane. But the biggest issue, as with the preventive board of censors, concerned the two police confidants. It is unacceptable, Lombardo was told, to imply that the Italian Police resort to informers as means to solve cases. Therefore, the informers must *not* be presented as such.

At this point, Petri was boiling with rage. He threatened to remove his name from the film. But nobody listened to him, and Lombardo proceeded according to the "suggestions" on the part of the armed forces. Overall, according to Petri,[13] *L'assassino* underwent ninety preventive modifications before the rating board officially reviewed it on March 25. Two days later, the film was given a screen certificate with a V.M.16 rating (forbidden to audiences under 16 years old) "because it features scenes not suitable to the personality of minors."[14] Its first public screening took place in Rome on April 1, 1961, at the prestigious Barberini venue.

Reviews were mostly positive. The noted Filippo Sacchi, in the weekly magazine *Epoca*, praised the narrative structure ("The method of shedding light gradually on a murder through episodes relating to previous facts is not new. But, if anything, the way of putting it together is, indeed, new") and the director's "remarkable perspective sagacity and cinematic spirit."[15] *Cinema 60*'s Mino Argentieri praised the "noteworthy mastery of the expressive medium," the "directorial measure," and the "freedom of inventive," although he judged the script too schematic and hasty in the psychological traits.[16] The *Corriere d'Informazione* wrote: "Petri is clearly a narrator: the setting is felicitous ... and the psychological nuances are rendered with finesse."[17] Even the biased *Cinema nuovo* (the most political Italian film magazine of the era) acknowledged *L'assassino*'s unusual quality and its "not negligible narrative skill," despite questioning the film's effectiveness in its analysis of police brutality because of its "high-level psychological methods ... rather than effective physical abuse"[18]—a pointless notation, given the modifications imposed on the script.

The critic for *Il Giorno*, Morando Morandini, was one of the few who mentioned its censorship issues. Petri wrote him a long letter to thank him and to stress the difficulties his film had met:

> You see, dear Morandini, the film's weak points have not been irremediably made worse by the intervention on the part of [General Inspector Gianni] De Tommasi's men: those weak points have always been in the film. The most serious matter is that this time censorship has acted against the very law which—arbitrarily, in my opinion—it is meant to defend. You know that the legal reasons for a film to be tampered with are limited to two very generic categories: defense of morality and of the public order. *L'assassino* has been tampered for far more mysterious reasons, and to seek logic in the censors' conduct toward this film means to fully enter the Kafkaesque mood which you found in the author's intentions.[19]

The director went to Milan to present the film and met critic Tullio Kezich, who had heard wonders about him from their mutual friend, poet Raffaello Baldini, another member of Santarcangelo di Romagna's Circle of Judgment. The two struck up a friendship and spent a couple of days together. Later Kezich took inspiration from the meeting for his short story *L'uomo di sfiducia*, and Petri was upset about it, possibly feeling that his trust had been betrayed. As the critic recalled, "he had a sensibility like one flayed alive, and saw ambushes everywhere."[20]

With over 251 million *lire* grossed at the Italian box-office, *L'assassino* was a moderate commercial success, allowing Titanus to cover the costs and giving Petri the chance to mount his second film. As he commented, "It was a period of euphoria in Italian cinema. Some debuts, mine included, lit up Lombardo with enthusiasm, and he thought of producing other filmmakers' debuts."[21] Mastroianni too was very fond of it: "It's a delightful movie. I found a poster of it in Hollywood at Martin Scorsese's place, where every room is filled with Italian movie posters, and this filled me with emotion and pride."[22] A Milan-based publishing house, Zibetti, even published the original draft of the script by initiative of Petri's assistant Giorgio Trentin, without Petri being aware of it. The book included a chronicle of the shooting.

L'assassino was one of the two Italian films selected for competition at the 1961 Berlin International Film Festival (the other being Antonioni's *La notte*, also starring Mastroianni), and received critical praise. *Film Quarterly's* Cynthia Grenier wrote that it "revealed an intelligent, imaginative film talent, well worth watching."[23] It was released in West Germany in October 1962. The following year it came out in the U.K. (the BBFC classified it on September 30, 1963), uncut and with an X certificate, gaining a very favorable review in *The Guardian*. "Elio Petri is a name worth remembering ... he is a director with something to say and the technical ability to say it convincingly," the reviewer noted. "He handles a difficult dramatic situation with admirable skill, gradually unfolding a plausible comment on life that manages to be unpretentious and interesting.... Altogether it is a film of unexpected maturity."[24]

Following a limited release in December 1963, Petri's debut came out in France (as *L'assassin*) in July 1964. It surfaced in the United States in August 1965, in a dubbed and trimmed version only 83 minutes long, released by Manson Distributing Corporation under the lurid title *The Lady Killer of Rome*, following Mastroianni's rise to stardom overseas. "Today's most exciting star in a new and provocative role!" the tagline promised. It opened in New York in June 1966, distributed by Pan World Pictures, and earned a condescending panning in *The New York Times*, the review's most significant trait being its author's belief that the film be a comedy:

> *The Lady Killer of Rome* brings us the Marcello Mastroianni of six years ago, and that's too bad. The film ... shows the Italian star as a personable fellow, but nothing near the actor he has since become. Abetted by two pretty actresses, Micheline Presle and Cristina Gaioni, he goes through this routine comedy which occasionally achieves a peak of faint amusement, in frozen style. It's a sort of poor man's *Dolce Vita*: a no-goodnik has two mistresses and when one gets murdered, he's the suspect. There are platitudes worthy of an Italian Edgar Guest, about life and love, and that's it. The cameraman passes the time trying out his lenses in shots reminiscent of early German cinema. One minute you are looking way up at something, the next way down, and then at other perspectives that do not add up to lasting art. Of course, the real murderer is—but on second thought, does it really matter?[25]

The Dark Side of the Boom

Even though Petri himself labeled it as a "post–Antonionian" film because of its theme of incommunicability,[26] akin to such works as *L'avventura* and *La notte*, *L'assassino* presents itself as a murder mystery of sorts, starting with its very title. It is, once again, an investigation. To Petri, such a narrative approach was the perfect counterpart to modern life.

> Detection is a form of experience.... Today's society justifies an investigative model of life with its tendency to paranoia, since interpersonal relationships are based on the uncertainty of other people's purposes.[27]

The whodunit structure displays the director's love for American cinema, and for Alfred Hitchcock's films in particular. Alfredo Martelli is a "wrong man" like Manny Balestrero in Hitchcock's 1956 film, and just like in *The Wrong Man* the protagonist's arrest under an accusation which turns out to be wrong leads to an existentialist investigation. But whereas Hitchcock focused on fate, chance and the limits of human justice, here the misadventure leads the protagonist to an examination of conscience. Martelli puts into question his life, his relationships, his way of living. In this, *L'assassino* is not dissimilar from Damiano Damiani's *Il rossetto* (1960), in the way it uses a crime story for social analysis; Damiani would do the same in the form of an inverted story in *Il sicario* (1961), another dark apologue on the Boom. But Petri's film employs the tools of the crime genre with much more confidence than its peers, starting with a tight narrative that unfolds over the course of twenty-four hours.

The story begins at dawn, as Alfredo returns home after a night out and leaves his car at the garage. The elegant opening dolly shot establishes the protagonist's social status: he is impeccably dressed, drives a fancy car, addresses the gas station attendant with the air of sufficiency reserved for the lower classes, and when he goes up the stairs that lead to his luxurious apartment he recalls a lord of the castle. Once inside, he looks out of the window which reflects his own image. He watches the city from a privileged position and contemplates himself doing so, in an act of narcissistic self-gratification.

The camera frames Alfredo from a lower angle, as if to emphasize his prestige, while he carefully hangs his elegant jacket, puts on a jazz record, sniffs a rose as if to savor one last memory of the night he has spent presumably with a woman, and prepares his bath. He appears to be a man with a fully satisfying, exciting existence. Which, as we realize immediately via a phone call with his fiancée Nicoletta (Cristina Gaioni), is actually a double life, based on lies. This house of cards proves illusory, while the clues Petri has given us in the first sequence take on an ambiguous meaning. Mirrors, a recurrent presence in the early scenes, stress Alfredo's self-satisfaction at his own social position, but at the same time they hint at his split essence, the surface of success hiding the side that he wants to be forgotten.

The "investigation" of *L'assassino* focuses on two themes that will become a constant in Petri's body of work, namely neurosis and power. If the former turns up in the awakening of Alfredo's guilty conscience and in the revelation of his tormented relationship with his past, his acquaintances and his family, the latter is represented by the observation of the relationship between the common citizen and the authorities. Just like Josef K. in *The Trial*, Alfredo is arrested and taken away by the police, with no explanation whatsoever. The way police officials wander around his apartment, touching things and snooping in wardrobes, is doubly upsetting, not just for the way Petri underlines the uncomfortableness of the ordinary man versus authority, who is allowed to trespass the limits of good manners, but because the intruders' attention seems to be devoted to the symbols of Alfredo's wealth, pushing his guilt to come to the surface. "You should be calm, if you have a clear conscience," a policeman points out.

The waiting room at the police station is depicted as an ironic reversal of Alfredo's apartment, with cheap paintings, uncomfortable chairs, a large window overlooking a squalid wall, and a mirror to which he is once again irresistibly attracted, not knowing that it is actually a two-way one, behind which the police are observing him. And whereas Martelli sells fakes, behind the commissioner's desk one can glimpse a reproduction of a painting by Giorgio Morandi.

The relationship between Alfredo and Commissioner Palumbo becomes a psychoanalytic one from the very first shot that encompasses both men. The commissioner is reflected in the two-way mirror behind which he is observing Alfredo, a carefully composed image which shows Petri's visual flair. Palumbo's questioning of the suspect is staged like a session of psychoanalysis, with the patient sitting and talking and the older policeman luring him into opening himself up. "We need to really understand who you are," the commissioner points out.

Little by little, Palumbo's questions proceed to undress Martelli of his elaborate mask and disguise by showing his hidden side and questioning his outward certainties. As Petri pointed out, his story was imbued with an ingredient unknown to existentialist writers—irony, and very biting indeed. Unlike the gray bank cashier Josef K., Alfredo is a son of the Boom, an ex-junk dealer who has climbed the ladder of success. As such, he is also a character molded from the core of the *commedia all'italiana*, an amiable rogue not dissimilar to, say, Vittorio Gassman in *Il sorpasso* (1962, Dino Risi) or certain types played by Alberto Sordi. He is arrogant with inferiors and servile with authority, and boasts about his business ("Do you know how much I can lose in one hour? I can lose millions...") to stress his belonging to the upper class. But underneath, he is a fake, and his proletarian manners, Roman accent, and petty cunningness turn up here and there beneath the accurate travesty.

Alfredo's claims to have attended the CSC to become an actor underline his habit of playing a part. Not only is he unscrupulous in his business, receiving cheap stolen furniture which he resells at high prices, but he also poses as an accountant to make his mother happy, even though he has no degree. He is duplicitous and exploitative, too. He has no qualms in betraying his best friend's trust and seducing his wife, and similarly abandons Adalgisa for a younger and richer woman. He points out that he never goes to bed with maids, yet he maliciously persuades the naïve Rosetta to strip off in front of an acquaintance who pretends to be a doctor, just to show off his power. Even his wealth is illusory, as he owed a great deal of money to the victim.

In an intriguing narrative choice, Petri juxtaposes two timelines, one objective (the twenty-four-hour span of Alfredo's incarceration) and one subjective (the flashes from his past). The flashbacks depicting Alfredo's real essence are not organized chronologically and jump back and forth in time, putting together pieces of Martelli's life as if in a puzzle. Each digression covers a side of his personality, but Petri is careful not to slip into a didactic or moralistic tone. As Sacchi noted, the flashbacks are characterized by their "indifference and ironically careless tone,"[28] hinting only indirectly at the protagonist's moral faults.

Overall, *L'assassino* already displays Petri's trademark eclecticism, and his "preoccupation with a cinema that must be politically engaged and aesthetically appealing."[29] Stylistically, the movie has a very different pacing than the typical Italian films. The scenes between Palumbo and Martelli are mostly developed in long takes, with Petri allowing the actors to move in the room as if on a stage and employing depth of field to underline the characters' reactions. Elsewhere in the film, there are dynamic cuts (as in Alfredo's arrival at the police station) or sudden fades-to-black introducing the flashbacks that punctuate the story, often told in a disjointed, nervous way which editor Ruggero Mastroianni compared to Godard's *À bout de souffle* (1960), although he claimed that he and the director hadn't seen it[30] (Godard's film opened in Italy in September 1960). It was this unusual choice that caused some remarks about the "somewhat raw, unfinished tone."[31]

L'assassino: **Alfredo (Marcello Mastroianni) maliciously persuades the naïve maid Rosetta (Giovanna Gagliardo) to be visited by an acquaintance who pretends to be a doctor.**

Petri's penchant for elaborate camera movements, a trait inherited from De Santis, is already in evidence. The scene of Martelli's interrogation on the terrace of Adalgisa's resort is an example, with the camera drawing tense prospective lines and enhancing background objects and surfaces. Carlo Di Palma rejected Petri's idea to shoot several sequences in 16mm,[32] but the director's taste for experimenting resulted in a daring, virtuoso three-minute long take which jumps in time from the past to the present and back. It starts in Adalgisa's bedroom, where she complains to Alfredo about his selfishness, before moving to the next room. Then a visitor arrives, and as the woman receives him, Alfredo leaves the room and goes to the bedroom, takes off his coat and lies on the bed. The camera pans right to reveal Palumbo, sitting in the same room. With a 360-degree turn, the camera returns to the nearby room, where the commissioner keeps questioning Martelli. Then it pans again leftward, following the commissioner and to the bedroom. Palumbo disappears and we are back on the night of the murder. Alfredo is joined by Adalgisa. They keep discussing and eventually start making out on the bed. This remarkable sequence shot is also notable for giving away the main clue for spotting the murderer. As Montaldo recalled, "it took us a whole day to shoot that scene, and Elio, always a big *capoccione*, was not willing to renounce these bizarre and amazing tricks for anything in the world. He was very careful about each and every detail."[33]

Besides the theme of the investigation, here adapted to the mystery genre, Petri's Neorealist roots can be seen in the flashback of Alfredo's youth. It depicts a cruel joke he played on his elderly anti–Fascist grandfather (an idea possibly coming from Guerra) in a bucolic scenario, a small country village and a river where the old man is fishing while Fascist squads are marching on a bridge nearby. Similarly, the minor characters retain a realistic regional quality, such as the bedridden junk dealer (who lives surrounded by antiques, mannequins, and assorted bric-a-brac), the two informers, or Rosetta the maid. The attention to realist setting is also noticeable in Alfredo's visit to the junk dealer, in a shack on a hill overlooking the city, a vision of the same barren and desolate outskirts which can be seen in many Italian films of the previous decade.

The influence of Fellini's cinema imbues the scene in which Alfredo's mother, a simple woman from the countryside, visits him. Instead of taking her to his home, Alfredo treats her to lunch at a restaurant by the sea where they are the only customers. The episode is patterned upon a similar one in *La dolce vita* (where it is the protagonist's father who comes to town, and his son takes him to a night club). But Petri develops the scene with a sober poetic tone, avoiding slipping into sentimentality. At the restaurant, Alfredo doesn't talk, she doesn't eat, he feigns consideration by offering to order expensive lobster, she sits sad and disappointed by her son's detached behavior. Then they stand on the shore, at twilight. "Have you seen, Alfredo? It's already night," she says.

Petri's attempt to get past Neorealism transpires in Alfredo's first meeting with Nicoletta, which is patently influenced by Antonioni's symbolic use of locations. It takes place in the museum of Roman ships in Nemi, outside Rome, destroyed by fire in 1944 during a bombing, which Alfredo, Adalgisa and Nicoletta are visiting. The huge and deserted museum echoes the ruinous state of Alfredo and Adalgisa's relationship, and soon she leaves, giving way to the other woman in Alfredo's life. Likewise, the episode of the

L'assassino: **Alfredo (Marcello Mastroianni) and his elderly mother (Lucia Raggi).**

suicidal man, shot at the Via Olimpica, makes good use of modern urban landscapes, amid tunnels, overbridges, and motorways.

On the other hand, the scenes featuring the two police informers, with their bold change in style, display Petri's predilection for the grotesque, as well as the film's blending of different acting styles. Compared with Mastroianni's effortless performance, and Randone's consummate theatrical skills made of small gestures and nuances, Ucci and Panelli—one tall and one short, both with strong dialectal accents and almost comical moves—seem to have come out of *Pinocchio*, for they recall the Fox and the Cat in Carlo Collodi's novel. They exchange glances and lines of dialogue, follow the protagonist in every corner of the ugly, filthy cell, whisper in his ear, take turns in their attempt to extract a confession from him. The grotesque is a matter of communication, a way to make the discourse more popular, as the director will acknowledge in *Indagine*. That is also the case with the scene in which Alfredo's acquaintances expose his faults, lies and petty crimes before an unseen interviewer, addressing themselves directly to the camera. It is the fruit of Martelli's feverish imagination, in which his guilty conscience is let loose.

As a *connoisseur* of detective stories, Petri doesn't treat the genre as a mere pretext, but immerses himself into its style and clichés, something which he will do again over the course of his career when dealing with crime stories, science fiction or Gothic. The viewer is left groping in the dark about the nature of Alfredo's alleged crime just as long as the suspect himself, and over the course of the film one is uncertain whether he is innocent or guilty. Clues and red herrings are carefully placed every now and then, and as Alfredo undergoes a series of interrogations in the police station, we briefly glimpse other suspects that turned up elsewhere in the story, one of whom will turn out to be the real murderer. In a clever move on Petri's side, the culprit's identity is hinted at in an oblique way before the commissioner's final explanation.

But the film does away also with the expected humanization of the police force. Unlike *Un maledetto imbroglio*, the audience is never asked to sympathize with Palumbo or his acolytes. The inherent hardheartedness at the core of police investigation, conducted on everyone as if they were the guilty party, presumably upset the censors the most. Such a grim depiction retains an outstanding power, precisely because of the unusual accuracy with which police procedural details are sketched, even after the tampering on the part of the censors.

As Petri pointed out, "those were the years of the Boom, of the easy and quick enrichments, and my protagonist was a man of proletarian origins who abandons every moral scruple for social advancement."[34] Alfredo's job as an antique dealer allows him to climb the social ladder and get in touch with the upper class. But the film displays an unusual acuteness in the portrayal of Adalgisa's character. She is a bourgeois woman who has managed to detach herself from her husband and become economically independent. "In those years, middle-class women in Italy started to enter the phase of the search for autonomy, but always within the *milieu* of the bourgeois experience,"[35] the director explained. But in a patriarchal society, a lonely, independent woman is a designated victim, and to the eyes of many her death represents a symbolic punishment.

Ultimately, Martelli's neurosis is in equal parts the result of his lack of political and social conscience and the fruit of his own Catholic roots. The grandson of an anti–Fascist, Alfredo claims he is disappointed by politics and is no longer registered with the PCI when speaking with the junk dealers (whom originally Petri had characterized as ex-factory workers forced to change jobs to survive). In fact, he has realized that being apolitical is the safest way. But he cannot escape his Catholic education. When he and Adalgisa see a man attempting suicide by throwing himself under a passing truck, he dismisses him as a drunk and mistakes his desperation for an act. In fact, Petri explained, Alfredo "cannot believe that someone can commit suicide, he has his Catholic conscience; he is fleeing the fact that there may be someone who wants to die."[36] As played by Mac Ronay, the man represents the dark side of the economic Boom, which people like Alfredo don't want to see. Silent and wide-eyed, he walks away like a ghost in the night. Soon, we'll find out he has thrown himself off a bridge.

Moreover, Alfredo is ashamed of his family. In a way, Palumbo becomes to him a surrogate of the absent father figure, who in the end will forgive the son: "He's a good boy," he patronizingly tells the press. By extension, he is also the Father par excellence, a severe but loving deity who has the authority to punish but ultimately absolves, because "the subject-authority relationship is a love relationship."[37] Petri will reprise and expand the theme in *Indagine*.

In underlining the similitude between the earthly and spiritual authorities in their influence and manipulation of the individual subject, Petri shows that the consequences are also similar. Like confession, the experience in jail seems to have drained Alfredo completely. On the dawn of the following day, he is so distraught that, like Josef K., he passively accepts whatever destiny may be in store for him; when he is released from his burden (he is asked to sign a register and told he is free) he is incredulous. But the ordeal has (apparently) awakened Alfredo's sensibility and made him more human. Once released, he meets another suspect, a homeless man who presumably has been submitted to the same police routine as he was, and he gives him some money as a gesture of pity. Later, he bursts out with an unstoppable cry.

The ending displays Petri's uncompromising political message. Palumbo's final judgment about Martelli to the press sounds paradoxical. Even though he is an innocent man as far as the law is concerned, the antique dealer is nevertheless morally guilty. And his atonement turns out to have been illusory. His soul-searching is automatic and merely superficial. Just like Meursault in Camus's novel, he is incapable of feelings.

This is evident in the film's epilogue, a late addition to the story which replaces the original and somewhat reassuring happy ending. In Petri and Guerra's outline, the protagonist returns home after his misadventure. His housemates come out of their flats and greet him. In his apartment he finds his fiancée expecting him. He asks her to marry him. "Her eyes were the first true heartening thing I saw that day, for they didn't make me feel alone," he concludes.

In the film, Alfredo's release from the police station and his climactic emotional outburst are followed by a coda set one year later. Martelli has resumed his old habits. He has a clandestine affair with Nicoletta, who is now married, and he hasn't lost his passion for fast and expensive cars. On the phone with the car dealer, attempting to profit off his reputation for a discount on the price, he quips: "Do you know who you are talking to? The lady killer!"

The moral catharsis doesn't happen and Martelli is ultimately guilty of "a more secret and uninterrupted guilt toward the next man," for, as Petri pointed out, he "doesn't have the moral principles he mimics anymore, just like the society in which he lives and which created him."[38]

THREE

Numbered Days

I giorni contati *(1962) and*
Nudi per vivere *(1964)*

A Plumber's Tale

In August 1961 Petri was already at work on his sophomore film, which he would describe as "a protest against the obsession of modern life: everyone runs, they rush, they are in a hurry, a hurry to get there ... but to reach what? A sad old age full of regrets for what has been sacrificed and lost."[1]

Cesare Conversi, a 53-year-old Roman plumber, feels lonely and useless after his wife's untimely passing. One day on a streetcar he witnesses the death by heart attack of another passenger who was about his age. The episode upsets Cesare deeply, and he becomes obsessed with the thought that his days are numbered. He leaves his job and decides to make up for lost time. He goes to airports, bath establishments and art exhibitions, which he never visited before. He sets out in search of affection and childhood memories: he meets with an old flame and takes a trip to the little village where he was born. But any attempt to embrace his vanished youth turns out a failure.

Not receiving any salary, Cesare soon runs out of money after lending a big sum to a young neighbor so that she wouldn't become a prostitute (she uses the money to buy a fancy wig instead). He becomes acquainted with Vinicio, a seedy character of the small Roman underworld who involves him in a grisly scam: a man will break Cesare's arm with a brick so as to simulate a car accident and they will collect the insurance money. But Cesare backs out at the last minute. Eventually he returns to work. One evening, Cesare is dozing off on a trip back home by streetcar. He is shaken by the controller, but does not answer...

Petri and Tonino Guerra had written the story for *I giorni contati* before *L'assassino*, but the project was not commercial enough for producers. There is no doubt the story touched intimate autobiographical chords with the director. As he recalled in one of his last letters to Giuseppe De Santis,

> I used to see my father coming home and in his weariness there was no joy. His face and limbs displayed only fatigue; slivers of tin had pierced his hands, his face was marked with burns, his skin had changed color. In a word, he bore no sign nor hope of redemption. There could be none. He was, in the classic sense, the embodiment of the worker.[2]

At first Amedeo Nazzari wanted to produce the film and star in it, but he changed his mind. Then Franco Cristaldi's Vides got involved but eventually sold the project to Titanus, who agreed to produce it on a small budget. In July 1961, during a convention labeled "Per un nuovo corso del cinema italiano" (For a new course of Italian cinema), Goffredo Lombardo announced his plan to focus on the production of artistically valuable and auteurist films, aiming at establishing his company as the most prestigious in the Italian industry, taking the place that in the previous decades had been that of Riccardo Gualino's Lux Film.

Lombardo's intention was also to promote a wave of films in the style of the French *Nouvelle Vague*, namely low-cost projects targeted to a selected home audience and to export as well. *I giorni contati* was one of several titles produced by Titanus-Metro, a joint venture between Lombardo's company (owning 51 percent of the shares) and Metro-Goldwyn-Mayer. Founded on May 10, 1961, with an initial capital of 30 million *lire*, Titanus-Metro intended to make films destined to the U.S. market. The deal was signed by MGM's representative Benjamin Melniker.

Petri developed the script for *I giorni contati* with Guerra and his old friend, actor and screenwriter Carlo Romano (who by then had become one of Italy's most famous voice actors) and completed a 203-page draft in June 1961. The commission that preliminarily examined the script didn't have any objection, save a notation on a brief scene by the river's edge involving Cesare and a prostitute, from which it is inferred that the man is impotent.

I giorni contati cost 185 million *lire* against an estimated budget of 203 million. Petri was paid 9,280,500 *lire* for directing. Guerra got 1,030,000 *lire* for the story, and 2,163,000 for the script (Romano got 2 million). Official papers did not list Petri as author of the story nor the script but included theater critic and scriptwriter Giorgio Prosperi, whose name is not featured in the credits, and who was paid 927,000 *lire*. Prosperi worked, often uncredited, on many important films including *Sodoma e Gomorra* (1962, Robert Aldrich), which would prove Lombardo's most hazardous bet. Petri himself was one of several writers involved in scripting the costly epic (as proven by a contract with Titanus dated 23 September 1960[3]), the others being Tonino Guerra, Ugo Guerra, Sandro Continenza, Pasquale Festa Campanile, Massimo Franciosa, and Prosperi. No one was credited on *Sodoma e Gomorra* except for Prosperi and Hugo Butler, who took care of the English language version, and Petri was probably more than happy with that.

For *I giorni contati*, the director surrounded himself with young and talented people. The cinematographer was 32-year-old Ennio Guarnieri, while the music score was entrusted to Ivan Vandor. Born in Hungary in 1932, Vandor had moved to Rome at an early age in 1938, and soon showed extraordinary musical qualities. Already an accomplished jazz saxophonist at sixteen, he had become one of the main attractions in the post-war Roman musical world and was the founder of the Roman New Orleans Jazz Band. In 1961 he had been awarded the first prize at an International Composers' Competition by SIMC (Italian Society of Contemporary Composition). Renzo Vespignani created the etchings for the opening credits.

The cast featured little-known names, except for Paolo Ferrari (as Vinicio) and Vittorio Caprioli (as an art merchant). Lando Buzzanca, then virtually unknown, played Cesare's son and was dubbed with a Roman accent. For the choice of the protagonist, an ordinary middle-aged man, Petri suggested three names to Lombardo: Totò, Jean Gabin, and Salvo Randone. In the early 1960s, even though he had been almost blind for several years, Totò was busier than ever. The bulk of his filmography consisted of quickly made comedies which relied mostly on his improvisational skills, sometimes with the great Neapolitan thesp acting as a bait and switch for the audience. But Totò was finally starting to gain a belated critical respect, after such films as Vittorio De Sica's *L'oro di Napoli* (1954) and Monicelli's *Risate di gioia*, and he would be hailed as a great dramatic actor after Pier Paolo Pasolini's *Uccellacci e uccellini* (1966). As Petri explained, "I thought of Totò not just because I saw him as fit for the role, but because Totò has practically been my master in aesthetics."[4] As a kid, Petri used to gain some money as a claque member in Roman theaters (claque being those audience members paid to clap, laugh and shout for encores during the shows), and had seen seven times the acclaimed musical show *Che ti sei messo in testa?* starring Totò and Anna Magnani, which opened in February 1944, while Rome was still occupied by the Nazis. Petri's film would have been Totò's first out-and-out dramatic role, but the comedian was too expensive for Lombardo. Ditto for Jean Gabin, who nonetheless would have brought a French participation to the project. As he did with *L'assassino*, the producer chose Randone, by far the cheapest of the trio. *I giorni contati* would be the Sicilian actor's only leading role in a movie and he was paid about 6,500,000 *lire*. On the set Petri would coddle his star, providing him his early morning breakfast of hot scarlet loaves and the "medicine"—that is, whisky—which Randone used to sip before his first scene of the day, accompanied with several pills to cure his hypochondria.[5]

I giorni contati was submitted to the rating board on January 19, 1962, and received the screening certificate on February 6. The board gave it a V.M.16 rating because of some scenes judged unsuitable for minors. It also demanded a couple of minor trimmings, namely that the words "mignotta" (whore) and "stronzo" (asshole) be eliminated in the scene in which Cesare is about to have his arm broken. The scene with the prostitute noticed by the preventive board remained in the film.

All in all, it was minimal tampering compared to what *L'assassino* had undergone. But Titanus kept the film shelved for a while. Petri was well determined to screen *I giorni contati* to as many people he could, outside the proper context of ordinary theatrical distribution. He knew that his film could play better to small, selected audiences who could understand the drama of Randone's character better. A news article reported: "With the three reels of his new film, *I giorni contati*, a portable projector and a movie operator, every morning Elio Petri goes around in factories and penitentiaries, where he shows his movie to workers, inmates and students."[6]

Meanwhile, there was room for more than just cinema in the director's heart. A few years earlier he had fallen for Georges and Ruta Sadoul's stepchild, French journalist Yvonne Baby, who had come to Rome in 1959 to write a piece on Cinecittà for *Le Monde*.[7] After this unfortunate idyll, Petri met the woman who would become his wife, Paola Pegoraro, the daughter of producer Lorenzo Pegoraro. "What struck me about him was his passion for politics, his passion for cinema, his passion for modern art, his passion for jazz," she would say. "In a word, his passion."[8]

Elio and Paola married on March 24, 1962. Marcello Mastroianni was the groom's best man. *I giorni contati* was to be screened a few days later in competition at the Mar del Plata Film Festival, in Argentina, and the newlyweds took advantage of it for their honeymoon, "corporate holiday-style, with a large party of filmmakers, scriptwriters, actors, critics," as Paola later described it.[9] Much to everyone's surprise, *I giorni contati* won the First Prize, beating Truffaut's *Jules et Jim* which got the award for Best

Salvo Randone (left) and Elio Petri on the set of *I giorni contati*.

Direction.[10] It was not just a wedding gift, but an auspicious sign as well, just a few days before its official release. The film finally opened on April 5, 1962, at the Palazzo Cinema in Genoa.

The critics hailed it almost unanimously. "Elio Petri is one of those young directors who have something to say," wrote *Cinema 60*. "In *L'assassino* Petri's mastery of the narrative technique was something more than the correct application of grammatical and syntactic rules: it was already style, inventiveness, command of the medium and its expressive instruments as well. These qualities shine even more in *I giorni contati* and are best used to depict a dense and problematic matter."[11] The newly founded bi-monthly *Cinema Domani* devoted ample room to the film, emphasizing how it "faces unseen and terrible aspects of the dehumanizing reality in today's world" and pairing it with *Jules et Jim* and *L'eclisse* as examples of the "new perspectives" in contemporary filmmaking, characterized by a "subversive charge … in the search for human tenderness which is … at the basis of our way of living—or surviving."[12] The journal published long excerpts from the screenplay, introduced by a note penned by Petri, who explained that "a movie, to me, is still a narrative gesture and therefore a way to communicate an idea to others; it is a form of knowledge of the world."[13] The more politicized *Cinema nuovo* compared the alienated plumber of Petri's film to Kafka's Josef K. and to the protagonist of Antonioni's *Il grido* (1957), praising the effective depiction of a country "that still lives as if during Fascism."[14]

The fact that Titanus was unsure of how to promote *I giorni contati* is made evident by the Italian poster. While conveying the film's dark edge with the stylized image of an hourglass seemingly sucking down in its lower empty half the protagonist, who is stuck in the middle, it is characterized by a caricaturish, comic book-like trait. The man is smiling and grabs a semi-naked young woman's ankle with his right hand and a chicken with his left. Then there are poker cards, a wine bottle, a bed, a car, a seaside view, a chirping bird, the sun. In retrospect, it seems the work of someone who is well aware of the story's downbeat nature but is camouflaging it as a comedy of sorts.

It didn't work. With slightly more than 52 million *lire* grossed, *I giorni contati* was an undisputed flop. Who would want to see a movie with no famous stars and centered on a middle aged, ordinary worker? Who would want to see a movie whose each and every frame hinted at the inescapable presence of death in every act of our daily life, in the enthusiastic days that surrounded the Italian economic renaissance? Moreover, despite the deal with Metro, it apparently had a very limited U.S. release (as *Days are Numbered*) and little circulation abroad.[15] A similar fate awaited the other five films produced by Titanus-Metro in 1962, namely Valerio Zurlini's *Cronaca familiare*, Franco Rossi's *Smog*, Folco Quilici's *Ti-Koyo e il suo pescecane*, Damiano Damiani's *L'isola di Arturo* and Nanni

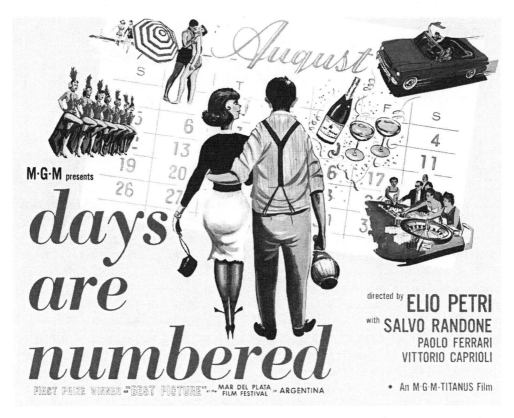

I giorni contati **had a limited U.S. release as** *Days Are Numbered.*

Loy's *Le quattro giornate di Napoli*. At best, they merely surfaced in a few arthouse the-aters overseas.

According to some,[16] the negative outcome of the deal with Metro had a part in Titanus's bankruptcy, in addition to the unfortunate commercial results of a couple of big-budget pictures which did not cover production costs, namely *Sodoma e Gomorra* and *Il gattopardo* (1963). In March 1963, Goffredo Lombardo announced that Titanus would stop producing films for at least a couple of years, focusing only on distribution. But it would be a virtually definitive halt instead.

"We are dead and all goes on as before..."

Whereas Alfredo Martelli was a typical product of the Boom, outwardly successful but gripped by an existential malaise, Cesare Conversi is the first of Petri's alienated pro-tagonists. A plumber who worked since the age of thirteen, at fifty-three Cesare already considers himself an old man, and one day he comes across the notion that he might die at any moment. All of a sudden, life appears to him as a useless routine spent waiting for the moment of departure.

It has been noted that the theme of *I giorni contati* bears resemblances to Vittorio De Sica's *Umberto D.* (1952), Ingmar Bergman's *Smultronstället* (a.k.a. *Wild Strawberries*, 1957) and Akira Kurosawa's *Ikiru* (1952). Petri loved *Umberto D.*, which however lacked *I giorni contati*'s social and political issues, but he wasn't particularly fond of Bergman's work (in the early 1970s, speaking with Jean A. Gili, he dismissed it as "kitsch, at least partly"[17]). Still, he acknowledged the influence:

> Without wanting to make comparisons, *Umberto D.* is a better film, but certainly *Wild Straw-berries* is richer: there's the idea of showing how a man lives with his time; on the contrary, in *Umberto D.* there's an old man who, because of his age, is now out of his time. There is a huge difference.[18]

Bergman's film opens with a gloomy nightmare which gives the egotistical professor Borg a sense of his impending end, and it is centered on the protagonist's almost mystical journey in his own past, to learn the mistakes he has made and atone. *I giorni contati* also opens with an omen, not in form of a dream but as a sketch of ordinary daily life. Cesare's quest for lost time is instead an obtuse rebellion to his social and historic condition, to "the division that separates economic time from existential time."[19] Hence, the medita-tion on old age leads to quite different territories from Bergman and De Sica's films. On the other hand, *Ikiru* is much closer to *I giorni contati* in the depiction of a man without qualities who finds in the awareness of death a means to redeem a colorless existence. The connection is merely casual, however, for Kurosawa's masterpiece was never released the-atrically in Italy and was aired on television only in the late 1980s.

Wild Strawberries ends with an affirmation of life, and *Ikiru* accompanies his protag-onist to an inner serenity exemplified by the unforgettable swing scene. Petri, a staunch materialist and a non-believer, is much more pessimistic, and his film focuses on the rela-tion between normality and abnormality, which will become one of the central themes in his cinema.

> Man lives, in his interiority, amid the spatter and debris of a continuous breaking of what's old; but he is protected by the armor of normalcy which the laws of productivity keep imposing on

him, or which he keeps imposing on himself. Hence, his status of madness in normalcy. Normalcy is a notion coming from the Judeo-Christian tradition which progress picked up ... and turned into a productive structure. But it is the source of malaise, illness, indifference, hysteria, schizophrenia. Just like the atom was split, man too is split. We live armor-clad and with the incessant and growing desire of releasing ourselves from our armor.[20]

Cesare's decision to stop working is met with incredulity, because it goes against normalcy and therefore against Cesare's own role in society. But each and every attempt at transgression he makes is rebuked by the invisible boundaries erected by society itself, be they moral, religious, juridical, economic.

Article 1 of the Italian Constitution defines Italy as "a democratic Republic funded on labor." But Cesare realizes that an entire life of labor has deprived him of many, many things. Now it is too late to make up for wasted time, and his attempts to discover, savor, or resume all the things he left behind over the years only make his situation harder to bear. The more of freedom he savors, the more of life he tastes, the more he feels void and lonely. Not only are his days numbered, but he is running out of money too. In the end, he cannot but conclude that "work doesn't make you think, in fact it chases thoughts away."

Cesare's return to work is a barely camouflaged defeat. He has to kneel down again, figuratively and literally, to fix other people's toilets, and now he is aware of the inescapability of his condition. The outside world is marveling at space enterprises, and near the end of the film a newspaper's front page tells of Russian astronaut Titov's return to Earth (Petri himself can be glimpsed in a blink-and-you'll-miss-it cameo as a man passing in front of the camera while Cesare is reading the newspaper). But, as the plumber bitterly quips while flushing a toilet, "This is my spaceship." In the rigidly hierarchical capitalist society those like Cesare are at the bottom of the pile and have no chance to escape their condition until they die. The film ends with a streetcar disappearing in the night with a deceased man on it, a poignant symbolic image which is at the core of Petri's cinema.

From the opening credits accompanied by Vespignani's etchings, *I giorni contati* is imbued with a tangible metaphysical anguish. Everything we do, we do it to exclude the thought of our mortality from our brains. Otherwise, life would be unbearable. Cesare's awareness starts when he actually witnesses the event of death—a guy like him, an ordinary middle-aged man, passing away unnoticed amid an indifferent crowd. From then on, every single thing reminds him of death and its ineluctability. He visits a cemetery and notices a gravestone of a man born the same day as him. He goes to see a doctor and foolishly asks him whether it is possible to forecast when he will die ("Did you take me for a fortune teller?" is the reply). While lying on his bed to rest he mimics the pose of a deceased person, his hands resting on his chest. On the street, he sees a man taking a horse to the slaughterhouse. One day at the beach his friends mistakenly believe he has drowned. "The one that should have died is alive!" someone says when he shows up. In the following scene, the plumber and his friends are sitting in a park. Around them there are children playing and couples making out, and everyone seems serene and happy. Cesare's dread comes out in an anguished speech:

Imagine! ... Had I really drowned.... More, imagine the three of us—we are dead. Look! Look! Look! You see? You see the people? The people have fun, all of them. They all have fun. We are dead and all goes on as before, without us!

Even though devoid of the explicit didactic quality of the director's later works, *I giorni contati* is a strongly political film, and pervaded by "a healthy melancholic vein, and a lively sense of humor"[21] which prevents it from falling into self-satisfied existential ruminations.

For one thing, Petri sharply defines the social context in which Cesare is caught. In one of the film's most amusing bits, he boasts to a boy about his job: "I'm a plumber. I'm a solderer, my friend.... A good trade! What do you think! You play around with the blowtorch! Pipes break down in house and then everyone's calling for you. Rich, poor, film stars, Ministers, Cardinals, you go in everyone's home!" But as a man of the working class, he is kept at a distance by the middle class he is serving.

In a scene brimming with pungent irony, Cesare enters an art museum on a whim, hoping that the experience will enhance him culturally. Inside, he is lost. He eyes the paintings with perplexity, unable to understand their artistic value. He chats with an art dealer and struggles to test his own taste for art. But the paintings he likes are dismissed by the other man with a mere gesture or a grimace.

> "It's beautiful, this one, eh!"
> "No."
> "Why not? Then how come I like it?"
> "Simply because *you* like it. What work do you do?"
> "What has that got to do with it? I'm a plumber."
> "So, you're a plumber. To each his craft."

The art dealer proceeds to give him a quick, patronizing lesson on life and art. He dismisses Cesare's neurosis ("See, yours is a modern problem. You're, without even knowing it, an existentialist"), depriving it of its political core. He invites him to his home to show him the works of an informal artist, which he says are much more interesting than the ones in the museum. But we soon find out that the true reason for the invitation is that the toilet needs to be fixed.

The sequence is witty in remarking on the distance between the bourgeoisie and the working class, with the former exploiting the latter. It also includes a stab at contemporary art. The informal artist's works are supposed to emphasize social issues. "You don't have to understand, just watch," the art dealer advises Cesare. But to the plumber (and to the viewer as well) those paintings seem little more than chaotic blots of ink on canvas. Cesare walks past the artist, who is painting white zebra-like lines on a black canvas. They look exactly like the street signs Cesare's friend Amilcare paints for a living.

Petri's sarcastic depiction of informal art relates to the polemic that had heated the Roman artistic world between figuratives and abstractionists, and it also stresses a key issue in the director's vision. Art, and cinema in particular, must convey worthwhile messages in a form to which anyone can relate. They must not be detached from popular culture, whereas the informal painter's works show the distance between artists and the people they are supposed to talk to.

It is not the film's only reference to the contemporary cultural world. In the opening scene, the dead man's face on the bus is covered with a newspaper, and a title in plain sight says: "Come Pasolini concilia cinema e letteratura" (How Pasolini merges cinema and literature). Petri's discourse touches some themes akin to Pasolini's work, such as the look at the sub proletarian world and the ongoing mutation that Italy was implacably undergoing.

Death and the Eternal City

Narratively and formally, *I giorni contati* is a step forward from *L'assassino*. There is no real plot to speak of, just a series of events, encounters, and brief scenes that accompany Cesare's parable, with an admirably free approach to storytelling. Petri often employs a hand-held camera in the outdoor scenes, shot in the luminous summer and slightly overexposed, in an attempt to retain the same immediacy as the *Nouvelle Vague* films. "The excessive brightness which in some scenes hits the lens and annoyingly hits the protagonist's eyes, even forcing him to protect them with his hand, aims to be an expression of a deeper discomfort with life and existential uncertainty."[22] Similarly, the off-center close-ups, which reject standard frame compositions, suggest a blurred, uncertain state of mind, a subjective feeling of dread and anguish which the audience grasps as well.

The director acknowledged the influence of contemporaneous French filmmakers, albeit with a polemic sting in the tail:

> The *Nouvelle Vague* helped us … to free ourselves from the camera complex. It broke many patterns and revealed their fragile staleness. In this sense, Resnais and Godard especially were extremely important. But their living in the myth of themselves, filming in the myth and wrapping themselves with literature is not a teaching. Rossellini was the first to make films with an advanced language, well before his French disciples.[23]

Many scenes are shot in long takes, with very few cuts interrupting the flow of the action, while others display a nervous pacing, with Ruggero Mastroianni's editing giving the film a syncopated rhythm. It stresses the director's attempt to "break the schemes … without using a pre-fabricated pattern. The old rules of moviemaking are wearing thin, especially because, like every form of schematism, they restrained the boost to invention. But trying to dictate new rules, or anti-rules, at all costs, means going back to square one."[24]

For instance, the sequence where Vinicio and his accomplices prepare to break Cesare's arm in a squalid basement comes as an unexpected change of pace. The man who has to perform the job, the "mazzolatore" (enforcer) arrives with a big smile on his face and starts giving Cesare instructions. He is a hulking Neapolitan and speaks in a mixture of Italian and dialect. Vinicio describes him as "very precise, like a surgeon." Cesare has to take off his jacket, kneel down and put his arm on a pair of bricks. Then they wrap his arm with a bandage. Vinicio keeps talking to Cesare, to distract him, while Cesare nervously looks around as the "mazzolatore" has disappeared from his field of vision. The enforcer moves like a predator, circling around his prey and then abruptly moving forward to strike the blow with a heavy iron. The sequence is almost unbearable for its tension and displays Petri's mastering of suspense, for until the very last moment we don't know what is going to happen to Cesare.

The film's style emphasizes its choice of locations, for there isn't a single scene shot in studio. Rome is a silent character throughout the story, a world which the protagonist explores as if he was seeing it for the first time. Early on in the film, Cesare pays a night visit to Amilcare, and a breathtaking high-angle crane shot onwards follows him as he walks past the Colosseum to meet his friend. Rome at night looks like a ghost city, and Guarnieri's black-and-white cinematography depicts the monumental remains as distant observers of the mortals' daily life struggle. The meetings between Cesare and Amilcare take place near imposing locations such as the Verano monumental cemetery or the Esquilino Obelisk, while the plumber and the prostitute seek intimacy at the Monte Testaccio, the "monte dei cocci" (shards mountain), a man-made hill made with smashed clay urns. It is yet another remnant of a distant past (the hill was originally a dumpsite in Ancient Rome for oil jars), another reminder of man's transient passage on this earth.

But there is another Rome, which Cesare is compelled to discover. A chaotic, ebullient city, the one he glimpses every day from the windows of the streetcar that takes him to work. Following a sudden impulse, he jumps on a kid's motorbike and follows a firemen's truck driving at full speed across town. The sweeping camera car sequence that follows, with several motorbikes following the truck, literally unveils a new world to his eyes, and to the viewer's as well. The firemen reach the place of the alleged fire, which turns out to be a series of bonfires lit as a gesture of protest by the inhabitants of the Borgata Gordiani. One of the poorest suburbs in Rome, it was created by Mussolini in 1928 as part of a housing program which involved the demolition of many houses in the center. Their inhabitants were forcibly moved to the new suburb, which soon became a ghetto of sorts, a symbol of marginality and an example of the hiatus between the social classes.

Borgata Gordiani hosted about 5,000 people living in decrepit and insalubrious huts, without running water, electricity, or toilets. Pasolini described it at length in his works, namely the 1955 novel *Ragazzi di vita* and his 1961 debut feature film *Accattone*. In *I giorni contati*, the inhabitants are protesting because of an invasion of ticks, and the scene is filmed in a documentary-like manner, with plenty of hand-held camera shots, but the effect is almost apocalyptic. In the harsh, overexposed light of a bright summer day, the Borgata looks like a hellish netherworld, amid smoke and the cries of the enraged inhabitants. By the early 1960s the Borgata was surrounded by huge housing condos, the result of the wild post-war urbanistic expansion. The tall buildings in the distance in the scene look like a mirage of well-being to the poor and exasperated inhabitants of that no man's land. The last huts in Borgata Gordiani were demolished only in 1980. Petri's political stance is clear without turning into preaching. Individual defeat reflects the downfall of an entire society, for any attempt of transforming the ongoing social reality is useless.

On the other hand, there are the emblematic places of the Boom, starting with the Fiumicino airport, inaugurated in January 1961. It was a symbol of internationality, a threshold to an unexplored and much more populated world, now within everyone's reach. While strolling around in the airport, Cesare watches in awe planes full of passengers take off and even attempts to embark on a flight which, he naively assumes, will make only a short trip all over town. Later he'll tell his friends: "How many human beings have I known in my life? One hundred? Two hundred? ... I've never met any Russian!" But the acquaintances he makes are unreliable, duplicitous, scheming or downright dangerous, whereas the people and places from his past are no longer like the images he preserved in his memory.

Such is the case with Giulia (Regina Bianchi), Cesare's old flame whom he notices during his trip to the Borgata Gordiani[25] and follows to her working place, the Cobianchi public baths.[26] He fleetingly attempts to resume the romantic entanglement of their youth despite the woman being married and with children, with an awkward date at a matinée venue. With its mixture of psychologic notations, realism and bitter irony, the scene is a gem, starting with Cesare's clumsy excuse to take Giulia to the movies. They laboriously make their way in the dark to their seats and he even bumps into a lonely spectator. Behind them, two teenagers are making out. Cesare feigns indifference, but when

Giulia notices them she finally realizes his intentions and walks away, incredulous and humiliated.

Likewise, when he travels to his home village—Oriolo Romano, a small hamlet outside Rome—the plumber finds a desolate place, inhabited only by elderly people. His acquaintances have died, and his childhood friend is a sad farmer who drowns depression in wine. These are the results of the dramatic changes in the post-war economy, with people abandoning the countryside for the big cities.

This juxtaposition of present and past further underlines the protagonist's desperation. Everywhere he looks, Cesare sees people who act like he once did, oblivious to the dread that makes his stomach crawl, and who think only about money, fun, and sex. He attempts to imitate them and take life as it comes, but to no avail. A wonderful scene has Cesare fleetingly attempt a clumsy dance step while leaving the beach where hundreds of young men and women are dancing to the sound of a pop tune (Nico Fidenco and Gianni Marchetti's hit single *Legata ad un granello di sabbia*). Randone's extraordinary performance perfectly synthesizes Cesare's regret, his fear of being ridiculed, his half-hearted effort at something he is incapable of feeling.

Elio Petri (left) directing Salvo Randone on the set of *I giorni contati.*

I giorni contati is characterized by a structure that would become typical of Petri's cinema, a dialectical discourse which juxtaposes a protagonist to society, and Randone's casting against type proves to be part of it. A cultured, middle-class man, Randone had never played a proletarian before. His "conservative psychological mentality" as Petri described it, gives Cesare further depth. Never before, in Italian cinema, had a working-class character been depicted in such a complex, multi-faceted manner.

> Many criticized the choice of Randone for *I giorni contati*; they couldn't understand why a bourgeois and cultured actor would play a plumber. But in my opinion a plumber can be Pirandellian and split, even though Pirandello has never written about a plumber. A worker is a character like every one of us, he suffers from inner splits, neuroses, lack of personality, escapes from himself, dreams, delusions. I needed an actor who could be all this, not an unarmed, naturalistic actor. Randone is not naturalistic; he lives in hallucination.[27]

Once again, as with *L'assassino*, Petri was consciously moving away from Neorealism into very different territories.

A Painter's Tale

> We make an appeal to filmmakers from all over the world, to those by profession and to those who, as film lovers, own a camera, even a 16mm one. We await from them the very latest news from the soul of men and especially from young people about peace.
>
> With the footage that we will gradually receive, we intend to create a "film about peace" which will be shown to people in the public squares if it won't be possible to release it in normal circuits.
>
> We do not ask you for films, but only for short excerpts ranging from 50 to 300 meters. It will be up to the editorial staff of the "Newsreel of peace" to put together each issue from time to time by editing the footage in the most effective way.[28]

This appeal, published in *Rinascita* in June 1962, was signed by Cesare Zavattini, and came at a time when the Cold War had almost reached a boiling point. The 1961 Berlin crisis, which led to the construction of the Berlin wall to stop the escapes of citizens to the Western side, had culminated with the chilling sight of the American and Russian tanks facing each other at Checkpoint Charlie on October 27, 1961. Such display of power showed how the world order was leaning on a balance more delicate than ever, like a man on a tightrope. In October 1962, the Cuban missile crisis would bring the world just one step from a nuclear war.

The result of Zavattini's appeal was a collective 16mm documentary, *Il cinegiornale della pace* (1963), signed by seven directors and with illustrious contributions from the likes of Mario Soldati and Jean-Paul Sartre.[29] Petri's name was nowhere to be found in the credits, but he had a part in the project's early stage, as a member of the artistic commission that would view and choose the footage for the newsreel, together with Renzo Vespignani, documentarist Cecilia Mangini, film critic Mino Argentieri, and philosopher Aldo Capitini. It had been Capitini who had organized the first Peace Walk from Perugia to Assisi in September 1961, where the multicolored peace flag turned up for the first time. Some years later Petri would collaborate again with Zavattini on a similar effort, *Cinegiornali liberi*.

Meanwhile, the director was busy with new projects. In 1962, he told film critic Vittorio Spinazzola he would like to make an openly political movie, "the portrait of a young

Italian politician," possibly Mario Alicata—a 44-year-old Communist MP who had also worked as a scriptwriter, namely on *Ossessione*—or Giulio Andreotti, or both. "A film in which the places and signs of Italian politics are the real ones," he specified, asking rhetorically, "Is there any producer in Italy willing to undertake such an enterprise?"[30] It sounded like a challenge, especially after all the trouble Petri had undergone with *L'assassino*, but in fact it was the early core of an idea which would reach maturation over a decade later, albeit in a much more complex way, with *Todo modo*.

Immediately after wrapping *I giorni contati*, Petri started preparing his next film, *Un amore lungo*, which he wanted to shoot in the summer of 1962. "It is the story of a great love, within the social frame of the last 15 years. Marcello Mastroianni will be the protagonist and will produce it in association with the director and Piero Notarianni," the press reported.[31] However, the project was soon dropped in favor of another one, with very different tones. In October 1962 the news came that Petri was prepping *Un tranquillo posto di campagna*, again to be starring Mastroianni (as soon as the actor would finish his work on the set of Fellini's mysterious new project, that is, *8½*) and Nadja Tiller.[32] It was loosely based on George Oliver Onions's 1911 short story *The Beckoning Fair One*, included in the best-selling 1960 anthology *Storie di fantasmi*, edited by Carlo Fruttero and Franco Lucentini.

In a letter to Ennio Della Nesta of Istituto Luce, Petri explained that he wanted to portray "the psychical damage produced by the mystifications of a badly lived well-being."[33] Moreover, he returned to the theme of painting, seen as "a contrapuntal dialectic between an artist's need to express himself or herself explicitly and publicly and the dynamics of the unconscious."[34] Whereas Onions' tale centered on an unsuccessful writer who loses inspiration, Petri and Tonino Guerra's story was about an abstractist painter named Marcello.

A detailed 36-page outline retained in the Elio Petri fund in Turin and consisting of 46 scenes gives a rather precise idea of the film's structure.[35] The story takes place in the Venetian area and starts at the Biennale. There, Marcello's lover and manager Giulia has cut a deal with an art merchant, who will pay a substantial monthly fee for a three-year exclusive. On a whim, Marcello claims that he needs to stay some time alone, in a quiet place in the country, to find new ideas and themes. He moves to an old, isolated farmhouse owned by an elderly widower. The man lives in the memory of his late wife Bianca, who had ended her days in an asylum, and he asks Marcello to paint her portrait, using an old photo as blueprint. Marcello finds out that Bianca was a nymphomaniac who indulged in orgies with local men together with her mother and had killed the baby she had had from her illicit affairs. He is visited by her ghost, who sabotages his work and provokes weird accidents, causing a sexual encounter with Giulia to end badly. Marcello starts to work on the portrait but finds out he is incapable of the task, and his obsession turns into madness. When Giulia pays him a visit with two merchants, Marcello kills and dismembers her.

However, the brief synopsis included in the ministerial papers shows that Petri and Guerra—who had been joined in writing the script by two prestigious names, Suso Cecchi D'Amico and novelist Goffredo Parise—had reshaped the story from its early draft. Characters were dropped (namely the elderly villa owner), new ones were introduced, and the backstory about the female ghost was rewritten from scratch. Lastly, the film would take place in a different setting (the Roman countryside), possibly due to budgetary reasons.

According to the new synopsis, Marcello moves to an old farmhouse outside Rome in the hope that the isolation helps his creativity. Even his lover Giulia will only visit him every now and then. Marcello's only company in his "quiet place in the country" is a young cleaning lady, Carmela, but once in a while a man named Attilio shows up, bringing some flowers to a nearby site. During the war Attilio had an affair with a young girl named Bianca, who allegedly died during a bombing. But Marcello finds out that in fact it was Attilio who murdered her out of jealousy. The man is arrested, but his story slowly upsets Marcello's mind. Obsessed with Bianca, the painter begins hearing strange noises and becomes convinced that the girl has come back to life. Giulia tries to help him, but to no avail. Marcello identifies Giulia with one of his persecutors, just like the art merchant who always demands the same type of works from him. Eventually Giulia disappears, and when the police show up to investigate, they find out a horrible truth: Marcello has killed and dismembered her.

The project, to be produced by Spa Cinematografica, had an estimated budget of 560 million *lire*, three times as much as *L'assassino* and *I giorni contati*. In addition to Mastroianni (who would be paid 100 million *lire*) and Tiller, the cast would include Salvo Randone (Attilio), Rosita Pisano (Carmela), Mario Feliciani (an art merchant) and Mario Brega (a butcher). The key role of Bianca had not yet been cast. The top-notch crew featured d.o.p. Gianni Di Venanzo, camera operator Pasqualino De Santis, editor Eraldo Da Roma, and production designer Nedo Azzini.

The preventive review of the script resulted in a favorable report. "The story, after a calm opening, dives fully into an atmosphere worthy of the *Série noire*," the commissioners noted, referring to the popular French crime paperbacks. "The script is written skillfully, punctuated with undoubtedly effective spectacular elements, and driven with the necessary 'acceleration' to the final solution."

On October 9, the production company presented the project and requested a 300 million *lire* state loan. Spa Cinematografica was in talks with Cocinor for an Italian-French co-production and was expecting a 180 million advance for the West German sales by Omnia Deutsche Film Export. Filming was due to start on November 5, 1962, and last till January 25, 1963, but in mid–November Spa Cinematografica informed the ministry that shooting had been delayed to early December. Meanwhile, the deal with Cocinor fell through, and the Italian company attempted to cut a coproduction deal with the Munich-based Eichberg Film and the Parisian Criterion Film. But it all came to nothing. According to Petri, at a certain point Mastroianni backed out, causing the project to halt.[36] Spa Cinematografica ended up in liquidation, and on March 28, 1963, it deposited an official act of renunciation to the production. Several months of preproduction had been wasted, and Petri had spent the whole winter of 1962 without working. Like Cesare, he had to *do* something.

Around the same time as Mastroianni was working on *8½*, he and his brother Ruggero had tried to involve Petri in a project which to call "bizarre" would be an understatement. *Necrofilia* (or *Il necrofilo*, according to other sources[37]) would be a spoof of the Roger Corman horror films starring Vincent Price which were all the rage at the box office. Mastroianni, who would play the lead, described it as "the story of a weird guy who, just like in American movies, keeps many corpses in the basement, including one which looks like Sophia Loren, another who looks like Lollobrigida.... I walk past them without giving them any importance and choose a teenage boy instead."[38] If the idea of a sexually promiscuous necrophile *à la L'orribile segreto del Dr. Hichcock* (and bisexual to boot) weren't bold enough to start with, Marcello and Ruggero came up with even more demented ones. "We had envisioned a pool full of blood sausages, bathrobes made with tripe, and two shady characters played by [Tino] Buazzelli and [Paolo] Panelli as body snatchers who stole bodies from a clinic basement. But Petri didn't even take the project into consideration."[39] Undaunted, the Mastroianni brothers came back with another, no less wacky story: *Los ruspantos*,[40] a Western spoof (at a time Sergio Leone hadn't yet come to the limelight) about two famished bandit brothers who become the terror of Mexican villages for their habit of breaking into houses and stealing food.[41]

Meanwhile, though, Petri was working on quite a different and secretive task. That's when Elio Montesti was born, a creature with one name and three heads, who lived for the short time span of one feature film.

The Strange Case of Elio Montesti

For many years, Elio Montesti was one of the best kept secrets in Italian cinema. The elusive director had helmed only one film, the notorious if little seen *Nudi per vivere*, a saucy report on the Parisian night life like many others that came out between the late 1950s and the mid–1960s like mushrooms after a night of rain, following the astonishing success of Alessandro Blasetti's *Europa di notte* (1959). Then Montesti had disappeared. Books on Italian cinema hesitated embarrassedly when (if ever) mentioning him. No date or place of birth, no certainty whether he was alive or dead.

But who was Elio Montesti? And what was he doing in Paris in the year 1963?

Elio Petri knew better. And Giuliano Montaldo, too. "Once a film historian called me to inquire about Montesti. He asked me if I knew how old he was. I replied, '112.' Because in that moment it was the sum of our ages: mine, Elio Petri's, and Giulio Questi's: Elio, 'Mont' as in Montaldo, 'esti' as in Questi."[42]

Montaldo and Petri had been friends since 1951. They first met during the shooting of *Achtung! Banditi!*, where Montaldo played the role of Commissioner Lorenzo, and a 22-year-old Elio showed up on the set, in his trademark plus-fours and with a shoebox in his hands, carrying the money raised from the comrades of Rome's section of the PCI to help finance Lizzani's film. In Montaldo's version of the Elio Montesti story, Petri wanted to help his father-in-law, producer Lorenzo Pegoraro, who was in financial difficulties. "To give him a hand, Elio proposed to me and Giulio Questi an extravagant idea. Since semi-documentary movies on various, let's say scandalous aspects of the night world were all the rage, he suggested we make a movie of that type, with the three of us shooting it, and sign it Elio Montesti."[43]

Giulio Questi's recollection of the events is slightly different.[44] In late 1962 he had worked for producer Alessandro Jacovoni on *Universo di notte*, a collection of nightclub numbers and stripteases on which Montaldo had collaborated too. Questi and Carlo Di Palma had shot risqué footage in the city's most notorious venues, and the experience had inspired Questi to put together another project along the same lines, which meant low-budget filmmaking and guaranteed box-office results. "Seeing that everyone was making money with these films, except me, I decided to gain something myself," he recalled in his memoir. "I knew all the behind-the-scenes and the secrets of the nightclubs."[45] He wrote an outline and went back to Rome, looking for associates … and involved Montaldo and Petri, both in severe need of money.

On February 15, 1963, the trio founded the company P3 G2 Cinematografica, yet another hint at the filmmaker's names (the two Gs were those of Giuliano and Giulio, while P3 was a wordplay on "Petri" which is spelled very similarly in Italian). Elio brought Pegoraro aboard as the general organizer with his company PEG Cinematografica. Questi claimed the idea of the collective alias as well. "It seemed absurd to sign with our own names a commercial picture which none of us was particularly fond of. I came up with Elio Montesti, the fusion of our own names into an unknown one."[46]

Questi's version seems the more believable, as his previous experience on *Universo di notte* would point at him as the ideal candidate for coming up with the idea for such a movie. But Petri owned a larger participation than both Montaldo and Questi in the P3 G2 company, with 180 shares instead of 135, while Pegoraro (who was also the chief executive) owned 270 shares, which hints at them as the initiators of the project.[47] What is certain, though, is that it seemed appetizing to all of them. It smelled of easy and quick money. Too good to be true.

The trio cut a distribution deal with Titanus, who would advance 30 million *lire*, and planned an eight-week shooting schedule (with five weeks in Paris alone) on a planned budget of 177,760,000 *lire*. But its financial difficulties caused Titanus to back out and forced them to cut the costs drastically. Filming, initially scheduled to start on February 25, 1963, was delayed to June 24, on an estimated budget of about 34 million *lire*. The three associates of P3 G2 decided that they would not take any remuneration but would split the profits.

After a couple of days in Rome, shooting footage of real-life characters (young lovers, beggars, etc.), the three directors traveled to Paris with two minuscule crews. The first one was comprised of Montaldo and Petri (who would be each other's assistant in turn) and four more people, including d.o.p. Giuseppe De Mitri. The second crew included Questi as director, Montaldo as his assistant, cinematographer Ennio Guarnieri and three more technicians.

Filming in Paris started on June 28. The trio concocted a tight schedule. They stayed in the same hotel and took turns with the first crew going out to shoot while the second rested and vice versa, working around the clock to stay on budget and shooting guerrilla-style, with no permits whatsoever. According to Montaldo, only Questi made an exception to the strict timing to shoot a scene at Baudelaire's grave: "He stayed a whole day there, waiting for the right light and shoot the scene the way he had it in mind."[48]

The Paris shoot went on until July 17, but Petri returned to Italy on July 6, to attend the 1st Trieste International Science Fiction Film Festival (where he was a member of the jury). In mid–July he would start filming *Peccato nel pomeriggio*, his episode of the omnibus comedy *Alta infedeltà*. On July 18, Montaldo and his crew moved to Nice to shoot at the local Casino, while Questi went back to Rome to film some of the juiciest nightclub scenes at the Istituto Luce studio. Montaldo joined him on July 21. They filmed the Lamine Touré ballet group scene from August 10 to 13, and the "sexual deviations" episodes from October 16 to 19. Petri was not involved in the latter scenes, for on those days he was on location in Vigevano, filming *Il maestro di Vigevano*. For his part, Montaldo himself turned up in an amusing cameo as a man standing atop a wardrobe and acting like a rooster while a woman is waiting below, dressed as a hen. They concocted an even weirder scene in which a man is waiting half-naked in a coffin, pretending to be dead; a half-naked prostitute comes in, lights the candles around the coffin and gets in it too. According to Montaldo, the production manager played the client.

The tentative title *Sexy Rififi (Una notte a Parigi)* (Sexy Rififi—A Night in Paris) was eventually changed to *Nudi per vivere* (Nude to Live). It was Questi's friend, the noted journalist Gian Carlo Fusco, who came up with the title:

> We used to meet him at Rosati's [Author's Note: a popular bar in Rome] because the moviola was at Fono Roma, just around the corner. After a couple of whiskies, we took Fusco to see the film, which we had just finished editing. We didn't have a clue about the title, and while the images rolled, he suddenly murmured: "Poor devils … nude to live." "Nude to live!" we cried. No title had sounded more appropriate to us.[49]

Fusco also wrote the commentary, recited by popular voice actors Nando Gazzolo and Pino Locchi, and Ivan Vandor provided the score.

On the surface, *Nudi per vivere* hardly differs from most "sexy night reports" of the era. It opens with tourist footage of Paris, while Fusco's narration adopts an ironic tone typical of his own reports on the mundane life in Rome, cracking jokes and passing witty observations. An eccentric journalist, scriptwriter and novelist who often collaborated with Tinto Brass, Fusco had already worked on a couple of *mondo*-type documentaries— *Io amo, tu ami…* (1961, Alessandro Blasetti) and *Mondo nudo* (1963, Francesco De Feo)— and would collaborate on several more similar flicks. Here, the commentary starts by quoting the poet André Rivoire ("Humanity is divided between Parisians and Zulus"), in quite a provocative way to begin the film at a time African nations were struggling for self-determination. The narration evokes the 1930s, the golden age of the Parisian night life, paired with archive footage featuring Josephine Baker, Maurice Chevalier and Edith Piaf, and the voice-over longs for a time when sex was surrounded by "candor and naivety" as opposed to a present characterized by "heavy sadness, fear, violence." It is all part of the game, of course, and the adoption of a moralistic tone allows the viewer to savor the risqué sequences without feeling guilty. As Questi put it, Fusco's commentary was, in short, "a banter of respectability's double moral standards."[50]

Nudi per vivere makes no secret of its tongue-in-cheek approach. The "interviews" with passers-by are patently fake, and poke fun at the would-be-documentary tone. The same can be said about some risqué bits which flirt with the grotesque and the bizarre and depict sex as a staged role play, often with macabre undertones. The necrophiliac sketch has a surreal taste which predates both *Belle de jour* (1967, Luis Buñuel) and *Ingrid sulla strada* (1973, Brunello Rondi). Other parts related to diverse weird aspects of Paris—an avant-garde show with a score by Chet Baker, homeless people in parks—add variety to the whole and are more in vein with the sociological satire of the "Mondo" movie genre. In the end, however, the tone is somber, and the ending, which deals with suicidal individuals making phone calls to a hotline, is downbeat. "When the sun goes up no one remembers the moon. The problems, the worries, the anxieties resurface," the voice-over comments. As Montaldo summed it up, "it was a very hard movie, not at all self-satisfied. It portrayed a sad, exploited world, even a bit famished. Rather than vice, with its titillating aspects, what came out was the brutality of that world."[51]

Overall, *Nudi per vivere* is a rather tricky work. Due to its collective nature, one is never sure whose voice is speaking. All three authors were or had been communists, but Questi's idea of cinema was poles apart from his politically committed companions. "In my films I never wanted to deal with explicitly political or social topics, or rather, I never had the vocation to do that," he stated.[52] Nevertheless the themes of sex as commodity and alienation are akin to Petri's sensitivity and predate his later work.

Italian 2-fogli manifesto for *Nudi per vivere*, directed by "Elio Montesti."

In his memoir, Giulio Questi recalled an awkward anecdote concerning his relationship with Petri. The three filmmakers were staying at a decaying hotel near Boulevard Saint-Germain, and Questi took advantage of a few hours' rest by having a hot bubble bath. While he was savoring the experience, Petri turned up in the room, ready to go out to film his scenes.

> He saw me, was struck dumb, then exploded, all red in the face, agitated, in a tirade against the corruption of morals, my morals, the bourgeois weaknesses, my own weakness, and the renunciation to moral and social commitment, etc. He could not stop. It was unbelievable and in fact I couldn't believe it, I thought he was kidding.... I didn't answer and limited myself to a sneer and an obscene gesture with my finger emerging from the bubble bath. We never talked again about it. I didn't want to ruin the work we had just started. But I thought long about this. The stiff moral of the Communist Party? Family education? Christ—he had agreed to come to Paris and make a movie about the sex industry! It couldn't be. But then, what? ... He was a sexually repressed individual who proceeded through symbols ... and who saw me, moved by a subtle and venomous grudge, as the negation of his efforts of virtue. Perhaps he even envied me.[53]

Questi's tale sounds a little exaggerated and any attempt to squeeze some deep significance out of it would be far-fetched at best. Montaldo, in fact, recalled how on the contrary Questi was by far the more "serious" of the trio during their Parisian stay, while he and Petri "had fun like crazies. We went at night shooting footage in nightclubs surreptitiously, because back then it was forbidden to enter a nightclub with a camera ... on some occasion we risked a lot ... once our d.o.p. Ennio Guarnieri got punched in the eye...."[54]

Could Petri indeed be just kidding? Other testimonies, such as Ennio Morricone's, stress the director's taste for pranks. Still, several of his acquaintances, including Pirro and Montaldo, pointed out Petri's "lay morality" and his insistence on lecturing his friends on the necessity of moral rectitude. Therefore, Questi's anecdote, albeit taken with a grain of salt, becomes yet another piece of the puzzle in light of the director's inner turmoil in his later years.

Submitted to the Board of censors on November 8, 1963, *Nudi per vivere* was initially denied the certificate for screening.[55] The motivation deserves to be reported at length:

> There cannot be any doubt that this is a product aimed at stimulating the sexual appetites of the audience. Under this aspect alone it would already surpass the limits of the sexy films, which unfortunately have found an easy market and concur to increase the danger of continuous decadence of mores, both in decency and sexual morality. But the film features also more worrying and damaging elements. With the exception of a limited number of scenes, in which the spectacular and choreographic aspects prevail and distract the viewer's attention from the dancers' nudity, all the other scenes, from beginning to end, are imbued with pornographic content which recalls and exalts the most vulgar sexual instincts, and can stimulate any tendencies to satisfy insane desires. And there is more: in addition to the effective sexual suggestion exerted by the innumerable scenes highlighting female nudity ... there are sequences, and not a few, where sexuality is associated with aggressiveness and violence, and therefore there is the real danger that they might arouse and exalt sado-masochistic tendencies, latent in the viewer's subconscious. Elsewhere in the film, even sadism and masochism are highlighted ... in a way which would be tolerable only if they were destined to a determined number of qualified people, for scientific purposes; again, other scenes describe seedy environments where sexual deviations and transvestism take place. The overall atmosphere is heavily unpleasant, not only because of these latest aspects, which are decidedly in contrast with normal bio-psychic values, and because of its prevailing dark tones, but also because of the deliberate degradation of any value in life, in terms of sexuality.

In appeal, the producer agreed to soften the tone of the voice-over and trim a few scenes, namely those depicting "sexual psychopathies," as well as one where a little girl dances the twist, for a total of almost nine minutes. Eventually *Nudi per vivere* was passed with a V.M.18 rating in December 1963, around the same time as Petri's "official" third feature film, *Il maestro di Vigevano*. It was released by Dear Film on February 28, 1964. Much to the filmmakers' enthusiasm, the initial revenues were outstanding, but the film was promptly seized for alleged obscenity.[56] The press applauded the "blow to the vulgar and demeaning market of eroticism in color"[57] and Pegoraro, as the producer, went to trial. As Montaldo commented, "instead of giving him a hand, we got him in trouble."[58]

Federico Fellini testified in Pegoraro's favor, defending his morality and honesty,[59] and the producer was acquitted, but the court demanded the seizure of three sequences, "Elle et lui," "Grand-Guignol," and "Boule noire," the latter featuring a nude black dancer.[60] *Nudi per vivere* returned to circulation in the summer of 1964 and was met with rather favorable reviews for that type of film. *L'Unità* described it as "a partially successful attempt at demystifying the erotic show business … the sequences display a dexterous, sometimes refined style."[61] *Il Messaggero* noticed the "well-made psychological investigation" and the "agile and witty commentary."[62] Fusco's contribution was praised by several other reviewers, as was the color photography. *Il Tempo* and *Il Globo* hinted at the true identity of the "three well-known filmmakers who preferred to hide themselves under the pseudonym,"[63] proving that in some quarters it was an open secret.

Then the film virtually disappeared, and today the only available copy is the one retained at the CSC. For many years, *Nudi per vivere* was not included in the authors' filmographies, and Petri never mentioned it in interviews.[64] It was Montaldo who broke the curtain of silence when interviewed in a 2005 biography, concluding: "In its own way, it's a *maudit* film. It contained the warning signs that that Montesti guy was a real pain in the ass and wouldn't have an easy life. In fact, he made only that movie and then vanished into thin air."[65]

FOUR

To Have and Have Not

Il maestro di Vigevano *(1963) and*
Peccato nel pomeriggio *(1964)*

Elio, Dino and I mostri

"The 'story' in movies ... is in crisis. Audiences have become bored by stories with a beginning, an end, a basic development and precise characters, and there are fewer and fewer people willing to waste two hours of their time taking interest in what might happen to strangers."[1] As a film critic of the period observed, the embrace of an episodic narrative was a common factor in Italian cinema of the early 1960s. Besides the narrative fragmentation of the travelogue "sexy documentaries" such as *Nudi per vivere*, another blatant example was the widespread diffusion of the anthology format, labeled as "cinema for lazy audiences" by Tommaso Chiaretti as early as 1954.[2]

Once again it was the pioneering work of Alessandro Blasetti, with the diptych *Altri tempi—Zibaldone n. 1* (1952) and *Tempi nostri—Zibaldone n. 2* (1954), that paved the way, but the format hit its peak in the early-to-mid 1960s, with seven titles produced in 1963, fourteen in 1964, and eleven in 1965. Anthology films were mostly collective works which saw the participation of famed directors—noted examples being *Boccaccio '70* (1962, Mario Monicelli, Federico Fellini, Luchino Visconti, Vittorio De Sica) or *Ro.Go.Pa.G.* (1963, Roberto Rossellini, Jean-Luc Godard, Pier Paolo Pasolini, Ugo Gregoretti)—and were usually comedies. They allowed producers to gather an array of popular actors, obtaining maximum exposure with less costs. Each actor would be under contract for a small period and paid in accordance, for a participation which was little more than an extended cameo with limited screen time.

Produced by Mario Cecchi Gori and released in Italy in October 1963, Dino Risi's *I mostri* stretched the anthology structure to paradoxical heights with a collection of twenty episodes, mostly brief sketches, all starring Vittorio Gassman and Ugo Tognazzi in a variety of roles. Compared with other anthologies of the decade, *I mostri* emphasized the grotesque element, with the two stars portraying a gallery of "monsters" (hence the Italian title) in Italian society, highlighting the misery of the lower classes and the cynicism of the *petit bourgeois*.

Elio Petri is one of several credited scriptwriters on *I mostri*, alongside Age & Scarpelli (Agenore Incrocci and Furio Scarpelli), Ruggero Maccari, Ettore Scola, and Risi, but in fact he had a key role in the genesis of the project, which dated to immediately after the ill-fated *Un tranquillo posto di campagna*.

59

I stayed all winter without any job. It was materially hard for me to go on like that. Unexpectedly, Dino De Laurentiis asked me to make a movie with Alberto Sordi. I always loved Sordi as a comedian, I think he is really an extraordinary Italian "mask." With Age and Scarpelli, we started thinking about an idea for a movie tailored for him.[3]

Sordi, Italy's most popular comedy actor, had signed an exclusive deal with De Laurentiis in December 1960 for three films a year, a hundred million *lire* a film, until January 1965.[4] Over the course of his career, Sordi had played many monstrous characters, in the moral sense of the term. So, why not have him play a whole series of monsters, all in one movie? As Petri described it, the original idea was even more thought-provoking than the finished film would be.

It was a collection of 15 or 16 episodes, all revolving around the monstrosity and cynicism of characters of the petty bourgeoisie and the middle class. It was a very strong political movie.... We collected 16 sketches and Sordi was to play 16 "monsters." After all, he has a talent for the expressionist caricature of the *petit bourgeois* ... among the characters there were a politician, Agnelli [Author's Note: Gianni Agnelli, head of FIAT], a surgeon....[5]

The project was in development during the months of April and May 1963, after the initial halt of *Nudi per vivere*. But De Laurentiis was not convinced about the script. Notably, he didn't like its political edge nor the scorching satire of the Christian Democrat elite. According to Incrocci, one evening he and Scarpelli read the entire script to the tycoon and his wife Silvana Mangano; she was laughing out loud all the time, while he was frowning: "I'd like to know what you find so funny about these sketches!"[6] Sordi was not convinced either. The idea of being depicted as a monster from beginning to end was disturbing to him, as all his characters moved along the risky path between sympathy and disgust, pity and contempt.

Then it was Petri's turn to be summoned at the producer's place, and the news wasn't good.

At the end of the meeting De Laurentiis told me: "You're a communist, go and ask Togliatti to produce this film!" Had I listened to my instinct, I would have gotten up and left, but I thought that this way I wouldn't find a job anymore and I needed to work. In that same period a team of scriptwriters were working on *Il maestro di Vigevano* with Risi, for Tognazzi to star, and were stalled. So, when De Laurentiis proposed that we switch projects, giving *I mostri* to them and taking over *Il maestro di Vigevano*, I accepted. After all, I liked the novel.[7]

A Thousand Factories, Not a Single Bookshop

Lucio Mastronardi (1930–1979) was a schoolteacher based in the Lombard town of Vigevano. The son of Southern immigrants, he was a solitary and introverted type, and he dreamed of being a writer. In his spare time, he wrote a novel, *Il calzolaio di Vigevano*, published in 1959, which gave him a certain notoriety, thanks also to a very favorable review by Eugenio Montale. The next year Mastronardi completed his second novel, also set in his hometown: *Il maestro di Vigevano*.

A town of shoe manufacturers in the province of Pavia, Vigevano was one of the symbols of the so-called Boom, the proof of the ongoing "Italian miracle." In January 1962 the noted reporter Giorgio Bocca had visited the town for what would become the first part of a vitriolic report on the economic renaissance of the province for the newspaper *Il Giorno*. Bocca's article was titled *Mille fabbriche, nessuna libreria* (A Thousand

Factories, not a Single Bookshop) and started like this: "Making money, for making money, for making money. If there are any other perspectives, I'm sorry but I haven't seen them. Citizens, 57,000. Factory workers, 25,000. Millionaires, battalions. Bookshops, not a single one."[8]

Luciano Mastronardi, Lucio's father, had been a schoolteacher too, but his anarchic ideas had cost him the expulsion from the school in 1921, near the dawn of Fascism. After the war, he was elected to the town council, as a member of the PCI, and became the Assessor for Education until 1956, causing disdain in the politically conservative town. In his novels, Lucio gave voice to the feelings his father had nourished for all the humiliations he and his family had suffered, and painted an enraged, merciless portrait of Vigevano and its inhabitants, depicting the mediocrity and squalor of the middle class, the egoism and careerism of the local teachers, the vulgarity and arrogance of the shoe manufacturers who had enriched themselves overnight. As Bocca himself had put it, "when it comes to taste and culture, the oh-so-liberal Vigevano is worse than ever."[9]

Il maestro di Vigevano is the story (told in the first person) of Antonio Mombelli, a primary school teacher married and with a son, whose salary is barely enough to make ends meet. His life is humdrum and squalid, his days are all alike. At school he is humiliated by the principal and has no real friends, at home his conjugal life with his wife Ada is devoid of love and passion. His only joy is his adolescent son, Rino. Ada keeps insisting that Mombelli leave his job and invest his savings in a family enterprise, a small shoe factory run by her and her brother. At first Antonio is reluctant, for he is afraid to lose the petty bourgeois respectability that his profession gives him, but eventually accepts. Soon, he and his family experience the inebriating smell of success. The factory provides them with an increasingly bigger income, and they can finally afford the small luxuries of bourgeois life. But disaster ensues after Mombelli boasts about his new-found wealth with his former colleagues and reveals some illegal gimmicks he and his wife have conceived to defraud the IRS. One of the schoolteachers denounces him to the tax office, and the authorities close down the shoe factory.

After Ada gives birth to their second son, who has red hair, Mombelli becomes convinced that the baby is not his own. Meanwhile, he has returned to teaching, and faces more humiliations from his principal. He often escapes from reality and finds solace in his own imaginary world. The child dies prematurely, but Mombelli is obsessed with his wife's cheating. He even follows her and her alleged lover to a motel, planning to kill them with a hammer, but doesn't have the courage to do it. Then Ada becomes ill and dies. On her deathbed, she tells Antonio that she has always been unfaithful to him and that not even Rino is his son. Now a widower, Mombelli is even more detached from reality. School life has become more grotesque than ever, with the other schoolteachers' only preoccupation being promotions and extra money. A fellow teacher commits suicide after being humiliated before his class, another one dies of a heart attack after learning of a promotion. The last blow to Mombelli's hopes is Rino's arrest for lewd behavior, which reveals that his son is homosexual. Rino is sent to reform school and Mombelli is pushed by a colleague to marry again with a fellow teacher, a fat, ugly and dumb woman who nevertheless has career prospects and family wealth.

It was Italo Calvino who prompted the prestigious Einaudi to publish *Il maestro di Vigevano*. "It is a book out of the ordinary, with a poetic force, a force of despair, a pitch-black view of humanity which becomes a poetic one," he told Mastronardi. "It will be an event."[10] Calvino was right. Released in May 1962, *Il maestro di Vigevano* immediately became a best seller. But Mastronardi's bleak depiction of life in the province made it a controversial work, as did the novelist's irascible temper, "endured with clenched teeth by a town which doesn't have much desire to joke about certain flaws."[11] His fellow citizens barely tolerated him, and their hostility became patent when Mastronardi was rushed to a mental clinic and later arrested after a heated argument with a conductor.[12] But his book's success was unstoppable. It entered the final for the prestigious Premio Strega and won another literary prize, the Premio Prato, prompting Dino De Laurentiis to purchase its rights. After being summoned to Rome by the producer, Mastronardi was so excited about the upcoming film adaptation that in a letter to Calvino he quipped: "The Boom has run over me!"

Sin in the Afternoon

The second half of 1963 was a very busy period for Petri. Before starting filming *Il maestro di Vigevano*, he signed a deal to direct an episode of *Alta infedeltà* (High Infidelity), an Italian-French anthology co-produced by Gianni Hecht Lucari's Documento Film. Back from Paris after the shooting of *Nudi per vivere*, in July 1963 Petri started prep work on *Peccato nel pomeriggio*, written by Age and Scarpelli. The other segments were to be directed by Nanni Loy (*Scandaloso*), Luciano Salce (*La sospirosa*) and Mario Monicelli (*Gente moderna*), respectively. Loy was eventually replaced by Franco Rossi.

As the title suggested, *Alta infedeltà* centered on the theme of conjugal betrayal. A common character of omnibus comedies was in fact the emphasis on eroticism. The new law on censorship pushed producers and directors to dare a bit more, with veiled sexual allusions and mild erotic situations which, although chaste by today's standards, were perceived as risqué at the time. Rossi's episode touched the theme of homosexuality, as a married man (Nino Manfredi) on holiday discovers that the handsome stranger (John Phillip Law) staying at their hotel is not courting his neglected wife as he thought, but him; Salce's dealt with a jealous woman (Monica Vitti) who ends up betraying her husband (Sergio Fantoni) with his best friend (Jean-Pierre Cassel). Monicelli's bit delved into the theme of honor, with a cheesemaker (Ugo Tognazzi) pushing his wife (Michèle Mercier) into the arms of an elderly acquaintance (Bernard Blier) to pay for his gambling debts, then regretting it, with humorous results.

Petri's episode is about a man and a woman who have a clandestine sexual adventure on a hot summer day in Rome. Giulio, a wealthy real estate developer, notices the beautiful Laura going shopping in the city center. He follows her to a café and unsuccessfully tries to pick her up. A phone call at work makes Giulio find out that the tax inspectorate is about to visit his office, forcing him to go back to work in a hurry. Yet, he finds Laura sitting in his car and takes her with him to his company's headquarters (located at EUR's trademark glass palace). While he is busy with his employers she strolls around maliciously, enticing the curiosity of a worker. Back from the office, Giulio takes Laura to a villa by the sea which he has built for his wife, who never wanted to visit it. Both are unhappily married and cannot find sexual solace with their partners. At the villa, Laura alternatively provokes and rejects Giulio, who is becoming more and more excited and nervous, but the prospected adultery seems destined not to happen because of the woman's indecision. Eventually she asks him to take her home, but during the drive back to Rome they spot a motel ("It looks like Arizona.... How exciting!" she purrs). The thought of consummating their affair in such a furtive manner is so exciting that Laura finally agrees to give herself to the man. In the evening, Giulio returns to his luxurious villa and learns that his wife has already come back. When they meet, we realize that the mysterious Laura is actually Giulio's wife, and that the whole sexual adventure was just an overcomplicated sex game to reinvigorate their marriage.

The two leads were Claire Bloom and French singer Charles Aznavour. At that time the 32-year-old British actress was in Italy with her husband Rod Steiger, who was working on a couple of films, Francesco Rosi's *Le mani sulla città* (1963) and Francesco Maselli's *Gli indifferenti* (1964). "Linguistically, there's no problem today. I used what little Italian I know. They help you," she told the *New York Times*, adding: "We had a good young director named Elio Petri—one to watch."[13] The casting of Aznavour, usually employed in dramatic roles, including *La tête contre les murs* (1959, Georges Franju), *Les Dragueurs* (1959, Jean-Pierre Mocky) and *Tirez sur le pianist* (1960, François Truffaut), was unusual but it proved felicitous in retrospect, for the small, thin and definitely not handsome singer makes for an amusing caricature of a bourgeois womanizer.

Running slightly over 20 minutes, *Peccato nel pomeriggio* is witty and entertaining. It overcomes the limits of its gimmick plot and turns into an amiable satire of Antonioni's "cinema of incommunicability." By then Antonioni was on the crest of the wave, attracting awards and critical praise, but also jokes because of its alleged boredom: a famous line

From left to right: **Elio Petri, Claire Bloom and Charles Aznavour on the set of** *Peccato nel pomeriggio.*

in *Il sorpasso* has Vittorio Gassman's character claiming: "Have you seen *L'eclisse*? It put me to sleep…." The game is patent from the credits sequence, a quick montage under the notes of Armando Trovajoli's sophisticated, piano-driven jazzy score. Petri depicts the two alleged strangers meeting and exchanging glances, the man following the woman amid the crowd, clumsily feigning nonchalance and self-assurance. The editing is tight, the shots are elegant and unusual: a zenithal one of Aznavour nervously following Bloom, extending his arm to touch the woman and missing her by inches is particularly striking. Even the costumes, rigidly monochromatic (she is dressed in black with a white hat, he has black shades, white jacket and black trousers), have a rarefied, minimalist elegance that evokes Antonioni's upper-class types. Petri explained he had initially tried to cast Antonioni's muse Monica Vitti in the lead, but the actress refused "because she understood my intentions."[14]

Throughout the episode, Petri stages elaborate shots that emphasize the relation between the characters and the architecture surrounding—and often symbolically dominating—them, in the way Antonioni did in *La notte* and *L'eclisse*. In the EUR scene, Bloom stands before the glass walls, her image reflected together with that of the skyscrapers around her. Then the camera frames her from below, in an extremely low angle shot, against the glass skyscraper towering over her and the blue sky. Only the tip of her hat protrudes in the shot as the human figure disappears against the surrounding architecture, as in the ending of *L'eclisse*. Later, in the deserted villa, a monster of concrete incongruously opening to a wild and deserted beach, the barren shapes and geometrical patterns frame the characters as if in a cage. Laura compares it to a luxury clinic. A long take follows Laura and Giulio as they walk from one large empty room to the next, amid fluctuating curtains (in which the man continuously gets tangled) and incongruous furniture such as a church kneeler, with Aznavour giving an amusingly clownish performance as the nervous and sweaty, and decidedly unattractive, lover. Their ridiculous banter echoes that of the anguished couples in Antonioni's cinema, adding a second degree of significance to the story.

Furio Scarpelli later dismissed the short film as not entirely successful: "Its intent was artificial because its target was unreal." In other words, satire was not centered on the mockery of existing types but on the "sophisticated spoof of a mere invention."[15] Still, *Peccato nel pomeriggio* doesn't just add up to a tongue-in-cheek mimicking of Antonioni's style and themes, but it allows Petri a semi-serious discourse on sexual neurosis in today's world which at times takes on political tones. Giulio and Laura's escapade takes the form of an elaborate performance, and their constant banter becomes a reinvention of a basic outline which leaves room for improvisation, in the attempt to escape the limits of the worn-off game of seduction. See, for instance, how the man's banal pick-up line "Have we met somewhere?" is met with open sarcasm by Laura. He goes back to his table and returns with a totally different approach. "Good, we are making progress," she replies. Rather than lovers, they look like two actors playing repertory and exploring their roles' possibilities.

The wealthy couple who can no longer have marital sex and are forced to wear masks to rekindle their mutual desire are the products of a society that has deprived them of their natural impulses. For Giulio this is the result of his role in the capitalist system. He is a crooked gear in a crooked society. For Laura it is in equal parts the effect of the Catholic heritage (evoked by the church kneeler in the villa by the sea: "This is never missing," she observes) and the hypocritical bourgeois moral, which must be transgressed to bring back the passion. Not by chance, it is the wife who leads the game, striving to overcome her inhibitions by playing the part of a modern, liberated woman. "Why don't you insist, you cretin? We must do it…" she begs Giulio, who at a certain point has given up trying. But adultery needs to be consumed in squalor ("I've never seen an uglier room," she says at the motel) and with a good dose of humiliation: "Tell me dirty words," she begs … only to be outraged when he calls her "Whore."

Nevertheless, transgression is only apparent, just like the adultery that has been acted out, and the dialogue reveals the void both spouses are trying to escape. Early in the story, Laura confesses: "You'll never understand what seven years of marriage mean…. Same husband, same friends, same issues … believe me, a deadly bore." The fact that she is actually telling this to her real husband gives their performance the tone of a psychoanalytic therapy, rather than a mere sex game. "Women are not steaks in which you stick a knife," she confesses while Giulio is busy eating spaghetti, "Steaks don't think, they don't react. But if they did, they would oppose, as I do. But I can't tell this to my husband." Her sneering line to Giulio, "Capitale corrotta, nazione infetta" (Corrupt capital, infected nation) quotes the title of a controversial report[16] on Rome's uncontrolled urbanistic expansion, hinting at an inner contempt toward his job of turning the city and its surroundings into a "forest of concrete" and his "disgusting passion for money."

But the alleged transgression must be paid for. In the end, when he returns home—a luxurious old-fashioned palace with a huge garden and pool, in stark contrast with the geometrical, rationalist villa by the sea he has built for Laura—Giulio discovers from the butler that his dinner will be a meager, low-fat one, by his wife's order, as if in atonement for his sins, both carnal and economic. As for Laura, she is suffering from a severe headache, a psychosomatic result of her "betrayal" … and she is wearing a night mask. To hide the *real* Laura, perhaps?

However, all the painful truths that have been uttered during their "performance" are now forgotten, and the utter emptiness of everyday conjugal life has taken the upper hand again, leaving behind only shame and regret. What remains is an empty simulacrum of marriage, with two people who must pretend to be strangers to share their feelings, and who start thinking that they should see a doctor to recover from their fixation.

Petri would develop the theme of sexual neurosis in his following works, with more explicit political nuances. Notably, the "Trilogy of neurosis" features couples staging erotic games to overwhelm boredom and sexual frustration and explores the theme of sex as an act of possession and power which mirrors the same mechanisms of the capitalistic system. See, in particular, *La proprietà non è più un furto*, where the butcher (Ugo Tognazzi) asks his lover/object Anita (Daria Nicolodi) to tell him he is the manliest, strongest, handsomest man in Rome, a scene which recalls a similar one in *Peccato nel pomeriggio* where Laura asks Giulio, "Say you're not my husband, say you're not him, say you're another, tell it to me!" "Sure, sure I'm another, more handsome, stronger, manlier…."

Even when he is working for hire, Petri does not forget to point out the "verticality of the social structure."[17] As Giulio admonishes Laura, she must indeed recover, otherwise she will have to get a job, "like all the normal people…." Here, the sting in the tail reminds us that it is precisely their upper-class status which allows the two protagonists to set up their elaborate performances. As for ordinary people, it is their daily job that makes them forget their inner issues (as with Cesare in *I giorni contati*), simply because it enslaves them. And slaves, like steaks, don't think and don't react.

The Economic Miracle

The publishing of *Il maestro di Vigevano* and the making and release of Petri's adaptation accompanied a turning point in the economic path of post-war Italy. The span of time between the summer of 1962 and 1964 marked the peak and the beginning of the decline of Italy's "economic miracle" which had started in 1958. The main symbol of the period was the A1, Italy's longest and most important highway. Its construction had begun in 1956, and the last stretch was opened in October 1965. With its 754 kilometers, A1 ran from Milan to Naples, through plains and mountains, overwhelming the country's geographical limitations—most notably the Apennine Mountains, a key element during the dramatic fight for the liberation against the Nazis after the Armistice—as well as the cultural ones. Italians called it "Autostrada del Sole" (Highway of the Sun). The sun was literal and symbolic, for it represented light, warmth and optimism. The A1 was like an umbilical cord uniting the North and the South, and bringing nourishment to a whole economy: tourism, industrial expansion, new possibilities for individuals and enterprises.

Italy was changing shape, with urban agglomerations growing rapidly around the big cities, industrial centers, and communication routes. Thanks to the new-found well-being, Italians were relishing such luxuries as the refrigerator (which as late as 1958 was owned only by 13 percent of Italian families) and the TV set. RAI-Radio Televisione Italiana started broadcasting in 1954, much later than in many other countries, and in 1960 only 20 percent of the families owned a television. But soon things would change. Ditto for motorbikes, cars, summer holidays at sea....

The nation seemed to savor the pleasures of a liberated society as well. In 1963 came the publication of Wilhelm Reich's 1936 essay *The Sexual Revolution*; the following year it was the turn of Mary McCarthy's novel *The Group*, merely one year after its U.S. release, and Herbert Marcuse's essay *Eros and Civilization*, a text which would prove immensely influential among young intellectuals. Social hierarchies and relations between generations were changing, too. But behind the surface the issues remained, although sometimes they were put aside like dust hidden underneath the carpet. As writer Alberto Arbasino put it, "in this conjuncture of boom and well-being, I keep bothering to think 'as if.' For instance, let's try and behave 'as if' we were living in an advanced civil society."[18]

The year of 1963 marked also the start of the so-called "*congiuntura*" (economic downturn) which would soon cause an inversion in tendency. The crisis highlighted the inner fragility of the economic miracle and one of its essential factors, the massive use of cheap labor. The phenomenon of mass emigration from the countryside to the big cities, and from the North to the South, had been masterfully depicted in Luchino Visconti's *Rocco e i suoi fratelli* (1960). The percentage of agricultural workers had decreased from 40 percent to 25 percent, meaning three million less individuals, while industry workers had risen from 32 percent to 40 percent. The economic miracle amplified the hiatus between the different classes, with the average industrial monthly salary being 70,000 *lire* against a vital minimum for family of 100,000 *lire*. This was the nation Mastronardi's novel and Petri's film attempted to portray.

Two Romans in Vigevano

Petri's involvement in *Peccato nel pomeriggio* brought further disagreements with De Laurentiis. On July 22 the producer sent him a letter, complaining: "I'm stunned by your carelessness regarding the commitments you have made with us."[19] Had the producer known about *Nudi per vivere*, he would have been even more dumbfounded. However, a 319-page shooting script for *Il maestro di Vigevano* was ready on August 30, although the director's handwritten corrections show that many details were still being ironed out until the very last minute.

De Laurentiis had wisely avoided involving Mastronardi in the adaptation, entrusting the work to Age & Scarpelli. The script discarded some digressions and episodes from the novel, toned down its desperation, and condensed its characters and mood—conveyed in the book through the inexhaustible first-person monologues of Mombelli, characterized by the liberal use of dialectal words—into a coherent story.

Some episodes lose the original edge they had in the novel and seem like lazy attempts at highlighting the comedy tone. For instance, the scene with Mombelli and his colleague Nanini spying upon a young couple having sex by the river, which in the book (with only Mombelli as the peeping tom) leads to a poetic, intimate meditation on the lost purity of an uncontaminated world, here is just a barely amusing episode with little extra value. Other passages retain Mastronardi's dazed depiction of a dumb and absurd world, such as in the scenes between Mombelli and the principal, who demands that the teachers make "dramatized" lessons, and the meeting with lawyer Racalmuto, who has invented a peculiar language made of numbers. Most notably, though, the script tries to normalize Mombelli's gradual descent into madness. Whereas Mastronardi gradually leads us inside the protagonist's mental obsession by way of his hallucinations and fixations, making the novel a study of human madness, Age & Scarpelli turn Mombelli into a dumb and naïve but ultimately sane character and drastically cut the references to his inner malaise.

The script was submitted to the General Direction of Cinematography with all the other papers, even though the new law on censorship no longer required preventive judgment on scripts. Still, the practice went on for several years as an unwritten rule, a sign of how slowly both the film industry and the bureaucracy were reacting to the changing times.

The ministry's response was very favorable, and the report read more like a review of sorts, littered with cultured references.

> "If the protagonist of Mastronardi's novel recalls ... the famous character of Topaze created by Pagnol,[20] it is unquestionable that the setting described in the book, the many characters and even the outlook on world and life ... rather evoke [Georges] Courteline.[21]... *Il maestro di Vigevano* is in any way a dignified work. In adapting it for the screen, even though they respected the novel's essence, the scriptwriters made an effort to spice up the story and draw all the possible spectacular effects from it.... It should make for an interesting film, both for its inner merits and for the prize obtained by the book and its ensuing success among Italian readers."

Immediately after wrapping *Peccato nel pomeriggio*, Petri moved to Vigevano with production designer Gastone Carsetti and started location scouting for the film.[22] Not surprisingly, the journalist from *L'Unità* who interviewed him described the director as "visibly fatigued."[23]

Il maestro di Vigevano cost 431 million *lire* (the initial budget was 450 million). Age and Scarpelli were paid 14,500,000 *lire* and Petri received 17,560,000 *lire*. De Laurentiis paired Sordi with Claire Bloom, marking Petri's second film in a row with the British actress. Sordi's fee was 37 million and Bloom's was 24,400,000. For the part of the bloated, hateful headmaster, professor Pereghi, who takes delight in verbally humiliating poor Mombelli, Petri had initially thought of Salvo Randone, but he had even considered Peter Lorre. Eventually he gave the role to actor and opera singer Vito De Taranto. Other secondary characters were played by solid dialectal thesps such as Piero Mazzarella and Guido Spadea, replacing Daniele Vargas and Gustavo D'Arpe as the vulgar factory owner Bugatti and as Mombelli's suicidal colleague Nanini, respectively. D'Arpe was eventually cast as Amiconi (initially to be played by veteran actor Annibale Ninchi).

As with *I giorni contati* and *Peccato nel pomeriggio*, Petri's assistant was Roberto "Berto" Pelosso. The director of photography was initially to be Armando Nannuzzi, but before filming started the veteran Otello Martelli took over. Martelli had worked with all

Il maestro di Vigevano: **Alberto Sordi between takes in Piazza Ducale di Vigevano, Pavia.**

the best Italian directors since the early 1920s and had lighted many De Santis and Fellini films, including *Riso amaro*, *Roma ore 11*, *La strada* and *La dolce vita*. Ruggero Mastroianni took care of the editing as usual, while another Fellini collaborator, Nino Rota, wrote the music score.

Initially slated for September 2, filming started in Vigevano on September 16, 1963, with the scene of Nanini's funeral. That same day, Mastronardi's father Luciano died of a heart attack, at 81.[24] Definitely not an event that bode well, especially for someone as superstitious as Alberto Sordi. The shoot was observed with nervous eyes not just by the local population, but also by the Ministry of Education, who unofficially recommended that the filmmakers depict the school system with "a light hand."[25]

Petri immediately showed his polemic vein when interviewed by *L'Unità*: "Why are newspapers so concerned when a new movie is about to start? In my opinion it would be better to follow the films more closely when they reach the screen instead of losing all the interest in them with one review."[26] A decade later, he would stress the same concept in what would become one of the most heated controversies of his career, following the release of *La proprietà non è più un furto*.

As for Mastronardi, he seemed moderately amused by the project despite not having taken part in the scriptwriting stage. While in Rome, he had met Sordi through his writer friend Luciano Bianciardi, the author of another grim novel on the Boom years, *La vita agra*, soon to be adapted by Carlo Lizzani and starring Ugo Tognazzi. "I immediately felt sympathy for him, also because Sordi was very interested in his new character," Mastronardi told the press. "In fact we discussed at length Antonio Mombelli and the human and social environment in which he moved, and overall I had the confirmation, as if proof were needed, that he would be the ideal actor for *Il maestro*."[27] Moreover, the novelist and Petri would maintain an amicable correspondence over the years.

During filming, Petri was constantly under pressure. Sordi was a tough nut to crack and his view on the character did not match the director's. Moreover, De Laurentiis was not too pleased with the dailies and sent directives from Rome by telegram. He insisted that Petri not print a scene more than twice and that the comedy angle be emphasized as much as possible. After watching footage of Sordi's character meeting his colleagues in Vigevano's main square and boasting about his new and successful job, the producer wrote:

> I have seen footage of the square—good but not funny—stop
> Remember that whenever possible it must absolutely be funny—greetings[28]

As expected, the shoot caused a sensation in Vigevano, but not in the sense commonly associated with the arrival of a film crew in a provincial town. On October 5, in a letter to Italo Calvino, Mastronardi observed: "Crazy things are happening over here for the movie. Hallucinating things. Each day a new one. Good stuff for short stories."[29] Among those "crazy things" there was a "small war" of sorts going on between the production, the Socialist mayor Corasmino Maretti, and the local Provveditore agli Studi (Responsible for the Ministry of Education), professor Bottaro, who hadn't allowed the crew to film some scenes inside the primary school despite the mayor's authorization.[30] The denial forced Petri to change the shooting schedule drastically and sabotaged his intent to make the film in the real locations described by Mastronardi. The incident caused a parliamentary interrogation on the part of a socialist MP and made clear that the hostility toward the writer was still high in places, especially in the education world.

For instance, the local Christian Democrat group chairman was one of the teachers portrayed in the book—needless to say, in less than flattering terms. And, as De Laurentiis
revealed, Bottaro himself had told him: "Dear sir, not only am I not allowing you to shoot
in Vigevano schools a movie based on a novel which offends the praiseworthy profession
of a teacher, but let me also tell you that I am waiting with joy for the day in which I'll
manage to chase Mastronardi away from Vigevano."[31]

De Laurentiis arranged the world premiere of Sordi's latest picture *Il boom*, directed
by Vittorio De Sica, to take place in Vigevano on September 24. It was not just a way
to secure the actor's presence, but also a publicity gimmick for the forthcoming movie
and a polite gesture toward the town. During the evening, Sordi thanked everyone—the
mayor, the citizens of Vigevano, the audience—except Bottaro. "But I want to let him
know," he added, "that this event is for charity to be devolved to the school patronage,
for the sins of the fathers shall not be visited upon their children."[32] Meanwhile, Mastronardi requested and obtained a transfer to the primary school in the nearby town of
Abbiategrasso.

As proved by Sordi's declarations on that night, the original script featured a different denouement than the one in the film. "Mine is a positive character," the actor specified. "After becoming a widower, he marries his principal's daughter and therefore he
willfully returns to school, to which he is sincerely devout."[33] In fact, Age and Scarpelli
had devised a "grotesquely optimistic, decently squalid ending,"[34] quite faithful to the

**Elio Petri and Claire Bloom at the world premiere of Vittorio De Sica's *Il boom*, starring
Alberto Sordi, and arranged in Vigevano by Dino De Laurentiis (September 24, 1963).**

book. They had conceived it as "incendiary and a bit bold … a pyrotechnic, didactic joke," perhaps more in tune with Sordi's previous film characters. Petri discarded it.

The crew left Vigevano on October 24[35] and moved to Rome to film the interiors at the De Laurentiis studios. Shooting was to be wrapped on November 23. Twenty days later, on December 13, *Il maestro di Vigevano* was ready to be submitted to the rating board. The commissioners demanded that a scene be trimmed, namely the sex encounter between a prostitute (Eva Magni) and a truck driver, prior to giving it an "all audiences" rating. The trimming had actually been proposed by production representative Luigi De Laurentiis (Dino's brother), worried that the film might get a V.M.14 rating. *Il maestro di Vigevano* premiered on December 24, 1963—not in Vigevano, as expected, but at the Delle Palme Cinema in Naples. It was De Laurentiis' private revenge against a town with which he never hit it off.

Despite its downbeat tone, *Il maestro di Vigevano* was launched as a comedy in tune with the Christmas holidays: "A true, cheerful, human, amusing and topical spectacle … it is funny, it is moving, it is interesting, it is curious, it is a novelty," newspaper ads promised.[36] Reviews were mixed. Despite the admittedly infelicitous casting of Claire Bloom, a very good actress but quite unconvincing as a Lombard lower-class woman—the price to be paid to De Laurentiis' ill-fated ambitions to reach an international audience—many perceived Sordi as the film's most critical issue. Alberto Moravia wrote:

> Sordi is a Roman actor, so he comes from a city which basically has remained plebeian-aristocratic … he gives us a portrayal of teacher Mombelli closer to Southern resignation than to the petty bourgeois fury of the North. His acting is certainly excellent for measure and subtlety; but since both the book and the film are in dialect after all, one notices all the time that his dialect is not that of Vigevano.[37]

Still, Moravia—who had been rather cold about *I giorni contati*—called *Il maestro di Vigevano* Petri's best film. He praised the way the director emphasized Mombelli's Dostoevsky-like quality, and the scenes depicting "with force and pity the psychological humiliation and pride, masochism and voiceless revolt of Mastronardi's hero."[38] On the other hand, Mario Soldati noticed similarities with Gogol' and Chekhov, and wrote: "In the final and most important scene … Sordi is at the top: he is heartbreaking and ridiculous, sublime and miserable, a cretin and a hero. Nothing is more modern; nothing is more futuristic and revolutionary."[39]

The film performed rather disappointingly at the box-office, with 578,141,000 *lire*: although still slightly better than *Il boom*, it was far worse than the over 847 million grossed by *I mostri*. Moreover, its circulation outside Italy was minimal. It was screened at the 1964 San Sebastian Festival, and reportedly distributed in Romania, opening in February 1966.

Alta infedeltà premiered a month after *Il maestro di Vigevano*, on January 22, 1964. The board of review had given it a V.M.18 rating because of "scenes and sequences not suitable to the particular sensibility of minors," and the producer appealed. The 2nd grade commission confirmed the rating, because of "the plot or approach of each episode, the many openly inappropriate scenes, and the language which in some points is even vulgar and scurrilous." Still, it did very good business in Italy, ending up at the 15th spot among the year's releases and grossing 834,359,000 million *lire*. It was the most successful among the omnibus features released in 1964, a year which seemed to be dominated by comedies, namely Vittorio De Sica's *Matrimonio all'italiana* and Franco and

Ciccio's spoofs (with 7 films among the year's 20 top grosses) ... until in September the world saw the release of Sergio Leone's *Per un pugno di dollari*.

Unlike *Il maestro di Vigevano*, *Alta infedeltà* became a profitable export entry. It was released in France on July 15 by Comacico and in West Germany on August 7. The following year it debuted overseas, distributed by Magna Pictures, and opened in New York on July 1, 1965, as *High Infidelity*. American reviews were suitably positive. *Variety* praised it for being "fast paced, modern, unprejudiced ... with adroit direction and popular performances.... Pic unspools smoothly and entertaining and everyone has a good time."[40] The *Morning Telegraph* called it "a passably bright, occasionally witty, and sometimes ironic treatise on the sin of adultery."[41] The *Chicago Tribune* labeled it a "cleverly wrought comedy ... heavily laced with O. Henryish surprises, and every nuance savored as if it was a spicy clam sauce,"[42] while *The Los Angeles Times* applauded its "Rabelaisian horseplay" and judged it "rife with surprise twists and turns ... cunningly written and performed."[43]

The *New York Times*' Eugene Archer had words of praise for *Peccato nel pomeriggio*. "The plot device in the second sketch is trickier, but *Sin in the Afternoon* has the benefit of a striking piece of direction by Elio Petri, a new name and one to watch.... Mr. Petri, with a technique as precise as Antonioni's but far more mobile, and his admirable actors turn this fragile fragment into an elegant tour de force."[44] To Richard L. Coe, in the *Washington Post, Times Herald*, the episode was "a genially updated telling of one of the oldest legends" and the whole film was "far better than most recent such."[45] *Chicago Tribune*'s Clifford Terry praised the leads' performances ("Miss Bloom, perhaps the loveliest actress in films today, again gives an intelligent and sensitive performance.... Aznavour is a hilarious study in frustration"[46]) and so did *The Los Angeles Times*' Philip K. Scheuer ("Charles Aznavour['s] ... expressions of alternate passion and puzzlement are hilarious to behold.... Miss Bloom's portrait of a frigid woman who makes teasing a torment is extraordinary."[47])

Alta infedeltà had its British theatrical debut in September 1967, through Miracle Films, uncut but with an X rating, as *High Infidelity* and with the alternate title *Sex in the Afternoon*. Over three years had passed from its Italian release.

Comedy or Tragedy?

Those who took part in *Il maestro di Vigevano* generally dismissed it as a disappointment. According to Agenore Incrocci, "it was an unhappy encounter between Sordi and Petri's personalities, and the book itself." For the scriptwriter, Sordi was not fully convinced about the project; moreover, being a Roman, he was a debatable choice for the role of a Lombard, better suited to Ugo Tognazzi, who was born just a hundred miles from Vigevano and could at least master the accent. Sordi's presence, in Incrocci's view, "alters the essence of the film, doesn't give it the needed balance."[48] Indeed, the actor's performance at times recalls the one in *Bravissimo* (1955, Luigi Filippo D'Amico) where he played a pathetic and penniless schoolteacher.

For his part, Sordi complained that Petri considered the novel "untouchable, a classic, like Dante Alighieri," whereas he felt the story and characters needed to be given a more realistic edge. "I had to play a role that convinced me only partially, so I can't say it was a happy experience," he concluded.[49]

It is possible that his reported dissatisfaction on the exclusive deal with De

Laurentiis played a part too.[50] Sordi had to renounce such important films as Pietro Germi's *Divorzio all'italiana* (1961) and *Il sorpasso* because of Dino's vetoes. In January 1965 the deal was not renewed, and soon Sordi began directing his own films, his debut behind the camera being *Fumo di Londra* (1966).

Petri himself labeled *Il maestro di Vigevano* a failure: "There are several things in it which are mine, things I really like, but overall I don't like the film."[51] He especially regretted not having a Lombard actor such as Dario Fo at his disposal, so as to work on the dialect the way Mastronardi's novel did. Moreover, he never got along with Sordi, who was too far removed from him, and not just politically:

> Sordi is maniacally negative, as a character…. In my opinion there is a contradiction between the image he wants to give of himself, which conversely is optimistic and let's say conformist, and his instinct for destruction … basically he is a nihilist, a right-wing nihilist, and this is what should come out. How could you harness him, then? It would almost be like censoring him. On *Il maestro di Vigevano* I had to be tough with him, also because it was not his type of role … and Sordi tended to overact.[52]

And yet, according to film critic Goffredo Fofi, what ultimately makes the film work is exactly

> Petri and Sordi's "distance" from the setting and its characters, which echo the novel's painful distance…. In *Il maestro di Vigevano* the conflict between director and actor (who said that they always have to get along well together?) gives strength to a character and setting which in the end turn out naturally ghastly.[53]

Upon its release, *Il maestro di Vigevano* has often been misinterpreted, based on the partially wrong concept that, given Sordi's presence, it was supposed to be a comedy. At least, that is what De Laurentiis thought it should be. Had the producer bothered to leaf through the book, he'd have realized that turning such a despairing portrayal of provincial life into a "funny" movie was out of the question. Petri himself was worried about the farcical tone of some passages, namely Mombelli's excessive ignorance, as shown by his annotations on the script.[54]

Nevertheless, the comedy parts benefit from the director's inclination toward the grotesque, as is the case with Mombelli's humiliations on the part of his pompous and hateful principal Pereghi. The script retains Mastronardi's use of dialogue to underline the characters' tics (a common trait with the *commedia all'italiana*), such as Pereghi speaking of himself in the plural ("When we were still a teacher…") and forcing Mombelli to stage a clumsy dramatized rendition of Columbus' discovery of America to the class, much to the pupils' delight at mocking the schoolteacher. In addition to that, the film adds a biting running gag, as Pereghi treats Mombelli like a dumb kid, interrupting words and phrases to have the latter complete them ("Because the teacher is a mis…? Because the teacher is a mis…?" "…sile!" "Missionary, teacher Mombelli! A missionary!").

De Taranto's over-the-top performance turns Pereghi into a predecessor to the representatives of the authorities that Petri would depict in his films of the 1970s, a monstrous embodiment of repression. His insistence on formalities and his willingness to demean his subjects have obvious fascist roots, as does his predilection for the bombastic poetry of Decadent writer Gabriele D'Annunzio. Pereghi, in short, is an updated version of the pre-war fascist hierarchy, and his very presence gives an idea of the retrograde school system, still stuck in the old regime's didactic methods. In a way, it is the typical situation Italy had been experiencing in the post–World War II era, with ex-Fascists still in the corridors of power and dictating the agenda according to pre-war rules. It had happened in the film business, with the likes of Nicola De Pirro and Annibale Scicluna Sorge, and in many other fields as well.

The many changes from the book notwithstanding, Petri sought to stay true to Mastronardi's intentions. What struck him the most was possibly the depiction of the main character's apathy and social alienation, and a passage of the novel reads like an anticipation of the director's "trilogy of neurosis." It is when Mombelli reflects on how he spent the week, as if he was doing a math problem:

> 168 hours have passed. Another Sunday is almost over. What did I do with these 168 hours?
> 25 hours I spent in school. 25 more I spent in private lessons, and that makes 50.
> About 60 hours were consumed in sleep.
> And the other 58?
> Half a dozen went into eating; a couple more went for the small actions, and 50 hours I consumed in my habits. Half an hour at the coffee bar before going to school; an hour at the coffee bar after dinner; an hour lying down after private lessons; the remaining hours talking with colleagues … until I wasted 168 hours.
> I realize my life is just a succession of wasted hours, of lost time.

Despite the script considerably toning down Mombelli's growing alienation, in Petri's view he becomes a gear in the capitalist system just like the director's future anti-heroes Lulù (*La classe operaia*) and Total (*La proprietà*). Mombelli is vaguely aware of his status and, at first, he tries to rebel against it, but his pride is soon overwhelmed by the desire to please his wife and by the lust for social revenge against his peers, which results in bitter humiliation. In the book he needlessly spends a huge sum of money to buy Rino a dress for Confirmation, only to have the boy give everything to a homeless gypsy kid who is poorer than him. In the film he gives back a loan to his wife's employer, paying it back from his own pocket, and then pretends to have been robbed of his paycheck to justify the lack of money, with pathetic results.

Mombelli's notions of honor and dignity are the kind of petit-bourgeois prejudices imposed on him by society, and his moral sense easily gives in to the "cynicism of capitalistic accumulation."[55] Eventually, he surrenders to the tidal wave, whereas those like his colleague Nanini, an idealistic soul who dreams of an idyllic return to nature, are destined to be crushed. Nanini's suicide (which in the book is caused by economic desperation and mental breakdown) is a fatal act of self-liberation, perhaps the only one left in a system which leaves no other choice to those who don't believe in miracles, economic or otherwise.

Ada, on the other hand, is the typical product of the consumer society, for she wants to work more to get more money and buy watches and fancy dresses to be fully realized as a woman. "If you'd have to think of another woman, how would you like her? Dressed poorly like me, or more elegant?" she asks her husband. She is a provincial version of Gustave Flaubert's Emma Bovary. But working in the factory first and then setting up her own workshop has devastating effects. The house becomes a surrogate factory, whose working rhythms dominate and constrain their life, destroying all remains of marital affection between her and her husband.

Like the novel, the film is very precise in depicting a society divided between the rich and the poor, and in emphasizing the fluidity brought by the Boom: thanks to the "economic miracle" it is possible to rise from one status to the upper one—at least momentarily. But this excludes those who are supposed to take care of culture and education. Being non-commodities, such values are neglected in the country of a thousand factories and zero bookshops.

In the end, the delusional miracle turns out to be a nightmare. Despite its many amusing touches, *Il maestro di Vigevano* shares the same anguished vision of death that is common in Petri's cinema and features two key characters destined to a violent demise, which in Ada's case underlines the impossibility of social and economic redemption. Petri not only reinvented her character by way of an existential light but managed to carry home a mature political discourse, "because no one would ever want to live in a society that, albeit economically evolved, lacks authentic, concrete bases for a full emancipation of the individual."[56]

The depiction of squalid and unsatisfying marital sex in Mastronardi's novel is toned down if not rejected altogether in the film, which omits also such details as the schoolteacher's fetishistic fixation on feet. But Petri hints quite well at Ada's sexual dissatisfaction, which causes a dramatic shift near the end, as the film cleverly reinvents one of the book's most grotesque episodes (Mombelli following his wife and her lover to a motel) into an unpredictably grim coda.

Stylistically, *Il maestro di Vigevano* is impeccable. Otello Martelli's photography is a standout. The interior scenes are characterized by a contrasty black-and-white, with vast dark zones and side lighting, while the exteriors feature many long shots that isolate the characters against the surroundings. In addition to complex camera movements and long takes in an expressive manner echoing Antonioni, Petri asked Martelli for unusual camera positions (such as zenithal or low-angle shots and Dutch angles) and the recourse to deep focus, in a display of technique that is poles apart from the usual stylistic laziness of the *commedia all'italiana*. The scene where Mombelli and his wife converse outside the factory where she works and Ada tells him that she wants to quit her job is a stunning anticipation of Petri's cinema to come. The camera pans along the factory gates, following Claire Bloom's syncopated moves, before dollying to discover the surroundings: a dirty ditch, the gate, and the plant. As some noted, it is already a bitter statement on the unhappy condition of the working class, eight years before *La classe operaia va in paradiso*.[57]

The director's penchant for elaborate camerawork results in some passages where Mombelli's petty dreams materialize. During a nervous argument with Ada on the way home, Antonio stops against a corrugated iron fence (note the detail of an obit behind him, a subtle omen of what will happen). When he turns, he sees Ada wearing a luxurious fur, lit by a heavenly light. Here, Petri employs the long take as he did in *L'assassino*, and even earlier in the script for *L'impiegato*, switching from reality to illusion within the same shot by way of tricky camera movements and mobile set props.

A similar trick can be found in the scene where Pereghi reproaches Mombelli for being late, and Antonio suddenly rebels, taking the principal by the lapel of his jacket and mortifying him in turn. The rebellion turns out to have been only imaginary, but once again Petri manages to release himself from the heavy burden of the *commedia all'italiana*, trespassing the limits of reality to create a parallel, delusional world, the first hint of a discourse that will reach its peak in *Un tranquillo posto di campagna*.

Another, very complex sequence, centered on the schoolteacher's fever-induced dreams, showcases not only the director's bold stylistic choices, but his preference for the grotesque as "sometimes a synonymous and sometimes a reagent to madness."[58] Besides highlighting his delusional conception of the conjugal bond as something magical,

Mombelli's nightmare allows the audience to read his foolishness, which causes his economic and personal ruin, in a more subtle way. In Petri's hands, the schoolteacher's stupidity becomes quite a different matter from the typical dumbness of the characters from the *commedia all'italiana*. It is, as Mario Soldati pointed out when reviewing the movie, "a studied, carved, suffered silliness—a symbolical one, in other words,"[59] which achieves a poetic tone. Eventually, as in the book, it becomes the sign of a deeper existential malaise.

In the ending—Petri's own choice as opposed to the script's paradoxical happy denouement—Mombelli's character reaches tragic heights. While driving away from the motel, Ada and her lover die in a car accident. At the police station, Mombelli reprises his schoolteacher role, proclaiming himself "*Maestro* Mombelli," and dictates to the commissioner a fake, embellished report on the circumstances that led to his wife's death, so as to cover up her betrayal. This final act of self-humiliation leads to a return to the fold—that is, to school, to the miserable life of being a poorly paid schoolteacher, to the daily harassing on the part of the principal, and to a future with no hope whatsoever. As with Cesare in *I giorni contati*, for Mombelli there is no other way but the admission of defeat.

For all its flaws, and even though basically a compromise between Petri's vision and the project he had inherited, *Il maestro di Vigevano* is one of the great Italian films about the Boom, alongside *Il sorpasso* and *La vita agra*. It virtually completes a trilogy which comprises *L'assassino* and *I giorni contati*, three works depicting early 1960s Italy with a depth and firmness that manage to go beyond the limits of the *commedia all'italiana*.

FIVE

POP!

La decima vittima *(1965)*

Sci-Fi, Italian Style

A longtime fan of science fiction, Elio Petri had been toying with the idea of making a sci-fi movie for years. In 1957 he had written a story with Luigi Vanzi and Enzo Provenzale, *I testimoni del nulla* (The Witnesses of Nothing), which he described as openly political. They offered it to Franco Cristaldi, but the project was shelved, for "in Italy we don't have a 'technical habit' to science fiction," the director pointed out. "The development of our society and the human phenomena that accompany it are starting to have a true 'modern' significance only recently."[1] Italians were discovering the genre's typical sense of wonder by way of popular literature and film. *Urania*, the series of sci-fi paperbacks launched by Mondadori along the line of their popular *Gialli*, had surfaced in 1952, and audiences were treated to a steady diet of American, British and Japanese films.

At that time, however, Italian producers were not yet ready to try their hand at the genre. *La morte viene dallo spazio* (1958, Paolo Heusch), largely considered Italy's first science fiction film, had flopped, and the first tentative efforts—Riccardo Freda and Mario Bava's *Caltiki il mostro immortale* (1959) and Antonio Margheriti's *Space Men* (1960) and *Il pianeta degli uomini spenti* (1961)—had been mostly ignored by the public. Producers would rather invest their money in sword-and-sandal or adventure flicks.

Petri's vision of science fiction was in tune with his political ideas, and he liked films with openly sociological and political undertones, such as *The Day the Earth Stood Still* (1951, Robert Wise) and *On the Beach* (1959, Stanley Kramer). As he stated in a 1962 interview in the magazine *Cinema Domani*,

> Science fiction is an ironic mirror of our fears toward the future, and in this sense, unfortunately, it has a rather extensive realistic basis. We see many aberrations around us, and unleash our fear for what might happen next by way of elegant, albeit horrendous, hypotheses. Through science fiction we paint a psychic picture of our times, and our pessimism is patent: I have never read a science fiction story which gave a portrait of the future devoid of fear and rooted in hope.[2]

Robert Sheckley's short story *Seventh Victim* was first published in 1953, in *Galaxy Science Fiction*. It depicts a future in which the government has legalized murder via the Big Hunt, a game devised as an outlet for human aggressiveness so as to prevent wars.

Participants are divided between "hunters" and "victims." The hunter is assigned a target (victim) and must track down and kill him or her. In turn, the victim must assassinate the hunter before the other does the same. After playing hunter, one must take turns as victim. Stanton Freelaine is an experienced player whose main goal is to enter the exclusive "Tens Club," a status earned by those who won ten rounds of the Big Hunt. Stanton is surprised to find out that his "seventh victim" is a woman, Janet-Marie. Moreover, she appears to be indifferent to her fate, almost resigned. Posing as a businessman, Freelaine approaches Janet-Marie to find out more about her, even though this puts him in danger. She tells him she is an aspiring actress who has failed her first mission as hunter, because she didn't have the courage to kill the victim, and now she is expecting inevitable death. Stanton and Janet-Marie spend some time together and he falls for her. He confesses being the assigned hunter and proposes to marry her. Janet-Marie kisses him and lights a cigarette, then shoots him with a gun concealed in the lighter. She can finally join the Tens Club…

Sheckley's short story was first translated into Italian the following year (as *Vittima n. 7*) in the fourth issue of *Galaxy*, one of several science-fiction magazines which saw the light in the mid-to-late 1950s. Then it appeared (as *La settima vittima*) in the anthology *Le meraviglie del possibile* (The Marvels of Possibility), published by Einaudi in November 1959. Edited by Carlo Fruttero and Sergio Solmi, it collected stories by H.G. Wells, A.E. Van Vogt, Fredric Brown, Isaac Asimov, Arthur C. Clarke, Richard Matheson, Ray Bradbury, Daniel Keyes and many others, and exposed a whole generation of readers to some of the greatest English language science fiction authors.

Le meraviglie del possibile was one of the most discussed books of the year. It brought science fiction from the newsstands to the bookshops, with a consideration and respect for the genre which many intellectuals found difficult to understand. "What strikes us in these short stories, as soon as one puts aside the technological gimmick and tests their substance, is their psychological poverty, their intellectual squalor," a reviewer wrote.[3] Petri thought differently. He immensely enjoyed the anthology, and considered adapting one of the short stories into a movie.

Initially the director had set his eyes on Daniel Keyes's *Flowers for Algernon*, about a mentally disabled man, Charlie Gordon, who undergoes an innovative surgical treatment to increase his intelligence. The surgery, perfected after experimenting with a laboratory mouse named Algernon, is a success. Charlie acquires the IQ of a genius, and quits his job as a factory janitor after discovering that his co-workers are scared by his new self and have signed a petition to have him fired. But, as he soon discovers, the effects of the treatment are temporary, and he is going to revert to his original state.

Petri had considered setting the story in a huge factory in Milan, so as to explore the social issues it raised, but he could not purchase the rights to it. "Mastroianni and I still hope that a certain American actor will sell the rights to the story, one day or the other," he told *Cinema Domani*.[4] The American actor was Cliff Robertson, who had starred in a TV adaptation, "The Two Worlds of Charlie Gordon," an episode of the television drama *The United States Steel Hour* aired on February 22, 1961. Robertson would reprise the role for the 1968 film *Charly* (which drew also from Keyes' 1966 novel, also titled *Flowers for Algernon*) which earned him the Academy Award as Best Actor.

Petri then opted for *Seventh Victim*, because, he explained, "I glimpsed a beautiful love story in it."[5]

La decima vittima, *from Page to Screen*

In late 1961 Petri wrote an adaptation of Sheckley's story with Suso Cecchi D'Amico and Tonino Guerra, but the film was postponed to April 1963.[6] News of the project being in development turned up immediately after the failure of *Un tranquillo posto di campagna*. Interviewed on the set of Monicelli's *I compagni*, Marcello Mastroianni passingly mentioned his involvement in the film, to be shot in Brasília and already titled *La decima vittima*.[7] But in the spring of 1963 Petri was also busy with the ill-fated collaboration with De Laurentiis on *I mostri*.

An early 12-page scenario,[8] not dated but presumably from the same period (and also titled *La decima vittima*), indeed sets the story in Brasília and is basically similar to Sheckley's tale. It opens with a series of seven eccentric murders taking place all over the globe—Sahara, the North Pole, an old Christian church, the jungle, a helicopter, a coffee bar, a stadium—to the indifference of onlookers and passers-by. All the murders are related to the Big Hunt. The protagonist, Alfredo Martini, receives communication that his next victim is a woman, advertising model Janet Frelaine. He flies to Brazil and then the story expands the original by exploring the growing attraction between Martini and Janet, with the man refusing to perform an easy task and gradually falling for her.

This early outline emphasizes the sexual angle, with a vision of a society where "no one has fallen in love in 200 years," children are born via artificial insemination and erotic tension is released through "outlets": a scene depicts, in a very explicit manner for the time, an encounter between Martini and a nurse who masturbates him and collects his semen for a sperm bank. Martini's falling for his victim results in the man experiencing psychosomatic symptoms such as palpitation and flushed cheeks and ears. He seeks advice from a psychoanalyst who diagnoses a "crack in his nervous balance."

The story bursts with satiric ideas such as a supermarket for hunters and preys, sporting all types of weapons and gadgets, and a scene in which Alfredo and Janet go to the movies and watch "old love stories that make the audience laugh out loud." It includes a subplot about Janet's mother, who lives in a sort of huge concentration camp together with "the tens of thousands of old people who are useless to society." There, the old have regressed to childlike status. The ending reprises Sheckley's coda, with a biting addition: Janet films Alfredo's death and after shooting him she turns to the camera and advertises a famous brand of tranquilizers. In the epilogue a crowd of black people carries her through the streets in glory, as if in a carnival. But she is crying…

Such an ambitious project needed a substantial budget. Titanus had purchased the rights to Sheckley's story, but after the company's financial breakdown Petri had to find another backer. Carlo Ponti initially refused to take part in it, but he was convinced by Mastroianni's involvement, which meant strong box-office potential. Reportedly, Ponti loathed science fiction. He decided to resort to an American scriptwriter to flesh out and reshape the project for the U.S. market.

In the spring of 1963, Petri exchanged some letters with Nate Monaster, who had submitted an outline out of Sheckley's story upon Ponti's request. In his first letter, dated May 9, Petri explained thoroughly the motives that pushed him to choose *Seventh Victim*:

> The story depicted a hypothesis—rather elegant but horrid—about the relations between the sexes as they will look in the future; starting from this the main theme gradually enlarged itself in order to show also the social aspects of the future, until it expressed—indirectly— also the psychological image of our posterities. The key of the story was ironic, but its nucleus

contained a love story which has been found, by all of us, nice and allusive. (In a certain way the relations between the sexes give utterance to a community like the relations between classes.) And, on top of it, sarcasm was hitting some commonplaces, very much in vogue nowadays, especially in Europe, meaning themes like the "incommunicability," the "eclipse of sentiments" and the "human loneliness." We were also interested in the narrative scheme of the story, which was that of a "suspense story," very much suitable for the modern audience, and congenial enough to the traditional motion picture story telling.[9]

He underlined his idea to center the love story upon "a contradiction so typical of today, that between a superstructure which tries to eliminate any sentimental remnants from human relations ... and the psychological and cultural structure which is somehow still romantic." He also stressed his intention of refreshing the suspenseful aspect of the plot (will the hunter kill his victim or not?) by depicting it "in a key of rather cynical comedy, in the spirit of a modern and witty apologue."

But Monaster was pushing the story in a very different direction. He focused on the theme of a world without wars, concocting a backstory in which a nation is forced by the psychological state of mind to organize one at all costs. The American scriptwriter devised a love triangle in which the male protagonist is torn between "a woman who is pushing him to kill and a girl who imposes him to revolt against the system."

This left Petri perplexed to say the least, as can be read between the lines of his letter:

> In order to amplify and to specify the "political" end of Sheckley's story—which is "political" only indirectly—your suggestions end up giving the love story only an ornamental character.... It remains a fact that our points of view concerning the making of the picture diverge in a rather spectacular manner, if I may say so, and I feel sorry for this, as it appears to me that, though taking two diverging ways, you and I wish to say the same thing.

Monaster's reply showed that they were definitely not on the same wavelength.

> There is much in your outline I would gratefully incorporate into my screenplay, but if I am to do so we must eliminate grim emotionless despair and offer hope. You express the wish that I develop your outline into a witty, ironical, amusing treatment incorporating the excitement of a thriller. In this wish I concur heartily. But I don't feel it should depict a joyless doomed *1984* society.[10]

Monaster suggested depicting Martini as "a new folk hero, the skillful, graceful killer whose virtuoso performances earn him ... the adulation of the cheering crowds," while Janet "should have millions of males vicariously anxious to accommodate her" whereas in Petri's outline she plaintively suggested an "outlet," as Monaster venomously quipped. The scriptwriter had reservations about the ending as well, which in his view inhibited the romantic side of the film for the sake of an unexpected tag.

In those hectic summer months Petri was working on *Nudi per vivere*. He was in the jury of the First International Science Fiction Festival in Trieste[11] and was about to shoot *Peccato nel pomeriggio*, before embarking on *Il maestro di Vigevano*. Newspapers announced that his sci-fi project was under development, but he was dealing with an American scriptwriter that had been imposed upon him and who was poles apart from him, literally and figuratively. One can sense his irritation in his reply to Monaster dated July 22—the same day Dino De Laurentiis reproached him for his lack of commitment on *Il maestro di Vigevano*—in which he pointed out:

> Mr. Ponti, Mr. Mastroianni and I would like to stress the thing we care about the most: the film that you have been entrusted with must be a rather faithful adaptation of Sheckley's story. We

all make the movie because we believe in Sheckley's story, and you must always keep this in mind. None of us wants to make a grey and monotonous film. We want to make a film which satirizes—in the funniest possible way—a society which is indeed grey and monotonous. The story we have chosen is exactly the amusing satire of a society without love.[12]

There is no trace of Monaster's reply in the Elio Petri archive, but it would be safe to infer that the two parts remained on different positions, for eventually the collaboration did not happen.

Mention of the project turned up again in the press in early 1964.[13] By then, a new collaborator came aboard: journalist and writer Ennio Flaiano, Fellini's frequent collaborator and a brilliant observer of post-war Italy. Flaiano had played with the science fiction genre in his 1954 short story (later a stage play) *Un marziano a Roma*, a bitter satire of the "Dolce Vita" as seen through the eyes of a Martian who lands in Rome in his flying saucer and becomes the sensation of the day. Soon, though, the Romans get tired of him. No longer an exciting novelty, he is gradually forgotten and even openly ridiculed. In the end, a passerby blows a raspberry at him.

Elio and Ennio got along very well. "Flaiano with me was really a delightful, enchanting man," the director recalled. "We spent wonderful hours doing nothing, and our conversations were about life, time passing by, other people, society, literature: everything, except work. Work, to him, was the last of topics. And this made him even more pleasant."[14] The scriptwriting trio (Petri, Flaiano, Guerra) became a quartet with ex-journalist Giorgio Salvioni, who would collaborate on De Santis's last film, *Un apprezzato professionista di sicuro avvenire* (1972). By that time, other filmmakers were becoming interested in sci-fi as means to a political discourse. Ugo Gregoretti had helmed the satiric *Omicron* (1963), starring Renato Salvatori, about a shapeless alien who takes possession of a worker's body in order to invade the Earth and is exploited by the factory owners because of his skills, and Tinto Brass had directed another alien invasion satire, *Il disco volante* (1964), produced by De Laurentiis and starring Alberto Sordi in four different roles (including a gay count).

While Petri was busy scripting *La settima vittima*, a tragic event shook the Italian Left. In August 1964, the secretary of the PCI Palmiro Togliatti was struck by a cerebral hemorrhage during a vacation in the Soviet Union, where he had met Leonid Brezhnev (who was about to succeed Khrushchev as the head of the USSR's Communist Party). He died a few days later in the city of Yalta, Crimea. Togliatti's funeral took place in Rome, on August 25, and a crowd of a million people followed the coffin from the PCI headquarters to Piazza San Giovanni and the Verano Cemetery. Petri, along with several other filmmakers—Gianni Amico, Libero Bizzarri, Francesco Maselli, Lino Micciché, Glauco Pellegrini, Sergio Tau, Paolo and Vittorio Taviani, Marco Zavattini, Valerio Zurlini and Giorgio Arlorio—filmed the ceremony. The footage ended up in the 40-minute documentary *L'Italia con Togliatti*.

In December 1964, the parliament voted for the election of the fifth President of the Republic, a few months after president Antonio Segni had suffered cerebral thrombosis, leading to his resignation. The parliament elected Giuseppe Saragat, after a balloting which lasted twelve days and twenty-one voting sessions. Petri followed it closely and took inspiration from it to develop the idea he had mentioned to Spinazzola in 1962, about a movie centered on a politician. He told *L'Unità*:

I have had in mind for a long time a feature film on the issue of power. I nurtured the idea when I watched the sessions for the election of Segni [in May 1962]. In these days the project has become more specific and there are good chances that I'll make it. It is not a documentary but a story that unfolds in the realm of political fantasy, keeping its feet on the ground and facing the issue of power, or rather of the "power vacuum" during a struggle of parties for the election of a President.... It is an attempt to define in poetic and satiric terms the great and decisive concreteness of the most fascinating abstraction, that of Power.... The title I have in mind for this modern fable on how a President is born—an imaginary President in an imaginary State—is in fact *Il vuoto di potere* (The Power Vacuum).[15]

The project never took off, but its mention proves that Petri was already considering molding his cinema in a more directly political shape, albeit with satiric elements. These would surface in his next work and would become prominent in his films of the following decade. Moreover, he explicitly stressed his idea of a committed cinema with spectacular values, which would entertain audiences while attempting to say something about the outside world.

Reportedly, the scriptwriting phase for *La decima vittima* was particularly elaborate. As Petri recalled, "Ponti neither wanted to make a movie with me nor a science fiction one ... but he did want to make a movie with Marcello. I worked on the script for a year and a half and arrived exhausted at the end, always with Ponti putting sticks in the wheel."[16]

In the April 1966 issue of *Films and Filming*, Saul Kahn wrote at length about the scriptwriting sessions, which evoked the way Petri used to work with De Santis:

The job took one year, including times when work was suspended and a three-month period in which four complete drafts were written. The four young writers created the script in group sessions where they would discuss the plot and character development. One would then volunteer to write the dialogue for the current scene, which he would read at the next meeting. "It was like archeology," reminisced Salvione [sic] during the shooting. "We started digging, and we never knew what we'd find."[17]

According to Kahn, early drafts moved in a very different direction from both the early outline and the final shooting script:

Mastroianni was, in the original, the hunter. After a grueling (legal) marriage to two hefty women.... Marcello sensed a weakening of the trigger finger, certain death for a professional assassin. He was then programmed for a homicidal battle with a cowboy type who would become governor of Texas if he could make Mastroianni his tenth kill. Desperate Marcello was haunted by the specter of a door-to-door vendor of suicide pills.[18]

As Petri told Jean A. Gili in the early 1970s, "it was not a movie about America, but about 'Americanism,' that is to say about cruelty, cruelty in intersubjective relationships. Ponti rejected this script and then he rejected another; without telling us, he had another script prepared by others."[19] Years later he returned to the subject, explaining that the producer "was having the script rewritten by two different teams including one with Garinei and Giovannini, and during filming an outline by Suso Cecchi D'Amico turned up."[20]

Pietro Garinei and Alessandro Giovannini were well-known playwrights who specialized in musicals, and their contribution was meant to add more comedy to the recipe, as was probably the case with future film director Luigi Magni, who is listed in production papers as another uncredited contributor. Mastroianni confirmed that Ponti pushed for the film to be more of a comedy, for he had pre-sold it as such to the American distributor.[21] Since Garinei and Giovannini worked on a parallel version of the script,

Petri never met them, and he never met another scriptwriter who claims to have had an important, if uncredited, role in the making.

Ernesto Gastaldi had always had a soft spot for science fiction: his novelette *Iperbole infinita* (1960) had been published in the *Urania* series, and he had penned some more sci-fi works, namely another novelette, *Tempo zero* (1960), and a couple of short stories, *Galassia in fuga* (1959) and *Una storia da non credere* (1961). But sci-fi had not caught on with the Italian movie industry and he had stuck to other genres, most notably the Gothic, cranking out scripts with admirable prolificacy.

In his amusing 1991 memoir *Voglio entrare nel cinema*, Gastaldi recalled the events that led him to participate in the making of Petri's film. He was reached on the phone by production organizer Jone Tuzi:

"You wanted to do that thing, how is that called, science fiction?"
I nodded on the phone while she went on.
"Ponti is making *Seventh Victim* but he doesn't like the script. I told him I knew someone who might fix it."[22]

Once in Ponti's office, according to Gastaldi, the producer handed him a screenplay telling him, "Look, in my opinion this is horse shit. We must start filming in fifteen days and I'm not shooting this stuff. You read it and then you suggest some changes. Here it is."[23] The scriptwriter's reaction upon reading it was not much different either.

Leafing through the pages of that unbelievable concoction I got pissed off. They tried to turn it [Sheckley's short story] into some sort of *commedia all'italiana*: a little bit of eroticism, a little bit of sentiment, some vulgarities … and a happy ending. And science fiction? Nothing, only the vague caricature of a future world, as if it was possible to poke fun at the (not yet) commonplaces of a genre that cinematically doesn't exist yet.[24]

Gastaldi claims that he practically rewrote the script from scratch in merely eight days, although Ponti was adamant that he had to stay incognito "or the authors will make a mess." The producer allegedly loved the result and told Petri and the others that an American specialist did in eight days what they couldn't do in eight months. Still, the scriptwriter's opinion about the film is vitriolic: "The damage was irreparable: no more science fiction in Italy. Every time I would propose a sci-fi story, they would bang on my nose this megacrap they called *La decima vittima*. To Petri, seven victims were not enough."[25]

However, Gastaldi's recollections must be taken with a grain of salt. For one thing, he implies that the title was changed at the eleventh hour, and the most likely explanation for this would be the Italian distribution of the German *krimi*, *Das siebente Opfer* (1964, Franz-Josef Gottlieb), which came out in April 1965 as *La settima vittima*, causing Ponti to come up with a different one. But the early draft kept at the Elio Petri fund is titled *La decima vittima*, proving that the change had already been made during preproduction. Moreover, Gastaldi depicts Ponti's intentions as the total opposite of what they were according to all other participants. Since the producer loathed science fiction, it is highly unlikely that he was happy with Gastaldi *adding* more sci-fi to a script which, in the latter's own words, sounded more like the *commedia all'italiana* the mogul was attempting to sell overseas. According to production papers, Gastaldi was paid 1,200,000 *lire* for his uncredited services, while Garinei and Giovannini were paid two million each and Magni one million, so it is likely that his contribution was not as extensive as he described.

Besides Ponti's reservations, the exhausting preproduction ordeal was also due to the Italian tycoon's difficulties in cutting a distribution deal abroad. Eventually Ponti found an American backer in Joseph E. Levine, and the project could move on. But the producer demanded that the film be set in Rome. According to Petri, the final draft was completed in thirty days. Indeed, news articles mentioned that the authors were still putting the finishing touches on it in late April 1965, barely a few weeks before shooting would commence.[26] "We had to turn everything upside down," the director complained. "It was not what we had in mind when working on the script, it had become the usual film about Rome.... For my part, I could only sketch schematic characters and introduce ... the satire of items in vogue at that time."[27]

The shooting script was noticeably different from Sheckley's short story, while keeping its basic premises, the Big Hunt giving its members free license to kill and the division between hunters and victims. But Petri and his team ultimately overturned the roles. The film starts with Caroline Meredith, a young and beautiful American, who dispatches her ninth opponent (a Chinese hunter) by way of her sexual charm. She is then assigned a victim, the last one before she reaches the "Tens Club" (called Decathon in the film). The adversary is an Italian, Marcello Poletti, who has won six games but plays the Big Hunt without any particular commitment, for he is overwhelmed by personal issues, namely a greedy ex-wife, Lidia, and an oppressive lover, Olga. Caroline approaches Marcello, pretending to be a reporter, and starts following him. She plans to stage the assassination at the Roman forum, so that the killing (broadcast and sponsored by a tea brand) will be a worldwide sensation. Marcello suspects Caroline to be his hunter, but he gradually falls for her...

La decima vittima was an Italian-French coproduction (respectively 80 percent and 20 percent) between Ponti's Compagnia Cinematografica Champion and the Paris-based Les Films Concordia, with an estimated budget of 500 million *lire*. Ponti sided Mastroianni with Ursula Andress, by then at the top of her popularity after her appearance as Honey Ryder in the first 007 film, *Dr. No* (1962, Terence Young). The Swiss actress's name was kept secret until the very end, although newspapers maliciously mentioned that the female lead would have a "license to kill" Mastroianni's character,[28] a reference to the Italian title of *Dr. No*, released in the peninsula as *Agente 007—Licenza di uccidere* (Agent 007—License to Kill).

As for supporting roles, Margaret Lee was originally considered as Olga, whereas Luciano Salce was to play Marcello's lawyer, Rossi, according to a cast list dating May 10. The same tentative cast included Antonio De Teffè (aka Anthony Steffen) as Rudy, Gastaldi's wife (and CSC graduate) Mara Chianetta as the "Head of the Erotic center," Ivo Garrani as an industrialist, Umberto D'Orsi as a "hunted man," Paolo Panelli (1st victim), Andrea Checchi (2nd victim), Gianrico Tedeschi (1st cop) and Romolo Valli (2nd cop).

None of these would appear in the film. By early June, Elsa Martinelli was cast as Olga, Salce's part went to Gastone Moschin (replaced in turn by Massimo Serato), while Milo Quesada came on board as Rudy and Luce Bonifassy replaced Michèle Girardon as Marcello's wife, Lidia, in accordance with co-production quotas. Salvo Randone, absent from early lists, was cast for a cameo appearance as the disfigured, maimed Professor. The crew included the prestigious d.o.p. Gianni Di Venanzo, art director Piero Poletto, and Petri's regular editor Ruggero Mastroianni. Piero Piccioni would compose the score.

With an overall cost of over 632 million *lire* (132 million over the planned budget),[29] *La decima vittima* was an expensive financial effort. Petri was paid 25 million *lire* for directing, while Mastroianni's fee was 45 million and Andress got 15,240,000. The board

From left to right: Elio Petri, Marcello Mastroianni, Elsa Martinelli, and Ursula Andress during the filming of *La decima vittima*, posing in one of the film's striking Op-Art sets.

which preventively examined the script pointed out its boldness and judged it "a bitter vision ... which not even the various comic and sentimental notes that punctuate the film manage to soften. In the end, at least for the reader, one has the strange feeling of having discovered something that was better left ignored."

The original shooting schedule, as envisioned in papers dated May 10, was of forty-seven days, from May 31 to July 24, 1965, with a six-day shoot in Africa, but it was soon expanded and altered. Filming started on June 7 in Rome. The shooting plan comprised fifty-one days, ending on August 6 with six days of exteriors in New York, but filming extended for over a month beyond schedule. The New York scenes were filmed in early September, with locations including the J. C. Penney building on upper Sixth Avenue and the South side ramp of the Grand Central Station; newspapers reported that Andress had suffered a small incident on the set, injuring her right arm while "shooting a dynamic scene," and showed pictures of Petri jokingly kissing the actress' bandaged forearm.[30]

Andress's presence garnered the film even more space in Italian newspapers, but Ponti's influence and Mastroianni's popularity granted ample coverage also in the American press. An article in the *New York Times* was accompanied by a set still of Petri posing with a radiant Marcello, Ursula Andress and Elsa Martinelli before one of the Op Art works featured in the film. The director, described in the text as "rotund and youthful," was careful to stress the movie's entertainment value beyond its grim premise: "A film must be made for an audience so we're coating the pill considerably. The surface action and all that should please the spectator. Then if he wants to dig below the surface, so much the better."[31] In addition to interviewing Mastroianni, the *Los Angeles Times* quoted Levine—billed as executive producer in the foreign version yet uncredited in Italian prints—trying to pass off the film as a James Bond–style extravaganza "loaded with lethal gimmicks and gadgets, including dynamite boots, a rapid-firing metal bra ...

and a toy beetle with a gun in its tail … the success of Fleming's secret agent has brought on a boom of spy, free-wheeler, dream-a-little, laugh-a-little hero movies both here and abroad."[32]

The very existence of *La decima vittima* signaled that something had changed in the commercial strategies of Italian cinema. The times when committed *auteur* films by the likes of Fellini, Visconti and Antonioni would become blockbusters were over. Only a couple of years earlier, Petri could spoof Antonioni in *Peccato nel pomeriggio*, but now the main reference would be the 007 franchise. The public's tastes were changing, audiences were crowding to see Westerns and spy flicks, and tycoons were trying to adapt themselves to that. According to many, including De Laurentiis, this was the public's reaction to an overdose of intellectual films. Marcello Mastroianni's transition from Fellini's alter ego to James Bond copycat (at least in newspaper headlines) was telling. It was the age of disengagement, and that is how *La decima vittima* would be perceived by the general public and critics alike. But was it really like that?

Tomorrow, Today

Petri's attempt at a "thinking man's science fiction film" took him along a similar path as those followed around the same time by Godard (*Alphaville*, released in France in May 1965) and Truffaut (*Fahrenheit 451*, released in September 1966). In the *Cinema Domani* interview, he had argued that

> a science fiction film can have realistic content … if the future it depicts has deep roots in the present and its essence. In the best science fiction stories, we can detect dreamlike or psycho-analytical realism, if one must yield to the temptation of playing with labels. As for the patterns and style, who can rule out that it is possible to shoot a science fiction film outdoors like *La terra trema*, with non-professional actors … like *Ladri di biciclette*, and with a hand-held Arriflex camera like *Shadows*?[33]

The original story's thin outline allowed for many digressions, and Petri used it to develop a philosophical tale, a Swiftian image of the future which looks like "tomorrow morning." The elements of social satire are equally distributed between the lines of dialogue and the visual rendition of the year 2000.

The results carry the vintage naïve taste of 1960s dystopian tales, such as in the depiction of computerized technology, with artificial intelligence taking the form of gigantic old-fashioned calculator machines, or when it is passingly mentioned that the Pope is American (the thought of a foreign Pope was very sci-fi like in the mid–1960s, but it would take only thirteen years before it actually happened, with Karol Wojtyla becoming John Paul II in 1978).

As a satire of mid–1960s Italy, *La decima vittima* dwells on the expected topics. One such is the irony on divorce (still not allowed in the country, and introduced only in 1970), a common theme in Italian cinema of the period. In 1965, Socialist PM Loris Fortuna submitted a draft law on the matter, followed by a campaign by the Radical Party to raise public awareness. The following year Alberto Sordi would write, direct, and star in a film on the issue, *Scusi, lei è favorevole o contrario?* (1966). But the humor in Petri's film comes from the paradox that in the future, despite all the technological novelties and such amoral pastimes as the Big Hunt, divorce still doesn't exist in such a deeply Catholic country as Italy. In fact, Marcello had to wait six years to have his marriage annulled by the Roman Rota, the highest appellate tribunal of the Catholic Church. "We're very religious," he explains. The Vatican still retains its influence in 21st century Rome. On the other hand, in Petri's futuristic vision, brothels (now named Relaxing Service Stations) are still active, unlike in 1960s Italy: the Merlin Law, which abolished them in 1958, had been a shocking event for the average Italian male.

Ditto for the stabs at bureaucracy. Italy in the year 2000 is an amass of red tape, lazy civil servants and obtuse regulations just as it is in 1965. But the most sarcastic segment is the one in which Caroline discovers Marcello's elderly parents, confined in a secret room equipped like the average Italian post-war homes with wooden furniture, carpets and old-style lamps. In a twist predating *Soylent Green* (1973, Richard O. Fleischer) and other dystopian fantasies, elderly people are being "collected" by the government and presumably eliminated. But Marcello, like many others, has refused to turn his parents over to the State. "In Italy we believe in the patriarchal family system," he explains. "We keep them hidden; we often fix them up to look like teenagers." And when Caroline marvels, "You really love them so much?" he replies curtly: "No. It's the obligation that bothers me." As in *L'assassino*, the ghosts of our past are still with us, hidden in a corner of our conscience, and despite the travesty of modernity, the core of Italian culture hasn't changed a bit. It is a startling vision of the present without any filters, frozen in time, which gives the measure of what *La decima vittima* might have been, had it been made the way Petri had devised it.

Flaiano's contribution can be glimpsed in the paradoxical slogans delivered, *1984*-style, by the female voice at the Hunt Ministry ("Live dangerously, but within the law," "Why control the births when we can increase the deaths?" and "One enemy a day will keep the doctor away") and in the amusing depiction of the "*tramontisti*" (sunset worshippers), the cult of which Marcello is the definitely unpassionate high priest. He climbs up a pedestal on the beach and delivers a prayer to the setting sun ("This last ray of light is reaching us from 149 million kilometers. Our father is leaving, we see him die with our own eyes…. But we can't despair. Our tears are purifying. They free us from the anguish of every day"), only to become the target of a rival faction, the "*neorealisti*" (neo-realists), in one of the film's best in-jokes. Another, also likely penned by Flaiano, has Marcello residing at "Lungotevere Fellini."

The director's moral stance is evident in the depiction of the intrusive mass media and advertising. The invective against the entertainment industry has a biting edge that predates Peter Watkins' satire on rock music as opium for the masses, *Privilege* (1967). Caroline wants to have Marcello's killing aired worldwide and replete with choreographic accompaniment, to advertise a tea brand ("Drink Tea Ming and you'll live longer!"), just like a commercial. But Marcello plans to do the same with Caroline, having her eaten by a crocodile live on TV while he advertises a soft drink ("With Coca 80 you always win!"). In today's consumer society, Petri underlines, television is a monster that feeds our worst impulses, a theme that would reach pessimistic extremes in his last film, *Buone notizie*. Here, the tone is lighter, and forcibly so due to Ponti's diktats, but such lines as "The idea of killing someone for publicity has always entertained me" are telling. The depiction of violence and death as spectacle is a surprising anticipatory theme that predates several dystopian works, namely Peter Watkins' *Gladiatorerna* (aka *The Gladiators*, 1969), Norman Jewison's *Rollerball* (1975), Robert Altman's *Quintet* (1979), Yves Boisset's *Le prix du danger* (1983, based on another Robert Sheckley story and similar in places to *La decima vittima*), Lucio Fulci's *I guerrieri dell'anno 2072* (1984) and Paul Michael Glaser's *The*

Running Man (1987, inspired by a Stephen King novel, albeit penned under the assumed name of Richard Bachman), up to the recent *Hunger Games* series.

Petri and his scriptwriters settled on many fast gags to emphasize the premise's vitriolic irony. An early one—a special pair of riding boots spiked with dynamite concealed in the heels, so that when the victim (a German Baron) clicks them in a military salute he is blown to smithereens—is virtually identical to one Riccardo Freda described when discussing one of his shelved projects, the grotesque anthology *Il dito di Dio*.[34] Some comedy bits are lighter than others, but the director often insists on black humor. An example is a hunter killing his victim (a young woman) in cold blood just before Marcello's eyes, outside the Hunt Ministry, after the poor woman has made one last desperate attempt to get Marcello's help by way of a passionate kiss. The omnipresent policemen inspect the hunter's credentials and report a regulation killing, before slapping him with a ticket for illegal parking. The mocking punchline notwithstanding, the scene is notable for the hardheartedness it conveys, not least on the protagonist's part.

In another scene a shooting takes place at an outside bar, only to be interrupted by a waiter (Pier Paolo Capponi, in an early film role) who alerts the opponents that a new regulation prohibits any shooting in the area. Then he takes away one of them by the ear, as if he were a disobedient kid. The other complains: "What kind of life is this? You can't shoot in hospitals, nor in restaurants, you can't shoot in churches nor at the barber's. You can't shoot at nursery schools ... you can't shoot anywhere anymore!" As Caroline points out, "In America there aren't many restrictions for hunters. Everyone can easily shoot wherever and whenever he wants to." The sequence is played in a lighter tone, almost as a passing joke, but the line has a sinister resonance even nowadays.

Overall, the humor is very much in the vein of *Dr. Strangelove*. Randone's Professor, a character possibly inspired by Peter Sellers' titular mad scientist in Stanley Kubrick's film, underlines Petri's preference for the grotesque. With his suede collar immobilizing his chin, steel teeth (a look evoking Peter Lorre's Dr. Gogol in Karl Freund's *Mad Love*), and metal hook,[35] he is a sinister figure who embodies society's death wish and its rigid selective rules. "The important thing is how one dies—as a rabbit, or as a Samurai?" he philosophizes. A very similar character, played by Gustavo D'Arpe, would turn up in Sergio Spina's pop/political satire *Fantabulous—La donna, il sesso e il superuomo* (1968), heavily influenced by *La decima vittima*.

As Saul Kahn remarked, at times the film's nightmarish vision comes close to Hannah Arendt's 1963 book essay *Eichmann in Jerusalem: A Report on the Banality of Evil*. Following and expanding the core of Sheckley's tale—which, like his other 1953 short story *The Monsters*, dealt with the shifting of civilized values—Petri explores the everyday cruelty of capitalism. "There are many victims in the film," he told Kahn. "Their deaths are antiseptic, bloodless ones—the bloodless homicide of love affairs, the moral deaths of commerce, etc. They are metaphors designed to make the point that everyday civilized life has almost reached the intensity of physical violence."[36]

A World of Surfaces

One of Petri's initial ideas was to shoot the film in the futuristic scenario of Brasília, the federal capital of Brazil founded in 1960. With its modernist architecture planned by Lúcio Costa, Oscar Niemeyer, Joaquim Cardozo and Roberto Burle Marx, it looked indeed like a vision from the future. The director's attention to existing architecture was in tune with his observation of Michelangelo Antonioni's films conveying science fiction elements by way of their visual style and setting. Because of Ponti's limitations, he had to make do with EUR, the residential and business district in the South area of Rome that the Fascist regime had started building in 1938, in view of the World Fair that should have taken place in 1942 but was cancelled due to World War II. With its marble statues and palaces openly inspired by Ancient Rome, EUR was to portray the official image of Fascist Rome, and as such it had been used by Italian cinema to evoke a distant past, such as in Riccardo Freda's *Teodora* (1954). But its blinding white buildings, wide open spaces and overall aloofness had also accompanied visions of the future, most notably in *L'ultimo uomo della terra* (aka *The Last Man on Earth*, 1964), an effective adaptation of Richard Matheson's novel *I Am Legend* starring Vincent Price. As Federico Fellini once put it, EUR "looks futuristic, but it is a future we already know, so it doesn't worry us because it is taken for granted, partly by sci-fi stories, partly by comics."[37]

Petri had already shot *Peccato nel pomeriggio* there, employing the familiar sight of the lake and the ENI Palace (or Glass Palace) in a way akin to the Antonioni mood he was spoofing, through the use of architecture as a mirror of the protagonist's feelings. In *La decima vittima* he and art director Piero Poletto—who around the same period worked on two more science fiction films partially shot at the EUR gardens, Antonio Margheriti's *I criminali della galassia* and *I diafanoidi vengono da Marte* (both released in 1966)—pulled out all the stops in their reinvention of the district. Existing locations are reimagined by way of colored transparent plexiglass and glass sheets which "soften and blur the limits between the object and the surrounding ambient," while the use of open spaces highlights the sense of emptiness of a depopulated world to the effect of "geometrical abstraction, an idealized city, De Chirico–style, where the presence of human beings seems, not by chance, an expendable surplus."[38]

An example is the scene where Caroline and Marcello first meet at an open space theater (designed by architect Adalberto Libera atop the Palace of Congresses) where the only other human figures are a pair of girls leaning against a wall and two saxophonists playing their instruments on cubic platforms. The musicians look like props themselves, while the motionless spectators bring to mind the enigmatic individuals in Alain Resnais' *L'année dernière á Marienbad* (1961).

The result is a Rome of the future which looks like a three-dimensional collage made with bits and pieces of ancient Rome (the Colosseum, the Temple of Venus, the Forum, the Temple of Janus) and the recent Fascist past (the EUR buildings). The ruins of an ancient civilization highlight the barbarism of an ultramodern society which resorts to man's basic instincts to keep citizens enslaved. It is a return to the past, a mocking denial of the progressive values of civilization. Beneath its glossy surface, Petri's depiction of "tomorrow morning" conveys a disenchanted pessimism.

The inner barbarism of the future as imagined in the film is underlined by the references to the foundation myth of Rome, with the fight to the death between the Horatii triplets and their enemy counterpart, the Curiatii from the nearby village of Alba Longa, to prevent a war (also the subject of a Bertolt Brecht play, *The Horatians and the Curiatians*). Even more telling, in this sense, is the recurring theme of gladiator games, an element to be reprised in many other dystopian films. Caroline's team plans to stage Marcello's death in the Colosseum ("The gladiators won't cost much, plus, ancient Rome always worked well on the American market"), and the scene at the Hunt Club features two gladiators fighting to the death for the audience's pleasure.

The contrast between the immaculate appearance and the terrible core is at the center of *La decima vittima*. Ordinary life is reduced to its basic impulses, violence and sex, and even religion has regressed to pagan adoration of the sun, a primitive symbol of life and light. Surfaces are clean, shiny and often reflective, hinting at a superficial, hollow world where people themselves have become objects and they don't even care about it.

Pop, Op, and Petri

In the summer of 1964 the Venice Biennale marked the definitive explosion of Pop Art. America presented the works of Robert Rauschenberg, Jasper Johns, Claes Oldenburg and Jim Dine. The 39-year-old Rauschenberg was awarded the Grand Prize. He was the first American to win it, causing ample controversy in Italy and Europe. His victory marked a defining moment, paving the way to a new approach to art, ironic and unconventional, which moved from the complex abstractness of action and informal painting to forms and colors influenced by advertising and comics, with bright surfaces and repetitive patterns. It was the birth of the "age of simulacrum" with banality and mass production elevated as art and popular icons as allegories of a time in which appearance was everything.

The Italian pavilion was no less exciting, with works by the most noted exponents of the so-called "Scuola di Piazza del Popolo," from the forerunners (Mimmo Rotella, Titina Maselli) to the younger ones (Mario Schifano, Giosetta Fioroni, Franco Angeli, Tano Festa). It showed a lively cultural *milieu* whose effects extended themselves in everyday life and commerce, marking a commercially fruitful era. The average man was discovering the pleasures of the "*bel design*" (beautiful design), with ordinary objects elevated as status symbols, such as the lamp designed by the Castiglioni brothers, or the Radio Cubo by Brionvega (now firmly exhibited at New York's MOMA). Living was easier with one's eyes open, if people were surrounded by beautiful objects.

Petri had visited the 1964 Biennale. His longtime friendship with Vespignani and the "Banda del Portonaccio" had made him acquire a taste for contemporary art, and he had begun to purchase paintings and design objects. His curious spirit was always looking for means of expression to portray the existing world and its contradictions. "I was very impressed by the revolutionary significance of 'pop' culture and I immediately thought of translating my feelings in cinematic terms," he later explained.[39] He had managed to include references to art in his previous films, from the Morandi painting glimpsed in a scene of *L'assassino* to the stab at informal painters in *I giorni contati*. Now he was going to make a whole film whose every frame was imbued with art.

Petri's accomplice was Piero Poletto, who had worked with Michelangelo Antonioni on *L'eclisse* and *Il deserto rosso* (1964). In the latter, Antonioni's outstanding use of color had turned the town of Ravenna and its surroundings into a portrayal of the tormented state of mind of Monica Vitti's character. With Poletto's help, Petri filled the sets with an array of faithful reproductions of avant-garde objects and works of art to rival anything ever seen in a motion picture, making *La decima vittima* "the world's first Pop Art film," as Kahn enthused.[40]

For one thing, the gargantuan bespectacled eye which covers an entire wall in

Marcello's apartment is a reproduction of Joe Tilson's painted wood construction *Look!*, also presented at the 1964 Biennale, with an addition that makes for a delightful sight gag, as the mechanical eye blinks rhythmically in the background as a tongue-in-cheek counterpart to the scene. Here, Poletto turns a sculpture into a work of kinetic art.

Lidia's villa, an ultramodern glass and concrete structure, looks like a museum exhibition littered with bizarre works of art amid bright red furniture and omnipresent lighting cubes, plus the incongruous presence of a flock of sheep. The chalk figures scattered around reference George Segal's sculptures (the one playing pinball hints at the artist's 1963 *Gottlieb's Wishing Well*), and another room in the house features three-dimensional Op Art works. As with the blinking eye, the chalk mannequins serve for a gag, as at one point, Mastroianni opens the back of one of them, revealing it to be the household safe.

But there's more. The targets in the "gym" evoke Jasper Johns' 1956 painting *Target with Plaster Cats*, and when Marcello's lawyer is speaking with him on the phone, in the background we can see a couple of gigantic panels from *Flash Gordon* and *Phantom*, recalling Roy Lichtenstein's works. The gigantic sign of Ming Tea erected in front of the Colosseum nods at Andy Warhol's reinterpretations of advertising icons, while Robert Rauschenberg lends his name to Marcello's early victim, Baron von Rauschenberg.

Likewise, the props seen in the film are actually existing commercial items in 1960s Italy, with minimal modifications. The cordless telephone used by Mastroianni's character and the car he drives are the "Ericofon" launched in 1954 by the Swedish brand Ericsson (here the only futuristic touch is the missing cord, an anticipation of things to come) and the Citroen DS (but with a transparent plexiglass top), respectively. The future as imagined by Petri retains an umbilical cord with the present, looking like a natural and perhaps inevitable evolution (or rather, de-evolution) instead of a totally groundless fantasy.

The film's pop quality extends to the costume design. Most characters wear black and white PVC skirts and suits, inspired by the French stylist André Courrèges's 1964 collection *Space-age-look*. Caroline is a notable exception. In her first meeting with Marcello, she is wearing a pink cyclamen blouse and trousers which stand out amid the black-dressed figures (including Marcello) and pale blue plastic furniture. Her appearance is a disruptive element, both figurative and emotionally, for she puts in danger Marcello's universe while questioning his way of life.

Comics are featured prominently as well, and not surprisingly given Marcello's inner boyishness. Indeed, there is a whole shelf full of them in his living room and he is reading one when Caroline first approaches him. Marcello's favorite comic is *L'uomo mascherato* (Lee Falk's *Phantom*), because "I'm a romantic," he says, and he owns a very rare 1935 issue of *Flash Gordon*. Marcello himself looks like a comic book character of sorts, perhaps one from the *fumetti neri*: when he takes his skull mask off, the ruthless Kriminal (the comic book of the same name started publication in August 1964) reveals himself as a handsome, square-jawed man with short, platinum blond hair.

Pop artists such as Roy Lichtenstein took inspiration from comic strips and often employed comic book style and elements such as balloons in their work (such as in Lichtenstein's celebrated painting *Drowning Girl*, 1963), and comics had begun to be taken seriously as an art form in Italy as well. In his seminal 1964 essay *Apocalittici e integrati* (Apocalyptic and Integrated), semiotician Umberto Eco began to investigate this form of popular entertainment with instruments formerly dedicated to "serious" literature, thus taking by surprise the stale intellectual Italian world. Italy's first magazine fully devoted to comics, *Linus*, started publication in April 1965. Presenting the works of Al Capp, George Harriman, Charles M. Schulz, Guido Crepax and other noted comic book authors and artists, together with monographic essays on the history of comics and its most important exponents, *Linus* (the name came from one of the characters in Schulz's *Peanuts* strips) was aimed at an audience of literate, intellectual readers.

Comics' growing cultural relevance is evoked in a tongue-in-cheek way as a complement to the world that the film depicts. An oft-quoted line elevates comics to the status of "classics," as Olga calls them in despair while Marcello's collection is seized alongside other valuable properties. In the future imagined by Petri, where the basic moral and cultural values have been forgotten or erased, comics have taken the place of literature. Mind you, it is not a cheap stab at *fumetti* on the part of some old-fashioned moralist complaining about their hollowness. Petri knew and loved comics, and was a keen reader of *Linus*, to the point of calling his beloved dog Snoopy. There is a dog in *La decima vittima* too, which Marcello is very fond of, but it is a mechanical toy named Tommaso: in tomorrow's dehumanized society the presence of pet animals has been erased too....

Far from being a paean to consumerist society, the use of Pop Art in *La decima vittima* is ferociously ironic in its playfulness, and the joke on comics as "classics" is part of the discourse on "aesthetic reversal,"[41] in turn linked with the one on the ongoing overturning of spiritual and cultural values. For all the spellbinding images, bodies and commodities that fill every frame of the film, crafted in pastel colors by Gianni Di Venanzo's exquisite photography, Petri is always careful to remind us "what man may someday make of himself in a world devoted to technological development at the expense of spiritual growth."[42]

Sex Is Comedy

With its wild concoction of genres—sci-fi, thriller, comedy, eroticism—*La decima vittima* too looks like a Pop Art collage. Even though sometimes it spins out of control, due in large part to its production vicissitudes, the result is something unique within Italian cinema of the era, and as such it predates a whole season of "Pop" cinema.

The opening scene sets the tone for Petri's vision. Pursued by her hunter (Chinese actor George Wang) through the streets of New York, Caroline (donning a black wig) takes refuge in the Masoch Club, where she performs a breathtaking strip act, wearing only a mask and costume of aqua and silver metal sequins. The hunter is so mesmerized by her moves that he drops his gun and agrees to take off her mask. At this point she shoots him dead with a double-barreled blast from the two small revolvers hidden in her bra, in an unforgettable sight gag.

The hand-held camera and low-angle shots give the scene a *Nouvelle Vague* taste, enhancing its realistic setting in contrast with the absurdity of the situation, a man chasing a woman and shooting at her amid indifferent passers-by and cops (whose only worry is that he has a license to kill...). All this is interspersed with the Masoch Club owner (Jacques Herlin) announcing the rules for the Big Hunt. The realistic exteriors then give way to the stylized Masoch Club set, with its white illuminated cubes on which Andress performs her striptease, and its audience dressed either in white or black. The result conveys an ambiguous playfulness that makes the spirit of Petri's adaptation immediately clear, both thematically and visually.

MARCELLO MASTROIANNI   URSULA ANDRESS

LA DIXIEME VICTIME

Un film de ELIO PETRI   EASTMANCOLOR   C. C. CHAMPION ROME
FILMS CONCORDIA PARIS

Ursula Andress (masked) performing a striptease in the opening sequence of *La decima vittima* (promotional still for the French release, *La dixième victime*).

Throughout the movie, the director makes use of comic book style shots to enhance a scene's momentum. Characters are framed against a monochromatic background or, as with the death of Baron von Rauschenberg, in front of a mirror. Caroline's duplicitousness is underlined in the scene after the sunset ceremony, when her features are reflected and cut out in a mirror. Later, when she lures Marcello in the trap at the Temple of Venus, their antagonism is echoed by their separation in the frame. Besides out-and-out comic adaptations such as *Kriminal* (1966, Umberto Lenzi), which even introduced comic book panels in the narrative, similar comic book-inspired visual choices would be reprised and enhanced in several films of the decade, namely Joseph Losey's *Modesty Blaise* (1966), Tinto Brass' *Yankee* (1966) and *Col cuore in gola* (1967), and Mino Guerrini's *Omicidio per appuntamento* (1967).

In *La decima vittima*, however, this is part of a more complex formal attitude which once again takes inspiration from art. According to Petri scholar Lucia Cardone, the film's visuals recall the works of Hard-edge artists such as Barnett Newman, Richard Smith and Kelly Noland, with their geometrical quality.[43] A constant motif is that of frames, grills, geometrical figures that enhance the futuristic look and symbolically hint at the characters' hard-heartedness.

Stylistically, *La decima vittima* oscillates between scenes shot with refined and complex camerawork and others characterized by the use of telephoto lens and zooms. Occasionally these look like time-saving tricks, but more often Petri uses these types of shots

as a rhythmic device to give his film a nervous edge, in a way more akin to contemporaneous genre cinema, a stylistic trait he would develop in *A ciascuno il suo*. The use of
stock footage as well is far from being just a lazy gimmick. Petri smuggles in the film
shots from a parade in communist China celebrating Mao, disguised as a celebration for a
hunter who entered the Decathon. The joke was probably lost on most spectators.

The story revolves around a battle of the sexes which echoes mythical motifs, with
Caroline hinting at Diana, the chaste Roman goddess of the hunt. With her aggressive
sexuality, Ursula Andress represents a shattering element in Petri's satire. "Even physically she's a type of woman that we can imagine as belonging to a near future,"[44] the director pointed out. From the opening scene she is in command, and constantly plays with
men's erotic fantasies only to turn them against her male opponents. During the strip-
tease at the Masoch Club her moves are hypnotic and predatory, and she never allows
men to take command of the situation. She allows herself to be touched by members of
the audience, only to slap them in the face in return, and after killing her hunter she takes
his tie as a souvenir, in a symbolic act of castration. Her breasts are, as Doris Wishman
would later have it, a deadly weapon, and the memorable double-barreled bra is, in Petri's
words, "a visual projection of the confusion between passion and aggression."[45]

On the other hand, when introducing Marcello dispatching his own victim at a
horse dressage, the director adopts a more relaxed, almost lazy tone, exemplified by the
long panning shot following him (framed from the waist below) as he carries the special
pair of boots for Baron von Rauschenberg. Marcello takes his victim's watch as souvenir,
and this time as well the gesture is revealing, for he is obsessed by the passing of time just
like Cesare in *I giorni contati*. Yet, instead of attempting to savor every bit of it, Marcello
opts for indolence, allowing the world around him to have the upper hand and taking refuge in such childish pastimes as reading comics and playing with his mechanical toy dog.
He is a grown-up kid in an adult's body, sexually immature and dependent on the whims
of his lover. In this sense, he prefigures other sexually childish characters in Petri's cinema, such as *A ciascuno il suo*'s Laurana, *Un tranquillo posto di campagna*'s Leonardo
Ferri, *Indagine*'s "Doctor" and *Todo modo*'s "M."

Petri's casting of Marcello Mastroianni has a nice sting in the way the director plays
with his star's screen persona. "Through the years of this decade no other actor has come
closer to what the ladies in the movie houses like to dream of as a Latin Lover," the *New
York Times* wrote in a long interview with Mastroianni around the time the movie was
released.[46] Petri was well aware of his skills and proceeded to draw for him a role that
would go against everyone's expectations, "Mastroianni is not a naturalistic actor," the
director explained. "Contrarily to the fashion created by the critics ... our true greatest
actors—Totò, Tognazzi, Volonté, Mastroianni, Randone—are antinaturalistic actors."[47]
A sentimentalist in an age of sadists, Mastroianni's character embodies "the ambivalent
image of inward impotence and predatory potency," as *Playboy Magazine* described him,
but he also emphasizes the core of Petri's satiric intentions, as underlined by the platinum
blonde Hamlet bob he dons, a show-stopping gimmick that recalls Welles's reinvention of
Rita Hayworth's look in *The Lady from Shanghai* (1947).

With its casual treatment of sexuality, *La decima vittima* is a refreshing take on one
of the main themes in dystopian sci-fi, as well as an anticipation of many other films on
the theme, from *Barbarella* (1968, Roger Vadim) to *THX 1138* (1971, George Lucas). An
example is the scene at the "Relaxing Service Station," a brothel where Marcello attempts
(but fails) to make love with a submissive, and perhaps robotic, prostitute (Swedish

actress Anita Sanders), an idea developed from the initial outline, when the protagonist released sexual tension through "outlets."

In its early stage as reported by Kahn, the script attempted some daring ideas such as Marcello's bigamy and his "weakening of the trigger finger." A hint at impotence which represented yet another stab at the male image of the protagonist, it was another issue common to Petri's antiheroes, who often reveal their neuroses through tics and psychosomatic pathologies (such as Total's unstoppable itch in *La proprietà non è più un furto*) related to troubled, insecure or patently immature sexuality, and Marcello is no exception.

Although barely sketched, the character of Marcello's wife Lidia has an ambiguous feel to it, enhanced by the actress' shaved eyebrows. In the scene where she watches Marcello and Caroline making out Petri hints at her lesbianism, thus giving her line about her relationship with Olga ("You even forced us to become friends with each other") a sexual innuendo.

But the director had to purge some of the more risqué bits. As shown by promotional pics in another article penned by Saul Kahn and published in the American magazine *Cinema*, in the Hunt Club scene Marcello and other licensed killers relax by shooting dancing girls with electronic rifles. When hit by the beam, the dancers light up in provocative poses.[48] The Freudian link between weapons and sex is in tune with one of the film's *leitmotifs*—men running around and handling their guns in plain sight, like a symbol of power. But this visual gag, also mentioned in the text, is nowhere to be found in the film. Ditto for another scene mentioned by Kahn in his piece for *Films and Filming*, which curiously predated Marina Abramović and Ulay's 1977 video performance *Light/Dark*:

> Petri had two bit players remain after other couples had left the dance floor. He staged a wicked slapping contest in which the boy and girl stolidly exchange smacks, expressing the thoroughgoing confusion of passion and aggression that characterizes their sick society.[49]

Similarly, lines of dialogue mentioned in the article, such as Caroline saying to Marcello, "Tell me more about my body ... it's the only thing I'm still curious about," have disappeared, together with such futuristic weapons as a "boomerang Beretta which fires back into the body of the person pulling the trigger" and a bullet-shooting camera which "makes murder a snap and provides the hunter with a souvenir photo of the victim during his last minutes alive,"[50] an idea Petri might have borrowed from *Peeping Tom* (1960, Michael Powell).

On November 22, 1965, *La decima vittima* was submitted to the rating board, which focused mainly on the alleged erotic content and judged that "even though with an ironic and satiric background, the plot revolves around the legalization of murder and the contempt for human life," thus giving it a V.M.18 rating (no minors allowed) that severely diminished its commercial potential.

The judgment was confirmed in appeal, possibly with even more severity. On December 22 the appeal commission underlined the "contempt for human life and the parody of some social values," the "language's continuous allusions to sexual facts and aphrodisiac tools," and the depiction of "acts of sexual provocation and intercourse clearly contrary to common decency," concluding that, "had the commission been invested with the judgment in first degree, it might have led to the total ban of the film from public screening."[51]

"Drink Ming Tea..."

According to Elsa Martinelli, who called it "a strange and extraordinary film," Petri had to reedit *La decima vittima* "according to the producer's will. Ponti didn't understand the film and every night, during the editing stage, he changed it his own way. There were tremendous fights between he and Petri."[52] Ponti's heavy tampering on the story to fit the tight garments of the *commedia all'italiana* is best exemplified by the ending. In Sheckley's denouement, the hero's demise mocked male chauvinism and its conception of the female as a passive, romantic creature, but it had a touch of ambiguity in the way it showed how archaic sentimentalism was being replaced by aseptic modernity.

Petri probably pictured the film's hero as a character from a Godard or a Ferreri film, a mixture of Jean-Paul Belmondo in *À bout de souffle* and Ugo Tognazzi in *Una storia moderna—L'ape regina* (1963) and devised an ending that suited this concept. In the climax, Marcello persuades Caroline to shoot him live on television during the Ming Tea commercial, a deliriously choreographed bit with Chinese kids, chorus girls in plastic suits and giant teacups, in what looks like a final act of surrender and a romantic sacrifice for love. "Drink Ming Tea and you'll live longer!" he happily says to the camera before being shot. The onlooking crowd applauds politely.

But, unbeknownst to the woman, the pistol hidden inside the man's mechanical toy dog, which he had given her as a gesture of trust, is loaded with blanks. Marcello reappears and shoots Caroline, in exchange for a double fee from the Ming Tea Company. In the end, he is the more callous of the duo. "When people are in love, they make mistakes..." he comments before shooting her. Then it's his turn to deliver the commercial's punchline. "She made a mistake. She didn't drink a double Ming Tea!"[53]

This would have been a perfect ending, just in line with Sheckley's story, and a pointed one too. Not so dissimilarly from *Divorzio all'italiana*, in a patriarchal society it is man who wins, reestablishing the order and echoing what Marcello's lawyer says to a potential customer, "I'll tell you, this year it's trendy to kill women." Petri's parable would have gained a bitter tone, for the protagonists' discovery of their mutual attraction and their revolt, not just against the consumerist system that is using them as bait for the masses, but against the dehumanization of sex as well, would turn out to be illusory.

But the frantic coda that follows—Caroline faking her own death, Olga and Lidia turning up to shoot Marcello, the shootout in the Forum near the Temple of Augustus, the two protagonists' escape and final wedding in an airplane—goes against the director's radical skepticism and destroys whatever moral point the story was to have had. The punchline looks botched as well, with the final shot of a bunch of flowers protruding from a gun being the result of post-production animation.

The original African ending would show Marcello and Caroline living in the wilderness like Adam and Eve, but Ponti did not want to pay for the extra transfer and imposed the current one. But some others were considered during scriptwriting. A particularly biting one had Marcello and Caroline get married in church and then keep hunting each other, "in the routine of middle-class family life, in a slow and reciprocal killing, day after day, unarmed but more and more inhuman."[54]

Petri was never satisfied with *La decima vittima*, and over the years he would return to the subject of its bungled denouement. "Were I allowed to make the film again, I'd

MARCELLO MASTROIANNI   URSULA ANDRESS

LA DIXIEME VICTIME

Un film de ELIO PETRI   EASTMANCOLOR   C. C. CHAMPION ROME
                                                     FILMS CONCORDIA PARIS

"Drink Ming Tea…" The human chase climaxes at the Colosseum, and Caroline (Ursula Andress) is about to shoot Marcello live on television while a ballet takes place (promotional still for the French release, *La dixième victime*).

probably end it as in Sheckley's story, with the man killed by the huntress." It was like an open wound which still bled and hurt. Once he explained: "If only you knew how much I sweated to convince the producer, and how much I suffered to adapt myself to that horrible clownish ending … but I couldn't handle it anymore, having to fight against everyone."[55]

"I'll tell you, this year it's trendy to kill women," the lawyer (Massimo Serato) tells Marcello (Marcello Mastroianni) in *La decima vittima*.

Surviving the Hunt

La decima vittima was released in Italy on December 3, 1965. Then the Big Hunt started, with Petri as the designated victim and the critics as hunters. Many argued that the "banal and well-known comic vein" dampened the effectiveness of many sequences.[56] *Cinema nuovo* called it "an example of how our most intelligent and shrewd filmmakers keep systematically losing precious opportunities," pointing out its "boredom, hollowness, pitifully stretched situations," and dismissing Mastroianni's performance as "incredibly uncomfortable and unconvincing." The reviewer's bias was evident in his remark that "before Petri's name, the film bears the mark of Carlo Ponti, whose ideas on cinema, and the means to impose them, are widely known."[57] *Cineforum* called it "disappointing" and noted how Petri had "lost himself in the game of irony, as elegant as an end in itself," blaming the "four different endings" as the "yield to commercial reasons and … to the need not to take too seriously a matter which to him has a force only if kept near the limit of paradox."[58]

No one bothered to analyze the many artistic references, let alone linger on the darker implications of Petri's discourse. Even the more sympathetic reviewers saw the film as a bow to commercial needs, as had in fact been *Nudi per vivere* and, partially, *Peccato nel pomeriggio*. Giovanni Grazzini urged Petri not to reproach himself, although he added that "after all, *La decima vittima* is not such a big treason that you must be ashamed of it."[59] Overall, critics seemed unable to understand the attempt to insert a sophisticated political discourse within an equally sophisticated formal context—that is, a marriage between commitment and spectacle.

A decade later, *La decima vittima* would be dismissed as "pure virtuosic embroidery," its visual style reduced to "ephemeral elegance,"[60] and overall labeled as a forgettable *divertissement*. Part of the problem was the Italian critics' diffidence, to say nothing of open hostility, toward genres, the consequence of an openly politicized approach which resulted in the inability to fully grasp the film's ambiguity. As Petri scholar Lucia Cardone put it,

> The sensuality of Petri's approach has ended up masquerading the polemic purpose and concealing the satiric intent. A film deliberately conceived as critical toward advertising, mass culture, and design, is read paradoxically as a glamour product, updated to the latest fashion tendencies. The narrative's snappy firmness, the sinuous style, and the skillful visual design ... have caused superficial judgments, as well as the labeling of *La decima vittima* as an elegant exercise in style.[61]

With little over 620 million *lire* grossed in the Italian market, *La decima vittima* was definitely not the hit Ponti had hoped for. Sergio Leone's *Per qualche dollaro in più* earned more than five times as much, with almost 3,500 million. However, the tycoon got what he wanted, with a wide distribution abroad and two million dollars in his pocket from Embassy Pictures, which released the picture in the United States and Canada in late December 1965 as *The 10th Victim* to mixed reviews. *The Washington Post*'s Richard L. Coe found the result "curiously pedestrian" and missing "the exact, cohesive tone such material demands."[62] *Newsweek* focused on "Ursula Andress's 21st century mammary musketry," but agreed that the film "isn't just sex play at all. It is bigger, better, funnier and vastly more important, a film that soars above the battle of the sexes to survey an entire war, the losing war being fought against violence in contemporary life."[63]

Frank Morriss of the Toronto-based *The Globe and Mail* labeled it "a mixture of George Orwell's *1984*, the James Bond books, and Pop Art," but dismissed it as missing its target, blaming the lack of humor or apt social comment, accusing Ponti and the script of "novelty for the sake of novelty," and singling out the ending as shallow and contrived. Morriss at least gave credit to Petri's direction for "keeping it moving from implausible moment to implausible moment with a kind of competence which sustains reasonable interest."[64] The film came out in the U.K. the following year, distributed by Anglo Embassy, with an A rating (the BBFC classified it on 8 August 1966).

La decima vittima would remain the director's only foray into science fiction: some time later, after the release of *A ciascuno il suo*, MGM agent Peter Witt sent him a Ray Bradbury script, which the director rejected for its lack of irony, resulting in the story being "too weighed down by easy prophecies, which face too many issues at once: fascism, racism, scientists' responsibility.... I am interested in a colder science fiction, less prophetic and funnier, which deals with the year 2168—ironically depicting 1968—instead of 1980 ... I'm more for Swift than H.G. Wells."[65] Some years later he embraced a more pessimistic view. He hypothesized that at the time being the only possible type of science fiction was the one hybridized with horror, "because of the cultural misanthropy of the general public and its 'delegates' ... the living look at posterity with antipathy."[66]

Around the same time, French producer Anatole Dauman of Argos Film, whom Petri met at Cannes, offered him an unidentified *fantastique*-related project, but once again he refused, explaining that he felt "more touched by reality, for many reasons—political, ideological, but above all, perhaps, for the good reason that reality, at present, is much more pervasive than *fantastique*."[67]

Overall, *La decima vittima* was a bitter experience for Petri, not least because it marked

The U.S. poster for *La decima vittima*, released as *The 10th Victim*, stressed the film's erotic and humorous content.

the end of his collaboration with Tonino Guerra. After the difficult scriptwriting stage, during which at one point he felt the writer had switched to Ponti's side, something had broken between them. Years later, he would say: "Tonino is a great friend to me, I respect and regard him very much, but our notion of things is different, both in art and society, and so we can work together only rarely."[68]

But the struggle against the tycoon, which marked his second experience of the kind after *Il maestro di Vigevano*, fortified Petri, as he later admitted: "One becomes a director by learning to deal with such powerful personalities as De Laurentiis and Ponti. There is a moment when one cannot run from producers, and this too is part of the job."[69]

Six

Death of an Intellectual
A ciascuno il suo *(1967)*

Getting His Hands Dirty

After *La decima vittima*, Petri's career seemed to stall despite his exposure abroad. It was partly because of the projects being submitted to him: "The offers of making films of the James Bond–007 genre started raining down upon me."[1] One such was from Marshall and Robert Naify. Marshall Naify was the president of Magna Pictures, which had successfully distributed *High Infidelity* in the States; he and his brother Robert co-owned the movie theater chain United California Theaters, where *La decima vittima* had been doing very well. The Naifys were interested in financing some pictures in partnership with Italian producer Maurizio Lodi-Fè and suggested that Petri submit several outlines.[2] Their requests were telling; they were interested in low-budget films (around 300,000 dollars each) to be shot in America and with "a good degree of physical action."

For his part, the director hadn't given up hope on *Flowers for Algernon*, and expressed interest also in adapting Bernard Malamud's 1957 novel *The Assistant*. He got in touch with agent Samuel W. Gelfman, who informed him that Malamud had decided to withdraw the rights to the novel from the movie market.

Eventually Petri got a job offer which to a committed filmmaker like him might have sounded like a provocation: to direct some TV ads for *Carosello*. One of the most popular TV programs in Italy, *Carosello* was a ten-minute collection of commercials broadcast at prime time after the newscast. The commercials, conceived as short films and themselves nicknamed "Caroselli," were usually witty and graced with animation and gags. For children, it was an appointment not to be missed, before going to bed. As Petri noted,

> *La decima vittima* had something, perhaps in the use of color, in the choice of decor, or something else, which made the advertising world in Milan go wild.... I knew that many filmmakers made Caroselli when in times of trouble.... Some directors, who were so rigorous in the choice of a movie, so much so that they had become sterile or unproductive in cinema, had revealed an almost Balzacian fertility thanks to the lucrative anonymity guaranteed by the advertising business.[3]

To paraphrase Oscar Wilde, one can resist everything except temptation. After all, he had already gone against his principles with the clandestine experience of *Nudi per vivere*, so why should he back away from a lucrative offer after so many comrades had accepted? So, he got to know Mario Belli, the creative for one of Italy's most powerful advertising agencies, CPV, a charismatic figure with the face of a prizefighter and the vocabulary of a psychoanalyst, who dressed all in black like a priest. "He charmed me," the director admitted.

Petri's first ad was for Shell extra-octane gasoline. It was titled *Al di là della mente* (Beyond the Mind) and retained the ironic sci-fi mood of his latest film. "The 'extra octanes' were superwomen all dressed in white. The normal fuel, the 'enemy,' were superwomen all dressed in black," Petri later recalled. "Those ten short films cost me an immense effort."[4] He had a princely budget at his disposal, which allowed for the use of a helicopter for some aerial shots, and for some prestigious collaborators as well. Antonio Margheriti took care of the special effects (all in just one day's work) and Gianni Polidori came aboard as art director. Shooting took place on the motorway to the Fiumicino airport and lasted two weeks. Two years later the priest-like Belli approached Petri again for another series of four short TV ads, this time for the furniture brand Salvarani, and once again he couldn't say no. As an old proverb says, To err is human, to persist is diabolical.

The theme of Petri's next tentative project, *La santa*, was exactly that of temptation and sin, as observed through the eyes of an atheist like him. In his memoir, Ugo Pirro mentions the project under the title *Suor Giacinta* (Sister Hyacintha) and describes it as "the tale of a rebel nun ... inspired by a true story." Their real-life model was Giacinta Marescotti (1585-1640; canonized in 1807), who took the vows after a disappointment in love and led an unorthodox life as a nun: she kept a private stock of extra food, wore a habit of the finest material, kept two novices as her private servants, and received and paid visits at will. Eventually, due to a severe illness, she underwent a spiritual crisis and completely changed her life. "There couldn't be anything more distant from us than a movie on a controversial religious figure," Pirro explained. "None of us was religious; perhaps what interested us about Sister Giacinta was her rebellion, as if we unconsciously felt ideally in seclusion and identified ourselves with that nun."[5]

For the role of Giacinta, Petri had gotten in touch with Ingrid Thulin.[6] Appearing as guest at the Taormina Film Festival, in August 1966, the Swedish actress confirmed that her next films would be with Italian directors, starting with Brunello Rondi's *Domani non siamo più qui*. Then she would work with Petri and Mauro Bolognini.[7] Filming for *La santa* was to begin in early September, but then the project was quietly dropped. According to Pirro, the script didn't go beyond an early outline stage. Petri's frustration resulted in a total change in direction.

> The Christian Democrat censorship had been blocking all things political for years. I couldn't stand it anymore; I was beginning to think that what I was doing was useless.... I had the neat sensation of where it would all end up, so I thought: "Enough with cinema made just for fun." ... I felt almost obliged to get my hands dirty.[8]

In October 1966, he was in Sicily shooting his next film, which had nothing to do with saints, took place in contemporary Italy, and bore an ambiguous, slightly menacing title: *A ciascuno il suo*. It was based on Leonardo Sciascia's novel of the same name.

The Sicilian writer had caused a sensation in 1961 with *Il giorno della civetta* (The Day of the Owl), the first book that openly depicted the Mafia in the form of a detective novel of sorts, loosely based on the true story of Accursio Miraglia, a communist trade unionist killed by Cosa Nostra in 1947. Sciascia reprised the same approach in *A ciascuno il suo*, an offbeat mystery inspired by the killing of a public security commissioner, Cataldo Tandoy, which took place on March 30, 1960, in Agrigento. Initially the murder had been labeled a crime of passion (Tandoy's wife was the lover of a powerful local

DC politician), but the investigation led to the Mafia. In fact, Tandoy had been conducting several inquiries on Cosa Nostra for some time, including one for the murder of Miraglia.

Published in February 1966, the book immediately became a best seller. Translated in English as *To Each His Own*, it has actually a more sarcastic significance, "To Each What He Deserves," which the plot fully clarifies in the end. It is set in the summer of 1964 in Sant'Anna, a small village in the heart of Sicily. The local pharmacist Manno receives an anonymous letter containing death threats. The man is well-liked by all the villagers and does not dabble in politics, and everyone thinks the letter is just a prank. Soon, however, Manno is murdered during a hunting party with a friend, Dr. Roscio, who is also killed, apparently for being in the wrong place at the wrong time. Professor Laurana, a shy and secluded schoolteacher, becomes obsessed with the double murder. By analyzing the anonymous missive, he finds out that it was compiled by cutting out fonts from the Vatican newspaper *L'Osservatore romano* (whose Latin motto is *Unicuique suum*, "To Each His Own"). Only two people in the village buy the newspaper, the parish priest and the archpriest. Laurana becomes convinced that the real target was Roscio, who had discovered the illicit affair between his wife Luisa and her cousin, the noted lawyer Rosello, the archpriest's nephew. If the affair had not ended, Roscio would have caused a scandal to break out on the basis of compromising documents on Rosello, who is affiliated with the Mafia. Smitten by Luisa, who is in cahoots with Rosello, Laurana is lured into a trap and killed. Eventually Luisa and Rosello get married. Everybody in the village knew about their affair.

The novel opens with a telling quote from Edgar Allan Poe's *The Murders in the Rue Morgue*: "But do not think that I am about to unveil a mystery or write a novel." The mystery structure, as so often with Sciascia, turns out to be illusory if not mocking. The detection is useless, the detective becomes the victim, the solution reveals a truth which everybody knew from the beginning except for the protagonist. "He was an idiot," the parish priest's curt judgment on poor Laurana, marks the novel's punchline.

The political content is just as important. Sciascia wanted to depict the failure of the center-left political alliance which had administered the island since 1964, when the Socialist Party joined the Christian Democrats. In the writer's words, "this event, destined to cause a radical change in Italian political life, was frustrated once more by the everlasting immutability of Italy's everlasting fascism. But the book has been interpreted as a story about the Mafia."[9]

A Cinema of Ideas

Petri and Ugo Pirro had taken separate paths after the unfilmed projects for De Santis, *L'uomo senza domenica* and *Pettotondo*. It was after *La decima vittima* that the two had started seeing each other again. "He was generous and moody, capable of long grudges, sudden outbursts, spites. And I think it was out of spite that I became his scriptwriter,"[10] Pirro wrote.

The two men took long walks, talking about books, films, politics, and life in general. And they started discussing the idea of making a movie together. Around the same time as the aborted *La santa*, they thought of adapting Piero Chiara's novel *La spartizione*, but the rights had already been sold and the book was made into a film by

Alberto Lattuada: *Venga a prendere il caffè da noi* (1970), starring Ugo Tognazzi. Eventually, they settled on *A ciascuno il suo*. Pirro stated he had read the novel before publishing and had thought of making a movie out of it with a cooperative, but the project never got off the ground.[11]

Despite Petri being an established filmmaker, nobody wanted to get their hands dirty with a story about the Mafia. *Il giorno della civetta* was still in limbo, the rights passing from one producer to the next without anyone daring to greenlight the movie.[12] The crisis of the film industry, in addition to such resounding events as the downfall of Titanus, had caused the disappearance of many small producers and opened the way to a monopolistic market, which would absorb only commercially safe films and reject riskier projects—those Petri liked to call "*cinema di idee*" (cinema of ideas).[13] According to Pirro, however, the diffidence around him and Petri was in no small part due to their political opinions. "It was as if both of us had been branded by the symbols of our ideas. We were aware of that and we had learned not to disown them out of opportunity," Pirro wrote. "Only a great commercial success would make all political prejudices fall, in spite even of the political and administrative censorship."[14]

So, Petri and Pirro had to risk. They needed a financier who was not fully part of the production system: a loose dog, enthusiastic and inexperienced. They found it in Giuseppe Zaccariello, a tile manufacturer based in the Emilian town of Sassuolo, who had been bitten by the film bug. His debut as producer had been a misstep and he was looking around for a second chance for his company Cemofilm. He had read Sciascia's novel and was enthusiastic about it. Luckily for Petri and Pirro, he didn't know, nor did he care, about market trends.

A ciascuno il suo was Zaccariello's second film as producer, in a career spawning fifteen years which comprised such titles as Roberto Faenza's *Escalation* (1968), Piero Schivazappa's *Femina ridens* (1969), Mario Bava's *Il rosso segno della follia* (1970) and *Reazione a catena* (1971), Rino Di Silvestro's *Le deportate della sezione speciale SS* (1976) and Aristide Massaccesi's *Duri a morire* (1979). The deal was signed in the spring of 1966.

The first scriptwriting meetings took place at Petri's house in Rome. He had moved to the district where he was born, not far from via de' Giubbonari, in an apartment on the fourth floor of a building without a lift. Pirro lived on the other side of the city, not exactly handy. Summer came, and Pirro moved to stay at the Petris' cabin at the so-called "Villaggio Tognazzi," a small residential complex on the Roman coast between the villages of Ostia and Torvaianica. Ugo Tognazzi had been one of the first to buy a chalet there, and many followed his example. The Boom had made Torvaianica a tourist center, and the proximity to the De Laurentiis studios attracted foreign actors who stayed there when shooting their films. Many people from the movie business spent their vacations at the Villaggio Tognazzi, and starting in 1967 Ugo Tognazzi organized a tennis tournament among celebrities there which soon became an out-and-out attraction.

In Torvaianica, Petri and Pirro used to work each day from ten a.m. to one p.m., then from three p.m. to sunset, sitting one in front of the other like two card players, Pirro handwriting and Petri beating on the typewriter like mad. The scriptwriter explained:

> We looked for a thread for the adaptation, then we started to write the scenes. In general … we don't use a "scaletta," a shooting script. We sometimes might use one for two or three scenes. At the beginning we never know what the ending is going to be like; we always leave the work somewhat open. We have an itinerary in mind, but we don't define it in every scene and every decision.[15]

To relax, they went to the beach nearby with Elio's beloved cocker spaniel dog, Snoopy. They chose the hours when the families and sunbathers had gone to lunch, to savor the peace and warmth of the deserted shore, all to themselves.

Pirro recalled his friend's sudden mood swings. Sometimes Elio was cheerful and expansive with the local acquaintances, and ready to laugh and joke; sometimes he was touchy and avoided company, and his moralistic side took over, just as Questi had noticed during the filming of *Nudi per vivere*. He would reprimand his friends for their promiscuous lifestyle and boast about his own monogamy. He was possessive toward Pirro, even demanding that he not stay out all night in Rome, as if both were athletes in seclusion. "Sometimes he gave the impression of restraining his instincts, but didn't always manage to, and you could tell it from some sudden admissions in which his repressed desires became the opportunity for foul verbal jokes."[16]

Zaccariello allowed Petri to cast the actors he wanted, such as Irene Papas as Luisa and Gabriele Ferzetti as Rosello. Neither was a marketable name. Papas was associated with foreign arthouse films such as Michael Cacoyannis' *Elektra* (1962) and *Zorba the Greek* (1964), but her latest work, Riccardo Freda's *Roger la Honte* (1966), had little commercial impact. Though just forty-two, Ferzetti was considered a has-been. His better days dated back to the previous decade, and after *L'avventura* he had collected mainly secondary parts. The cast was rounded out by such reliable stage thesps as Salvo Randone (as the elderly blind professor Roscio), Mario Scaccia (the parish priest), Leopoldo Trieste (a communist MP) and Luigi Pistilli (Manno, the pharmacist).

For the role of Laurana, Petri cast a 33-year-old Milanese actor he had noticed in *Le quattro giornate di Napoli* and who had impressed him for his intense screen presence, Gian Maria Volonté. After his supporting turns in Sergio Leone's *Per un pugno di dollari* and *Per qualche dollaro in più*, Mario Monicelli's *L'armata Brancaleone* (1965), and Damiano Damiani's *La strega in amore* and *Quien sabe?* (both 1966) Volonté had become a recognizable face, but not a popular name at the box-office. But he and Petri were politically close, although Volonté was still affiliated to the PCI. "It is very difficult to work with people who don't have the same ideas as you,"[17] the director pointed out when commenting such a bold casting choice, possibly referring to his difficult experience with Alberto Sordi. Volonté was paid very little, about seven million *lire*. Pirro recalls that when he told Documento Film's Gianni Hecht Lucari the names of the three leads, the other replied that they had a surefire flop in their hands.

Pre-production was not devoid of trouble. Petri found out that Dino De Laurentiis was attempting to buy the project from Cemofilm and replace him as director. The experience on *Il maestro di Vigevano* had borne grudges, not least because their opposite political ideas. To discourage the tycoon, Petri wrote a letter to ANAC, complaining about De Laurentiis's move. Born in 1950, after the dissolution of ACCI, chaired by Cesare Zavattini, ANAC (Associazione Nazionale Autori Cinematografici) gathered filmmakers and scriptwriters, unlike similar European associations. Its statute comprised cultural and political purposes, in order to preserve freedom of expression. Petri's letter had the desired effect on Dino.

Shooting took place mostly in the town of Cefalù, on the Northern coast, about one hour from Palermo. Petri chose it because of its imposing cathedral, which gave "a sense of the authority's command."[18] *A ciascuno il suo* marked the first collaboration between the director and Luigi Kuveiller. It was production supervisor Claudio Mancini—who had to give up working on the film due to previous commitments with Francesco Rosi—who recommended the 40-year-old Kuveiller, an expert cameraman who had never been a director of photography before. A quiet man who seldom talked and used to sit very calmly with his Toscano cigar in his mouth, Kuveiller would become Petri's trusted d.o.p. on the director's following films. Make-up artist Pierantonio Mecacci, another Petri regular, recalled: "From that moment, Luigi used to ask, 'Elio, when is the next film?' 'In three months.' And so, he organized his schedule. They were extremely close."[19]

A ciascuno il suo was not only the start of a new phase in both Petri and Volonté's career, but also the beginning of a long friendship and the first of four collaborations between the director and the actor. Volonté's performance, much more controlled and subdued than in his following films with Petri, hits just the right notes and is one of the film's highlights. Still, according to Paola Pegoraro Petri, at first it was very difficult for the actor to "enter" the role:

> Gian Maria had the impression that in Elio's mind his role had been written for Mastroianni. Marcello and Elio knew each other since they were kids, their bond was stronger, they were more similar, both from Rome, whereas Gian Maria came from the North and was rather touchy. To Gian Maria, it was a new type of role. At the beginning of the shooting he had some reservations, he was nervous. But the result was excellent.[20]

The two got along very well together during shooting but had a big argument during post-production. The mercurial Volonté could be very distressing and provocative in his attitude, and Petri was not one to let provocations pass by. The argument had a somewhat humorous ending, though. As Pirro recalled, "Elio ran after him with a stick, but bumped into a chair and broke his little toe."[21]

An Unconventional "Giallo"

Petri was adamant that the choice of *A ciascuno il suo* came out of frustration due to the current political situation, and the novel was just what he needed. "In those pages, Sciascia described in a very lucid way the political world in Southern Italy, the various forces and the stakes, the relationship between the Church and the Democrazia Cristiana. And the role of the intellectual, frustrated and castrated. I was interested also in the fact that the murderer in the end is the winner because he belongs to the ruling class."[22]

During filming, newspapers described *A ciascuno il suo* as "hot stuff." When interviewed on the set, Petri explained that he had used the book as an outline and had focused on the character of Laurana, "a cultured intellectual who, despite his intelligence, doesn't understand the reality that surrounds him and unveils before his eyes, the same reality which others can decipher. Basically … he can understand the past and the future, but he has a veiled, opaque stare on the present, hence his orientation to abstract himself from life."[23] Still, perhaps as a diplomatic move, the director stressed that he did not want to make a movie about the Mafia, "but only tell a densely suspenseful story centered on a certain harsh reality of the isle."[24]

Speaking to the newspaper *Il Popolo*, he was even more explicit:

> The very fact of being able to make such a movie—which, besides its suspense mechanism, aims to be an exposé—in a democratic climate, looks to me like an act of trust. However, let there be no mistake: I want to point out that *mine*, in a certain sense, will not be a political film.[25]

Petri and Pirro had sent the script to Sciascia beforehand. The novelist replied a few days later, telling them that there was little left of Sicily and of his book in it, and sarcastically suggested them to shoot the movie in another region, Puglia.[26] Moreover, Sciascia's friend, critic Aldo Marcovecchio, sent them a list of remarks and suggestions so as to stay more faithful to the novel. This prompted Petri's irate response to Marcovecchio's "insults"[27] as well as a letter to Sciascia, who graciously apologized for his friend's intervention.

It was the beginning of a tight and very polite correspondence, with the two exchanging fourteen letters between August 1966 and January 1968.[28] Petri (who addressed the writer with a familiar "*tu*" instead of the formal "*lei*") invited Sciascia on the set, and told him he was trying his very best to do justice to the source material: "Rest assured I'll make every effort to make a good movie out of your novel, and a successful one too."[29]

The director's respect and admiration for the novelist were sincere. He even paid homage to him in the film, in the scene when Laurana interrogates a student about Sciascia's 1964 novel-essay *Morte dell'inquisitore* (aka *Death of an Inquisitor*). But Sciascia didn't conceal his disappointment about Petri's interview in *Il Popolo*: "I trust … you will make a good movie, but in any case, that movie will have nothing to do with my story. My personal regret … mainly concerns your intention of not making a political movie. I only write to be political, and the news that my story will be a pretext *not to be* political cannot fill me with joy, as you will surely understand."

The director's reply, dated September 10, made very clear what he meant:

> I don't think there is the need to underline that the choice of adapting your novel is fairly bold nowadays. We could undoubtedly make even bolder films…. I'm content with making this one…. I wanted to make an unconventional *giallo*…. I wanted to make a political yet not didactic film, and your book provided me with the chance because, even though it is "political" from the first line to the last, it is never awkwardly so…. With the term "political," I mean every film which presents itself openly, massively as a pamphlet or as a political theorem. That is, as a work where a political thesis—which in this sense is propaganda—prevails on (or hangs over) the research.

The correspondence reveals also the director's interest in the story mechanism. Most of Sciascia's novels revolve around a mystery plot that serves a political theme, and *A ciascuno il suo* is no exception. As an avid mystery reader, Petri's will to make an "unconventional *giallo*" was the spark that would ignite several of his following works, conceived as eccentric enigmas where the final twist is puzzling if not openly mocking in its refusal of genre rules and mechanisms (see *Un tranquillo posto di campagna*, *Todo modo*, *Buone notizie*, even the unmade *Chi illumina la grande notte*). It would also allow him to address his discourse to the largest possible audience.

Petri and Pirro decided to expand and emphasize that side of the story by stressing its contradictory, maze-like quality, which mirrored the "complexity and political darkness of that period."[30] Starting, it must be added, with the title itself and its ambiguous meanings. On the surface, the movie is about a crime of passion, two lovers getting rid of the woman's husband by misdirecting the authorities on the designated victim, by way of the anonymous letter to the pharmacist. But this oblique scheme reflects also a whole mentality, a tortuous way to proceed which Petri would masterfully pin down as the main trait of the Democrazia Cristiana politicians in *Todo modo*.

The enigma in *A ciascuno il suo* is apparently played by the rules, through the revealing detail that Laurana notices in the anonymous letter, a Latin motto which solicits his own expertise. He immediately realizes that the fonts were cut out of the *Osservatore Romano*, but his devotion to the investigation proves delusional, for he is blind to the solution. It is not so much a matter of who had access to the newspaper but the deeper metaphorical significance of it, the indissoluble tie between Mafia, politics and the Church. Laurana, this provincial would-be Auguste Dupin who embarks on his investigation as if it were a brainteaser, and who believes that his learning raises him above the others, is too focused on details to notice the bigger picture. Even though he thinks of himself as upright, the professor is widely considered an outsider by the civic consensus—or even, as the final line in the book states, an idiot. In the end, he comes out almost as a sexually repressed version of the photographer in Antonioni's *Blow-up*, and equally powerless when it comes to deciphering reality. But *A ciascuno il suo* is as anti-conformist as Antonioni's film in rejecting the much-anticipated happy ending, and therefore denying to viewers the catharsis they expect. This very sting in the tail would become a key element in the political cinema to come.

Moreover, Petri and Pirro had the mystery unfold not amid nights, shadows and fogs as the *film noir* tradition would have had, but under the blinding Sicilian sun. As the scriptwriter explained, they sought what Roland Barthes would call the "hidden meaning" of Sciascia's novel and found it in the sunny Mediterranean setting, which they used as a paradox to portray the story's dark essence, its duality. The shiny surface paradoxically emphasizes the shadowy mentality, the ambiguity of gestures and words. On the other hand, it metaphorically blinds poor Laurana, who cannot see what is in plain view (the affair between Rosello and Luisa, the woman's complicity in the murder, his own fate) just like the missive in Poe's *The Purloined Letter*.

The theme of blindness stands out also in the character of professor Roscio, whom Laurana meets in Palermo. The blind optometrist—a reference to Jorge Luis Borges, a writer whose work bears many similarities to Sciascia's—is a key character in the film. In a scene littered with surrealistic traits, namely the eyes drawn on wood panels all around his living room, Roscio enigmatically warns Laurana about Luisa, whose beauty he cannot see but whose nature he understands very well, unlike the sad professor: "When we were kids, we used to call them 'bed-worthy.'" It is a warning bell, in a house literally filled with warning bells (for the suspicious old man "always wants to know where we are," as Luisa explains), to which Laurana doesn't listen.

The absence of the police is another infringement of the rules. "It was a special crime novel, with a dead man and no cops,"[31] Pirro quipped. The State and its authority are far away, spying and observing from a distance (as in the funeral scene) and eventually proving ineffective. In such an environment the Mafia can act undisturbed. It must be noted that neither the book nor the film ever mentions the Mafia explicitly. This led some to assert that "overall, *A ciascuno il suo* is not a 'mafia movie' but a black comedy on the bourgeois, Sicilian and Italian alike … which owes more to *Divorzio all'italiana* than to *In nome della legge*."[32] But this very absence is the core of Sciascia and Petri's discourse. The Mafia is, so to speak, the elephant in the room. It is "It who must not be named," to paraphrase Lovecraft. Its presence, its influence and its way of thinking imbue every frame of the story. In fact, Rosello can plan and execute the murder and get away with it precisely because he is a Mafioso.

Italian cinema initially portrayed Mafia in an idealized manner. Pietro Germi's *In nome della legge* (1949) was a sort of Sicilian Western, openly influenced by John Ford's cinema. It portrayed the members of the Mafia as criminals, but also (and especially) as

A ciascuno il suo: **The elderly, blind professor Roscio (Salvo Randone, right) warns professor Paolo Laurana (Gian Maria Volonté).**

"men of honor" who act according to unwritten and ancient rules, "immersed in myth and destined to remain in myth for decades."[33] Germi's vision of Sicily was mythical too, but even though his portrayal of the land and its inhabitants was spectacular and poetic, it clashed with the reality of facts. His Mafia men, who quoted Aristotle and preached loyalty and honor like Medieval knights, were worlds apart from those who, in accordance with the landowners, had sent the bandit Salvatore Giuliano to shoot at the peasants during the Labor Day parade at the Portella della Ginestra massacre on May 1, 1947.

Officially, the Mafia was something of a taboo. The Christian Democrat government denied its existence despite evidence proving otherwise. Similarly, cinema offered a euphemistic view of the phenomenon in such works as *Gli inesorabili* (1950, Camillo Mastrocinque), starring Charles Vanel in a role of sage Mafioso similar to the one he had played in Germi's film, and *I mafiosi* (1959, Roberto Mauri), an unbelievable concoction where the Mafia people are the *good* guys, defenders of the weak and the poor against the rich. Moreover, the rigid censorship prevented movies from addressing controversial figures such as Salvatore Giuliano: *Turri il bandito* (1950, Enzo Trapani) was very liberally inspired by true facts, while the more faithful *I fuorilegge* (1950, Aldo Vergano) was heavily tampered with and altered. Even *Vento del sud,* which Petri had co-written, was basically a lurid, old-style melodrama. Another, much more daring project Petri had been involved with was *La mafia* (1959), scripted with Luciano Vincenzoni and to be produced by Giovanni Addessi's company Era Cinematografica. But it remained unproduced.

It was only with Francesco Rosi's *Salvatore Giuliano* (1962) that Italian cinema finally portrayed the Mafia without alibis nor concessions to the popular imagery. But with the notable exception of Alberto Lattuada's *Mafioso* (1962), over the following years the term was usually delivered in a parodic context, as in the comedies starring Franco Franchi and Ciccio Ingrassia (usually nicknamed "mafiosi," as in *Due mafiosi nel Far West*, 1964) and related to the same old-style, reassuring vision of Cosa Nostra as a phenomenon confined to the rural and backward areas of Sicily.

Petri's Mafia does not consist of men on horseback with a Basque hat and a shotgun like those romantically depicted by Germi. When the story moves to Palermo, Sicily's capital, the first thing we see is two young thugs planting a bomb inside a car in broad daylight. "Chicago … it's like Chicago around here!" Laurana's communist MP friend complains, as a crowd gathers around the wreck. "You know, when I come here it feels like I'm in Texas, or Dallas…."

Rosello too is a different kind of Mafia man. One who is at home in the corridors of power, is friends with the local politicians and has connections with the most dangerous men of Cosa Nostra. One who is clean and respectable. A citizen above suspicion, who "would walk over corpses to get where he wants to be." He is an amoral and smart bourgeois who prospers in an unholy alliance with the Christian Democrats and the Church, "in league with the Socialists while the Communists are already giving him the wink," as a line of dialogue states.

In a biting political allusion, a scene has Laurana reading *Moby Dick*, the story of one man's obsession with a gigantic white whale. In Italy, the Democrazia Cristiana was commonly referred to as "la balena bianca," the white whale, and even though it is not made explicit, Rosello's politician friend is obviously a Christian Democrat. But as Petri noted, ultimately the one truly responsible for the events that followed is the archpriest Don Rosello, who looked after his nephew and Luisa and has always been aware of their longtime affair. "We must resign ourselves…. What else can we do but hope that poor pharmacist goes to hell," he tells Laurana, referring to Manno having an extra-conjugal affair, a chilling line which sums up the position of the Church, in covering for the culprits and blaming the victims.

It is a whole system of thought that allows the Mafia to prosper. Therefore, all the characters in the film are part of it, including the communist MP and even Laurana, whose mistrust of the authorities leads to his own demise. The blind old Roscio embodies the essence of the Mafioso mentality. "Some things are best left in the obscurity you find them in," he warns the professor, hinting at the symbolic blindness to the outside world that nurtures the privileged classes' self-preservation.

In the end, the truth is buried (as Laurana will be) under secrecy, fear, and hypocrisy. The police cannot but embrace the "official narration" of the facts. "They are like brother and sister," an officer comments about Rosello and Luisa. "Is that what they say?" the commissioner inquires. "They say it and it's true," is the reply. Or, to put it differently, *it is true because they say it.*

"He was an idiot!"

In an essay he penned on the book and the film, Petri pointed out he had made *A ciascuno il suo* especially because it was "the sensual and ironic portrait of a humanistic and sexually incompetent intellectual. For me, the political aspect of the book consisted essentially in this mingling of sex with the whole of reality."[34] He was smitten by the "sensuous" quality of Sciascia's work, both in the prose and in the novel's core, Luisa's seduction of Laurana which leads to his demise. "Sciascia is a prude.… But he is also sensual. Or better still, his sensuality consists of his prudishness, which is a stylistic one, a verbal one, but it is also a form of reticence about things and about the 'words' used for the senses."[35]

Luisa appears only a few times in the story, and Sciascia is very skillful in describing the professor's growing attraction to her with sparse, effective touches. She is always dressed in black as widows are required to do in Sicily in mourning for their departed husbands, thus seemingly rejecting any form of male desire. And yet her attire acquires a fetishistic, morbidly erotic quality. Small and (ostensibly) involuntary acts and gestures reveal her sensuality, with fleeting visions of her body and details of her clothing. One such moment takes place as Luisa kneels before her husband's grave and briefly displays the "abundant, languishing nudity of a Delacroix odalisque," the white flash of her thigh standing out against the black stockings. Ironically, during a bus trip to town with the woman, Laurana has a small chat with her and finds out she is a moron, but "the more his judgment of her became scathing and merciless," the more her physical closeness provokes "a painful desire" in him.

Petri and Pirro expanded Luisa's role and turned the fleeting, mysterious creature whom Sciascia described as "evil in its incarnation, in its sexual darkness and splendor," into an earthier, maternal figure, as opposed to the acerbic sensuality of the pharmacist's lover, the Lolita-esque Rosina (Luciana Scalise). Unlike in the book, Luisa's complicity in her husband's murder is explicitly underlined. A misogynist joke Laurana overhears in the film goes as follows: "What animal keeps its beak underground? The widow!" It is a macabre wordplay on the word "*becco*" ("beak" but also "cheated husband"). And it is Luisa who lures Laurana into the final death trap … and underground as well, as an explosion buries the professor under tons of rocks. Woman as a menacing attraction for a sexually immature man—one of Petri's recurrent themes—was already at the core of *La decima vittima*, and Luisa turns out a more effective and ruthless incarnation of the victim/huntress in Robert Sheckley's story. Yet, to Laurana, Luisa is as enigmatic and faceted as the Picasso painting we glimpse behind her in her late husband's study.

From the scene of her late husband's funeral, when Luisa's fainting exposes her legs and reveals her black stockings, *A ciascuno il suo* emphasizes this picture of sexual repression and the duplicity of its unwritten codes. To the director, in fact, she is "both object and victim of a sexual, death-driven desire."[36] Luisa literally becomes an erotic ghost in the scene at old Roscio's house. For once devoid of her black mourning uniform, wearing an elegant transparent blouse and pearl necklace, she appears and disappears in mirrors and balconies while Laurana is talking to her father-in-law. She is a fleeting presence who nevertheless dominates the scene.

In his letters to Sciascia, Petri openly admitted that he somewhat identified with the doomed protagonist: "Will you laugh if I tell you that I feel a bit like Laurana?" Indeed, in the film, Laurana is described as a disillusioned ex-communist, like Petri. "Do you always vote for the party?" his MP friend asks. "Yes, but it keeps getting harder." But there was more than that, and the director explained the reasons of such identification at length. "The thing I cared the most about in the film was the portrait of an intellectual detached from reality—humanly, politically and even sexually isolated. The film is a sort of self-portrait of an intellectual."[37]

In Gian Maria Volonté's masterful incarnation, Paolo Laurana is a boy in the body of

A Sicilian funeral: Laurana (Gian Maria Volonté, left), the voluptuous widow Luisa Roscio (Irene Papas) and her cousin, Rosello (Gabriele Ferzetti, right) in *A ciascuno il suo.*

an adult man. He lives with his overprotective mother and his octogenarian grandma and has childish habits. He travels by train for he cannot drive, eats ice cream and reads comic strips. His friends call him "Paolino" as if he were a kid. He comes across as inhibited, unmanly, whiny. Like several other Petri characters, Laurana's sexual immaturity results in social and political naivety, for "the acceptance of one's own sexual role comprises also the acceptance of one's social role."[38] As he himself admits, Laurana is abstracted (in one of the film's best puns, his mother misinterprets the term as "distracted"), and he walks through the world without ever raising his eyes to look around him, immersed as he is in the pages of the books that give him a complex yet ultimately ineffectual vision of that same world. He is culturally autistic, so to speak. In his bedroom there are portraits of Marcel Proust (incidentally, Sciascia loathed Proust), who wrote his greatest novel as a recluse in his own soundproof bedroom, and Antonio Gramsci, the great communist intellectual who ended his days in prison. But there is also a poster of Marilyn Monroe, an ideal female model for someone who lives in a world of fantasies. "These are the ritual fetish images for a certain type of Leftist intellectual," Petri commented.[39]

Laurana's sexual ineptitude is made explicit right from the beginning. When Luisa faints at the funeral, it is he who attempts to cover her exposed legs. As the police watch the footage, someone asks about him: "How does he get along with the women?" The reply is: "Well, he's a man for sure, but he might be impotent." Whenever he is close to Luisa, Laurana feels nervous, sweaty, dizzy. Once again, in Petri's cinema neurosis (here, more precisely, sexual ineptitude) takes on psychosomatic forms.

Later in the film, Laurana desperately and clumsily attempts a sexual pass at Luisa on the beach, lying on top of her, his hand between her thighs. Absent from the book, it synthesizes the protagonist's immature eroticism and his pathetic attempt to replicate what a "real man" does to a woman. Laurana's incapability to seduce Luisa, his awkward and even ridiculous behavior with her, his sexual failure, become the symbolic depiction of his obtuse misunderstanding of the bigger picture. As Petri put it, "Laurana is sexually incompetent; thus, he is also politically incompetent."[40]

"Professor, how do you live? What do you do?" the parish priest asks him while playing chess, before giving him checkmate. "How come you ignore everything in your village? The time of the poets with their heads in the clouds is over." Indeed, it is, and Laurana's spectacular demise takes place by way of dynamite, as the professor is blown up in a *solfatara* (a sulphur mine). The scene "disturbed" Sciascia, as the writer remarked in a letter to the director, because he saw it as something extraneous to the Sicilian way of killing (ironically, the U.S. release would be titled *We Still Kill the Old Way*), noting how in a venue in Milan the Sicilians in the audience were booing while the Milanese applauded.[41] It is actually a nod to Orson Welles' film version of *The Trial* (1962), in which Josef K. (Anthony Perkins) is executed in a similar explosion (in Kafka's novel he is stabbed to death). Like Josef K., in the end Laurana seemingly accepts his fate with resignation. It is one of several references to Kafka's work in Petri's *oeuvre*, starting with *L'assassino* and up to the project of adapting the short story *In der Strafkolonie* (aka *In the Penal Colony*). For the abstracted *and* distracted intellectual, who used to seclude himself in his own room, burying himself alive among his books, it is a grimly sarcastic comeuppance.

Zooming in on the Mafia

As noted by Petri scholar Gabriele Rigola, in the director's view political commitment "can (and perhaps must) be found in the folds of the story and in the language, and does not express itself solely through militancy."[42] The filmic language of *A ciascuno il suo* is definitely popular in its exploration of the genre structure and mechanics, while keeping an extraordinary formal variety and richness. But it is also a way to carry home the film's political essence.

Stylistically, *A ciascuno il suo* is characterized by great visual dynamism, mostly expressed by the repeated use of the zoom and the telephoto lens. By the mid–1960s, the zoom was relegated mostly to genre filmmaking, such as spy films and Westerns, even though noted filmmakers such as Rossellini had adopted it as a stylistic trait from its advent. Petri admitted that such a choice was partially due to the hurried shooting schedule, adding: "I wanted the audience to recognize in Sicily a much wider South, without borders, a South that was the same as many other countries."[43] In exterior scenes, the stylistic device somehow makes *A ciascuno il suo* similar to the contemporaneous Westerns, with the camera zooming in on barren landscapes scorched by the sun.

But throughout the story the zoom becomes a much more complex narrative tool. Petri often uses it at the end of a scene, as the camera closes in on an apparently insignificant detail, such as the small paper cut from the anonymous letter in Laurana's hands as the professor notices the Latin motto. The zooms focus on a newspaper, a person in a corner, a man's sunglasses, a fly on a wall. Here, Petri seems to mimic Laurana's tendency to focus on details while overlooking the context. The effect is bewildering. We find ourselves in a world reeking with allusions, where every single object or gesture might have a hidden or implied significance.

Sometimes, on the other hand, a zoom-out is used at the beginning of a sequence. Petri introduces a key sequence by following Rosello's hand as he enters a club and greets his fellow members, shaking hands or benevolently pinching someone's cheek, before the camera zooms out on the man. Here, the zoom testifies to the lawyer's privileged place as a Mafioso, allowing us to catch what Laurana cannot fully grasp yet.

Brusquely (and violently) moving to or from a detail, the zoom has a destabilizing force. It is revealing of an outside presence, an unseen but omniscient observer, who accompanies the viewer and urges him to see and understand things. For instance, Laurana's attraction to Luisa is immediately evident, as he can't take his eyes off of her when she enters the church during the funeral, or when he meets her outside a church, even before a single word is spoken between them.

The use of the telephoto lens conveys a voyeuristic quality, which becomes explicit in the scenes where the police spy on the suspects from behind a closed window, a moment destined to become a cliché in subsequent mafia movies. Overall, it predates the "totalizing and pervasive vision of power and of Italy's mysteries which will dominate political cinema and mafia-related films in the years to come."[44] But such a visual choice acquires a moral significance, as in the masterful sequence of Manno's murder during the hunting party, with the killers and the victims observed from a distance, flattened against the landscape. Viewers feel like witnesses and thus accomplices to the crime, while the zoom underlines the most uneasy details, such as Roscio's bloody hand raising in a gesture of surrender, vainly asking for mercy before he is dispatched by the faceless hitmen.

The zoom is one of several stylistic traits that Petri employs to stress the mystery angle while subtly subverting it. The insistent close-ups of body parts, hands and feet, are influenced by a groundbreaking thriller such as *The Ipcress File* (1965, Sidney J. Furie). Interiors feature vivid colors, sometimes bright and unrealistic as Bava would have had (note the red light next to Laurana's telephone). The hand-held camera can either highlight an action sequence (as in the frantic car chase in Palermo, which begins with a POV shot of Laurana getting in a taxi) or underline Laurana's emotional turmoil before Luisa during their encounter at Roscio's house. Cuts are often abrupt, sometimes in jarring contrast with Luis Bacalov's romantic, orchestral score.

But the zoom is also a stylish embellishment that becomes part of the film's visual panache. Paired with tracking and panning shots, it turns the ever-moving camera into a fountain pen which describes scenes and events with elaborate touches that are the visual correspondent to Sciascia's baroque, literate prose. A splendid example is the scene where Laurana returns to Cefalù after his stay in Palermo and arrives in the main square, where Rosello and the other notables are reading their newspapers. Shot in a long take, with the camera tracking sideways, focusing on one character and then to the next as they move and deliver their lines as pawns in a chess game, and then eventually backtracking in the opposite direction as Laurana leaves from where he came, it is an example of Petri's mastery of the medium.

Kuveiller's outstanding cinematography and Bacalov's score also highlight another key factor, the director's recourse to caricaturish and grotesque elements, starting with the sweaty mailman carrying the anonymous letter in the opening scene, accompanied by a descending four-note figure. When the police film Roscio's funeral and the commissioner asks who the various bystanders are, the town dignities are all fat, unpleasant, wearing dark shades and suits, looking pompous and hypocritical. Manno's widow is an ugly woman with a shadow of moustache on her upper lip, like Daniela Rocca's character in *Divorzio all'italiana*. These are the kind of characters Petri was aiming to depict in his idea for *I mostri*, and they underline the subterranean thread between *A ciascuno il suo* and the *commedia all'italiana*, revisited through a scathing political view.

Under the blinding sun, a comedy of characters unfolds, filled with folkloristic details which emphasize Sicily's most stereotypical elements. People eat ice cream and snow cones all the time; men put grease in their hair and wear suit and tie in the scorching heat; villagers sit outside bars, smoking, sweating and playing cards; at funerals and weddings, they gather like old gossips and discuss murder, cuckoldry and money ("Two hitmen cost more than a car, an apartment!"). Burials become collective recitals accompanied by marching bands. Cheated husbands are mocked with the offensive gesture of the "devil horns," symbolizing cuckoldry. Old men spy from behind fences and look away when someone addresses them. The whole island seems frozen in time, tied to centuries-old rituals and mores which underline Sciascia's concept of mental immutability. The Mafia is first and foremost a state of mind.

The ending, following Laurana's demise, is Petri's unrepentant sting in the tail. A long line of black limos arrives at a cathedral. It looks like a funeral, at first. Are the local people giving the last goodbye to the poor professor? Not at all. This is a wedding. Rosello and Luisa are getting married, and Don Rosello himself is celebrating the wedding. All the big shots are gathered to pay homage to the newlyweds, including Manno's widow. They all look happy and cheerful. The locals comment upon the scene, and it becomes obvious that everyone knew about the affair and the truth behind Roscio's murder as well. They are not outraged, though, but admiring: "They created a real masterpiece!"

So, everyone knew, except Laurana. "Poor innocent, he didn't know a thing." "He was an idiot," someone replies contemptuously, reprising the book's final words. But Petri's own visual punchline is even more effective. The newlyweds enter the church, followed by a crowd of guests. The camera is placed inside the sacred building, and a frontal short-focus shot shows an indistinct mass of silhouettes advancing toward us, regally, implacably. Gradually they fill the screen, obscuring the light until it goes dark. It is the nastiest of bad endings imaginable.

"Bravo bravo Elio sei proprio bravo"

A ciascuno il suo was ready for release in early 1967. In January Irene Papas flew to Rome for a private screening,[45] and Cemofilm submitted the film to the board of review on February 8. Three days later, the 3rd section opted for a V.M.18 rating because "regardless of the story's intents, the protagonists' cynical behavior and the milieu's passive complicity are explicit and looming, and so are the planning and diabolical execution of three murders. All this is contraindicated for the particular sensibility of the developmental age of said minors."

The producer appealed such a far-fetched motivation, but on March 11 the second-degree commission confirmed the verdict by majority, although three members were favorable to changing the rating to a milder V.M.14. It was clear from the beginning that the film was likely to cause a stir. In fact, a week before the official release, its poster was seized by the police headquarters in Rome, who judged it "offensive to public decency."[46] The offending item was a pictorial rendition of Laurana's sexual pass at Luisa, with Gian Maria Volonté and Irene Papas' characters lying on the sand, the man on top and kissing the woman as she tries to reject him.

The seizure gave way to a heated political controversy. The Socialist politician Giuseppe Amadei submitted an inquiry to the Christian Democrat Minister of Interior Paolo Emilio Taviani "in order to know the reasons for the extraordinary and sudden procedure."[47] In fact, the poster had been seized a mere thirty minutes after its placement and without any written order. A similar inquiry came from the Christian Democrat Agostino Greggi and involved the Ministers of Justice and of Tourism and Spectacle.

Distributed by Ugo Santalucia's Panta Cinematografica, *A ciascuno il suo* hit the venues on February 24, 1967. Petri received appraisal from many colleagues. Ennio Flaiano sent him an enthusiastic telegram: "Finally a theme approached with great lucidity strength and artistic conscience." Federico Fellini too sent a telegram, declaring that the movie had "excited, moved, enthused" him. "*Bravo bravo Elio sei proprio bravo*" (Good, good, Elio, you're really good), he concluded.[48] Critics, especially leftist ones, were far, far colder.

A notorious panning appeared in the magazine *Cinema & Film*, signed by the 27-year-old Maurizio Ponzi, an aspiring filmmaker who had been Pasolini's assistant and had directed a few documentaries. It started as follows:

A ciascuno il suo: Laurana clumsily attempts a sexual pass at Luisa on a beach. The scene inspired the film's official poster, which was considered "offensive to public decency" and seized.

A first reaction toward this movie could be silence.... The silence of those who love cinema too much, unfortunately, to delight in harsh criticism. The silence of those who think it's easy to underline the dazzling ugliness of a film by Petri, Fulci or Sollima. The silence of those who hold the reader in too high esteem to give him a lesson of good cinematic taste.... But ... silence can be, if not guilty, at least ambiguous; and contempt, if untold, becomes useless. So, we are compelled—as we did in the last issue with *La battaglia di Algeri*—to discuss Elio Petri's *A ciascuno il suo* and exhume this Z-grade filmmaker—long since set aside among the many in Italian cinema—to clarify, warn, specify.[49]

As Ponzi recalled, "Two years later, at an ANAC meeting, Petri asked someone to show him who I was. Once outside, he took me by the chest and slammed me against the wall! Many years later we met again in Milan and became close friends. Petri is an adorable man, the contrary of what one might imagine, and very sweet."[50] Ponzi claimed that the panning was mainly a polemic on the use of the zoom lens, which, as the review argues, "alters reality, in the literal sense of the word. This is not bad in a fantastic film, on the contrary ... but it is in a film which aims at being an exposé."

But such objections are highly debatable, for the use of the zoom in *A ciascuno il suo* has a stylistic, narrative and symbolic urge. Over the following years leftist critics would often attack Petri, among many other things, for his stylistic choices: they saw the expressionist deformation of reality as an "authoritarian technique" which brought a façade of formal complexity but prevented viewers from having a clean understanding of the political issues at stake, "in a repertoire of stylistic elements employed without any consideration of their specificity." In short, style was perceived as a synonym of constraint, with an aesthetic zeal which evoked Jacques Rivette's violent bashing of Gillo Pontecorvo's *Kapò* (1960) as "worthy of the most profound contempt"[51] for having chosen to make a forward tracking shot in the film's most harrowing scene, in turn echoing Jean-Luc Godard's oft-quoted axiom about tracking shots being "a question of morality."[52]

What is most striking about Ponzi's review nowadays is the contempt toward Lucio Fulci and Sergio Sollima, whose work is dismissed with such scorn as to make one understand the attention (or rather, lack thereof) given to genre filmmaking in the period. The same contempt is reserved for Petri, labeled a "Z-grade" hack who aims at a politically committed film while indulging in the lurid tricks associated with genre cinema. As Ponzi conceded, "like the Italian Westerns ... the film knows how to keep the viewer alert for 90 minutes, because it knows how to dose the color effects, the music and the acting in pleasant shifts from 'truth' (horrible, repugnant) to false appearances (the chromaticity of landscapes and costumes)." In short, its cinematic effectiveness and aim for spectacle were reduced to faults, and *A ciascuno il suo* was labeled as "fake just because it seems real ... and unwillingly racist, because it reduces Sicily to a cliché."[53]

After the film's release, Leonardo Sciascia expressed his appreciation to Petri while sticking to his original position in a letter dated March 10: "My prediction that you would make a great movie, yet different from the book, has come true."[54] Their subsequent correspondence includes interesting bits of information. In June 1967 the novelist told Petri that he was considering making a story about a "man who kills judges."[55] This would become the novel *Il contesto*, published in 1971 and adapted into a film by Francesco Rosi in 1976 with *Cadaveri eccellenti*. In turn, Petri mentioned his interest in adapting another eccentric mystery novel, Geoffrey Holiday Hall's *The End Is Known*, which Sciascia liked too. Both men considered also the possibility of working together on an original story to be made into a film, but the collaboration never materialized. As the disheartened director wrote, "Such is cinema. I feel a great despondency if I think that when I'll turn fifty or sixty, I'll always have to face the same problems. How can you convince a producer that a story is good, if not <u>after</u> turning it into a movie?"[56] The tentatively titled *Un delitto* was developed solely by Sciascia into the short story *Gioco di società* and published in December 1967.[57]

Despite a somewhat inadequate advertising launch, which prompted Petri to send a rather polemical telegram to Santalucia, complaining about the latter's "disinterest" and the "lack of any form of usual publicity,"[58] *A ciascuno il suo* was a solid commercial success. It grossed over 407 million *lire* and was nominated for several Nastri d'Argento awards. It won four, for Best Direction (beating Pasolini's *Edipo Re* and Paolo and Vittorio Taviani's *I sovversivi*), Best Script, Best Lead Actor (Volonté) and Best Supporting Actor (Ferzetti).[59] It also won the San Fedele prize, awarded by a jury comprising some of Italy's most noted sculptors and painters.[60] It did worse outside Italy. Released in the German-speaking areas of Switzerland as *Zwei Särge auf Bestellung* (Two Coffins by Order), it stayed in Zurich cinemas for only five days.[61] Still, its success caught Petri and Pirro partially off-guard, "as if we were discovering the power of our film for the first time together with the audience," as the scriptwriter put it.[62]

The best was yet to come. *A ciascuno il suo* was selected for competition at the 1967 Cannes Film Festival, and for both Petri and Pirro it was the first time at the prestigious event at the French Riviera. *Blow-up* was the big favorite, but there were many competitors. The festival took place amidst scandals and controversies. For one thing, the screening of Joseph Strick's *Ulysses* was interrupted after the director protested because his work had been arbitrarily censored, and Strick retired it from competition. The response to *A ciascuno il suo* on the part of the critics and the audience alike was favorable. As Mario Soldati summarized it, the film "has only one fault, but unforgivable for specialized critics of the festival: it's not boring and on the contrary (even worse!) it grabs the viewer's interest with an engrossing suspense...."[63]

Petri, Volonté and Papas attended a spirited press conference which started with a journalist asking the director: "Considering this and your previous works, it seems that you are a violent individual. Is the impression well founded?" Petri admirably kept a straight face. "On the contrary. I'm not a violent person at all. If anything, the society in which we live is violent: despite its technological progress, in some ways, it's still medieval."[64] Another French reporter asked Petri about the relevance of a scene in which the camera lingers on a fly on a door. "Does that insistence have a symbolical meaning? Do flies have a particular importance in Sicily...?" The question aroused hilarity in the audience, but for all its goofiness it underlined the way the film was perceived by the foreign press. Some compared the final wedding to Buñuel, a director whom Petri admitted knowing very little, having seen only two of his films. As for Volonté, he stayed faithful to his political commitment and underlined the film's anticlerical aspects, something the Italian press sought to minimize.

Eventually *A ciascuno il suo* won the prize for Best Screenplay, while the Grand Prix went to *Blow-up*. It was quite possibly a small concession to the two Italian jury members, director Alessandro Blasetti and film critic Gian Luigi Rondi. But it granted the film a worldwide theatrical distribution. United Artists released it in the United Kingdom, West Germany and Japan, while the Lithuanian-born producer and executive Ilya Lopert took care of the U.S. release through his company Lopert Pictures Corporation, in February 1968. According to a 1973 article/interview in *Cinéaste* magazine, "the film was well received critically, but did such poor business during its New York run that it never received a national release."[65] It also came out in France the following year, in the fatal month of May 1968, and in many other European countries as well.[66] Its success gave way to the making of *Il giorno della civetta*, directed by Damiano Damiani, a more traditional film about the Mafia, also scripted by Pirro and even more unfaithful to the book than Petri's. This time, Sciascia had no objections, though.

A ciascuno il suo was a key film for its time. Not just because of its subject, but because of the way Petri and Pirro approached it, by aiming at a narrative and formal compromise between exposé and character study, civic pledge and murder mystery, the drive of indignation and the need for a commercially viable product. In short, between politics and spectacle, as the director synthesized: "I was trying to create a 'popular' relationship between cinema and people."[67]

With its exuberant aesthetic and thematic boldness, *A ciascuno il suo* fit in a new phase for Italian cinema, in which a new generation of authors—namely, Marco Bellocchio, Bernardo Bertolucci, Paolo and Vittorio Taviani, Marco Ferreri, Carmelo Bene, Liliana Cavani—were working on film language, bringing to "a deflagration and stirring of expressive forms, stereotypes (which were overturned and became vehicles for new meanings) and mirror games which had never occurred before in our cinema," as Carlo Lizzani put it.[68]

After a time when social awareness seemed asleep, the limelight had been taken by disengaged products, and political messages were being delivered within unusual contexts, such as the political Westerns directed by Lizzani (*Requiescant*, 1966) and those scripted by Franco Solinas, such as Damiano Damiani's *Quien Sabe?* or Sergio Sollima's *La resa dei conti* (1966)—the kind of films that critics like Ponzi snubbed or treated patronizingly. *A ciascuno il suo* was the right film at the right moment, and it caught something new in the air. A general impatience, perhaps, or rather the feeling that something was about to change, and that the time for "poets with their heads in the clouds" was definitely over. Ordinary people—students, workers—were rediscovering a word that seemed forgotten: commitment.

SEVEN

A Portrait of the Artist as a Schizoid Man

Un tranquillo posto di campagna *(1968)*

Unmade Projects, 1967–1968

While presenting *A ciascuno il suo* to the press, Petri was already cooking up new projects. He announced he was working on two new scripts, one of them with Ennio Flaiano. "The title perhaps is not very commercial, but I like it very much: *Affettuoso rapporto su una donna da cui forse vorremmo essere amati.*"[1]

He was definitely correct about the uncommercial nature of the torrential title—a trait soon to become a trademark of Lina Wertmüller films—which translates into "Affectionate report on a woman by whom perhaps we would want to be loved." He described the story as "the analysis of the relationship that exists today between women's emotional world and their participation in the economic life."

Petri and Flaiano worked on the story, initially titled *L'italiana*, from November 26, 1966, to January 21, 1967. The results are a sketchy outline plus several notes and memos on some key scenes.[2] The story begins in an exclusive residential area in a pine wood, with pretentious-looking villas and well-kept gardens full of flowers with garish colors. As for its inhabitants, "all of them are inside their own fences, like prisoners, and indulge in their hobbies, generally gardening. All employ weed whackers, very noisy electric lawnmowers or automatic sprinklers, attempting to recreate the alienating conditions of the city in the countryside." From the striking opening, the theme of alienation is made explicit by way of a strong visual idea that looks like a Pop Art painting come to life.

A series of scenes laconically marked as chapters of a book ("The Lunch," "Love," "Shopping," "The Good Deed," etc.) describe the life of a wealthy married couple with children, whose empty daily routine is mercilessly sketched beneath its idyllic appearance. At dinner, with her husband's associate and his wife, their conversation is banal and void. After the guests leave, they remain alone. "He pretends to want to make love. She rejects him." Her main distraction is shopping, for she is a "prisoner of commodities."

At first glance, *L'italiana* looked like a story of conjugal betrayal, Antonioni-style, paired with a biting look at the ongoing property speculations taking place around Rome. In order to "make a good deed" for their *au pair* girl, who has been seduced and impregnated by a young construction worker, the wife meets him and tries to convince him to be good to the maid. But they end up in bed instead. He asks to meet her husband and proposes to him a commercial deal. The two men agree to defraud the local administration via an ambitious housing project, but a scandal ensues and the construction worker takes all the blame, while the husband emerges unscathed. In the end, the lady finds out she is pregnant too. Who is the father? She doesn't know. She leaves her husband and her lover. And she starts buying things for her new baby.

Petri's notes shed light on the director's creative method. He and Flaiano would exchange thoughts about scenes, characters, sometimes even just lines of dialogue, details or images they wanted to keep in the film. Petri would then examine the material thoroughly, discarding or reshaping ideas and interrogating himself on their effectiveness and meaning. In his notes he summarized the theme of the film as follows:

> Woman is the key of consumerist society. It is she who directs the common process of buying goods, those indispensable for survival, those that make life more comfortable, and also the totally superfluous ones. On the one hand, commodities alienate; on the other they are loaded with symbolic significance, related to sexuality. Therefore, the film should be a sort of conjunction of two themes: that of woman as consumer of goods, and that of woman who no longer perceives family as the only and typical center of her sentimental journey.... Ennio asks: "Is this movie an investigation?" I say "Yes."

Hence the subsequent, lengthy title.

Petri was considering a non-linear, episodic narrative, through the female protagonist's point of view. To stress the theme of woman as consumer, he considered the idea of punctuating the story with "dozens of scenes of domestic appliances being purchased," and images of shop windows, supermarkets, store counters, assorted advertising. As for the second main theme, the crisis of traditional family, there would be "dozens of love scenes with different men, all younger than her." As the director synthesized, "She buys everything she can, so she feels she is more complete; she has sex as often as she can, so she feels she is more complete."

To Flaiano, who suggested the titles *Scene della vita di una donna* (Scenes from a Woman's Life), *Questa donna* (This Woman) or *Questa donna innamorata* (This Woman in Love), "sexual conflict between males and females is born from this simple disagreement: woman consents to pleasure only to be able to sleep with the man she loves, whereas man, once he has satisfied his pleasure, falls back into the routine of duties and friends. Woman loves deeply and wants the man next to her, whereas he wants the woman to be available, which is substantially different."

The story would not be devoid of irony. Sexual symbols would be depicted through objects—cars, planes, etcetera—and by the way the characters *avoid* talking about sex. One of Flaiano's ideas was a scene set in a bookshop where the lady meets an intellectual who is playing pinball "because pinball means onanism." He also proposed making the protagonist a kleptomaniac (an idea suggested by *Marnie*, perhaps?) and frigid, for "a sexually complete woman is not successful in the movies."

But Petri was well aware of the issues such a project involved. "There are two types of risks. One, and I can tell without even having seen it, is making a movie like Pietro Germi's *Signore & signori*, cheaply moralistic, sexophobic, misogynist, Catholic." The other danger was ending up with something in the vein of Claude Lelouch's *Un homme et une femme* (also 1966), "that is, the *petit bourgeois* meta-love story ... with feelings above everything else, a risk which pushes the characters toward a sort of social limbo ... devoid of any sociological relevance or implication."

For the female lead, he was considering an actress "with an exotic beauty, not a prototype like those we find on the female magazines," a bit like the bossa nova singer Astrud Gilberto.[3] News that Marcello Mastroianni had signed a contract for the film turned up in April,[4] and while in Cannes the director confirmed that his upcoming work would star Mastroianni "at the center of a story about family relationships."[5] But, as Petri admitted in his notes, the project quickly lost its urgency, and he and Flaiano never got around to writing a proper script. "In the attempt to give an order, a line, a sense of veri-similitude to the things we said, we have been slipping toward a middle-class story. And I think we'll never be good enough to escape this risk, because both Ennio and I are immersed in a moralistic stickiness, bourgeois-type...."

Nowadays some observations on the main character's psychology (such as her fear of being a nymphomaniac) sound clumsy. But one must keep in mind the social climate of the period, the ever-growing changes in mores and bourgeois women's growing detachment from the patriarchal family model. Perhaps Petri was feeling the danger of being left behind with a story which might be old by the time it would reach the screens. And he most certainly knew that he could not offer a convincing solution to the protagonist's issues. Which once again proves his deep respect for his characters, De Santis' greatest legacy to him.

As for the second project, the intriguingly titled *Nostra signora Metredina* (Our Lady Methedrine), which he was scripting with Ugo Pirro and to star Marcello Mastroianni, he explained:

> It's the story of a politician who uses this drug often in order to endure the fatigue of his role. The powerful medication will lead the protagonist to find himself again on the one hand, and to lose himself on the other.[6]

The brief description fed to the press was understated to say the least. From the very first scene, the eight-page outline[7] displays a satirical tone targeted at the country's main party. The protagonist, Pilato, is a Christian Democrat MP who lives a parsimonious and chaste life in a convent, worthy of a Franciscan monk. But in fact he is duplicitous and unscrupulous, and after he finds out about an attempt to overturn the party hierarchies by way of listing its members in alphabetical order (the move is designed against a powerful politician named Zazo), he does his best to take advantage of it by way of blackmail and assorted schemes.

But the stress is too much. Following an embarrassing meeting with his fiancée Lucia (who is worried about Pilato's virility, for they have never had sex), Pilato has a breakdown during a ping-pong match. A mysterious man offers him a pill with miraculous reinvigorating properties, which turns out to be methedrine. The drug has unexpected side effects, though: it turns Pilato into a sex maniac who nevertheless is content with stealing his victims' panties. But it also provokes a crisis of conscience which leads him to abandon his plans. He has a drug-induced dream of "a ministry headed by Christ, to whom he submits an infinite list of renovating proposals." The dream is filled with erotic imagery as well, such as Pilato's obsession for panties and the recurring presence of phallic objects such as cannons and tanks.

Once the drug effect is over, Pilato is reduced to an apathetic, indifferent individual, marginalized by his own party. He has to take more methedrine. By now addicted to it, he believes that "only chemistry can give the world a new political conscience" and has visions of a parliament where it is mandatory for MPs to take hallucinogenic drugs. In the end it turns out that methedrine was part of a plan by the secret service to test Pilato's reliability, but now he is totally out of control. Driven by some sort of evangelical yearning, Pilato runs away and goes around preaching. He speaks with factory workers, housewives, pensioners and students, asking advice on how to be a good politician. Eventually he is caught in a park, while trying to explain his credo to a crowd of children. He is carrying a suitcase full of panties. In the last scene we find Pilato at work as gardener "in the convent of ex-politicians."

Even though openly mocking and punctuated with comic book-like imagery—such as the mysterious secret agents, all dressed in black and sporting thin mustaches, who follow the politicians everywhere, and Pilato's drug-induced visions of "pink and polka-dot tanks"—Petri's satire of the DC and its practices was scathing. In a scene, for instance, Pilato goes to an asylum and corrupts the head doctor in order to buy the inmates' votes. As he leaves, a fellow party member is arriving there with the same intent. Even more violent was the allusion to the politicians' hypocritical sexual mores: Pilato is clearly impotent and possibly a closet homosexual, and his drug-induced behavior highlights his fetishistic tendencies.[8]

In June 1967 Petri submitted *Nostra signora Metredina* to Ilya Lopert but with no success. Over a year later, in October 1968, he offered it to Alberto Grimaldi, to no avail. Nobody wanted to have anything to do with it.[9] But the director would reprise many ideas in his following works, most notably in *Todo modo*. Moreover, *Nostra signora Metredina* marks a turning point in Petri's *oeuvre*: from the depiction of neurosis portrayed in existentialist terms, as in his early films, he reached a point where he described out-and-out schizophrenia, "but trying to depict schizophrenia as the basis of normalcy, that is to say as the content of reality itself."[10]

A similar theme can be found in another unproduced project, *Le cose* (Things), which Petri summarized as "the story of a love consumed by consumerist society." It revolves around a young couple, Marco and Lucrezia, so ordinary they seem to have come out of a pop song. But while setting up everything for the wedding, they are ensnared by the desire to possess. "Everything they <u>can</u> possess seems infinitely less beautiful, less true, less tangible than what they <u>cannot</u> possess." They get married but find themselves dissatisfied. They feel the unstoppable urge to have what they cannot have. Soon they become "an infernal couple who need to change their car, fridge or television even twice a week." Their house is bursting with washing machines, TV sets and other appliances. They dismantle them as kids would do with new toys, just to see what's inside. They have a top-notch American-style kitchen but eat only canned food. They incur heavy debts to pay for all the things they buy. Eventually Marco, who works in an insurance company, becomes a murderer to benefit from insurance policies and get enough money to purchase new commodities. But their love gradually dies too, strangled by preoccupations, envies and desires.

A satire on consumerism told as a wild black comedy, and openly influenced by Georges Perec's 1965 novel of the same name (*Les choses. Une histoire des années soixante*) which had a very similar plot, *Le cose* had in itself the seeds of what would become *La proprietà non è più un furto*, with its idea of a pathological relationship with things. Moreover, despite their being outside the law, the two protagonists are just as much part of the capitalist system as ordinary consumers, similarly to the thieves depicted in the 1973 film.

A three-page outline for *Le cose* is dated June 14, 1967.[11] Petri told Flaiano the idea and he liked it, for, as the director quipped, "unlike Ugo, he's not against murders."

The director also sketched a scene in which Marco and Lucrezia are watching a shop window with all kinds of ultramodern sanitary facilities. "They look like sculptures," Marco notices. "To be placed in the garden." Petri submitted the outline for *Le cose* to Ital-Noleggio in August. The project was greenlit and the company was willing to pay a five million *lire* advance, but ultimately it was shelved.

Petri was also toying with other ideas, namely the adaptation of Bertolt Brecht's posthumous novel *Die Geschäfte des Herrn Julius Caesar* (aka *The Business Affairs of Mr. Julius Caesar*), with Vittorio Gassman as Caesar[12]; a movie loosely based on a true story "about the city's racism toward the suburbs" called *L'idiota*[13]; and another inspired by the notorious story of Walburga Oesterreich and Otto Sanhuber, the "attic lover." Petri had already convinced Vanessa Redgrave and Franco Nero to star in the latter as the wife and her lover, while Michel Piccoli would play the husband, but he discarded the project when he found out in Cannes that Paramount was producing a movie on the same subject, *The Bliss of Mrs. Blossom*.[14]

In the summer of 1967, contradictory bits of information turned up about Petri's next work. After the shelving of *Affettuoso rapporto ...* and *Nostra signora Metredina*, news leaked that he was the most likely candidate to direct *Sequestro di persona*, written by Pirro and starring Franco Nero and Anna Karina, about the kidnapping business in Sardinia.[15] The film was eventually made by Gianfranco Mingozzi, and with Charlotte Rampling alongside Nero.

Around the same period, Petri considered adapting Alexander Klüge's shocking 1962 short story *Ein Liebesversuch* (A Love Experiment), under the tentative title *Esperimento d'amore*. It is a fictional interrogation of doctors who have conducted experiments on prisoners in concentration camps. In order to test whether sterilization by X-ray treatment had been successful, they try and make a female test patient conceive. The woman had had a love affair with a Jewish prisoner who is still alive, so the two are put in a cell together in and kept under observation through a peephole. They are expected to have sex, but nothing happens. The doctors and guards try to instigate "love" from the outside: they install red lights, give them champagne, spray the couple with cold water in the hope that the need for warmth will drive them together. After a week, the doctors give up, and the couple are shot.

During the months of September and October 1967 Petri was in talks with Ital-Noleggio's Mario Gallo for the possibility of an Italian-British co-production starring Vanessa Redgrave, and even mentioned it in a letter to Leonardo Sciascia.[16] As far as early May 1968 he was still interested in purchasing the rights to the story.[17] Kluge's tale—a fictional interrogation of the doctors who conducted the experiment—was never adapted to the big screen, but it would prove influential to future German filmmakers: Christian Petzold mentioned it as one of the inspiration for his acclaimed 2014 film, *Phoenix*.[18]

Eventually Petri decided to resume a script dating from several years back, *Un tranquillo posto di campagna*. Around 1964, while his career was stalling during the exhausting scriptwriting work for *La decima vittima*, he had attempted to restart the project and sent the first draft of the script to Istituto Luce's Ennio Della Nesta, together with a treatment for *L'uomo nero*. He pointed out that many changes needed to be made to both. In late 1967, after cutting a deal with Alberto Grimaldi's PEA, Petri went on to revise his old script with the help of Luciano Vincenzoni. His intention was to describe the situation of modern man as a split entity, the product of a society which is just as disjointed.

There is an out-and-out schizophrenia of the modern man. For instance, I believe I'm a schizoid myself, for I profess ideas which are typical of the revolutionary leftist circles, and yet I am part of the capitalistic system, for I'm exploiting workers—not directly, in the economic sense, but in terms of privilege, of the pay, and that's the same. At the moment it is just a moral issue, but it's a schizophrenic situation. The same can be said about the reporter ... who writes according to the directives from "above" although he doesn't share them; same about the factory worker divided between his will for revolutionary action and the obligation to keep up with the rhythm of the capitalist mode of production. In my opinion, this is not alienation: it is a split, on a clinical ground.[19]

For the main role Petri needed a younger actor than Mastroianni and a "lighter" one than Volonté. Someone fascinating and with an innate self-ironic vein. Franco Nero represented the ideal choice. Petri and the actor had known each other for a while.

In 1966 I was in a car with Paola Petri and her husband.... I had been offered a Western, *Django*. I told Elio Petri: "Elio, I am an actor coming from the Piccolo Teatro in Milan. Why should I do a Western?" And this was his answer: "Who knows you?" I said: "No one." "Then do it. You have nothing to lose." And that was the first helpful advice Elio Petri gave me.[20]

After the success of *Django* (1966), the handsome 27-year-old actor had become a highly marketable name in Italy and abroad, and his love story with Vanessa Redgrave had made the headlines. Petri had already considered pairing Nero and Redgrave for *The Attic Lover*, and he stuck to the idea for what would become their second movie together after *Camelot* (1967), so as to exploit their chemistry to the film's benefit. Moreover, he claimed he preferred to work with foreign actresses, for "Italian ones easily become all like Alberto Sordi: they are always afraid of looking ugly, or not very effective, they don't want to shoot this or that scene...."[21]

The film being an Italian-French co-production between PEA and its French counterpart led to the casting of Georges Géret (in the role Petri had originally devised for Salvo Randone) and Madeleine Damien (as Wanda's mother). The rest of the cast featured lesser-known names (including a cameo of Brit writer and film correspondent John Francis Lane as an asylum attendant) and a couple of female beginners. The enticing Wanda was played by the blonde Gabriella Grimaldi (real name Gabriella Boccardo), while Rita Calderoni, soon to become one of the icons of Italian sexy horror, turned up in the small role of Egle the maid. Petri's dog Snoopy had a brief cameo in the final scene.

News that Franco Nero and Vanessa Redgrave would star in *Un tranquillo posto di campagna* came out a few days before shooting started on April 1, 1968.[22] The British actress made no mystery of her political commitment and claimed to suffer the same contradictions that Petri would emphasize in the film. "I'm convinced that the world must change, that something is going to happen from which radical transformations will ensue. To me, this is a relief and a source of concern at the same time. In fact, I'm a bourgeois, and even though I loathe the bourgeoisie I am inevitably part of it."[23]

Her words were prophetic. While Petri and the crew relocated to Northern Italy for the twelve weeks of filming, with interiors in and around a villa in the Veneto region—not far from where Marcello Mastroianni was shooting De Sica's *Amanti* (1968), resulting in the actor's frequent visits on the set—and exteriors in Milan, all eyes were set on France. After the events of May 1968, the world would no longer be the same.

An Erotic Ghost Story

Tentatively titled *Un tranquillo posto di campagna (La paura)*, the new version soon lost its subtitle and underwent at least two different drafts, from a 315-page one to a 212-page one, both dated 1967[24] and sensibly different from the 1962 script. Names were changed (and the ghost was renamed Wanda in a nod to Leopold von Sacher-Masoch's novella *Venus in Furs*) and the ending was overturned. The original denouement gave way to a violent climax which turns out to be the product of the protagonist's now totally deranged mind, followed by a sneering epilogue set in an asylum. But Petri's major intervention was in the relationship between the artist and his manager/lover Flavia. The loosening of censorship allowed for the sexual theme to come to the foreground, imbuing the tale with strong erotic overtones.

Petri and Vincenzoni's version centers on a successful Pop Art painter, Leonardo Ferri, whose inspiration is channeled by the art market. He must oblige by producing commercially viable works. But he is developing a neurosis, torn as he is between the search for true art and moneymaking. This neurosis takes on sexual forms, by way of nightmares in which he is Flavia's victim. Ferri retires in a country villa but he is upset by strange phenomena. He learns the story of the young and sexually uninhibited Countess Wanda, who allegedly died in a bombing during the war, and becomes obsessed by it. A man named Attilio brings flowers to the spot where she died, and Leonardo befriends him. Attilio tells the painter that he was one of Wanda's lovers and shows him their "secret room" with a double-sided mirror through which Wanda's mother spied on her daughter's affairs. After visiting the elderly woman, Ferri becomes convinced that Wanda's ghost is still haunting the place and is hostile toward Flavia, who—in one of the few elements retained from Oliver Onions' story—is the victim of weird accidents whenever she shows up at the villa. He sets up a séance which leads to a surprising revelation: it was Attilio who murdered Wanda. He had caught her with a German soldier and savagely killed the man, then he and the girl had buried the body just before a bombing took place. Wanda had survived the attack, but Attilio killed her immediately afterwards, crazed with jealousy. The revelation drives Ferri mad. He kills and dismembers Flavia, or at least that's what he believes. In the end, we find him locked up in an asylum, happily working on new paintings and released from his neurosis. As a madman, he is now fully integrated into the system. Flavia, who is still alive and well, sells his works to art collectors for high prices.

In a letter to French producer Anatole Dauman, Petri described *Un tranquillo posto di campagna* as "a modern-day *À rebours*,"[25] referring to Joris-Karl Huysmans' 1874 novel of the same name about an eccentric aesthete who retreats to a secluded house in the countryside to spend his time in meditation. Indeed, Ferri aims to be a Romantic artist, and his escapist fantasies take on Romantic forms. Like his 18th century predecessors who painted for their muse, he becomes enamored of a lady ghost whom he sees as the sole reason for living in a world where money is the only recognized value and urge. In fact, he is less a romantic hero than an out-and-out victim, tortured and exploited by the system he feeds with his successful paintings.

In Petri's vision, art has lost its original significance in today's world. He summarized the story as follows:

> A painter practices art as it was practiced in previous centuries, without realizing that such art is dead. A painter sees that his paintings are totally commodified, as it should be in this type

of society, and requires that they are not…. He becomes mad, crushed by this contradiction of demanding that his paintings be not merchandise but works of art in a society in which this is no longer possible. A work of art is commodity, and nothing else.[26]

In the original version of *Un tranquillo posto di campagna*, he explored at length the dichotomy between figurative and abstract art, picking up where he left off in *I giorni contati*. The opening scenes, set at the Biennale, portrayed the art world in a disillusioned manner, highlighting the artists' fashionable status, and the protagonist, Marcello M., was described as a vain, self-confident type, whose rejection of figurative art hid his artistic limits. Much of the 1962 script focused on the artist's failed attempt to paint a portrait of the dead woman, upon her widower's request. He was an abstractionist who created large canvases akin to Lucio Fontana's "Tagli" (cuts) but had no real talent. The ghost openly mocked him, functioning as an embodiment of his own conscience: "She tells him that he is a buffoon, he is not Picasso as he thinks, he is not even a real painter."[27] Eventually, out of desperation, Marcello repeatedly slashed the canvas with his awkward sketches. The art merchants were enthusiastic about the result, commenting about his "rejection of the figurative," in a sarcastic stab at the emptiness of the art world.

The rewriting of the protagonist into a Pop artist was not merely Petri adapting himself to the new fads but the sign of his ongoing meditation on contemporary art. In 1964 he visited the Biennale and was very much impressed by the works of the American artists. To him, Pop Art was "an even more advanced degree of desperation of the Romantic artist in the face of the recovery of his own experiences and his relationship with reality."[28]

To prepare for the movie, Petri got in touch with Neo-Dada painter Jim Dine and traveled to the United States to shoot a 16mm short film on him, in order to portray his working method (which Franco Nero's character would reprise) and study the artist's gestures and personality at work. The footage shows Dine in the act of painting twelve canvases that appear in the film as well. "There was a lot of schizophrenia in this infuriated relationship with objects that he wanted to incorporate into his work; the 'Pop' artist carries out a sort of constant stealing in order to start expressing something again. There is a terrible despair in this little film," the director commented.[29]

Whereas the 1962 version showed a protagonist who slowly discovers his malaise, similarly to what happened in *L'assassino*, Leonardo's schizophrenia manifests itself already in the opening scenes. We see him half-naked and tied to a chair, on a stage of sorts, while Flavia comes home and proceeds to surround him with all the hi-tech electric appliances she has just purchased. He releases himself, follows her into the bathroom and kills her.

It is a hallucinatory dream, the first of many that punctuate the story, and it immediately makes it clear that Leonardo's inner self is split. He sees himself in various states of impotence, either tied or wheelchair-bound, with Flavia as his nurse, captor or torturer, and his hallucinations have a violent content, turning his sexual impulses into homicidal ones. The grotesque tone somehow evokes Nino Manfredi's naïve fantasies in *L'impiegato*, which at some point took the form of a murder depicted in the way a photonovel would. But Petri was also reprising some ideas from *L'italiana*, namely the insistence on woman as consumerist and the emphasis on the appliances Flavia buys in the opening scenes of the film.

Ferri envisions himself as a prisoner, straight from the beginning. He seems uninterested in money, loathes the pleasures of consumerism, is spiteful of bourgeois rituals,

Painter Jim Dine (left), Franco Nero (center) and Elio Petri on the set of *Un tranquillo posto di campagna*.

happenings[30] and commodities, both in his look and social attitudes. Yet he is incapable of detaching himself from them. His loft is littered with consumerist symbols, most notably a huge Coca-Cola dispenser. He too is a producer and a consumer, willing or not.

The artist's inner split manifests itself when he "sees" another version of himself, free and joyful, a vision which drives him to the idyllic "quiet place in the country." There, Leonardo takes refuge among the ghosts of the romantic culture, in the warm colors and the timelessness of the countryside as opposed to the alienating, abstract shapes and frantic productive rhythm of the city. Wanda is a "ghost of art" as Ferri idealized it, and the painter's seclusion in the country is the attempted return to a state of childish innocence, a way to cleanse and purify his mind and therefore renew his creativity.

Soon, though, the virginal Wanda turns out to be quite different from the image Leonardo had of her. Likewise, his romanticized countryside shelter is invaded by the items of progress, such as a dishwasher (in which he will wash his brushes and later the knives he has used to "kill" Flavia). Ferri himself cannot resist transforming the place according to his own distorted vision. In one of the film's most striking scenes he has the trees near the place where Wanda died painted red, turning them into works of art—and, it is implied, causing them to die because of the paint. Man yearns for nature but cannot resist its indifference. Hence, he attempts to control it.

Leonardo's infatuation with the ghost—who sabotages his work, destroying one of his canvases in a night rage and making colors fly everywhere as in an action painting session—results in his attempts to turn Wanda's photographs into works of art. As in the 1962 version, Ferri is incapable of figurative painting, so he resorts to Warhol-style reproductions and coloristic variations. But these copies do not retain the same magic aura as the original. At some point, Walter Benjamin's 1935 essay *The Work of Art in the Age of Mechanical Reproduction* can be spotted in a shot, underlining Petri's discourse.

Un tranquillo posto di campagna brims with artistic references, not as mere flourishes but as part of the message. Ferri's opening dream is staged like a body art performance, and his obsession with leaving his marks or imprints on the canvas recalls the work of Yves Klein. In both cases the emphasis on the human body as an integral part of the creative process hints at the artist's desperate attempt to reaffirm his personality, his uniqueness, and therefore his work's authenticity. This occurs at a time when, as noted by Benjamin, mechanical reproduction has devalued a work of art of its aura (that is, its unique aesthetic authority), which is absent from the mechanically produced copy.

With their use of arrows, numbers, magnified typeface, the opening credits recall the early works of Jannis Kounellis, and are interspersed with images of several famous works of art, including Goya's *El tres de mayo de 1808 en Madrid*, the *Presumed Portrait of Gabrielle d'Estrées and Her Sister, the Duchess of Villars* attributed to the School of Fontainebleau, Francis Bacon's *Study after Velázquez's Portrait of Pope Innocent X*, and Ingres's *La Grande Odalisque*. But the most notable presences are Jacques-Louis David's unfinished *Madame Récamier*, which depicts a woman sitting on a sofa, and its Surrealist reinterpretation by René Magritte, *Madame Récamier by David*. Magritte painted it in 1951, replicating David's Neoclassical colors and fine detail brushwork, but replacing the main subject of the painting, Madame Récamier, with an L-shaped coffin. Juliette Récamier was one of the most beautiful women of the late 1700s and early 1800s, and David portrayed her as a vestal virgin of her time. Magritte's substitution highlights the transience of beauty and life.

These two works turn up again in the scene—Petri's favorite in the film—where Leonardo pays a visit to Wanda's elderly and half-demented mother and sees her replaced by a coffin which looks exactly like the one in Magritte's painting, thus further underlining Ferri's obsession. "You can feel the horror of art in the movie," Petri argued. "It's not true that art is reassuring. It can also be horrifying. The Sistine Chapel is horrifying, for it is inhabited by the ghosts of our sinfulness and by death. That's what great art is like. Reassuring art does not exist."[31]

The theme of art as merchandising predates such recent, diverse titles as *The Square* (2017, Ruben Östlund) and *Velvet Buzzsaw* (2019, Dan Gilroy), with their vampire-like merchants and spoiled artists; moreover, the sarcastic ending anticipates Alberto Cavallone's *Blue Movie* (1978), which also features a barter of an unusual kind, with a caged model exchanging her excrements (stored inside cigarette packets and Coca-Cola cans) for Coca-Cola and canned food. But the nature of Ferri's alienation takes on a wider perspective. In an early scene he watches a slideshow, a series of images which are alternatively erotic and gruesome. Pictures of naked women, scenes from the Vietnam war, starving children, capital executions, a tank in the streets of Prague. It's a concept Petri will reprise in *Buone notizie*, where Giancarlo Giannini's character is bombarded and brainwashed by all kinds of images from the ever-present TV sets at work and at home. Here, Ferri is totally oblivious to the outside world and its issues. Not only is the artist unable to speak to the public, as in *I giorni contati*, but he no longer has the political, revolutionary function he once had.

Keeping up with a thread that had become more and more explicit, from *Peccato nel pomeriggio* to *La decima vittima* and *A ciascuno il suo*, *Un tranquillo posto di campagna* explores one of the central themes in Petri's work, male sexuality torn between norm and transgression. In both versions of the story, the protagonist displays somewhat immature behavior, which in the 1962 script manifests itself by way of childish whims and poses: Marcello behaves like a spoiled child and his lover is a motherly figure who either goes along with him or reproaches him. In the film, this relationship is openly depicted as a deranged mother-son one, as when Flavia tells Leonardo "Come to mommy, come!" The changes from the 1962 version result in a drastic change for Flavia's character. Depicted as a potential victim in Ferri's dreams, she eventually turns out to be yet another huntress who manipulates the man and reduces him to impotence for good.

Petri's depiction of the commodification of sex came at a time when the market was flooded by erotic publications. In December 1966 publisher Rosario "Saro" Balsamo launched *Men*, the nation's true first adults-only magazine. It was followed several months later by *Playmen*, Italy's answer to *Playboy*, funded by Balsamo's wife Adelina Tattilo, who would become the leading publisher in the field. Initially included in *Men*, the photonovel *Supersex* was later launched as an autonomous publication, paired with the equally saucy *Sexybell*.[32] It is one of the sexy magazines Leonardo consumes avidly—a step forward from the comics Marcello reads in *La decima vittima*—, further underlining his childlike sexuality. Ferri reads aloud the balloons and makes funny voices, while Flavia attempts to arouse him by wearing sexy lingerie and donning the same make-up as the one displayed by the scantily-clad models. But it is only in the country, away from the

Un tranquillo posto di campagna: **Flavia (Vanessa Redgrave) and Edoardo (Franco Nero) reading an erotic photonovel.**

city's alienating rhythms, that the artist's libido erupts again, at the sight of the maid's rustic and spontaneous sexuality, her sweaty neck, her bra and her exposed thighs. But once again he focuses on an erotic phantom instead of a real woman.

Ferri is driven to imaginary objects of desire, just as he cannot connect anymore with the outside world by way of his art, which in turn is imbued with his own sexual issues. Marcello's cut canvas in the 1962 draft conveyed sexual innuendo, and this becomes more explicit in the filmed version, where Leonardo's inability to produce new work is related to impotence. In the epilogue, Ferri glues stylized wood vulvas over the many small paintings that adorn his asylum cell. Finally, he has found the missing object his huge canvas lacked. But in the meantime he has devoted himself to producing a series of barely distinguishable copies. The asylum nurse gives him erotic magazines in exchange for his works. His creativity is now released, yet he is once and for all the prisoner of his erotic fantasies, and of the mass production system as well.

Experimenting and Improvising

The film's inner core demanded that both the narrative and the form be experimental, in line with Ferri's art, so as to better convey his neurosis. It was a risky move on Petri's part, and one which alienated many viewers expecting a more traditional thriller (which the 1962 version ultimately was). He was aware of the danger of falling into avant-garde pretensions, but he also knew that an idea's clarity is the antidote to formal and narrative fragmentation.

Un tranquillo posto di campagna approaches the Gothic genre and its tropes in a highly distinctive manner. Petri revisits the Fantastic and its rules with a stylistic verve that pushes even further the visual ideas of his previous films. For one thing, he reprises a trick he had explored in *L'assassino* and *Il maestro di Vigevano*, where he mixed past and present, reality and hallucination within the same sequence by way of complex long takes. Here, Leonardo experiences past events which take place before his eyes, in the same shot. At one point he appears in the midst of a field, and suddenly several partisans turn up around him, transporting us to the year 1945. After Attilio shows Ferri a room with a double-sided mirror from where he spied on Wanda and recalls killing the German soldier who was making love to her, the ensuing flashback is introduced with no cuts. And it is Attilio's older self who smashes the soldier's head with a shovel, while Ferri is right by his side, witnessing the murder. To further add to the disorientation, the painter even briefly identifies himself with the victim, his face full of blood—or is it the dementedly jealous Attilio who sees him like that?

This daring narrative approach breathes new life into typical ghost story material, such as the appearance of the red-dressed ghost or the séance that preludes Ferri's final rampage. The scene of Wanda riding her bicycle along the villa's corridors, announced by the bicycle bell, is a moment worthy of Mario Bava, with the camera conveying the almost tangible nature of the ghost and its fleetingness. The séance, introduced by an elaborate long take, features the expected overhead shots of the participants' hands on the table, but Petri engulfs it in darkness, and the close-ups of the actors' barely distinguishable faces give it an unnerving quality. Even the sparse use of on-screen violence and *grand guignol* effects is subtly misleading. The climax in which Ferri apparently kills and dismembers Flavia with a set of huge knives, played by way of ellipsis and quick shots of (seemingly) blood dripping from a table and blood-soaked wraps stuffed in the refrigerator, is a case in point. Petri convinces us that we have seen more than we actually have, for when the cops open the fridge, they do not find human body parts, but a huge sheet stained with red paint.

Luigi Kuveiller's cinematography moves in a direction akin to Godard, Resnais and Robbe-Grillet, as well as to Bergman's latest works, subverting the rules of traditional storytelling. The camerawork project a sense of disorientation, with abrupt changes of focus and quick panning shots. Images become almost indecipherable at times, amid blots of color and out-of-focus shapes. All this is further emphasized by Ruggero Mastroianni's fractured editing. Soon, viewers are losing grip of reality just as Leonardo Ferri is.

For the score Petri wanted something just as outside the box. He recruited Ennio Morricone and got what he wanted, for the composer resorted to the services of the "Gruppo di Improvvisazione Nuova Consonanza." Formed in 1964 by avant-garde composer Franco Evangelisti, a pioneer of electronic music, GINC was the offspring of the Roman association Nuova Consonanza, born in 1959, which by the mid–1960s had become the most important European association of contemporary music. The ensemble practiced improvisation, with influences ranging from Giacinto Scelsi to John Cage, and Evangelisti labeled it as "the first and only group formed by composers who are also performers." On its first public exhibition at the 3rd Festival di Nuova Consonanza in 1965, GINC's line-up was a cosmopolitan collective of foreign musicians based in Rome, featuring American composer Larry Austin, two more American multi-instrumentalists (John Eaton and John Heineman), German keyboardist Roland Kayn, plus two jazz musicians, clarinetist William O. Smith and Ivan Vandor, the latter responsible for the score for *I giorni contati*.

Ennio Morricone had become part of GINC in 1966, together with Frederic Rzewski and Mario Bertoncini, at the time the group recorded their debut namesake album for RCA. Eaton and Smith had already left. Even though each member's roles were not predetermined, given the improvisational nature of the music, Morricone mainly focused on trumpet. "The music we made was improvised starting from targeted exercises: we used to play eager for months and months on very precise parameters, we recorded ourselves, in the evening we listened to the tapes and criticized each other. It was painstaking."[33] The album landed on the American market in 1967, rebaptized "The Private Sea of Dreams," credited to Il Gruppo and displaying a lysergic cover sleeve. RCA promoted it as "improvisational mood music for modern dream extensions" and liberally changed the compositions' titles so as to please psychedelia fans. In a way, it was the type of marketing process Petri described in his film.

The result of GINC's work on the film is outstanding. Music takes a similar function as the accompaniment during the silent era, but the effect is disorienting, almost cacophonous. The rhythmical music consists of isolated piano notes and sparse sounds such as chimes, reed sounds and reverberations, accompanied by assorted amplified noises made with found objects, while in the background one can hear a distorted hiss which hints at the protagonist's mental disorder. As Morricone recalled,

> I remember one episode in which The Group responded to the protagonist, who suddenly poured his colors all over the desk, by bursting into "sliding" scales and arpeggios rapidly falling like muddled sonorous waterfalls.
>
> Nobody conducted; each of us reacted in our own personal way, yet we were constantly aware of the collective rules we had preestablished. Another element that made this experience

unique was that we improvised under Petri's attentive supervision; he would interact with us by saying, "Ah, I like this, ah, this is good…."

We aimed to obtain the nuances that he judged best fit; in this way the director gradually gained control over the outcome of our improvisation.[34]

The fact that Morricone alone is credited with the score is puzzling, given GINC's nature and especially the central role of Evangelisti and his concept that the composer is also the performer. According to the credits GINC's members become mere performers of the distressing suite whose fragments are scattered all over the film. Still, the score remains a key moment in Morricone's *oeuvre* and it predates a new phase in his career. The Roman composer and GINC would team up again for Enzo G. Castellari's *Gli occhi freddi della paura* (1971).

"Dear Morricone, I want you to know that I have always changed the composer for each of my films. So, this will be the first and the last we will do together,"[35] Petri had told him upon their first encounter. He would change his mind, for Morricone would score all of his following works.

"A film against women which women like"

Un tranquillo posto di campagna was submitted to the rating board on November 5, 1968. Once again, its controversial nature resulted in a troublesome experience with the censors. Submitting a film to the board was often a matter of strategic trimmings and negotiations between both sides. Petri and Grimaldi underlined that their work was not "aimed at commercial purposes" and were adamant that they would not perform any cuts. On November 12, the board allowed it a certificate for public screening and gave it a V.M.18 rating by majority, "for the various sequences depicting the protagonist's states of mental excitement are of a gruesome and shocking nature." But two members voted for the ban, and their motivation must be read to be believed.

> The minority expresses a contrary opinion to the concession of the screening certificate, for the film depicts the depraved and exasperated sexuality of a madman. This results in acts of sadomasochism and sadism mixed with erotic necrophilia and it is portrayed in such an explicit manner that it is in contemptuous contrast with the most elementary rules of public decency.

Grimaldi was worried that the film might be seized by the magistrates upon release, and asked the director to cut a scene where Vanessa Redgrave's nude bottom appeared. Petri replied that he didn't see an offense to decency in any image of the film and entrusted the final decision to the producer.[36] The scene stayed in the film and *Un tranquillo posto di campagna* was not seized.

Still, the tagline, "Un film contro le donne che piace alle donne" (A film against women which women like), added fuel to the fire of the controversy and rode its alleged misogynist undercurrent, while the advertising campaign—which the director didn't like—attempted to market it as an erotic thriller, complete with the recommendation of not entering the venue during the last ten minutes. However, at 387,358,000 *lire*, revenues were not up to expectations.

Critics were moderately favorable. The *Corriere d'Informazione* mentioned Poe, Antonioni, Carlos Fuentes and Fellini as the "closest cultural background."[37] Giovanni Grazzini, in the *Corriere della Sera*, pointed out the story's dual nature.

If the film goes zigzag, it's not because its ideological satire is badly aimed, but because Petri has chosen a double-track tale. On the first … he boldly attempts a type of cinema Godard-style, with little dialogue, stylized … in which the form overlaps very well with the significance, and the idea of our neurotic times springs from intense imagery and obsessive mockery. The second, featuring echoes of Hitchcock and Antonioni, is just a ghost story … told with great skill and effective suspense which, however, is only casually centered on that "Pop" Leonardo. So, eventually, the tale is a bit rickety, and the scary movie plays the lion's share compared with the analysis of an intellectual's crisis.[38]

The expected bias against the horror genre did not prevent the reviewer from pointing out the director's "visual intelligence, which Petri has to the highest degree," and calling the film "one of the most gratifying examples of how the photographic look, the sequences' pacing, the thrilling use of color, the whole stylistic outfit of a very skilled filmmaker sew together two separate movies' stumps by way of constant figurative invention."[39]

Other reviews were less complimentary. According to *La Stampa*, the film proved that "if telling one's dreams is boring, depicting madness on screen is even more so," and the reviewer blamed the "acute but very rickety narrative" and the "headache-inducing camerawork." He also dismissed Nero's casting and labeled the result as a "fairly respectable spectacle … polished in the images, the colors, the sound," halfway between Bergman and late 19th century Italian novelist Antonio Fogazzaro, author of the seminal Gothic novel *Malombra*.[40]

Specialized film magazines attacked *Un tranquillo posto di campagna* with rabid relish. The heavily politicized *Cinema 60* called it a pathetic "supermarket of mystification … by a filmmaker who still thinks he is addressing a kindergarten,"[41] and, as Maurizio Ponzi had done in his infamous review for *A ciascuno il suo*, wrote that it would have deserved silence. Instead, the reviewer went on panning the film (and the critics who had praised it) for two whole pages. *Filmcritica* dismissed it with just one sentence as "the most worthless example of kitsch, a massacre of a wonderful actress."[42]

Selected for competition at the 1969 Berlin Film Festival, *Un tranquillo posto di campagna* was awarded a Silver Bear (a tie-in with four other films[43]), with a special mention to the photographic and chromatic results achieved by Kuveiller. It was released in France on August 14, 1969, by Les Artistes Associés as *Un coin tranquille à la campagne*, to meagre box-office results (30,119 spectators).

The film's thriller elements and its two stars facilitated distribution abroad. The April 1969 issue of *Playboy* announced *A Quiet Place in the Country* in a pictorial three-page article dedicated to Vanessa Redgrave which promoted the "comely and contentious" actress's latest two "far-out films" (the other being Karel Reisz's *Isadora*), emphasizing the erotic content with several nude pictures from its boldest moments.[44] However, Petri's film opened overseas only the following year, on August 28, 1970, in New York City, to obtuse reviews: "Mental aberration is merely exploited in it—not defined," wrote *Motion Picture Daily*'s Richard Gertner,[45] who mistook it for just another bizarre but ultimately unsuccessful genre offering ("odd camera angles, bizarre op-art sets, and weird color and optical effects"), proving how the core of the story could easily be lost on an audience expecting a more straightforward cinematic experience.

It took several more months before the film was distributed in the United Kingdom. Even though the BBFC provided an X certificate on September 28, 1970, *A Quiet Place in the Country* came out in theaters only the following May. *Films and Filming*'s Gordon Cow judged it "reminiscent of numerous precepts, although not daunted by any of them in its presentation of a ghostly threat," but complained that "amid his intelligent intentions and filmic ruses … the director reaches too far and topples into absurdity" and that the film "does make a dangerous welter of its sexual and violent connotations which do as much as the lamentable English dialogue to shatter the fragile shell. It ought to have been a delicate work, irradiated with sudden shocks. Instead it goes hammer and tintinnabulating tongs at the sensibilities."[46]

Un tranquillo posto di campagna feels very much like a product of the era as well as a turning point for its director. In the portrait of a bourgeois artist who has attempted to "revolutionize the forms and formulas" and who has become a prisoner of mass production, one can sense Petri's own attempt to release himself from labels and ties. Was he making movies that were *useful* to the audience? Was his own work worth something within a society which turned all forms of art into commercial fare?

In a way, the film's narrative and formal excesses allowed Petri to let loose his wilder and more experimental side, and its radical rethinking from its early stages was like a symbolic farewell to his own past. After that he would be ready to start again on a new direction. "It was at this moment that I decided to make only political films."[47]

Franco Nero, Vanessa Redgrave and Elio Petri on the set of *Un tranquillo posto di campagna*.

EIGHT

Repression Is Civilization

Indagine su un cittadino al di sopra di ogni sospetto *(1970) and* Ipotesi sulla morte di G. Pinelli *(1970)*

Prelude: Free Newsreels

Around the same time as the release of *Un tranquillo posto di campagna*, Petri was involved in another project stemming from Zavattini's mind, *Cinegiornali liberi* (Free Newsreels), eleven short films conceived as independent newsreels on important social and political themes and aimed at a different audience than the standard moviegoers. The first, *Cinegiornale libero di Roma n°1*, was shot at Zavattini's own apartment, where several directors (Marco Bellocchio, Liliana Cavani, Salvatore Samperi, Romano Scavolini and others) had gathered to discuss the topic, "Is cinema over?"

The project involved other noted filmmakers. Ugo Gregoretti's *Apollon: una fabbrica occupata* (1969), about a printing house occupied by the workers, featured narration by Gian Maria Volonté. Petri's contribution was *Cinegiornale libero di Roma n° xyz*,[1] the only one without any directing credits. Shot on a cold day in late 1968, it is a twenty-minute interview (in French) of May 1968 student leader Daniel Cohn-Bendit. The location is telling: Petri and Cohn-Bendit (with Ugo Pirro assisting in the conversation) are standing in Piazza San Pietro, in the Vatican. Soon, they are interrupted by the police and turned away. The interview continues in the nearby Via della Conciliazione and touches upon various topics: the political situation in France, the relationship between the students' movement and the leftist parties, the economic and political power of the Church. The camera often moves away from the two men, zooming in on the San Pietro dome as if to highlight the sense of their words. Meanwhile, a small crowd has gathered around Petri and his interlocutor. The interview itself is more of a debate, with the two men discussing passionately, surrounded by curious bystanders who don't understand a word of what they are saying. The documentary ends with a witty visual pun, half-De Sica, half-Fellini: the sight of nuns and priests coming and going along Via della Conciliazione, and the Pope blessing the crowd after Mass from the Piazza San Pietro balcony.

The *Cinegiornali liberi* give an idea of the new climate surrounding Italian cinema. For many filmmakers it had become imperative to put their political commitment into practice, in an attempt to use their status as a way to channel the ideas of the 1968 protest movements and take an active part in reshaping society.

Crime Without Punishment

The year of 1969 was a troubled year for Gian Maria Volonté. He had undergone a deep personal and professional crisis after the end of his love affair with actress Carla Gravina and a sensational gesture that had upset the Italian film world. Just days before shooting started, he had backed out of Giuseppe Patroni Griffi's *Metti, una sera a cena*, announcing that he would abandon acting for good: he gave back the advance and was replaced by Tony Musante, but the producer Euro International Film sued him for breach of contract. The events of 1968 had affected him deeply, and his political commitment had made him reconsider the essence of his job. He would no longer act in disengaged films or accept roles just for money. Whenever he would make a movie, it would be a meaningful political work. Volonté also renounced a princely contract (250 million *lire* for four films in two years) with Dino De Laurentiis and got involved in the heavily politicized street performances of the ensemble Teatro di Strada (rebaptized "Teatro di Provocazione Politica"), becoming its leader and director.

At that time, Elio Petri was toying with different projects. He got in touch with French novelist Michel Tournier regarding the possibility of adapting his 1967 novel *Vendredi ou les Limbes du Pacifique* (aka *Friday, or the Other Island*), a reworking of Daniel Defoe's *Robinson Crusoe* which won the Grand Prix du Roman.[2] Tournier's philosophical novel overturns the colonialist premise of the original: Robinson doesn't transform the wild island into an organized space by way of his own rationality and industriousness; on the contrary, the savage native Friday drives him to a complete regression to the "natural" state, until the white man embraces an authentic, primitive existential dimension. In the wake of the revolutionary anti–Colonialist movements of the 1960s, it was a thought-provoking project. However, in December 1969 Tournier informed Petri that the chances of making a film from his novel had waned.[3]

Petri was also intrigued by the Teatro di Strada, which had caused a sensation in Rome. His idea was to use that form of spontaneous performance to portray the political and social mood, by way of a Brechtian storyline. Volonté was thrilled about it, but neither he, nor Petri or Pirro managed to find a convincing narrative structure.

But Ugo Pirro had an ace up his sleeve. One day, on his way home, he had gotten stuck in a traffic jam, one of the many that happened daily in Rome. The city with more children than cars which Petri had known as a child, in the days after World War II, had rapidly expanded with new districts popping up in the outskirts. The Grande Raccordo Anulare, the motorway ring surrounding Rome which so many citizens used for their daily drive to work and back, looked like a hellish circle, filled day and night with smog and vehicles, not unlike its apocalyptic rendition in Fellini's *Toby Dammit*. That day, Pirro noticed one of the cars preceding him, driven by a man of indefinable age with a young woman by his side. The car suddenly veered to the left, in the emergency lane, and gained some advantage on the other vehicles that were proceeding at a crawl. It was a showy but useless maneuver, not to mention one prohibited by the road code; it looked like the driver wanted to impress the woman and display his power. Pirro found himself fantasizing that the man was a policeman, someone who considered himself above the law, and who wanted to show his impunity to the lady as an act of transgression.

Back home, Pirro started thinking of a story. A man murders his lover and leaves clues that reveal him as the guilty party, in a perverted reversal of Dostoevsky's novel,

Crime and Punishment. But he is not simply a murderer: he is a high police official, and his challenging acts are motivated by the will to test his own authority and prove that he is not subject to the law he is called to enforce.

> This is the contradiction in which every individual who is invested with some kind of power lives. To be called to enforce the law, to impose penalties on those who break it, and at the same time to be pushed to break it himself, either to gain a personal advantage or for the sake of power itself.[4]

Pirro's story was affected by the ongoing climate of tension. On March 1, 1968, a clash had taken place between the students and the police at Valle Giulia, in Rome, after the cops had cleared the Faculty of Architecture at the Sapienza University from those who were occupying the building and 4,000 people had gathered to march across the campus. The clash resulted in 148 injured among the armed forces and 478 among the students. Four were arrested and 228 were held in police custody.

The "Battle of Valle Giulia" catalyzed the attention of the cultural world on the student protest movement and exposed the existence of extremist groups (both far-left and far-right) against the institutions. But the growing reaction against the authorities, often identified with the police, involved not just the students but the middle class as well. The clashes between students and cops became more frequent, and Pirro himself witnessed one just outside Petri's house. "I saw some teenagers, their face covered with handkerchiefs and an amused, provocative air, chased by cops wearing helmet, shield and truncheon. The youths were running away laughing, they were having fun…. I felt on the side of the chased teens and helped them hide in a doorway while I misled the cops, giving them false indications."[5]

At first, Petri was not fully convinced about the story Pirro provided. He liked its crime angle but didn't want to make a movie that relied on the iconography of 1968. But the project on the Teatro di Strada just didn't gel. One evening, after yet another useless discussion, Pirro briefly told Volonté his story about the "citizen above suspicion" and the actor's response was so enthusiastic that Petri decided to carry out the project on the spot.

Once again, as with *A ciascuno il suo*, the problem was to find a backer. In April 1969 Petri got in touch with Columbia Pictures' John Whalley and sent him an estimated budget, but the attempt at a deal was unsuccessful. "No one wanted to produce that movie," Federico Pantanella recalled.[6] In 1967, the 30-year-old Pantanella—an ex-car dealer who sold Lancia automobiles in the wealthy Parioli district—his childhood friend Daniele Senatore and an attorney, Ferruccio Ferrara, had founded Vera Film. The name was a homage to Ferrara's wife, Vera, and the noted painter Mario Fattori designed the logo. Their first film was Peter Wood's *In Search of Gregory* (1969), an English/Italian coproduction starring Julie Christie. Soon after, Ferrara left the company. When Petri knocked on their door, Pantanella and Senatore jumped at the opportunity.

Pantanella was Vera's CEO and took care of the administration. At first Volonté didn't want to have anything to do with him. "I was never allowed to set foot on the set because when Gian Maria heard I was one of the producers, he said, 'I'm not going to do the film.' Why? Because Carla Gravina and I had become a couple for a year, and she had been his lover. Later, however, we became friends."

The intervention of Marina Cicogna's production and distribution company Euro International Film was fundamental to overcome the financial difficulties that Vera encountered at the beginning. In the meantime, Costa-Gavras' *Z* (1969)—released in Italy in late May 1969 with the alluring subtitle *L'orgia del potere* (The Orgy of Power) right after its screening at the Cannes Film Festival, which had resulted in the Jury Prize for the director and the award for Best Actor to Jean-Louis Trintignant—was doing well at the box-office, proving that there was a market for politically committed cinema.

As a condition for the deal, Euro imposed Florinda Bolkan for the role of Augusta Terzi, instead of Monica Vitti. News that the 28-year-old actress would be in the cast of Petri's next work came out in the press in July 1969.[7] Bolkan, a Brazilian hostess with no film experience, had been introduced to the movie business by countess Cicogna, her lover and a member of the Italian jet-set. Luchino Visconti noticed the exotic, stunning-looking Bolkan and gave her a small part in his new film, *La caduta degli dei*. After a handful of appearances, her breakthrough role in *Metti, una sera a cena* earned her a special prize at the 1969 David di Donatello awards. Bolkan's fee was 30 million *lire*, two million more than Volonté's. As a result of the lawsuit regarding *Metti, una sera a cena*, Cicogna had signed a new deal with the actor for three films, two to be directed by Petri and one by Jean-Pierre Melville, *Le cercle rouge* (1970). "A large part of the money we paid him actually came from Euro Film, after an arrangement they made," Pantanella recalled.

Over the summer, Petri and Pirro retired at the Villaggio Tognazzi in Torvaianica, where Pirro had rented a chalet too, and worked hard on the script. The director's hermit-like, moody attitude was worlds apart from the scriptwriter's more buoyant lifestyle, but they made a perfect scriptwriting pair. "Our work finally made us happy and it was a strange feeling. We enjoyed shaping with nastiness the character of the murderous commissioner," Pirro recalled. "We were full of optimism and ideas to the point of deluding ourselves that our country was changing for good, and we felt a special happiness that paradoxically stemmed from the built-up anger.... Sometimes it looked like the script was writing itself."[8]

Petri came up with one of the most provocative ideas: the murderer would deliberately leave his fingerprints everywhere so as not just to challenge the law, but to deny it. Pirro added the surreal ending in which the Chief of Police and the other high officials gather at the protagonist's house, threatening him and finally persuading him to confess that he is innocent. Being an emissary of Power, he simply cannot be guilty.

Shooting for *Indagine su un cittadino al di sopra di ogni sospetto* started on August 22, 1969. It was accompanied by unconcealed curiosity on the part of the press, and the scarce bits of information about its storyline, not to mention its striking title, resulted in speculations about its political content. Before filming even began, some newspapers pointed out alleged similarities between the plot and the "Scirè case."[9] Nicola Scirè was an ex-deputy commissioner involved in illegal gambling dens, who gave himself up in June 1969. The scandal was widely covered by newspapers,[10] but neither Petri nor Pirro ever considered it as a source of inspiration. "We had already written our screenplay when people started talking about him," the scriptwriter pointed out.[11]

In giving coverage to the filming, the press underlined Volonté's comeback.[12] Petri's film was his second effort after Jean-Luc Godard's controversial "*gauchiste* Spaghetti Western" *Le Vent d'Est*. The cast also featured Salvo Randone, again playing a plumber as in *I giorni contati*, the great stage thespian Gianni Santuccio as the Chief of Police (Santuccio would soon play another authoritarian, devilish figure in Tonino Cervi's *Il delitto del diavolo*), Arturo Dominici (Iavutic in Bava's *La maschera del demonio*), Massimo Foschi and Orazio Orlando. The latter, as Brigader Biglia, replaced Paolo Graziosi, Petri's first choice for the role, who dismissed the script as reactionary, claiming that he would not wear a policeman's uniform in a film that glorified the armed forces. As Pirro put it, "he simply confused his character with the film's meaning."[13]

Volonté's new partner Armenia Balducci joined the crew as script supervisor, and the actor involved other members of the Teatro di Strada in the filming, to give them economic help and have their support on a difficult project. Lorenzo Magnolia, credited as assistant director, took part also in rewriting some lines of dialogue.

> With Gian Maria, scripts were never accurate. We used to discuss the character and his lines. The dialogue was often changed … if you compare the original script with the final draft there are many changes. The speech the commissioner gives when he is promoted from head of the mobile squad to chief of the political office is full of slogans, and I wrote those myself two hours before shooting, in agreement with Gian Maria and with Petri's approval.[14]

The director, who loved improvisation, used to give actors hints so that they would add an unexpected twist to a scene. When shooting the flashback sequence on the Torvaianica beach in which Bolkan and Volonté are having an argument, he told the actress, unbeknownst to her partner, to put sand in his mouth when he least expected it. Similarly, he instructed Bolkan to come out with an unscripted line during the car scene inspired by the one that suggested Pirro the idea for the film: "Show your badge to the officer! Tell him you are an important man, frighten him!" As Cicogna explained, "all these spur-of-the-moment scenes amused Elio very much."[15]

Volonté was Petri's ideal other half before the camera. To him, acting was like the work of "an investigator who gathers all possible information concerning the question in which he's interested. My preparation is done therefore on a more journalistic level than a dramatic one, and it is based on the same material that the screenwriter gathers and uses to build the story."[16]

The estimated cost for *Indagine su un cittadino al di sopra di ogni sospetto* was between 240 and 260 million, but the film went over budget. In order to complete it, Pantanella gave his company shares as warranty, and Senatore's father—an ex-army general who had made a fortune after the war by cleaning up minefields—provided the rest of the money. Eventually Pantanella was ousted from Vera Film and his name doesn't even appear in the credits. "Wherever I'd go, there was always someone who came up with this story about *Indagine*, because in the biz everybody knew I produced it too."

Intermezzo #1: Tension

After the Battle of Valle Giulia, Pier Paolo Pasolini wrote a much-discussed poem, *Il PCI ai giovani*, which included the notorious line, "*Quando ieri a Valle Giulia avete fatto a botte / coi poliziotti / io simpatizzavo coi poliziotti. / Perché i poliziotti sono figli di poveri.*" (When yesterday in Valle Giulia you came to blows / with the cops / I sympathized with the cops / Because cops are sons of the poor.) The provoking affirmation—which over the years has been repeatedly misquoted and misinterpreted—meant to underline how cops, often coming from working class families, were themselves exploited just like the other workers, unlike the bourgeois brats on the other side of the barricade.

And then, look at how they dress them: like clowns,
with that rough cloth that stinks of rations,
the orderly room, and people. Worst of all, naturally,
is the psychological state to which they are reduced
(for roughly 40,000 *lire* a month);
… At Valle Giulia, yesterday we have thus had a fragment
of class conflict; and you, my friends (even though on the side
of reason), were the rich,
while the policemen (who were in the
wrong) were poor. A nice victory, then,
yours!

In open contrast with the PCI, who treated them as a genuine political force, the poet was in fact urging the students to join forces with the workers' movement. To him, the revolutionary sections of the bourgeoisie had to identify with the revolutionary sections of the working class and peasantry, or else their protest would lack a truly revolutionary dimension. Eventually, this is what happened during the so-called "Hot Autumn," a series of large strikes in the factories of Northern Italy that followed the student rallies of 1968. Gradually the protests—occupations, strikes, marches—shifted from the universities to the plants, as the student movement joined the workers who demanded salary raises and a new law governing the working conditions. The expiry of the three-year contracts for metalworkers was the spark that ignited the flame. Between September and December 1969 over five million workers, belonging not just to the industry but also to agriculture, trade and other areas, began protesting in the streets.

The strikes took place in a climate of unrest. Several months earlier, in April 1969, two people lost their lives during a general strike in Pirro's hometown, Battipaglia, killed by stray bullets shot by the armed forces. One of the victims was hit while looking out of her window on the third floor. A wave of popular rage ensued, with twelve million people protesting in the streets all over Italy and the police charging against the crowd in Rome, Florence and Milan.

This spontaneous uprising caused a dramatic reaction, and a series of terrorist acts took place over the following months. On April 25 (the day when Italy celebrates its liberation from Nazi domination by the Allied troops) a bomb blasted at the Milan fair, and seven more exploded on trains in August 1969. All of these were immediately labeled by the authorities and the press as anarchic acts germinated within the far left, but there emerged evidence that the bombs had been planted by terrorists related to the far-right group Ordine Nuovo.

Then, on December 12, 1969, at 4:37 p.m., a bomb went off in the headquarters of the Banca Nazionale dell'Agricoltura (National Agrarian Bank) in Piazza Fontana, in the center of Milan, causing sixteen dead and eighty-eight injured. There were four more terrorist attacks on that day. Another unexploded bomb was found in Milan, in another bank in Piazza della Scala, and three more detonated in Rome that afternoon, injuring sixteen people. Immediately after the events, the President of the Republic, Giuseppe Saragat, announced his intention of declaring a state of emergency in the country, while the Minister of the Interior Franco Restivo claimed that investigations would be conducted "in all directions."

That night, the police arrested eighty-four suspects, including an anarchist named Giuseppe Pinelli. According to the law, a suspect could be held in police custody for a maximum of 48 hours. The suspects were released as soon as their alibis were verified, but Pinelli was kept in jail for three days. On December 15, around midnight, Giuseppe Pinelli fell to his death from the window of the tiny office on the fourth floor where he was being interrogated. The family was alerted by the journalists: when his wife Licia called the police station to ask why no one had informed her, the reply was, "We didn't have the time."

Pinelli's funeral took place on December 20. About 3,000 people attended. It was a clear sign that the attempt to pin the bombing on the anarchists wasn't succeeding. The Police superintendent, Marcello Guida, claimed that the deceased had committed suicide, throwing himself out of the window while yelling "È la fine dell'anarchia!" ("It's the end of anarchy!"). Licia Pinelli denounced him for defamation. Then she denounced Commissioner Luigi Calabresi and all the police officials who were in the office on the night of December 15 for voluntary manslaughter, kidnapping, private violence and abuse of authority. Petri and Pirro (but not Volonté) were among the 757 signatories of a petition for the formal expulsion of the police officials involved in the Pinelli case, first published in the weekly magazine *L'Espresso* on June 13, 1971.

The official inquiry ended on October 27, 1975, with a dismissal. The magistrate excluded both suicide and homicide and concluded that the anarchist's death had been caused by an "active illness." All the suspects were acquitted.

More bombings took place over the following years, the most notorious being the ones in Brescia's Piazza della Loggia (May 28, 1974), which caused eight victims and 100 injured during a union rally; on the Italicus train (August 4, 1974), with twelve victims and 105 injured; and at the Bologna train station (August 2, 1980), with eighty-five victims and about 200 injured. A leading opinion is that the bombings were part of a political sidetracking concocted in order to set in motion an authoritarian turn by way of false flag operations and agent provocateurs, in a so-called "Strategy of Tension."

The trial for the train bombs of 1969 ended with the condemnation of neo-fascists Franco Freda and Giovanni Ventura, both members of Ordine Nuovo. In 1987 Ventura and ex-secret service agent Guido Giannettini were acquitted for insufficient evidence in the massacre of Piazza Fontana. Another member of Ordine Nuovo and ex-secret agent, Carlo Digilio, who confessed having built the bomb, received immunity from prosecution by becoming a witness for the state. In 2005 the Court of Cassation stated that the Piazza Fontana bombing was carried out by a "subversive group set in Padua and affiliated to Ordine Nuovo," led by Freda and Ventura. However, these could no longer be put on trial because they had been irrevocably acquitted by the Court of Assizes of Appeal in Bari.[17] The trial for the Bologna massacre ended with a sentence of life imprisonment for Francesca Mambro and Valerio "Giusva" Fioravanti,[18] and with a 30-year sentence for Luigi Ciavardini. All were affiliated with the neo-fascist organization NAR. Other trials, such as that for the Italicus bombing, ended with acquittals for insufficient evidence.

"They're going to arrest you!"

"I wanted to make a film against the police,"[19] Petri later said about *Indagine*. It was a film born out of anger, a reaction to the frustration of having to deal with punitive if not persecutory authorities. Italians had still in them the memory of the Fascist era, when police forces were synonymous with violence and danger, and the blackshirts subjected dissident citizens to severe beatings or forced them to drink large quantities of castor oil (a laxative), a humiliation that showed Fascism's cruelly mocking side. But police brutality had continued after the war, and violent methods were the preferred way to control public order. Minister of the Interior Mario Scelba (who liked to be called "Minister of the Police") had given the armed forces a political direction, with paramilitary elements and brutality as a rule against spontaneous protests and strikes, which resulted in many deaths among peasants and workers. As Petri explained, "I agreed only partially with Pasolini's poem on cops, because as a kid I had been a systematic victim of those 'sons of the poor' and I took so many blows without ever striking back."[20] But there was more than that. Police forces used methods of intimidation against political enemies, such as administrative measures applied on the basis of mere suspicion, bypassing the constitutional limits and displaying their power above the law. This is what Petri wanted to show in his film as well.

It was a bold move at a difficult time. The Piazza Fontana bombing took place right after shooting had been wrapped. In a chilling coincidence, a bomb blasts off in a scene of Petri's film as well. The bombing takes place inside the police station, and dozens of young students are arrested and brutally interrogated. "Do not tolerate them anymore!" Volonté's character says to the Chief of Police. And that is exactly what happened.

The turn of the screw that ensued, with all the leftist movements being the object of constant attention on the part of the armed forces, led the authors to believe their film would either be banned or seized immediately upon release. On the night Petri finished the mixing, a private screening for some ANAC members took place. Petri's recollection is vivid: "Zavattini was the first to see the movie, with Bernardo Bertolucci. As soon as the lights turned on in the projection room, he whispered to me: 'They're going to arrest you!'"[21]

To find some political support, Petri and Pirro decided it would be better to show *Indagine* around in advance and screened it for the vice-secretary of the Socialist party Giacomo Mancini and other MPs. Mancini didn't like it, especially the line of dialogue in which the commissioner claims to have voted Socialist to convince a student he is interrogating to confess. It seemed the worst time ever to release such an explosive film. A political crisis was maturing, and premier Mariano Rumor's days as the chief of government were numbered. It was going to be the fourth government crisis in less than two years.

One evening Petri and Pirro were at a restaurant, having dinner with Luchino Visconti, when film critic Gian Luigi Rondi showed up. He was very alarmed. He believed that in the likely event that *Indagine* was seized, a political storm would ensue, and Rumor's position would be weakened. Rondi arranged a private screening for high police officials at Euro International. Marina Cicogna showed up at the end and asked for their opinion, but everyone got away as fast as he could, for fear of being spotted by the press.

Indagine su un cittadino al di sopra di ogni sospetto was submitted to the board of review on February 2, 1970. The screening had a deep effect on the committee, much to Cicogna's surprise: "Back then, maybe because I was young, maybe because I didn't have a great political consciousness, I only saw it as a beautiful film which was going to be commercially successful. I realized it was politically explosive only at the screening for the board. It left everyone quite upset."[22] The board gave it a V.M.14 rating because of the "erotic scenes with allusions to sadism and foul language," a tame verdict which didn't let anyone foresee what would come next.

On February 7 Mariano Rumor resigned. The first page editorial in the *Corriere della*

Sera, titled *Tutto incerto* (Everything uncertain), commented sharply: "There is no reason to hide what the nation senses infinitely better than its political class, locked in an hermetic and undecipherable struggle for power ... the government crisis that began yesterday ... is little less than a crisis in the dark."[23]

Indagine opened on February 12 in Milan. The audience consisted mostly of police officials. As the lights turned on, they left the venue in a rage. Four days later, the Chief Prosecutor of the Republic in Milan, Enrico De Peppo, opened a judicial inquiry on the film, following a denunciation on the part of the Carabinieri. The article reporting the news added that allegedly "someone in the Palace of Justice has found elements susceptible of legitimating a trial for contempt to the police."[24]

"I've seen Petri's film yesterday. It's a good movie. From an artistic point of view, I can say I liked it. For the rest, I'll refer to my superiors," the magistrate commented.[25] Contrary to everyone's fears, the investigation was archived within a week by State prosecutor Giovanni Caizzi, who argued that

> one must keep in mind the continuous grotesque deformation of situations and characters ... therefore, there cannot be inferred an offensive or derisive interpretation, because the grotesque is the chosen form to express criticism, albeit mordant, in an intelligible way at a fictional level.[26]

Petri framed the decision and hung it in his study, just as he had done with the rejection letter from the CSC.

Despite the archiving of the denunciation, its mere existence was proof of the tense period the nation was undergoing. This veiled attempt at repression could not stop the film's extraordinary success. In Rome, Pirro recalled, the crowd in front and around the cinema caused a traffic jam, and two extra daily screenings had to be added. Everybody wanted to see the most talked-about movie of the year. The weekly magazine *L'Europeo* even organized a roundtable discussion between the authors and the police commanders-in-chief. "They came to defend themselves and we found ourselves playing the role of the accusers," Pirro commented. The result, in his own words, was "eight pages of embarrassing justifications."[27]

Just as *A ciascuno il suo*, *Indagine* was the right film at exactly the right time. It ended up at the third spot among Italian releases of the year (after De Sica's *I girasoli* and Luigi Zampa's anthology comedy *Contestazione generale*) for a total gross of 1,456,000,000 *lire*. At the end of August 1971, it was still in the box-office Top Ten. It became the most successful film in Petri's career.

Critical reception was mixed. The heavily ideologized leftist film magazines, such as *Cinema nuovo* and *Filmcritica*, strongly panned the contrast between its thought-provoking message and its form, seen as the result of commercial compromise, and therefore conservative. "*Indagine* is not a film about the police but the clinical-farcical portrait of a cop," *Cinema nuovo* wrote, complaining that it had "nothing to do with critical analysis and political exposé, which have been reduced to heavy and coarse didactic intrusions" within a story built totally in function of the main character. The reviewer concluded blaming "our filmmakers' impotence to face with a minimum of honesty and strictness the political discussions that they assume to open," and labeling the film a "socio-psychoanalytic mess" which made one regret American filmmakers such as Welles, Dassin, and Huston.[28] However, in the quarterly cultural review *Quaderni Piacentini*, Goffredo Fofi acknowledged its relevance in relation to the recent events.

He called it "good, and important," praising the narrative construction and the formal polish, "not annoying and overdrawn as in *A ciascuno il suo*," but wrote that its limit was "essentially being a non–Marxist film" and dismissed the depiction of left-wing characters, especially the students, as "amorphous figures."[29]

On the other hand, right-wing newspapers such as *Il Giornale d'Italia* accused Petri of being an agitprop who used the camera as a weapon and had made a "political, party-political, agitator movie" against the Roman police and supporting Maoist students.[30] But center and left-wing newspapers and periodicals were fulsome in praise of the film's narrative and formal qualities. *Rinascita* called it "the first truthful, frank and honest movie about an institution which until now was cinematically unquestionable."[31] In his review for the *Corriere della Sera*, Giovanni Grazzini compared it favorably to "certain mocking Eastern European films, especially Czech and Hungarian, devoted to the analysis of the arbitrariness involved in the use of authority." He concluded: "Let's mark this date in red: whether you like the movie or not, this is the first time Italian cinema throws itself headlong into the depiction of the police environment … it's difficult to deny that the film's release … represents an important step forward to a more adult society."[32]

To film historian Gian Piero Brunetta, the enormous success of *Indagine* relied on its ability to unify the audience, inventing "a system of communication which puts in motion emotional and cognitive functions shared by fathers and sons. It is a film that responded to the Italian middle class's need to move left."[33] Even more importantly, Petri had managed a unique achievement: a non-conformist, challenging movie in the form of a perfectly accomplished spectacle which stood within the framework of commercial cinema, yet employed its rules and elements in a thought-provoking, subversive and demystifying manner.

Citizen Petri

The opening credits—white on a black backdrop, with no musical accompaniment—are stark, intimidating. A sign warns us that all characters and events are fictitious, and any similarity is purely coincidental.

Then, the film opens on a luminous sunny day, to the sound of a Southern-style mandolin melody. A man—elegantly dressed in white shirt, cream-colored suit and pale blue tie—is waiting outside an old elegant building opposite the Synagogue. He looks nervous and doesn't want to be seen. A young woman appears from behind a window curtain, smiling at him in an open invitation.

The man enters the building and into an elegant apartment, exotically furnished in Liberty style. He has his own key. The woman—beautiful, black-haired, wearing a 1920s style see-through nightgown—welcomes him with a kiss. "How will you kill me this time?" she asks. "I'll slit your throat," he replies.

He undresses silently and folds his clothes methodically while she is waiting for him in bed, under black silk sheets. In bed she moves on top of him, but her sensual movements suddenly halt as she stiffens in what at first looks like an orgasmic spasm. The man emerges from underneath the sheets, his face and chest partly covered in blood. He has a razorblade in his hand. He has slit her throat with it, just as he announced.

The murderer's ensuing actions are contradictory. He takes a shower, puts on his clothes, and then proceeds to scatter clues all over the place. He takes the woman's jewels but leaves her money in full sight. He drinks some liquor and leaves his fingerprints on the bottle and glass. He even places a fiber of blue silk torn from his tie under the victim's fingernail. Then he makes an anonymous phone call to the police, reporting the murder and without even caring to camouflage his voice. He is arrogant, contemptuous, authoritarian. He calls the policeman on the other end an idiot. Before leaving he picks a couple of champagne bottles from the fridge. Then he goes to work. We find out that he is a policeman, and not an ordinary one. He is the former chief of the Homicide Squad, and he has just been promoted to the Political squad.

After an idiosyncratic whodunit such as *A ciascuno il suo*, Petri and Pirro adopted the form of what in crime fiction is commonly referred to as inverted detective story or "howcatchem," for we witness the murder at the beginning and follow the investigation from the perpetrator's point of view, and what remains to be unveiled is the reason why he committed it. The format is the opposite of the whodunit and "the suspense mechanism conveys the sense of anguish which stems from the search for truth,"[34] the director explained. But he and Pirro engraved the plot within a complex, thought-provoking narrative which proceeds to frustrate the viewer's expectations and elicits the audience's attention. In fact, "it doesn't simply aim at producing a purely spectacular tension ... but an active awareness, for the surprise and bewilderment elicited by the commissioner's increasingly contradictory and paradoxical behavior should push the audience to critically question its origin and significance."[35] In other words, Petri's approach is dialectic, and once again he uses genre trappings to convey a point that is not merely fed to the audience, but requires the latter's active participation.

For one thing, the commissioner is never called by name during the film. To everybody he is the "Doctor," a common usage in Italy when someone addresses to a person of an upper social category. Depriving the protagonist of a name means turning him into a symbolic figure who performs actions that in turn carry a symbolic resonance.

The film moves along two directives. One follows the Doctor's disconcerting strategy: he scatters around clues that lead to him as the culprit, as he confesses on tape, "not to mislead the investigations but to try out my being *above suspicion*." The second consists of six lengthy flashbacks interspersed in the narrative which shed light on his relationship with the victim. The flashbacks are not in chronological order, but they turn up, as in *L'assassino*, because of the sudden analogy with present events, and are seen through the protagonist's point of view. They are ingeniously inserted into the plot, sometimes even popping up unexpectedly in the middle of a sequence (as in the interrogation of Augusta's husband) which resumes at the end of the digression. Like pieces of a puzzle, they provide a different side to the story, revealing the motives behind the murder and the protagonist's psychology.

The Doctor's actions follow a tortuous path. First, he attempts to pinpoint the murder to the victim's homosexual husband (Massimo Foschi). But after the man has been arrested, he personally intervenes to clear him, and even sends the police an anonymous package with clearing evidence, for "when you make an innocent being condemned, your being above suspicion is not proven." Then he proceeds to direct the investigation on himself. Eventually, after a dramatic confrontation with a young anarchist student who has seen him on the premises after the murder, he writes a confession.

The protagonist's behavior throughout the film is ultimately split. He meticulously plants clues of his culpability and then he proceeds to cover, deny or destroy the evidence he has left. In doing so, he merely exercises the power that comes from his own status. On the one hand, he challenges authority. On the other, he seeks atonement. He goes so far as openly proclaiming to his colleagues: "We are all innocent here. In here the only guilty one … is me!" But it must be underlined that he is not moved by a personal interest of any kind. His challenge is ultimately motivated by the need to test, albeit through different means, "the defense and reinforcing of the authority before a rampant wave of political and social protest."[36]

This becomes evident in one of the film's most discussed and openly political scenes, the rabid speech he delivers after his promotion to an audience which encompasses Petri himself in a blink-and-you'll-miss-it cameo. The Doctor claims that "underneath every criminal hides a subversive person, underneath every subversive individual there hides a criminal," thus theorizing the equality of common criminality and "organized subversion." Both, in fact, "have the same objective even if they use different methods. They want to *upset the social order*." He spits out statistics to uphold his claim, indifferently pairing actual crimes, immoral behavior, protests and strikes, and eventually concludes:

> Use of freedom is a constant threat to the traditional powers and the constituted authorities. Use of freedom makes any citizen a judge and prevents the free use of our functions! We defend the law which has to be unchangeable and engraved in time! The people are immature, the city is sick. Others have the task of educating and curing this. We have the duty to repress it! Repression is our vaccine! Repression is civilization!

The Doctor's words are patterned on Mussolini's speeches, namely one dated 26 May 1927, in which the dictator exalted race and Italy as a new "Imperial force," claiming that "the police must be not only respected but honored" and that "man, before feeling the need for culture, felt the need for orderliness. It can be said that the policeman preceded the professor in history, because if there are not hands armed with handcuffs, laws become dead letters."

Fathers and Sons

Indagine was not the first Italian film to portray a bad cop. In 1951, Fernando Cerchio directed the gripping crime drama *Il bivio*, starring Raf Vallone, the story of an ex-war hero who is also the head of a criminal gang. He manages to join the mobile squad so as to mislead his colleagues about the robberies performed by his men. But Cerchio's film was a tale of moral redemption, as Vallone's character eventually sacrifices himself in order to secure his gang to his fellow policemen. Nothing of this can be found in Petri's film, which depicts a very different kind of cop, a power figure closer to Captain Hank Quinlan in *Touch of Evil* (1958, Orson Welles) than to the commissioner played by Tomas Milian in *Banditi a Milano* (1968, Carlo Lizzani), even though both Petri and Lizzani partly took inspiration from Luigi Calabresi.

The political content of *Indagine* is very much upfront throughout, and several lines of dialogue refer to actual events. In an early scene the Doctor and Biglia comment upon the title on the front page of the newspaper *Paese Sera*, "Agente spara" (Agent shoots):

"He fired by mistake, of course."
"That is the more probable version."

Most allusions are imbued with sarcastic humor. The bombing at the police station results in dozens of young left-wing protesters being incarcerated. One of the police officials observes that "in two hours, four groups have formed. Fortunately, they are divided, otherwise it would be difficult for us." The reference to the political division within the Left and the many extra-parliamentary groups that formed after 1968 is all too evident. In another scene, policemen are reporting the number of political writings on the city walls praising Stalin, Mao, Ho Chi Minh and other political leaders. One notes that "in 1956, however, there were only a hundred writings for Stalin." 1956 was not only the year the USSR invaded Hungary, but also the year when the 20th Congress of the Soviet Communist Party took place, with Khrushchev's shocking denunciation of Stalin's cult of personality. The police official concludes that in 1958 there were "500 writings *against* Stalin. Obviously, on orders from above, these were not removed."

Much of the film's strength comes exactly from its boldness, its will to laugh in the face of authority by mixing acute political observations with biting sarcasm. It was something unimaginable, if one thinks that *Totò e Carolina*, a comedy directed in 1953 by Mario Monicelli and starring Totò as a cop, underwent a censorship ordeal because of its humorous depiction of policemen. The film eventually came out in 1955 after many cuts and changes. Petri himself had learned the lesson the hard way with *L'assassino*.

Indagine was in many ways a filiation of sorts of Petri's debut, its demonic, perverse reversal, imbued with a Kafka-esque feel and with the police becoming the secular arm of an authoritarian Power. Petri even included an in-joke reference to the early film's vicissitudes in the scene where the housemaid asks the Doctor to use felt flaps when stepping on the freshly cleaned floor of his own apartment. Besides the parallel plot centered on the killing of a woman, both works have a similar flashback structure, and both revolve around a psychological character study, which in the case of *Indagine* results in the story working at different levels. The film is not merely a discourse on authority and power, but also on the inner split that power causes on those who exert it. After the tormented painter in *Un tranquillo posto di campagna*, neurotic behavior manifests itself in strict connection with the social structure, and "the character's pathological status reveals tendencies latent in the so-called normality."[37]

In shaping the protagonist's neurosis, Petri took inspiration from the works of Wilhelm Reich, most notably *The Mass Psychology of Fascism* (1933) and its parallels between the authoritarian state and patriarchal family. He insisted that his film focused "on the description of an inner mechanism, common to those who exert power and the subjects alike. Each has his own slice of power and tends to exert it in an authoritarian way, because inside ourselves we have the concept of a repressive society which continually demands a paternal presence."[38] Exerting authority becomes an unconscious impersonation of the father figure. Repression—either fascist or on the part of a police force of a democratic state—is a degeneration of the paternal authority. "The father is forced to punish, even violently, to convince the sons that certain things are necessary ... however, when the father goes beyond this duty, it's because he wants to take hold of his sons ... he wants to model them according to his own conception of existence."[39]

But one cannot be a father without being a son, and the authoritarian figure is itself childish because in turn it is in need of a higher, more powerful figure to be reassured (or even punished) by. The Doctor is openly childlike in his essence. He is strong, cocky, arrogant with subordinates, suspects, common citizens who are intimidated by his power. While celebrating his promotion, he mockingly harasses one of his subordinates, the unctuous, dumb-looking middle-aged Panunzio (Aldo Rendine), yet another in Petri's gallery of monsters. He openly teases his colleagues and reacts with disgust to their sycophancy. "Enough of this praise. This isn't the Carnival season!" he curtly replies to the adulatory words of his successor Mangani (Arturo Dominici). Later in the film he purportedly confronts Mangani in a corridor, speaking out loud so that everyone around can overhear, so as to publicly humiliate him.

On the other hand, the Doctor is weak, spineless, servile with his higher-ups. He is ceremonious with the clergy and approaches the Chief of Police with reverence, uttering the laid-back greeting "Ciao" as if it was a privilege the other has allowed him. He barely dares to look his superior straight in the eyes, and confesses to him his liaison with Augusta just like a pubescent kid would reveal his first sexual experience to his father. "How was she? Good?" is the reply. The Chief of Police "becomes the indulgent father who enjoys his son's carousing and thereby welcomes him to 'the club.'"[40]

An example of the protagonist's dual essence can be seen in his confrontation with the two students. In the first one, the Doctor plays the patriarchal father, who reaffirms his authority by punishing his rebel offspring, but at the same time offering comprehension. He forces the student to choose between sitting straight on his knees (the typical act of submission to a higher authority) or drinking a liter of saltwater if he wants to stand up. Both acts have the symbolic quality of exemplary punishments, the kind a severe father would administer in a backward patriarchal society.

At the same time, the Doctor coaxes the student. First, he claims he politically sides with him, then he depicts himself as a spiritual authority, thus a merciful one:

> Student, I don't want to imprison you. We are not the Gestapo or the SS. We are the police of a democratic country.... We are pleased when we avoid sentencing a citizen ... you are not a horse, you're a democratic citizen.... What is democracy? It's the beginning of Socialism. I, for example, vote Socialist. I am your confessor; they all have spoken to me!

It is basically the same situation he had recited during one of his encounters with Augusta, when explaining how interrogations are conducted.

> "Imagine that you're to face terrible hours, cruel questions, deception, extortion. You'll remember parts of your life you have forgotten about. You'll remember the shameful images from your life. You'll be thinking I am able to know all about you. The State provides all means necessary to know an individual.... I will convince you I know all about you, to provoke a complex of guilt.... Tell me the more shameful things. Confess your weakness and little daily shames. Only then I will forgive you."
>
> "I understand. You treat them as children."
>
> "Everyone comes back to childhood, when confronted with the established authority. I represent the power. The law.... All laws known and unknown. The suspect reverts to being a child. I become the father, an unassailable model. I assume the position of God and of the conscience. It is a setup to discover secret and profound feelings."

In the second confrontation the roles are reversed. The scene is shot like a Western duel of sorts, with words instead of guns, as the two adversaries advance from the opposite sides of the room and keep yelling at each other. But the young anarchist Antonio Pace shows no fear of authority whatsoever. He is the first and the only one who openly tells the protagonist that he knows he is the killer, adding: "A murdering criminal directing the repression. It is perfect!" The son shouting out his rebellion to the older man's face represents the breaking of a taboo, the symbolic killing of the father figure, the "unassailable model." It is the Doctor's turn to be humiliated and ridiculed through the reversal of similar situations throughout the film.

Sergio Tramonti, now a renowned production designer who took his first steps in the movie business as an actor, played Pace. He recalled the intensity that the scene demanded of the performers and the way real-life events imbued each and every line and act.

> Prior to shooting the scene, Petri had me drink seven coffees in a row and told me to attack the commissioner verbally and not let him talk. "You must tell him what he hasn't already asked yet!" … Gian Maria gave me great advice on my acting. He told me not to be merely emotional, but to … take inspiration from the leaders of student assemblies, who were able to guide the movement as true politicians. Because, he added, my character was a solitary anarchist who one day would become a leader.[41]

This leads to the Doctor writing a confession letter. According to film historian Alberto Tovaglieri, this is not merely the umpteenth display of the man's inner split between will of transgression and need to be punished, but the consequence of his confrontation with Pace, "the devastating awareness of having unintentionally given the 'subversives' a powerful point in favor of their challenge against power."[42] His contemptuous words to Mangani underline the implications of his act: "You'll never understand the meaning of my gestures and of my sacrifice, by which I want to affirm the concept of authority in its purest form."

It must be noted, however, that Pace is not depicted as a positive character. In many ways, he is the protagonist's *doppelgänger*, as Petri implies in the early moment where they first come face to face at Augusta Terzi's gate. Even though he is a key witness to the crime, Pace seems more interested in weakening his adversary's authority ("For the next action I'll phone you! You're in my powers!") than in having him incriminated, because it is easier to believe that *all* the political oppressors are criminals too. It is the same concept the Doctor had expressed in his own speech when pairing common criminals and subversives. In the end, Pace displays "a conception of the primacy of power on law and democracy which is as cynical and Machiavellian as the commissioner's."[43]

The film climaxes with a dream sequence which lays bare Petri's use of the grotesque to highlight his vision. It is not immediately clear that this is a dream, though, and the strength of *Indagine* is that, after all we have witnessed about the exercise of power and authority, and its ambiguous and self-protective nature, what is happening looks like a believable conclusion, the odd jarring detail notwithstanding. In fact, the sequence was not originally devised as such, but Petri and Pirro turned it into a dream to make sure there would be no problems with such a bold ending. Paradoxically, the added ambiguity resulted in an even stronger impact on the audience.

The Doctor dreams that the authorities show up at his place. One expects them to be confrontational against him, yet their attitude is mocking and patronizing. The Chief of Police treats him like a disobedient child, grabbing him by the ear and jokingly forcing him to eat a handful of salt, in a reversal of the student interrogation scene. Then, as the Doctor enumerates all the bits of evidence against him, the others reject them one by one. He tries to justify his acts, to which the Chief of Police explains to him his condition:

> "In that moment I didn't know if I should confess the crime or use my small powers to cover up the traces."
>
> "You have had a dissociation, a neurosis. However, it is a contracted illness due to the prolonged use of power. It is an illness common to a lot of powerful persons in our little society."

The more the Doctor insists on his own culpability, the more the others become angry and peremptory in rebuffing it. Eventually, in a mordant parody of the real beatings the suspects undergo during custody, the commissioner's colleagues start beating and kicking him until he surrenders and admits his own innocence. The black sheep finally atones for his sins and is allowed forgiveness. The Chief of Police grabs him by the ear jokingly, like a spoiled child who needs to be reprimanded. The Doctor is ready to resume his original place in the pack, alerting his "brothers" and his "father" about the ongoing fight against the enemy.

The sequence is revealed to be a dream, Petri's camera showing the Doctor lying on the bed, his short black socks—which Augusta had sneeringly compared to those of a priest—well in evidence. Then, real-life events enroll as he had dreamt, with the authorities arriving in a black limousine. They come in. Not a word is spoken, only ambiguous glances are exchanged. The film ends with an enigmatic gesture absent from the dream. The commissioner lowers the blinds, engulfing himself and his interlocutors in semi-darkness and once again obstructing the viewers' sight. Will he be arrested, or, as in his dream, will he be welcomed back as a prodigal son?

The quote from *The Trial* that seals such an ambiguous ending seems to hint at the latter option: "Whatever we may think of him, he is a servant of the Law, and therefore belongs to the Law, and that places him beyond human judgement." Most notably, Petri's film conveys "the elusiveness, the indefinability, the indisputable arbitrariness of the lord in Kafka's *The Castle* or the judge in *The Trial*: that is, Power seen as inaccessible or unimpeachable."[44]

As with *A ciascuno il suo*, the final scene is a ceremony of sorts, and the shot of the Chief of Police and his men entering the Doctor's apartment is exactly the same as in the other film. It is a symbolical return to order, the recreation of an enlarged family who must remain united in order to beat an enemy who denies authority and fights "against the powers and against God." Both the Mafia-embedded Sicilian upper class and the repressive authorities have the nature and the structure of the patriarchal family, and this is what makes them so powerful, and terrible.

Incompetents and Libertines

Like many of Petri's characters, the Doctor has developed an immature sexuality. Augusta calls him "sexually incompetent," the same definition the director gave of Laurana. This doesn't mean that sexual psychopathy is the *cause* of authoritarian tendencies, as a superficial reading would infer. In fact, Petri tried to underline the role of sexuality in revealing such tendencies as well as in the dynamics of power. In doing so, he drew from philosopher and psychoanalyst Norman O. Brown's *Love's Body*,[45] a book which developed psychoanalysis toward "a rather curious (and radical) brand of religious mysticism"[46] and discussed the metaphorical quality of the erotic language, stating that "everything is symbolic ... including the sexual act."

The Doctor gets excited by staging and photographing the aftermath of sado-sexual murders with Augusta posing as the victim, in a liaison that looks more like a child's play, not unlike the one between Ferri and Flavia in *Un tranquillo posto di campagna* (in a scene, Augusta is making up her eyes just as Vanessa Redgrave's character did in the 1968 film). At one point, during one of their *mises-en-scène*, Augusta asks him if he was excited by the spectacle of murdered women, and the Doctor becomes embarrassed like a little kid as he confesses that he was "excited by a certain detail" which he is "ashamed to say."

Augusta Terzi (Florinda Bolkan) posing as a victim of a sexual murder in one of the macabre pictures staged by her lover in *Indagine su un cittadino al di sopra di ogni sospetto*.

"You make love like a child because you are a child!" she mocks him. Words that mark her fate, together with his discovery that she has another lover, younger and much more sexually capable than him. Her murder is the result of the protagonist's investigation of his own sexuality, which has led him to discover his impotence—that is, the impotence of authority. "She has become the enemy, the witness of his weakness and his sexual inadequacy," Petri explained. "Thus he has to destroy the proof of this impotence so that authority can rule again."[47] But Augusta has also grasped the core of his neurosis: his childish illusion about the omnipotence of power. "Power needs irresponsible citizens…. Those who believe that a representative of power is a superior being and that socio-political institutions are immutable, are immature," the director argued. "But even more perversely immature are those who let them believe it—that is, those who have the power."[48]

But there is more. Augusta Terzi is a smart, independent, uninhibited woman who lives in an elegant Art Nouveau apartment and chooses the men she likes. She is a free spirit, free as the bird depicted on the curtain behind which she is first glimpsed (later she paints her eye with a peacock motif) or like a butterfly, which she evokes when she welcomes the Doctor in the opening scene. Her movements throughout the film are elegant and unpredictable like a ballet. She literally dances around the man, a mysterious and alluring image of seduction that makes her the most fascinating and enigmatic female presence in Petri's cinema. Augusta rejects the role assigned to women in a patriarchal society. It was she, we learn, who made the first move, luring the Doctor to her apartment and making him her lover. "I don't spend money on women," he awkwardly replies to her advances, for he cannot move past the duality between a mother-type and a whore. During their affair, she gradually proves she has the power while deluding him that he is the dominating one, as in their S/M routine. She fools him, she mocks him, she catches him off-guard. And she manipulates his ego, suggesting that he might use his authority in ways he has never envisaged.

Eventually, even though she is used to having wealthy and powerful lovers and is fascinated and excited by authority, Augusta sides with the "enemy" by giving herself to the young and penniless student Antonio Pace, who is "young, beautiful and even revolutionary." She humiliates the Doctor not just as a man, by deriding his virility, but as a man *of power*, for her very existence is a transgression against the rules he represents. And this is what ultimately leads to her murder. On the one hand the Doctor is intrigued by her disobedience to the rules, which leads him to experience the thrill of exerting power outside the limits of the law; on the other, he sees her as the enemy, for she is openly contemptuous of authority while he firmly believes that any transgression must be aimed at reinforcing it.

In *La decima vittima*, Petri subtly referred to violence against women with a chilling line about female sacrifices being "in style." Here, Augusta predicts, "I'll be raped and killed—that's my destiny." Descriptions of gruesome sex murders are casually dropped throughout the film, with women being victims of vicious assaults that hint at male violence related to sexual frustration. These acts have seemingly become the norm and have turned into the inspiration for the commissioner's snapshots of Augusta, a homemade replica of the type of pics to be found in sex magazines and photonovels.

After death, Augusta Terzi will be sneered at and humiliated by males. The Doctor describes her to journalist Patané as having "the velvety skin of a courtesan of this low empire" and insists that he mention her habit of not wearing panties, a morbid detail for the readers. Later, discussing with his colleagues, he claims that "in this city, not only whores are killed but also the order and the social equilibrium," and it is quite clear who is the "whore" he is alluding to. The other cops talk about Augusta with a mixture of contempt and envy for her uninhibited lifestyle, and she is repeatedly dismissed as a "libertine, D'Annunzio-style" by men who hide their libertine inclinations behind a moralizing façade. Self-repression is civilization, too.

In Petri and Pirro's venomous gibe at the hypocrisy of authorities, Gabriele D'Annunzio is mentioned as a symbol of moral decadence if pinpointed to a woman, whereas he is elected as a role model by men of power. Petri had already targeted the Decadentist writer in *Il maestro di Vigevano* ("D'Annunzio has always made me puke! He was hollow! He was bombastic! ... I don't care shit about D'Annunzio!" Mombelli's colleague bursts out). Here, the fascist Chief of Police has a picture of the "one-eyed seer" in his office. As the director explained,

> Why did I put a reference to D'Annunzio in my film? That's simple: because D'Annunzio represents the decadent side of the authoritarian fascist system, to which the aggressive side must be added. You couldn't explain Mussolini without D'Annunzio, just as you couldn't explain De Gaulle without Malraux.[49]

The D'Annunzio reference alludes also to the relationship between latent homosexuality and fascism, as Petri confirmed to *Cinéaste* magazine, "especially insofar as it is from the mechanism of sadomasochism that authoritarianism draws its strength. Of this sadomasochism, latent homosexuality is only a symptom. It is also clear that the superego wants to make love to the ego and dominate it."[50]

The film is clearly divided into two halves, with the past being dominated by

Augusta, whereas the present takes place in the austere, misogynist, all-male universe of the armed forces, the only female presences being the commissioner's cleaning lady (a middle-aged, asexual, motherly figure) and two vulgar prostitutes escorted by their ugly-looking pimp (Vincenzo Falanga, *I giorni contati*'s "mazzolatore") in a police office. In such a world homosexuality is openly mocked (see the cops' cruel jokes at the expense of Augusta's queer husband), but comradeship hints at an ambiguous complicity. The confrontations between the Doctor and the fatherly Chief of Police are all a matter of ambiguous glances and smiles, affectionate gestures and male bonding, sharing indiscreet sexual confidences while puffing on a cigar. Boys will be boys.

The Comedy of Power

In the collective memory, *Indagine* is often identified with Gian Maria Volonté's extraordinary personification as the "citizen above suspicion." The actor modeled his character on very precise references: "The way he walks, his attitudes, his language, even the way he combs his hair, relate to a precise tradition which in Italy goes back to the time of the Bourbons. Nowadays the remnants of this tradition are often found in ministries."[51] The accent Volonté came up with is particularly effective, "a singular and very felicitous central-southern lingo with inflections ranging from the mocking to the hysterical: a sort of effective phonetics of power" which contributed to giving his character "an almost metaphysical dimension." According to film critic Lino Miccichè, in fact, "with the sneer of his smile, the defiance of his look, the insolence of his gait, the violence of his action, the sinuosity of his persuasion, the Doctor ends up acquiring a more universal significance than he seemingly has at first sight."[52]

During filming Volonté and Petri often discussed about the protagonist's nature and the film's political content. Volonté was convinced that his character was a downright mean Fascist, whereas Petri's view was more subdued and gave the Doctor an ambiguous aura, something which the actor didn't consider in his political vision, as his friend Marlisa Trombetta pointed out.[53]

Upon the film's release, Volonté's no-holds-barred performance caught some critics off-guard for its ostensibly caricaturish traits. "Snobbish, intellectual cinema requires 'understatement,'" was the director's reply. "But, unfortunately, reality *is* caricaturish and I believe that cinema should stress this, even if it means resorting to very popular forms; it should not fear sliding into kitsch."[54]

This was evident also in the choice of some types in secondary roles, from Panunzio to the delegation of authorities that show up at the Doctor's place. The perceived connection with *commedia all'italiana* was one of the traits that provoked irate reactions from the leftist critics. It was a somewhat simplistic labeling, for Italian comedy often managed to bring to light the contradictions between the individual's existential reality and his social façade, characterized by the dramatic gap between desire and deprivation.[55] Here, the insistence on theatricality is essential to Petri's discourse, and aims at an antinaturalistic effect which is actually the opposite of the *commedia all'italiana*'s Neorealist roots. The director openly called it "Brechtian ... in the presentation of the characters, in their relationship with the audience, in their observing themselves critically."[56]

Every gesture the Doctor makes and the way he uses his voice convey an overt theatricality that depicts the character's inner split. The theme of performance is recurrent, from the S/M tableaux he reenacts with Augusta to the confrontation with Pace, when the Doctor strategically places his seat at one end of the room to achieve the desired effect and behaves like an actor practicing his moves. The interrogations themselves are in fact mini-shows in which the cop plays indeed a role—he dons the father mask, as he explains.

Sometimes the Doctor even bursts into extemporaneous bouts of impromptu mimicry, such as when he cruelly imitates Augusta's effeminate husband, dons a fake Roman accent in his anonymous phone call to Patané, or impersonates a flamboyant theatrical producer to persuade a meek plumber to purchase all the ties in a shop ("The title of the show is *50 Blue Ties for 50 Big Babies...*"). His official "mask" is a mixture of arrogance and disdain for the next man which sometimes gives way to condescending buffoonery, such as when he openly winks to his colleague while mocking poor Panunzio, the embodiment of the average Italian who will do everything to please his superior. The Doctor expects that the others laugh at his jokes, just as he expects that they lower their eyes when he scolds them. The exercise of power becomes a mind game focused on soliciting his interlocutors' responses at will, according to his whims.

Petri's depiction of the arrogance of authority takes on darkly humorous tones. When he makes the anonymous phone call to Patané, giving him bits of information only the murderer would know, the Doctor barely conceals his own voice; but when the reporter confronts him and tells him he recognized it, he simply threatens to stop giving him privileged information, thus effectively silencing him. Similarly, he preventively confronts Panunzio with an incriminating file on the latter's cousin, a communist activist;

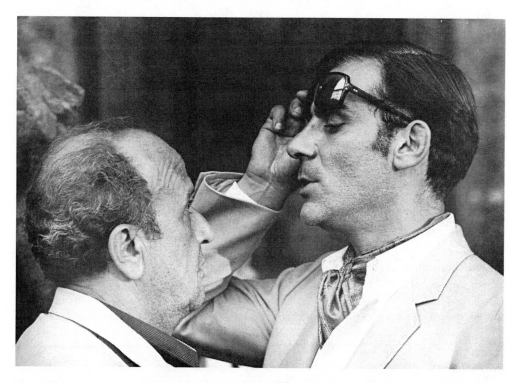

The Doctor (Gian Maria Volonté, right) confesses the murder to a meek plumber (Salvo Randone, left) in *Indagine su un cittadino al di sopra di ogni sospetto.*

later, when briefing him on the lab results, the intimidated Panunzio will offer all sorts of far-fetched explanations for the presence of the Doctor's fingerprints all over the crime scene. The scene in the lab, set among huge sheets of enlarged fingerprints, borders on the surreal, as Panunzio unctuously comes up with one justification after the other to deny the obvious. The Doctor is so inebriated by his own power that he eventually swoons.

The Doctor goes so far as allowing his subordinate Biglia to search his apartment (but again he does so in the certainty that his cleaning lady won't let Biglia in) and, after persuading the plumber to buy the ties, he even reveals himself to the man as Augusta Terzi's murderer, urging him to go to the police and denounce him. Upon hearing these words, his interlocutor almost faints, just like the Doctor did in the lab scene. Then we see the plumber's face as reflected in the Doctor's mirrored lens, a visual nod to a similar scene in *A ciascuno il suo* (where Laurana's face was reflected in Rosello's shades) which underlines the power gap between the two men.

At the police station, the plumber—detained for an exhausting interrogation, verbally abused and humiliated—quickly retracts his testimony when he finds out that the man he has denounced is the same one who is interrogating him. Here, as Millicent Marcus noted, "raw power and the sheer force of institutional authority" enable the protagonist to "prevail over a man armed with unequivocal evidence of his guilt."[57] The victimized citizens adhere to their role and don't even dare to rebel, which makes them the object of further vexations. Petri here addresses the average man's distrust of the authorities while sarcastically confirming its soundness, for "the State has such a distrust of citizens that all institutions tend to control and surveillance."[58]

Visually, *Indagine* is characterized by recurring images of assorted barriers (gates, sheets, curtains, veils) which partly blur the sight, evoking repression, obstruction,

The Doctor (Gian Maria Volonté) stands before enlargements of his own fingerprints.

dissimulation, but also hinting at the protagonist's convoluted mind, in parallel with the intricate narrative. Petri often observes the characters from a distance but employs short-focus lenses which either crush them against the backdrop or highlight their close-ups. The camera never stops moving, its intoxicating dynamism at times bordering on dizziness. In the scenes set in the police station it either follows or backtracks the Doctor advancing across the corridors as if to underline his authority, a stylistic figure that recalls Kubrick's use of the tracking shot, here sometimes paired with the zoom.

Elsewhere, a voyeuristic quality emerges. In the first scene in Augusta's apartment, the camera restlessly explores and investigates objects and gestures, picking up details, suggesting hidden analogies, exploring unusual perspectives, unveiling puzzling elements. See, for instance, the subtle way in which Petri depicts the murder. The Doctor sneakily extracts a razorblade from his trousers, hides it between his lips and gets in the bed where his unaware victim awaits him. But it is all so discreet, shot in a long take without any close-up, that most viewers won't notice it upon first viewing. Unlike in *A ciascuno il suo*, when the camera closes in on the characters by way of the repeated use of the zoom, here Kuveiller opts for crude lens changes (a trick already employed in *Un tranquillo posto di campagna*), as in the scene of Augusta's husband being harassed by the cops. The device gives a visual correspondent of the brutality being perpetrated on screen.

This array of visual nuances results in an incessant challenge of our perception of reality, which is deformed and questioned until its contradictory essence comes out. This is further highlighted by the use of locations. For one thing, the Doctor's transgression is symbolically underlined by the site where the murder takes place. The building where Augusta lives is located in front of the Synagogue and has two female figures representing Justice and Science sculpted on the façade, while the Jewish temple displays the Decalogue on its front wall. These evoke the pillars of society he is putting to the test, human and divine law.

Likewise, Carlo Egidi's sets highlight the protagonist's duality, by juxtaposing Augusta's fascinatingly extravagant, Liberty style apartment and the Doctor's ultramodern, cold-looking, sparsely furnished one (Petri shot the latter scenes in a Brutalist villa designed by the noted architect Francesco Berarducci). Moreover, the scenes at the police station are characterized by slightly futuristic sets which have a menacing yet subtly grotesque quality. There is a room full of fingerprint enlargements hanging from the ceiling like sheets hanging out to dry, a huge underground archive filled with dossiers ("Here are the communists, partisans, Trotskyists, Maoists and anarchists…") and an ultramodern room replete with an electronic brain—an image reminiscent of *La decima vittima*—which fills the Doctor with childlike enthusiasm, like a kid with a new toy. "The revolution from America has arrived!" he enthuses. Petri and his collaborators resorted to inventiveness when depicting the telephone exchange center beneath the police headquarters—an image borrowed from the opening scene of *Nostra signora Metredina*—as a "powerful, obscure, unknown organism in which hundreds of men listen to other men,"[59] yet the result on screen is impressively plausible, and it caused a sensation upon the film's release.

But *Indagine* would not be the same without Ennio Morricone's score. The composer sought to follow Petri's critical vision and "intensify it with the necessary musical means, drawing on experiments and themes pervaded by subversive elements."[60] He wrote two very different pieces for the film. One, which scores the flashbacks with Volonté and

Bolkan, has a ternary, sensuous rhythm, whereas for the main theme Morricone wanted "the perverseness of the film to clearly emerge." He came up with a "folksy and perverse tango," melodically and harmonically ambiguous yet instantly memorable. As soon as he finished it, the composer realized its similarity with the theme he had written for Henri Verneuil's *Le clan des Siciliens* (1969). Both were in fact derived from Johann Sebastian Bach's *Fugue in A Minor* BWC 543.

The choice of timbres and instruments is fundamental. The main theme is characterized by a combination of classic and popular elements, namely the use of mandolin (an instrument related to the Southern Italian tradition and to folk music), which nevertheless is played as if it were a harpsichord to baroque effects, and a classical guitar. Morricone added an off-tune piano and bassoons, "aiming to obtain intestinal, extremely vulgar timbres." Then he added a synthesized ostinato characterized by an acid timbre.

Moreover, the arrangement features rhythmically unpredictable inserts by such diverse instruments as the *marranzano* or Jew's harp (typical of Sicilian tradition, and a nod to the protagonist's roots), soprano saxophone and electric bass, which allude to the Doctor's fractured psyche and its neurotic, contradictory impulses. The execution is deliberately imprecise and unpolished, so as "to evoke the shadiness conveyed by the images."

Overall, it is one of Morricone's greatest achievements. Stanley Kubrick was so impressed by it that he got in touch with Morricone to work on *A Clockwork Orange* (1971), but the composer turned down the offer.[61]

To better explain his personal and working relationship with Petri, Morricone recalled an amusing anecdote about the test-screening of *Indagine*:

> I recorded the cues and handed them in to him. He insisted that I not attend the mixing sessions of the film, and I complied without resistance. In those years it was normal for me not to attend the mixing sessions, as I believed they ought to follow the director's taste. He called me in afterward to ask for my opinion on what he had done. We went into the projection room, the lights went off, and the screening began. Something wasn't right from the very first scene, up until Florinda Bolkan's character's murder. The music was different from the one I had composed for the film, and instead came from *Comandamenti per un gangster* (1968), a rather cheap movie for which I had composed easy-listening music....
>
> I looked at him horrified and clueless. From time to time he hinted at me as if to imply that he liked that music better.
>
> During the murder scene he told me, "Ennio, listen to how well it fits!"
>
> It was absurd, an incredible agony for me: a director who contested the music of a composer in that way....
>
> When the first reel was finished, the lights went on and I was in pieces, devastated, petrified. Elio came closer and asked me, "So, what do you think?"
>
> I pulled myself together and replied, "Well, if you're happy with it, what can I say...."
>
> He topped it off by adding with absolute conviction, "It is perfect, isn't it?"
>
> I was speechless and did not know what to answer. I thought that, all in all, it was a necessary compromise, he was the director and if that was his will, what else was I supposed to do?
>
> I swallowed, and I tried to find some energy to reply, but before I could utter a syllable, Elio patted me on the back, shook me with both hands, and in Roman dialect said, "*A Morrico'* ... You always take the bait! You wrote the best music ever for this film and you should punch me in the face for such a prank!" Just like that.
>
> It was a prank, but I had no clue. He confessed he had been concocting it for a while. It was a big blow; this was Petri's nature.[62]

Intermezzo #2: Death of an Anarchist

The heavy climate hovering over the country after the Piazza Fontana bombing brought winds of repression and led to the reinforcement of right-wing forces. As Petri told Jean A. Gili, "it was necessary to give a lesson to the workers, it was necessary to limit their demands significantly from a qualitative point of view, it was absolutely necessary to defend the rights of proprietors and bourgeois exploiters."[63]

All this pushed him and Pirro to create the "Comitato Cineasti Italiani contro la Repressione" (Italian Cineastes Committee Against Repression), a collective of film-makers, actors, and assorted film workers from ANAC and AACI[64] which included Bernardo Bertolucci, Marco Bellocchio, Liliana Cavani, Nelo Risi, Nanni Loy, Marco Ferreri, Damiano Damiani, Luchino Visconti, and others. Their aim was to document the ongoing repression against the protest movements. Petri shot hundreds of meters of footage depicting headquarters of small Marxist groups, assemblies, protest marches, clashes with the police. Sometimes it was not just the cops who would obstruct the shoot but the militants themselves, who were tending more and more toward secrecy. Political extremism was taking on worrying tones.

The Committee set out to make five films dedicated to Giuseppe Pinelli. The only ones who completed the task were Petri and Nelo Risi, and the results were later combined as *Documenti su Giuseppe Pinelli*. The rest of the footage was never edited.

Risi's one-hour *Giuseppe Pinelli. Materiale di lavoro n. 1* (Giuseppe Pinelli. Work Material #1) features interviews with those who knew Pinelli and those who were arrested and kept in the police headquarters with him after the Piazza Fontana bombing. It also includes the public trial staged by the anarchists in Milan to exonerate Pinelli from any accusation.

Petri's contribution, *Materiale n. 2—Ipotesi sulla morte di G. Pinelli* (Material #2. Hypotheses on the Death of G. Pinelli) runs just eleven minutes. Shot in black and white on 16mm, it was made without a proper script and with the collaborative effort of a crew which included Gian Maria Volonté, actors Renzo Montagnani and Luigi Diberti, d.o.p. Luigi Kuveiller, and special effects artist Carlo Rambaldi—all of them working for free.

The film takes place in a small room made to represent Luigi Calabresi's office where Pinelli was being questioned when he died. The sparse furniture includes a chair, a table, and a picture of the President of the Republic on the wall. It starts with a man shutting a clapperboard that reads "Pinelli—1ª versione" (Pinelli—1st version). Five actors turn up before the camera, including Volonté (wearing a mustache, jeans and a black short-sleeved shirt). He explains:

> We are a group of show business workers. Our purpose is to recreate through the use of our specific means—actors, directors, technicians—the three official versions, that is, those endorsed by the magistrates, of the alleged suicide of anarchist Pinelli.

The *mise-en-scène* is openly didactic, with Volonté reading from a list of notes, addressing the camera and interviewing the other actors about the circumstances under which the tragedy occurred. The camera zooms in and out, focusing on this or that actor as they speak. Each version (except for the last segment) consists of a long take, with no cuts.

Still, *Ipotesi* is permeated by a gritty irony. Volonté (who plays one of the cops) specifies that Calabresi was known "among the Milanese leftist ambients" as "Commissario

CIA." The actors meticulously light up cigarettes, as everyone in the office was supposed to be smoking at the time of Pinelli's death. The reconstructions underline the implausibility and contradictions of the official truths. Yet the actors take their roles very seriously. As Diberti recalled, "In those years and relating to that specific event, it couldn't have been otherwise. We thought it could be useful so that people would not be gullible, lazy, passive or whatever regarding what the official narration stated."[65]

In Version #1, the police officers are supposed to be talking about their business, oblivious of Pinelli getting up from the chair a few feet away, stretching and going to the window. "They say that I, anarchist Pinelli, threw myself out of the window with a feline jump," the actor says as he does just that. The camera returns to Volonté and the others, turning back as if in a daze. Volonté underlines that the expression "feline jump" was actually used in the official report.

Version #2 has the policemen standing in different parts of the room. Unlike the first version, they actually see Pinelli jump. "They say that I, anarchist Pinelli, got up to stretch. Then I slowly went to the window as if to catch a breath of fresh air…." This time two officers attempt to stop him but, unbelievably, they don't manage to despite being next to him. "Why did he jump?" one asks. "We didn't make it," Volonté concludes. "Despite the four officials' zeal, anarchist Pinelli managed to reach the courtyard."

Version #3. "I, anarchist Pinelli, got up to stretch out. Then I slowly went to the window as if to catch a breath of fresh air…." Again, the four men attempt to stop him but in vain. "I missed him by a hair," Montagnani says. "I was left holding his shoe," he adds, showing the shoe he still has in his hand. But, as Volonté points out, Pinelli's body was found with *both* shoes on. Montagnani looks at the shoe, incredulous.

After the three versions, a fourth section, titled *Titoli Pinelli* (Headlines—Pinelli) has the actors read various newspapers headlines on the anarchist's "accidental" death, plus excerpts from *La strage di Stato*, a booklet published by a group of leftist militants soon after the fact. The last passage is a recollection from another anarchist, who recalls that Calabresi was nicknamed "Commissario Finestra" (Commissioner Window), for when interrogating a suspect, he and his agents taunted the man to jump out the open widow behind him. Volonté symbolically shuts the window.

The fifth and last segment, *Versione Frezzi*, has Volonté read an excerpt from Giampaolo Pansa's book *Le bombe di Milano*, on the death of Romeo Frezzi, an anarchist who died during an interrogation in 1897 in similar circumstances as Pinelli. The official report labeled the demise as a suicide, but the autopsy showed that the man had been beaten to death by the police. The actors reenact the episode. Then the "policemen" give their version. "It was an accident at work." "He committed suicide." "It is true," Volonté concludes, "he committed suicide." He and the others take the body and throw it out the window. This is the only scene that features a cut, a shot from "outside the window" before the anarchist's body is thrown out of it. The last shot has Volonté again address the camera, saying: "Pino Pinelli, the last in a long line of suicidal anarchists."

The end credits list all the names involved in the project,[66] even though it was materially Petri who made the short film. "It meant that all the signatories, even though they had not concretely collaborated on the film, considered themselves as supportive. If the law would intervene, we would all go to jail. It would be necessary to put all of us on trial."[67]

Documenti su Giuseppe Pinelli did not have a proper theatrical distribution. It was screened in alternative venues such as PCI sections, union headquarters, student assemblies. But *Ipotesi* was picked up by French producer Claude Nedjar who distributed it, devoid of credits, as a short film accompanying Yolande DuLuart's documentary *Angela Davis: Portrait of a Revolutionary* (1972), much to Petri's disdain.

Ipotesi is one of the most relevant reactions to Giuseppe Pinelli's death on the part of the intellectual world. Other contributions were Dario Fo's stage play *Morte acciden-tale di un anarchico* (1970), and painter Enrico Baj's monumental three-dimensional col-lage *I funerali dell'anarchico Pinelli* (1972). Both works faced censorship issues: eventually, Fo had to move the setting to 1920s America, while the exposition of Baj's work, initially set for May 1972, was cancelled after the murder of commissioner Calabresi. The collage was exposed in various European cities, but never found a permanent exposition venue in Milan.

A Movie Above Suspicion?

The Cannes Film Festival seemed the ideal international limelight for *Indagine*. Still, rumors were circulating that Petri's film was "not welcome" and that Festival direc-tor Fravret Le Bret would choose Ettore Scola's *Dramma della gelosia* and Franco Brusa-ti's *I tulipani di Haarlem* for the competition instead.[68] Eventually, *Indagine* made it into the selection (together with a fourth Italian title, Mauro Bolognini's *Metello*) and was screened on May 3, 1970, receiving a warm response from the audience.[69] Even though Volonté didn't show up in Cannes, the crowded press conference took place in an unreal mood. Petri spoke at length about the film's meaning and its political resonance, and in Pirro's recollection French director Claude Autant-Lara intervened to say that in France it would be impossible to make a movie like *Indagine*, because of its sheer subversive charge and the power of its images.[70] The hall erupted in a long applause.

The Grand Prix went to Robert Altman's *MASH*, while *Indagine* won the Grand Prize of the Jury and the FIPRESCI prize (assigned by the International Federation of Film Critics). Columbia Pictures purchased the worldwide distribution rights (with the exception of Italy) in perpetuity for a modest sum, and according to Pirro the proprietors of the film never saw a dollar after the advance.[71]

Released in France in October 1970 as *Enquete sur un citoyen au-dessus de tout soupçon*, the film was seen by 670,610 spectators. *L'Avant-Scène Cinéma* put it on its cover[72] and *Positif* published a lengthy interview with Petri.[73] But even though crit-ics emphasized its controversial and bold topic, not everyone grasped its deep political stance, and some reviewers were uncomfortable with its polemic virulence. *France Soir*'s Robert Chazal wrote: "Love stories are losing ground in favor of stories of hate. This is certainly not a healthy sign."[74]

Indagine's critical impact abroad was such that the Svenska Filminstitutet (Septem-ber 1970) and the French Cinémathèque organized retrospectives on the director. Of course, its content prevented a release in Spain, where it came out only in July 1975, near the end of the Franco regime, as *Investigación sobre un ciudadano libre de toda sospecha*. It proved a success, with 668,156 tickets sold.

The Cannes prize was just the beginning of a long series of awards. That July, Volo-nté won the Grolla d'Oro as Best Actor, and in October *Indagine* was judged Best Film and Volonté Best Actor, at the Globo d'Oro (Golden Globe) ceremony, a prize awarded by the International Press Association in Italy (Dario Argento won as Best Debuting Direc-tor). In December it was selected as the Italian candidate for the Academy Awards.

Despite the ongoing worldwide critical recognition, to many leftists the film's commercial success was proof that Petri was a servant of the Capital, and therefore a sellout. When asked by a reporter about his movie being labeled as politically indifferent, "because there is nothing that amuses Italians like bad-mouthing the police," Petri reclaimed the exceptional box-office results of his film as part of its political weight.

The stunning Hungarian poster for *Indagine su un cittadino al di sopra di ogni sospetto.*

For the first time a film which talks about the police institution in a critical way has not been charged with defamation. Now, this is a precedent. So, I think that political indifference doesn't create precedents, it never moves anything. Whereas in a very small part *Indagine* did move something.... I believe it is a popular film and, as such, a political film. I think that *Indagine*'s political content has come out mostly because of the support of a large audience.[75]

With *Indagine*, Elio Petri created more than a film and achieved more than a commercial phenomenon. He did create a precedent, a path for other filmmakers to follow, even though its epigones did not have the same boldness. A couple of months later, reviewing Piero Zuffi's *Colpo rovente*, the story of a cop who investigates the death of a rich Mafioso and who in the end turns out to be the killer, the *Corriere della Sera* noted that it had a bold denouement similar to Petri's film.[76] But *Colpo rovente*, scripted by Ennio Flaiano, was set in the States, hence its political impact was definitely lesser.

The commercial success of *Indagine* led also to the typical phenomenon of titles imitating it, with words such as investigation, inquiry, confession, in evidence. Rolf Olsen's *Das Stundenhotel von St. Pauli* came out in Italy as *Inchiesta di un procuratore su un albergo di tolleranza* (An Attorney's Inquiry on a Brothel Hotel), and Marcel Carné's *Les Assassins de l'ordre* became *Inchiesta su un delitto della polizia* (Inquiry on a Police Murder). Damiano Damiani's 1971 political crime film about the connection between the Mafia and the institutions, inspired by a controversial real-life magistrate figure, bore the torrential title *Confessione di un commissario di polizia al Procuratore della Repubblica*. As Damiani admitted, "At that time it was dangerous, revolutionary even, to talk about these things. My film likely got made because of the precedent of *Indagine*."[77]

With "his propensity for social commentary and sociological investigation," Petri was now widely considered the "number one of political cinema,"[78] a thread which by the early 1970s had become a staple of the Italian film industry, thanks to such filmmakers as Rosi, Montaldo, and Damiani. But there was more than that. With his polemic verve and his non-aligned political stances, Petri became an influential voice, which would often find space in newspapers even outside the realm of film chronicles. And his work proved more complex and multi-faceted than, say, Costa-Gavras' vibrant, Oscar-winning *j'accuse* about the political horror of right-wing Greece.

But with that title came many responsibilities. Even foreign crime films were now read with Petri's work as a point of comparison. Reviewing *The French Connection* (1971), Giovanni Grazzini argued that "William Friedkin is neither a moralist nor a polemist like Petri."[79] *The French Connection* would be one of the blueprints of the upcoming Italian crime genre, in which cop characters would usually take on opposite characteristics as in Petri's film.

Indagine proved a powerful influence on the forthcoming *poliziotteschi* as well. Ironically, though, Petri's film is in many ways the latter's dark half. The Doctor is definitely one step aside from the stereotype of cinema detectives as "stoic embodiments of the conscience of the world, the 'right ones' as opposed to the decay of morals and the disintegration of moral codes."[80] As if to get rid of *Indagine*'s uncomfortable shadow, the new centurions of Italian crime cinema would adopt frugal lifestyles: no love affairs, indifference—if not contempt—for power and career, while the authorities would be seen as hostile and unattainable. Distrust of power, the expression of a centuries-old popular wariness, would however be devoid of Petri's biting political discourse. For all its extraordinary influence on Italian popular culture (to limit it to cinema would be diminishing) and its weight in the country's political debate, *Indagine* was—and still is—something unique.

Coda: *The Investigation That Never Was*

In April 1986, news came that the Cannon Group was developing a remake of *Indagine*. The project was part of Cannon's attempt to diversify their offer by producing prestigious movies such as Andrei Konchalovsky's *Runaway Train* and Robert Altman's *Fool for Love*. It was announced just in time to promote sales at the upcoming Cannes Marché, as *The Investigation*. Paul Schrader would script it and Konchalovsky was attached to direct as part of a five-picture deal with Menahem Golan and Yoram Globus's company, as soon as he mounted the opera *Eugene Onegin* at La Scala. Al Pacino was rumored to star.[81]

Schrader completed a sixteen-page treatment on July 8, 1986, a first draft on September 19, and a 105-page revised draft of the script on May 8, 1987. All were simply titled *Investigation*.

The treatment is preceded by an eloquent writer's note which in the end echoes the famous one in the Rolling Stones' album *Let It Bleed*:

> Everything about *Investigation*—writing, directing, acting, scoring, editing—must be brash, bold. All flash. For the moment. Nothing sitting still; nothing dripping below the surface. All to music. This is not the style of a drama, not the style of expose. But the rules are changing; by dancing on the surface, by pretending to be about nothing. *Investigation* can disguise its true identity—a political broadside in the form of a polaroid. Thomas Nash via rock and roll. This script should be read with the music *loud*.

Schrader goes a long way to shape the character akin to the original one ("His walk presumes order in the space through which it moves, creates an allusion of order if none exists") and describing him as an Italian American type. But he gives Petri's nameless Doctor a name, Jude Mazzo ("Hey, Jude. It's a name you remember."). The Big Bopper's song "Chantilly Lace" turning up every once in a while as a musical leitmotif attempts to echo Petri's use of Morricone's score. A screenwriter's note specifies that "the choice of pop source music (with the exception of 'Chantilly Lace') is indicative, not proscriptive. Jude is the product of rock and roll, more Presley than politics."

The treatment and script open with the Kafka citation (actually misquoted as "He's a servant of the law and eludes justice"), thus putting their cards on the table from the very beginning, and follow the original outline rather closely, replete with the flashback structure, even reprising several lines of dialogue to the letter, starting with the most famous one: "So, how will you kill me today?" "I'll slit your throat." But Schrader relocates the action to Washington, D.C., and devises a new context to the story, with the city plagued by a series of terrorist bombings and Mazzo, former Assistant Attorney General, being appointed the head of a new anti-terrorist agency (and thus nicknamed "the Anti-Terrorist Czar"). The script provides a quick background to the protagonist, in a TV montage of clips that depict Mazzo's rise to fame. Overall, *Investigation* works like a glossy, realistic thriller, replete with tight dialogue and more procedural mumbo-jumbo than in Petri's film.

But there are issues. The victim's role in the story is deprived of its original meaning and seen through a one-dimensional, misogynistic perspective. The paper-thin Karin Schreiber (a twentyish north-European model) turns out a sluttish type and a terrorist sympathizer. Schrader pairs Mazzo's affair with Karin with him gradually turning from dorky to self-assured, thus losing another key point. The Doctor was *always* a self-assured type, and Augusta Terzi made his façade creak and show his childish side.

The role of Antonio Pace is badly rewritten too. Here, it is a young Italian terrorist, Ria (a *very* unlikely name for an Italian male, incidentally), who was in cahoots with Karin. Jude has been meaning to pin the murder on him from the beginning. On the other hand, the episode with the plumber is drastically revised. Jude, camouflaged with sunglasses and baseball hat, goes to the Missoni store and buys a new tie to replace the other. The clerk recognizes him but then changes his version during the interrogation. The episode loses the edge of the original, where the Doctor openly confessed to the meek plumber played by Salvo Randone that he was the murderer and urging him to go and denounce him.

Tellingly, one of the differences with Petri's film is the scene where Jude discovers Karin's affair with Ria, which takes place in her apartment. She makes Jude hide in the closet with an excuse, and then proceeds to have sex with the other man on the bed, making sure that Jude watches and listens. This preposterous sexual humiliation—which prompts Jude's tortuous homicidal plan—gives a measure of Schrader's simplification of the main character's issues. The new adaptation reduces the original's ambiguousness and symbolic pregnancy into something far more banal and realistic, turning the Doctor's schizophrenic split into Jude's delusions of grandeur, all rockstar poses and spoiled kid provocations.

Originally, Schrader had added a couple of scenes in the treatment to show Jude's power games that he discarded in the script. In one, Mazzo seduces a congressman's wife in Georgetown just to try out his power; later, he picks up a hooker and takes her with him to a *Time* magazine photo session just to see if the reporters will make questions about her. However, the script features a needless action sequence in which, after a bombing, Jude jumps into a burning truck and finds evidence of a planned attack on the White House. This leads to his appearance at the *Phil Donahue Show*, with his popularity reaching a peak, and even a *Time* magazine cover.

The political angle reveals Schrader's agenda. Take Mazzo's speech: "Just as the early years of this century demanded a new law enforcement bureau, the FBI, so these difficult times require a new, independent anti-terrorist agency.... The United States shouldn't hide from the terrorists—they don't respect cowardice or vacillation...." In retrospect, this might have worked better in the wake of 9/11, after the Patriot Act and its restrictions to individual freedom, but in the late 1980s it would have sounded a bit forced. Still, the transition from Fascist police striving to repress the post–1968 students' movement in Petri's film to a task force fighting terrorism deprives the story of its thought-provoking punch—so strictly entangled with the Italian situation of the period and the "Strategy of Tension"—and turns it into a well-meaning but rather predictable political parable. Similarly, the interrogation scene discards the Doctor's sneering monologue on democracy and socialism and takes on Biblical tones, even (mis) quoting Oliver Wendell Holmes ("The great act of faith is when man decides he is not God"). Unlike Petri, Schrader never addresses the repressive nature of power nor does he depict the police as a whole as an instrument of repression to "carry out the wishes of the political and economic powers of the bourgeois state,"[82] but merely shows Mazzo as a deranged servant of democracy. Hence, his discourse loses the edge that made the original unique. Significantly, the Doctor's original motto "Repression is civilization" is nowhere to be found, replaced by one more in tune with Reagan's America ("The Law is the answer! America is back!").

Speaking of which, there are a couple of lines that hint at Schrader's target, the then-current GOP administration: "The president views movies seriously," the Attorney General wisecracks, and during a TV interview on the *Phil Donahue Show* Mazzo name-drops Reagan among his heroes, together with JFK, Martin Luther King, Lee Iacocca … and Walt Disney. This angle becomes clear in the third act, when Mazzo meets with a group of wealthy and powerful Republican supporters who explain their idea to have him as the new presidential candidate ("You got a New Decade vibe. You might just be the man for the Nineties.")

Even the ending loses its ambiguity. Compared with Petri's use of the grotesque through the gimmick of the Doctor's dream, here the final confrontation between the hero and the authorities sounds just silly. After forcing Mazzo to confess his innocence, a party chairman tells him: "You've got a great future. Just smile!" From that we infer that Jude Mazzo will become a political puppet to be maneuvered by the gray GOP eminencies.

Shooting for *Investigation* was to start in October 1987 and the film was slated to premiere at Cannes in 1988. But Al Pacino had not yet signed the contract, and his backing out led to the project falling apart. It was briefly resurrected in the 1990s, when Jodie Foster's company Egg Pictures purchased the rights. Sidney Lumet was attached to direct, but it did not go beyond preproduction, and perhaps it is just as well.

NINE

Working Class Anti-Hero
La classe operaia va in paradiso *(1971)*

A Hot Autumn

In 1970 industrial occupation reached its all-time peak in Italy, with 42 percent of the total labor force in the country. FIAT alone employed about 140,000 workers. The increase concerned primarily car and household appliance plants, which operated on assembly lines and recruited large masses of unqualified workers from the South. These were detached from their family and cultural roots, lacked specific abilities and were given a limited function within the automatized production process.[1] It was a different type of laborer, whom Marxist thinker Mario Tronti labeled "*operaio massa*" (mass factory worker) in his 1966 book *Operai e capitale*. This was a well-known figure overseas—think of Charles Chaplin's character in *Modern Times* (1936)—after Fordism had applied Frederick Winslow Taylor's theories to the technology of industrial assembly line. In Italy, this type of job organization had been virtually unknown before the economic Boom. Industrial expansion resulted also in the reorganization of unions and in the attempt to raise awareness in the working class.

In the 1960s, Tronti and other Marxist thinkers gave birth to a utopian current, *operaismo* (workerism), focused on the working class as the key agent to overcome the capitalistic system. To them, the "*operaio massa*" and the factory represent the subject and the place where capitalism exposes its inner contradiction: each worker has a small part in producing a commodity which he is then solicited to purchase, thus becoming a consumer. Therefore, he is doubly exploited. Tronti described the "*operaio massa*" as some sort of Pagan race, without faith or morality, subject to capitalist exploitation and to the alienation of the assembly line, without emotional or cultural roots. By achieving awareness of their condition, the "*operaio massa*" could bring radical and spontaneous struggle inside and outside the factory, bypassing the unions and the reformist left-wing parties, and giving way to a revolutionary process. Workerist theories led to the birth of radical, extra-parliamentary left-wing groups, such as Potere Operaio (Workers' Power, usually abbreviated as Pot.Op.), who operated in the big factories of the North to raise the workers' awareness and demand better working conditions. A typical slogan was "More income, less work!"

The traumatic experience in many industrial plants reduced workers to automatons in a restless race for productivity and resulted in stress, sudden bursts of violence, anger, nervous breakdowns, bouts of depression, even madness. The general dissatisfaction and the growing diffusion of the workerist theories resulted in many spontaneous strikes and in a wave of mobilization in factories. What the protesters asked were not just better wages, but an improvement of the working conditions: more rights, and therefore more contractual power. The wave of strikes and struggles in Italy was longer and more intense than in other European countries and conveyed a blatant distrust in labor unions and their moderate stances. Strikes resulted often in violent clashes with the police and saw also the participation of the students' movement.

On November 28, 1969, the same day the Rolling Stones released their *Let It Bleed* album, 100,000 factory workers gathered in Rome from all over Italy for a rally. They manifested for the renovation of their collective contract. Despite the palpable tension in a year of clashes and struggles, no one was harmed.

> The demonstration erupted in a crescendo of noises—cowbells, drums, whistles, megaphones—that disturbed the order of a city accustomed to ignoring the sacrifices, the marginalization, the physical and mental wear of factory life. But it was also a party, a moment of liberation from the bond and the discipline of assembly line work, an expression of self in the slogans shouted and written on the boards.... There wasn't a single broken glass that day. 100,000 steelworkers had taken possession of the city and paraded for hours without any accident. From the post-war period till today there had never been rallies in Rome ... a powerful, ordered and determined workers' procession made an impression. The steelworkers were beginning to be relevant.[2]

The parade led to the signing of a collective deal in January 1970, and the following May saw the promulgation of the "Workers' Statute, "[3] that is the "rules on the protection of the freedom and dignity of workers and of trade union freedom and union activity in the workplace, and rules on the public employment service." The Statute granted workers a series of prerogatives, including a highly innovative feature: Article 18 provided the mechanism for reinstatement after a dismissal had been declared unlawful. But the huge rally in Rome had awakened the whole cultural world. As union leader and Socialist politician Ottaviano Del Turco would later write, "some simply came down from their terraces, others seemed to soothe their sense of guilt by raising their fist in the air.... Elio Petri and Ugo Pirro were not content with just raising their fists. They started working on a film story."[4]

The Loneliness of the Assembly Line Mass Worker

Right after the release of *Indagine*, Petri stated that "the only type of cinema worth making today is political cinema." But he also specified that political films must not be "against the audience.... I want to hold on to communicability, which is fundamental, especially in a popular art such as cinema which is also a social occurrence for people to be together. I don't think it's time for pseudo-cultural riddles, which moreover are decades behind literature and painting."[5]

Indagine's success at Cannes led to offers from abroad, centered on vaguely similar stories—that is, crime scripts with a socio-political angle and possibly spiced with sexual content. The subject choices give an idea of how the film was perceived in some circles. In June 1970 producer Danton J. Rissner of Warner Bros. sent Petri a copy of Hans Habe's novel *Das Netz* (aka *The Poisoned Stream*),[6] about a reporter who discovers the identity of a sex murderer and attempts to capitalize on the discovery by sheltering the man and asking him to write his memoirs for his magazine. Petri curtly rejected the idea. The book was made into a film in 1975 by German director Manfred Purzer, as *Das Netz*, starring Mel Ferrer and Klaus Kinski. In late July, Si Litvinoff sent him *The Man with the Chocolate Egg*,[7] a script based on John Noone's 1967 novel of the same name, about a young British soldier who steals grenades from his army outfit and gives them to his brother, the leader of a terrorist group. Petri allegedly liked the script but thought it would be more appropriate for an American filmmaker. Raphael Etkes proposed to him Nicolas Freeling's 1963 novel *Gun Before Butter*, which had raised Orson Welles' interest as well.[8]

Even though he could have easily ridden the wave of *Indagine*'s popularity, Petri was moving in a totally different direction. Presenting the film to the press, he mentioned his next project, tentatively titled *Il premio della bontà* (The Reward of Goodness) and centered on a group of factory workers in Northern Italy. The protagonist would be "a young woman who undergoes many ordeals due to the misunderstandings that rise from a common and honest meaning of goodness."[9] Petri would write it with Ugo Pirro, and the film would star Ottavia Piccolo and Gian Maria Volonté.[10] It was, he explained, a way to hark back to the themes of *I giorni contati* and sum up his "relationships with others through a more direct, less paradoxical analysis of reality. In short, I would like to confront my own pessimism with more direct personal experiences."[11]

Il premio della bontà was not the only project Petri was considering. Others were a movie on piracy, seen as navigating hippie communities before their time, and one about a company of Neapolitan stage comedians in dire straits who decide to renovate their old-fashioned repertoire to retrieve their audience.[12] He also mentioned the idea of a film about "a politician of the Catholic left," tentatively titled *Informazione sulla classe politica al potere*,[13] proof that he was still toying with the concept he had told Spinazzola back in 1962. Another project he had been considering was the adaptation of a 1963 novel by Albanian poet Ismail Kadaré, *Il generale dell'armata morta* (The General of the Dead Army), about an Italian general and a priest who return to Albania 20 years after the end of World War II to collect the remains of their countrymen who died during the 1940 military campaign.[14] Petri had contacted director Vladimir Kasaj as early as May 1970 about the possibility of adapting it.[15] Kadaré's novel was eventually made into a film in 1983 by the noted director of photography Luciano Tovoli, in his only directorial effort, and starring Marcello Mastroianni and Michel Piccoli, the actors Petri had in mind for the roles.

These projects were all dropped, but the idea of a film about factory workers was drastically reshaped. Petri, Pirro and Kuveiller made an inquiry into the workers' struggles at the FATME plant in Rome, near Cinecittà, interviewing the personnel and filming the strikes. "Our intention was to film everything and make a document to distribute in the workers' circles, in the assemblies that took place in schools and elsewhere, as we had done with *Ipotesi sulla morte di G. Pinelli*, while at the same time checking closely some of our working outlines."[16] The footage is lost, but the inquiry was very useful. "We wanted to understand, to enter a world we only knew from a cultural point of view," Pirro argued. "We lacked precise and direct knowledge of it."[17]

While filming at FATME, Petri and his crew watched the students from Pot.Op. take action *in opposition* to the union. It was a new stage in the ongoing conflict between the workers and the industrialists, and it pushed the struggle to a higher level. A Pot.Op. member attempted to halt the shoot, claiming that the filmmakers would have to pay to film in order to finance their struggle. In those days, protests were even more vibrant, for a worker who adhered to Pot.Op. had been fired and his fellow workers were fighting for him to be reinstated. The event gave Petri and Pirro the idea for a story, and the worker, a certain Timperi, was the blueprint for the protagonist.

The film would be about a 31-year-old workaholic pieceworker, Ludovico "Lulù" Massa, who has been in a factory for half of his life. He works eight hours a day, six days a week, fifty weeks a year. His whole existence revolves around his job, and he is so obsessed with productivity that he can't even have sex with his lover anymore. He is deaf to the unions' struggles and labels those who demand better working conditions as idlers. Employers use his efficiency as a term of comparison for the other workers' productivity (or lack thereof), which makes him unpopular.

After an incident at the lathe which results in the amputation of his forefinger, Lulù becomes aware of his condition: he is exploited by the capitalist system. He becomes one of the most rebellious workers in the factory and leads his companions in a strike which results in a violent clash with the police. As a result, Lulù is fired, but the union has him reinstated with the other agitators. But now he is at the assembly line, working under even worse conditions than before.

Petri and Pirro prepared for the movie meticulously, conducting interviews with various workers. They wanted their film to be as honest as possible, and perfectly understandable for the average viewer: "We had to make the rate and piecework issues obvious to an audience that was unaware of them, and make them understand how piecework was the provocative agent of the film's tragic conflict."[18]

As for Volonté, he dedicated himself to the role with his customary perfectionism:

> My preparation is done … on a more journalistic level than a dramatic one, and it is based on the same material that the scriptwriter gathers and uses to build the story.… I spoke at length with factory workers about the specific illnesses for their condition, such as neurosis, deforming arthritis, lung infections.… Then I move to a kind of critical-analytical research of the character and his psychology, which brings me to establish the general attitude I must have throughout the film. Then there's the normal dialectic relationship that must take place between the actor and the director.[19]

After the outstanding success of *Indagine*, many producers stepped up to finance Petri's next project. One of them was Dino De Laurentiis. On the insistence of Dino's right-hand man Bruno Todini, Petri sent the tycoon the script. Unsurprisingly, De Laurentiis backed out. He wasn't the least bit interested in a film about a factory worker. Franco Cristaldi backed out too. It was Marina Cicogna's Euro who accepted the challenge.

Principal photography started in December 1970. Petri was determined not to shoot in a studio. At the beginning he had sought to make the movie in Rome, but found many doors shut. Then he headed North to locate a suitable plant for the shoot, but as soon as the owners heard his name they backed out. It was thanks to the union that he finally found one in the Lombard town of Novara: the elevator factory Falconi, which in that period was under controlled administration and was occupied by the personnel.[20] The script wasn't even finished but "to make the movie, it was absolutely necessary to enter the plant on December 12, because on December 31 the judge would declare bankruptcy and with bankruptcy there would no longer be the possibility to shoot inside it."[21]

The production rented the building from the court and hired Falconi workers and students as extras. Paradoxically, the unemployed laborers became extras in a film about their issues and struggles, and, as Pirro noticed, they would have to "pretend to do what they had been doing for a living, and repeat the same gestures of a whole lifetime, without producing anything." On top of that, the plant did not have an assembly line, and art director Dante Ferretti had to build a prop. "Cinema turns fake into plausible," the script-writer quipped.[22]

With the exception of Volonté and Salvo Randone (once again in a minor but key role, as Militina, an elderly worker gone crazy), the cast featured little-known stage actors. Mariangela Melato had been only in a handful of movies, such as Zampa's *Contestazione generale*, Marco Vicario's *Il prete sposato* and Pupi Avati's supernatural drama *Thomas … gli indemoniati* (all 1970). It was musician Lino Patruno who recommended her to the director for the role of Lulù's lover, Lidia: "One day I accompanied my friend Gian Maria Volonté to Novara, and Elio Petri asked me: 'Since you do theater, could you name an actress who speaks Milanese dialect?' and I: 'Mariangela Melato, she's 100% Milanese.' And a few days later she was called on the set."[23] Petri had already cast another actress from the Piccolo Teatro in Milan, Liliana Zoboli, but as soon as he saw Melato he realized she was perfect. Melato arrived in Novara one cold winter morning and found the crew amassed in a bedroom around a bed with a man in it. It was Volonté. Petri told her to get in the bed in her nightgown and join her partner beneath the sheets for the scene. Mariangela's feet and hands were ice cold, and the actor flinched. "Sorry, Mr. Volonté," she apologized. The actor's curt reply was: "Forget the 'Mr.' No problem, let's go on." At the end of the first take Petri told the crew: "Ok, print this, see you tomorrow!"[24] To Melato, it was the beginning of an exciting, if exhausting, adventure:

> At that time I was in a stage play in Rome, doing *Alleluia brava gente* at the Sistina Theater, and so I had to travel back and forth all the time: during the day I was on the set and in the evening I had to be back in time for the show. And it was like hell, but a wonderful one, because Elio was such a great artist. Besides his extraordinary skills as a director I was struck by his ability as an editor. He would edit bits of film that he had just shot in a brilliant manner. He became one of my dearest friends.[25]

Luigi Diberti was an ex-FIAT worker turned actor, who had been in Luca Ronconi's groundbreaking stage play *Orlando Furioso* alongside Melato and had made his film debut in *I visionari* (1968) directed by none other than *A ciascuno il suo*'s staunchest enemy, Maurizio Ponzi. But there were other talented beginners in the cast. The 21-year-old Corrado Solari, as the Maoist saboteur, impressed production manager Claudio Mancini, who suggested to Sergio Leone to cast him in *Giù la testa* (1971) as one of Rod Steiger's family. Solari would turn up as the killer in *Sbatti il mostro in prima pagina* (1972, Marco Bellocchio) and in several *poliziotteschi*, usually in villain roles. Last but not least, the debuting Flavio Bucci was taking his first steps on screen thanks to Gian Maria Volonté. Bucci had paid him a visit as soon as he arrived in Rome from his hometown Turin:

> I went to Gian Maria's place in Vicolo del Moro, in the Trastevere district. Without a word, he took me to Botteghe Oscure, to join the [Communist] Party. Then, a little later, we found ourselves together at the assembly line…. "*Er capoccione*," Big Head, that's what they called Petri in the movie business. Small body and big head, bursting with ideas. He was like a second father to me. But, oh, did he beat me. If he saw you tired or listless on the set, he filled you with punches and curses. He even beat Volonté, who was crazier and bigger than him.[26]

The crew stayed in Novara for a couple of months. True to his commitment, Volonté convinced the others to take part in local rallies, namely a vigil of protest on New Year's Eve outside the penitentiary of the nearby town of Verbania, where two union activists had been detained for eighty days,[27] and the occupation of the Novara city hall on

January 9. Newspapers followed the shoot with a mixture of curiosity and perplexity and interviewed local people in the hope of learning more about the film, whose plot was still a secret. The caretaker at Falconi told the *Corriere d'Informazione* that Petri and his crew "showed up early in the morning, with two or three trucks with all their equipment and got on to work immediately, with few words. They were dressed like the real factory workers … many of whom earned a few *lire* as extras, which is convenient in such a difficult time. Once they forgot the script here, and I gave it a read at night. It's all about work, there is no drama."[28]

Most of the drama actually took place off-screen. Unlike *Indagine*, the filming was very turbulent. As Marina Cicogna recalled, "I got angry with all of them, a little less with Elio because he was milder than Pirro and Volonté. The film became a sort of political manifesto … each word was put on the balance to assess whether it was purist or not."[29] Even though Volonté would later call Petri "the director who has the least hierarchical conception of cinematic work, and the one who establishes the best dialectic relations with all of his crew members," turning a movie into "a collective effort where everyone contributes ideas,"[30] his own attitude on set was often polemic and antagonistic. Pirro later claimed that he had insisted that the film be engrossing and enthralling during the scriptwriting sessions,[31] but Volonté was an orthodox member of the Communist Party, and his political commitment extended to the way his character should speak and act on the set.

Due partly to the aforementioned timing issues, the second half of the script had been left "open" and was constantly revised on the set. Scenes were written in large part the evening before shooting them, leaving room for last-minute changes. This resulted in frequent clashes between Volonté, Petri and Pirro. Once, the actor even threatened to leave the set because of some lines of dialogue, namely the slogan "Lotta dura senza paura" (Hard Fight Without Fright) which the workers would yell in a scene. Volonté objected that the slogan belonged to the leftist extra-parliamentary group Lotta Continua, not to the PCI. A small uprising ensued. On another occasion, Volonté and Pirro almost got into a fight at dinner, and the actor accused the scriptwriter of making a film against the Communist Party. Pirro replied by threatening to hit him on the head with a hammer.[32]

Conversely, Volonté got along very well with the other actors. Luigi Diberti recalled how he behaved fraternally with his colleagues and was always prodigal with advice, without egoism. One such example was a sex scene between Volonté and first-time actress Mietta Albertini, who played Adalgisa. She was very nervous, and Volonté, who didn't like shooting love scenes either, had the idea of having it take place in a car instead of a hotel room, to highlight both characters' discomfort. Even the ending was left open until the last minute. According to Marina Cicogna, Petri shot three different versions but eventually chose the one that seemed the more plausible from the start.[33]

By February 1971, when the crew left Novara, newspapers reported the title as being either *La classe operaia va in vacanza* (The Working Class Goes on Vacation)[34] and *Operai in paradiso*.[35] But, as shown by on-set pictures portraying the clapboard, the shooting title had always been *La classe operaia va in paradiso* since the beginning. According to Pirro, it was inspired by a Soviet film released in Italy as *L'Armata Rossa va in paradiso*,[36] but there appears to be no movie with such a title.

In a late March interview, conducted while he was still busy working on the interior shooting, the director labeled his new movie as "a triple somersault." Noting that

Elio Petri (left) and actor Donato Castellaneta (right) on the set of *La classe operaia va in paradiso*.

"the factory and the factory workers are emblematic cases who represent us all, because all of us have the problem of production, even intellectuals," Petri explained: "I schematically identified two driving currents among the forces acting in today's history—a utopian and a mediating one. The protagonist is divided between this typical schematization of modern life: utopia—that is, revolutionary change, 'everything right away'—and mediation, that is, gradual change." The director quoted Karl Marx: "To be radical is to grasp things by the root. And the root of man is man himself. Radical political cinema cannot but focus on the root of things, and therefore of man. Workers are the human root of society, an example of the human condition." But Petri was well aware of the risk that his discourse might become intellectualistic and elitist. "A political film must be made in a popular form; it must have the maximum communication. Therefore, the triple somersault consists in telling a hard story in a popular form. Maybe with this triple somersault I'm going to break my back."[37]

Oscar ... and Edgar

Petri's fears would soon be soothed. *Indagine* had been distributed overseas by the end of 1970 as *Investigation of a Citizen Above Suspicion* and premiered in New York City on December 20, while it opened in Los Angeles in February 1971. Critical reception was mixed. Judith Crist, in *New York*, hailed it as "a stunning Kafkaesque political thriller,"[38] while *Show* called it, rather puzzlingly, "Petri's latest in a series of futuristic films about the present" but judged it his "most interesting picture to date ... although decidedly inferior to Costa-Gavras' *The Confession* ... some of the contrivances are facile and annoying, and the camera work is a trifle hyperactive, but the philosophical insinuations are absorbing and certain liberal stances are gorgeously mocked."[39] On the other hand, the noted Stanley Kauffmann panned it in *The New Republic*:

> That picture with the long title arrives from Italy decorated with several prizes and an epigraph from Kafka. They don't help. *Investigation* makes strenuous efforts at allegorical resonance, but is fuzzy throughout and finally fizzles.... The symbols are vivid and promising, but, as is often the case with allegory, they arrest more immediate attention than they finally justify.

Kauffmann criticized the film's theme of sexuality related to politics, arguing that "it sinks the symbolic ship.... It is one subject to show the magical effect of allegory; it is quite another to show power as a substitute for sexual potency." He also slammed the direction and acting:

> Elio Petri ... has become a man of flash and filigree. Some of his early work had simple, direct address, but the same curious thing has happened to him that has happened to two other Italian directors who, like Petri, are political radicals, Pasolini and Bertolucci: they have all moved from concerned art to arty concerns. Petri's last previous film, *A Quiet Place in the Country*, was as sterile a farrago of audio-visual smartness as *Performance*.... Here there are still traces of psychedelic whoring, but in addition, almost every sequence is lacquered with obtrusive egocentric pride in the way it looks.... And the performance of the inspector, by Gian Maria Volonté, is in quite the wrong vein. He is strident and vulgar, with no conviction of the cold pseudo-Nietzschean mind that would concoct such a scheme, with no steel edge in his tone. The part needed Mastroianni or Gabriele Ferzetti ... or Massimo Girotti. Volonté is just a coarse, bullying cop, and he helps a lot to put the picture at a far remove, where we see what was intended but what does not arrive.[40]

Reviews like this give an idea of the way Italian cinema was not only known superficially, but often misunderstood in its essence, as the mention of the director's early films and the comparison with Pasolini and Bertolucci reveal.

If Kauffmann at least made his point clear, albeit debatable, *Films in Review* was downright obtuse. Besides calling it "badly written, acted and directed," the anonymous reviewer not only completely missed the point of the film, but added insult to injury noting that "*every* political party or faction likes to allege the security chief of its opposition is a kook or worse, and this film milks that propaganda ploy with a fervor that may delight Italian workers-&-peasants but will make the politically sophisticated smile." If this bit of patronizing were not enough, the politically sophisticated author added: "Signor Petri ... is said to be a Communist—of what stripe it's impossible to tell from his film. Stalinist, pre–Stalinist, post–Stalinist, Trotskyite, Maoist? My guess is he takes his ideological light-&-leading from whatever faction is currently in the saddle of the Italian Communist Party."[41]

Still, the film made an impression overseas, no doubt due to Columbia's clever marketing in addition to its growing international resonance. On March 6, 1971, the President of the Academy of Motion Pictures Daniel Taradash sent Petri a telegram communicating that *Indagine* was among the five titles nominated for the Foreign Language Film Award.[42] The ceremony took place on April 16, 1971, and *Indagine* won the Academy Award for Best Foreign Film. It was a bold choice on the part of the Academy, but Petri was well aware of the ambiguity of his position. On the one hand he was on top of the world; on the other, he was dangerously exposed to political attacks from those who took this victory as proof that his film was a commercial compromise.

Winning an Oscar … might cast shadows even on a film such as *Indagine*, which has been recognized as a bold denunciation of a certain type of society…. Evidently the facts narrated by *Indagine* are shared by a large part of American society…. And we mustn't forget that the Oscar jury members, even though they are conditioned in the choice of the films to be awarded by a thousand political and commercial reasons, have always had a very different attitude when assigning prizes to foreign films … and have always tried to choose avant-garde, intransigent films.[43]

The director received the news while in Rome, and so did Marina Cicogna, who had underestimated the chances of the film. When the plane tickets and the invitation for the ceremony had arrived, Elio had decided not to go, without hesitation, despite Paola's attempts to change his mind. He told her that he would never win anyway. And so, on that night, it was French actress Leslie Caron, who had absolutely nothing to do with *Indagine*, who took to the stage and received the statue for Best Foreign Film. Petri celebrated in Cinecittà, where he was finishing post-production for *La classe operaia*. "Go get three bottles of sparkling wine," he told Claudio Mancini, who recalled: "We sat at a table and made a toast. And that was that…. He didn't like all that publicity."[44]

The winning season was not over yet. In July *Indagine* won the Silver Ribbon for Best Film and Best Actor, and the following month it was awarded a special prize at the Moscow Film Festival, won by Damiani's *Confessione*. But according to those who knew him, the prize Elio cherished the most was the 1971 Edgar Allan Poe Award for Best Motion Picture Screenplay. For a passionate mystery reader like him, it was a career high point.

"Burn this film!"

La classe operaia was submitted to the rating board on September 7, 1971. At first the censors asked Petri to trim

Paola Pegoraro Petri and Elio Petri in the garden of their home. This promotional pic was distributed to the press after the news of *Indagine su un cittadino al di sopra di ogni sospetto* winning the Oscar for Best Foreign Film.

severely the sex scene between Lulù and Adalgisa, namely the part starting from Lulù's line "È finita" (It's over). The director refused, and the commission gave the film a V.M.18 rating, with a detailed yet blatantly specious motivation centered on foul language (namely, Lulù's line "Paradise is here," referred to Adalgisa's vagina). The production appealed and on September 30 the Appeal Board changed the rating to a V.M.14.

Petri and Pirro previewed the film to the central committee of the FIOM, the metal workers' union, to lukewarm response. None in the audience seemed ready to deal with the issues it raised, and the screening was followed by a brief and awkward debate.[45]

The events of 1968 had had strong repercussions on Italy's most important film event, the Venice Film Festival. The many protests during that year's edition led to the decision to abolish all prizes: from 1969 to 1979 the Mostra del Cinema was a non-competitive event as it had been in its first edition in 1932. But the decision to extend the commissarial management of the Biennale provoked many complaints against the Statute, which dated back to the Fascist era, and which "even the blindest have judged authoritarian, patronizing and bureaucratic."[46]

In 1971 Gian Luigi Rondi (affiliated with the DC since 1948 and a longtime friend of Giulio Andreotti) was designated vice-commissioner of the Biennale, against the unions' advice. Rondi formed a committee of experts which included noted directors (Blasetti, De Sica, Fellini, Visconti, Zeffirelli, Zurlini) and critics (among them Tommaso Chiaretti), in the aim of giving life to what he himself called an "emergency edition" of the Festival. But the associations of authors, ANAC and AACI, confirmed their "non-collaboration" in order to solicit a new Statute. Some, like Marco Ferreri, suggested that a strike of film workers be proclaimed during the Festival. Even though he was on good terms with Rondi, Petri agreed to sign a "non-collaboration" document, together with many other filmmakers—including Ferreri, the Taviani brothers, Bellocchio, Cavani, Giraldi, Loy, and Maselli—in which they stated that their works would not take part in the next edition of the Festival.

As a protest gesture, Petri allowed *La classe operaia* to be screened as the closing event at the 6th "Mostra internazionale del cinema libero" (International Exposition of Free Cinema) in Porretta Terme, near Bologna, in October. On that occasion, he argued with Luchino Visconti, who had sided with Rondi as member of the experts committee for the Venice Film Festival: "Visconti said that he would like to speak with me, that I'm a 'good fellow,' but he cannot because he doesn't have time. But he should find some of his precious time and come to Porretta, and see how a new festival can be made, full of hundreds of 'good fellows' like me and even better than me, since I'm already a middle-aged man." In praising the refusal of "eccentricity, rituals and prima donna behavior" as opposed to Venice's commercial attitude, he added: "The authors who deserted Venice did it exactly because Venice on the one hand, and Porretta and Pesaro on the other, stand for two different ways of conceiving society and cinema."[47] Visconti's reply: "I always held Elio in esteem and admired him, many times I proved my friendship and appreciated his work. If now he prefers the Porretta Festival to the others, let him stick to Porretta and I'll stick to Venice and Moscow, Cannes and Berlin. Fact is, what Elio Petri wants to teach me, I've known a long time before him."[48]

The argument between Petri and Visconti—himself a communist who had experienced first-hand censorship and commercial setbacks—is significant of the debate among Italian directors in post–1968 cinema. Whereas Petri was widely labeled as the champion of political filmmaking, a definition which included such diverse names as Maselli,

Cavani, Rosi and Damiani, others were perplexed about this new tendency. "I'm not convinced by this crude way of facing issues outside any expressive research," Michelangelo Antonioni argued. "Early Russian classics were first and foremost extraordinary films in this respect. Today, on the contrary, the superficial violence of political cinema's impact, instead of undermining bourgeois consciences, absolves them."[49]

It had been a bad, stressful summer for Petri, as he confided to his friend Marco Ferronato,[50] and the Porretta events did not make it better. The screening of *La classe operaia* was followed by a heated debate, and the film was contested by both the far-left trade unionists and the avant-garde militant cineastes. Jean-Marie Straub took the microphone and yelled that all the copies of the film must be burned, because it was a reactionary work.[51]

"I remember it as if it was now," Petri wrote seven years later,

> because Straub's words were so painful to me. They made me wonder if from his point of view an artist like Straub could be right, and that indeed somebody could find that way of making movies absolutely despicable. But the fanaticism that exuded from Straub's words and ideas, and even from the grim and upset expression on his face and his livid complexion ... and the stupid intolerance of his desire of burning ... soon cured my doubts. I thought that if my film had in itself something that could offend such a fanatic, a Swiss chalet Calvinist, it was certainly something anti-fanatic and anti-intolerant. Bad, if you like, but positive.[52]

A Tool Named Lulù

To quote film historian Lino Micciché,

> In Italian cinema, which nonetheless has a traditionally left-wing political view, the working class is the great absentee. After the intense Neorealist years, when it was often depicted as "the people" and class analysis was almost always replaced by populist summary (Visconti's *La terra trema* being one of the few exceptions) it disappeared from the screen.... *La classe operaia va in paradiso* is therefore virtually the first wide-ranging film which brings to the screen the factory workers, seen within the class struggle. And it sets the story in the heart of this conflict: the factory. An absolute first time in Italian cinema, and not only that.[53]

As Petri told Jean A. Gili, he made the film because he wanted to "tear down certain barriers which relegated collectivity to the borders of *auteur* films. The folk had quite simply disappeared from the screen or were used as the starting point for light dialectal comedies. That humorous aspect, although it derives from the Italian popular tradition, eventually cancelled the simple historical facts because of the absence ... of class conscience."[54]

In the mid–1950s, filmmakers such as Germi and Antonioni had put workers at the center of their films—*Il ferroviere* (1956) and *L'uomo di paglia* (1958); and *Il grido* (1957), respectively—but chose an existentialist perspective instead of focusing on the relationship between factory work and private life. Whereas other works, such as Mario Monicelli's *Renzo e Luciana* (from the anthology *Boccaccio '70*, 1962) filtered the discourse through a comedy angle. Direct antecedents of *La classe operaia* can be traced back to Visconti's *Rocco e i suoi fratelli*, Monicelli's *I compagni*, and Ugo Gregoretti's *I nuovi angeli* (1962) and *Omicron*. But Petri's film bypasses every social and historical discourse, unlike Visconti and Monicelli (*I compagni* focused on late 1800s factory strikes) and sticks to reality without any genre travesty, unlike Gregoretti's sci-fi apologue. *I nuovi angeli*—an anthology comedy in a fake inquiry style which includes a brief episode set in a Milanese plant and centered on assembly lines, pieceworking and timekeeping—is the closest to Petri's film, but reduces its discourse on the alienation of factory workers to a handful of minutes.

At the same time, though, Petri rejected the idea of making an idealized portrait of the factory worker. In particular, he pointed out to have

> put aside all Soviet iconography, all the trappings of socialist realism usually invoked in films about workers, and any attempt to propagandize. The main character is split into many parts—as we all are—and he has only a partial understanding of what is happening. Within him are all the forces that exist outside of him, he is made up of them. Inside the main character all the other characters are present. He is all these things at the same time: a Stakhanovist, a slave to the boss, interested in production for its own sake, a TV watcher, an anarchist, middle class, a revolutionary, a trade unionist—as we all are.[55]

The film starts with a close-up of Lulù, waking in the middle of the night in a sweat after a bad dream. He looks around, and through his eyes we see his bedroom, filled with cheap embellishments such as the pennant of a football team, a plush toy, and a kitschy ornamental gondola. It is an ordinary bedroom, for a man who has no interests in life, no education, and no aesthetic taste. The alarm clock sounds at 6:30 a.m. and Lulù, far from reinvigorated, is nervous and moody. "It's the cranium," he complains. He is so affected by his condition that he thinks of his own body as a plant, as he tells his partner Lidia and her son Arturo:

> In the brain there is the central headquarters, it decides, makes projects, programs, and gives the go-ahead to production … man lines up and sets in motion … arms, legs, mouth, eyes, tongue, everything … it starts to move until … it takes up food, which is the raw material. One: man works in order to eat. The food goes down, here is the machine that crunches it, and it's ready for exit. The same as in a factory. Man and factory are the same! A factory that produces shit! … Imagine if it had a price … everyone nice and happy with their assured income … instead they don't know where to put it … it pollutes waters, smells … and you, Arturo, you'll be forced to eat it when you're a man.

Lulù's opening monologue touches a recurring theme in Italian cinema of the period. Excrement as symbol for goods turns up in lines of dialogue which are often indebted to that in Petri's film, albeit with a more blatant humorous vein. On the one hand we have the nihilistic wisdom of Rambo (Tomas Milian), who in *Il giustiziere sfida la città* (1975, Umberto Lenzi) philosophizes "Life's a hole: we are born from a hole, eat from a hole, shit from a hole and end up in a hole," and the proletarian rage of Sergio Marazzi "er Monnezza" (also Milian) in *La banda del gobbo* (1977, also by Lenzi): "You bet that the day shit becomes gold, we poor fellas will be born without an asshole?!" On the other, we have the harrowing "Circle of Shit" in *Salò o le 120 giornate di Sodoma* (1975) and the graphic excesses of *Blue Movie*, where the nihilistic mockery of consumerism's "product for use" urgency and the exploitation of the working classes takes on provocatively, paradoxical forms.[56]

In *La classe operaia*, the metaphor of man as a "shit factory" is at the service of Lulù's inner turmoil and his growing dissatisfaction which he nonetheless accepts, for he cannot conceive a different way to live except competition with his fellow workers. "Everyone's on the racing track, we're all running here … there's not much else to do here. Since we have to work, let's work," he says. And when his colleague Bassi (Luigi Diberti) tells him he's going to die on the machine, he replies. "What difference does it make?" Not by chance, Lulù's surname is Massa, a blatant reference to Tronti's theory of the "*operaio massa.*"

And yet, Lulù Massa is not the mirror image of the "*operaio massa*" as described by Tronti. Petri and Pirro rebuffed the latter's idealistic, apologetic approach, which resulted in the workers being depicted as a modern-day version of Jean-Jacques Rousseau's "noble savage." "In my opinion, to make a film about a factory worker is like making a film about any other human being. Whereas back then—and still today—the factory worker was considered a saint, a martyr,"[57] Petri later argued. In fact, Lulù is far from being a likeable character. He is shabby, sweaty, grumpy, illiterate, and immature. He labels Southerners as "Africans," is unsympathetic to his fellow workers (who in turn despise him), and an ass-kisser with the employers. As he himself admits, "I'm already in another world. Think only about the piece, the rest doesn't matter."

"No way of fixing it!"

Lulù's inner split is best exemplified by the sudden cut from the close-ups of him at work, frenetically operating the machine, and his spent, dull expression at home, in front of his TV set. In his free time, away from the plant, he is lost, an empty carcass of a man. The accident at work takes place after his fellow workers have provoked Lulù. Blinded by rage, he loses control of his pitch-perfect productive rhythm and his finger is amputated (off-screen) by the machinery. The event puts in motion an inner reaction which has Lulù move from childish self-pity to rage and eventually to the first glimpses of self-consciousness, as the symptoms of his illness—such as his obsessive attention to lining up the cutlery—become evident to him as well.

To emphasize Lulù's state, Petri and Pirro concocted a dialectical contrast between him and an elderly worker, Militina, who ended up in a mental hospital and is fully aware of his situation. By confronting Militina, it is as if Lulù is confronting his inner self. For one thing, it is Militina who makes Lulù aware that he doesn't even know what he is producing.

Lulù's encounter with Militina pushes the symbolic and metaphysical elements to the extreme. The fool is a figure reminiscent of Italian popular theater and literature since the Middle Ages, the depositary of truth hidden behind the shield of lunacy. Militina can also be seen as an elder version of *I giorni contati*'s Cesare, not least because he is played by the same actor. But he's not a pathetic figure: dressed in raw wool, unshaven, his eyes spirited, he is a living nightmare. Cesare's dumbfounded reaction to the awareness of his own mortality has given room to a demented wisdom. "It's others who decide when one should become mad ... but I fooled them," he tells Lulù. His madness was born out of an act of rebellion:

> I met the engineer, I grabbed him by the collar and said: "What the hell are we making in this factory ... what the hell is this shit for?" ... If they didn't take me away, I would really have strangled him. But this, Lulù, is not madness, because a man, a man had the right to know what he's doing, what it's for...

Madness is the only way one can escape his predetermined role. It is a revolutionary gesture in a society based on conformity. As Petri underlined, Militina "is the true revolutionary, for he understood that there is something, not only outside but inside our heads as well, to tear down."[58] In fact, Militina is reading Raffaello Giovagnoli's novel *Spartaco*, about the revolutionary slave who rebelled against his masters, exalted by the PCI (a novelization of Giovagnoli's novel was released in the party's weekly magazine *Vie nuove* in 1952), and tears off pages from it. Lulù has brought him "that little book you asked me about," Mao Tse-tung's *Little Red Book*.

Militina tries to explain to Lulù that their alienation has a dual nature, for it doesn't just relate to factory work, but to the products of his work as well. The market dictates the rules, and everybody, rich and poor alike, employers and employees, "owners and slaves," are subject to it.

> You see them? You see all those over there? They were all workers, peasants, unskilled laborers, builders, policemen, land office employees, gravediggers, accountants, attendants, drivers, 1st, 2nd, 3rd class workers, even 6th, 8th and 16th ... the rich crazies are not here, they're hidden in private clinics. Of course, it's understandable—just imagine if poor people realized that even the rich go crazy! It would make them cry, wouldn't it? ... Lulù, it's the money, it all starts there ... we're part of the same group, owners and slaves. Money, *l'argent*.... We become mad because we have too little, and they because they have too much. And so, in this hell, on this planet full of hospitals, lunatic asylums, cemeteries, factories, barracks and buses, the brain slowly runs away. It goes on strike....

As Militina argues, the factory and the asylum are one and the same, "only that at night they don't let me out." When Lulù asks him how he realized he was going crazy, the elderly man explains that at home he started dreaming he was in the factory, and put the cutlery "straight, in line, you know, like soldiers," exactly like Lulù does. Later in the film, the factory psychiatrist who visits Lulù—and who is more concerned about the latter's prowess at work than his mental health—shows the same symptoms. Lulù chuckles at the sight: Militina was right after all, and madness is spreading throughout. As Militina explains to Lulù while pointing at the other inmates (who in turn keep singing restlessly the same jingles Lulù is fed by TV every evening), alienation is a mandatory condition in today's society. Moreover, it is society's purpose to produce alienated citizens. When Lulù goes to pick up Arturo at school he tells him, "You all look like little factory workers," and the camera pans along the school gate exactly as it does along the factory fences.

Lulù's rebellion, it must be pointed out, does not come from political awareness but from existential anguish. He has realized he is going crazy and must do something about it. This results first in his opposition to the factory rules he once dutifully followed, by keeping a deliberately slow production rhythm and then in his challenging attitude during the interview with the psychiatrist. Another confrontational encounter with a student significantly nicknamed "Carlo Marx" turns out to be the last straw.

The students are a constant presence outside the plant. They distribute leaflets which the workers throw away, and they keep shouting their slogans on the megaphone to what seems a deaf crowd: "Comrades, it's eight in the morning. When you will come out it will already be dark. Today the sun won't shine for you!" Incidentally, their slogans such as "More income, less work!" are those typical of Potere Operaio. But Lulù is deaf, even intolerant to all this. It is only when the student asks him, "What is this, life? Is this life?" that he finally starts to realize his state.

All this climaxes in Lulù's impromptu speech to his fellow workers, which crowns him as their new leader, and in him leading a small minority of workers to strike, *de facto* breaking the union unity. Once an extremist of production, he becomes an extremist of revolution, as the director quipped.[59] Lulù picks up from the words of "Carlo Marx" and, in a mixture of sarcasm and desperation, pictures the same concept of life as hell he has learned from Militina:

> I don't know what to call you—workmen, comrades, workers ... the student, the student out-side said that we come in when it's dark and leave when it's dark. What sort of life is ours? Whilst we're at it, why don't we double the piecework? Huh? Then we can work on Sunday too, maybe we could work throughout the night. Actually, maybe we could bring in our children and wives.... We force the children to work whilst our wives stuff a sandwich in our mouths, and we just go on and on without a break, on and on! We go on for these four damn *lire*, until we die! And so, from this hell, always with no break, we pass directly to that other hell, which is the same thing anyway.

The speech ends with Lulù finally admitting what he has become—a machine—and screaming out his alienation. "I am a pulley, I am a bolt, a screw, I am a transmission belt, I am a pump! But now this pump is broken and there's no way of fixing it!"

Sex and the Machine

Once again in Petri's cinema, neurosis takes on a sexual form as well. At home, Lulù is too spent to make love to Lidia. "Do you think I have a machine between my legs?" he justifies himself, unconsciously hinting to his alienated state: after all he has become a machine. His reaction to her complaints is violent and childish, showing his sexual immaturity. At one point he even threatens to stick a fork in her belly and she replies it is the only thing he would be able to stick in her, a moment which evokes the scene in *Peccato nel pomeriggio* where Laura complained that women are not steaks in which to stick a knife. But Lulù also seeks comfort with her like a child, crying about his fellow work-ers' contempt for him. In turn, after he has lost his finger, Lidia behaves as a mother con-soling her little son.

Lulù sublimates his frustrated sex drive in his working ambience and manages to achieve a tireless, pitch-perfect working rhythm by concentrating on a fellow female worker's bum. He is not the only one, though. Another worker has a poster of a naked woman taped on his piece of machinery. Productivity has become a surrogate for orgasm, and not by chance the plant manager tells the workers to "treat the machine you have been given with love. Take care of it." The camera shows the workers' hands caressing the steel metal surface of the machineries as if they were female bodies, and one cannot help but think of drill sergeant Hartman having the marines give their rifle their girlfriend's name in *Full Metal Jacket* (1987). "All the repressions of our childhood are used by soci-ety to make us into instruments of production," Petri explained, referring to Wilhelm Reich's theories on the link between sexuality and politics. "When a worker is a slave to a machine, his sexuality is being employed in the rhythm of production."[60]

Whereas the amputation of the forefinger has a Freudian significance to it, being comparable to castration, as Lulù himself acknowledges with the psychiatrist, his rebel-lion against the system has the side effect of stirring up his dormant libido. His voice changes too, becoming deeper, as if the accident has awakened another him (Volo-nté acknowledged it was Petri's idea). But Lulù's awkward sex encounter with Adal-gisa, his young colleague whose bum was his fixed idea while piece working, is depicted with pungent irony. It takes place in Lulù's small Fiat runabout, inside an abandoned plant, in snowy mid-winter, and is one of the clumsiest and least erotic sex scenes in cinema history, and all the more realistic and punchier for that. Adalgisa is a virgin, she is scared, and she has no clue on how to move during sex. He tries to teach her, the way he would operate machinery. But their physical chemistry is non-existent, their movements are uncoordinated, and inside the car it's so cold that they drink whisky to warm up. Her dirty foot pushes against the windshield, he fills his mouth with her hair, their bodies bump into each other and into the car's parts—the steering wheel, the gear shift, the handbrake. They are like two workers who cannot achieve the right productive rhythm. Mietta Albertini recalled that Petri gave her and Volonté different instruction for the scene, unbeknownst to each other, so as to heighten the sense of unease and embarrassment.

When it's over, both get dressed in a hurry, clinching their teeth from the cold. Lulù boasts about his car ("I've had it for a year, but I still look at it"), Adalgisa complains she hasn't felt anything. "Is this love?" she asks. Lulù replies that women start "feeling something" when they turn thirty. "You should even pay me for this job," he concludes.

Far from being played just for laughs, the scene is a bitter observation on the state of human relationships in a capitalist society, where the working methods are perfected to the best of productivity but the basic mechanics of sex are still primitive and often unsatisfying, not to mention exploitative. "Women are the basis of the social pyramid," Petri noted. "They are the objects of both sexual and economic exploitation."[61] Adalgisa is aware of her condition, whereas Lidia, the hairdresser who proclaims she will never be a communist ("because I'm for freedom") and votes for the DC, is not. She molds her identity through the different wigs she wears throughout the movie, for she too is a victim of a society that imposes predetermined female models (Lulù calls her "tinned meat" at one point) and status symbols such as the mink coat she yearns for. Lidia's surrendering to the consumerist values is similar to Ada's in *Il maestro di Vigevano*, for here as well the working class lives in misery but imitates its exploiter. As Melato observed, "the character was unpleasant, but I think I gave it a twist, and turned this dumb hairdresser who wants her mink coat into a rather understandable and humane figure."[62]

"*Picture of a clown … 10 hours' work*"

In Gian Maria Volonté's extraordinary incarnation, Lulù becomes a tragic clown, a modern-day version of the factory worker in *Modern Times*, whose mimicry he evokes in his tireless, obtuse movements at work. As with *Indagine*, the use of language is crucial. The Sicilian accent and syntactical structure of the previous film here give way to a mixture of strong Lombard accent and dialectal phrases and terms which allowed Petri to achieve what he hadn't managed to on *Il maestro di Vigevano*. As the director put it, Lulù is "someone who can no longer speak dialect but doesn't yet speak Italian well."[63]

The actor's meticulous work on his voice and accent is an added value to the character, and his tone sometimes gets close to falsetto, like that of a geld. Volonté claimed it was his favorite film because of the "very fruitful relationship of collaboration and dialectic exchange,"[64] although, according to Claudio Mancini, Petri was not always satisfied with some of his lead actor's nuances: "One day there was an argument: 'Don't act like Sordi!'"[65] In its virtuoso handling of the whole emotional spectrum, Volonté's depiction of Lulù is truly one of the most memorable performances in Italian cinema, and even more so if one compares it to the actor's equally strong but completely different portrayal of

Enrico Mattei in Francesco Rosi's *Il caso Mattei* (1972), which gives an idea of the astonishing complexity of Volonté's acting.

Given Petri's claim that "Inside the main character all the other characters are present," it is no surprise that the coworkers are just briefly sketched, sometimes even nameless. Still, the film presents various worker types, and all quite believable. The most notable one is Bassi, who lives with Lulù's ex-wife and child. He helped create the union in the factory but now stands powerless against the more violent protesters. But there are also a couple of timekeepers (the freaky-looking Guerrino Crivello and Ezio Marano) who are contemptuously called "leeches" by the others, for their duty is to control and increase productivity, regardless of anything else.

The factory owner is patently a self-made man who still speaks in dialect and presents himself as a benevolent patriarchal figure. He evokes the "spirit of collaboration between us which had made our factory a jewel, in which the interests of the workers and capital are combined." The reference to "*our* factory" (echoing the principal's use of "we" in *Il maestro di Vigevano*) is a rhetorical artifice that harks back to early capitalism, when the owner presented himself as a worker and was perceived as such.

Petri purportedly depicted both the students and the unionists as schematic. "It's a sector of the Left which is also a sector of our conscience: the former represent all and everything, the latter represent good sense. Both forces are virtually symbolic of our mental construction; but they should, I believe, put in motion a dialectic process between them."[66]

The depiction of the contradictions within the Left caused many arguments. The union trade representative (Gino Pernice) relies on the standard answers his party has conceived for the workers and is afraid of taking stances on his own. But—just as the young protesters in *Indagine* looked unappealing and ineffectual—the students come out as windbags, abstractly intellectual and detached from everyday issues. Their attempt to raise the workers' awareness and join forces against the employers is sincere, as is their analysis of "the average proletarian" who is "exploited in the factory but models himself on the examples given to him on television, newspapers, cinema." But this is all too obviously coming from someone who belongs to a totally different world. The gap between their revolutionary slogans and impenetrable reasoning and the workers' raw existential drama is patent. As Lulù tells Lidia, "If you heard how they talk … you won't understand a word!" The students push the laborers to rebellion, but after Lulù is fired they abandon him to his destiny: to them, it's the working class that matters, not the individual worker. When Lulù, desperate after being fired, goes to look for the bearded student who called him a slave and opened his eyes, and asks him what he has to do now, the other replies:

> I don't care. Do whatever you like. There are a thousand ways to live…. Stay here with us. Now you're unemployed, you can do what you like. Anyway, you can always find something to eat…. If you feel like it, you can even be a full-time activist!

Once jobless, Lulù finds out he has no longer a place in the capitalist chain. He is no longer a productive individual nor an active consumer. He has lost his identity. Not even Militina can soothe his desperation. Lulù's second visit to the lunatic asylum brings the consciousness that his attempt to escape his condition has proven vain. "If you want to become mad, believe me, you have to return to the factory. I became mad in the factory!" Militina jokes. Then, in a gesture whose meaning will become clear only in the final scene, the elderly man vainly attempts to break down a wall.

Alone in his flat, desperate, Lulù makes an inventory of the many useless items he purchased thanks to his Stakhanovism in the hope of selling them:

Dark small table with foreign stamp, 30 hours' work ... 5,000 *lire*. Picture of a clown, 10 hours' work ... 24,000 *lire*. Puppets ... 5,000. Radio and book, *I promessi sposi* ... 10,000 in Switzerland, 15,000 in Milan.... Crystal vase with plastic ... 2,000 lire. This one even brings bad luck. Various animals ... prizes.... If I meet that guy who had the idea to make all this stuff.... Wizard in the kitchen opens cans ... prepares mayonnaise ... sharpens knives.... Four alarm clocks? Who knows why?

The worthless riches of the working class are like the colored beads the early pioneers gave the Indians. Rarely has the horror of induced needs been displayed with such lucid precision.

Frustrated and impotent, Lulù gives vent to his rage against an inflatable Scrooge McDuck doll. His pathetic fury against the doll, which ends with the latter deflating, leads to an illusory but useless victory against a symbolic enemy, but it also hints at the man's utter powerlessness. Devoid of his job, of his only aim in life, Lulù himself has become a deflated doll.

"If there's a wall to knock down we knock it down!"

In commenting on the film's structure, Petri explained:

Alienation is a void, the absence of a whole fragment of our personality; through schizophrenia we can put into movement, both inside and outside ourselves, a series of fragments and organize a debate inside us. It is what I sought to express with *La classe operaia va in paradiso* ... there is a unity that breaks and recomposes into another unity, which in turn splits into several other unities which then meet up. The film is like that until the end when unity is found, but in slavery.[67]

In fact, the film provides only an illusion of a happy ending. Lidia comes back to live with Lulù, and he is hired again thanks to the union. But when his fellow workers show up at his flat to tell him he can return to work, he looks stunned. "To him it is like the announcement of a friend's death."[68]

Moreover, Lulù and the other "mutineers" are downgraded and placed at the assembly line. Together, but each for himself, in an even more alienating job which consists of the same repeated gestures over and over, while the incessant noise doesn't even allow them to talk to each other. Instead, they yell, and their words are misheard and misinterpreted by one another. Petri's depiction of the collective and fragmented line of workers is an allegory of the Left's incapacity to find a common ground and speak the same language. But it is also a reflection of man's irrecoverable inner split.

The final scene is deliberately ambiguous. At the assembly line, Lulù tells his fellow workers of a dream he had, thus marking yet another similarity with *Indagine*, which closed on a dream sequence. This time, though, the dream is told through the protagonist's words.

Previously impermeable to metaphysics ("Paradise is here!" he exclaimed, touching Adalgisa between her thighs), Lulù has experienced a nocturnal vision of the afterlife, inspired by his second visit to Militina. In his dream he is dead, buried, and Militina joins him. In front of them there is a wall. "He says, let's break everything and go inside!

Yeah, let's break everything and take over paradise!" Lulù has "a tremendous vision.... There was a guy with his head in one place and his body 10 meters away...." The workers break in, Militina makes a breach in a wall (as he attempted to do in the asylum) and leads the others inside. On the other side of the wall, there is a thick fog. Amid the fog, Lulù explains, he sees Militina. Then another worker, without a finger: himself. And then all the others, amid the fog.

"But what does it mean?" Bassi asks.

"It means that if there's a wall to knock down we knock it down!"

At first it looks like a call to arms, but upon his fellow workers' insistence to learn more about the dream, Lulù becomes uncertain and eventually contradicts himself. "Look, even I wasn't there ... there was no one there!"

The symbolic content of Lulù's vision is complex. If the wall refers to alienation, then the "tremendous vision" of the disembodied worker alludes to Lulù's comprehension of its effects on the workers' physical and psychic integrity; but the fog on the other side from which their doubles emerge seems to suggest that, even after the "wall" has fallen under revolutionary action, the workers will still have to come to terms with their own split inner self in everyday life. As someone said, revolution begins in the bathroom mirror.

Paradise means freedom, and Lulù's dream is a vision of social, spiritual, and interior renewal. But, indeed, for the time being revolution is just a dream and no one understands what it means. Meanwhile all the walls, both real and symbolic, material

From left to right: Gian Maria Volonté, Elio Petri and Luigi Diberti rehearsing a scene for _La classe operaia va in paradiso_.

and psychic, are still firm and sound. And every worker is still a prisoner of his own alienation.

At the assembly line, the workers' gestures become more and more frenetic …

A Political Film for the Masses

In a way, *La classe operaia* is a spurious offspring of *I giorni contati*, for it shares the same basic issues, such as the relationship of man with time, both in the existential and productive sense. Lulù claims he gets bored in the factory, "So I work, what else am I supposed to do?" Yet he doesn't even know what he produces. When he rebels against the slavery of production, he tells the employers, "You'll have to give me back everything you stole from me," an existential claim which recalls Cesare's attempt to make up for all the lost time in the 1962 film. Both works carry an autobiographical memory, too. Petri recalled his visits to the Nardi workshop where his father worked, and where "the working conditions were medieval … it was like watching someone work in a mythological cavern."[69]

The film expands the theme of neurosis and schizophrenia, which had become the main center of Petri's work starting with *Un tranquillo posto di campagna*. After the artist and the bureaucrat, it was the turn of the employee, the proletarian, whose position inside the capitalist society feeds his own neurosis. He is part of the productive chain, but he is also forced to become a consumer, thus feeding the system that exploits him. Leonardo Ferri and Lulù are not so distant despite their different jobs. Whereas Ferri fed his imagination with sex magazines and slideshows, Lulù leafs through sports newspapers. He fills his flat with useless items and spends his evening hours in a semi-comatose state, watching TV programs which seemingly consist only of advertising, such as *Carosello*. Incidentally, television would become a prominent presence in *Buone notizie*.

The depiction of factory life at the turn of the decade, replete with the conflicting influences of the union and the students' movement, is precise. See, for instance, the unions' slogans centered on negotiation ("Piecework should be paid more! More pieces, more money") in stark contrast with the students' radical position against piecework ("Less pieces, more money, less work!"). But if Petri's Neorealist background resulted in a meticulous research that reprised Zavattini's idea of cinema as "stalking of reality," *La classe operaia* is by no means a Neorealist film. Petri wasn't interested in the pure and simple portrayal of reality. He needed to inject a creative input, which here is both narrative and formal.

As he pointed out,

> Cinema is not for an elite, but for the masses. The acting and the use of camera must be a spectacular one. We as well have to take into account the rich, popular tradition which is the basis of the Italian theater and cinema, and of Fellini, of course, in particular.[70]

This approach is evident in the film's elaborate, engrossing camerawork and frame composition. The camera sticks to Lulù's face in extreme close-ups and observes his body with an attention to facial and body tics which recalls the *commedia all'italiana* (note the shots of Lulù preparing for work, stretching his arms and legs like an athlete before the race). But it also hovers over the mass of workers walking past the factory gates by way of elegant crane shots, becoming some sort of an invisible presence, an eye which is too sucked into and dragged along by that human flow, a sight which bears similarities with the marching slaves scene in *Metropolis* (1927). On the other hand, the long shot of the workers running in the snowy woods after clashing with the police is a striking pictorial image that evokes Flemish Renaissance paintings by Pieter Bruegel the Elder.

The editing is tight and restless, providing a visual counterpoint to the factory's unexhausted productive cycle, most memorably during Lulù's obsessive litany: "A piece, a bum, a piece, a bum." The sight of gates opening and closing as well as the recurring shots from behind the fences suggest the symbolic equation of factory and prison. But Petri goes beyond such a simple analogy and adds interesting nuances to it. He compares the workers' entrance in the plant to that of actors entering a stage through a curtain of sorts, as if a performance is about to take place, and litters the environment surrounding Lulù with grotesque touches which function as Brechtian counterparts to the story. The imposing statue of a worker towers over the driveway to the factory; the gates are equipped with an alarm device called "The Impartial" (again, shades of *I nuovi angeli*) which chooses random workers for after-work frisks in order to check whether they stole pieces from the plant; the factory walls are decorated *La decima vittima*-style, with colored Plexiglas sheets and Pop Art–style paintings, most notably a gigantic hand pointing its forefinger to the ground, in an ironic reference to the finger Lulù will lose; the psychiatrist's office has its walls filled with illustrations depicting everyday objects which the workers are asked to recognize as if they were kids in nursery school. After all, as Lulù acknowledges, "this is a job even a monkey could do." Later on, he notices a newspaper article reading, "Chimpanzee really believes is a man." Who is the monkey, who is the man?

Most notably, an omnipresent voice accompanies the laborers like a Big Brother of sorts, welcoming them as they enter ("Good morning, workers! The director wishes you good work!") and giving advice ("Your health depends on your relationship with your machine. Respect its needs and don't forget that a machine in good condition means a productive one") which have a paradoxical, sarcastic quality. The employees must keep the machine in "good condition" but they themselves are not. An elderly worker has a prostate problem and is threatened with a fine because he sits instead of standing up, therefore producing half as much as the others.

Ennio Morricone's score is one of his boldest, most brilliant ever. It puts to good use his avant-garde experiments of the previous decade while retaining a peculiar, dramatic melodic quality which openly draws from *Indagine*, on Petri's own request. It features ample use of electronic sounds produced by the Synket, combined with reverberated effects obtained with a palm-muted electric guitar, to evoke the loud, deafening noises of an industrial press; then it gradually morphs into a rousing, if jarring, horn-driven march (possibly a reference to the protest rallies of the period) in which the metallic noises become a rhythmic element.

The theme starts with a sequence of C-minor string chords in close root position voicing. Apparently, such compact and hammering staccatos—sort of evoking the sound of metal casting—seem disorganized, as if the machinery itself was gradually igniting. A melody played by the trombone unwinds over these dark chords; its sound in that range and with those dynamics is meant to be unpleasant to the ear; the melody was to evoke the human voice, the voice of the workers, who are increasingly brutalized by their life in the factory.

Over the boorish force of the trombone I layered a contrasting element which returns three times in the piece. It is a solo violin playing a poetic and transcendent melody. Still, there is nothing to fantasize about, as the machinery strikes ever stronger at each repetition. Alongside the trombone, the low register of the contrabassoons produces a rather visceral effect, just as the bassoons did in *Indagine su un cittadino al di sopra di ogni sospetto*.[71]

Petri employs Morricone's score on different levels—a counterpoint to the action, a commentary, a dramatic punctuation, a mocking memento. But his work on sound can also be seen in the scene where, while Lulù is busy working and explaining his credo to another colleague ("Think only of the piece ... a piece, a bum, a piece..."), the workers start wreaking havoc in the plant, smashing lights and audio speakers. But we hear no sound: we are inside Lulù's mind, and he is too concentrated on his job to allow the outside world to filter in. And it is to him that the camera plunges back after following the sabotaging acts, in an exquisitely staged dolly shot which gives a measure of Petri's refined technique while conveying a precise significance.

The strike sequence catapults the viewer from Lulù's private microcosm to the outside world, and at the same time it summarizes the film's style and scope. The image of Lulù clinging to the windscreen of the factory owner's car is clownish at first, but it leads to a chaotic escalation. The police escort the owner inside the plant, some workers burn his car and the cops beat the strikers savagely, all this rendered in a series of tightly edited long shots, close-ups, panning and dolly shots, to the rousing pace of Morricone's score. Suddenly, a small episode acquires a wider significance. In Petri's cinema, the urge to tell (and sometimes to yell) never overcomes the style but rather employs it to better drive the point home.

Politics vs. Spectacle

In a season dominated by *Continuavano a chiamarlo Trinità* (over six billion *lire* grossed at the box-office), *La classe operaia* made 1,460,233,000 *lire*, not as much as *Indagine* but a very satisfying result for such a problematic work. It ended up at the 22nd spot among Italian releases. However, it was scarcely distributed in Southern Italy. According to Lietta Tornabuoni, "South of Naples it has been rarely if ever screened."[72]

The film's echo somehow led to the making of several movies with similar settings and protagonists. Still, only Ettore Scola's *Trevico-Torino—Viaggio nel Fiat-Nam* (1973) depicted the workers' struggles. Others focused on social satire, such as *Il sindacalista* (1972, Luciano Salce), starring Lando Buzzanca; on the grotesque, namely *Mimì metallurgico ferito nell'onore* (1972, Lina Wertmüller), starring Giancarlo Giannini and Mariangela Melato; on melodrama, as did *Delitto d'amore* (1974, Luigi Comencini), starring Giuliano Gemma and scripted by Pirro. The most interesting of the lot was Monicelli's *Romanzo popolare* (1974), starring Ugo Tognazzi, Ornella Muti and Michele Placido, which evoked its proletarian setting from the very title and depicted the world of the Southern immigrants employed in Milan factories with anthropological precision.

Critics were once again divided. Giovanni Grazzini judged *La classe operaia* "one of the most fruitful" films of the year and "among the best of the new Italian cinema."[73] Lino Miccichè praised it as one of the season's best alongside *Il conformista* (1970) and *Morte a Venezia* (1971).[74] But the leftist militant critics destroyed Petri's film with an unprecedented rage. The anonymous reviewer in the quarterly *Ombre rosse* wrote: "I wouldn't have reproached the authors, had they told the story of a worker, a social comedy, or something equivalent to their means. What disgusts me is their slapdash attitude, the unawareness of their own limits. They made a film on the contradictions of a factory worker today according to a petty bourgeois perspective, with second-rate metaphysics and fifth-rate psychoanalysis."[75] Goffredo Fofi, in *Quaderni Piacentini*, accused Volonté of hamming without restraints in a way "that even Charles Laughton would have found excessive" and labeled the result "as noisy and inarticulate as its lead. It is not sufficiently sociological, nor sufficiently psychological, neither comedy nor drama, and most of all absolutely not political..."[76]

As Volonté argued, "*La classe operaia va in paradiso* is a dialectical movie, not a propaganda film,"[77] something critics could (or would) not understand. Most reviews focused on the film's political discourse and ignored its stylistic and narrative choices. It was exactly the opposite of what had happened with *La decima vittima*, where the style had befuddled the critics to the point that no one grasped the content. For instance, *Cinema nuovo* complained about the depiction of the students, labeling it as "old" and blaming the director for not distinguishing between the various groups. Moreover, the review rejected the ending, which didn't underline the "will to fight" of the working class.[78]

Another topic brought up by critics was the film's entertainment factor. Some called it a cynical attempt to exploit the success of Petri's previous work by employing the same formula (but with the *commedia all'italiana* instead of *giallo*...). Being a film about a social issue depicted (also) by way of comedy elements, it was judged a commercial compromise, and therefore condemned in the name of a bigger necessity of realism and adherence to activist political cinema.

A telling passage gives an idea of what the term "political cinema" meant to many: "A cinema which should ... qualify by its commitment to make the audience think instead of resorting to the weapons of suggestion and emotional involvement."[79] A vision poles apart from the director's. To the average militant critic, Petri's idea of cinema as spectacle, and therefore naturally destined to a wide audience, seemed as incomprehensible as hieroglyphics.

As film historian Claudio Bisoni underlined,[80] there were three basic issues that made critics mad at Petri. In their view the film lacked class analysis, and therefore was not authentically Marxist. Moreover, the director was interested in alienation instead of class conscience: Lulù was too stupid a character, and the analysis of his situation was considered too simplistic and politically apathetic. Finally, Petri's pessimism was inconceivable to Marxist critics who firmly believed in revolution and the rise of Socialism and saw the working class as the motor of history. The final scene of *La classe operaia*, with its surrendering to the metaphysical and the irrational, was simply impossible to digest.

The Working Class Goes to Cannes

The year 1972 started with another vigil of protest. This time, Petri, Pirro and Volonté took part in a solidarity vigil outside the Regina Coeli penitentiary in Rome, to protest against the detention of anarchist Pietro Valpreda, who had been arrested after the Piazza Fontana bombing, presented to the public as the "monster bomber," and was still awaiting judgment.[81] The trial started on February 23, 1972, and Valpreda was eventually acquitted in 1987 by the Supreme Court of Cassation for lack of evidence.

That January producer Alfredo Bini announced a collective feature film about pollution, *Sporco mondo* (Dirty World), to be shot in various countries with the participation of many noted filmmakers: Visconti, Lizzani, Pontecorvo, Damiani, Vancini, De Sica, Rossellini, Bergman, and Petri. "It's not a documentary, but a film that will discuss the various aspects of the tragedy of pollution."[82] Unfortunately the project never took form.

In late February the news that Petri and Pirro had been nominated in the Best Original Screenplay category for *Indagine* for the upcoming Academy Awards came rather unexpectedly, as the film had already won an Oscar in the previous edition. The prize went to Paddy Chayefsky for *The Hospital*, while De Sica's *Il giardino dei Finzi Contini* won as Best Foreign Film. Once again, Petri did not attend.

La classe operaia entered the official competition at the 1972 Cannes Film Festival, representing Italy together with *Il caso Mattei*, also starring Volonté, and *Mimì metallurgico ferito nell'onore*, co-starring Melato. It was screened on May 16, and the response was just as warm as the one reserved for *Indagine*.

During an animated press conference, Petri explained that he wanted to raise the issue of the conditions of the working class, "taken as symbol of the most general human and social condition in Italy and in the world," and make a plea to "break down the wall of incomprehension that divides us all. We all live in ghettoes, both as classes and as populations. We must revise the concept of today's world, founded on money...."[83]

The atmosphere became heated when a journalist asked him whether he would accept a prize, and after the director's affirmative answer ("Why not, if it is useful to spread the ideas expressed in my work?"), another one objected why in Cannes and not in Venice. Petri replied that he would never accept a prize from a festival directed "by a critic who collaborates with a right-wing newspaper," alluding to Rondi. It all deteriorated in a dispute after a French journalist argued that the film was contradictory, since it attacked the type of alienating assembly-line factory work which in turn was exalted as Stakhanovist in the Communist regimes with which the director sympathized. Petri rebuffed the criticism: "The issue of productivity does not exist in Russia. Over there, there are other types of issues, such as freedom." At this point the press conference wholly degenerated into a passionate political debate, without any reference to the film itself. Which, as Petri later confessed, amused him very much.[84]

Despite such competitors as *Jeremiah Johnson* (Sydney Pollack), *Slaughterhouse-Five* (George Roy Hill), *The Visitors* (Elia Kazan), *Solaris* (Andrei Tarkovsky), and *Red Psalm* (Miklós Jancsó), *La classe operaia* won the Grand Prix du Festival (which replaced the Palme d'Or from 1964 to 1974), in a tie-in with *Il caso Mattei*. The prize confirmed both the centrality of Petri's work in contemporary European cinema and the importance of the political attitude shared by such filmmakers as he and Rosi, although *Il caso Mattei* (the story of Enrico Mattei, the president of ENI, killed in a suspect plane crash in 1962) was characterized by a semi-documentary tone which was quite the opposite of Petri's approach; Petri later compared Rosi's cold, detached style to that "of a great Hemingwayan reporter."[85] Both films gained from Volonté's extraordinary performances, and the actor was given a special mention for his outstanding work. Ironically, in both films he was playing a "servant" (Lulù) and a "master" (Mattei), respectively.

The jury's verdict elicited mixed reactions among critics. *Positif*'s Michel Ciment was indignant:

> The ridiculous splitting of the highest prize between *La classe operaia va in paradiso* and *Il caso Mattei* makes no sense. There is a gap between Petri's coarse satire, confused and sensationalist, and Rosi's film, so deserving of the Palme d'Or, which is supposedly meant to be awarded

to an outstanding film-director, one in full possession of his faculties, and to an ambitious and accomplished work.[86]

To Jean A. Gili, on the contrary, the verdict "underlined the extraordinary capacity of Italian cinema to analyze through opposite means, either from the standpoint of the ordinary citizen or that of the man of power ... the socio-political dysfunction of

Italian poster for *La classe operaia va in paradiso*.

transalpine society."[87] Moreover, as John Michalczyk noted, Petri's film anticipated a new tendency to explore the tension of the proletariat, not just in Italy but both in European and American cinema as well, with such titles as Marin Karmitz's *Coup pour coup* (aka *Blow for Blow*, 1972), Andrzej Waida's *Czlowiek z marmuru* (aka *Man of Marble*, 1977) and *Czlowiek z zelaza* (aka *Man of Iron*, 1981), Paul Schrader's *Blue Collar* (1978) and Martin Ritt's *Norma Rae* (1979), although "few have the sting of *La classe operaia*; few raise the *cri d'alarme* so stridently."[88]

The Cannes victory led to a not-so-successful French release, as *La classe ouvrière va au paradis*, with 192,092 spectators (*Il caso Mattei* had over 617,000). In Spain the film came out only after the end of the Franco regime, in December 1977, as *La clase obrera va al paraiso*, and was seen by 35,000 spectators. Unlike *Indagine*, it didn't have a proper release overseas, and surfaced in New York City only in May 1975.

Introducing the Parisian première, a couple of weeks after the Cannes Festival, the director faced leftist protesters, irritated by the "bourgeois laurels" put over his head. The Italian militant left did not like the film either: Petri's depiction of the counterculture and his view of the unions was vitriolic and hit where it hurt the most. "The film is not aimed at convincing those who already have my political and ideological convictions," he stressed. "Rather, it tries, through a dialectical process, to reach those who are still outsiders to these ideas."[89] In doing so, he had made the most sincerely political film he could make. And this cost him a lot. Those who had saluted him after *Indagine* as the undisputed champion of Italian political cinema saw him as a traitor.

> Everyone has been polemical against my film: trade unionists, leftist students, intellectuals, Communist leaders, Maoists. Each of them wanted a work that would support their own reasons. Whereas this is a movie about the working class.[90]

Elio Petri was well aware of his difficult position. He was a successful filmmaker, perfectly integrated in the system, who was making "protest films" which grossed money and were awarded prizes at Festivals and even by the symbol of the enemy itself, Hollywood. As an intellectual, he definitely suffered from this paradoxical condition, as an interview of the period revealed. "It remains to be seen whether we who are trying to work through the system in order to raise the consciousness of the audience, in spite of the ability of the system to absorb everything, are doing the right thing."[91]

TEN

The Thief, the Actor, the Butcher and His Lover

La proprietà non è più un furto *(1973)*

Thieves and Masters

During the memorable press conference at the 1972 Cannes Film Festival, Petri announced that in September he would start filming his next work, *Ladri e padroni* (Thieves and Masters). The tentative title made no mystery that the director intended to keep on making committed, provocative works centered on the contradictions and issues of modern-day life. The film, scripted with Ugo Pirro, would be "an analysis of property and its consequences on society."[1]

The term "padroni" (masters) was among the most frequently used in that period. It evoked a long history of submission, from the Southern landlords in pre–Union Italy to the factory owners against whom the workers were protesting in the streets. But not just that. In the view of the militant left, the Marxist dialectic between exploiters and exploited characterized other fields as well. The previous year, Goffredo Fofi—possibly the most passionate and belligerent left-wing critic in the country—had published *Il cinema italiano: servi e padroni* (Italian Cinema: Servants and Masters), a self-described "pamphlet on the directors' opportunisms and escapes, the miseries and conditionings of the movie business."

In September 1972, Petri and other renowned filmmakers (Pasolini, Maselli, Rosi) showed up in Venice to back up the "Giornate del Cinema Italiano," the "alternative" film festival organized in the city center by ANAC and AACI in opposition to the "official" one (held at the Lido, an island in the Venice lagoon). After fighting for the abolition of prizes, filmmakers were trying to renovate the whole film festival concept from scratch. It was all part of a painful and often confused attempt to call into question the authoritarian core of the film industry, which resulted in some sort of "endless mass group therapy,"[2] in Petri's own words. It also led to the breaking of years-long friendships. One such was that between Petri and Ennio Flaiano, who dedicated one of his notoriously scorching columns in the *Corriere della Sera* to the alternative festival. "Among the idealists, before whom I bow, there are also individuals who are now established, distinguished, initiated to the most comfortable well-being, and embittered only by the demeanor of the tax authorities," he wrote. Flaiano's sarcasm aimed at the authors' request that the steel workers support the "Giornate." "Steel workers must have a good temper," he quipped. "Not only do they do a tough job, and not even well-paid these days, but they also jump to the rescue of the wealthy; and this is good, because the rich must be helped, we already have too many poor."[3] Flaiano had a fatal heart attack just a couple of months later, in November 1972. Petri always regretted that they did not reconcile.[4]

As expected, the "Giornate" caused a stir. Producers, distributors and theater owners attempted to sabotage it. For one thing, Ferreri's *La cagna* (1972), starring Marcello Mastroianni and Catherine Deneuve, was released in mid–August, a few weeks before its Venetian screening at the "Giornate," the act labeled as an *"intrigo padronale"* (masters' conspiracy) by *L'Unità*.[5] The most anticipated event was the screening of Jean-Luc Godard and Jean-Pierre Gorin's new film, the last effort of the Dziga Vertov group, *Tout va bien*, starring Yves Montand and Jane Fonda, initially destined to the Venice Film Festival. Godard and Morin's about-turn caused Italian co-producer Edmondo Amati to ask for the film to be seized.[6] But when the Venice customs inspected Godard's baggage, they found boxes of chocolates instead of film reels. It was reportedly Gian Maria Volonté who in the meantime had flown to Paris to pick up the reels and back to Saint Tropez, then sailed to Genoa on his yacht to bypass the customs.[7] This adventurous travel ignited Flaiano's venomous allusion to "directors and actors devoting themselves to *coups de main* and commando-like actions, as in the years of war, to smuggle and transport a movie, even jeopardizing their personal yachts."[8]

Volonté denied that the daring exploit had actually happened, and eventually *Tout va bien* was not screened, but Godard showed up at the "Giornate" and attended a heated, confrontational debate, during which he was openly challenged by the audience. Petri himself reportedly yelled at him: "Rondi ti aspetta!" (Rondi is waiting for you!).[9] *Tout va bien* was released in Italy in November as *Crepa padrone, tutto va bene* (Die, Master, Everything is Fine), which probably prompted Petri and Pirro to rename their new project. They opted for an even more thought-provoking one, a biting wordplay on 19th century French anarchist Pierre-Joseph Proudhon's famous slogan "Property is theft!" Their next film would be titled *La proprietà non è più un furto*, Property Is No Longer a Theft.

From Marxism to Mandrakism

Petri wanted to make a movie about property, "an analysis of what can be considered a natural, legitimate sense of property or ownership … as opposed to the excessive, pathological sense of property."[10] He wanted to make a movie about thieves. He wanted to make a movie about actors, whom he considered akin to thieves for both lived pretending to be other people. He wanted to make a movie about theft as performance, "a secret show which in the making unveils the role of property."[11] And he wanted to make a movie about today's society, "which absorbs everything and turns it back into consumerism."[12] All these crammed into one.

La proprietà was conceived as the last part of a trilogy, after *Indagine* and *La classe operaia*. It dealt with themes already explored in the previous two films, namely the relationship between citizen and power, and the one between the individual and productivity, respectively. As Petri explained, "these are three faces of the human condition: first power, then work, now property…"[13] The meditation on property had already been at the center of *Le cose*, the project he had sketched in mid–1967, and the new script retained some of those ideas.

La proprietà non è più un furto: **Total (Flavio Bucci) and the cause of his neurosis—money (Jugoslavian fotobusta).**

Petri and Pirro concocted a story about a young bank accountant, Total, who quits his job because of a bizarre allergy, an uncontrollable itch that manifests itself in the presence of money. Converted to the ideology of "Marxism—Mandrakism," Total becomes a thief and sets out to persecute only one victim, a wealthy butcher who is a client of his bank. The butcher himself is a crook who cheats on the weight of the meat he sells, owns a clandestine abattoir with underpaid workers and is even an abusive developer. Total doesn't steal money from the butcher but deprives him of symbolic items which make him what he is: his knife, his hat, his jewelry, his car, his lover. In turn, the butcher takes advantage of the theft and cheats the insurance company, demanding a higher indemnity. He and Total thus become accomplices of sorts.

Total turns into some kind of actor who repeats the same performance over and over. He even seeks help from a professional burglar, Albertone, who moonlights as a stage thespian. But Total finds out that thieves as well act within a strictly hierarchic structure which mirrors that of capitalist society and functions according to the laws of the market, just like bourgeois economy. Albertone's arrest and ensuing death from a heart attack at the police station mark the beginning of the end for Total. First, the butcher tries to corrupt him, but to no avail; then, he kills Total with his own hands.

The central concept dealt with Petri's own malaise. As an established filmmaker, he had reached economic well-being. He lived in a beautiful penthouse on the Lungotevere, collected paintings and *objets d'art*, and owned a fancy car. And he felt guilty about that. "Sometimes Elio felt ashamed of what he owned, he hid his not-so proletarian car so that his friends, his comrades, would not know, and wouldn't have the chance to mock his contradictions," Pirro recalled.[14] It looked as if he was making a movie out of spite and resentment, to exorcise the demons and the contradictions that he was experiencing, namely the struggle between his egalitarian fervor and his hard-earned wealth.

In the summer of 1972, Petri and Pirro moved to Torvaianica to write the script. This time the work would be much longer and problematic than in their earlier collaborations: a 114-page draft of the script retained at Rome's CSC library, and dated September 5, 1972, is fairly different from the finished film, and includes several ideas, characters and sub-plots that were dropped altogether.[15] In a 1973 interview with Jean A. Gili, Pirro claimed it took a year overall to shape the story and screenplay, although this time prep work did not include investigation in the field.

> We didn't conduct research on thieves, for it wasn't the truth about thieves' world that we were interested in. From a dramatic viewpoint, what we were interested in was the notion of offense: if one has power, he can commit an offense and receive immunity, offenses don't exist; if he hasn't power, he is punished for the slightest offense. Starting from works about total institutions and the issue of social exclusion in contemporary society, we tried to define the social privilege that comes with property ownership.[16]

Producers threw up their hands upon hearing the title. In 1972 Italy, amid terrorist groups fighting and killing for their ideal of destroying capitalist society, financing a movie that basically spat at money and material wealth seemed a suicidal move. As Pirro put it,

> There was on the part of many authors the purpose of challenging and provoking censorship. But making a movie against property, no—that was an intolerable, subversive gesture, which touched something buried inside all of us, of which we were not fully aware. In a sense, it was a demolishing game which turned against us as well, an unconscious act of self-accusation because of those small properties we both had acquired, the only sign of a well-being which never stopped surprising us.[17]

Eventually Petri set a deal for an Italian/French co-production. The film would be financed by Quasars Film Company, a newly founded enterprise headed by production manager Claudio Mancini and Franco Committeri, with participation from the Paris-based Labrador Films. Titanus would take care of the distribution. Mancini had first met Petri through Giuliano Montaldo, with whom he had started as production assistant, and was initially to work on *Nudi per vivere*. He and Petri had become friends, and Mancini had been production supervisor on *La decima vittima* and production manager on *La classe operaia*. His recollection of Petri is telling: "He was a communist who was miles ahead, but he was also middle-class. He bought houses, he had family, had a balcony at the opera. He had certain things that we call middle-class, but he was still a world apart."

Mancini got to produce *La proprietà* under curious circumstances:

> There is a story behind that film. He had given it to Mars … an American company. Mars called me to do a film with Damiano Damiani, *Los torturadores*, and so I left for Mexico. But there were problems making it, it was a bit too costly…. Then I saw that Elio was working on a project. I talked about it with Committeri, whom I was setting up a company with. "Why don't we do this film?" Elio agreed, because the Americans wouldn't let him.[18]

Mancini's version seems faulty, for Mars Produzione was in fact an Italian company that had financed, among others, Bertolucci's *Il conformista* (1970). But a telegram from Dino De Laurentiis (possibly dated February 1972) mentions a verbal agreement between him and Petri, with the director committing to make his next movie with the tycoon but failing to show up in his office to sign the deal.[19] It seems that Petri was not enthusiastic about the possibility of working with the man who once had attempted to take *A ciascuno il suo* away from him.

After the disputes during the making of *La classe operaia*, Gian Maria Volonté was not to be part of the project. He, Petri and Pirro were going their separate ways. Just a few months earlier Paolo Grassi, the co-founder and head of the Piccolo Teatro in Milan, had vainly tried to put the three men together for a project which never went beyond a vague idea.

Ugo Tognazzi's chalet in Torvaianica was near Petri's, and the actor often paid visit to his neighbor during the scriptwriting stage. He was eager to work with him. "I'd give an arm to make that movie," he once told Mancini. Given that Committeri was also Tognazzi's administrative representative, it was a deal made in heaven. Tognazzi used to get 85 million *lire* a film, but Mancini set a deal with him for 65 million. "And you can keep your arm!" he quipped.

Petri modeled the role of the butcher on the actor. "What Elio liked about Tognazzi was his shameless vulgarity," Pirro explained.[20] However, the director wouldn't want any risk after all the trouble with Volonté on *La classe operaia*. When Tognazzi demanded to be listed in his contract as co-author of the script, Petri sent an official letter to Mancini requesting that he cast someone else.[21] Tognazzi abandoned any pretense. "Ugo didn't say a word. He was game," Mancini confirmed. "He didn't misbehave at all. He did his very best. He believed in that character."[22]

In a way, it was a complementary role to the one Tognazzi was to play in Marco Ferreri's *La Grande bouffe*, shot in February 1973 and set to make a controversial debut at the 1973 Cannes Film Festival. In both movies he portrayed a character obsessed with food and sex, just as Tognazzi—a self-styled amateur chef and notorious womanizer—was in real life. Moreover, in Ferreri's film Tognazzi played a restaurant owner and chef who brings his set of knives with him to cook at the villa where he and his friends will die during a non-stop orgy of food and sex. Knives have a symbolic significance in Petri's film as well, and similarly hint at the character's virility and power.

But compared to the gluttonous, childlike Ugo who in *La Grande bouffe* dies while eating a gigantic breast-shaped pudding and being masturbated by a motherly woman (Andréa Ferréol), the unnamed butcher of Petri's film was a more unpleasant character, rustic and vulgar, violent and possessive, constantly over-the-top. "Your veins must explode! Concentrate, don't be afraid to exaggerate, he is an Expressionist character, not a naturalistic one," Petri would tell him.[23] During filming he made the butcher even more vulgar, in the way he looked, dressed, behaved, and even in the objects with which he surrounded himself.[24]

Tognazzi stressed the differences between the two directors:

> Petri demands a certain style of acting, not naturalness. The actor must be an actor, he mustn't "live" the film. And he is very skilled with the camera, he moves it a lot and this forces you to roll up your sleeves and repeat the same scene many times, from this or that point of view. Then there's the political issue. Ferreri's films are political too, of course, because for him standing against certain types of abuse or hypocrisies comes as natural as breathing, whereas Petri's films are purposely political. I'm not saying Petri is not in good faith, of course he is … he's been a communist all his life, a true communist….[25]

Total was played by the 26-year-old Flavio Bucci, who had made his screen debut in *La classe operaia*. Bucci's casting was unusual, and not because he was practically a newcomer. Bucci wasn't good looking but had a rather weird and perturbing face, with eyes like a bird, a long nose, his complexion pale and unhealthy. A rebel without a cause, and with plentiful anger inside him. An outsider. Just what Petri needed.

As Anita, the butcher's lover, the 23-year-old Daria Nicolodi was another relatively unknown name. The granddaughter of renowned composer Alfredo Casella, she had appeared only in Rosi's *Uomini contro* (1970) and Carmelo Bene's *Salomé* (1972), whereas the TV show *Babau*, in which she took part in 1970, had been shelved due to its scandalous nature. Petri molded the aristocratic-looking, pale-skinned actress into a working class, vulgar "woman-object," the kind someone like the butcher would show around like a trophy. Or like a side of beef.

For both actors, the film represented an impressive calling card. Bucci was awarded a Globo d'Oro by the foreign press as Best Newcomer Actor,[26] went on to play secondary roles in *L'ultimo treno della notte* (1975, Aldo Lado) and *Suspiria* (1977, Dario Argento) and had his breakthrough role in the TV mini-series *Ligabue* (1977, Salvatore Nocita), a biopic of controversial naïve painter Antonio Ligabue. Gian Maria Volonté, who helped him make his debut, was always highly appreciative of him: "I'm sure that, had Bucci's father emigrated to America, nowadays Bucci would be like Travolta or Stallone."[27] Nicolodi's next film would be *Profondo rosso* (1975), and she and Argento became romantically involved.

Besides Salvo Randone, in his last appearance in a Petri film as Total's father, the cast featured some distinguished stage thesps: Mario Scaccia (the parish priest of *A ciascuno il suo*) as the actor-cum-thief Albertone, Orazio Orlando (*Indagine*'s brigadier Biglia) as brigadier Pirelli, and Luigi Proietti as "Paco the Argentinian," a fellow thief who delivers a scorching monologue during Albertone's funeral. A couple of French actors turned up in small roles for coproduction quotas, namely Julien Guiomar (the bank director) and Jacques Herlin (a bank clerk).

Claudio Mancini had a cameo as a bank robber who is assaulted and reduced to impotence by guard dogs in an early scene. But he was a constant presence on the set, supervising expenditures and solving issues on the spot. Production had to be interrupted for twenty days after Petri was hospitalized in a private clinic, to recover from the stress which had caused the chain-smoking director a nicotine intoxication. "He fell ill during the dubbing, so I oversaw that," Mancini explained. "The doctor told him to go for walks, as he had a heart problem. So, sometimes I went to his place on the Lungotevere and we would walk to Castel Sant'Angelo and back."[28]

Petri definitely felt the pressure after the success of his previous films, as well as the challenge to live up to expectations. Yet, unlike with *La classe operaia*, very few news reports accompanied the shooting. In retrospect, it was the calm before the storm.

Private Vices, Public Debates

La proprietà had its world première at the 1973 Berlin Film Festival. The delay caused by the three-week halt had resulted in rushed post-production work: just days before the Berlin debut, Petri was still busy mixing the film in the studio. Interviewed by the *Corriere della Sera*, he maintained his disdain toward festivals: "I don't like the mundane context ... and the prizes. What's the point of being in competition with other people?

Are those who don't take part in the festivals and don't win any prize, less worthy than me? Are their works inferior to mine?"[29]

Petri's third time in Berlin would prove controversial. The July 2 screening began with a 25-minute delay, for the print had reached Germany at the very last minute. Reports that the film had "shaken" the audience and had received warm applause[30] led Italian correspondents to label it as the favorite for the Golden Bear. The award went to Satyajit Ray's *Ashani Sanket* (aka *Distant Thunder*) instead, a verdict that left the audience cold if not openly dissenting.[31] *La proprietà* did not win any prize. Despite the public's favorable reception, the German press was severe with it, and the Italian correspondent for the weekly magazine *Il Mondo*, Francesco Savio, dismissed it in a few venomous lines: "Given the tyranny of space, it will be better to wait until the film is released in Italy to talk about it with due completeness. Unless we are spared this small calamity."[32]

La proprietà would face similar negative reactions at the "Giornate del cinema italiano" the following September, anticipated by a negative review penned by Petri's good friend, Mino Argentieri, which appeared out of the blue in August in *Rinascita*. The director was caught off-guard: "It had the tone of a punishment directed against me and, at the same time, it seemed to be a cue for the readers of *Rinascita*, to prepare and alert them."[33]

Gian Luigi Rondi, whose mandate as vice commissioner of the Biennale had expired at the end of 1972, had officially resigned in February 1973 after the parliament's failure to approve a new statute,[34] and the Venice Film Festival did not take place that year, causing noticeable economic damage to the city. Unsurprisingly, the heavily politicized "Giornate" was organized in a red-hot atmosphere. The screening of *La Grande bouffe* was prohibited for censorship reasons, there was a failed attempt to set on fire the headquarters of the communist newspaper *il manifesto*, and two venues were cleared out after false alarms provoked by anonymous phone calls. On top of that, the screenings were followed by fierce debates between filmmakers and the audience. As Pirro recalled,

> For the first time Italian directors found themselves face to face with audiences who were not at all impressed by their interlocutors' fame. Ferreri, Loy, Comencini, Petri were literally assaulted with questions brimming with sarcasm and negative judgments bordering on insult. Most of the time there was no actual discussion, there were no objections raised, but everyone and everything were condemned without appeal. Protest, rejection, mockery, offense, were all spectacularized in an involuntarily carnival-like climate.[35]

As a reporter commented, "the 'Giornate' debates are becoming more and more nervous and aggressive. It is as if interventions were urged by an exasperated need of debate, clarification, dialectical discharge."[36] Following the screening of *Il fiore delle mille e una notte*, the third part in his "Trilogy of Life," Pier Paolo Pasolini was verbally attacked by several spectators during a heated argument that lasted over two hours and focused on his "cultural responsibility" for having "suggested nudity as a commercial solution" to Italian cinema. He asserted his right to find in nudity and eroticism the vital momentum lost in the ongoing political crisis and to use sexuality as a means to fight the overpowering mass culture. He later pointed out that the public was interested only in the message without even caring about the form, thus showing scarce respect for the filmmakers' work.

As for Petri, the only scene in *La proprietà* that raised applause was Daria Nicolodi's monologue, which the feminists in the venue approved unconditionally. Yet, during the ensuing debate, many claimed that his film did not carry enough "classist and challenging messages" and soon the confrontation took on harsh tones. At one point, Petri got mad with a spectator who accused him of being in bad faith. In rejecting the protests from the far-left groups, the director stated: "I'm an outraged, nauseated man. I wanted to provoke. That's intentional.... It has been said that the film is too pessimistic. Well, I say, let's have a look around. What reasons do we have to be optimistic in a society like ours?"[37]

Some years later, recalling that period, he was both ironic and disillusioned:

> Dozens of times, during public debates about our films, we were insulted, mocked, put at the center of Chinese-style trials, someone almost lapidated. Well, we went to those encounters without ever backing out, even though we knew what awaited us, with a comical inclination to martyrdom.... We indeed wanted all this, well aware that our role carried the mark of quality but also that of privilege, and that in some way, even petty, we had to pay for it.[38]

Property Is No Longer Obscene

La proprietà non è più un furto was submitted to the rating board right before the Berlin festival. It passed with a V.M.18 rating because of "the insistent vulgar expressions and scenes of sexual encounters portrayed with excessive realism." Still, two members voted against its release and considered it detrimental to public decency.

Released on October 4, 1973, the film was seized twelve days later in Genoa by order of the local general attorney Mario Calabrese.[39] It went like this: as with any new release, two Carabinieri entered the venue and viewed the film; then they wrote down a detailed report for obscenity, denouncing the movie as well as Petri, Tognazzi, Bucci and Nicolodi for "diffusion of obscene content." The incriminating scenes were four, namely a sex encounter between Tognazzi and Nicolodi, about a minute and a half long; an "anomalous sex scene" in a movie theater; a group sex scene (possibly, Total and Albertone's rape attempt on Anita); and, lastly, Nicolodi's monologue. The deputy prosecutor, Dr. Jacone, expressed his contrary opinion in a note to Calabrese: "No obscenity. Considering the film's content, the complaint takes on ideological aspects." Between the lines, one could guess that the act was prompted by other motives, namely the depiction of the armed forces, embodied by Orazio Orlando's character.

Nevertheless, Calabrese didn't take into consideration Jacone's opinion and, after personally viewing *La proprietà*, signed the seizure order. The judge with jurisdiction was the magistrate in Venice, for the first screening had taken place during the "Giornate." But Calabrese, with a juridically debatable move, labeled the film as "body of evidence" and thus demanded its seizure nevertheless, taking it out of circulation in the Genoa territory. It was yet another turn of the screw in the recurring habit of seizing films, usually the consequence of a denunciation by a private citizen, and not by the armed forces. "This time censorship was entrusted to the Carabinieri," many commented.[40] Petri defended himself eloquently: "I challenge every person of common sense to consider those scenes obscene or even erotic."[41]

The Venice magistrate judged *La proprietà* as not obscene,[42] but the film was seized again the following day in Benevento.[43] The national syndicate of film critics (SGNCI) denounced the "absurdity of the current state of cinema in Italy, where a motion picture which has obtained the certificate for public screening from a commission which includes magistrates as well, can then be put on trial and retired from circulation," and expressed their solidarity to Petri.[44] The memory of the vicissitudes of *I racconti di Canterbury* and *Ultimo tango a Parigi* was still vivid. Pasolini's film—first rejected by the board, then given a V.M.18 rating—had won the Golden Bear at the 1972 Berlin Film Festival and had been screened at the "Giornate" in Venice. It was seized in October 1972, and even though the reports of obscenity had been dismissed it returned to circulation only in December 1973, after Pasolini and producer Alberto Grimaldi had been acquitted in appeal. Bertolucci's film suffered a far worse fate: it was seized in December 1972, acquitted in first grade but condemned in appeal in June 1973. The judgment was annulled for technical reasons and a second appeal trial ensued, which ended with condemnation on November 20, 1974. The Court of Cassation confirmed the ruling on 29 January 1976, and *Ultimo tango a Parigi* was condemned to be destroyed.

As a commentator noted, "So many scandalous films are screened ... without judges batting an eyelid. One would say that the commercial purpose exonerates questionable filmmakers, whereas severity and indignation occur as soon as one notices the purpose of giving viewers a non-conformist portrayal of today's reality."[45] For his part, Tognazzi (who would soon face another seizure for obscenity for *La Grande bouffe*, released in Italy in December 1973) commented: "These bourgeois who write anonymous letters have so many skeletons in their closet.... It's useless that they complain because they see Daria Nicolodi doing things to me when at home their wife does the same thing to them, and if she doesn't, they pay a prostitute to do it."[46]

The seizure actually improved the film's box-office potential. *La proprietà non è più un furto* was difficult to promote because of its political nature, its allegoric narrative, and its overall bleakness. Nevertheless, Titanus labeled it as an erotic comedy, relying on Tognazzi's presence and on the "scandalous" sex scenes. The film grossed 1,451,300,000 *lire*, a bit less than Visconti's *Ludwig*, and ended up at the 27th spot among Italian releases of the year: the box-office champion was *Malizia*, starring Laura Antonelli, with over 5,500 million. As Claudio Mancini put it, *La proprietà* "became a success because deep down Italians are dirty!"[47] Whereas Luigi Magni's *La Tosca*, the film Committeri and Mancini had set their hopes on, released around the same time, was a resounding flop.

In December 1973, Bompiani published a 171-page novelization as part of its "Ombre rosse" series.[48] Credited to Petri and Pirro, it appears to be based on yet another draft of the script and features several differences from the film. The cover depicted two frames from a sex scene between the butcher and Anita, a move which undoubtedly helped sales.

A free screening of *La proprietà* took place at Paris' Latin Quarter in late November and many spectators were left outside the venue.[49] However, upon its release in France next year, on October 16, 1974, as *La propriété, c'est plus le vol*, it totalized only 20,737 admissions (*La Grande bouffe* attracted over 2,800,000 spectators). It surfaced in Spain only several years later, in December 1980, as *El amargo deseo de la propriedad*, distributed by Regia Films Arturo Gonzalez. It was seen by 12,419 spectators.

Criticizing the Critics

Over the past decade, Petri had often kept a dialectical relationship with film critics, writing letters to thank them for their words of praise or to reply to some off-target observations. With some exceptions (such as his first tête-à-tête with Maurizio Ponzi) he had always been open to criticism, but in later years his attitude had become more tense, following several heavily politicized and sometimes downright hostile analyses. *La proprietà* marked another turn of the screw.

The response after the Venetian screening had been tepid to say the least, and reviews were almost uniformly negative. As *L'Unità* pointed out, "this time, the confrontation and clash of opinions were accompanied by an element of exasperation, almost of mutual intolerance.... It was like a sign of unease, that each side was attempting to unleash on the other."[50] But there was more. Whereas the director's previous works, and especially *La classe operaia*, had been attacked by specialized film magazines and praised by most newspapers, now the latter as well reacted negatively.

Petri was furious. He gave several interviews to major newspapers in which he attacked the critics, claiming that they had slammed his film out of prejudice, and remarking that they would never undertake self-criticism. Speaking with *La Stampa*'s Lietta Tornabuoni, he contested "the methods and the function" of said critics and argued that "even film criticism can become a barony. Film critics, like noted surgeons or powerful professors, run the risk of subtracting all the time they spend ensuring their own status from the actual examination and understanding of films." He pointed out that during festivals critics would watch three films a day and write reviews in a hurry, adding:

> How can one have the time to think, to ponder the judgment, to dedicate to a film the attention it sometimes deserves? Film criticism becomes an assembly line of sorts. An intellectual activity punctuated by the clock; a cultural function conditioned by minutes. How is that possible? I never understood such a haste. What need is there to review a movie the day following its opening? Who said it is indispensable? ... Is it a culturally effective service? ... We have reconsidered so many traditions and habits over these years, and pointed out their errors and shortcomings; why not reexamine the times and modes of film and theatrical criticism? ... It is inevitable that, when critics are forced to express themselves in a small and predetermined space, they will adopt perfunctory labels which sometimes are lacking meaning.... It is fatal that reviewers, either in doubt or in a hurry, will take refuge in anodyne adjectives: "singular," "disconcerting," "curious," "unusual." But, are these critical judgments? ... Critics demand a difficult cinema, but they pretend to understand it immediately, as if a movie were a bullet.... You make a stylistic and narrative effort because you want as vast an audience as possible to understand what you want to say, and they accuse you of bad faith, political apathy, commercial sellout.[51]

The piece, eloquently titled "Criticando la critica" (Criticizing the Critics) caused a fuss, as did a similar interview published the same day in another hugely popular newspaper, *Il Giorno*.[52] Francesco Savio replied to Petri's attack with an open letter on the pages of *Il Mondo*, in which he refused to review the film as a gesture of protest:

> Such a polemic will never have me as an interlocutor. That's because, dear Petri, I won't talk about your film.... Having watched *La proprietà non è più un furto* three times, I won't say ... "I advise you against going to see Petri's latest film." No. I will mail this open letter in a hurry, I will leave to my few readers the judgment on said work, and I'll run away unexhausted to defend my faltering "barony."[53]

Then it was Ugo Pirro's turn to take part in the debate. He wrote some outspoken articles (signed UP) in the communist newspaper *il manifesto*, in which he stood alongside Petri, accused Savio of retaliating against the director, and attacked the whole category of critics, blaming them for sitting on top of a pyramid while the public would be incarcerated at the bottom. The pyramid "would deserve not to be overturned but destroyed, so that the public, the reader, the spectator, the author, the critic might finally act on equal terms."[54]

The argument spread on the pages of film magazines. *Cinema 60* accused Petri of choosing the wrong targets: "Why charge head-on against windmills instead of turning against those who have the money and therefore real power in cinema as well?"[55] Oreste Del Buono, in *L'Europeo*, objected that Petri had attacked the critics with the same haste as the critics had attacked his movie.[56] The echo of the debate even reached the front page of the *Corriere della Sera*.[57] The dispute lasted for over a year and culminated in a two-day convention in Ferrara, in November 1974, which newspapers pictured as an armistice between critics and filmmakers.[58] Petri had a different view, though. "The authors, albeit physically present, didn't say much of anything: only the critics talked. However, despite lots of talk, things didn't change."[59]

Freud Meets Brecht

The opening credits of *La proprietà non è più un furto* roll over an outstanding Expressionist-like painting panel by Renzo Vespignani, which depicts the film's main characters. Their faces are deformed and transfigured with greed, hatred, rage, meanness. One of the faces is split into two, a male and a female half. Flying and flaming banknotes surround them. There is no musical accompaniment in the traditional sense, but an assembly of weird, hissing, echoing male voices (actually the same one filtered, doubled, layered) reciting the forms of the verb "to have." "Io ho, ho, ho … tu hai, hai, hai … egli ha, ha, ha … io, io, io, io … noi, noi, noi … essi hanno" (I have, have, have … you have, have, have … he has, has, has … I, I, I, I … we, we, we … they have). The effect is at once chilling, disquieting, perversely sexual, with the verb "ho" sounding like a climax. But at the same time, these voices recall a dying man's gasps.

Then Total appears, surrounded by utter darkness, like an actor on an empty stage, illuminated by an unreal spotlight, in close-up. He addresses the audience, breaking the fourth wall and describing his character.

> I, accountant Total, am no different from you, and you are no different from me. We are equal in our needs and unequal in the way we satisfy them. I know that I'll never be able to have any more than I have now until the day I die. But none of you will be able to have more than you have now either. Many of you will certainly have more than me, while many of you have less. And in the struggle, whether legal or illegal, to obtain what we don't have, many people fall ill with shameful diseases. Their bodies fill up with sores, inside and out. Many others drop dead. They are excluded, destroyed, transformed. They become beasts, stones, dead trees, worms. That's how envy is born, and in this envy class hatred is hidden. It is born out of egoism, which makes it innocuous. Egoism is the fundamental sentiment of the religion of property. I feel that this condition is becoming intolerable and I know that many of you feel the same way.

At the end of his speech, a sudden dolly movement frames him in an overhead shot. Total is engulfed in darkness. It is as if he disappeared in the dark venue, mingling with the audience. Then, the story begins.

Throughout the movie, each of the main characters will turn up in similar interludes, staged in a theatrical manner reminiscent of *Die Dreigroschenoper* (aka *The Threepenny Opera*). Critics pointed out analogies with other works by Brecht, such as *Im Dickicht der Städte* (aka *In the Jungle of Cities*), for the metaphysical nature of the struggle between the protagonists.[60] These entr'actes introduce different chapters of the story and have the function of underlining each character's nature and unveiling their roles, according to a dialectic model that goes far beyond what Petri had attempted in *La classe operaia*. The director knew and appreciated Brecht's *Lehrstücke* (Learning-plays), in which the German playwright had brought further some concepts and techniques from his epic theatre and had explored the didactic possibilities of acting and playing roles. The Brechtian influence would characterize also the director's following works, namely *Todo modo* and partly *Le mani sporche.*

But Petri was not content with merely replicating the "distancing effect" (*Verfremdungseffekt*, also known as "alienation effect" or "estrangement effect") theorized by the playwright. In Brecht's works the actors break the fourth wall, address the spectators and thus hinder the audience from identifying with the characters subconsciously, pushing it to a critical approach to the story. The interludes in *La proprietà* function also as a peek into a private hell, the "secret chamber" of greed and envy, as the director put it, which reeks with "the miasmas that exhale from our subconscious."[61] They give the viewer the "sense of ineluctability in which the characters live and have lived. The character who speaks about himself shows that he has very clear ideas on what he is; despite this, he cannot change."[62]

The novelization adopts a different tone, as the various characters turn up one after another as narrators, telling the events from their point of view, whereas in the film the subjectivity is limited to the interludes while the story is told objectively. This must be the result of Petri's last-minute change of heart, for Pirro recalled the narration as being based on this very idea. "Each part of the story was seen from a different perspective. From A to C it was the thief's point of view, from D to F it was the butcher's and so on, hence the perspective was continually overturned…. Our dream was to merge Freud and Brecht."[63]

La proprietà marks a further step in Petri's transgression of Neorealist canons, according to his credo that "reality equals symbol and metaphor and therefore it must never be repeated flatly and schematically."[64] To Jean A. Gili,

> the film doesn't tell a dramatic continuity but juxtaposes a certain number of situations which put into practice Brecht's concept as defined by Walter Benjamin…: "Brecht has given up on wide-ranging actions." And so, he managed to transform the relationship between the scene and the audience…. Not only do these monologues interrupt the audience's participation in the way of Brecht's "songs," but in addition to that they create a similar relationship between the character on screen and the spectator in the venue.[65]

Moreover, as Gili noted,[66] the whole film is based on a series of dualities whose terms are strictly related, such as property and theft, or church and police. As a quote by Paul Valéry which opened the early draft of the script made it clear, one cannot exist without the other: "*Le loup dépend de l'agneau qui dépend de l'herbe. L'herbe est relativement défendue par le loup. Le carnivore protège les herbes (qui le nourrissement indirectement).*" Likewise, the story plays with the juxtaposition of the stylized and the redundant, the void and the chaotic. Morricone's score, littered with fuzz guitars and dramatic strings, is once again fully in tune with the film's targets and mood.

Even more than in the previous films in the "trilogy of neurosis," the story becomes a philosophical tale in which each scene is conceived, staged and played first and foremost for its emblematic significance. Characters either have symbolic names (Total's name hints at the "totalizing" nature of his desire) or no name at all (the butcher, like the Doctor in *Indagine*, is characterized by his social status) and exist in a symbolic universe, characterized by the blind race to profit, by egoism, and envy. In Pirro's recollection, Petri pushed the metaphoric elements of the story as far as he could, in "a resentful vision of wealth and life … as if he had a personal matter with money."[67]

One such choice was to have the bank where Total works (called "The Most Holy Trinity") depicted as a temple devoted to the deity of money, possibly a nod to an infamous passage in Louis Ferdinand Céline's 1932 novel *Voyage au bout de la nuit* (aka *Journey to the End of the Night*) which imagined Manhattan as the new Holy Land devoted to the divine omnipotence of the dollar:

> This was the priceless district ... the gold district: Manhattan. You can enter it only on foot, like a church.... It's a district filled with gold, like a miracle, and through the doors you can actually hear the miracle, the sound of dollars being crumpled, for the Dollar is always too light, a genuine Holy Ghost, more precious than blood.... When the faithful enter a bank, don't think that they can help themselves as they please. Far from it. In speaking to Dollar, they mumble words through a little grill; that's their confessional.... They don't swallow the Host, they put it on their hearts.[68]

As Mancini recalled, "In Piazza del Collegio Romano there was a little church that wasn't used anymore. But it still looked like a church. Elio wanted to use that for the bank, as money is religion."[69] On the wall, the Eye of Providence towers over the clerks and the crowd of customers/believers who come in for the daily celebration, for, as the director put it, "the capital is now a metaphysical entity much more elusive than the concept of God."[70]

Production designer Gianni Polidori devised other striking set pieces. The butcher shop has marble walls like a church or a court of justice (or a morgue!), and they are covered with slogans such as "Man is a carnivorous animal." The butcher serves customers from a raised platform which recalls an altar from where he performs a rite, dispensing meat instead of hosts as communion. Or, perhaps, a tribunal in which he, as the judge, decides who to serve and serve not, and administers justice by way of his scale (which is fixed). On the other hand, the butcher's apartment, decorated with kitsch wallpaper and marble panels and furnished with erotic paintings and expensive objects in bad taste (a counterpart to the cheap, kitschy ornaments in Lulù's flat) is like a mirror in which he can constantly see what he has become. Wealth, for the enriched, serves to enhance one's own self-esteem. It gives the illusion of good taste; it creates the simulacrum of a "good life" as the uncultured butcher thinks a rich man like him would lead.

La proprietà displays a visual density that brings to mind *La decima vittima* and *Un tranquillo posto di campagna* but moves in a very different direction. Luigi Kuveiller's outstanding photography depicts a livid world of suffocating primary colors or utter darkness, where faces emerge either with ghastly paleness or red-blood rage. The camerawork is superb, with plenty of complex camera movements and long takes. Mancini enthused: "Petri made tracking shots with stops you could hardly feel, and used a similar tracking shot for the reverse shot. There was no monitor back then. He had everything up here, in his head. He had brain and memory. He was so good."[71]

In addition to the director's elaborate dollies, the camera often sticks to the faces in insistent close-ups, as if observing the characters through the magnifying lens of an entomologist. Dario Argento would hire Kuveiller for *Profondo rosso*, a film heavily influenced by *La proprietà* in several aspects: the cinematography, the estranging camera movements, the emphasis on fetish objects, the use of locations, and the overall theatricality; and check out also Total's disguise in the jewel robbery scene, as well as Daria Nicolodi's heavy make-up, bright red lipstick and pearl necklace (not to mention that elevator...).

The theme of performance is carried on throughout the film. The aforementioned interludes are as many theatrical speeches, and so is Paco's funeral eulogy before an audience of thieves. The presence of the audience is underlined also in the scene at the butcher shop: in the establishing shot Tognazzi's character is cutting the meat atop a platform which evokes a stage while customers are watching his movements intently, as if hypnotized. After Total has stolen his knife, the butcher walks away from stage like a whimsical thespian who refuses to perform for the night.

Performance consists not just of speeches but of acts as well. When he comes home, early in the film, Total already behaves like a thief, looking around suspiciously, erasing his fingerprints, picking locks. He is like an actor rehearsing before opening night. His stealing is more like a series of impromptu performance art pieces, similar to Situationist actions. And each act deserves a proper disguise, costume, or identity. When Total shows up at the butcher's flat to rob the jewels, he looks like some weird *giallo* maniac, a stocking over his face, black hat and raincoat; later he turns up at his adversary's shop wearing a pair of motorbike sunglasses that recall a mask; at the police station, he meets brigadier Pirelli dressed as a priest, and when he recruits Albertone he pretends to be the butcher. In his attempt to escape neurosis, he becomes someone else, dropping a mask and donning a different one.

Anita's sexual encounters with the butcher are staged as performances as well. "I'm used to doing things, to moving around, dancing, touching…" she tells Total. During sex, she has to deliver predetermined lines and even put a stocking on her face at some point. It seems her lover's pleasure derives more from her performance than from sex itself.

Another blatant reference to performance occurs when the butcher and Anita attend an exposition of security devices presented as an amusement park's funhouse. The participants enter the exhibition space while an intermittent sign warns "Difenditi" (Defend yourself) and walk through a series of doors while their guide explains the virtues of the various bolts and alarm systems. Then several brief vignettes take place on stages illuminated by spotlights, as the vendor introduces various items. A masked man with a machine gun shoots at the onlookers through a bulletproof glass; a masked thief (looking every bit like Diabolik) attempts to steal a luxury car equipped with a sophisticated anti-theft device, only to be reduced to unconsciousness by gas erupting from the inside ("For a premium you can have poison gas too!" the vendor explains); then the visitors come across an array of weapons hanging from the ceiling like some sort of modern art piece; lastly, the Diabolik-type performer demonstrates the impenetrability of a security door.

The scene is reminiscent of the funeral art exposition in Dario Argento's *4 mosche di velluto grigio* (1971) but Petri possibly took the idea from the supermarket for hunters and preys depicted in the early draft of *La decima vittima*. Even the ironic emphasis on advertising (starting with the slogan "Help us to protect you") and the scene's vaguely futuristic pop look are in tune with the 1965 film.

Last but not least, one of the main characters in the film, Albertone, is indeed an actor who moonlights as a thief, or vice versa. In the original script, he was to deliver a speech, which Petri discarded as too explicit a variation on the theme of performance:

> I am an actor; therefore, I am a thief. The actor steals other people's identities in the crazy dream of finding out who he is…. The thief does nothing but act as best he can the role of the honest man, like everyone … and at night he even blends in with the animal world. He is a rat, a cat, a monkey, a mole, a hyena … a chameleon.

"To be or to have? That is the question…"

Total proudly claims to be a "Marxist–Mandrakist." The reference to Lee Falk's *Mandrake* (whose image can be seen in Total's bedroom, next to those of Karl Marx as well as various primates) is not merely a joke sparked by Petri's interest in Pop Art and comics. It is rather the result of a meditation on the value of Marxist thought in today's society. Like Mandrake, Total performs acts of magic, making the butcher's knife, hat, and car disappear. The items he steals are not for his own pleasure or greed, though—unlike his father, who craves the things consumerism associates with wealth, such as caviar. "It is as if, by refusing possession, Total rejects not only the middle class but society, the world, reality as it has been understood for centuries."[72] As his father warns him, quoting linguist Nicolò Tommaseo, "what distinguishes one thing from another is property.… If you steal, you are confusing things, and confusing their owners … and a property-owner mustn't be confused with a non-property-owner."

Total's Marxism-Mandrakism is therefore a symbolic act of rebellion against the slavery of property in capitalist society. Accordingly, his first act after he resigns is burning a banknote, much to the horror of the bank director ("You're committing sacrilege!"). Later, he throws stolen money in the toilet and flushes it away.

Money's specificity is that it is absolutely equivalent to any other commodity, it is the fungible good par excellence, for "to belong to everyone, money mustn't belong to anyone, not even to itself."[73] A passage in the novelization makes Total's aim clear. "I watched the stolen jars for a long time. I compared them to other jars I had honestly purchased in the last days of my slavery to money. They were perfectly identical.… No difference existed, since stolen objects do not differ from purchased ones, just as the money earned has the same nominal value as the money robbed, cheated or won at the gaming table."[74]

Total's rebellion is also directed against his father, an ex-bank clerk who always keeps a hat on because "he took it off too many times before the rich and the powerful" (as the novelization explains), and it takes the form of a symbolic reversal of roles.

Petri had already depicted a troubled father/son relationship in *I giorni contati*, where Cesare's son attempted to make his rebellious dad change his mind and go back to work, representing the call of normality, the voice of reason. In *A ciascuno il suo*, Randone played another father figure who was symbolically blind and said of himself: "A father is always guilty, always responsible." In *La proprietà*, the father/son duality is openly symbolic. Both *Indagine* and *La classe operaia* dealt with the paternal essence of authoritarianism, be it the police official or the factory owner, and depicted rebellious figures who challenged it. Here, though, the father embodies an authority figure that has lost its grip. He is elderly, shabby, idiotic. In Petri's experience, it was Togliatti's PCI that had revealed its paternalizing, authoritarian essence, causing him to come out of it. He himself was a "rebel son" who no longer had respect for his "father."

But the father/son relationship takes on a psychoanalytical significance as well. The young son represents the Ego while the old man represents the Super-Ego, the prone obedience to the rules. This is exemplified by his use of proverbs and mottos. When he claims "*Proprietas est sacra*," a Latin motto meaning "Property Is Sacred," Total replies quoting other maxims such as "Credere, obbedire, combattere," (Believe, Obey, Fight: the most famous Fascist slogan) to underline the vacuity of such platitudes. Another symbolic element in this respect is the big old vocabulary the elderly man keeps by his side and feverishly leafs through (a nod to *L'italiana*, where the protagonist looked in a vocabulary to

Total (Flavio Bucci, right) and his father (Salvo Randone) discuss the value of money in *La pro-prietà non è più un furto* (Jugoslavian fotobusta).

find the meaning of the term "nymphomaniac"). "Stealing, more than a crime, is a mistake," he claims, quoting the French 19th century politician Talleyrand.

The Super-Ego struggles to annihilate any tendency toward transgression and the overturning of the social order, just like the police does in *Indagine*. When Total asks him how much money they have in the bank, his reply is "As much as we deserve." It is through dialectics that Total exposes the faults in his father's reasoning, hence taking over the role of the father while the old man becomes like a son who is to be taught and educated:

> TOTAL: So that thing ... what's it called?
> FATHER: Money.
> TOTAL: ... it's a prize?
> FATHER: Yes.
> TOTAL: A prize for what, goddammit? For honesty?
> FATHER: Maybe...
> TOTAL: So, in your opinion we are dishonest. Thieves. Because we've never had a cent!

Like other characters in Petri's cinema, Total's father is deliberately oblivious of the truth. He benefits from his son's petty thefts (the caviar jars Total brings him home) but keeps denying their real origin, for his petit bourgeois morality prevents it. His stubborn denial of evidence recalls both Martelli's dismissal of the suicidal man as a fake in *L'assassino*, and Mombelli's obstinacy in giving back the loan to his wife's employer in *Il maestro di Vigevano*. But he eventually puts aside such petty moral rules to savor the acquired well-being.

In turn, Albertone becomes briefly a surrogate father figure: he and Total look very much alike and share the same wide-eyed, bird-like stare and beaked nose. The middle-aged actor-thief teaches his pupil how to move in the world of illegality, but he too ends up a disappointment. "You were born to be a slave!" Total hisses after he finds out the fence pays Albertone a cut-rate price for the furs they have stolen. His mentor is subject to the same duties and humiliations as his father is.

For the sake of his discourse, Petri depicts money's neurotic effects on the individual, bearing in mind Marx's words in the *Economic and Philosophic Manuscripts of 1844*: "It transforms fidelity into infidelity, love into hate, hate into love, virtue into vice, vice into virtue, servant into master, master into servant, idiocy into intelligence, and intelligence into idiocy."

Neurosis reveals itself as an uncontrollable psychosomatic itch[75] which forces Total to wear driving gloves at work. It is the umpteenth sign of man's inner split: Total craves money but he literally can't handle it. Such a split manifests itself through behavior and language as well. In an early, absurdist dialogue with his father, Total is unable to utter the term "money" and doesn't remember "that word that means that you possess something" (in *I giorni contati*, Cesare had a slip of the tongue and could not utter the word "cancer"), while his father cannot conjugate "to have":

> TOTAL: I can't remember that word which means that you possess something. A son, a house, a plot of land, a car, a wife…
> FATHER: The verb "to be," an auxiliary verb. I am, you are, he is, I was…. That's it, I was. No, no, no, no. I had! That's it. I had. I had, we had, we had, you had, if they had, they had, we had, having had, they had … all being conjugations of the verb "having."
> TOTAL: "To have." Conjugations of the verb "to have."
> FATHER: Yes, yes. This indicates possession of things. That's it, "to have." "To have" can be simple or conjugated. Of course. I … I *habbing*, I *hab*, he *habs*, he *habs*, we *hab*, we will *hab*…
> TOTAL: No more, for God's sake! We don't have a bean. I don't have, you don't have….
> HE has. Dammit, he sure does have. He has us. He possesses us. He has, he possesses shops, houses, cars, women, houseboys, and … that thing, money, by the sackful, by the cartload….

Total's father confusing the verbs "to have" and "to be" is the thematic core of the film. "To the bourgeois moral, the two things get confused, and it's in this confusion that illness is located."[76] Petri and Pirro proceed to lay bare the misunderstanding between "to have" and "to be," with the instruments of Brechtian dialectics. People believe that "to have" means "to be," and the ensuing struggle to get what one doesn't have (and doesn't need) results in alienation. Total's acts against the butcher follow a coherent symbolic path. He doesn't just steal the icons of his wealth and power, but each time in doing so he deprives him of "a connotation, a piece of his personal history, a fetish of his daily routine."[77] If property defines personality, and we are what we have (or *because* of what we have), Total is attempting to dispossess the butcher of his identity, piece by piece, and create himself one (even more so in the early draft of the script, where he became the butcher's *doppelgänger*). But the equation is fallacious, as Total discovers: "I'd like to be *and* to have, but I know that it's impossible, and this is my illness." It is not merely a matter of "the more you have the less you are," but of "not being even though not having."[78]

Petri doesn't just elaborate on Mackie Messer's oft-repeated quote in *The Threepenny Opera*, "What's picking a lock compared to buying shares? What's breaking into a bank compared to founding one?" He goes beyond the didactic juxtaposition of actual thieves such as Albertone, who operate against the law, with those who operate under the cover of legality. This would imply a mere overturn of moral values and turn Total into some kind of a Robin Hood figure, which he is not. In fact, Total's opening monologue makes it clear that he indeed craves property, just like the butcher does. Alienation is the result of the continuous struggle to grab what one doesn't have and doesn't need, a *totalizing* desire which knows no satisfaction. As the butcher admits in his own entr'acte,

> What will I do with all this money I accumulate, now that I'm in a position, as I have been for some time, to take care of all the needs I have in life? Well, I'll use it to make more. And even more. Millions, billions. Because my fundamental need is to get richer.

The choice of making Total's adversary a butcher was violently criticized by some Marxist critics, who judged it too simplistic a symbol of capitalistic accumulation. Petri replied that he wanted to depict "not an abstract exploiter but someone who, under certain aspects, is actually useful"[79] and at the same time someone who literally has blood on his hands. The novelization explicitly depicts the butcher as a criminal (as a butcher boy he raped his employer's daughter and married her) and an unpunished assassin (he killed a thief in his shop and got away with a self-defense verdict). As the butcher tells Total, "If it weren't for me, you would all have to go into the forests and hunt for prey in order to eat." No surprise that sometimes he looks like a primitive dressed in modern clothes. Such regression is spiritual as well. The butcher is a superstitious man who believes in bad luck and the evil eye and keeps his first knife as a fetish of good luck, the symbol of his fortune just like Scrooge McDuck's Number One Dime.

In creating the character, Petri and Pirro had probably in mind Giovanni Verga's short story *La roba* (The Stuff) and its protagonist, Mazzarò, a small farmer who accumulates great wealth, driven by his never-ending greed. The story ends with a chilling punchline. On the verge of death, Mazzarò starts killing all his farm animals, crying *"Roba mia, vientene con me!"* ("My stuff, you come with me!") Here, the butcher confesses: "But despite everything I'm not happy. No, because I, just like money, would like to be immortal." Later, in a monologue to be found only in the novelization, he concludes:

> What the fuck does "everything" mean? In my opinion, "everything" doesn't exist. It might seem I do have everything, and yet, lo and behold, it seems to me I'm naked. Mine is an "everything" that to me is nothing, and the more I have the more I want, the more I have the less I think I have.[80]

The Butcher's Meat

The religious symbolism connected to money and wealth is even more sarcastic, considering that *La proprietà* depicts a humanity obsessed with material goods. It is a materialistic world in the meanest sense of the term, in which people have regressed to a primitive state and follow their basic instincts, behaving like animals.

The novelization underlines such analogy with frequent similarities between the characters and various beasts: the butcher is described as a "rich predator" and compared to a lion, Total's father to a monkey, two guards look like hound dogs. The film, however, relies on the actors' features and expressions. But Petri suggests the parallel between money and meat (which satisfies the most basic of needs, hunger) from the beginning, when the butcher brings filets and steaks to the bank employees; this is brought to overly didactic terms in the novelization, where Total compares money to a dead edible animal, thus explaining further his disgust for it.

The human body itself is a commodity, similar to the slabs of beef, steaks and filets that the butcher slaughters, cuts and sells. Daria Nicolodi recites her monologue with her legs open, in a provocative sexual offer, to underline her condition of object for the male.

> I feel like a thing. I am a thing. Actually, many things. Tits, thighs, belly, mouth. I am many pieces, many pieces of a thing, and I live like a vase full of holes. They took me from my home just like they'd take a can of tomatoes. And now I'm here. But if I wasn't here, I'd be somewhere else. In another shop, in another house, in another neighborhood, or even sitting in the cinema like you are. But they'd always open me up like a can of tomatoes, with a can opener, with their dick, or even without it, with their fingers. And I laugh. Why do I laugh? I laugh because you're like me, but you act like nothing's happened.

Anita is treated like a thing by her "owner," who exposes her in full sight in his shop like a cup in a trophy case, forcing her to wear heavy make-up, tight-fitting shirts and miniskirts. And when Total "steals" her, she follows him meekly, passively. "I belong to his shop," she tells him. She is a tool, an exploited worker who exists solely to satisfy her master's pleasure and soothe his anger. Anita eventually becomes aware of this, and in the novelization, it is made explicit that this happens after Total kidnaps her: "Before, I didn't really know what I was," she reflects. But hers is a condition of utter powerlessness and resignation. "Sometimes I become like a worker and he's like a machine that I have to operate," she admits.

Petri's discourse extends to the commodification of the female body in current cinema. The scene in which the butcher forces Anita to perform fellatio on him in a theater

La proprietà non è più un furto: Total (Flavio Bucci) kidnaps Anita (Daria Nicolodi) (Jugoslavian fotobusta).

during the screening of an adult movie amid a raincoat crowd of lonely masturbators and promiscuous couples is not just an ideal counterpart to the matinee movie theater scene in *I giorni contati*, but also a pitch-perfect depiction of second-run venues circa 1973. The film-within-a-film is likely footage shot for the occasion and not a pre-existing film; the image of a woman's hand grabbing and ripping a sheet in the throes of orgasm is a humorous side note to the director's point.

Sexuality, a theme constantly imbuing Petri's work, becomes a central element in *La proprietà*. Ugo Pirro related such choices to the director's own inner contradictions.

> A man of great decency, afflicted with a moralism of political and proletarian origin, only in his films Petri abandoned himself to his instincts. He allowed himself to be overwhelmed by their subversive charge and offered a view of sexual relationships in which ease and ruthlessness of the depiction, mockery and complacency were torture instruments he used on himself.[81]

Around that time, Petri was very interested in the works of Sade and Bataille, and the depiction of such a degrading master/servant relationship unveils a punitive (and self-punitive) view of sexuality close to the chilling vision of Pasolini's *Salò*. The butcher, who surrounds himself with erotic paintings, sculptures and drawings, employs sex as a display of power. He puts his hands between Anita's legs like Lulù did with Adalgisa in *La classe operaia*, but whereas the latter's gesture was the expression of a primitive, uneducated sexuality, the butcher's is an arrogant reaffirmation of property. As such, it demands a reaction on the part of the woman, an acknowledgment of her being wholly subject to him. She duly obliges, feigning pleasure to please her master. Later, when Total grabs her crotch, she reacts the same way, as if out of a conditioned reflex.

The erotic scenes have a funereal essence. They are mortuary and repetitive rites, devoid of joy. The woman is always on top of the man and recites her lines according to his wishes. Each individual lives the experience separately. Their bodies are together, their minds and feelings are not. For the butcher, Petri pointed out, "sex is a tool, carnal love is only a mechanic succession of gestures."[82]

The casting of the slender, androgynous Daria Nicolodi was a brilliant touch: her elegant, delicate beauty underlines her character's constant humiliations. When Anita attempts a joke by putting on her head the stocking Total had used to conceal his features, the butcher gets excited and has sex with her, demanding Anita to scream "Stop thief!" during the act. (As brigadier Pirelli told the butcher, "You can't enjoy your riches without some fear of having them stolen.") The scene caused lots of fuss because of the actress's ample nudity, but the overall effect is less erotic than perturbing, in no small part due to Nicolodi's disquieting grimaces, which force viewers to consider its degrading essence.

Another controversial scene depicts the butcher and Anita having sex on the bed. After an establishing shot, with the woman seen from behind, what follows is a succession of close-ups of the characters' faces, and once again the scene unfolds like a duet, a call-and-response in a crescendo that accompanies the man to orgasm. He asks Anita a series of rhetorical questions that gratify his ego and manhood. She replies joylessly, looking bored as if she was saying those words for the umpteenth time, and, in the end, she bursts out crying.

> —Who's the smartest of all?—You!—Who's the manliest?—You!—Who's the strongest?— You!—Who's the handsomest man of all?—You!—Who's the greatest butcher in all of Rome?— You!—Who's got the most beautiful dick in all of Rome?—You!—The biggest?—You!—The

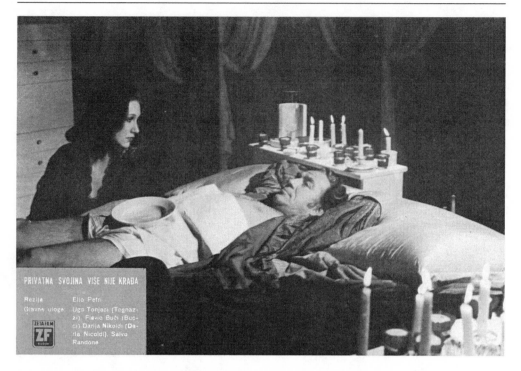

La proprietà non è più un furto: Anita (Daria Nicolodi) and her lover, the Butcher (Ugo Tognazzi) (Jugoslavian fotobusta).

most powerful?—You!—Who's the most envied?—You!—Who's the luckiest?—You!—Who pays the least in taxes? ... Who's the king of Rome?—You are!—And who's the most pitiful person in the world?—It's me!

But the butcher's arrogant display of power, which manifests itself in the physical and psychological coercion of his partner, hides an immature, even ambiguous sexuality, a common theme in Petri's cinema. This is much more evident in the novelization, where, after forcing Anita to have sex with him with the stocking on her face, he asks himself: "Why did I have her put on a mask like that? Maybe I think I can rape the thief through her?"

On the other hand, Total is apparently asexual, at least at the beginning. In the novelization he suffers from premature ejaculation (as will the protagonist of *Chi illumina la grande notte*), a trait discarded in the film. After performing his first act of stealing he becomes self-assured, for property encourages his aggressiveness and his sexual urges as well. He kidnaps Anita as an act of retaliation against the butcher but he treats her exactly like his enemy does, partly because he wants her to achieve awareness of what she is, but partly because, by stealing the butcher's "things," he is driven to *become* him. His attempt to take the butcher's place fails, though, and he cannot go all the way and rape her. He, too, is sexually incompetent, like Laurana and the Doctor. In the novelization, however, Total *does* rape the woman, and, as Anita points out, "I realized that he had done to me, so to speak, what he wanted to do to him," a line which further stresses the subterranean sexual attraction between the two male adversaries.

The theme of sexual ambiguity is carried out in the film through the character of Albertone. Besides having two jobs—and therefore a dual personality—he is also bisexual. He is accompanied by the kind of low-life youth that Pasolini used to merge with and he touches their crotch just like the butcher does with Anita's. He, too, is a property-owner.

In the umpteenth duality depicted in the film, Albertone appears on stage in a typical sketch in Roman vaudeville, here imbued with symbolic values. In his stage dress, half-male and half-female, Albertone evokes the androgynous creatures described by Aristophanes in Plato's *Symposium*. He touches his body and looks surprised, even scared when finding out he has a male organ, as if he just discovered his true identity. Ultimately, he is putting on stage his own inner split.

Subverting Comedy

As Pirro explained, *La proprietà* was the result of an exhausting scriptwriting effort. "We were facing unprecedented difficulties … work was really hard, all the more so as we wanted to get away from certain cinematic models while remaining attached to an Italian cultural tradition."[83] As Ugo Tognazzi put it,

> *La proprietà non è più un furto* is an important movie—actually it is *two* important movies. An Expressionist film in which characters tell their reasons in turn, or rather deliver their sermons as if from a tribune, a balcony … and a naturalist, even Neorealist film, with a bit of *commedia all'italiana* … we'll have to see if the two films stand together…[84]

Even more so than in *La classe operaia*, here Petri employs themes and types that belong to comedy, only to subvert its mechanism and rules. The protagonist being a thief recalls such classics of Italian cinema as *Guardie e ladri* (1951, Mario Monicelli, Steno) and *I soliti ignoti* (1958, Mario Monicelli), with their patent sympathy for outcasts; but the characters' unpleasant traits reveal them as variations on the concept of "monsters" which imbued the original idea for *I mostri*. Moreover, Petri's use of the grotesque bypasses the emphatic side of Italian comedy, which urges viewers to identify with the protagonists. In fact, Bucci's bird-like face and stare make for one of the less photogenic heroes in Italian mainstream cinema. As Total confesses in the novelization, "I would like the spectators to start hating me, to judge me repulsive."

Even though its basic plot evokes the classic *commedia dell'arte*, with a rebellious servant mocking and humiliating a wealthy master, *La proprietà* does not elicit amusement, but stops laughter cold. It is as if the film itself is donning a mask to fool the viewers.

As usual, Petri worked painstakingly on the use of language, a key feature of the *commedia all'italiana*, in which dialectal terms, regional accents, popular sayings serve to depict the characters and their behavior. Ditto for vulgarity, employed as a means to both elicit laughter and better characterize the protagonists. *La proprietà* reeks with vulgarity, in the character's words and behavior. "It is also a film about vulgarity," Petri noted; "the vulgarity of the bourgeois life system is present in all things … vulgarity is now the distinctive sign of everything…. From a certain point of view, vulgarity is an improvement: things reveal themselves with their true face."[85]

Accordingly, during shooting the director changed several lines from the screenplay and made them cruder, to stress this vision of moral decay. For Albertone's on-stage monologue, he replaced the original speech with a sonnet in Roman dialect by the 18th century poet Gioacchino Belli, *Er padre de li Santi* (The Father of Saints), which consists of a long enunciation of all the various synonyms for the male sexual organ. The choice upset Pirro, who attributed it to Petri's inner turmoil, "as if a long-repressed contradiction was about to explode inside him, a split between his desires and the obsessive normality of conjugal life."[86] Nevertheless, the result acquires a symbolic weight, and predates the use of foul language in *Buone notizie*. As such, it turns into a way to unveil the character's neurosis.

But language serves also a subtler function. It is often employed because of its rhythmic fluency, namely in the duets between Total and his father, centered on the impossibility for words to convey the anguish of alienation, and in Pirelli's monologue, where the list of acts from which the policeman gets his satisfaction is like a tongue twister of sorts, constructed by the terms' phonetic assonance. In this sense, *La proprietà* comes closer to the experimental, and openly Brechtian, films by Carmelo Bene rather than the type of dialogue penned by Age & Scarpelli.

The contravention to the rules of comedy is carried further with the acting. Flavio Bucci's Total has the wide-eyed craziness of a mad jester, and his uncontrolled itch whenever he is near money—initially played for laughs, with the character assuming puppet-like poses to scratch himself—becomes a truly unnerving sight. Similarly, Total's recurring disguises—including the priest-dressing scene, the closest thing in the film to proper comedy—become more and more the sign of a fractured identity. As Petri noted, Total "never feels the joy of transgression." His acts rarely feel liberating and rather convey a sense of desperation. Later, the director labeled *La proprietà* as "a movie on the birth of desperation amid the Left."[87]

Similarly, Ugo Tognazzi's over-the-top characterization of the butcher, replete with phony Roman accent, which some criticized as they did with Alberto Sordi's inflection in *Il maestro di Vigevano*, seems to border on caricature, and the opening scenes at the bank apparently lead in the same direction. But soon the character's unpleasantness takes over. He is a proletarian who has risen from his status and now, dressed in his flashy suits, looks at the masses from a privileged position, both in his shop and at home. Whereas Total is thin and weakly, he is strong and well-fed, for his body "conveys also the abject health of the executioner."[88]

Viewers, who were treated to the somewhat humorous crescendo of the first half, were at odds. The more the story goes on, the less there is to chuckle about, let alone to grin. During scripting the director wrote in his personal notes that the film was turning out "too dark" and the result confirms his feeling. The pessimism of *La classe operaia* had become even more extreme and anguished.

Cops and Robbers

The strength of *La proprietà*, and at the same time its more difficult aspect to swallow, is represented by the lengths to which Petri carries its central paradox. The characters' various perspectives, apparently so different, turn out to be almost identical. As Jean A. Gili put it, "owners and thieves have interests in common, even class interests to defend; therefore, they are not different but in the eyes of the law."[89] Speaking of which, the unctuous brigadier Pirelli is an even more scathing caricature than the Doctor in *Indagine*, a servant of the Capital who proclaims his own alienation in explicit terms:

> I ... stand guard against human hatred. I've been working to keep order for 20 years. But I fear that this order, this harmony is impossible to achieve in a life founded on inequality. To make

up for this, I get plenty of satisfaction elsewhere. I investigate, arrest, interrogate, misrepresent, coerce, affirm, deny, exercise cruelty, acquire, set up, tear down, and take over parts of people's lives, some important, some less so. And so, I'm consumed with pessimism and console myself with the egotistical nature of my privileges—first and foremost the freedom to arrest whoever I want. Arresting people is a wonderful thing....

This is one of the most explicit political moments in the film. Petri compares police procedure to robbing other people's immaterial possessions—their dignity, freedom, secrets, rights, even their life. As in *Indagine*, the police keep files with the subjects' political and sexual tendencies ("Sadistic atheist, blasphemer.... Communist, Trotskyist and masochist..."). The cops kidnap, beat and torture the suspects, and the scene in which Albertone dies during questioning evokes the memory of Giuseppe Pinelli. All this unsettled the authorities much more than the sex scenes and possibly prompted the film's seizure, together with such lines of dialogue as Pirelli's admission that "These days no one believes us ... not even our own people."

Petri repeatedly, and sarcastically, hints at the closeness between the repressive armed forces and the Church. The police station is located next to a cathedral; when Pirelli accompanies Total, dressed as a priest, to his archive, he remarks, "We've got our faithful flock, too ... our jurisdictions follow parallel paths ... in fact our jurisdictions, despite their differences, share the same goal ... maintaining order." Talking to the butcher, Pirelli tells him, "You need to trust me like you'd trust a priest during confession." The police's reactionary essence comes out in Pirelli's line of dialogue which echoes the Doctor's speech in *Indagine*: "Without us, theft is no longer theft. It becomes a right, the law, and thieves become revolutionaries." But Pirelli, as a servant of the law, is not impartial. Some people are more equal than others, and he must bow to them, as painful and humiliating as it is. The whistling voices in Morricone's score accompany the end of his visit to the butcher's house with the line "Voi avete" (You have).

The film's most provocative concept is that order and disorder, justice and illegality are all part of the same system. Night watchmen are in cahoots with low-life burglars just like the police are in league with grand scale thieves. Even thieves are exploited like factory workers, not by employers but by fences—who set the rules of the clandestine market in the very same way as the butcher does when selling meat—and they lack any class conscience.

At Albertone's funeral, a crowd of thieves is gathered around the coffin. One of them, Paco "the Argentinian," delivers a speech:

> Friends, comrades, colleagues, and rivals. What would the world be without us? Think about it. How many of these bastards who call themselves honest men would end up in the gutter? ... What would locksmiths do without thieves? And lock factories? And shutter factories? And all the bank workers, the night guards, the police, the Carabinieri? People who make doors and windows? Inventors of anti-theft devices, always trying to perfect their work? And the porters, the lawyers, the judges, the prison guards and governors? What about the night watchmen? The insurance men and the police dogs? What would they all do without us? Think about it, my friends, think about it. How many people would be out of a job if all of us took revenge against this ungrateful society, if all of us together, at the same time, decided to stop stealing? The nation's economy would crumble.... Society owes its established order and social equilibrium to us. Because we, stealing under cover of darkness, cover up and justify the thieves who operate under cover of legality.

The monologue (absent from the novelization) is further proof of Petri's radical approach. Paco is a Brechtian character who has no other function in the story. He is the court jester who is allowed to tell inconvenient truths. His speech touches various points and ends on a paradoxical note. It is not a eulogy of thieves. On the contrary, theft, and thieves, are themselves part of the capitalistic system. They make the economy move and thrive. As Paco explains, property and theft are two sides of the same coin. They belong in the same economic structure and are equally necessary to its survival and prosperity. The character embraces the instruments of rhetorical discourse, which is the main device to influence someone's perception of reality. Through speech, the orator guides the audience to an interpretative outcome that serves his rhetorical goal.[90]

Paco's evoking of a thieves' strike as a utopian, catastrophic event conveys the disillusion of someone who does not believe in radical social overturn anymore. As the butcher tells Total,

> Is there a written or unwritten law against making money from industry or commerce? No. Religion, perhaps? My dear friend, religion tells us not to commit adultery, not to kill, not to cause offence, not to steal, but doesn't mention getting rich.... And to get rich you have to cause offence, overpower, rob, etcetera.... I'm a property owner. And to make a property owner like me give up everything, there would have to be a revolution. Which there isn't.

Just as Cesare, in *I giorni contati*, could not escape his status of worker, here Total's attempt to break the rules (and roles) of society is doomed to defeat. Not only his efforts to make a common front with other thieves are a failure, but his one-man revolution ends in tragedy. The System always wins, either by incorporating the rebel cells or destroying them. First the butcher tries in vain to use dialectics to convince him, then he attempts to bribe him. When corruption proves useless, he strangles Total with his bare hands, a sacrificial act which turns this would-be Mackie Messer into a symbolic slaughtering lamb.

In the very last scene—an eerie yet merely casual similarity with the most famous moment of Kurosawa's *Ikiru*, and another similarity with an early draft of *La decima vittima*, which showed elderly people regressing to prepubescent status—Total's father is swinging on a swing in the same stylized netherworld as the other characters, mumbling only a line: "My son was like a father to me...."

If, to Petri, the PCI was like an ideal father figure, the final image of *La proprietà* hints at a father/party that has failed and, devoid of its offspring's utopian ideas (those heralded by the student movement in 1968), has become an orphan, talking to itself, detached from the outside world. Unlike Lulù and his fellow workers, there is not even hope for a heaven of sorts, but only a limbo, a black abyss, "the historical void that is middle-class existence."[91]

But the scene allows for another, even more pessimistic interpretation. Petri once admitted: "The struggle between the butcher-master and accountant Total is inside me just as I believe it is inside each and every one of us."[92] It is the conflict between the revolutionary side, which naively believes the system can be destroyed by way of a miracle or an act of magic (hence, Marxism-Mandrakism!), and the side which is jealous of its own privileges and will fight to preserve them. And in this inner struggle, it is the moral side that succumbs, together with the ideals and delusions for a better world. The old man's mourning of his lost son is therefore our own regret for what we once were and now have lost for good.

Overall, *La proprietà non è più un furto* is a singularly split film. It is a bold and daring work which encompasses theatrical elements and is populated by negative and even hateful characters that are almost repellent to the viewer; but it aims also to be a useful film for the general public, just like Petri and Pirro's previous efforts were. It desperately wants to communicate, pushing the political and psychoanalytic content even further, both in style and content, even though what it does communicate is an utter lack of hope. But it seems also a public act of purification and penitence. It hints at an inner, deeper dissatisfaction, a split between desire and everyday norm on the part of its director. Its contradictions are Petri's as well. It is the work of a moralist who fears he is falling victim to temptation and cannot see any way out.

ELEVEN

Maudit

Todo modo *(1976)*

Mio padre *and Other Unfilmed Projects*

When interviewed in Venice, after the controversial screening of *La proprietà*, Petri admitted he was tempted to stop working for a while. "I feel an indefinable sadness, the consequence of the conflict with my profession."[1] He told the interviewer he had no immediate projects for the future, except for a vague idea about a movie on the religiousness of Italians.

Just a few months earlier, on the eve of the film's Berlin premiere, things seemed very different, and Petri had agreed to discuss his future projects. He was considering adapting an outline by Gore Vidal, centered on "provocation as an endemic fact in every society. A political, modern tale which embraces many world events of our times, from the Watergate scandal to CIA operations."[2]

Vidal's 14-page outline, *The Pope Must Die*,[3] was about a ruthless CIA agent provocateur, John Malerba—who moonlights as an author of popular James Bondish paperbacks—arriving in Rome on a mission: the polls for the next elections show that the Communists and the Socialists will gain the majority, and Malerba has a complex plan to help the declining Fascist party win the elections. He befriends Celestino, a young, uneducated and naive Maoist who is disillusioned with the Communist Party, and starts manipulating him. Malerba persuades Celestino to kill the secretary of the PCI, but causes the attempt to fail at the last minute: as it turns out, he has a much more daring plan. He convinces Celestino that to accomplish his mission he must kill the Pope instead, for the Pontiff is going to endorse a Fascist government (whereas, having bugged the Vatican, Malerba knows it is going to be quite the opposite). Everything goes just as planned: Malerba has Celestino shoot the Pope, then he immediately dispatches him and succeeds in having the public opinion blame the Communists, by way of a diary which he has made Celestino keep, in which the gullible assassin exposed his credo. Malerba returns to the U.S., flying first class and drinking champagne just like at the beginning. The End.

The plot evokes political thrillers such as *The Day of the Jackal* (1973), with a good dose of nasty irony in its crescendo, Vidal juxtaposing the buildup with excerpts from Malerba's novels, with their watered-down depiction of spy work aping 007 flicks. But the core of the story is openly political. Malerba is described as someone who "in his days ... has made history, this fact is not in doubt, but what history is sometimes a question." Vidal evokes some of the crucial events in the last twenty years of American history as the result of CIA secret ops, namely the overthrowing of Guatemalan president Jacobo Arbenz Guzmán, the Bay of Pigs, and the assassination of JFK. In evoking the latter it covers similar ground as the Dalton Trumbo-scripted *Executive Action* (released in November 1973), and includes a flashback in which Malerba himself pulls the trigger and "we see the head of the President explode."

But the story has several elements akin to Petri's cinema as well. Not only does it refer to the Strategy of Tension, but it portrays a grim picture of the Roman fascist bourgeoisie and its environments: the head of the Fascist party is a nasty caricature, "a cool, gentle, compassionate seeming man with a wife, five children, and a number of remarkably handsome young men in constant attendance as bodyguards and secretaries, masseurs and lovers," like a modern-day Roman emperor. Vidal was ready to pen *Caligula*, evidently. But Malerba himself is an interesting character, a split protagonist with a baroque personality who often resorts to camouflages and disguises (even dressing up as a priest, like Total in *La proprietà*) and who revels in violent and erotic fantasies, dictating into a machine pulpy spy stories in which his alter ego kills commies by the dozen and makes love to beautiful women. This inner world provides a counterpoint which evokes Petri's own script for *L'impiegato*; the act of creation to which Malerba is addicted is mirrored in the diary entries he dictates to Celestino, making him the perfect scapegoat.

Still, one month after mentioning the project to the press, in July Petri wrote Mickey Knox (who had offered him to direct the film) that even though Vidal's story was excellent, he felt he would not be the right director.[4] He was intimidated by the scope of the project and felt inadequate, not least because he didn't speak English and the script, dialogue and actors would necessarily be American. Vidal had suggested Paul Newman or Mastroianni for the role of Malerba, and the elaborate story called for a big financial investment. For all its thought-provoking political nuances, *The Pope Must Die* looked like a big, expensive American thriller, one more suited to a Hollywood studio.

It was Ugo Pirro who inherited the project. In the summer of 1977, he wrote the script with Yves Boisset, who was to direct it. Boisset's *L'attentat* (1972), inspired by the Ben Barka case and co-starring Gian Maria Volonté, featured a crime novelist who is also a ruthless CIA agent, played by Roy Scheider. Claude Jaeger and Serge Silberman were to be the producers. James Coburn was in talks to play the lead but eventually he turned it down.[5] The following year, Pirro told *L'Espresso* that the project (retitled *Oscuri delitti nell'estremo Occidente*, Obscure Murders in the Far West) had been shelved "because the common idea within the Italian film industry is that it would be better not to deal with anything political, especially if it's a dangerous topic."[6]

The Venetian debates and the controversy surrounding *La proprietà* marked the end of Petri's association with Ugo Pirro. There were no clashes or arguments, but the two drifted away from each other. No talks were made about new projects, and the director behaved rather coldly on the mundane occasions when the two came across each other.

Despite his statement about his willingness to rest for a while, Petri kept his hands busy, exploring different paths. One such was stage direction. Playwright Angelo Dallagiacoma proposed that he direct his play *Una storia emiliana*,[7] and Petri himself penned an outline for *Giacobbe o elaborazione di una ossessione* (Jacob, or the Elaboration of an Obsession), a thought-provoking piece set in a correctional center "where the servants and masters of the domineering ideology are forged by way of masochistic exercises," and characterized by a marked Sadean vein and obscene imagery. "The body of Giacobbe, the protagonist (and that of his brethren) is orthopedically bent, that is, it becomes … exchange value: the tongue serves to lick those who hold the vestige of Power, the arsehole to welcome them."[8]

Throughout 1974, Petri involved playwright and critic Enzo Siciliano in the story of the relationship between a young priest who is undergoing a vocational crisis and has fallen for a young widow, and an older con man who disguises himself as a clergyman to defraud the old parishioners and steal their savings. The latter worms his way into the priest's world and replaces him as a charismatic figure among the parishioners. The young priest kills the fake one, but the murder turns him into a concealer in turn. Was it the story about religiousness Petri had mentioned the previous year? His idea was to explore the controversial state of the Church, split between old habits and new demands, and he considered riffing on the paradoxical elements of the story, such as the recurring theme of confession.

While developing the outline, Petri suggested that Siciliano read a couple of novels, Georges Bernanos' *Un crime* and Georges Bataille's *L'abbé C.* (published in Italy only in 1973) for inspiration. The latter, set during World War II in occupied France, is centered on two twins, one a priest and the other a libertine. However, the project ended up shelved. Ditto for an adaptation of Carlo Cassola's novel *Gisella*. Others didn't go beyond a rough outline or brief sketches. This was the case with *L'italiana* (no connection with the 1967 story penned with Flaiano), for which Petri considered also a couple of alternate titles, *La donna ideale* (The Ideal Woman) and *Mamma sorella sposa* (Mom Sister Bride). The five-page outline dated May 9, 1974,[9] is actually a short story of sorts, as was the director's custom. It is the sarcastic first-person monologue of a Southern girl, Armida, who takes part in a contest for the Ideal Italian Woman, upon suggestion of her husband Leandro. "You are the pure Italian, the perfect Mediterranean woman…. Juno, Venus and Minerva all in one … and even a Madonna," he has told her. But Armida has an affair with Leandro's best friend, Gilberto, who also thinks she is the perfect woman. Armida prepares for the contest with Leandro as her trainer, on various specialties: cooking, housekeeping, childcare, sex, morality, good sense, and so on. She is so obsessed with the prize that she plans to kill either her competitor Anita or the jury president, a noted writer named Calabresi (a namesake of Commissioner Calabresi, incidentally).

A modern-day variation on the classic myth of Paris, the apple and the snake, the sketch lacks any real narrative progression. It is accompanied by a brief memo in which the director put down his thoughts on the theme, with his usual dialectic method: "It's good to make a movie about the female condition, but we need an idea. First of all, we must choose the point of view: from the man or the woman's side? … The objection to the idea of a film about woman in a man's life is that it's inevitably patronizing and always male-centered." This is the reason that had possibly prompted Petri to abandon another, earlier project, *Identification*, written with Lucile Laks, about an upper class woman who investigates on the attempted suicide of a female friend.[10]

Petri's working diary shows that in late August 1974 he had taken the project in a different direction, starting with a new title, once again almost identical to the one he had developed with Flaiano, *Affettuoso rapporto su una donna da cui vorremmo essere amati, forse*. He and his co-writer Franco Solinas wanted to reflect on a theme that had regained strength with the growing debate surrounding the feminist movement and its "liberationist" theories. Both rejected the schematism of such stances and believed that the feminists' determination to supersede the male revealed traces of neurosis or psychosis. Still, Petri was convinced that women were indeed among the designated victims in a society based on exploitation of man by man.

The project seemingly developed into an anthology of sorts, a series of sixteen potential stories (a suicide, a young woman's education, a sacrificial murder, an impossible journey abroad, a relocation, pregnancy...), all centering around female characters who undertake a quest or undergo a transformation, either accepted or rejected, for "the dominant theme in a woman's life is *change* from a biological or social status to another." Petri's idea was to portray a desperate female character who unconsciously lives the same general crisis as society as a whole. Woman is split between the passive biological function to which she has always been confined and the active one that her socio-economic needs urge. On the one hand, she is still tied to traditional values (motherhood, companionship, sexual submissiveness), on the other she is oriented toward male standards. The ongoing crisis of values results in the loss of her own role, but she fails to attain a new identity. Petri's idea, in short, was to depict a character who would be

> woman and, at the same time, man, and not because this is what biology wants, but because this is what society wants. Ours is an *unfulfilled* character, for her role is still incomplete and it will take on some decisive traits exclusively through radical social mutations.... Such a confused conscience of being still a social hybrid and almost a natural hybrid ... cannot but give her a painful sense of inferiority.

It was a similar path as the one Petri designed for Lulù in *La classe operaia*, and he was ultimately aware of that when he argued in the same pages that desperation, inferiority and uncertainty were common to the whole of human society.

In August 1974 the director sketched another project, very different in tone and theme: a four-page outline, *Mio padre ovvero L'amicizia* (My Father, Or Friendship), so titled "because we are children of the situation and of the human beings depicted in the film. Those issues which were the basis of human relationships at that time are still ours as well."[11]

The story takes place during Fascism. A communist worker, Comunardo, is arrested, condemned and sent to confinement on an island where other "subversives" are secluded. There, he befriends another exile, a solitary man named Martini. One day the other exiles tell Comunardo that he mustn't socialize with Martini, who resigned from the Communist party and proclaims himself an anarchist. Comunardo obliges, but Martini (obsessed by his wife's infidelity) comes looking for him after receiving a letter from the woman where she confesses her betrayal. Comunardo tries to console Martini, but the other exiles condemn his act of human solidarity.

A new rule makes the Fascist salute mandatory on the isle. The exiles protest against it and Martini is one of the most resolute and brave. He is sentenced to one month's confinement. When he comes out, Comunardo is the only one who stays near him, but both men have now been excluded by the others. Then, a dramatic event ensues: an old antifascist attempts suicide, jumping into the sea. The authorities try to pass the act off as an escape attempt and condemn the dying man to one year's imprisonment. He dies in jail. His funeral turns into an assembly where a comrade's right to kill himself is discussed. Comunardo, who defends such a desperate gesture, is expelled from the party. He pays a visit to Martini expecting consolation. However, much to his surprise, Martini finds Comunardo's expulsion logical and coherent. Eventually, "Comunardo realizes that friendship, on which he leaned to prove that antifascists … mustn't give up to sectarianism, has become impossible to achieve concretely."

The pessimistic apologue deals with personal and political themes. One cannot but think of Petri's own exit from the PCI and his subsequent feeling of isolation. Moreover, the depiction of a fractured opposition, torn between unreasonable dogmatism and individual and ineffective rebellion, reflects his view on the state of the Italian Left, with the Communist party being unable to deal with dissidents' voices.

Throughout 1974, Petri considered other projects as well. Between December 1973 and April 1974, the noted Peruvian novelist Manuel Scorza—exiled in Paris for his political commitment with the indigenous Peruvian communities—sent him a couple of original stories, *La Persecution* (The Persecution) and *A la sombra del sol* (Under the Shadow of the Sun),[12] but there is no record of Petri's response. On the other hand, the director considered adapting Vladimir Nabokov's novel *Despair* (later made into a film in 1978 by Rainer Werner Fassbinder and starring Dirk Bogarde) and got in touch with the Russian writer's son, Dmitri, who asked for a $1,500 advance for a six-month option on the book.[13] Once again Petri was intrigued by an idiosyncratic crime story which became the pretext for a reflection on the fallacious perception of one's own self. In Nabokov's novel, a wealthy industrialist named Hermann meets a homeless man, Felix, whom he believes is his dead ringer. He persuades Felix to dress up as him and then kills him in order to collect the insurance money. Hermann thinks he has accomplished the perfect crime, but he is delusional: it turns out the two men had no resemblance at all, and Hermann will be captured by the police. Petri gave up the project, but the theme of the *doppelgänger* would turn up again in the unmade *Chi illumina la grande notte*.

In November 1974, a news article briefly evoked the director's past. Lucio Mastronardi had attempted suicide, throwing himself out of a fifth-floor balcony. "Why did you save me? I wanted to die," he told rescuers.[14] Slightly more than a decade had passed, and *Il maestro di Vigevano* looked like a relic from another era, for all those involved. Mastronardi and Petri had kept in touch over the years, but lately the novelist had suffered another nervous breakdown and his mental state was deteriorating. In August of that year, he had half-jokingly proposed to Petri to make a movie from his third novel, *Il meridionale di Vigevano*.[15] In retrospect it looked like a call for help. Mastronardi would drown himself in April 1979.

In a transitional period marked by Petri's declining critical fortunes, the news of a monography on him was surprising, even more so considering that it was published in France. Unlike other Italian filmmakers, in fact, Petri was not the object of a huge cult beyond the Alps, and the Cannes award to *La classe operaia* had left many perplexed. The volume, simply titled *Elio Petri*, was a collection of critical essays preceded by a lengthy career interview with the director and one with Ugo Pirro. It was edited by Jean A. Gili, a film critic based at the University of Nice and a long-time admirer of Petri's work. He and Petri had gotten in touch in late 1971 for an interview and struck up a friendship. Gili would become the director's most dedicated scholar.

On January 22, 1975, prime minister Aldo Moro attended, in his capacity of university professor, an open session of the Constitutional Court which examined a request of unconstitutionality concerning a seizure of an allegedly obscene film: namely, Mac Ahlberg's *Nanà 70* (Nana, 1970), acquitted on first grade in 1972 but still seized. Petri was among the audience, together with other filmmakers, including Rosi, Zampa, and Comencini.[16] The situation recalled one that took place a decade earlier, when Petri attended the session for voting for the President of the Republic, to gather inspiration for the unmade *Il vuoto di potere*. Sitting just a few feet away from the Italian prime minister, in his mind the director was molding the idea of his most openly political and belligerent film to date. It would be based on a novel published just weeks earlier and it would mark his second screen encounter with the work of Leonardo Sciascia.

Murder as a Spiritual Exercise

In the summer of 1970, Sciascia stayed for a week at a hotel outside the Sicilian village of Zafferana Etnea, near Catania, where he would attend a literary event. The hotel was run by Salesian friars, and each evening the novelist could witness a rather singular sight. Many individuals walked quickly across the large square outside the premises, reciting the rosary. They were former Salesian students doing spiritual exercises. Sciascia noticed that most of them were notable exponents of the Democrazia Cristiana. The non-stop coming and going, the voices mechanically reciting prayers, the sudden turnabouts, reminded him of Dante's *Inferno*, precisely the chasm of thieves.[17] That sight gave him the idea for a new book. What if a murder is committed right during the spiritual exercises, and someone reciting the rosary suddenly drops dead?

It was only three years later that Sciascia put the idea into motion. Every summer, he moved to his country house and devoted himself to writing a new book on the basis of his notes, outlines and assorted ideas. He was a methodic writer, with a constant output of four pages a day, with few corrections and rarely, if ever, any rewrites. He was determined to write a book on theoretical physicist Ettore Majorana, who had mysteriously disappeared in 1938, but as soon as he put a white sheet in his typewriter, he realized he was going to write another one, a detective story with a murder taking place during spiritual exercises.

During the summer of 1973, Sciascia wrote half of the novel, which the following year he vaguely described as "on Catholics, on the politics of Catholics; the other half of *Il contesto*."[18] He was referring to his 1971 novel, the story "about the man who kills judges" he had once mentioned to Petri. Sciascia completed the book in September 1974 and sent the manuscript to Italo Calvino. The illustrious novelist's response was admired:

> At first, I was a bit impatient, with all those priests, all those Masses and all that theology. But from the murder on I got hooked on it, because of the mystery as well as of the hellish vision of Christian Democrat Italy, which is as strong as has ever been written on the subject. Now, it is precisely the novel it takes to tell what Christian Democrat Italy has been and still is, and no one's been able to write it before you.[19]

Such a powerful work had to have a powerful title. Sciascia discarded the tentative *Esercizi spirituali*, a nod to Ignatius of Loyola's *Spiritual Exercises*, a set of meditations and prayers published in 1548. Instead, he used a direct quote from the Basque theologian and co-founder of the Jesuits: "*Todo modo para buscar y hallar la voluntad divina.*" (One must use every means to seek and find the Divine Will). Initially *Todo modo, todo modo, todo modo*, the title became *Todo modo* when the book hit the streets in December 1974.

The story is told in the first person by a famous painter, whose name is never mentioned. While driving around in the countryside, looking for some peace and quiet, he notices a street sign to the Zafer Hermitage (a nod to Zafferana Etnea, although the novel doesn't contain any geographical reference) and decides to have a look around. The hermitage has been turned into a hotel run by an enigmatic priest, Don Gaetano, and is currently hosting a spiritual retreat for members of the ruling class. The painter is allowed to stay, but a murder takes place during the rosary. The victim is a corrupt ex-senator, and almost everyone is a suspect, save for Don Gaetano and the narrator. A second murder ensues, the victim being a noted lawyer, and magistrate Scalambri shows up to investigate. Scalambri, an ex-schoolmate of the painter, asks him for help, and the narrator solves the mystery, although the solution is not revealed. The next day Don Gaetano is found dead in the woods, apparently a suicide. The investigation ends and the hotel is cleared. The narrator claims he murdered Don Gaetano but Scalambri doesn't take him seriously and concludes that one always has to look for the motive behind a killing, otherwise everyone becomes a potential suspect. The book ends with a long quote from André Gide's novel *Les caves du Vatican*, Sciascia's acknowledged inspiration.[20]

In *Todo modo* the Sicilian writer employed the mystery element "in an inverted sense, because a *giallo* without a solution in fact is not a *giallo*," as he pointed out, adding, "but one must keep in mind that mine is a game, a joke, a parody." Exactly, one might add, as *Il contesto* (subtitled *Una parodia*), which Francesco Rosi adapted for the screen a few months after the publication of *Todo modo*: shooting for the film (released as *Cadaveri eccellenti*) started in Naples on April 7, 1975.[21]

The mystery structure offered Sciascia "a reading key for reality and the instruments to construe its absurdity"[22] while the parody element served as a filter, a trick to have the freedom to address controversial topics, like a jester in a king's court. "One must joke about the things he fears, or hates, or loves," he wrote, "so as to release oneself from fear, or to better love them."[23]

Here, it was the context that mattered, pushing critics to read *Todo modo* as a *roman à clef*. The allusions to the Christian Democrats were all too evident. Don Gaetano was an embodiment of the DC and its power, and the murders hinted at the party's inexorable decline amid corruption, scandals and the growing strength of the Left. In the end, Don Gaetano's death looked like a prophecy of the end of the party's supremacy in the nation's political life.

Moro and the "Third Phase"

The year of 1974 was a critical year for the Democrazia Cristiana. The "battle" against the 1970 divorce law climaxed with the May 12 and 13 referendum and ended with a burning defeat for then-secretary Amintore Fanfani. The administrative elections, on June 15, marked another halt. A few months earlier, the voting age had been changed by law from 21 to 18 years, one of the consequences of the students' protests of the previous seasons. The electoral campaign had been littered with violent episodes on both sides, including terrorist actions by the Neofascists on the one hand and the Brigate Rosse and NAP (Nuclei Armati Proletari) on the other. Newspapers were filled with reports of protests (often violent) from extra-parliamentary groups, and several clandestine and independent "cells" developed from the more extremist parts of the Left. As historian Guido Crainz pointed out, these cells were formed by "very young people, initiated to politics during the gloomy years of the 'Strategy of Tension' and therefore inclined to mistrust the Republic's democracy and emphasize 'military' forms of politics."[24]

The June 1974 elections saw a noticeable drop in votes for the DC. It remained the country's leading party, with 35.3 percent of voters, but the PCI was very close, with 33.4 percent. The 12 percent hiatus of the 1972 regional elections (where the two main parties had 38.7 percent and 27.1 percent, respectively) was now less than 2 percent. Newspapers compared the results to an "earthquake." The PCI was now too strong a political force to stay at the opposition. The *Corriere della Sera* interpreted the vote as "a desire for novelty"[25] and added that the PCI's victory, "so huge, so diffused, was not predictable. As had happened with the referendum, now we discover a different country ... this is a reformist vote."[26]

Thirteen months later, in July 1975, reporters were allowed for the first time to follow the DC's National Congress through a closed-circuit television. Aldo Moro gave a controversial speech in which he coined the expression "*terza fase*" (third phase). The previous two phases in the history of the DC had characterized post–World War II history, first with a Centralist government (in which it either was the only party or led a coalition of centrist forces) and then, starting in 1963, with a Centrist-left coalition, with the active participation of the PSI. The third phase would mark, in Moro's own words, "the fall of the moral and political barrier" of anti–Communism. In Moro's intentions, it would lead not just to a coalition with the PCI but to a radical reconstruction of the DC itself. "It is difficult to foresee what will happen. The future is not in our hands anymore, in part," he argued. "Democrazia Cristiana must be reconstituted and I hope that it will be reborn free from the arrogance of power."[27]

Moro's speech acknowledged the image of the ruling class that resulted from the popular vote. Politicians were perceived as mummies who had held power undisturbed for almost 30 years. And indeed, many party members were septuagenarians who had preserved their seat in Parliament for decades. Not by chance, *Cadaveri eccellenti* would open with symbolic images of mummified bodies.

The speech was met with hostility by the party. Benito Zaccagnini, elected (with many white papers) as the new secretary, was on Moro's side for a coalition with the PCI, but the rightist faction, led by Andreotti, was strongly contrarian. Discontent spread among the allies as well. Moro's "third phase" was the specular image of the "democratic alliance" PCI secretary Enrico Berlinguer had proposed in 1973. Thanks also to the wide emergence of newer members, especially after 1968, the Italian Communist Party was turning into a younger, moderate political force, by now detached from the influence of Moscow. In August, speaking with U.S. President Gerald Ford, Moro had insisted on the mutation of the PCI: "What you must remember is that not everyone who votes Communist is in fact a communist. Most of them are also in favor of freedom and liberty."[28]

The inner struggle within the DC led rapidly to a government crisis, enhanced by the economic one that had caused monetary inflation to rise over 20 percent. The year 1976 opened with dark clouds hanging on the fourth Moro government. The prime minister resigned on January 7, officially opening the crisis. The President of the Republic, Giovanni Leone, entrusted him with the formation of a new government, but weeks passed without a solution. Eventually, Moro had to settle on a government formed only by the DC which stayed in charge a mere two months, amid general protests and armed terrorist actions.

Social conflicts were becoming more and more radical and violent. On March 25, a general strike took place throughout the nation. The following weeks saw sabotages, fires, bombings. Moro's resignation seemed more and more a matter of weeks. It would mean the inevitable snap elections, which many feared would be the most dramatic in Italy's history.[29] Elio Petri's new film was going to add fuel to the fire.

"M"

The DC appeared fleetingly in *La proprietà*. In a scene, the butcher is watching TV and Giulio Andreotti turns up in a newscast while giving an award to a "commendatore." It was the only allusion to Italy's government in the film. *Todo modo* would be a totally different, and much more explicit affair.

Petri read Sciascia's novel at the end of 1974, right after it was published, and was immediately struck by it. He already mentioned it as his upcoming project in a letter to Jean A. Gili dated December 16, 1974.[30] The book's anti–Catholic polemic was just what he needed to channel the rage against the Democrazia Cristiana he had been nurturing since adolescence.

It was the rosary scene that prompted him to adapt the novel for the screen: "This extremely theatrical scene appeared to me, the first time I read *Todo modo*, as an appalling, even pitiful metaphor of Christian Democratic power exerted by its politicians, who were like prisoners inside a dark and obsessive labyrinth."[31] It touched personal chords as well. In his early teens, Elio had participated in a week of spiritual exercises in a convent, headed by

a rather crazy priest, wild-eyed, a Jesuit who spoke while waving a big crucifix and who scared us by continually evoking before our eyes the specters of agony and death. I recall that at night, to shake off the malaise that he put on us during the day, we gathered in our rooms, smoking and playing cards: we were already split, like the DC politicians in Sciascia's novel.[32]

When Gili interviewed him on the set, in February 1976, Petri claimed: "The book, in and of itself, is an imperfect one, but it is great because of its imperfections. Why? Because you don't really know if it's an essay or a dialogue, if it's drama or philosophy."[33] This allowed him to alter Sciascia's novel liberally while keeping its stimulating ambiguity. He took a few elements (the hermitage, the spiritual exercises, the murder during the rosary, the characters of Don Gaetano and Scalambri) and discarded others. One such was the relationship between Don Gaetano and the painter, who are basically doubles of each other. Petri saw it as an obstacle to his goal, which was essentially political. "I wanted to make a film against the party that governed Italy for thirty years and shipwrecked the country, politically and culturally," he stressed.[34]

Accordingly, he created a totally new plot, taking Sciascia's concept to paradoxical extremes and making explicit what was barely sketched and subtly hinted at. Most notably, he replaced the lay artist with a new character absent from the book, who became the film's focus and narrative center, opposed to Don Gaetano: a party leader referred to as "M" whose name is never uttered, but whose personality and demeanor are patterned after those of Aldo Moro.

To many leftists, the rise of Moro on the political scene as Prime Minister in 1963— the first government to include Socialists—was a glimmer of hope after the political aggressiveness of his predecessors. Moro's approach was propositional, and he was open to dialogue with political adversaries. But to Petri his regency coincided with "the decomposition of institutions, and at the same time with the definitive consolidation … of the cultural bases of consumerist society."[35] The director's intent was clear:

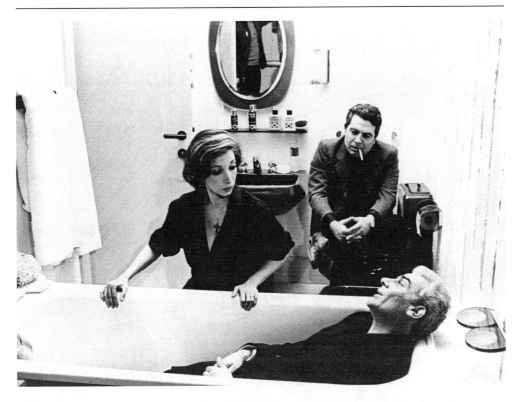

Filming *Todo modo*: Mariangela Melato, Elio Petri and Gian Maria Volonté rehearsing a scene.

For many years Moro carried his power like a cross on his shoulders, and the torment of this sort of exhausting spiritual exercise was clear in his emaciated face, in his somewhat lost behavior, in the bitter grimace of his mouth, in his sickly gaze. He took onto himself the impossible endeavor of mediating between the utopian and the wheeler-dealer souls of his party, between his party and the leftist parties, between the poor and the rich, between the exploited and the exploiters. As the cross of mediation weighed on him more and more, it looked as if it could crush him at any moment.[36]

Petri's adaptation starts during a mysterious epidemic that is spreading all over Italy. The streets are littered with Red Cross tents offering help to the infected. A limo is carrying "M" to the Zafer hermitage, an ultramodern structure in reinforced concrete which looks like a bunker, surrounded by a huge park of maritime pines. "M" descends into the catacombs underneath the hermitage and starts praying in Latin, in a conceited suffering manner. There he is reached by Don Gaetano. The two men share compromising secrets, and "M" mentions an incriminating letter he has received about the corrupt priest. "M" is an overly pious man, almost effeminate, and with affected manners. Don Gaetano is patently disgusted by him. In his room, "M" meets with his wife Giacinta (another character created specifically for the film). Their relationship is morbid and asexual, more akin to mother and son.

Other politicians start arriving at the hermitage to perform the spiritual exercises over the course of three days. It soon transpires that the meeting is actually a pretext for a political rendezvous within the party, which must renovate its structure deeply in order to maintain power in the country. The politicians (all of them ugly, elderly, unpleasant looking) can't stop arguing, accusing and taunting each other. All are waiting for a powerful party member (called "Him") to show up. Don Gaetano's sermons are spiteful and openly accusing of the party's corrupt ways. "M"'s opening speech is met with either approval or hostility. The party is clearly split into two.

Soon, someone starts killing off the politicians. One is murdered in his room; another is shot dead in a crowded area while all those present are frantically reciting the rosary. On the second day "Him"—"M"'s biggest adversary—shows up. A magistrate, Scalambri, turns up to investigate, but the party's code of silence proves a severe obstacle. More murders ensue: first Voltrano, a homosexual who collected incriminating evidence against everyone in the party, and then "Him" are found dead. CIA agents take "M" away, dressed as a priest, to a secret hideout in the catacombs. There, "M" meets with Scalambri and tells him he has found out that the killings follow a bizarre pattern: the victims all headed state agencies whose acronyms, combined together, form the phrase "*Todo modo para buscar la voluntad divina*." To prevent further killings, a meeting takes place in which every survivor must tell the names of all the organizations he controls, which soon descends into chaos: everyone is involved in myriad such agencies (and benefitting of princely earnings) which in turn are all connected to one another. So, everyone is a potential victim. Eventually, Don Gaetano is found dead, apparently he has killed himself. In his room there is a secret archive with plenty of incriminating dossiers. The case is seemingly solved.

On the morning of the third day, "M" prepares to leave Zafer. Giacinta spitefully tells him that she knows everything, for Don Gaetano told her the name of the murderer. The place is empty. In the huge atrium, all the other politicians' suitcases are gathered for their departure. "M" walks in the park and an apocalyptic sight appears before his eyes. Thousands of paper sheets are strewn across the landscape. They are Don Gaetano's dossiers on his fellow party members. And each dossier leads to a dead body, like Tom Thumb's breadcrumbs. It is a massacre.

Bodies pop up by the dozen, including Scalambri's. They are arranged in grotesque poses, even piled one on top of the other, in a hellish vision. CIA hitmen wander around the park. "M" at first pretends not to see anything and walks among the macabre exhibition as if in a state of trance. Then he starts collecting the pieces of compromising evidence, in a desperate attempt to save appearances. He was clearly part of the conspiracy, possibly carried out by the CIA, to exterminate the party cadres and start anew. But the palingenesis cannot take place without "M"'s death. Eventually, he comes across his own picture, at the end of a path covered with top secret dossiers.

"M" kneels down, raises his eyes to the sky and starts praying to the Holy Father. His driver, who happens to be a secret agent too, pulls out a gun, steps behind "M" and aims at his head. The camera slowly rises away from "M." The driver shoots. The sound of church bells accompanies the end credits.

Making Todo modo

Petri adapted the novel with the collaboration of Roberto "Berto" Pelosso (who had been his assistant on *I giorni contati*, *Peccato nel pomeriggio*, *Il maestro di Vigevano* and *La decima vittima*), and asked the advice of his friend, University professor Marco Ferronato, for bibliographic information on Ignatius of Loyola. Ferronato is credited as consultant on the film.

The first draft of the script was completed on the evening of Monday, May 19, 1975. In a note dated May 27, Petri wrote that he had typewritten it and prepared seven copies. "Those who read it are Ruggero [Mastroianni], [Enzo] Siciliano, [Franco] Reggiani, Claudio M. [Mancini], [Alberto] Grimaldi, [Domenico] Naldini, [Mario] Di Biase, and of course Paola and Dante [Ferretti]."[37]

Petri felt confident that he would start shooting in September, but his optimism proved excessive. The Italian production system was based on the so-called "guaranteed minimum," with distributors giving producers an advance sum based on the expected box-office figures. Alberto Grimaldi was willing to produce *Todo modo* but could not find any distributor willing to advance the money. No one wanted to have anything to do with it. On August 26, 1975, a disheartened Petri wrote:

> Fact is, I can't yet say that the film won't be made. But if it will be made, how will I get to work, under what conditions? I'll write down the list of distributors that have rejected the project so far: United Artists, Twentieth Century–Fox, Warner Bros., Titanus, Gaumont…. My mistake: wanting to make this kind of cinema with big producers, with capitals that increase dramatically the objective difficulties … and result in censorship, apparently commercial yet basically political. Capital is censorship…. It is the master. It is impossible to reverse the roles. It is the defeat of a certain type of cinema, which I call political or political-popular. *Polpop, poppol …* ahi, ahi, ahi. Goodbye *polpop*, goodbye *poppol*.[38]

As he later complained,

> There are difficulties. Mostly practical ones. Nowadays distributors demand eroticism, and so they are scared even of *Todo modo*, which nevertheless addresses a popular theme, has a *giallo* mechanism and is made according to very grotesque and lively schemes … they say it is too countercurrent. It is easier for them to extort billions from the audience by rummaging in their genitals….[39]

After Grimaldi backed out, Petri cut a deal with Daniele Senatore. It was only through the involvement of Warner (one of the many who had rejected the project at first) that Senatore found the necessary backing. To produce *Cadaveri eccellenti*, Grimaldi had to make a similar move and resort to United Artists. Claudio Mancini too had been doing prep work on *Todo modo*, even though his name doesn't appear in the credits. "I had advised against doing it, and eventually I couldn't do it. I was working with Sergio Leone … my daughter worked on it. Years later I bumped into Senatore, who told me: 'My father disowned me for that film. I should have listened to you….'"[40]

In his memoir, Ugo Pirro claims that Senatore and associate producer Francesco Genesi tried to convince Petri to hire him to revise the script, possibly to soothe its core.[41] But the director did not oblige. On the contrary, he reshaped the screenplay according to the elections and their aftermath, well determined to make it as close to the political climate as possible. In a diary note dated September 25, 1975, he wrote: "We must revise *Todo modo* and take into account the results of the June 15 vote, but proceeding from the assumption that it was indeed a historical date, yet only in the long term."[42]

While working on the film, the director was considering other projects. One such was an adaptation of Evan S. Connell's 1966 novel *The Diary of a Rapist*, whose rights were owned by Franco Nero, and to be produced by Alberto Grimaldi. Another was an unspecified project for Senatore, mentioned in a letter dated August 12, 1975, as *Papa Borgia*.[43] A third project from this period involved Franco Nero, with whom Petri had remained friends. Sometime in 1971, when the actor was shooting Duccio Tessari's *Viva la muerte … tua!* in Spain, Elio and Paola had paid him a visit, and Nero's dancing skills had inspired the director with an impromptu inspiration:

> I remember one night there was some music and I started dancing with the actress, Marilù Tolo … and I was dancing so well … when I was young I could dance well, and I even participated in competitions. And Elio goes: "Franco, I have the movie for you. The story of a small-town dancer who dances with the old ladies in the dance halls."[44]

The idea never materialized, but some years later Nero asked Petri to write a film to do together. "He wrote a wonderful screenplay, titled *L'ostaggio*. I showed it to the greatest screenwriter ever, Robert Bolt," Nero explained. "I still have a twelve-page note from this great screenwriter where he criticizes Elio's script, but loves it so much. He both loves and criticizes it."[45] Set in South America in 19th century and almost entirely focused on just two characters, *L'ostaggio* was the story of a virgin girl who must cross a desert to marry an army captain. But a political prisoner, escaped from a prison camp, takes her hostage, and the encounter will have unexpected consequences for both. According to Nero, Gillo Pontecorvo read the script and decided to direct it himself. There is indeed a 58-page treatment retained in the Pontecorvo fund at Turin's AMNC, signed by Petri's screenwriter friend Franco Reggiani, suggesting that Petri actually put down a basic outline which he passed to Reggiani for development. But the project halted. "Pontecorvo wasted two or three years of our time, because in his whole life Gillo made four or five feature films…."[46] In recent years Franco Nero has repeatedly claimed he wants to direct the movie as a homage to Petri, setting the story in the present (as suggested by Bolt) and with Vittorio Storaro as d.o.p.[47]; however, unbeknownst to the actor, the film already exists. After Pontecorvo backed out of *L'ostaggio* to make *Ogro* (1979), Reggiani recycled the same plot for the script of *Fuga scabrosamente pericolosa*, shot in Colombia in 1980 by Nello Rossati, starring Eleonora Vallone and Rodrigo Obregón, and released in Italy only in 1985.

To take a break from the troubled preproduction of *Todo modo*, Petri went on vacation in Sardinia. There he probably had a laugh at the news that the praetor in Palermo, Vincenzo Salmieri, had seized Super 8 tapes of *La decima vittima* in the midst of a personal crusade for common decency which made it into the news in the midst of a sleepy, hot August.[48] The motivation for the seizure was the sight of a bikini-clad Ursula Andress on the box cover.

News of Petri preparing *Todo modo* started filtering into the press in the summer of 1975. The protagonist would be Gian Maria Volonté, on his fourth film with the director. "Shooting should begin in autumn and I hope I'll find a way to be in this film,"[49] the actor commented. True to his commitment, he had reduced his film appearances and accepted only roles in openly political works. After starring in Miguel Littin's *Actas de Marusia*, in June 1975 Volonté had run for the local administrative elections in the Lazio region with the PCI and had been elected regional councilor but resigned after just six months. "I cannot be an actor and take care of the cultural issues in the region at the same time," he explained.[50]

Among the reasons for his resignation there was his upcoming film with Petri. As usual, Volonté prepared meticulously for the role, and curtly replied to those who questioned his choice:

> Today, even being an actor is being political. Cinema is a great means of mass communication. We must manage to make political movies which are not ambiguous and are capable of

winning over the audience, and we must be able to have them distributed everywhere. Or else, movie theaters will keep screening commercial films instead of those that promote culture.[51]

The cast comprised many prestigious names, such as Mariangela Melato as Giacinta, Marcello Mastroianni as Don Gaetano, Renato Salvatori (*Poveri ma belli, I soliti ignoti, Rocco e i suoi fratelli*) as Scalambri, Franco Citti (*Accattone* and many other Pasolini films) as "M"'s driver and Michel Piccoli as "Him"—a role patterned on Giulio Andreotti, as the make-up, square frames, and combed back black wig underline.

Piccoli and the director knew each other since the late 1960s and had become close friends. "Apparently he was a great *bon vivant*, but he was full of anguish,"[52] the French actor recalled. During the making of *Todo modo* he and Petri attempted to put together *Settore privato* (Private Sector), based on French stage critic Paul Léautaud's private diaries (*Journal particulier*), published in Italy in 1968. Léautaud was one of the most unique figures in the 20th century, notorious for his scathing judgments on his contemporaries and his libertine lifestyle. He kept a meticulous chronicle of his life in his diaries. Piccoli's company Les Films 66 would purchase the rights to the book from the Parisian Animal Protection Society (to which the eccentric writer had left them) and he would star and coproduce the film. *Settore privato* was a project Petri was quite fond of, but it ended up in the long list of unproduced ones.

A great fan of the comedy duo Franco Franchi and Ciccio Ingrassia, Petri cast the latter as the unctuous Voltrano. It was not Ingrassia's first dramatic role—he had appeared in *La violenza: quinto potere* (1972, Florestano Vancini) and in Fellini's *Amarcord*

Michel Piccoli as "Him," a character modeled on politician Giulio Andreotti, in *Todo modo*.

(1973)—but certainly not one audiences would associate with the popular comedian. Petri had also planned to cast Luigi Diberti, but the delays in the production caused conflicting schedules with Diberti's stage commitments.

Filming for *Todo modo* started in December 1975 in Cinecittà. Petri asked production designer Dante Ferretti to envision the Zafer Hermitage as an underground resort built next to Christian catacombs. "It gives the idea of how today's 'last Christians' carry out their avidity and compare it with the conditioned reflex that religion has become to them.... A contemporary hell which recalls regime architecture in its cold technocratic modernism."[53]

The mood was gloomy, or at least Petri's was, judging from his answers to Jean A. Gili, who interviewed him on the set on February 8, 1976. The director still had a chip on his shoulder against critics, whom he said were "part of a system even without realizing it." He went on at length lamenting their obsessional mania, their single-mindedness, their short-sighted culture, and complained that his early works had been praised by communist critics only because his own statements were communist friendly, and not because of the films' inner qualities. "There are so many ambiguities concerning criticism that, personally, it no longer interests me."[54]

Despite a series of strikes among Cinecittà workers, which caused a halt in the shoot in January,[55] the following month news articles reported that *Todo modo* was to be screened at the next Cannes Film Festival together with *Cadaveri eccellenti* and Visconti's *L'innocente*.[56] It would be the ideal showcase for such a highly anticipated work. Having already won the Grand Prix, Petri claimed that he would take his film out of competition.[57] Eventually, however, *Todo modo* was not among the titles screened in Cannes in 1976.

Mingus

Always one to think big, Senatore decided that such a daring film must have a score just as bold. He and *L'Unità*'s music critic Filippo Bianchi suggested the use of jazz music to convey the story's feel and message. Petri was perplexed to say the least, for he had in mind something in the vein of Olivier Messiaen's "Oiseaux exotiques" (1955–1956) and "Catalogue d'oiseaux" (1956–1958), but he obliged. The choice of double bassist and pianist Charles Mingus seemed ideal. His overt political commitment had resulted in one of his most famous compositions, "Meditations on Integration," as well as in provocatively titled pieces such as "Remember Rockefeller at Attica" and "Free Cell Block F, 'Tis Nazi USA" (both released in 1975, on the albums *Changes One* and *Changes Two*, respectively).

Mingus was not new to the film industry. He had studied with Lloyd Reese and had appeared as an extra in *Road to Zanzibar* (1941, Victor Schertzinger), where he was edited out of the final cut, and *Higher and Higher* (1943, Tim Whelan). He had appeared also in the British film *All Night Long* (1962, Basil Dearden) playing a new composition, "Peggy's Blue Skylight." Mingus had had a chance to try his hand at a film score in 1958, when John Cassavetes had asked him to write the music for *Shadows*, but his score was eventually deleted and replaced with improv sax solos by Shafi Hadi.

Involving Mingus in *Todo modo* seemed also a sly marketing choice for foreign distribution. In fact, the artist was under contract to the record company Atlantic, part of the Warner Bros holding. But Mingus was very popular in Italy as well. He had first played there in 1964, and between 1974 and 1975 he had often played gigs all over the country, with an outstanding response from the public resulting in audiences of 10,000 people.

Senatore and Petri got in touch with Mingus in late 1975, possibly during his exhibition at the Bologna International Jazz Festival on November 15, and Bianchi flew to New York to discuss with the musician about the type of score that was expected of him. But, as the critic recalled,

> I immediately and dramatically discovered that Mingus was a mystic. Not only did he have no feeling of derision or satire against the deity or the Church, but, on the contrary, he claimed that his music was inspired directly by God. To me, this revelation meant an appalling displacement from all our assumptions, and therefore an uphill battle from the very beginning. Anyway, possibly because Mingus, like many Americans, saw Italian cinema's expressive value in a mythical light, he seemed very interested in the job, even though he had trouble understanding the explanations I gave him about the film: these things were so removed from him....[58]

A letter to Petri dated January 15, 1976, and signed by Mingus and his wife Susan Graham proves that he was already at work on the score. He already met the director and was struck by his "warmth and openness ... in spite of the language barrier."[59] Through Bianchi, Petri had suggested that Mingus listen to Messiaen's music. But "Catalogue d'oiseaux" left him upset, for he found many similarities with his groundbreaking 1955 composition, "Revelations (First Movement)." "Mingus was convinced that the Messiaen piece had been copied from his composition, or at least that 'Revelations' had been the inspiration for 'Catalogue d'oiseaux,'" Bianchi recalled. "We doubted that Mingus was telling the truth. Petri made him listen to it so that Mingus would take inspiration to write the score for the film, and now it turned out that Messiaen had taken inspiration from Mingus to write that piece."[60] To prove his point, Mingus sent a tape to Bianchi and Petri with the recording of "Revelations" played on his turntable and captured by a microphone from the loudspeakers, apologizing for the background noises ... including the barking of his dog. When he heard it, Bianchi had to agree with Mingus. However, as Italian musicologist and Mingus scholar Stefano Zenni pointed out, it was just an amazing coincidence, for both compositions were written around the same time and Mingus' record was issued later, so Messiaen couldn't have heard it.

In late March 1976, the American musician arrived in Rome. He took advantage of the visit to play four gigs at Rome's Music Inn,[61] with basically the same lineup that had played on the two *Changes* albums: Mingus on double bass, George Adams on tenor saxophone, Jack Walrath on trumpet, and Dannie Richmond on drums. The only variation in the lineup was pianist Danny Mixon instead of Don Pullen.[62]

The band recorded the bulk of the music for *Todo modo* at the Umiliani Studio on March 29 and 30. Mingus had brought from the States about 45 minutes of usable music which he was willing to modify according to necessities. "Being the film a parable on a 'confessional' party, Mingus thought the organ was in theme," Bianchi commented.[63] The artist had asked his friend Buddy Collette to help him with the orchestration and direction, but Collette didn't show up. The quintet (with Mixon on organ instead of piano) was joined by a handful of Italian musicians, chosen by musical assistant Nino Dei: namely, Anastasio Del Bono (horn and oboe), Pasquale Sabatelli (bassoon), Quarto Maltoni (contralto sax), Dino Piana (trombone).[64]

Composer and multi-instrumentalist Roberto Laneri, who had attended the musician's unorthodox classes on contemporary composition at the UCSD,[65] was recruited to play bass clarinet. "I was at RCA playing film music, I don't know which. And someone came and said: 'There's a phone call for you.' It was Mingus, who had heard I was in Rome. He was recording and told me: 'If you want to play with us, come over.' I picked up my instruments, took a taxi and to another studio, and we recorded."[66] When Mingus found out that Maltoni was a good reader but not an improviser, he asked for a soloist. Filippo Bianchi called 19-year-old alto saxophonist Giancarlo Maurino, who couldn't read music but was a very talented player. Maurino played all the improv contralto sax solos in the recording.

Mingus hadn't seen a single frame of *Todo modo* but worked only on the basis of Petri and Senatore's indications. He was very upset about it, so Senatore invited him on the set. Then they had lunch together and Petri agreed to show Mingus some footage. A third session was held on April 1 at Dirmaphon Studio, where a screen was available. There, Mingus and Adams (on flute) recorded an improvised duet whilst watching excerpts from the film, possibly "M"'s confession to Don Gaetano.

However, Mingus' music is nowhere to be found in the film. According to Filippo Bianchi, Petri came up with excuses for he was not quite convinced with such a choice from the beginning. "He said that he didn't like the type of orchestration, that he would have wanted a score with a contemporary academic feeling whereas Mingus had proposed one with bassoon, trumpet, horn, organ etc. which, we didn't quite understand on what basis, had been judged aprioristically unfit for the film. But that music was wonderful."[67]

In Bianchi's recollection, Petri invited Renzo Arbore, a well-known disc-jockey, musician, and TV and radio host (and Mariangela Melato's fiancé at the time) and had him listen to Mingus' score. "Arbore claimed that it was second-hand music made by assembling old material recycled for the occasion, and which in any case did not fit the atmosphere of the film. This was enough to convince Petri to sack Mingus."[68] In a radio interview on January 13, 2005, during the radio program *Hollywood Party*, Arbore vehemently denied this story.[69] According to Stefano Zenni, the reason behind Petri's choice was that Mingus' music only partly fit the film. The parts he played with Adams while seeing the footage at Dirmaphon Studio would suit perfectly the Volonté/Mastroianni scene, and the opening theme plays great under the title sequence. Other parts don't quite work, even though the music is beautiful and inventive throughout.

Eventually, Petri called on Ennio Morricone, who put together in just a few days a Messiaen-inspired score. Mingus left Rome without knowing that his work had been rejected.[70] The music he recorded for *Todo modo* can be heard on the B-side of his 1978 album *Cumbia & Jazz Fusion*: a 22-minute piece titled "Music for 'Todo Modo,'" with Senatore credited as producer. The opening section evokes the early minutes of "Revelations," but the piece soon takes on other directions. As Mingus' biographer Krin Gabbard noted, "typically, whatever is happening at the beginning of Mingus' compositions bears little resemblance to what happens later."[71] According to Sue Mingus, "Music for 'Todo Modo'" was her husband's favorite listening in the last, painful months of his life. He was proud of it.[72]

The troubled story of the score for *Todo modo* echoes the destiny that would loom over the film itself. The controversy began well before anyone had seen a single frame. In her column in the *Corriere della Sera*, Lietta Tornabuoni anticipated that the character Volonté played in the film was described in the director's notes as "a politician affected by latent homosexuality and religious mania … his relationship with his wife Giacinta, who behaves with him like his mother, is incestuous … this relationship serves to depict a current form of infantile regression of a certain type of Italian male."[73] Tornabuoni reported the scandalized reaction of politician Franco Evangelisti ("I feel insulted in my Christian Democrat virility") and added: "He is particularly outraged by the physical depiction studied by Petri and Volonté for the character of the eminent Democrazia Cristiana politician in the film: a grey man, with grey clothes and grey hair, priest-like gait, tired gesturing, dampened eloquence, his head always a bit oblique. 'And the name starts with the initial "M." Got the hint?'"[74] Everybody did. Long before the film opened, everyone knew that Gian Maria Volonté was portraying what looked like a ferocious caricature of prime minister Aldo Moro.

Massacre Time

In late April 1976, days before the official release of *Todo modo*, a front-page article in the nation's most important newspaper reported Petri's alarmed complaint about "pressures" to stop its distribution. With national political elections scheduled for June 20 and 21, *Todo modo* was seen as a bomb about to blast. "I've been told this nice story from someone in the U.S.," Petri told the *Corriere della Sera*:

> A so-called high personality of the Democrazia Cristiana got in touch with Dino De Laurentiis through a Christian Democrat leader of the Italian producers' association. De Laurentiis, who has now settled in the U.S. but has always been a sympathizer of the DC, was asked to intervene with the president of Warner Brothers, the co-producer of *Todo modo*, and have him notice how untimely it would be on the part of an American company to release in Italy such a movie at election time. And De Laurentiis promptly executed the diplomatic mission.[75]

Petri added that the mission had been accomplished, given that Warner would retire *Todo modo* from circulation before May 30 and re-release it again in September. From a commercial viewpoint, with barely one month's time in theaters, this would mean a sure-fire box-office flop. It was not, Petri pointed out, the only difficulty he had had: despite being based on a best-selling novel, being directed by a well-known and successful filmmaker and featuring an all-star cast, the project had had trouble finding financing, and even faced unexpected issues during the shooting at Cinecittà, where Petri struggled to rent the studio. Why all these acts of hostility?

> Because the film tells about the spiritual exercises of Christian Democrat politicians who haven't got anything spiritual in them anymore. Because it's not an anti–Catholic film: the accuser of the political class is a priest. Because in its own way it's a religious film: it denounces the utter split in the party between the religious ideas it professes and the political behavior it practices. In the end, perhaps for the first time, there are no mediations. Things and people are called by their names.[76]

However, regarding the film's most controversial character, Petri mischievously suggested a second—and by all means even more provocative—explanation to the initial "M." "It can relate to so many words, such as mother, or else *Mörder*, which means murderer in German and was the title of a famous Fritz Lang film."[77]

The debate became more heated on *Todo modo*'s opening week. The Italian producers' association denied any intervention to prevent its circulation[78] and De Laurentiis curtly refuted the director's accusations. "Petri thinks that we must have the same ideas as him. He doesn't accept that others can democratically think in a different way," the producer replied. "I want to clarify that no one ever called me from Rome about that matter … to elaborate further would only mean free publicity for Petri's film. But I think that it would be more serious if communists had their propaganda financed by Moscow or Peking instead of the corrupt American capitalists," he added sarcastically. During the interview, he never mentioned the film's title nor the company that produced it. But he left with a poisonous sting in the tail, quoting a phrase Ennio Flaiano allegedly told Petri during the 1971 Venice Film Festival: "Dear comrade, I would so much like to be a communist like you, but I'm too poor to afford this luxury."[79] Although fake—neither Flaiano nor anyone else had addressed Petri like that—the line went to the heart of the director's controversial position in Italian cinema: a communist filmmaker who made political films but was "guilty" of making successful ones. The son of a coppersmith had become a wealthy, important personality, and this attack to his well-being hit where it hurt the most.

Todo modo came out in Italy on April 30, 1976. That same day Aldo Moro resigned, putting an end to the Italian Republic's sixth legislature. The President of the Republic would then dissolve parliament and call for new elections. In Lietta Tornabuoni's report of Todo modo's screening before the rating board, the description of Petri's descent in the ministry's subterranean belly to the projection room where board members would watch the movie, echoed its characters' descent in the underground hermitage where they would meet their end. And the image of Petri's hearing before the committee gave an idea of the mortifying atmosphere that reigned in the ministry, with filmmakers and producers behaving like schoolboys in front of an exam board. "The censorship committee is standing in half circle, mature ladies and gentlemen with curious stares, and half-smiles of paternalistic encouragement. The Todo modo people are standing in front of them, trying to remain adult."[80] After reporting Petri's embarrassment before the commission when having to explain the message of his film and the final decision—the committee rated it V.M.14 because of images of blood-covered corpses—Tornabuoni ended the piece with the words from an unnamed member: "Congratulations, you have made a very strong film. It won't last a week; they're going to seize it straight away."[81]

Incredibly, it didn't happen. However, a couple of months later an association named "Difesa Uomo-Natura" denounced Petri for public insult to the head of the government.[82] It happened on June 24, a few days after the new elections. The denunciation was quite peculiar, for, as the renowned jurist Giovanni Conso noted, such acts by private citizens were usually motivated by a film's alleged obscenity. Moreover, Conso argued, it had no juridical ground. "In short, Elio Petri should be sufficiently calm about the fate of his film. The procedure will never start, or, in the worst-case scenario, it will halt soon."[83]

The June 1976 vote photographed a polarized nation: the DC got 38.7 percent of the votes, the PCI got 34.3 percent. As Guido Crainz synthesized, "the DC invoked consensus to avoid overtaking, and must therefore prevent or delay the PCI's entry in the government, whereas the PCI had long since taken a path that precluded a clash with the DC: therefore it was exposed to conditionings, delays, and to the most diverse forms of wearing out."[84]

Communists did not become part of the new government. Not least because at the second G7 summit in Puerto Rico, the major Western world leaders had decided not to lend money to Italy in that eventuality. This led to a tragicomedy of sorts, with the choice of Giulio Andreotti as Prime Minister: a technical move made to reassure the allies, balance the situation, and calm the markets. Moro stood behind, in the shadows. The DC

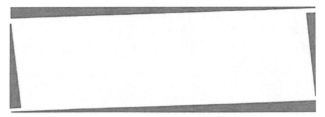

The Italian locandina for *Todo modo* attempted to sell the film as an ordinary *giallo*—which it definitely wasn't.

gradually caught the PCI in a "death embrace," involving it in government policies so as to smooth its edges and defuse its aims, just as it had done with PSI in 1963.

To many who had voted Communist, it was more than a disappointment. It was mockery. Despite having reached an outstanding result, the nation's second biggest political force had been reduced to powerlessness, forced to bow to the decisions coming from the Christian Democrats. The apocalyptic scenario painted by Petri had not taken place, after all: the DC had not ended in self-destruction but had been reborn from its ashes. The general climate in the nation was gloomier than ever. "It's a time of suspension," Petri wrote to Jean A. Gili. "Everything appears swollen with something which cannot, doesn't want to or doesn't know how to burst. The appearance of Italian society in these days is like that of certain pregnant women—big, staring, deformed, livid. It carries an old baby in its womb, perhaps already dead."[85]

"Mr. Petri is like Goebbels"

Critics were waiting for *Todo modo* with their weapons well-oiled and knives between their teeth. Panning reviews ensued, openly spoiling the ending and invariably focusing on the identity between Volonté's character and Aldo Moro. There were also violently contrarian readers' letters to the press, even accusing it of making involuntary propaganda for the DC.[86] *L'Espresso* hosted a debate on the film and its depiction of the DC with Petri, journalists Aniello Coppola and Giampaolo Pansa, and the Christian Democrat Minister for Tourism and Spectacle, Adolfo Sarti.[87]

Even critics who in the past had been very supportive toward the director panned the film. Lino Micciché wrote:

> The lack of dialectics, the excessive over-the-top tone, the expressionistic incontinence, the crudeness in alluding, the continuous mockery—not to mention the hopelessly bad things, such as the whole part about Giacinta … a true psychopolitical mess—make this spectacle justifiably unacceptable to Christian Democrat spectators and uselessly consoling to non–Christian Democrat ones, and therefore politically ineffective too.[88]

News articles attempted to mount the controversy by noting the many differences between the novel and the movie, but Sciascia was adamant: "I don't care about other people's films' literal faithfulness to my books. I care about substantial faithfulness to the idea which is the book's starting point. Judging from the reactions the film has provoked even before its release, I guess this faithfulness can be found in Petri's film."[89]

Among the critical response to *Todo modo*, one stood out. Francesco Savio, who had ignited the angry controversy following *La proprietà*, wrote a self-styled "farewell letter to Elio Petri" in his last column for *Il Mondo*. Returning to the theme of the "barony of critics," Savio bitterly remarked that, in fact, his was "a precarious and difficult job neither more nor less than yours, dear Petri." Savio had many reservations about the movie ("its generous and vivid intentions are not matched by adequate expressive results"), but decided indeed to linger on the analogy between the author and the critic, with some illuminating passages:

> Once a film is finished, its author gets rid of it, breaks away from it. To the critic, that's impossible. He keeps pondering by himself, like a mirror from which no image is cancelled, about all that a film hasn't said, the abstruse and opaque images left between the folds of each sequence…. I am sure you will make more films, and you will carry on your discourse on

power and conscience, dear Petri, while I, at the moment, don't know if I'll ever find space and chances to engage with other people's films. People will say: Who cares about the critic, it's the director (and his *oeuvre*) that we must care and worry about. Now you see, dear Petri, how specious was the controversy that divided us three years ago. What does the page matter, compared with the peremptory lightning of the image? The more the critic is struggling, a bit dizzy, consuming his eyes, the more the latter transfixes our memory and settles there forever.[90]

That was indeed Savio's last film review. On October 28, following a quarrel with his lover, he put his head in the oven and killed himself.

As for the Christian Democrats, an interview with MP Bartolo Ciccardini (who had only seen a short clip of the film on TV) reported in the newspaper *La Repubblica* is telling:

> Mr. Petri is like Goebbels, this film is like *Süss l'ebreo* [Author's note: *Jud Süß*, 1940, by Veit Harlan, an infamous anti–Semitic Nazi propaganda film]. This film has only a precedent, that of Nazis against Jews. It is an uneducated and partisan contortion of the Democrazia Cristiana, and an incitement to civil war. Let's be clear: there may be ten thieves among us Christian Democrats, and it is legitimate, in the play of democracy, to send the Christian Democrats to the opposition in parliament. But this hate, this mendacity, the logic of this film, is terrible. If you follow this logic, you arrive at concentration camps. You should realize that this film takes you to the ghetto.[91]

Todo modo ended up at the 68th spot among Italian films released in 1976, its box-office gross amounting to 856 million *lire*, lost amid much less ambitious genre fare, while *Cadaveri eccellenti* grossed more than two billion. It was also ignored at the annual ceremonies: on June 28, Mastroianni and Melato won the Grolla d'Oro award, but for the whole of their films released during the 1975–1976 season, without any mention of *Todo modo*. The only other prize awarded to the film was that to Ciccio Ingrassia as Best Supporting Actor by the National Syndicate of Film Journalists. Volonté's performance was ignored, and he was quickly marginalized: it would take a year and a half before audiences could see him again in an Italian film, Damiano Damiani's *Io ho paura*, released in October 1977.

Todo modo's commercial life abroad was hardly noticeable. That October it was screened in Tbilisi, Georgia, at a convention on Italian and Russian cinema,[92] and the following month it turned up at the second edition of the Paris International Film Festival, leading to a January 1977 French release. It was seen by 51,178 spectators. It was one of its few showcases outside Italy: in October 1977 it played at the Chicago International Film Festival, but it surfaced in New York venues only in December 1979. It came out in Spain on June 16, 1978, distributed by Continental Cinematográfica, and was seen by 16,592 spectators.

Masters and Sinners

"Mine is not just a political work, but a call for the need to renew the way of doing politics,"[93] Petri claimed upon the film's release. The result nurtures a complex ambiguity, riddled as it is with symbols and allusions. The director defined it as "a work on the split between ideas and behavior, on the hell of political power, on the wearing out of certain principles, like a big metaphysical ballad destined to make the audience think and elicit conscious anguish in them."[94]

As Alfredo Rossi pointed out, *Todo modo* is a "condensation, a clot of phantoms that awaited, in diverse ways, to take form."[95] First and foremost, it is littered with more or less open references to the DC and its main exponents. The setting itself, the huge park with Mediterranean pines where the hermitage is located, evokes a key moment in the party's history, the congress which took place between 14 and 17 March 1959, at the Domus Mariae, a Dorothean convent just outside Rome, after the then-secretary and head of the government Amintore Fanfani had resigned, in disagreement with his party. There, over the course of 72 hours, a heated struggle between the DC's main currents ensued, namely Fanfani's supporters and the dissidents (nicknamed "Dorotheans"). It ended with Aldo Moro being elected as the new secretary. Ironically, Moro's positions then, as opposed to Fanfani's, were against an agreement with the Socialists, which took place only four years later.

Petri stated that he took inspiration from Sigmund Freud's posthumous book *Thomas Woodrow Wilson: A Psychological Study* to shape the main character.[96] Published in 1967 but actually written in 1930 by the then-septuagenarian father of psychoanalysis and his friend, the American ambassador to France and longtime Wilson adversary William C. Bullitt, it was a controversial biography of the late U.S. President which combined Freud's psychological insights and Bullitt's own records. Panned upon release as "a mischievous and preposterous joke, a sort of caricature of the worst that has come from psychoanalytic dialogue, or else an awful and unrelenting slander,"[97] it nevertheless struck Petri. This says a lot, for he and Bullitt likely shared the same acrimony toward their *bête noire*.

Another likely influence was *Berlinguer e il professore*, a novel published in early 1975 by Rizzoli, initially signed "Anonimo" (Anonymous). In less than six months it sold over half a million copies and caused a fuss: some even thought that Berlinguer himself had penned it. Only in 1976 did the noted *Corriere della Sera* journalist Gianfranco Piazzesi step in to reveal himself as the author. Set in the year 2000, *Berlinguer e il professore* was an ironic dystopian tale that depicted the results of the "historic compromise" between the DC and the PCI. Among other things, Piazzesi imagined that all the major DC party members had been murdered one by one. Only Moro was left alive.

But Petri reprised several elements also from *Nostra signora Metredina*, which he had described as an attempt to channel the rage he felt against the Democrazia Cristiana. Both stories adopt an openly satirical tone and deal with the description of the politicians' hypocritical pious attitude. Pilato, the main character in *Nostra signora Metredina*, is in many ways a predecessor to "M." He lives in a convent like a monk, goes to church every morning (like Moro did) and practices chastity, but he watches porn films in his princely villa, and his frustration (both political and sexual) manifests in sudden crying fits. In *Nostra signora Metredina* all the politicians have funny surnames, devise Machiavellian schemes, and their language is "abstruse and with no connection whatsoever with reality, at least common knowledge reality," just like in the 1976 film, to the point that Don Gaetano urges them to "create … a language which will bring you closer to God." *Nostra signora Metredina* revolves around a surreptitious conflict between the party's various currents which echoes *Todo modo*'s struggle for power, replete with blackmailing attempts, corruption at all levels, espionage, surveillance and intelligence work. Last but not least, the relationship between Pilato and his chauffeur Arturo, who turns out to be a secret agent, predates the one between "M" and the driver.

With such premises, it's no surprise *Todo modo* displays a moral fervor comparable to that of the spiritual exercises conceived by Loyola. Petri devised the film "exactly as if it were a spiritual exercise, even in the police investigation assimilated into the exercise."[98] The director knew and cited Roland Barthes' 1971 essay *Sade, Fourier, Loyola*, in which the French semiotician labeled Loyola's ecstatic discipline as sadistic in its rituality and capricious repetition. And it is from Barthes' reading that Petri developed the idea of a literal *mise-en-scène* of Hell in which sinners are confined while attempting to get closer to God through the word.

The whodunit structure reprises and expands that of Sciascia's novel. It was a necessary choice, the director explained, to portray "the climate of horrible mystery in which we are forced to live. Since '68 we live in some kind of bad, stupid, vulgar *giallo* novel whose threads are held by politicians and magistrates, and often by cops and journalists…."[99] The offbeat conspiracy plot and apocalyptic undertones make *Todo modo* akin to *Cadaveri eccellenti*, which describes a coup d'état on the part of the Right. Rosi's film too starts in a catacomb, hinting at a similar mortuary and grotesque tone. But it ultimately tries to reconnect to contemporary Italian reality: Rosi shot the opening inside a real catacomb, the Catacombe dei Cappuccini in Palermo, and included semi-documentary footage of clashes in the street. Petri resorted to extreme stylization instead. *Todo modo*'s characters lock themselves away from the outside world, and the whole film has an unreal, theatrical quality to it.

The insistence on penitence and punishment, the association between physical pain and mystical ecstasy, the description of a self-secluded ambient which is basically a prison, and the depiction of a stylized but harrowing violence also bring to mind Franz Kafka's short story *In the Penal Colony*, which Petri considered adapting in the late 1970s, possibly encompassing the themes of *Giacobbe*. On the other hand, the duality between vice and virtue, as well as of spirit and flesh, owes a debt to Sade and Bataille's work. Petri reprised themes from *L'Abbé C.* which had imbued his collaboration with Siciliano, most notably in the character of Don Gaetano and in the element of confession.

In addition to its literary and philosophical implications, Petri's "loose adaptation" of Sciascia's novel (as the credits stress) displays interesting film influences, with echoes of *L'année dernière à Marienbad* and Luis Buñuel's *El ángel exterminador* (1962) in the use of spaces. On top of that, the film delves deeply into the apocalyptic, mortuary tone that characterized Italian cinema of the period. Its portrayal of an enclosed microcosm where a *jeu de massacre* takes place makes it a worthy successor to *La Grande bouffe* and especially *Salò o le 120 giornate di Sodoma*, another film which revisited Sade's philosophy as filtered through Barthes, and which Petri loved. "It is a magnificent film that no one understood," he noted. "Apparently, it's because people did not want to accept a film so pure in its provocation, so provocative in its purity. Pasolini thought he was making a provocative film, and in reality, he made a very poetic film, one that is provocative only because it's poetic."[100]

As with *Salò*, *Todo modo* is divided into chapters. These mark the passing of the three days of the Ignatian exercises (First Day, Second Day, Third Day) and indicate the various meditations that Don Gaetano does against the politicians. This gives the story an overtly metaphysical tone, for Pasolini's "circles" (of manias, shit, and blood) preceded by an "Anteinferno" are mirrored in Petri's film by the meditations on Sin and on the Cross. The two films are inhabited by characters who pursue a form of spiritual enhancement by way of penitence, which in *Salò* takes the form of rigid norms of sexual behavior, following an obsessive combinatory organization. *Todo modo* even features a dining scene at the refectory, in which the participants decide to abstain from food, which echoes the infamous excrement-eating scene in Pasolini's film.

But there is more. In one of his most controversial articles, published about one year before his death, Pasolini wrote:

> I know. I know the names of those responsible for what will come to be known as a "military coup d'état" (and this, in reality, is a series of "instituted military coups d'états" systematized for the protection of power). I know the names of those responsible for the massacre of Milan on 12th December 1969. I know the names of those responsible for the massacres of Brescia and Bologna in the first months of 1974.... I know all these names and know all the facts (the attempts on the institutions, and the slaughters) which they've become guilty of. I know. But I do not have the proof. I don't even have clues.[101]

With *Todo modo*, Petri was paraphrasing Pasolini's oft-quoted words and putting them into film. He, too, could claim that he knew but had no proof. Therefore, he chose not to give the names but to show the faces and made them recognizable. But he went one step (or two) further. He organized a macabre, Swiftian apologue which put on show "the metaphor of the death without resurrection of a party and the debacle of a ruling class."[102]

Upon the film's release, Sciascia noted:

> It has a Catholic, Biblical gloominess. It is the apocalypse of the DC because, in fact ... the DC has sinned against the spirit. In the end, *Todo modo* is a Pasolinian film, for the trial that Pasolini wanted and could not bring to court against the Christian Democrat ruling class, today it is Petri who's accomplishing it. And it is a trial that sounds like a capital execution ... there is no better Democrazia Cristiana which distinguishes itself from the worse, a Moro who stands out better than a Fanfani. There is only one Democrazia Cristiana, and the Italian people must decide to come to terms with it, definitively and radically.[103]

"Mistero Buffo"

Alberto Moravia labeled *Todo modo* as part of a new genre which he called "didactic-ritualistic," comprising of such titles as *La Grande bouffe*, *Cadaveri eccellenti*, Valerio Zurlini's *Il deserto dei Tartari* and *Salò*.

> These films are carried out as moral fables or allegories in which the story supports a more or less precise and educational meaning. We might as well call them "cinematic mysteries" because of their symbolic and ritual pace and their didactic will.... These films are not realistic, for the events they depict are not meant to be descriptions of reality but depictions of ideological, moralistic, sociological, philosophical schemes.[104]

Indeed, Petri conceived *Todo modo* as "a kind of political and theatrical '*mistero*.'"[105] The term "mistero" (mystery) here refers to Middle Age mystery plays (from the Latin *mysterium*, ceremony), centered on the representation of Bible stories told in a didactic way. A recent and very successful reinvention of the *misteri* had been Dario Fo's 1969 one-man-show *Mistero buffo* (Comic Mystery), which recreated the irreverent quality of popular Medieval theater through a series of monologues inspired by the apocryphal Gospels. Fo's intention was to look at the present with the instruments of history and culture in order to judge it better, and Petri was following a similar path.

The theatrical quality of *Todo modo* can be seen first and foremost in the film's structure and its use of space and time, with the action condensed over the course of three days and in a confined location. In Parisian playhouses, where mystery plays were presented in the 15th century (earlier they were performed outside churches, at fairs, in public places or even in the streets or fields), the stage was divided into three sections, representing Paradise, the Holy Land, and Hell. Petri demanded of production designer Dante Ferretti an extraordinary effort to convey his vision of a symbolic representation of the netherworld—which in turn echoes a much more recent predecessor, Jean-Paul Sartre's 1944 play *Huis Clos* (aka *No Exit*). Ferretti's sets make the Zafer Hermitage a chilling vision of Hell, with its walls and ceilings of reinforced concrete hanging over the characters as if to crush them, its labyrinthine underground corridors, white statues scattered all over and depicting scenes from the Bible or figures of saints as shaped by some demented sculptor. The rooms are white and bare, with wooden beds and seats, and suggest a frugality which underlines the party members' hypocrisy, while the nearby catacombs add a surreal touch with the incongruous mixture of centuries-old and postmodernist design.

Mystery plays were one of the forms of the grotesque in medieval culture. They involved the use of masks to dramatize the characters as much as possible, and as a warning to the audience, such as masks depicting Satan or other demons. In Petri's film, the actors' performances are not just overly theatrical, but in Gian Maria Volonté's case one can properly speak of a "mask" the actor is wearing throughout the film, depicting a real-life politician.

In *Todo modo*, Volonté takes to another level Petri's discourse on masks and performance, which had found its most explicit expression in *La proprietà*. The actor's dedication to his craft reaches disturbing heights, and his embodiment of Moro is a literal interpretation of Petri's words about the Christian Democrat leader carrying a symbolical cross on his shoulders. Throughout the film he walks and moves as if hampered by a crushing weight, a burden that prevents him from adopting an erect posture. He never faces the camera and barely looks the others in the eyes.

As the director recalled,

> During shooting … he became evanescent, he walked as if on clouds, talked in a low voice, didn't look anyone in the eyes, he was totally focused on Moro. His was an exceptionally intense concentration effort.… I scrapped the first two days of filming for *Todo modo*, in agreement with the producer and Volonté himself, because his likeness with Aldo Moro was nauseating, embarrassing.… In that portrait there came out all the insidiousness, the shrewdness of the politician.[106]

Discussing the film, Sciascia told a reporter that a newspaper picture of Moro getting ready for a TV program, with greasepaint and face powder, had immediately made him think of Volonté. He had realized that the film carried out a paradox, "a reversal of reality: as if it weren't Volonté who put makeup on his face to look like Moro … but rather it was Moro who tried to look like Volonté in the film."[107] The actor would portray Moro on screen again in Giuseppe Ferrara's *Il caso Moro* (1986).

Stylistically, *Todo modo* is an extraordinary achievement. Even more so than *La proprietà*, Luigi Kuveiller's lighting enhances the film's stylized theatricality. It looms over the actors, who are lit from above and often move in semi-darkness, with eerie violet glass windows being often the only color element in the black and grey compositions. The camera almost never stops moving. It ascends and descends with surprisingly fluid and unexpected dolly movements, like some invisible death angel beating its wings on human misery and then flying away in disgust; it sticks to the characters' faces in insistent close-ups and often observes them from behind their shoulders, like an unseen judge that never leaves them for a moment (as in the amazing scene at the refectory with the dialogue between "M" and Don Gaetano on good and bad priests and the appearance of the creepy Voltrano); it pans right and left during Don Gaetano's enraged speeches, following the priest's moves from one microphone to the other, as if hypnotized by his eloquence. Overall, it transcends the story's claustrophobic mood and displays the director's attention to style as a means to convey the message in the most spectacularly effective manner.

Petri's penchant for contemporary art can be seen in the sculptures popping up here and there, with the white chalk statues of Christ and saints revisited through a contemporary eye hovering in the corners or on the walls behind the characters and giving the sets a metaphysical, De Chirico–like quality. There is even a nod to comic books, namely the many issues of *Linus* glimpsed in Don Gaetano's room. In addition to being an inside joke (and a nod to Mastroianni's character in *La decima vittima*) the sight gag was a passing reference to the book: in one of the early pages the concierge at Zafer is reading *Linus*.

For all its gloominess and spite, *Todo modo* is a darkly humorous film. The term, of course, must be taken with a grain of salt. Petri highlights the ridiculous and the grotesque and elicits a grimace of disgust in the viewer rather than laughter. He once said that "a Franchi and Ingrassia film is much funnier and more painful"[108] than any *commedia all'italiana*, and the casting of Ingrassia for a character who is as physically repellent as he is ludicrous is telling. Like *Salò*, *Todo modo* is an atrociously comical work. Whereas Pasolini's film was populated by monsters who enjoyed telling jokes to their victims, here the act of murder itself becomes a joke, played by an invisible (but definitely human) entity on these hopelessly silly and despicable characters.

The first homicide, early in the film, creates a mood of suspense and anticipation, but Petri overturns expectations and turns the body count into a macabre farce. The introduction of farce was another typical element in mystery plays and often accompanied the appearances of the Devil, who was subjected to the cruelest indignities.[109] Here, bodies turn up in increasingly grotesque poses and places. They are found leaning on doors, hidden under beds, sewn into garbage bags or preserved into reliquaries like obscene parodies of embalmed saints. They are often naked or semi-naked, their buttocks exposed in post-mortem outrage that deprives them of any dignity, for they don't deserve it.

Petri goes a long way to portray on screen the cryptic language of politicians, filled with allusions, metaphors and (in "M"'s case) adverbs, but he also uses it to satirize the very essence of the Democrazia Cristiana. "To Christian Democratic power, what matters is not reality but appearance. It doesn't matter how one is but how he appears to other people's eyes."[110]

Satire often takes the form of double meanings in dialogue. For instance, Voltrano's declaration of his will to fast on the first day at Zafer becomes the pretext for a declaration of membership to one current or the other, as the various politicians split between those who will fast and those who won't. Likewise, when reenacting the murder during the collective rosary, Scalambri tries to figure out who was standing to "M"'s right, and the sequence takes on an absurdist political innuendo, as the various party members misinterpret the magistrate's request and start accusing each other of being either at the (political) left or right of their leader. "M" himself admits: "I confuse the right with the left … this anomaly has given rise to many misunderstandings."

In Petri's line of law enforcers, Scalambri is another step down from the self-important and childish Doctor of *Indagine* and the unctuous Brigadier Pirelli of *La proprietà*. A freemason, not baptized, irremediably stupid, he is clueless about what is going on (as "M" suggests, he has been summoned to Zafer just *because of that*), and in

Todo modo: M (Gian Maria Volonté), his chauffeur (Franco Citti) and one of the victims (Piero Nuti).

the end he is dispatched too. If *Cadaveri eccellenti*'s Rogas is an honest cop who gets killed because he knows too much, Scalambri is just an expendable servant of the State, a "useful idiot."

Whereas Sciascia's novel used the whodunit plot in a self-styled parodic way, creating an engrossing riddle only to deny its solution, here the alleged key to the solution becomes a nonsensical, madcap charade.

M: Someone wants to send us a message, a warning, a signal…

SCALAMBRI: What? … Please explain. I don't understand.

M: It's easier than it seems. Look. Read what's written beside the name of the first victim…. Scaglia…. Ifim…. Rate…. Ortis…. Vicipu…. Do you know what all these strange words mean?

SCALABRI: They're acronyms. And I presume each one stands for a corporation or institution the victim had an interest in.

M: Well done!

SCALAMBRI: And?

M: And? I can assure you that all these strange words. ISNAN … REACA … DOBRA … CICA … ANAU … ANASARDA … Together, separate, multiplied, divided, they form the following sentence: "Todo modo para buscar la voluntad divina!"

SCALAMBRI: What does it mean?

M: A saying of Saint Ignatius, it means: "Every means to find the divine will."

This is all too patently a preposterous justification on the part of "M," who indeed believes that every means must be used in politics, murder included. The scene in which he explains his tortuous theory to the idiotic Scalambri like a teacher would do with a dumb kid is a knowing nod to the comedy duets between Totò and Peppino De Filippo, or Franchi and Ingrassia, as the politician and the cop literally become a vaudeville duo doing their routine. Petri had attempted something similar in *Il maestro di Vigevano*, in the scene where principal Pereghi humiliates poor Mombelli ("Because the teacher is a mis…? Because a teacher is a mis…?" "…sile!" "Missionary, teacher Mombelli! A missionary!"). Here, as well, the comical becomes a way to read the living hell of his own time, "a crisis of a way of life, so deep that it marks the passage from one civilization to the next."[111]

Mortification of the Flesh

Todo modo overflows with didactic dialogue and religious symbolism. "I wish I were last," "M" says upon being informed he is the first to show up at Zafer. It is an allusion to the Gospel's passage, "So the last shall be first, and the first last: or many be called, but few chosen" (Matthew 20:16). Indeed, he will be the last to be called, and the last to die.

"I think I have a mission to accomplish," "M" tells Don Gaetano. He sees himself not just as a martyr, but as Christ himself, and so does Giacinta. The camera even frames them in a perverse parody of the sacred image of the Virgin Mary with her child, with "M" breastfeeding on her. Don Gaetano ironically asks him if he has stigmata, and during the reciting of the rosary at one point "M" has to stop because something (a nail) punctured his foot. And his final walk in the park is at the same time a Way of the Cross and a reference to the betrayal in the garden of Gethsemane, with his trusted driver acting as his personal Judas.

Religion, politics, and sexuality are inextricably linked. "M" believes he has a cancer "where temptation is stronger," and admits he is basically impotent when explaining to Don Gaetano that he is never able to fulfill the many political projects he dreams of. "It is like an erection that never happens," he concludes. His chaste relationship with Giacinta is characterized by bizarre sexual surrogates. They kneel down together for a prayer according to Ignatius' exercises, rhythmically breathing in synch. The act makes both excited, and she offers him her breast to suckle. Later, Giacinta confesses to Don Gaetano that she and her husband don't have intimate relations anymore. "I'm like Italy, and to me he's Cavour…. And I can't…. I can't make love to Cavour, to Garibaldi, Metternich, Disraeli or De Gaulle! And to me he is Christ on high…. I let him suckle me, so he'll become strong. But a mother cannot make love to her own son."

"M" and Don Gaetano act as if there is a deep unspoken bond between them. Petri hints at the attraction between the two emblems of power, "its two faces during these last thirty years, bonded by a complicity based on the blackmail of hell, of faith, of the fear of death."[112] But their relationship has a sadomasochistic edge to it. "M" acts in an almost effeminate way, as shown by his habit of touching Don Gaetano's cheek and shoulder, while the priest cruelly mocks the politician, telling him that he would look better dressed as a priest: "It's a bit like being a woman. In the summer, the breeze enters under the genitals … you can go without briefs. Priests are half-men and half-women." Later, "M" will indeed dress up as a priest to escape the massacre. The comparison with the clergy evokes the scene in *Indagine* where Augusta tells the Doctor that he has "black short socks like a priest … at least a priest smells of incense." In both films such comparisons are used to diminish the interlocutor's masculinity.

Several party members are explicitly addressed as homosexual or mocked for their lack of virility. After Voltrano is found dead, covered with panties (yet another reference to *Nostra signora Metredina*), "M" labels him as a "culetto allegro" (pansy), and the body of "Him" is arranged in a humiliating position, with his trousers down and no underwear. The allusions to homosexuality or scarce manhood are a sneering unveiling of the characters' repressed essence. This is best exemplified in the scene where Voltrano strips naked before the other party members and shows the scars of the self-flagellations to which he submits himself, only to be reproached by "M": "Censor yourself!" As Petri explained, "A moralist doesn't see any other moral but the sexual one, and gets mad at the idea of not being able to carry out the transgression he condemns … to me, there is only one moral to defend: everything which is committed against the collectivity, that is immoral."[113]

In Mastroianni's masterful incarnation, Don Gaetano is a Sadean character. He defines himself "a bad, very bad priest" and claims, "The Church's triumph over the centuries is due to bad priests. Their wickedness serves to confirm and glorify sanctity." It is up to Don Gaetano to denounce the chasm between the religious ideas that the politicians profess and their corrupt behavior. Mysterious and powerful, saintly and devilish, he is divided between a preaching anger against those who surround him and the awareness of his own corruption. And his inner split is even more dramatic for in his heart he knows that, to quote Marx, God is dead.

Even though he had already played a priest twice, in *La moglie del prete* (1970, Dino Risi) and *Rappresaglia* (aka *Massacre in Rome*, 1973, George Pan Cosmatos), Mastroianni was very attached to the role, because, he claimed, "for the first time I have been entrusted with a different character from those I was accustomed to playing. This strong, tremendous, diabolical priest was a good thing for an actor, and in fact I did it with great passion."[114] His performance struck also a young press officer and aspiring director, Anna Maria Tatò.

> One day I got a phone call from Elio Petri. He had just finished shooting *Todo modo* and … he was worried about the ostracism that he envisaged it would meet. "I would like you to organize a screening with all the trimmings of an event." I accepted and immediately set to work: I invited many intellectuals and newspaper editors, and while the images ran on the screen, two things happened…. On the one hand, I felt the spectators' discomfort: they moved in their armchair as if they were suffering. "This movie will bomb," I told myself. And then, for the first time, Marcello appeared to me in a different light. On screen, especially in the rosary scene, he had a kind of fever on him, a kind of inner strength. I was dazzled.[115]

The two became a couple that very night and stayed together until Mastroianni's death in 1996.

Martyrdom

In the film's key scene, "M" goes to Don Gaetano to confess, but the meeting becomes a brutal session of analysis in which, through Petri's dialectic method, both men come to terms with what they truly are. "You're like other men. Do you love power?" Don Gaetano asks. "Yes, magmatically," is the answer, replete with one of those adverbs "M" seemingly cannot do without. "Can you give it up?" the priest insists. "To whom? There's no one better," the politician replies, betraying his own arrogance hidden beneath the surface modesty. He tells the priest that he has a mission to accomplish, but Don Gaetano's reply is scathing:

> DON GAETANO: You're like the rest. You follow their example. Stop faking.
> M: No, I'm not like the rest. I'm different! I'm not greedy or arrogant. I'm not a hypocrite. I'm an honest person. I don't steal. I keep my word…. Tell me that I'm not like the rest.
> DON GAETANO: You're like your voters: cynical and savage. Follow your mandate; we'll fall together. You and your rich impostors, who keep you in power, to save them from the poor. And I, with my stupid flock, innocent and sinful, who expect from me the viaticum for the next life.
> M: You don't love me anymore…. Confess me … for the last time. I have the feeling this is our last meeting.
> DON GAETANO: No. I couldn't give you absolution…
> M: Think what we represent, what we are.
> DON GAETANO: You cry like a sniveling woman.
> M: To continue, I need your absolution. What are we without you, and you without us?
> DON GAETANO: *Non possumus* (We cannot).

Don Gaetano's refusal to give "M" absolution—itself a Sadean gesture—is like Petri's own sentence and preludes the execution of the judgment in the film's bold, inflammatory epilogue.

As Petri explained in a self-penned essay on the film, the ending was "the inevitable consequence of 'M's own veritable vocation for martyrdom, and it seemed to me that, among the murders that occur throughout the spiritual exercises, the final and

Todo modo: **bodies are piled one on top of the other, in the hellish, grotesque climax.**

most significant one had to be his own murder, even insinuating that he, himself, was the instigator."[116]

Franco Citti had played Oedipus in Pasolini's *Edipo re*, and the scene of the chauffeur shooting "M" recalls the symbolic killing of a father. But it is devoid of any pity or empathy toward the victim: on the contrary, it ends on an open mocking tone with a parody of the Ascension, as the demise of "M" is saluted by heavenly bells. "M" the sacrificial lamb is only a whiny little man who believes he is Jesus but is actually a Judas. After his mission is accomplished, he is no longer useful. The powers that be will find another puppet and pull its strings as ever.

The director compared the dead politicians to the herd of swine cited in Luke's Gospel, when Jesus casts out demons, quoted in Dostoevsky's *The Demons*. Likewise, Petri's Christian Democrats seem destined to slaughter. As he quipped, "Are these the 'demons' of the Right?"[117] But his corrosive *De Profundis* for the country's leading party hardly camouflages the author's pessimism. "Who has any hope left nowadays? Not the middle-class, who knows it cannot keep ruling with impunity and shamelessly, and not the working class, who is forced to cooperate or at least to cohabit by its sense of reality."[118] In the director's view, the whole system is plagued and there is no cure, as suggested by the opening images. The individual neuroses of his previous film have given way to a collective one, the farcical drama of a party split between its claimed ideals and its true essence, and of a whole nation whose hopes for a better future have degenerated into anger and violence. And there is no way of fixing it.

TWELVE

"Unsalvageable!"
Le mani sporche *(1978)*

Of Men and Monkeys: Zoo

The fall of 1976 saw the government launch severe austerity measures to face the dramatic economic crisis, including the rise of gasoline prices, phone and electricity rates. More strikes ensued. Communist militants found themselves in an uncomfortable position because of the PCI's moderate response, a result of the party's adherence to the "historic compromise" theorized by Moro and Berlinguer. The first government in thirty years with some (albeit marginal) responsibility on the part of the PCI was demanding more sacrifices than ever. Workers were resigned, disillusioned, furious. How could "their" leaders take sides with such Draconian measures, while dropping the previous demands and pretending not to see the widespread corruption among the lines of the DC? "First changes, then sacrifices," was a common slogan. Even though Berlinguer defended the position of the PCI as a necessary stance to avoid "the decadence of a civilization, the ruin of the country,"[1] the dream of a democratic alliance had turned sour and was rapidly accelerating the lacerations in the social tissue.

For Petri, it was time to move on and perhaps take a breath of fresh air after the bitter and exhausting experience of *Todo modo*. He had been toying with the idea of directing a theatrical play for a long time, and in September the news came that he would put on stage a version of Plautus's comedy *Amphitryon*, with singer Milva as the female lead, Alcmena, during the next season of Turin's prestigious Teatro Stabile.[2] Rehearsals were scheduled from January 24 to February 17, and the play was to go on stage from March 18 to April 7, 1977. It was an ambitious project, and Petri was one of several well-known directors involved with Teatro Stabile, together with Giorgio Strehler, Mario Missiroli, and Giorgio Albertazzi. But the theater underwent many financial issues during the season, and dramatic cuts had to be made. Eventually, Petri was replaced by Flavio Ambrosini.

However, even though his debut as stage director didn't happen, Petri stayed away from sets for the whole of 1977. He didn't even take part in *I nuovi mostri*, the sequel to *I mostri* directed by Mario Monicelli, Dino Risi and Ettore Scola, and put together to help financially veteran scriptwriter Ugo Guerra, who was gravely ill. It was not a sabbatical year, though, as he seemed incapable of stopping from thinking about new projects. But it had always been difficult to find backers, even after the Oscar and the Cannes award; now it was becoming harder than ever.

After *Todo modo*, Petri had been working steadily on a new, ambitious project titled *Zoo*. Daniele Senatore had sent the outline to Jack Nicholson, who expressed his interest in it. In a letter dated 9 November 1976, he wrote: "It seems to me that it could become a film in which I would want to play the lead,"[3] although he pointed out that due to previous engagements and to the actual writing of the script, they would not be able to start shooting until a year from then. In the meantime, Petri lost touch with Senatore, who at that time had put up shop in New York with Giulio Questi for an ambitious project, *Sierra Nevada*.[4] After trying in vain to reach him for over a month, by late January 1977 Petri ended their collaboration and Alberto Grimaldi's PEA took over as producer. News about the film—described as a humorous parable about the relationship between man and animals—started appearing in Italian newspapers in February 1977.[5]

The early 29-page outline for *Zoo* retained in the Elio Petri fund is basically a short story set over the course of one day and told in the first person. On a sudden whim, the unnamed narrator visits the huge Berlin zoo. He is soon overwhelmed by the place's wildness, the violent odor of animal urine and feces. "I realized that it was the smell of the jungle." He joins a group of elderly ladies who laugh at the captive animals and stop before the gorilla cage for a picnic, observing in awe as the primate mates with his female partner. Following an unstoppable urge, "a terrible need to affirm something, to give a peremptory sign of my presence," the man exposes his genitals to the ladies. After their scandalized reaction, he runs away and climbs up a tree with "the velocity and agility of a monkey." Unbeknownst to him, a typist named Annelise is watching him from the nearby Mercedes high-rise.

Hiding from his pursuers, the man reflects on his gesture. "Yes, I had done something absurd, unexpected, against my education and my nature, undoubtedly. But I was forced to admit that never, ever in my life I had felt, even for a few burning instants, such a feeling of vitality." But as he watches the caged animals, such as a female gorilla named Bella and her captivity-born offspring Fred, he realizes that he himself is a prisoner.

> Suddenly I felt infinitely close to the animals in captivity, to the point that I saw myself in their place…. I was in a cage. My cage. And inside the cage, more cages. All the cages in my life were in front of me … my mother's living room, my primary school class … the room where I work, in the big building made of cages where many others live like me, and the bedroom where I lived during the first months of my wedding, the same room where something broke.

Meanwhile, the zoo guards have arrested an innocent homeless man and the old ladies are beating him, believing he is the exhibitionist. Suddenly, the protagonist realizes a young woman is watching him. It is Annelise. He feels the urge to expose himself again, but—much to his surprise—she is not scandalized. A strange complicity is born between them. Annelise confesses to being anorexic and shows him a panther in her cage. The big black feline too refuses to eat food and is surrounded by rotten carcasses.

Annelise pushes the man to expose himself again to other visitors. He obliges, but he starts feeling like her prisoner. Meanwhile he keeps observing the visitors, who have the tendency to talk to the animals.

> Their speeches are actually soliloquies, rants about their life, confessions addressed to beings who have to listen because of their own condition. They are usually elderly men and women who have been pushed by the city, their families and society to the utmost solitude…. They have no other hope but to talk to wild animals. And they talk about everything, their lost illusions, their solitary life, and they can lie even to a caged animal…

The man and Annelise get to a dancing hall inside the zoo. They dance and talk. She seems attracted to his diversity. "Tell me about you," she says. "Since this morning I'm not the same. And I still don't know who I am," he replies. But he confesses that his exhibitionistic fit has allowed him to find his own self, albeit for just a brief moment. "In my life I have been what the others wanted me to be," he reflects. "All the others, even the few who claimed they loved me. These are the worst, because they manipulated me according to their love inclination."

Annelise encourages the man to expose himself over and over. His newfound freedom "seems more and more like a new form of imprisonment." Eventually he escapes and hides atop a tree. Night falls, visitors leave, the zoo closes. "Everyone had returned to their cages. Now I was definitely an animal." But at night another type of fauna populates the zoo. Exiles, hippies, globetrotters, homeless men. The rejects of society, who have no other place to sleep. The protagonist makes acquaintance with some of them. "I feel safe here," an elderly beggar tells him.

In the epilogue, the narrator steals the caretaker's key and enters Bella and Fred's cage. He takes off his clothes and starts playing with Fred. "Now I'm waiting for the first visitors," are his last words.

The ill-fated *Todo modo* had not dampened Petri's creativity. *Zoo* was a thought-provoking, brave philosophical fable, riddled with symbols and ambitious in scope, about the modern Western world seen as a gigantic cage which molds man's identity at will, predetermines role models and destroys any attempt at rebellion. With this emblematic story, the director was trying once again to analyze the relationship between individual and social schizophrenia. To feel free again, the only chance seems to be a return to wildness—yet, an illusory one, for once the protagonist has stripped bare of all his clothes, as well as of all social conventions, he has nothing left to go to but a cage, and becomes part of a dysfunctional gorilla family unit. The punchline vaguely recalls the ending of Philippe de Broca's pacifist satire *Le Roi de Coeur* (aka *King of Hearts*, 1966), in which Alan Bates's character strips nude and voluntarily enters an asylum to escape the horrors of World War I, whereas the choice of Jack Nicholson hints at another symbolical tale of men and cages, *One Flew Over the Cuckoo's Nest* (1975, Miloš Forman). Petri was envisioning using the actor's penchant for histrionic acting as he had done with Gian Maria Volonté in his previous films.

The comparison between men and caged animals brings one step further ideas barely sketched in *La classe operaia*, where madmen cling to the asylum bars like monkeys, and *La proprietà* (more evidently in the novelization), where the characters were often compared to beasts. Moreover, the theme of regression to a wild, primitive state echoes Petri's interest in adapting Michel Tournier's similarly themed novel, *Vendredi*. But *Zoo* also conveys another of the director's crucial themes, troubled and/or unresolved sexual issues. The narrator's obsession with his own member predates *Buone notizie* (which features a scene where the protagonist exposes his penis to a female colleague who is not the least bit scandalized) and hints at the crisis of the male that would be at the center of the latter film. Overall, *Zoo* is every bit as unpleasant as Petri's later works, and it exudes a sense of uneasiness that borders on downright desperation.

Looking for a U.S. backer, in May Petri got in touch with producer Danton J. Rissner and sent him a copy of the Italian script. On July 4, 1977, he left for Los Angeles and stayed in California (and briefly in Mexico) for a whole month to work on the English version of the treatment and pre-scenario with American scriptwriter and *Newsweek* film critic Paul D. Zimmerman. Then he spent a few days in London for other working commitments, and while in Britain he contacted Twentieth Century–Fox Vice President Sanford Lieberson for a possible coproduction deal. By early August he and Zimmerman penned an extended 37-page treatment, and they completed a 205-page first draft of the script by mid–September.[6]

The story had gradually metamorphosed from the thin early synopsis into a more eventful outline. Given Nicholson's interest the setting was changed into an American one. Moreover, the script added a better defined array of characters (including the protagonist's wife), a substantial backstory and a slightly different ending. The hero, now called Bruce Grimes, is a businessman working in real estate on the verge of closing an important deal, who pays a visit to the zoo in order to delay the meeting and cut a better deal with his client, but the gambit backfires completely. In fact, when he calls his client, he learns that the latter is going to close the deal with someone else from his office, for, he says, "You guys are all a dime a dozen."

Stunned and broken, Grimes realizes that he has practically destroyed his own career. He wanders around the zoo, exposes himself before the elderly ladies and flees, as in the early outline. Another man—a fastidious teacher—is arrested in his place and kept at the security office. Grimes is filled with guilt and sets out to be discovered in order to have the teacher released. This is when the meeting with the girl previously known as Annelise takes place. In the final script, the character is modeled into an uninhibited and rather unhinged girl who has been in a skin flick, is into astrology and works nights at a motel, living off leftovers from people's plates.

Petri and Zimmerman fleshed out the plot, introducing new characters and episodes. Grimes calls a psychiatrist who becomes interested in his case and sets out to reach him at the zoo. To kill time, Grimes watches a movie at the children's zoo and learns that a number of old zoos used to exhibit people as well—Indians, Eskimos, freaks. The conversation with the psychiatrist appropriately takes place before the gorilla cage, with Grimes lying down on a bench as if it was a couch and the shrink sitting behind him. The psychiatrist is then called to the security office, where the teacher is in a demented state and has become convinced that he is the exhibitionist. This leads to a twist in pure Petri style:

> The psychiatrist is furious at our hero. Considers him an imposter pretending to be an exhibitionist…. The hero insists that the other is the imposter. He is very angry and jealous. The imposter is stealing his identity. But the psychiatrist abandons him. He has found a more interesting case.

After another exhibitionist act gone wrong, Grimes spots his wife amid the zoo crowd. He slips away from her and into the arena where the seal show is held. There, the seals' routine reminds him of critical episodes in his life, through a series of flashbacks intercut with the present that give us a full picture of the character and relate to the early outline where the protagonist reflected on the many cages in his own life. The flashbacks relate to religion, school, work, sex and marriage, success and competitiveness.

Eventually Grimes bumps into his wife, who's mad at him. The deal has gone wrong, his boss is furious, everyone is looking for him. Grimes confesses what he has done, by way of one of Petri's typical dialectic schemes. "He talks about what is natural and perverted, showing his wife that, in the world of the animals, there is no such thing as a perversion. He gets her to agree that man is essentially an animal. He talks about the many forms of exhibitionism … actors, politicians, girls at the beach are all exhibitionists." She is outraged at the revelation, but she too has a secret to share. "For years, she tells him, she has repressed her own urges so as to protect his career. She has led a model life. Now that he has ruined his career, she is free to indulge her own secret desire. She is and has always been a secret kleptomaniac."

Grimes remains alone and spends the night at the zoo. The scene in which he makes acquaintance with the homeless man and the other people who converge there after closing time is replaced by a nightmare in which the other characters chase him as if he were a wild animal and shoot him with a tranquilizer gun.

The next morning Grimes goes to the men's room, shaves and gets himself ready for his new job. He presents himself to the zoologist and offers himself to be exhibited. "He would want a salary of $60,000, medical care, life insurance, room and board of course, and two weeks a year out of the sight of the crowds."

In the epilogue, a tour bus approaches an enclosure. We find Grimes, naked, in his local habitat, a small house with one wall missing.

> "I am native to Southern California," he tells the tour. "I am six feet tall, 180 pounds. I eat six pounds of food per day. I am the most adaptable of all animals, and the most dangerous…."
> There is a large crowd around him, some taunting him. The hero is very happy in his role. A keeper enters with his food. It is his wife. He has everything he needs. He smiles.

The new ending was perhaps not up to Petri's original one, but still packed a punch. The treatment and script managed to convey the original ideas and put new ones on the table. For instance, he had in mind a breakneck opening montage which recapitulated the evolutionary development in a series of dissolves. Moreover, Grimes' growing mental unbalance would surface on screen through his visions. In a scene he watches a traffic jam in the nearby highway and sees animals at the wheel instead of people. His sexual insecurity is depicted in a surreal flashback in which, after making love to his future wife for the first time, he asks her how many lovers she had in her life. She begins an incredible catalog of men, each of whom materializes in her room as she speaks. He asks how good he is in relation to them and she gives him a mortifying answer. Then, in a montage, we see him making love to her like an athlete training for the Olympics. His wife doesn't care who's "the best," but he does. Eventually, Grimes envisions himself as an athlete on a podium, his wife awarding him a gold medal before an applauding crowd.

Overall, the script has its share of flaws. The psychiatrist, described as "a pure Freudian," is little more than a caricature, and some passages seem a bit forced or exceedingly didactic, such as making Grimes' wife a repressed kleptomaniac (like in the 1967 unproduced project, *L'italiana*). One wonders how Petri would have managed to get away with the theme of exhibitionism and male nudity (the scene at the security office describes the teacher "holding the women at a distance with his cock in his hand, like a machine gun"). Still, *Zoo* looked like the comeback project that would give him back prominent status, in Italy and abroad.

Petri briefly flew back to America in October, and around the same time the weekly *L'Espresso* published a lengthy interview in which he discussed the film, to be shot in San Diego. Two months later *Zoo* (described as "about the condition of today's man, about our own cages") was still in development.[7] But the project gradually fell apart, even though in a letter dated May 1978 Zimmerman expressed his intention to resume work on it.[8] Nicholson was no longer available, as he was working on *The Shining*, and eventually *Zoo* went to join the long list of Petri's unmade films.

The frustrating preproduction work for *Zoo* caused other projects to be dropped. *Quartetto* (Quartet) dealt with the love tangles amid the four components of a string quartet, "a maze in which each road leads back irreparably to the same theme, that is, unquenchable love."[9] Willing to experiment with music and narrative structure, Petri had envisioned building the tale around a musical leitmotif, Leoš Janáček's String Quartet No. 1 "Kreutzer Sonata" inspired by Tolstoy's novella of the same name. *Quartetto* marked a change of direction, a withdrawal to private themes which hinted at the director's disillusionment with the political-popular film. Another idea he briefly considered was a modern-day retelling—to script with Zimmerman's help—of Adolphe d'Ennery and Eugène Cormon's novel *Les deux orphelines*, which had already inspired many films, the most recent a 1976 adaptation by Leopoldo Savona.

During his forced inactivity, Petri found the time to give a hand to Robert Altman, whom he once labeled as "a pop artist in the revolutionary sense of the term, a popular artist who never loses sight of the general nature of events."[10] Altman stopped for several days in Rome in May to conduct casting for his upcoming film and oversee the Italian dubbing of *3 Women* (1977). Petri was the dubbing director along with Luigi Proietti, whom Altman cast in *A Wedding* (1978).[11]

That summer also brought terrible news regarding Gian Maria Volonté. His younger brother Claudio was himself an actor under the alias Claudio Camaso, although he had never reached Gian Maria's fame. On July 26, Claudio was about to leave for Tunisia for a film and had brought a gift to his little daughter, at the clothes shop in which his wife Verena Baer worked. They were separated and about to divorce. A violent argument ensued between them in the central Campo de' Fiori square, in front of a small crowd. Claudio was half-drunk, and at a certain point he took out a jackknife. A 27-year-old electrician and amateur actor, Vincenzo Mazza, stepped forward to stop him. Claudio turned back and stabbed him to death.[12]

The news caused a storm. Claudio Volonté fled immediately after the fact. After ten days on the lam he gave himself to the cops, claiming that he had killed Mazza accidentally, and that he was tormented by remorse. On September 16, he hung himself in jail.[13] Petri, who had returned to Rome at the end of August, was among those attending the funeral[14] alongside the heart-broken Gian Maria, who had learned of the tragedy while on a boat trip through the Mediterranean Sea.

The Ghost of Stalin

In November 1977, Elio Petri appeared in the unusual role of the interviewer in the TV program *L'attenzione critica*. The show celebrated Alberto Moravia's 70th birthday with a small group of guest interviewers selected to discuss specific topics with the noted writer. Petri, who had known Moravia since the early post-war days when they often bumped into each other in Rome venues, asked him about his relationship with cinema.

The appearance in *L'attenzione critica* anticipated Petri's directorial debut on the small screen. By the end of the year, news came that he was about to film an adaptation of Jean-Paul Sartre's 1948 play, *Les mains sales* (Dirty Hands), starring Marcello Mastroianni, following a proposal from Rai Uno. The news came as a surprise given Petri's open hostility toward the medium. In a 1968 interview in *Il Giorno*, he had spoken scathingly against television, calling it "the new ally of vulgarity, even more penetrating and conditioning than cinema ... for it arrives even in the nursery and the bedroom."[15]

Still, lately he had been considering working for the small screen, given also the increasing difficulty of putting together a new film. There had been contacts in the past: he had been invited to direct a TV adaptation of Italo Calvino's *Fiabe italiane*, a collection of fairytales from the Italian rural tradition. "At the beginning I was rather cold, but then I read the book and was fascinated by it. But my growing enthusiasm was met with a growing disinterest on the part of those who proposed the project," he explained. "I think they got scared because I told them about what thrilled me, that is, the ferociousness of rural tradition."[16]

Another ambitious project was a five-hour made-for-TV movie on Mussolini, coproduced by MCA and NBC, and written by Age & Scarpelli with consultancy by historian Renzo De Felice.[17] RAI Corporation's Daniele Pachetti and Daniele Senatore were interested in it. The tentative cost was esteemed as twenty million dollars, and Petri claimed that he envisaged Marlon Brando playing Mussolini. But he had also toyed with the idea of a TV-movie based on the crimes of Dr. Marcel Petiot, the notorious French serial killer who had been executed in 1946.[18] Other ideas were a film for Rai Due based on Moravia's "four visions of Rome" based on the novelist's books—"1930s Rome, Rome during the war, the Rome of alienation, the Rome of madness"[19]—and a TV movie on the theme of violence, which Petri submitted to the head of Rai Due, Massimo Fichera, in March 1978.[20] All these were eventually dropped.

It was Paolo Valmarana who finally convinced the director to try his hand at the small screen. A former film critic, Valmarana (1928–1984) was one of RAI's most audacious executives. In 1976 he had been appointed to produce and purchase films for Rai Uno, and during his stint he financed works by the likes of Ermanno Olmi, Paolo and Vittorio Taviani, Gianni Amelio. He and Petri had been friends for a long time despite their opposite political ideas, Valmarana being a staunch Christian Democrat.

Les mains sales takes place in the fictional Eastern European country of Illyria, an ally of Nazi Germany, during the last days of World War II. Illyria is on the verge of being annexed to the Eastern Bloc. The Communist Party leader Hoederer is negotiating a political alliance with other non–Socialist forces to form a joint resistance group opposing the Nazis and set the stage for a post-war coalition government. The other Communist leaders, including Louis and Olga, consider Hoederer a traitor, and entrust the young and immature Hugo Barine with his assassination. Hugo and his wife Jessica move into Hoederer's place, and Hugo becomes his secretary. Just as he is about to perform the killing, a bomb explodes. Nobody is hurt but Hugo realizes the party doesn't trust him. He is so furious that he gets drunk. Olga, who threw the bomb, pays Hugo a visit and warns him to do his duty, for party members are getting impatient. Jessica, unhappy with her marriage and secretly attracted to Hoederer, learns that her husband is going to assassinate him the next day.

But Hugo as well has succumbed to Hoederer's charm. He feels Hoederer can help him sort out his internal conflicts, and the older man promises that he will mentor him. They discuss the leader's political strategy. Hoederer's plan is to have the Communist party support a right-wing government, in order for the most unpopular policies to be implemented by his adversaries and set the path for the Communists to take over in the future. Hugo, who believes the party is to remain pure and not ally with anyone, rejects such a disenchanted scheme. He pulls out his pistol and is about to shoot Hoederer, but ultimately he desists and leaves. Then Jessica turns up and tells Hoederer that she loves him. They kiss. Hugo catches them in the act and shoots Hoederer.

The story is told via a lengthy flashback. Hugo, released after serving two years in jail for Hoederer's murder, goes to Olga's place. There she reveals him that the party is planning to kill him. Olga, who is attracted to Hugo, asks the other leaders to give her a few hours to speak with the young man, whom she believes is "salvageable," and find out whether Hoederer's murder was political or a crime of passion. After Hugo's tale, Olga reveals that the party has eventually adopted the late Hoederer's line and formed an alliance with the other forces, on Moscow's orders. In fact, Hoederer's initiative was merely premature, and the party eliminated him only to adopt his plan later. Now that Hoederer has been rehabilitated as a great leader, Hugo realizes that his murder was useless. He leaves the house and faces the assassins awaiting him. His final words are: "Unsalvageable!"

Sartre's play openly alluded to the assassination of Leon Trotsky, killed on August 20, 1940, in Mexico City (where he lived in exile) by NKVD agent Ramón Mercader, upon Stalin's order. Through his lover and under a false identity, Mercader had managed to become acquainted with Trotsky, posing as a sympathizer, so as to earn his trust and have the chance to strike. In 1972 Joseph Losey made the story into a film, *The Assassination of Trotsky*, starring Richard Burton (as Trotsky) and Alain Delon (as Mercader).

Upon its debut on stage, the play caused a controversy and its author was accused of anti–Communism. A Soviet critic wrote: "For thirty pieces of silver and a plate of American lentils, Jean-Paul Sartre sold whatever honor and honesty he had left." As Petri recalled, "the communists rejected what they believed were visceral lies, whereas the anti-communists exploited the drama for their own political agenda."[21]

Sartre's aim was actually to denounce the lack of democracy and the contradictions of Stalin's regime compared with the socialist ideals of freedom. But in 1948 to criticize Stalin so explicitly as Sartre did was taboo for a communist militant, and the misunderstanding about its message ended up weighing over *Les mains sales*. Despite vehement attacks from the French Communist Party, the play was a great success, but Sartre decided to retire it, and for sixteen years he vetoed it from being put on stage again. A film version was produced in 1951, starring Pierre Brasseur and Daniel Gélin, but upon its release in France communists threatened the venues screening it.

The play was staged again in 1964, by Turin's Teatro Stabile, with the action no longer unfolding in Illyria but in Hungary. By then, Sartre had defined himself a "critical fellow traveler" of the Communist party and added that the characteristic situation of the intellectual "fellow traveler" is one of tension between criticism and discipline.[22]

Petri himself had long been a "critical fellow traveler" of the Italian Communist Party. Making *Le mani sporche* represented a "penance" of sorts for being "an ex-young Stalinist man, and now also ex-young man, who in the Cold War years was induced to see Sartre as the devil, and Fadeyev as God."[23] He referred to Soviet writer Alexander Fadeyev, who in 1948 had violently attacked Sartre, calling him a "hyena with a fountain pen."[24] For a long time, as an orthodox communist, Petri had avoided reading *Les mains sales*. He eventually did in 1956, when he still owned the PCI card but was now openly critical of it. For the TV adaptation he chose to respect the original text to the letter:

Its melodramatic twists, schematic conflicts, emblematic characters are in the style of the period, and they are inherent to Sartre's conception that history and existence form a tangle that produces dramatic events. It is the existential content, besides the political one, which makes the play so interesting.[25]

In highlighting the existentialist essence of Sartre's text, Petri sought to underline its affinities with the work of Dostoevsky, such as Hugo choosing as a battle name "Raskolnikov" after the main character in *Crime and Punishment* and bearing the same kind of nihilistic urge as Stavrogin in *The Demons*. He also highlighted Hugo's neurotic tendencies and, most notably, the relationship between him and Hoederer, a development of the themes Sartre explored in his acclaimed short story *L'enfance d'un chef* (aka *The Childhood of a Leader*). As Petri explained, "I don't know whether Sartre was aware of the latent homosexuality in the bond between a man who sacrificed his virility and narcissism to the party and was left with the body of an old, aged animal, and the young man, still sexually undecided and so full of himself."[26]

But there was more. Valmarana recalled that the director kept a portrait of Stalin behind his desk, painted by the noted artist Giacomo Porzano, which had an obvious symbolic meaning. "Stalin was like Uranus who devours his children, he was the father whom you must kill in order to survive."[27] A big portrait of the Russian dictator can also be glimpsed in a scene of *La classe operaia*, when Lulù opens his apartment closet to reveal a bunch of old and useless things amassed inside, an allusion to a long-gone past. "A museum," he labels it.

In a letter to film critic Alfredo Rossi dated March 21, 1978, Petri was adamant about his intentions: "I'm going to make *Le mani sporche*, within certain limits, as if it was a Stalinist version of *Todo modo*."[28] So, in a sense, it was a way to reprise the theme of his previous film, this time facing the skeleton in the closet that every Italian communist was afraid to talk about. Sartre's drama revolved around the same crushing political mechanism as his version of Sciascia's book, with the Communist Party instead of the Christian Democrats.

Lastly, the discourse on Stalinism tied back to a couple of old, unmade projects. Petri had been trying in vain for over a decade to make *Un amore lungo*, a story set in a Roman section of the PCI, which he claimed "had something in common with Sartre's drama, namely the analysis of the relationship between morals and politics as well as of the psychological roots of Stalinism, observed in everyday life."[29] Adapting *Le mani sporche* allowed him to reprise some themes from that unmade script. Another abandoned project was *Stalin è morto?* (Is Stalin Dead?), which he had proposed to Franco Cristaldi before even making his debut behind the camera, following the events of the 20th Congress of the Soviet Communist Party.[30] "Today, *Le mani sporche* is a replacement of that idea. And it could be titled *Stalin non è morto* (Stalin's Not Dead)."[31]

To stress his point, he added two scenes at the beginning and end, filmed at the Teatro Gerolamo in Milan, which underlined the theatrical nature of the work and marked his sole intervention on its original structure. As *Le mani sporche* begins, we see Hugo, carrying a suitcase, crossing the auditorium, filled with young spectators, and reaching the stage. The camera lingers on an elderly man sitting in a box, wearing a military outfit. His features are unmistakably those of Stalin.

The closing scene marks the return to the theme of performance by way of an ironic gimmick. Hugo is shot dead outside Olga's door by the party killers. He falls down and dies while the curtain is quickly drawn. But his arm pokes through the curtain. The actor realizes his mistake and quickly retracts it. The lights turn on again and the cast gathers on stage at the end of the show to receive the public's applause. The audience is divided, though: half of them applaud enthusiastically, the other half whistle and boo. Slogans and insults can be heard. The curtain is drawn again. Then, in a POV shot from behind the stage, the camera looks out on the empty audience. The lights go out. Everyone has left, except for one person. Stalin is still sitting in his box. He gets up and takes one last puff from his cigarette. The screen goes dark. The image couldn't be clearer. Stalin has devoured his children and died, but his ghost still lingers, hovering on the living and the dead, the past and the present. And it's the last to leave.

"A strike against the heart of the state"

On the morning of March 16, Leonardo Sciascia had an appointment with a painter friend. He took a taxi. The driver was very agitated. Sciascia never listened to the radio, so he was not aware of the events that had happened earlier that morning. It was the driver who told him.

March 16, 1978, was the day the members of the new cabinet led by Giulio Andreotti were to undergo the required confidence vote in Parliament at 10 a.m. It was a delicate moment for the nation. After months of mediation with Enrico Berlinguer, Aldo Moro had convinced the PCI to take part in the parliamentary majority and back the new cabinet. It would be the first time in Italian history. But the vote was uncertain, for many Communist MPs were dubious about the composition of Andreotti's cabinet. On the other hand, Moro had been criticized by his own party members, who opposed his political move, and his authority was somehow cracked by the ongoing Lockheed bribery scandal. On that day, several newspapers reported rumors that he was the mysterious politician—nicknamed "Antelope Kobbler"—bribed by the American company.

Moro left his house at about 9 a.m. and got in the back seat of his Fiat 130 car. The president's trusted collaborator, marshal Oreste Leonardi, was in the front seat next to the carabinieri official at the wheel, Domenico Ricci. An Alfa Romeo Alfetta with three more bodyguards—Francesco Zizzi, Giulio Rivera and Raffaele Iozzino—followed them. The two vehicles entered Via Mario Fani, a downhill street in the Trionfale neighborhood, in the North Area of Rome. There, the Brigate Rosse had set up their ambush.

Near the end of Via Fani, a Fiat 128 car driven by terrorist Mario Moretti was parked near a crossroads with Via Stresa, waiting for a signal from the BR lookout Rita Algranati. As Moro's car approached, Moretti suddenly cut off its path, causing the Fiat 130 to bump into its rear and remain blocked between it and the Alfetta that followed. A second terrorist vehicle, a Fiat 128 with two more Red Brigades in it (Alvaro Lojacono and Alessio Casimirri) blocked the Alfetta from behind. Four terrorists armed with machine guns and machine pistols and wearing Alitalia airline uniforms in order to avoid friendly fire—presumably Valerio Morucci, Raffaele Fiore, Prospero Gallinari and Franco Bonisoli—turned up from behind nearby bushes, approached the cars and let out a storm of bullets against the Fiat 130 at close range, killing the five carabinieri. Only one of Moro's men had the time to fire his weapon but was immediately dispatched. Another Red Brigade, Barbara Balzerani, blocked the other end of the road so that no car would enter via Fani during the shootout.

Moro, unharmed, was taken out of the car by Fiore and Moretti, who put him on a Fiat 132 driven by Bruno Seghetti and fled at full speed. The other terrorists followed in two more cars. The surprise attack had lasted just three minutes, from 9:02 to 9:05 a.m. Ninety-one bullets had been fired.

Dirty Hands, Dirty Conscience

Rehearsals for *Le mani sporche* started on March 6, 1978, and filming began on April 3 at the Centro Telecinematografico Culturale,[32] in the outskirts of Milan, in a climate which the director labeled "*todomodesco*" (*Todo mod*o-esque).[33] Speaking of which, Daniele Senatore—still based in New York—was in touch with Petri for a U.S. release of *Todo modo* (on this occasion Petri considered making some cuts) to be screened in Los Angeles by the end of April. But after Moro's kidnapping he changed his mind: "I think it's very negative to try a release of this film at this moment. I'll decline the distributor's offer. Maybe in the future the film can circulate without creating the issues it creates today."[34]

Shooting for *Le mani sporche* lasted sixty-one days, until June 10, followed by the extra shooting at the Teatro Girolamo. Newspapers and magazine reports betrayed a certain curiosity, and many sensed Petri's career was at a turning point. Film historian Fernaldo Di Giammatteo noted how the director had "seemingly ground to a halt. His restlessness has grown, his fury has deviated to grotesque tones and is going in circles convulsively. What can come out of this is either intense maturity or rabid dispersion."[35]

For the role of Hoederer, Petri called on his old friend Marcello Mastroianni, who, like him, was on his first experience on the small screen. Mastroianni wasn't too fond of the play either: "The text didn't have great literary qualities, but Petri, with his directorial genius, managed to give rhythm and suspense to it," he later recalled.[36] Alongside Mastroianni, Petri cast Giovanni Visentin as Hugo, upon the advice of his friend Franco Giraldi; the rest of the cast featured noted stage actors such as Massimo Foschi (in his second film with the director after *Indagine*) as Prince Paul, Omero Antonutti as Karsky, Anna Maria Gherardi as Olga, and the experienced voice actor Pietro Biondi as Louis. For the role of Hugo's wife, Jessica, Petri cast the 22-year-old Giuliana De Sio, chosen over Monica Guerritore.[37] Born in Salerno in 1956, De Sio was the younger sister of singer Teresa De Sio. She had started acting through her friend Teresa Ann Savoy, after an experience in a hippie commune, and had had her breakthrough role in the 1977 mini-series *Una donna*. *Le mani sporche* was her second appearance on the small screen.

"Elio was a person of great existential and intellectual severity, but without the boredom of severe people. He was strict but also funny, likeable, flexible, although only regarding certain things," the actress recalled. "Politically, for example, he just couldn't accept the state of things. Because of all this, I liked him very much."[38] The director worked thoroughly on De Sio's performance.

> My character had to be very feminine, bourgeois, frivolous, someone who wanted to have fun. By then I was a tomboy, a half-hippie, and ideologically I was against the idea of the perfectly dressed woman in 1940s style. I still wore pigtails and he wanted me to wear high heels, which I had never done before.... He was very harsh toward me and taught me to get into character almost by force. And he put into me an eroticism, a sex appeal which I didn't have or didn't know I had.[39]

During filming, Petri kept a constant strong emotional mood on the set, in order to have his actors give their best performance, sometimes even having an argument with someone out of the blue so as to avoid a release of tension. But the result was astounding.

"I've never seen a TV crew so involved with the director," De Sio admitted. "Usually TV crews move with the same nonchalance from vaudeville to Ibsen, they don't give a damn. After ten days shooting with Elio, I've seen Sartre's book going from hand to hand on the set, passed on by cameramen and technicians. Elio had managed to raise their awareness, speaking about Sartre with everyone, every day before filming."[40] Petri also wrote a long essay on Sartre's play and the reasons behind the new adaptation, a testimony to his attachment to the project.

The director—reportedly paid 18 million *lire* for the job[41]—was well aware of the issues he would face working in television. "It is very difficult to adapt to the working methods of RAI-TV. I feel like a handicraftsman could feel, someone like my father, a coppersmith, who is put forcibly at FIAT's assembly line. Every minute I feel like leaving. But I'm too involved now."[42] The film was shot with electronic cams: three cameras which also simultaneously recorded on tape. Petri's old friend Renzo Vespignani was the artistic consultant, while Ennio Morricone composed the music. He later claimed it was the TV work he was most proud of.[43]

Le mani sporche went well beyond the estimated budget and shooting schedule, and its making was quite laborious. At first Petri worked with all three cameras shooting at once, a time-saving method as was habitual on television, but then he opted to use only one camera and employ long takes instead, a more elaborate and costly choice but necessary to give the film a more vibrant rhythm and make it stand out from the typical made-for-TV products. His trademark complex camerawork characterizes many scenes and as in *L'assassino* and *Un tranquillo posto di campagna* the elegant transitions from the present to the past take place without cuts. In a film shot entirely within interiors, Petri's artistic taste manifests itself with a brilliant scenic idea: at the beginning, when Hugo arrives in the theater and at Olga's house, the curtains open and a huge reproduction of René Magritte's painting *L'empire des lumières* dominates the stage. The Surrealistic, uncanny confusion of light and darkness in Magritte's masterpiece can be seen as a metaphor for the contrast of ideas that characterizes the party's different currents and their obscure maneuvers.

As he had done in *I giorni contati* and *Indagine*, Petri had a brief cameo, and not a casual one. During the first installment, after the end of a party meeting, Louis dismisses some of the participants, who walk down a flight of stairs. The third and last to leave, with a hat in his hand, is Elio Petri. Like the other comrades, he salutes Louis with his raised fist, then shakes his hand and looks him in the eyes, with a knowing look and the shadow of a smile in his face. Did that smile hide a deeper significance, perhaps the memory of how, many years earlier, he was indeed a communist militant?

Always faithful to his idea of democratic confrontation, Petri was aiming to raise a debate with *Le mani sporche*, unafraid of the consequences, whatever they might be. He had attempted to do so with *Todo modo*, but his film had been virtually buried, like a dissenting voice to be silenced. So, he would raise his voice, again, and try once more. Some days before shooting started, he and Mastroianni held a press conference to illustrate the exceptionality of the effort, and possibly to shake off their heads the feeling of doom that was covering the country like a dark cape. "It is too easy to identify Hoederer with Berlinguer," he pointed out, "and Hugo with a Red Brigade terrorist. But the play is not about that."[44] Once again, as in *Todo modo*, a central point in Petri's vision was the duplicity of the characters, "who are all politically in bad faith."[45]

But the core of the play had an even more personal and deeper resonance to Petri, for it portrayed one of his most heartfelt themes, the symbolical killing of the father. Once, as a young man, he would probably take Hugo's side as the rebel son. Now, given also Visentin's over-the-top impersonation of the young revolutionary (an even more unpleasant character than Total in *La proprietà*), he would rather see himself on Hoederer's side. As Valmarana put it,

> Elio wanted to discuss and said that was the reason for choosing Sartre's work and his own reading of it; he had some views to argue, which were not entirely Sartre's. He wasn't so much interested in the text's reference to Trotsky's assassination ... rather, he was interested in the cold and cynical way the party leaders take their decisions.... And he was interested also in the contradiction of the two positions, Hugo's abstract idealism, feverish but cold, versus Hoederer's realistic pragmatism, calm but hot-blooded. But unlike Sartre, who saw a scission in those two characters, and who in '68 would be implicitly on Hugo's part, Petri's choice was different. He was not against pragmatism. His choice between purity (Hugo) and compromise (Hoederer) is neat. He is for Hoederer, and in fact he cast one of his dearest friends in the role. He is for the "dirty hands" if they lead to a project and allow it to be made. Hoederer is human and Hugo is not. Hoederer has a project of life, he thinks the world can be changed. Hugo has a project of death, he doesn't want to change. He only wants to destroy.[46]

Killing the Father

The shooting of *Le mani sporche* was accompanied by the ongoing news of Moro's imprisonment and the ensuing political turmoil. The whole nation was in a state of shock, as if paralyzed by such a traumatic event. Over the following weeks, events followed one another in a frenzied, sometimes chaotic manner, with the unsuccessful investigations to locate Moro's hideout, the prisoner's letters to his family and fellow politicians, and the Brigate Rosse's "Communications" (nine overall) which explained the political motives behind the kidnapping.

On April 16, Communication no. 6 announced that Moro had been sentenced to death as result of a "people's trial." After the Pope's public appeal to release the hostage "without conditions," the Brigate Rosse proposed to exchange him for thirteen imprisoned terrorists. A dramatic debate between political factions followed on which stance to take. Some, such as the PSI led by Bettino Craxi, were willing to negotiate, whereas others—including most of the Christian Democrats and the PCI—were against it, for any negotiation would be a sign of weakness and a legitimization of terrorist violence. The latter faction prevailed.

With Communication no. 9, on May 6, the BR declared that they would "conclude the battle begun on March 16 by executing the sentence to which Aldo Moro has been condemned." On May 9, Moro's body was found in the back trunk of a Red Renault 4 in via Caetani, near the PCI headquarters in Via delle Botteghe Oscure and not far from Piazza del Gesù, where the DC had its own H.Q.

Marcello Mastroianni recalled that many reporters ran to the studio to interview Elio Petri on that day, since in *Todo modo* he had announced and depicted Moro's death. "Petri underwent turbulent days," he explained. "He felt almost responsible, guilty."[47]

He was not the only one. Some years later, in a 1982 interview, Sciascia confided:

> I had written *Il contesto* and *Todo modo*, and I must confess that I felt somehow responsible for what had happened. Not because I had inspired other people's actions, but because I had imagined, I had drawn conclusions of what might happen on the basis of what had happened.

I started to be afraid of imagination. If ten years earlier I'd been told that Moro would change my life, I'd have laughed. But it was like that. After Moro's death I don't feel free to imagine anymore. I'm afraid to tell things that might happen in the future.[48]

As Adolfo Bioy Casares once wrote, everything a man's fantasy can imagine, might and will happen. Sciascia admitted that he fully understood his own book only through Petri's adaptation. As for Petri, he was immediately listed among those morally responsible for the killing. After all, hadn't he imagined it and put it on film?

French critic Pierre Billard was explicit in his accusations. In an article published in the May 1 issue of the conservative weekly magazine *Le Point*, he wrote:

After being Neorealist, Italian cinema remains the most realist in the world. It derives effectiveness, prestige, and a legitimate fierceness from it…. Enthusiastic, sincere, generous, Italian filmmakers inspire admiration and envy. But in the terrible crisis that Italy is currently facing, do they have clean hands? Are they above suspicion? It is not certain. What do Italian filmmakers denounce in their films? Police excesses, judicial shortcomings, landlords' abuses, notables' bribery, party corruption, secret services' plots, moral and religious hypocrisy, social inequality…. But in the last several years, and especially today, Italy is facing a specific evil: the challenge from terrorist groups who … put in peril the institutions and the nation's very existence. When did Italian filmmakers condemn these terrorist groups? Never. Which films did they make about the recruiting, training, and organizing of these fanatic criminals? None…. A singular absence, an extraordinary silence on the part of such lucid, realistic, courageous artists!

Billard's sarcastic attack was aimed at specific targets. He mentioned *Cadaveri eccellenti*, *Io ho paura*, *Todo modo*, Dino Risi's *Mordi e fuggi* (1973), the collective anthology comedy *Signore e signori buonanotte* (1976) and Mario Monicelli's *Un borghese piccolo piccolo* (1977). And he concluded:

Italian filmmakers speak of assassinations, but what guilty parties do they point their finger at? Always three: the police, who investigate improperly, the magistrates, who judge improperly, and the victim, who complains improperly, and is not even such an innocent victim. And the murderers? Never seen nor heard. They are of no interest to Italian cinema. Strange dialectics! These filmmakers are often socialist or communist. But why do they ignore the existence of the Brigate Rosse, whose harmfulness their parties denounce so

Todo modo's final scene was a chilling anticipation of the murder of Aldo Moro, kidnapped and killed by the Brigate Rosse in 1978.

virulently? How can it be explained that nowadays they are, objectively, innocent accomplices of the Brigate Rosse, by contributing to undermine Italian people's pale trust in the State's authority and institutions? If tomorrow a new Fascism, either white or red, should rise from the collapse of democracy, what part of responsibility would Italian filmmakers have?[49]

L'Espresso translated Billard's piece and dedicated a lengthy article to the polemic, with a roundtable discussion between Billard, Petri, Pirro, and Damiano Damiani. The magazine also reported the news that the Christian Democrat MP Giuseppe Costamagna had asked the president of the Chamber, Pietro Ingrao, to promote an investigation into the bankrolling that allowed Petri to make *Todo modo*: a sign, as the writer noted, that the prophecy of a "grand carnage" of the nation's leading party had shaken many people deeply.[50]

Francesco Rosi, who was busy shooting *Cristo si è fermato a Eboli*, sent a scathing open letter to the magazine in which he accused Billard of an "overwhelming urge to start a witch-hunt."[51] As for the others, Pirro and Damiani were trenchant in refuting the allegation, while Petri replied:

> The BR phenomenon has come to the fore very recently, but the issue exists and Billard's question is legitimate. But why is it so difficult to answer it? Because the rise of the so-called left-wing terrorism has created a disorientation among filmmakers as well. But the problem is another: Italy's wrongdoings are always the same, the ones we always exposed. And the BR only confirm this…. I am against the BR, but at the same time I think the biggest problem now is not the BR but the huge wave of displaced, unemployed, unhappy young people whom we feel are siding with the BR. The BR are only the tip of the iceberg.[52]

The director was adamant in noting that he had indeed been criticizing the Left for some years. Not only he was making *Le mani sporche*, but he had made *La proprietà*, where Total's "Marxism-Mandrakism" and his acts against the butcher were a metaphor for the birth of desperation among the Left. "Now, perhaps, that metaphor would be clear. What fault do we have if people cannot 'read' movies? Making a movie on the BR today would be like making a movie on Robin Hood."[53]

The debate ended with Billard partially softening his original views. But he ended with another provocative observation: "The satirical-critical tradition of Italian cinema was born in contact with another historical and political reality. Now that this reality has changed, we need other forms of criticism, other forms of analysis. Perhaps Italian cinema hasn't perfected these new forms yet."[54] For his part, Petri agreed.

Hoederer Equals Berlinguer?

Le mani sporche was aired on TV in the prime-time slot, as a three-part mini-series, on November 14, 15 and 19, 1978. According to Valmarana, the broadcast was preceded, a few days earlier, by a veto from Sartre himself (or someone for him) despite a previous and formal authorization.[55]

Petri's expectations about the Communist Party's reaction were amply satisfied. The film reignited the director's controversy with the PCI, with an intense exchange between him and politician Gian Carlo Pajetta on the pages of the newspaper *Paese Sera*, which, according to Petri, reached even more heated heights in private.[56] *L'Unità* accused the film of being instrumental for an attack on the party, with a scathing front-page column titled "La storia dal buco della serratura" (History as seen from a keyhole).

We have a rather clear idea of how *Le mani sporche* was intended—or rather, pretended—to be presented to the public. That is, a depiction, good for yesterday, today and tomorrow, of history and politics as a "tragicomedy" behind closed doors: a ruthless, illusory, mendacious and even ridiculous game, played by a few over the heads and at the expense of the people.... To Sartre, in 1948, communists were the subject for drama, debate, polemic, critical adherence or motivated dissent. To Petri, in 1978, they are the object of a spectacle too obviously serviceable to a transitory political game.[57]

Petri later observed that "in 1978 the PCI was part of the majority with the Christian Democrats, and Hugo's ideas must sound rather unpleasant to their hypersensitive ears. But in some ways, Hugo's ideas were also those of many communists who refused the concept of historical compromise."[58] As ex-communist philosopher Lucio Colletti, who had signed with Petri the "Manifesto dei 101," pointed out, "communist politics, back then but very often today as well, is not presented for what it is, that is, politics, but—by way of rhetoric and propaganda—as 'ethic,' that is, the whole of the actions that the 'good guys' take against the 'villains.' Being rhetoric, this way of presenting things is naturally hypocritical, and cannot stand that things be called by their own name."[59] This is what Petri had done, and his ex-comrades did not like it at all.

But *Le mani sporche* caused perplexities even outside the left. In reviewing it in the *Corriere della Sera*, novelist and critic Alberto Bevilacqua questioned the choice of a play which, as the director had acknowledged, had its share of issues and weaknesses.

Why Petri has chosen *Le mani sporche* for his TV debut is still not clear to us.... Perhaps, between the lines, he sensed the possibility of using it to read actual themes? The accusation of embourgeoisement to the Communist Party, its lack of revolutionary tension? Hoederer equals Berlinguer? A discourse on terrorism? If that was the intent, it doesn't add up. *Le mani sporche*, surely explosive stuff in 1948, nowadays looks dated, imbued with nihilism and approximation. A lot of irons in the fire—too many: explanations of today's ideas with the pretext of yesterday's ideas; the attempt of turning certain situations into metaphors and allude to others; dramatic tension; desire of alignment.[60]

In many ways, *Le mani sporche* was Petri's most personal and heartfelt work, the one in which he laid bare his ideological distress, his communist roots and the impossibility of coping with the party's politics, his personal torment and increasing pessimism. As he confessed to his friend and scholar, film critic Alfredo Rossi,

Can I say I'm a communist? Sincerely ... I can't, and not just because none of the communist chapels think I am, but also because, in my old experience as a militant, being a communist means accepting a party discipline, somehow sacrificing one's own subjectivity to the party reasons, and living the party minute-by-minute—and I'm not accepting this. More or less, I live like an upper-middle-class man, my day is completely detached from sociality, and my turmoil, if there is any, is only interior ... in short, what's my life got to do with communism? My life is that of a more or less troubled, more or less split bourgeois who was a member of a revolutionary party in his youth, who lived the fall of revolutionary hopes, and who saw the entire society in which he lived degrade with that fall. And who now cannot identify himself any longer with any of the political forces who evoke communism.... Some will say that many communists live their lives exactly like me, if not worse, and no doubt ever touches them that a communist might live differently. But what can I do if people don't want to look at their own face and see what they really are?[61]

But once again his work was met with open hostility and quickly forgotten.

For both sides, Elio Petri was now unsalvageable.

Thirteen

Before Dying
Buone notizie *(1979)*

Good News, Bad News

Until some time ago, I believed that making certain films might be useful to people and so every time I felt there was something useful to do I threw myself into the fray … lately, the situation has deteriorated to the point that you don't even see what might be useful anymore. Until some time ago, making a movie just for me seemed an egotistical gesture. I've made my latest films even suffering a bit, because I didn't have fun making them, but I was following my own discourse on usefulness.[1]

Petri's words, from a 1980 interview, were significant of the mood surrounding what would be his last feature film. In a certain way, he was detaching himself from his last three works, conceived and directed in a social and political climate that had seen him slip gradually from a central position to a somewhat marginal one. As he himself concluded, "Often, it seems to me I'm not even part of Italian cinema."

His political view was just as disenchanted. After witnessing the PCI distancing itself from the 1968 Movement, the party's obsessive search for an alliance with the DC seemed delusional to him. "Only the petit bourgeoisie—that is, people who haven't lived on their skin, physically and psychologically, exploitation and alienation—can nourish the illusion that the masters will make compromises on the basic issues. Unless such compromises are utterly profitable for the masters themselves."[2] The apocalyptic prophecy of *Todo modo* had not become true. On the contrary, the PCI's subordinate position had given new life and credibility to the Christian Democrats. "I cannot even consider myself a fellow traveler," he concluded, paraphrasing Sartre. He was not alone in that. The June 3, 1979, elections saw the PCI lose 4 percent, while the DC retained almost the totality of voters. The Communist party's detachment from the masses had resulted in the masses detaching themselves from the party.

After the controversial experience of *Le mani sporche*, Petri considered another made-for-TV work, an adaptation of Kafka's *In the Penal Colony*. He also received several offers he did not take into consideration. Novelist and poet Tommaso di Ciaula[3] proposed to him adapting his book *Tuta blu* (Blue Collar), the autobiographical tale of a Southern worker that had caused a sensation upon its release and was heavily criticized by the unions. Swiss filmmaker and producer Werner Zeindler of Elite Films asked him to direct a movie based on Jacques Chessex's 1975 novel *L'Ardent royaume*.[4] But he was also in talks to adapt *La vita interiore*, based on Alberto Moravia's best-selling novel of the same name published in 1978.[5] Despite his friendship with Moravia, Petri turned the offer down.[6] It was not just the result of a growing indecision on which path to take. According to Alfredo Rossi, the refusal was the consequence of a "pact with himself to bring to the surface, at all costs ... and all the risks, his secret and marginal self, his own phantoms."[7] And, one might add, a sign of a deeper existential crisis.

In fact, there was more that tormented Petri's heart, and it wasn't politics.

The director's working relationship with Giuliana De Sio during *Le mani sporche* had often resulted in heated arguments, and De Sio pictured herself as the scapegoat. But something deeper started growing between them. "We used to go out together after *Le mani sporche*. We used to see Marcello too, then, after a year and a half, something clicked, and we became a couple," De Sio recalled.[8]

The abrupt affair with the actress caused a traumatic change in Petri's life. He left his wife and moved away from his luxurious attic on Lungotevere Mellini, full of books, paintings, and *objets d'art*. After a brief stay in Fiano at Franco Giraldi's house, he moved to his mother's place, an apartment on the third floor of a modest house in the popular district of Bravetta. Gianni Amelio, who paid him a visit with Valmarana, recalled the latter's vain attempts to lighten the director's dark mood. "In that small living room ... he looked like a recluse.... an intellectual who brought on himself, like a cross, all the world's ills; a man who rejected serenity as if it was a guilt, restless and embittered."[9]

The year of 1979 saw Petri return to the big screen with a new project, *Le buone notizie ovvero la personalità della vittima* (The Good News, or the Personality of the Victim) which eventually became *Buone notizie*. For the first time, he was the sole author of the script, a sign that the story delved into very personal issues. *Buone notizie* was a definite change of pace from *Todo modo*, and overall from the author's overtly political output of the decade. "Intellectuals stick to their own formulas just like some entrepreneurs specialize in the making of a certain product,"[10] he observed. Was it a way to go against the market's expectations? Or to let loose his own demons, changing the focus from the wider fresco to a smaller sketch? "I made this film just for the sheer pleasure of making it. I took notes and wrote it on my own."[11]

Originally titled *Prima di morire* (Before Dying), it was conceived in Milan, while Petri was filming *Le mani sporche* and rereading the works of Sartre and Wittgenstein. The two philosophers' reflections on the private sphere elicited in him a number of notes and thoughts about life in today's society. The object of Petri's meditation was the triumph of the petit bourgeois ideology in the Western civilization: "The middle class has won with respect to the things obtained, but rather than a victory it is a regression to childhood," he wrote, observing how the newly found well-being had caused a withdrawal into the private sphere, self-narcissism, and a morbid attention to biological and sexual needs. At one point he even considered using as a title a verse from T.S. Eliot's poem *Little Gidding*, *...e i bambini tra i rami del melo* (...and the children in the apple tree), to stress this child-like regression, because "the head of a petit bourgeois is full yet empty; it is a sounding board of a void echoing with questions that accompany the investigation of the real, of the social, the search for one's own identity since childhood ... we will never know what life is, for we refuse to measure ourselves with its own rhythm, which is biological. Our doubts thus become senseless and absolute, prenatal or preagonal."[12]

Prima di morire took shape as a numbered series of sketches about a middle-aged man confronting himself with love, sex, solitude and other issues. Its embryonic form, broken and episodic, close to a succession of comic strips, sought to capture the alternance between the dramatic, the ridiculous, the grotesque. Petri modeled the protagonist on his cinematic alter ego Marcello Mastroianni, who was to coproduce the film, but he had second thoughts that led him to rewrite the script drastically. The second draft, *La personalità della vittima*, maintained the spirit of the original but sought to distance itself from the central discourse, first of all by making the protagonist younger. As Petri later explained, "Mastroianni could have been mistaken for a man on the verge of old age and afraid of death. A 40-year-old individual is more clearly a victim and a sick man."[13]

For the starring role, the director opted for the 37-year-old Giancarlo Giannini, a versatile actor who could veer easily from comedy to drama, and who had displayed a remarkable talent in such films as *Dramma della gelosia (tutti i particolari in cronaca)* (1970, Ettore Scola), and in several films by Lina Wertmüller, such as *Mimì metallurgico ferito nell'onore, Travolti da un insolito destino nell'azzurro mare d'agosto* (1974) and especially *Pasqualino settebellezze* (1975), where he played a despicable, wily Camorrist who ends up in a concentration camp during World War II. Giannini had always wanted to work with Petri, and circa 1977 had suggested they make a movie together, an adaptation of Giulio Castelli's 1973 novel *Il fascistibile*, about a young man who is injured during a robbery and undergoes a physical and psychic transformation, becoming a fascist. Anthony Burgess, who was living in Italy at that time, wrote the adaptation, but the project was eventually shelved by producer Vincenzo Labella. Still, a collaboration between Petri and Giannini was written in the stars. "He called me one night, around eleven, and he told me: 'I have to talk to you.' It was, let's say, a year before *Buone notizie*," the actor recalled. "He read to me a few short pages of notes he had taken and told me: 'I want to make this movie with you.' Because I wanted to make it too, we set out to produce it together."[14]

This time, in fact, Petri opted for an unusual venture, and he and Giannini set up their own production company. Over the course of his career the director had worked with moguls such as Ponti and De Laurentiis, but also with unorthodox producers such as Zaccariello. After *Todo modo*, he wanted freedom more than anything else. As Giannini explained, "We decided not to worry about government assistance. If we didn't get it, too bad. We were our own producers, so we could take some risks.... We knew we weren't working on something that would be a big success, but whatever it would be, it would be something different."[15] For distribution, the actor got in touch with his friends at Medusa Distribuzione, who had financed some of his previous films, and managed to obtain an advance. Medusa specialized in comedies, and as the actor recalled, there was only one concern about the project: "'Giancarlo, will this film make people laugh?' they asked me..."[16]

"The distributor gave us 605 million *lire*," Petri explained; "the film cost exactly that sum. We got paid well below our market fee."[17] The crisis of the national film industry was under everyone's gaze, and the glory days of the early 1970s, when Italian cinema was at the top of its game, internationally revered and critically recognized, seemed far away.

"It is an unusual film, a strange, funny, ironic story, different from all the other movies I did," Giannini told an interviewer when asked about the plot. "If I were to label it, I'd say it is a tragedy in the form of a comedy, but it's difficult to pin down."[18] As had occurred with Ugo Tognazzi, who spoke of *La proprietà* as a comedy, perhaps as a way to protect his work on the film, Giannini's words reveal how Petri's cinema was pursuing a path totally its own, through a story which the director himself described as "evanescent and tortuous."[19]

Buone notizie centers on an unnamed television functionary at RAI, referred to in the script simply as "Uomo," Man. He sits all day in his office in front of six TV monitors which broadcast all the programs of the day. What exactly is his job? He is so accustomed to watching television that he sees reality as filtered through it. When he comes home, he keeps watching television. He has an estranged wife, Fedora, who loves him more than he does. He is obsessed with sex and seeks extramarital affairs, but his efforts to seduce his female colleague Tignetti result in humiliation, and his attempt to make love to Fedora's best friend, Benedetta, is a failure.

One day the Man meets an old friend, Gualtiero Milano, who asks him for help. Gualtiero, a hypochondriac, believes someone wants to kill him. His wife Ada convinces the Man to help her hospitalize Gualtiero in a clinic to cure him from what appears to be a nervous breakdown. Then the Man learns from TV that Gualtiero has been murdered. The police believe it could have been a mistake, for a politician was hospitalized in the same clinic. At the funeral, Fedora, who is pregnant, confesses that she had an affair with Gualtiero, who is the father of the child she is carrying. Back at the office, the Man finds out that the deceased has left an envelope for him, with the words "Do not open" on it. He opens it. Inside, there are many stickers, each with the words "Do not open" on it....

Filming for *Buone notizie* took place in the summer of 1979 and principal photography was wrapped by mid–August.[20] Michel Piccoli, who was initially to play Gualtiero, was replaced by the noted stage actor Paolo Bonacelli, one of the "Excellencies" in *Salò*. The main female roles went to Ángela Molina (Fedora), Aurore Clément (Ada), Ombretta Colli (Tignetti), Ritza Brown (Benedetta). Paola Petri was Molina's agent and suggested the Spanish actress to the director, who had noticed her in Buñuel's *Cet obscur objet du désir* (1977) and in Luigi Comencini's *L'ingorgo* (1979). Clément was a friend of the family, while Petri cast Colli upon suggestion from her husband, singer-songwriter, playwright and stage actor Giorgio Gaber, whom he had first considered for a role.[21] Pasolini's fetish actor Ninetto Davoli had a cameo as one of the man's colleagues. Upon suggestion of Gianni Amelio, Petri hired Tonino Nardi as director of photography. "He needed a young, fast d.o.p., who could light a scene with few resources," Amelio explained.[22]

Shooting on location in Rome, Petri had to face many issues. He needed to film some scenes outside a huge building at EUR but was denied the permits, and had a hard time convincing the authorities to let him shoot inside the Verano monumental cemetery. As usual, he was very vocal in his complaints. "You can't make movies in Rome anymore! It's a catastrophe. Everything is hostile, everyone is diffident. All are asking lots of money ... for a while now this city has been acting in a very arrogant way toward cinema."[23]

It was not just Cinecittà facing a crisis. In September, the news came that ENPALS, a pension fund for employees in the entertainment industry, could not pay the expected pensions for its 35,000 members. These included many famous actors and directors, counting Petri, but the most affected would be the unknown soldiers. As Nino Manfredi put it, "an actor like me can still keep working without a pension, but what about the weaker ones, those who work in the entertainment industry and who must work at least sixty days a year, or else they lose medical assistance too? They don't even have the right to fall ill, but just to die."[24] After thirty years living above their possibilities, it suddenly looked like the people in the movie business were facing an abyss: fewer and fewer films were being made, box-office grosses were tumbling, second and third-run theaters were reconverting into red-light venues or, worse, supermarkets or parking lots.

Excerpts from *Buone notizie* were screened in October at the annual "Incontri internazionali del cinema" in Sorrento. Intervening during a convention held to discuss the current economic crisis and hemorrhage of spectators, Petri accused his own category in very pessimistic terms. "The values of professionalism have fallen into disuse, amid general disaffection, and if filmmakers do not love cinema anymore, tell me why spectators should. Our disaffection has been passed over to the audiences."[25]

The director was adamant that he had not made a commercial film. "I don't know how it will do at the box-office. I don't give a damn," he commented. "I had fun."[26] Medusa apparently knew better and—with a move not dissimilar to De Laurentiis' with *Il maestro di Vigevano*—opted for a blatant gimmick, leaning on Giancarlo Giannini's fame as a comedian and shamelessly promoting *Buone notizie* as an unconventional, yet exhilarating comedy ("A lucid, ironic, sharp Petri, with many laughs and some bitter grimace"), replete with a tagline announcing, "Woody Allen leaves … here comes GIANNINI!" Another tagline sold the movie as an erotic comedy of sorts: "My wife, my lover, my secretary, my friend's wife, my wife's girlfriend … all with the same vice! The year's most sophisticated comedy!"

After its world premiere on November 23, 1979, at the Firenze Cinema Festival, *Buone notizie* opened at the 7th spot in Roman venues, but soon dropped to the 9th spot before disappearing. Petri and Giannini went on a promotional tour with several presentations all over Italy that lasted almost three months,[27] something the director had never done before. Both knew that it was a difficult film which needed to be explained to audiences. To Giannini, it was a chance to know Petri better and form a closer bond. On stage, the director was very aggressive. The arguments with the critics over the years had forged him to a point when he would no longer consider being diplomatic. "He said exactly what he thought," Giannini recalled. "He told everyone they were idiots."[28]

Buone notizie was not nearly the commercial disaster that some described. With 379 million *lire*, it ended up at the 70th spot among Italy's seasonal releases, grossing more than genre films such as *The Fog*, *Phantasm* and *Cannibal Holocaust*, or auteur works such as Pontecorvo's *Ogro* and Polanski's *Tess*. Still, not enough to recover costs.

The film elicited varied reactions from critics. Some were dumbfounded. "Here's a movie that leaves you stunned," the *Corriere della Sera*'s Giovanni Grazzini wrote, admitting that "one cannot quite figure where it wants to end up."[29] Morando Morandini, in *Il Giorno*, labeled it "one of those films that the English call 'arty,' not as artificial but as pseudo-artistic." Petri didn't take it well, as Giannini recalled. "I remember he downright told Morandini that he was an ignoramus. 'You allow yourself to talk about my movie, but in reviewing one of my previous films you mistook a Van Gogh for a Picasso. You should stop talking, you're only good enough to be a priest, go be a priest!'"[30]

Once again, film magazines attacked Petri with an ideological fury bordering on hysteria. *Cinema nuovo* called *Buone notizie* ambiguous and moralistic,[31] *Cineforum* labeled it as downright squalid.[32] Other reviewers were moderately praising, most notably Alberto Moravia, who wrote: "the film, which at first seems disconcerting and absurd, in the end comes together … in a coherent and unitarian structure and significance."[33]

Overall, as film historian Alberto Pezzotta observed, "in the reception of the time *Buone notizie* appears to be an 'average' film,"[34] as proven by the attempt to "normalize" it on the part of both critics and the audience. As such, it was not the "film *maudit*"

The Italian poster for *Buone notizie* misleadingly advertised it as a comedy.

that *Todo modo* had become and was gradually absorbed in the Italian production of the period without much debate. To many, Petri had become a "has been" of sorts, and it was as if without the red cape of a blatant political target (the police, the factory, capitalism, the Christian Democrats) his work was not important enough to deserve a more in-depth analysis.

That's Entertainment...

"It is a film on the *societé du spectacle*,"[35] Petri said about *Buone notizie*, referencing to Guy Debord's mammoth 1967 opus of the same name (aka *The Society of the Spectacle*), published in Italy in 1968 and made into an experimental film by Debord himself in 1973. That same year, Petri had observed: "I have read Guy Debord and *La societé du spectacle*. But if we take this path, we must destroy everything that surrounds us. Everything is spectacle: a shop window, a walk, a way of looking, of dressing. It's man that loves spectacle. Accepting spectacle means accepting one's own condition."[36]

Several years later he was even more trenchant:

> In the society of entertainment, the entertainment of life disappeared. What's left is only the entertainment itself that was organized, programmed, and elaborated by society to give us the impression that we're still alive, while we actually haven't been for a while. I believe reality doesn't exist anymore.... I believe ours is a simulacrum of life. Our love is a simulacrum of love. Our culture is a simulacrum of culture. We mime feelings we don't even feel anymore, just like Pavlov's animals. Even death is in the natural order of this non-living.[37]

With the unnamed protagonist, Petri wanted to depict the ordinary middle-class man, who abandoned every aspiration, both cultural and political, and locked himself in a cage, looking at the outside world through the filter of television, "the driving belt of dominion, the power of power, the surrogate of all existing things."[38] *Buone notizie* is one of the first Italian films to attempt an in-depth analysis of the cultural mutation that television was bringing into every home, and fully explore its uncontrollable rise and its newfound centrality in the lives of Italians after the boom of private networks.

On August 10, 1974, "Firenze Libera" had started its transmissions, breaking the monopoly of RAI-TV. With sentence no. 202 of July 28, 1976, the Constitutional Court agreed that State monopoly over local broadcasting was unconstitutional. It stated that local broadcasting channels were legitimate, for there were no dangers of private monopolies or oligopolies, and it demanded the institution of a law system in order to protect the public service and thus prevent the insurgence of such. This sentence led to the so-called "deregulation phase": the liberalization of public broadcasting paved the way for a competition that, in the absence of any regulator, would prove overwhelming.

Petri's disdain for television was well-known. "Television provides extracts of life that are inoculated not intravenously, but anally, through suppositories,"[39] he once quipped, and in *La classe operaia* he had depicted it as an hypnotizing device, the bluish light from its screen feebly illuminating the workers and their families sitting in the darkness of their kitchens and living rooms, and feeding them non-stop advertising.

When introducing *Buone notizie* to the press, the director went on at length speaking about TV, a "magnetizing object which substitutes itself for reality, steals our life from us, populates our imagination with menacing phantoms. A surrogate of life which turns us into a new type of monks in the seclusion of images. If you will, you can live in your house, all alone as in a convent cell, you and your TV set."[40] It is another kind of neurosis, a dissociation. Not living life but watching it.

The analogy between the contemporary "television man" and cloistered monks works on many levels. It gives the idea of the dramatic detachment from reality Petri was noting around him, but it also sheds light on the director's own fears and issues while connecting to the visual mood of *Todo modo*. For someone as obsessed as he was with the idea of mortality, a particularly disturbing function of television was as a memento of human transience. Lonelier than ever, television man was reduced to watching a constant reminder of his own mortality, for the "good news" is the contemporary version of the old monastic rule, "remember that you have to die." And, as the protagonist says, "Dying scares me shitless…. I'm afraid at the table, in the toilet, at the movies, in the office. Fear comes without warning…." His friend Gualtiero, on the other hand, has projected these irrational fears into the belief of a conspiracy against him.

Petri had thought of the alternate title *La stanza delle buone notizie* (The room of the good news), which refers to the living room where TV sets are usually placed, but also to the office where Giannini's character watches six TV screens arranged like a video wall and transmitting all kind of images at the same time. The scene recalls the one in *Un tranquillo posto di campagna* where Ferri is watching a slideshow made of erotic images interspersed with gruesome ones, feeding on them in a sort of trance.

Here, the Man is apparently reading Gabriel Chevalier's satiric novel *Clochemerle*, but later on it turns out he is just *pretending* to read the book, which is turned upside down. Throughout the film, the same book will always be open more or less around the same page. The Man is not really reading, but using it as a shield of sorts to pretend he is immune from the TV virus, which he isn't. Like the slaves in Plato's cave, chained to a wall and facing another blank wall, he is watching a simulacrum of life and pretending that those shadows are reality. In a brief moment of awareness, he complains he hasn't seen a sunset in years…

Petri, always a careful observer of contemporary art, was well aware of video art, from the early pioneering Fluxus artists of the 1950s to the works of David Hall, who in 1976 had curated the first video installations exhibition at London's Tate Gallery. The "video wall" in his film, albeit possibly hampered by the low budget which allowed only for six television sets, becomes literally an eye on the world. As Pezzotta observed, the classics of 20th century painting that appear in the film, such as Georges Braque's dove or Picasso's *Guernica*, "seem dull artifacts of a past that is now mute, whereas the so-called 'small screen' is an invasive window on reality which Petri depicts as a technological Pandora's box."[41]

The idea of the video wall had been in Petri's mind for quite some time. In the early draft for *La proprietà non è più un furto*, Anita is infected by Total's "illness" and steals three TV sets which she places before her in the living room: "I function as a robot," she says; "my only form of spiritual nourishment comes from those little robots that are televisions." And the sketched outline for *Le cose* featured a passage in which the protagonists "watch six TV sets at the same time, all airing the same stupid program." *Condominium*, a 1967 treatment he co-wrote with Nicola Badalucco, is set in a luxurious building, with slices of life characterized by the ubiquitous presence of TV sets. The tone is hyperbolic, apocalyptic. It is as if everyone is hypnotized by television while the streets are covered with abandoned dead bodies. A young couple, Mazia and Milo, the only ones who don't own a TV, finally buy one. They turn it on and are bombarded by images of catastrophes and calamities, including dead Russians and Chinese on the moon.

> Mazia and Milo are fascinated by the eruption of this river of disasters into their house. Mazia and Milo take the TV set in their bedroom. The girl tries to excite her husband, but without success. They fall asleep, exhausted by the tragedies seen on TV and by their vain attempts to make love. For the first time in their conjugal life, one of them hasn't had the strength to reply to the other's sexual call.[42]

In the early scenes of *Buone notizie*, with the reiteration of the same image (the TV announcer played by Ritza Brown), the video wall becomes a piece of Warholian art, a reflection on repetition which is somehow reassuring, aseptic. Then, chaos ensues. The images on screen are violent, erotic, confused, contradictory. Petri blends fiction and reality by way of newsreels, documentaries, stock footage (with a new audio commentary superimposed), plus expressly recreated scenes (such as a fake news report and footage with a magician, shot by Berto Pelosso) in a frenzied hodge-podge which predates the themes of video art. Images are chosen for their symbolic significance: the "good news" is, sarcastically, deaths, killings, natural disasters, pollution, terrorist acts, mixed with images of sports events, political personalities, excerpts from films. In the epilogue, the screens are all blank, with white noise static snow.

Petri includes footage from films in the Medusa catalog, namely Umberto Lenzi's *Il giustiziere sfida la città* (1975) and a bit from Sergio Martino's *La montagna del dio cannibale* (aka *Slave of the Cannibal God*, 1978), in which Ursula Andress is captured by the cannibals. Besides the obvious in-joke—given Andress' role in *La decima vittima*, not to mention the late seizure of the film's Super 8 tapes in 1975—the juxtaposition of the actress' nude body to the images of starving African children acquires a provocative, disturbing quality. Petri is not merely criticizing one of Italian cinema's most notoriously exploitative subgenres, the cannibal film, but he is exposing how both images—the nude actress in a movie, the real dying child—have ultimately the same spectacular value in the "society of spectacle." Reality is reduced to an endless supply of commodified images. A punitive society immerses individuals in a universe of danger and uncertainty in order to stimulate their basic needs, which they satisfy mechanically: "Eating without being hungry, working without producing nor feeling realized, looking at a book without reading, making love without emotion nor pleasure, speaking without saying, dying without pain."[43]

A Surreal Apocalypse

Buone notizie is programmatically unpleasant and inscrutable. It was Petri's own rebellion against a society which wants everything to be pleasant and smooth, including political commitment. "Why do I make films like that?" he commented. "Evidently because of a neat feeling that we have come to a point where all the premises that there were when I was a kid have truly been frustrated."

His bewilderment before such an anguishing present was common to several Italian directors. Critic Callisto Cosulich later suggested that *Buone notizie* be compared with other products of the era that conveyed the same anguish and impending dread by way of exemplary tales, namely *L'ingorgo*, set during a huge traffic jam outside Rome, Fellini's *Prova d'orchestra* (1979), with its wrecking ball demolishing the walls and exposing the orchestra players to the outside world, Risi's *Caro papà* (1979), where a wealthy father discovers that his son is a terrorist who is planning to murder him, and the Taviani brothers' *Il prato* (1979), which depicted a young man's illusory retreat in the countryside.[44] Whereas 1968 caused a flourishing of politically-themed films in the form of apologues—from Bertolucci's *Partner* (1968) to Tinto Brass' *L'urlo* (1970), from Roberto Faenza's *H2S* (1969) to Liliana Cavani's *I cannibali* (1970)—the next decade's backflow caused a sense of inadequacy to face reality and the need to reprise similar narrative forms.

Petri's film revolves around a bizarrely obscure plot which once again gives away the director's love for the mystery genre as well as his habit of going against clichés. In fact, the many questions scattered throughout the story will never have any proper answer or will have several contradictory ones. Is Gualtiero simply paranoiac, or is someone actually attempting to kill him? What do the anonymous threats left in his answering machine mean? Who will dispatch him, and why? Is his murder a tragic (but ridiculous) mistake on the part of the killer(s) attempting to assassinate a politician instead? We will never know, nor does the film leave any clue to help us. When the Man asks Gualtiero who his persecutors are, the other replies: "You'll never know. Another mystery!" As Petri once wrote, "questions are lunatic, just like the reality that produces them."[45]

Buone notizie conveys an overall apocalyptic mood which reconnects to *Todo modo* but is rendered in a Surrealist way. "It must be like a Magritte painting," he once told Giannini.[46] The result is his most Buñuelian work, and not just because of the presence of Ángela Molina: as with *Cet obscur objet du désir* the film depicts a society on the verge of breakdown. It starts with a blackout, which symbolically plunges the protagonist into darkness ("They are turning us into cavemen," he mutters in despair), and ends with a bomb alarm which causes the RAI building to be evacuated. But besides the terrorist menace hovering over the city—a common feature also in comedies, such as Carlo Verdone's *Un sacco bello* (1980), and proof that Italian filmmakers had started dealing with the issue—Petri depicts a city landscape which looks like the modern-day counterpart to the decadent late Roman empire, metaphorically in ruins, where pompous Fascist monuments stand out as an ironic contrast to the human misery that surrounds them.

Petri's surreal apocalypse takes place amidst the general indifference. People are aggressive and angry. Some fight, some steal, some go around with menacing guard dogs.[47] The traffic is chaotic. Ambulance and police sirens continually pop up in the background, together with a non-stop cacophony of car honks. Drug addicts shoot heroin in public view. Rome is flooded with trash. Garbage bags turn up at every angle, echoing the dossiers scattered all over the park in *Todo modo*'s final scene. But all this is accepted as normal. No one ever removes the piles of trash, but people just walk around them in ballets. No one cares about a dead body popping up inside an empty fountain either.

Humanity has seemingly regressed to a childlike state. After a bomb alarm at RAI, the employees run in the park like children after school. They lie on the grass, some start playing soccer, others take advantage of the situation to make out. An ice cream truck arrives and everyone gathers around it. This motif is underlined by the toy instruments with which the Man plays puerile melodies and by Ennio Morricone's score, which sounds at times like a sarcastic, macabre merry-go-round.

The low budget is reflected by the stylistic choices. As Amelio observed, "figuratively, *Buone notizie* doesn't look like any of Petri's previous films."[48] The director did not give up entirely on his use of complex camerawork and long takes, as in the sequence of the Man's arrival at the clinic after Gualtiero's murder, but overall the film is much more static than its predecessors, and the contrast with *Todo modo*'s elaborate dollies and tracking shots is evident. Moreover, Tonino Nardi's luminous, sunny photography is quite different from Kuveiller's multifaceted color palettes, and TV images sometimes fill the screen with their ugly blurring colors. Compared with the symbolic, at times almost abstract approach of *La proprietà* and especially *Todo modo*, this time Petri resolutely opted for a hyper-realistic tone—that is, art as the precise depiction of reality as seen through his eyes—to portray what he described as a "lack of reality."[49]

"Everything is possible!"

Petri's hyper-realistic approach results in the depiction of sexuality and obscene imagery in a way that goes far beyond the "scandalous" *La proprietà non è più un furto*. As Pezzotta noted, it is "a specific and original aspect, which blends high-level language and methods of a cinema which would be restrictive to label as 'genre,' and which embraces a grey area ranging from mainstream to popular cinema. Once again, Petri employs codified languages in an unpredictable and disturbing manner."[50] Despite its V.M.14 rating, *Buone notizie* includes graphic hardcore footage which apparently passed unnoticed by the rating board. At Gualtiero's flat, the Man views vintage porn photographs through a stereoscope. Later in the film, he is watching TV in his living room while arguing with his wife, and shocking footage from a S/M gay porn film pops up on television. A man has a chain extracted from his anus while the protagonist comments, more amazed than disgusted: "Fedora, look … incredible. You believe it? I don't. It's not possible!" To which she replies, without even looking: "No, I do believe it. Everything is possible!" Immediately after we see a contortionist performing self-fellatio (as in Charles Matton's 1976 erotic/fantasy extravaganza, *Spermula*). As Pezzotta argues, "the inclusion of said images shows the erosion of the limits of the visible in a society of spectacle where everything is allowed … and becomes emblematic of the status of the obscene and its normalization."[51]

As with the film-within-a-film in *La proprietà*, Petri's choice of images was telling. Even at a time as 1979, when private networks were broadcasting hardcore porn late at night, no TV channel would have dared to show such shocking footage. In fact, the scene has a strong symbolic meaning, and embraces the evolution of the concept of "common decency" and obscenity.

In 1962 the new law on censorship had redesigned the limits of intervention on the part of the rating board, while the evolution of mores and sexual liberation had contributed to redefine the limits of what could be shown on screen. At the same time, it had been the magistrates who had taken over in the battle for the common decency by seizing "obscene" films. In 1964 *Nudi per vivere*, with its mild strip-tease scenes and caricatural vignettes about sexual perversions, could be labeled as such, but just a few years later the mere thought would be ridiculous. In 1973, *La proprietà* got a V.M.18 rating and was seized because of a few simulated sex scenes. By 1979, the situation was again very different.

Sexuality in Italian cinema had blossomed throughout the decade and in different media, and the passage from softcore to hardcore porn had undergone several stages. The appearance of film magazines and photonovels with erotic content, such as *Cinesex*, which hosted more explicit photo versions of sequences tampered with by the censors, highlighted the common practice of shooting more risqué material for the sex scenes. It was on paper, in magazines such as *Le Ore* and in pocket comics such as those published by Edifumetto, that the graphic depiction of sexual acts finally surfaced. Shooting graphic hardcore inserts for the foreign markets had been a common practice since the early 1970s for many filmmakers, as was adding explicit inserts to the movie in the form of an "extra reel" delivered to venue patrons, who would use it at will. By the end of the decade hardcore was all over the place.

The board of review was still rejecting the graphic depiction of sexual scenes, even when it came in the form of respectable, auteur films such as *Ai no korida* (aka *In the Realm of the Senses*, 1976, Nagisa Oshima), but sometimes some footage escaped their vigilant eyes. Examples are the hardcore film the fence is watching on TV in a scene of Pasquale Squitieri's *L'ambizioso* (1975), and the one seen in Marco Bellocchio's *Marcia trionfale* (1976). Both can barely be glimpsed by an attentive eye, but they are definitely there. Another case is the depiction of the male organ in erect or semi-erect state. Take, for instance, the harrowing finale of Marco Ferreri's *L'ultima donna* (1976), or Bernardo Bertolucci's *Novecento* (1976), which includes a non-simulated scene in which actress Stefania Casini is holding Robert De Niro and Gérard Depardieu's members in her hands.

The creation of a proper "red-light circuit" specialized in screening sex movies finally brought hardcore porn to the surface. The first "red-light" theater, the "Majestic Sexy Movie," opened in Milan in November 1977. By 1980 the number of these venues had grown to fifty. Soon the bridge would be officially crossed, and the Italian hardcore porn industry would come out in the open. And yet, tamer versions were still being submitted to the board in order to obtain screening certificates, whereas explicit cuts ended up in theaters. In the meantime, private TV networks used to air softcore and pornographic films late at night, allowing consumers to watch forbidden images in quiet domestic isolation and becoming "a decisive instrument in the creation of mass voyeurism."[52]

Petri's view of pornography was not a narrowly moralistic one, although he was well aware of the earthquake that the outbreak of hardcore would mean, economy-wise, for the Italian film industry, especially for the many venues that would soon embrace porn. But there was more. At a time when erotic imagery was repressed, sexuality on screen could still be seen as a subversive, taboo-breaking act, and as such it was vital to the message of such works as Pasolini's "Trilogy of Life," *La Grande bouffe* and *La proprietà non è più un furto*. But by the time Petri was making *Buone notizie* graphic sex was just another commodity. And, as such, it marked yet another source of alienation in its consumers.

"Cazzo!"

In addition to the existential theme of alienation and the socio-political discourse on contemporary society, *Buone notizie* focuses on a more private and intimate issue, the crisis of the male. As the director acknowledged, "a constant theme in my films is that of immaturity, pregenitality, sexual incompetence, incapability to accept one's own sexuality all the way in all its values, for we are only what others and society want us to be, regarding sex."[53]

The Man is the last in a line of immature protagonists in Petri's cinema, from the obtuse Mombelli to the lazy Marcello Poletti, from the clumsy Professor Laurana to the schizophrenic Leonardo Ferri, from the sexually incompetent Doctor to the sexually alienated Lulù, from the self-important butcher to the repressed "M." Petri possibly drew elements from another undeveloped project, *Eros O.* (an ironic reference to *Histoire D'O*) centered on a man named Eros Olivieri who is obsessed with sex and claims: "My life is so banal I cannot do anything but make love, with anyone, anywhere, in any way.... I accepted my mediocrity in exchange for more and more vivacious results in the field of eroticism."[54]

The Man and Gualtiero are like two halves of a split personality, both with barely hidden autobiographical traits. On the one hand there is the Man. He is cynical, disillusioned, tired of his job and family. He is undergoing sexual turmoil and suffers from bouts of panic. On the other hand, there is Gualtiero, who lives in a luxurious apartment filled with books and *objets d'art*, likes to stroll along the Lungotevere with his dog, no longer thinks of himself as a communist and has (apparently) given up on sexual impulses. He is content with masturbation and indulges his sweet tooth. He suffers from Peter Pan syndrome, lives in the shade of the past, and rejects the idea of getting old.

The Man's insecurity is patent from the opening blackout scene, as he gropes around with his lighter in the dark apartment, which has become "a tomb, a sepulcher." "I feel as if I were a ghost," he says. The sudden lack of electricity, which results in the appliances (including television) not working, gives him a glimpse of what he really has become. But it also briefly brings back the lost sexual urge ("Let's make love like two ghosts..." he tells Fedora). Then we see him at work, boringly watching the non-stop images on his video wall and transmitting empty instructions by phone which make him sound like a robot.

The succession of the two sequences at home and in the office recalls the opening of *La classe operaia*, when we observed Lulù first in his family environment and then at work. The Man is no less alienated than Lulù. His sex life with his estranged spouse is, in his own words, "squalid and occasional," and like Lulù he projects his frustrated libido at work. Lulù focused on Adalgisa's bum while piece working, here the Man gets up from his chair with a massive erection upon hearing of the umpteenth terrorist acts and watching images of chaos and destruction. (Petri cleverly juxtaposes the Man's erection with Gualtiero holding a gun inside his coat pocket, which looks just like another erection, in the following scene.) He then approaches Tignetti, asking her to "make love once, before dying," with much less successful results than Lulù.

Once again, language is a key to penetrate the characters and their neuroses. Language was also what had intrigued Petri when he was to direct *Amphytrion* on stage, with the indomitable force of Plautus' Latin, its mixture of coarse plebeian expressions and elegant rhythmic structure. *Buone notizie* encompasses a similar use of the spoken lingo. As with sexuality, four-letter words on screen had been liberalized over the years. Just a decade earlier, critics had deplored the frequency with which the characters uttered the insult "figlio di puttana" (Son of a bitch) in *Il buono, il brutto, il cattivo* (1966) and moviegoers reacted amusedly to foul language during screenings of *I giorni dell'ira* (1967).[55] But by the mid–1970s, another taboo had fallen. Cesare Zavattini had been the first to utter the term "*cazzo*" (a profane word like "fuck" in English, but literally a vulgar appellative of the male sexual organ) on the radio, on October 25, 1976 ("And now I'm gonna say a word nobody has ever said before on the radio.... Cazzo!"), causing a fuss. Foul language was more and more diffuse in everyday life, and much criticized by the feminist movement, who labeled it as fascist and sexist (as do the women in the film).

Buone notizie literally bursts with vulgar dialogue. In *La proprietà*, Petri had Mario Scaccia deliver a sonnet about the various appellatives of the male organ. Here, Giannini's

Ángela Molina and Giancarlo Giannini in an Italian fotobusta for *Buone notizie*.

language is constantly gross and his lines invariably include "cazzo." While in bed with Fedora, who reproaches him for this very reason, he delivers a whole monologue on the theme:

> It's true, I'm trivial. I know it … fucking well! But shit, what the fuck can I do? That's how I talk. Yes, I'm perfectly aware that I should talk differently…. But the trivialities come out by themselves. If I keep them in … fuck! It's like obeying an inner police force … it's censorship! I mean, fuck, that's not right. Shit … fuck … cock … ass—you see? As they come to mind, they come to mouth. They're like a comma, like a semicolon, a parenthesis, a period, paragraph. But this is a lie. Not a fuckin' word is true! For instance, if I analyze myself while I say "*cazzo*" … I don't mean "comma." If I say "*cazzo*," I mean just that, "CAZZO."

The monologue works in a dual way. On the one hand, it is a bait to the audience, a "funny" bit to laugh at, if only for the mere flood of four-letter words erupting from Giannini's mouth like in a stream of consciousness. On the other, Petri is exploring the problematic ways his character's sexuality manifests itself. It is as if, by uttering the word "cazzo," the Man is exhibiting his own member, in a continuous burst of sexist chauvinism. He is an evolution of the exhibitionist in *Zoo*, who boasted about his virility with Annelise ("Look at it, take a good look. You like it, don't you? It's yours, it's ours. It's strong, it's beautiful, it's hard!") who in turn looked indifferent to it.

Here, the Man's wife calls him a fascist, and fascists have always had the myth of virility. But when he does expose his penis to Tignetti he is actually worried, insecure. "Too short? Too long? Lacks character? Too aggressive?" It is the exact opposite of the butcher's arrogant questions to Anita during sex in *La proprietà*, when he forces her to tell him that he has "the biggest cock in Rome." This makes clear what the Man means when he explains, "I need this trivialism to defend myself…" whereas Gualtiero has to carry a gun (a phallic symbol which he hides in his crotch) to defend himself.

In *Un tranquillo posto di campagna*, Leonardo Ferri has become so addicted to erotic magazines that he can no longer have an ordinary sexual relationship. He projects his desires into S/M fantasies and resorts to romantic passion only with an impossible object of desire, a ghost. Here, the Man is so bombarded with depictions of sex that his masculinity falls to pieces and he is forced to lean on obscene language as a way to reaffirm his heterosexuality, while becoming more and more conscious that it is just a social construct. "Between 13 and 20 years of age I resorted to these shocking words … so that people wouldn't see the real me … my true self," he confesses while pathetically attempting to seduce Benedetta. "My heart was soft, gentle. I was afraid they'd crush it."

As with his previous films, Petri subverts the mechanisms of genre in several ways. *Buone notizie*'s narrative, so scattered and all over the place, is patterned on the satirical comic strips the director was familiar with from *Linus*, and perhaps it was exactly that which made some think of Woody Allen as a term of comparison besides the analogies with Giannini's neurotic behavior. This rhapsodic structure also brings to mind the early works by Nanni Moretti (*Io sono un autarchico*, 1977; *Ecce bombo*, 1978), where the story is presented in the form of quick and barely related vignettes. In a way, it is as if the director was reacting to Billard's words about Italian cinema's lack of "other forms of criticism, other forms of analysis."[56]

Even though *Buone notizie* presents itself as a comedy, Petri's handling of humor takes the form of quick in-jokes that border on the grotesque. One such is the recurring gag about Gualtiero's book on masturbation[57] which he takes to the clinic and which a policeman is seen reading after his death. The subtle distortion of everyday life can be seen in the frequent appearances of men with dogs, or in the recurring sight gag of the garbage bags scattered all over. The director indulges in his mockery of authority figures: the commissioner (Franco Iavarone) who interrogates the Man is yet another addition in Petri's gallery of petty servants of the law. The grotesque is also a central element in the male leads' performances, as with Giannini's grimaces and self-satisfied vulgarities. However, according to the actor, when he came back to another work commitment to put the finishing touches to his dubbing, he found out that Petri had excised "all those things that made my character a bit funnier,"[58] further evidence of how the director wanted to let down audience expectations.

Giannini's presence led some critics to pinpoint his role as "the same he played in many Lina Wertmüller films, the selfish, narrow-minded, vulgar, sexist man."[59] But Petri's Man is much more than that. In a way, he is the problematic descendant of the chauvinist male in the *commedia all'italiana*, who always ends up defeated and humiliated. Giannini's character in *Buone notizie* is the exact opposite of the virile, macho ones he played in such films as *Paolo il caldo* (1973, Marco Vicario) or *Travolti da un insolito destino nell'azzurro mare d'agosto* and, as Pezzotta noted, is actually closer to the ones he embodied in Dino Risi's anthology comedy *Sessomatto* (1973), that is, "various heterosexual characters whose desires are doomed to be frustrated."[60] The humiliations he faces mark a turn of the screw in the usual practices of the late *commedia all'italiana* and show Petri's subversive handling of the genre, with the target of the jokes being the very audience at which *Buone notizie* is supposedly aimed.

An example comes early in the film, when the Man asks Tignetti, "Why is it I don't appeal to women?" He is uttering the same secret question so many men ask themselves after feeling rejected. "Do you like yourself?" she provocatively asks in return. "Very much ... no, not at all," he admits. "Then why should women like you?" is the reply.

The film portrays different female types who elicit the protagonist's desire but ultimately let him down. In *La classe operaia*, Lulù had an unsatisfied but dumb lover and a virgin colleague whom he deflowered in a hasty and awkward intercourse. But his male pride was safe, for he dealt with an inexperienced woman who knew nothing about sexuality. Whereas *La proprietà*'s Anita was in her own words a thing, a sex object to be opened like a can of tomatoes. *Buone notizie*'s women are liberated and smart, like *Indagine*'s Augusta Terzi. They sunbathe topless and have no qualms about showing their bodies. They take the initiative and are not content with mediocre sexual performance. They make the Man uncomfortable. "When I'm near one of you," he confesses, "I'm not well, I feel uneasy. It is maddening, unbearable. You know why? Because I'm eyed as if I was something strange, different, from another space."

The actresses' frequent nude scenes look like a mockery of the Man's shortcomings rather than a treat for the audience's voyeurism. A case in point is the picnic scene at sea in the trailer. He is sitting at the table after lunch with Fedora and Benedetta, and both women have their breasts exposed. Then they play hide-and-seek amid the dunes and he takes advantage of the childish game to attempt a clumsy and unsuccessful pass at Benedetta which echoes Laurana's in *A ciascuno il suo*. The nudes underline a liberated view of gender relationships on the part of the women while emphasizing the Man's utilitarian, puerile sexist view, doomed to failure. *La Géante*, a big, Surrealistic, painting by René Magritte which turns up in Gualtiero's flat, synthesizes this condition: a gigantic nude woman, her pubic hair and breasts exposed in a provocative pose, is observed by a tiny, Lilliputian man seen from behind. The protagonist watches the painting in awe, perplexed. He doesn't quite realize that the painting is about him—a man crushed by the fear of the feminine.

Likewise, the sex scenes mark a sabotage of the typical erotic comedy stuff for the reversal of roles they stage. The Man wants to change places in bed with Fedora, then he challengingly asks her: "Want to play the male? Go on, mount me.... Being the man isn't easy!" But she goes beyond his expectations and tries to penetrate him anally with her finger (Petri was probably thinking of an infamous scene in *Ultimo tango a Parigi* when Marlon Brando's character invites Maria Schneider's to do just that). After his awkward attempt to protect himself she mocks him: "You wanted 'male,' what did you expect?" In the early draft, *Prima di morire*, the scene ended in a different way, with the protagonist forcing Fedora to masturbate him, an exhibition of power (with echoes of *Salò*, where slaves must learn how to masturbate a man and exercise on a wooden mannequin) which was at odds with the film's tone.

In the clinic, it is Ada who seduces the Man and takes the initiative, taking off his clothes and forcing him to stay still. Petri films the woman licking his nipples, a reversal of a typical moment in erotic cinema which serves both as a subversion of the public's expectations and an underlining of the protagonist's loss of masculinity. Moreover, the Man refuses Ada's attempt to perform fellatio on him, which brings the attempted lovemaking to a sudden, early halt. His protective gesture—a recurring tic in the character—hints at a fear of castration, an act often depicted in Italian cinema of the period.[61]

Whereas the scene in which the Man exposes his genitals to Tignetti is a symbolic castration, in the end he faces a paradoxical retaliation. At Gualtiero's funeral, he finds out that he is not the father of the son his wife is expecting, as Fedora reveals in tears that she betrayed him with his late best friend, and now she is pregnant with Gualtiero's child. The scene, one of the most ferocious in Petri's *oeuvre*, recalls a passage in Mastronardi's *Il maestro di Vigevano* (discarded in the film) when the dying Ada confesses to Mombelli that Rino is not his son. The denial of fatherhood is the biggest humiliation to the Italian male. Not only has he become a "cornuto" (cuckold), but someone else has replaced him in his primary function of impregnating the female. But there is more. Whereas Fedora made love to Gualtiero because, she tells her husband, "It was like being with another you," in turn Gualtiero made love to Fedora because he saw his friend (the Man) in her, a dialogue which echoes a similar moment in *La proprietà*'s novelization. The protagonist learns he was the object of another man's desire. His certitudes are crushed for good.

In 1974, in his notes on *L'italiana*, Petri had noted that "the crisis of the male is in the discovery of bisexuality in the social side as well."[62] Regarding *Buone notizie*, he was adamant that the relationship between Giannini and Bonacelli's characters must be interpreted as an unexpressed homosexual one, as in *Le mani sporche*. Gualtiero is vaguely effeminate, and the Man is immediately suspicious about his friend's sexual orientation ("Gualtiero…. Gualtiero … you're not a queer, are you?") but he himself is pinpointed by Benedetta as a closet case after his humiliating sexual fiasco: "You know why you think '*cazzo*'? Probably because you like *cazzo*!" a line echoing Fedora's sneering invitation, "If you want to try with a man, go right ahead." In his apartment, littered with reassuring heterosexual imagery, Gualtiero packs female clothes in his suitcase and then leads his friend into dancing an interminable waltz (a nod to Bertolucci's "last tango"?) in which Giannini's character plays the female role, just as in bed with Fedora. Then, in the clinic, Gualtiero kisses the Man on the mouth, much to his embarrassment, and Ada tells the protagonist she is jealous of his relationship with her husband. After Gualtiero's death, the commissioner tells the Man that the murder looks like "una storia di froci" (a love affair among faggots).

But all this must be read via a psychoanalytic interpretation, as can be inferred from the extraordinary waltz scene, one of the best in Petri's cinema. "It's nice to dance among men," Gualtiero explains. "*It's like dancing with oneself.*" They keep dancing for hours in the huge, well-lit room, until the Man falls on the floor, exhausted, in the warm light of the sunset beneath the curtains. Later, when Fedora justifies her betrayal by telling her husband that Gualtiero was like "another you," Petri hints once more at the main character's inner dissociation. This gives further resonance to the aforementioned inclusion of the disturbing gay S/M imagery the Man watches on TV in his own living room. Is he coming to terms with his other, hidden self, embodied by Gualtiero? The Man is a direct filiation of Lulù and Total, and as such he is dissociated to the point of schizophrenia. Here, his "true self" is literally split into two separate characters.

This inner dissociation pushes the two male halves to take opposite paths. Gualtiero passively allows his wife to hospitalize him and submit him to electroshock. He retires in bed, in a return to a prepubescent state (he cannot even speak properly) and waits for the end to come. After witnessing his alter ego's symbolic death, the Man comes to terms with his own defeat. His power role in bed has been overturned, his virility has been derided, his place as the man of the house has been usurped. But this finally forces him to face his own feelings, those he had always put aside in a far corner of his soul. The sunset he briefly glimpses after reconciling with his wife represents an epiphany, a fleeting grasp of understanding after a life spent in a cave. But, after a moment, it is already gone. It is a tiny glimmer of hope, but it is definitely there.

Overall, *Buone notizie* turns out to be a reflection not only on the collapse of society, but on the crisis of the male, like other important films of the period, namely Fellini's *Casanova* (1976) and *La città delle donne* (1980). But instead of focusing on the anxieties of aging, in Petri's film such inadequacy takes the form of a return to adolescence, to the clumsiness and fears of puberty: "You're like a stubborn little boy," Ada tells the Man while stripping him. The incapacity to understand women is caused by one's incapacity of understanding his own self, and his own sexuality as well. Hence, the incompatibility between sex (dirty, forbidden, shameful) and love (pure and spiritual). And the film's circular ending shows that any attempt at bypassing this impasse is doomed to failure.

"Do not open..."

In a story stuffed with riddles, symbols and clues, the denouement is just as enigmatic. After another bomb alarm, the workers run out of the RAI building and go to the park, like the little children at play they are. Some play soccer, some make out, an ice-cream truck comes by. The Man sits on a bench, completely indifferent to the outside world (a woman is being robbed of her purse and screaming just behind him), and frantically opens the envelope Gualtiero has left for him, with the line "*Da non aprire*" on it. A final act of transgression to a prohibition that stresses his childish nature. Inside, he finds many white pieces of paper, each with the line "Da non aprire." Why "do not open"? "What" must not be opened? It is one last mockery and a symbolic depiction of the Man's inner void. As much as he wants to know who he is, he will never know it. The warning not to open means that it is useless to search for answers and epitomizes Petri's words about the "full but yet empty" head and the void that welcomes one's search for his own identity.

"Hysteria, which in individuals has a sexual origin, in a society comes from unexploded revolutions,"[63] the director commented, and *Buone notizie* depicts a society which has become hysterical in the maximum grade, where the characters' sexual frustration is reflected in the collectivity's collapse. The society depicted in *Buone notizie* is one whose days are numbered.

FOURTEEN

The Long Night

The American Clock

"You see, I consider cinema as the remnant of another culture, and this makes me love it even more than the indispensable," Petri told an interviewer in 1980. He went on, explaining his romantic and pessimistic vision. "A movie is made because someone has an idea, a simple idea. This idea can be vulgar, commercial, but it is born outside the direct interests of power. A group of people gather together and try to make a film. They don't submit their idea to any approval.... This is why spectators might not like it, but especially power doesn't.... Nobody wants to save cinema. It is obsolete. Television's better: there you can reach the true power over the masses."[1] Such a disenchanted view echoed that of the painter who looks desperately for romanticism in *Un tranquillo posto di campagna*, and was in no small part the result of frustration for not being able to finalize his projects, now that the economic situation of Italian cinema was more dramatic than ever.

Right after the release of *Buone notizie*, Petri seemed to be finally on the verge of making *Un amore lungo*, which he described as the first love story of his career.[2] But once again he had to desist. Other ideas remained on the shelf. One, possibly in the same vein as the outlines for *L'italiana* penned in August 1974, was a story about a virgin girl who wakes up one morning with the idea of losing her virginity. She goes out to find the right man and has many encounters, no one proving satisfactory. At the end of the day she returns home, still a virgin.[3] Another, possibly an evolution of the idea for a film on Mussolini dating back to 1977, was a movie about the relationship between Hitler and the Duce, read through an unusual perspective, as if it were the story of two lovers. Petri would have liked to have Alec Guinness or Peter Sellers as Hitler, and Alberto Sordi as the Italian dictator, and his aim was to explore the way the weaker partner (Hitler, who at the beginning of his rise was fascinated by Mussolini's public persona, to the point of asking him for some autographed photos) gradually became the stronger one, and vice versa: "Little by little, in Mussolini's mind, Hitler ended up having a more distressing and obsessive role, like that of a lover who's too exclusive and persecutory."[4] Most likely, the project didn't go beyond a vague outline, but in late 1981 the director was still listing a made-for-TV film on fascism (to be released in a theatrical version as well) among his forthcoming projects. Meanwhile, he kept attending conventions in which the "death of cinema" was a sinister, recurring theme.[5]

Nevertheless, Petri kept himself busy writing. He penned some short stories for *Nuovi argomenti*, the prestigious quarterly magazine founded in 1953 by Alberto

Carocci and Alberto Moravia. He also resumed his old critic habits, writing reviews for Ugo Tognazzi's monthly magazine on gastronomy and wine, *Nuova Cucina*. His column was called *Cinefagia* and then *Cinema nel piatto*, and his reviews were littered with wordplay and culinary metaphors. In 1980 he was a jury member at the 28th San Sebastian Film Festival.

A project dated 1980 which remained at an early stage was *Autobus*, the story of the daily life of a bus driver in Rome. As customary with Petri, it was told in the first person in the form of a monologue. It starts with the protagonist addressing the director, in what sounds like a declaration of poetics:

> Dear friend, since you make movies, why don't you make a movie on a guy like me? Do not complain if people don't go to the movies anymore, for you always make them watch the same stuff. People want movies to talk

A portrait of Elio Petri circa 1980.

about them and the way they live, or not live, and not about dreams.

The narrator pictures the bus as a steamer sailing through the ocean ("for the big cities, such as Rome, are huge, foamy oceans where it is dangerous and fearful to venture"), and describes the varied humanity that catches it every day, "all these people with the burden of their problems on their back." The bus becomes a microcosm, a symbol of society, even a metaphor of life itself, and the driver thinks of himself as a figure of responsibility. But alienation turns up. Like Cesare the plumber, Ferri, Lulù or Total, the driver too is on the verge of a breakdown: "During the long hours at the wheel, which I must embrace like a lover, whereas it's a plastic thing, sometimes my brain starts boiling," he says.

There is no real plot to speak of, only a series of briefly sketched characters and events. Some are amusing, some are melancholic, and some are downright grim, such as a young cop trying to arrest three terrorists on the bus and being killed. "It's true, the audience wants brutal emotions, big events," the driver concludes, "but the audience is made also of those who catch the bus, and maybe they would like to watch a movie like this, and see how they are, without fictions nor embellishments…. Anyway, sooner or later they'll make a movie set on a bus. I'm positive about that." Had Petri lived a longer life, he would have been amused to watch Jim Jarmusch's *Paterson* (2016), whose protagonist has some traits that recall *Autobus*'s unnamed driver-philosopher.

Autobus suggests the director's deep love for the city of Rome, described like a woman, its most famous monuments and sights portrayed like parts of the female body.

"No beautiful woman was ever mistreated like Rome," the narrator adds, complaining about its urban metamorphosis after the construction boom. The ending, with the driver's dream of abandoning the streets in the outskirts and driving through the open fields, just for fun, conveys a nostalgia for a time long gone, and gives way to Petri's poetic sensibility. If *Autobus* is the closest thing to Neorealism he ever conceived since his early days as a scriptwriter, it is imbued with a kind of magic realism that is closer to Zavattini than anything else. Petri submitted it to producers Franco Poccioni and Felice Colajacono of Medusa Distribuzione in February 1980, with the hope that such a type of non-commercial cinema be still possible. But his hopes were in vain.[6]

In September 1980, news came that Petri would try his hand at stage directing. After the aborted experience with *Amphytrion* he had kept looking around for suitable plays. Among those he considered between 1978 and 1979 there were Tennessee Williams' *Vieux Carré* and a couple by Aurel Baranga. After *Buone notizie* he was initially attached to put on stage Curzio Malaparte's *Das Kapital* starring Mario Maranzana as Karl Marx, at the Teatro Metastasio in Prato.[7] It was Maranzana who eventually directed *Das Kapital* in 1981.

The play Petri chose for his directorial stage debut was Arthur Miller's *The American Clock*, which had premiered in May at the Spoleto Festival U.S.A. in South Carolina. He would stage it for its European première in Genoa, with a cast featuring Ferruccio De Ceresa, Eros Pagni, Marzia Ubaldi, Claudio Gora, Camillo Milli and Ugo Maria Morosi.[8]

Miller's play, inspired by Studs Terkel's book *Hard Times: An Oral History of the Great Depression*, was set in the 1930s, and depicted the story of the Baum family, basically focusing on three characters—Moe, the father; Rose, the mother; and Lee, their son—struggling to survive after losing all their wealth. The "clock" marked the moment of the Wall Street crash and metaphorically a defining moment not just in American history, but in the very essence of America as a concept, not just as a nation. Narrated by the would-be writer Lee, the play had an autobiographical connotation, echoing the vicissitudes of the Miller family.

The American Clock faced a disappointing reaction upon its Broadway debut, on November 11, 1980, at the Biltmore Theatre, directed by Vivian Matalon and with Miller's sister Joan Copeland as Rose. It closed on November 30, after just twelve performances and eleven previews. According to Miller, its failure was to be blamed on several factors, including a misguided staging of the play and his own "capitulation to pressures to rewrite the material in ways that conformed to conventional expectations but robbed the work of its true voice."[9]

The news of the Broadway fiasco took Petri and Ivo Chiesa, the director of the Teatro Stabile, off-guard. "Evidently there is a general barbarization that is affecting Broadway too," Petri commented. "It's an old-fashioned play, but very beautiful, very poetic, which recalls imagery from a different era and a different society, which people evidently don't want to remember."[10] However, they decided to stick to the version seen at the Spoleto festival, rather than the Broadway one, which Miller had almost completely rewritten. Moreover, Italian translator Gerardo Guerrieri added several inserts from Terkel's book, with Miller's approval.

L'orologio americano opened on January 24, 1981, at the Duse Theatre in Genoa, with Lino Capolicchio as Lee, Ferruccio De Ceresa as Moe, and Marzia Ubaldi as Rose; among the rest of the cast, Eros Pagni played many secondary roles, in a standout chameleon-like performance. Petri's *mise-en-scène*, with art direction by Dario Ferretti (whom the director asked to take inspiration from Pop Art[11]), costume design by Barbara Mastroianni and music by Piero Piccioni, highlighted chaos and confusion. The spectator's eye was captured by an empty space at the center of the stage, which was occupied in turn with varied objects, many of them emblematic and outdated, such as a big refrigerator or a gramophone, with the Manhattan skyline in the background. For such an ambitious play, with eighteen actors playing about fifty characters, it was a decidedly troublesome opening night, plagued by an hour-long blackout. A scene included a radio message by Roosevelt, prerecorded by an actor, which could not be transmitted. So, Petri managed to enroll Giorgio Albertazzi, who was doing another play in a theater nearby, to read Roosevelt's monologue instead, live and in contemporary clothes, before the audience. It was a touch of improvisation that made the event more spontaneous and livelier. Curtains came down at one in the morning.

The gradual awakening of Lee's political conscience touched autobiographical keys in the director, whereas on the other hand the Baums' descent from well-being to poverty was an upside-down mirror of his own rise to fame. But to Petri the play's thematic center was the point where America went through a totally different way to produce and conceive life, that is, consumerism. "It is the same path us Italians have started,"[12] he argued. This reflection somewhat evoked Pasolini's theories on consumerism as a manipulation of the masses, which transformed the essence of Italians, and it reconnected to Petri's earlier approximations on the subject, such as the unmade *Le cose*. Finally, to him, directing Miller's play was also a late homage to Luchino Visconti, and an ideal reconciliation. In the past there had been arguments between them, such as the debate regarding the 1971 Venice Film Festival, but it had been Visconti's stage directions which had taught Elio to love theater at a young age, such as his 1951 production of Miller's *Death of a Salesman*.

L'orologio americano included many references to Petri's beloved Hollywood movies. *L'Unità*'s Aggeo Savioli noted that the scene of a farm auction in Iowa brought to mind John Ford's masterpiece *The Grapes of Wrath* (1940), while a dancing duet was "the affectionate recreation of a performance by a very young Judy Garland and Mickey Rooney."[13] Reviews were mostly positive, albeit noticing the play's didactic and sentimental quality, "a bit of Piscator, a bit of Brecht, a bit of Thornton Wilder." Petri's direction was judged "brilliant, fluid, but rather superficial: it doesn't linger, doesn't single out, doesn't underline enough"[14] the play's key points.

Based on a True Story

After *L'orologio americano*, Petri kept his hands busy on several new projects. One such was transforming *Roma ore 11* into a stage play. Another was a made-for-TV version of Carlo Castellaneta's 1975 novel *Notti e nebbie*, the story of a Fascist commissioner in Milan during the last days of the Republic of Salò. Like many other directors, the choice of television was more of a necessity given the constant hemorrhage of spectators in cinemas. Bellocchio, Sollima, Lattuada, Lizzani, Tovoli (with *Il generale dell'armata morta*) and Brusati were all preparing films for Rai Due. Petri was rumored to be attached to *Notti e nebbie*,[15] in August 1981, but the project stalled. The book was eventually adapted for the screen by Castellaneta himself in 1984 and directed by Marco Tullio Giordana. According to Paolo Valmarana, Petri even considered adapting Arthur Koestler's 1940 novel *Darkness at Noon*, another controversial work centered on Stalin's purges, and even more radical than *Les mains sales*. However, none of these materialized, and a similar destiny awaited an ambitious project tentatively titled *I figli di Colombo* (The Sons of Columbus), which showed Petri's idea of television as a didactic instrument. It would consist of a series of films made by prominent Italian and Italian American filmmakers, each focusing on a noted Italian personality who contributed, either positively or negatively, to the history of the United States. After their theatrical run, the films would be screened on TV as part of a long program of forty or fifty installments, "a complete spectacle of historical, cultural and social analysis of a great human adventure."[16]

Often in Naples to follow Giuliana De Sio's theatrical tour, Petri used to walk around the city for hours. Once he met a common acquaintance of his and Pirro. Occasionally the director and the scriptwriter had bumped into each other at some art exhibition and chatted for a while, but never about movies. It was as if they considered their collaboration over for good by mutual agreement. That day in Naples, Petri told their common friend to tell Pirro that he would never find a director as good as him again, and in turn he would never find a scriptwriter like Pirro again.[17]

Petri's stay in Naples possibly prompted him to pen *Ninni*, an unproduced 120-page script dated 1980 and based on a true story that happened in the city. On October 9, 1979, a hitman had killed bus driver Filomeno Napolitano and wounded off-duty carabinieri official Raffaele Russo who had tried to disarm him. After a brief chase he was killed by two law officers, Brigadier Savino and an off-duty public security agent, Salvatore Recci.[18] It turned out that the killer was an ordinary surveyor by the name Enrico Gay, married and with two little children, who moonlighted as a hired hitman to pay for his hobbies, such as collecting weapons. The murder was an honor killing: Napolitano's son had run away with the daughter of a rich and powerful neighbor, but the bus driver had objected to the shotgun wedding.

The director was struck by an article in *L'Unità* which summarized the incredible story, arguing how "the rules of Mafia and Camorra were applied to a story worthy of a Neapolitan *sceneggiata*." The article pointed out the existence of

> a submerged criminality which is often linked with a submerged economy; there is a custom in certain environments, which is anchored to old prejudices—offended honor, shotgun wedding—but reacts according to patterns, schemes and methods typical of big organized crime. The "*borghese piccolo piccolo*"[19] learns the big criminal's macabre lesson, in a mimesis which cannot be casual and is the result of too many impunities: get organized and you will get away with it.[20]

Petri collected newspaper clips about the "killer surveyor" and reconstructed the events meticulously, keeping the characters' true names and changing only slightly that of the killer, whom he renamed Francesco Bay. In a way, it was a return to the days of *Roma ore 11* and *Giorni d'amore* and an attempt to portray reality through a more direct look, leaving aside the Brechtian drift of his latest works. The script for *Ninni* is characterized by a matter-of-fact approach which at times recalls Francesco Rosi's cinema, but in the end it proves coherent with Petri's vision and themes.[21]

Ninni's early scenes introduce Napolitano and Francesco Bay (or "Ninni" as his wife calls him). The opening section conveys a disquieting suspense by juxtaposing the daily routine of the meek middle-aged bus driver, the faceless hitman's acts as he prepares to meet and kill his victim, and the actions of the other men involved in the shooting, Russo and Recci. Ninni shoots Filomeno several times and mortally wounds Russo. He flees, pursued by the cops, and the following chase takes place amid alleys and courtyards, as

Ninni's escape is followed by the residents who observe the action from their windows and balconies like a silent chorus. Two cops finally entrap the man in a blind alley and shoot him. The engrossing crescendo of the first part is akin to Italian crime films of the period, replete with abrupt violence and tight action scenes. Petri was once again relying on genre elements to better make his point, but he would never passively follow its clichés.

What follows after Ninni's death is an investigation which evokes the director's Neo-realist roots. The police find a picture of Filomeno on the killer's body, evidence that he didn't know the victim and was a hired hand. The script then follows police major Costa and deputy prosecutor Di Giovanni as they put together, piece by piece, the story behind the killing. The investigation brings to the surface an individual malaise and offers a complex sociological picture as well. In the end, *Ninni* becomes yet another reflection on the average man's neurosis, which leads to a schizophrenic split. The titular character is an immature, childlike individual who collected weapons and Mickey Mouse comics and built toy gun replicas with his children. It turns out that every now and then Ninni fell ill at work, and during these periods of illness he led his second life as a hitman.

On the surface, the depiction of Naples is not dissimilar to the one seen in many crime films of the period. A scene in which a varied crowd watches as police motorboats chase smugglers in the gulf looks like something out of a Mario Merola flick ("The smuggler always wins," a street urchin proudly claims). But Petri's analysis lays bare the duplicity of a "crazy city" where "everything has two faces." The most openly political scenes are those set in the construction site where Ninni worked. A new road is being constructed, but it already looks dilapidated. "We have been working here three years and built fifteen kilometers…" someone says. People discuss the Red Brigades and some believe terrorists could purify a rotten society: "Sometimes I don't feel like condemning them." It looks like Petri still had in mind the debate with Billard.

But the reality surrounding Ninni's story shows that each and every one is a pawn in a general state of corruption and degradation. A teenage girl named Carmosina, whom we have seen throughout the story looking out the window near Napolitano's house, stands out. Her father, an ignorant and violent farmer, paid Ninni four million *lire* to kill Filomeno, whose son he wrongly believed had taken her virginity, whereas in fact she had been raped by her own cousin. "You see, my father wants to think I'm the Virgin Mary," she tells the police, "Whereas I'm a girl who likes to make love." Carmosina is smart and intelligent, but she is a prisoner of a retrograde family. And she knows very well that any rebellion would be useless. "Sometimes I think I'll kill myself," she says, and when they ask her why she has dropped out of school, she sarcastically replies: "Shall I get my GED, then a degree, and marry a doctor, an engineer, a professor?"

In the end, Di Giovanni labels Filomeno's murder as "an idiotic killing … a killing performed by idiot children," for the big picture is that of an environment dominated by ignorance, envy, puerile thinking that has allowed a small argument between two families to degenerate into murder, with no one bothering to pacify the quarrelers. But Costa's reply is fatalistic: "A carabinieri official is not a priest. And life must follow its course…."

As with *La classe operaia*, the script ends with the recollection of a dream. Ninni's widow tells her mother-in-law that she dreamt her deceased husband was driving around in the brand-new car he had purchased after his last hit and looking for a psychiatrist. But they all cost too much and he could not afford it…

Night Approaches

Finally, it seemed that Petri was about to return behind the camera with a project destined for the big screen, *Chi illumina la grande notte* (Who Lights the Long Night), co-written with a young film critic and scriptwriter, Franco Ferrini. Born in La Spezia in 1944, Ferrini had penned a couple of genre scripts in the mid-to-late 1970s (*Poliziotti violenti* and *Enigma rosso*), but his first important job assignment had been for Alberto Lattuada, with *La cicala*. Ferrini sent Petri an outline for a thriller through his friend Umberto Angelucci, the director's assistant on *Buone notizie*. Petri was not too impressed by it, but he and the scriptwriter met and became friends. Both loved cinema and spent some time together strolling around Rome and discussing films.

Ferrini had just read a novel by Australian writer Estelle Thompson, *Hunter in the Dark* (1978; published in January 1980 in the *Giallo Mondadori* series as *Cacciatore nel buio*) and was very impressed by its opening. A blind man at the bus stop starts a conversation with a little girl. Suddenly, a car stops, someone comes out and kidnaps the girl, who is later found murdered. No one bothers about the blind man, as if he did not exist. His ego is deeply wounded, and he starts investigating with the help of his former fiancée. The rest of the novel was quite banal, but both Ferrini and Petri thought the opening could be a good starting point for a movie. They started writing the script in Torvaianica, at the Villaggio Tognazzi, where Elio had moved, the place where all his scripts with Ugo Pirro were born. A major influence was Hitchcock's *North by Northwest* (1959), for its story about a man involved in an intrigue much bigger than him. *Chi illumina la grande notte* would be a return to genre cinema as means for an existential discourse, with the story of a small theater owner who must pass off as blind in order to escape death and finds himself involved in international spy intrigue.

The story raised the interest of producer Gianfranco Piccioli of Hera International Film. Piccioli had recently financed Sergio Citti's *Casotto* (1977) and *Due pezzi di pane* (1979) with his company Parva Cinematografica, co-owned by Mauro Berardi. He and Petri had gotten in touch in the summer of 1979, when Piccioli attempted to involve him, Bellocchio and Citti in a tentative production enterprise. The trio were to write together three scripts which they would direct separately. The three films would be shot back-to-back with one director of photography, one production designer, the same crew and studio, same print and development lab. According to Piccioli, this would lead to substantial saving on production costs, with just one billion *lire* budget for the three pictures combined. According to *L'Unità*, "the three authors ... were enthusiastic" and "met periodically to study the formula more deeply ... the three films would be shot in 21 weeks overall."[22] The project never materialized, although Citti's idea on a story about hunger eventually became *Il minestrone* (1981).

Work on *Chi illumina* went on in fits and starts. Ferrini would come to Torvaianica, sometimes spend the night there, and the two would eat together the meals that Petri's mother had prepared. "But it was complicated," Ferrini explained. "Elio had a strange relationship with his scriptwriting partner. He said he could no longer work with Ugo Pirro, who had become like a bookmaker, always on the phone for contacts or requests for collaboration.... Moreover, he had an attitude toward cinema which I couldn't understand nor share.... 'Cinema is dead,' he used to say, and he believed it."[23]

Petri and Ferrini completed the first draft of the script in the fall of 1980, before Petri's stage commitment with *L'orologio americano*. When interviewed in *L'Unità*, in

October 1980, the director announced that he would start shooting next April, with Marcello Mastroianni in the lead, and described the film as "a *giallo*, but it's not simply an obsession of mine. Here as well I think the mystery is largely reflecting current events." He also anticipated a subsequent project for the small screen, a series of telefilms to be titled *Cronache italiane*.[24]

In the spring of 1981, after the end of Petri's stage commitments with Miller's play, the director and Ferrini wrote a second draft, and an article in the July issue of *Screen International* mentioned Max von Sydow and Hanna Schygulla as part of the tentative cast.[25] But filming was postponed over and over. Petri was unhappy with Ferrini taking other commitments, namely *Nessuno è perfetto*, directed by Pasquale Festa Campanile. "Elio considered it a betrayal, both personally and professionally, since it was a comedy. But scriptwriting had been going on for too long."[26] Ferrini then accepted Sergio Leone's offer to work on *C'era una volta in America*. He didn't tell Petri, who found out about it from another scriptwriter, Enrico Medioli. Before starting work on Leone's film, Ferrini came up with an ending which Petri dismissed scornfully as something along the lines of *Segretissimo*, Mondadori's paperback spy series. This led to the inevitable breakup.

In late 1981 Piccioli associated with Giorgio Nocella's Iter Films to produce the film, and Sergio Donati came aboard to revise the script. Donati recalled in his memoir: "He came to me with ... a dazed, expressionist script, of a leaden and desperate pessimism. But the initial idea was terrific.... I told him that the script was terrible, but the start was worthy of Hitchcock. Petri replied that he came looking for me exactly because of that, because of my 'American-style' approach."[27]

Donati remembered his collaboration with Petri with sincere enthusiasm: "Writing for Elio was a thrilling experience. He had a tremendous intellectual honesty; he didn't allow you any trick of the trade, but he was also able to catch every nuance of a page. He had great respect for other people's work." After the asphyxiating collaborations with the likes of Pirro and Ferrini, this time the director opted for a more relaxed approach: he used to leave his notes to Donati's draft in the scriptwriter's mailbox and wait at the bar around the corner as Donati studied them, then they would discuss them together.

Due to scheduling conflicts Mastroianni had to give up the role, and Petri settled for Ugo Tognazzi in the lead. Tognazzi did not hide his enthusiasm:

> Cinema is an industry that obeys the market laws and the audience, and so you make movies because you have to. Among those you are offered, sometimes there is one which you like in particular. It doesn't mean it's going to be your most successful film, but it can help make your job less trivial, less squalid.... This is one of those films which I really like to be part of. Sometimes it does happen.[28]

Shooting was slated to begin in November or December 1981 with Rai Due coproducing. The cast would feature Marie-Christine Barrault and Sandra Monteleoni (seen in Ferreri's *Ciao maschio* and currently shooting Antonioni's *Identificazione di una donna*).[29] But it was postponed once more, as the latest draft of the script was yet to be completed, and the new date of January 1982 seemed unlikely for a series of practical reasons. As Petri confessed to agent France Degand in a letter dating 21 October 1981, his situation was becoming difficult, and the forced inactivity was weighing heavily on him, not just psychologically but economically as well.[30]

Besides *Chi illumina la grande notte*, the director was bringing on projects on several fronts. He was to put on stage again *L'orologio americano* in Rome for a series of performances between March and April 1982, with several changes from the Genoa opening. He was also going to develop a series of six films for the small screen, based on real-life facts and set in Naples, Rome and the Venetian region, respectively. They likely were the *Cronache italiane* mentioned in a previous interview, with the Naples-based episode being *Ninni*.[31]

Moreover, in the Summer of 1981 Petri had been trying to develop a project with French executive producer Dominique Antoine (of Marthe Mercadier Promotion) in collaboration with TF1, based on Philippe Saint-Gil's novel *Le Vendredi des banquiers*, about the corruption within the French bank system. Bruno Tardon would adapt it for the screen with Petri's supervision. The producer delivered a draft contract in October 1981, stating that shooting would take place in France during the first half of the following year, starring Jacques Perrin and Ugo Tognazzi.[32] But the ongoing postponement of *Chi illumina la grande notte* marked an early halt for the project, and by December 1981 Petri confessed to Gili: "I don't want to do it. The novel is too bad, too bad to be made into a film: its clumsiness penetrates everywhere and would certainly imbue the film."[33]

In the Spring of 1982, Petri announced that filming for *Chi illumina la grande notte* would finally start next June and that the cast would also include Eddie Constantine, with Gaumont Italia becoming involved in the financing.[34] "It will be a metaphor on what is visible and what is not, on what they want us to see, and what they don't; a metaphor on cinema as well, then. An adventure movie, but also a reflection on cinema."[35]

Right after finishing *Chi illumina la grande notte*, he would start working on another film to be shot in France, *La mort du prince*, starring Gérard Depardieu and Jean Carmet and inspired by the notorious De Broglie affair. The director had been collecting material on it since the late 1970s, when he had met some reporters from the French magazine *Le Canard Enchaîné* who insisted that he make the movie. The noted Jean Aurenche would collaborate on the script.

The wealthy French prince Jean De Broglie, a former government minister of Italian ancestry and the co-founder of ex-president of the Republic Valéry Giscard d'Estaing's political party, was killed by three shots fired from a passing car as he was leaving his financial adviser's office, on December 24, 1976. At first it seemed a political killing, but in fact there turned out to be economic motives, as the prince had made a loan to his financial adviser that would not have to be repaid if he died. But it also turned out that the police and even the Minister of the Interior knew well in advance that De Broglie was going to be murdered but they didn't raise a finger to save him. The De Broglie affair contributed to the fall of Giscard d'Estaing, who lost the elections to François Mitterrand in May 1981. On paper, it seemed a no-holds-barred political thriller which Petri wanted to focus on the relationship between a police inspector and an informer, played by Carmet and Depardieu, respectively. But in private he told Gili his reservations about the project: "As you know, I don't think it will be so easy to find the money for such a scorching film: France is not Italy, through thick and thin…. There, all films are made for 12-year-old kids."[36]

Chi illumina la grande notte was also a way for Petri to rethink his own approach to cinema, in times of political and cultural carelessness, the so-called "*riflusso*" (backflow) which in his view had caused

> a persecution against political cinema…. The first move comes from the political forces, who privilege television in the choice among mass communication media for obvious reasons, since it's more controllable than newspapers and cinema. So, we witness an adventurous

"Americanization," an enormous cultural damage which was born from a precise choice. Accordingly, the level of competitiveness has dropped, and we all have to reckon with television. It is the "cinema of attention" (let's not call it "political" anymore) which suffers the most from this situation.[37]

When asked about the state of Italian cinema, the director, sincere as ever, could not hide his pessimism.

It is hard to make one's way in the crowd of superficial films, consumeristic symbols just like cars, stupid and bad movies like the current Italian ones, so distressingly provincial that they are incomprehensible abroad and seem to come from an obscure planet.... For many years Italian cinema has been cutting edge worldwide, thanks also (modesty aside) to my generation: and now should we watch helplessly this anthropological and cultural devastation?[38]

Night Falls

Elio Petri's passing came unexpectedly to those who, just a few months earlier, had read such passionate words and marveled at the intriguing list of projects the director had mentioned. But he had been ill for some time, in the spirit and in the body. He spent his time between his mother's house and the villa by the sea where he and Ugo Pirro used to write scripts, and where he and Giuliana De Sio would meet, far from indiscreet eyes. But he couldn't cope with his situation. He wrote his friend Jean A. Gili: "What have I become? I really don't know anymore. Indecision, as you know, has thoroughly consumed my identity.... I feel I resemble each day more an adolescent, and this feeling is certainly reinforced by the fact I'm living with my mother, which truly brought me forty years back in time."[39]

Goffredo Fofi recalled bumping into Petri in Rome, one summer day of 1981, and spending an evening with him and friends at Giuseppe De Santis' house in Fiano Romano, a small village outside Rome. Petri had come across his old friend and mentor one day, by chance, after many years. They had resumed contacts and Elio would often drive the 40 kilometers from Rome to Fiano to pay visit to "Peppe," who had become the older brother he never had. On that occasion he picked up Fofi, another old acquaintance from the days of *Nudi per vivere* (at the time the critic was based in Paris) and an early admirer of his work who had become a vibrant adversary over time. Elio nevertheless held him in esteem, unlike many other critics. At De Santis' place, Fofi recalled, Petri suddenly burst out crying, in an open-hearted confession. "He felt bad, very bad, because after splitting with his wife he had fallen in love with an actress much younger than him, and their relationship was neurotically difficult. He had tried, to no avail, to seek advice and comfort from his wife."[40]

Ugo Pirro hadn't seen Petri in a while. He knew the director had turned into some kind of a misanthrope, isolating himself in a sullen solitude and excluding even his closest friends. Now Elio Petri was an embittered man, and his extraordinary vitality had vanished.

The crisis of his marriage must have shattered him, changed him. He had remained a lower-class guy, and that transgression which he couldn't avoid, that sudden and surprising event which was in contradiction with all his insistently enunciated principles, must have tortured him to the point of torment. How many times did he reproach his friends because of their disorderly lives, how many times did he publicly declare himself being a monogamist! So, feeling in such an open contradiction with his own moral principles must have been his most painful and obscure illness.[41]

Giuliana De Sio is adamant that Petri's bitterness was mostly a reaction to his being marginalized. He had become an outcast in Italian cinema. The critical interest in his work was almost non-existent and limited to his films of the early 1970s, the one exception being a monograph written by Alfredo Rossi and published in 1980. His attitude toward critics was more polemic and disillusioned than ever. An interview published in the March–April 1982 issue of *Cinemasessanta*—founded and edited by Mino Argentieri—was eloquently titled "Ci rimproverate ma non ci avete mai difeso" ("You reproach us, but you have never defended us"). The interview, dated early 1981 and centering mostly on Petri's stage work on *The American Clock*, saw him return to the theme of making political films in the early 1970s:

> The directors most preoccupied with, and dedicated to, political film found themselves attacked more aggressively by the critics, censored by the parties, and generally regarded with suspicion, from [ultra-leftist magazine] *Lotta Continua* to the conservative press. We made our films only because we believed in them, without anyone else's help.... We were attacked from all sides.[42]

He recalled the infamous episode in Porretta Terme when Jean-Marie Straub demanded that *La classe operaia* be burned. "No one came forth to call such a man crazy," he remarked. "How can you [critics] regret the mediocre political sensibilities of today's Italian filmmakers when you never fought for, never took sides with those who tried to keep talking about politics despite a thousand obstacles?"[43]

The interviewed was accompanied by a polemic "side note" signed by Argentieri, which read like a throwback from 1973 and the debate following *La proprietà*. The critic wrote: "It would bother us if Petri alludes to certain judgments by critics who weren't always laudatory toward his films.... we would not want the most fierce accusations to be fueled by the intolerance in the face of a friendly criticism, but not willing to give up its role."[44] Petri replied with a lengthy open letter to Argentieri, in which he stated:

> You see, I won't at all rule out that some searing lashes of the whip or other summary punishments occasionally inflicted on me—whether with a frivolous smile, knowing academicism, or the customary recklessness of critical terrorism—have left some traces on me. But I must ask: why shouldn't they have? ... My "resentment," if you want to call it that, is not about some fruitless collection of compliments. I might say that it is essentially against myself, since I feel no less responsible about this situation than the others.... But I can't help addressing it also against those individuals and political forces who, in the past, had shown great interest in all the problems concerning cinema. In light of today's facts, the interest and solidarity of that time appear instrumental and propagandistic.[45]

A couple of autobiographical short stories published in early 1982 in the magazine *Nuovi Argomenti*, directed by his friend Enzo Siciliano, bitterly analyzed Petri's own condition, with ample resort to sarcasm.

The self-explanatorily titled *Ex* was about an ex-communist who had left the party twenty-five years earlier but "never stopped looking at his ex-party as something that went beyond politics and ideology." With his typical scorching sincerity, Petri wrote: "'Ex' had been kicked out of the Communist party because he had published ... some critiques on the USSR.... But today, twenty-five years later, the whole party has detached itself from the USSR. Now, why not admit without couth that this party is formed entirely by ex-communists?" His disillusionment touched deeper issues, both personal and universal. "A father, a mother, the sons cannot become anything else.... And yet, a family can become an ex-family ... it's not true that a river and a sea cannot become an ex-river, an ex-sea. Many rivers aren't rivers anymore and many seas aren't seas anymore, but only huge masses of infected sludge.... Earth can become an ex-planet at any minute, if only a handful of ex-men decide it."

The surreal *Breve incontro* (Brief Encounter) is even more explicit. Structured like a script for a short film and replete with indications of shots and camera movements, it is the most self-reflexive of Petri's works, a meditation on his own relationship with cinema and on the growing difficulties, not just economic, of making a movie. Petri lays bare his doubts, his insecurities, his unhappiness with painful earnestness, and composes a beautiful ode to the cinema of his childhood, paying homage to such masters as Ford, Lubitsch, Von Stroheim, and to old classics like *The Jazz Singer* and *I Am a Fugitive from a Chain Gang*. Once again, the method he uses is dialectic, and the non-stop dialogue becomes a psychoanalytic *tête-à-tête* between himself and his alter ego, embodied by an old Mitchell movie camera. The story is told through the latter's subjective point of view.

Breve incontro starts with the camera following "a middle-aged man dressed in gray like actor Elisha Cook, Jr. in *The Big Sleep*," amid a crowd of youngsters all looking at shop windows for a famous brand of boots in the central Via del Corso. The man is Elio Petri, whose name throughout the story is replaced by his social security number, PTRRCL-29H29H501C. The man tries to chase the camera away: "We have nothing more to say to each other." He is disenchanted, even resigned: "I realized that I was getting old when I started to go to the movies as a duty.... I guess that to make films and watch them one must be young, very young, maybe even a child, and must have the energy to dream."

The camera asks him why other noted filmmakers keep making films. His reply is ironic: Antonioni can't grow up; Fellini is in love with Cinecittà ("It's his mother, his psychoanalyst, his amniotic liquid"); Bertolucci is a poet whose films are love letters to the camera; and Rosi is "a case of rare optimism. He staunchly believes that you can inform the world." But most filmmakers aren't like that.

> A director's work is so unrealistic, so superfluous, that if he doesn't believe in something, he will never find the energy to shoot a film. In a world so highly specialized as ours, a director's is the most non-specialized profession. A director is not an actor, nor a writer, nor a photographer, nor a dancer, nor a painter, nor an editor: he is nothing. Or, in other words: he is a failed writer, a failed painter, a failed politician, etcetera. So he believes in order to acquire credibility. His specialization is to believe. He believes in an idea, in a school of thought, in an aesthetic principle, or, what do I know, in money; yes, many directors believe in money, though they won't say it. They specialize in money.

PTRRCL admits he too has a soft spot for money, but he's just not good at making it. He then goes on listing the cost per day of a camera, of 35mm film, of printing and developing. "I cannot afford it. That's why I don't love you anymore."

The camera snaps back that these are only excuses. "Don't blame it on others: on the producers' vulgarity, the distributors' illiteracy, the movie theater owners' greediness, the audience's unpreparedness, in short on the whole of society. Just say you're not good."

The camera advises him to try and tell "a light, funny, tasty, and optimistic story. Maybe add a few bad words and a fart here and there if you want to be sure of success. The formula is always the same." Then, in the most bitingly political passage, the camera quotes a speech by Senator Oscar Luigi Scalfaro, who had been Undersecretary of Spectacle in the 1950s. Infamous for his staunch moralism and his crusades against obscenity, which resulted in many films being heavily censored, Scalfaro had once synthetized the role of cinema as simple entertainment for the masses which does not present "the torment of complex feelings" and whose only aim is to alleviate the strains of the day and offer a "happier outlook on life." Words like Scalfaro's had accompanied the end of Neorealism in the early 1950s and the film industry's shift toward noncommitted products, a situation not unlike the current one, with movie screens invaded by pleasant and optimistic, simple-minded stuff.

PTRRCL replies that after all the things he has seen and experienced over the course of his life he cannot help but think of sad and dramatic stories, and pessimistic, even desperate metaphors.

> In the past, these stories would have been considered dialectic, but today there is no need for dialectics. Now we must hide and conform. Everyone rejects pessimism because we went beyond it, we entered a pure void.

All of a sudden, the man notices something and orders the camera to pan left. "Come on, do as I say, I'm still a director after all." The camera pans to a window shop with several cameras on display "like in a small, shimmering zoo." He points out that the camera is getting old too, because the new video cameras "work with a film that loses and regains its virginity at will.... You're like me, you're not electronic or telematic, you're not informatic.... You were born in 1895 ... you are eighty-six years old, but this century burns through means of production at a crazy speed, so you're as obsolete as a wool-winder or a lithographic stone."

The contrast between Petri and contemporary cinema is summed up when he notices a woman crying at a bus stop and orders the camera to zoom in on her. But the camera turns in another direction, where two women are laughing. "See, that's the thing," PTRRCL comments. "If I have to choose between two women, one laughing and the other crying, I would choose the one who is crying."

Before leaving, the man instructs the camera to film him like in an old Hollywood ending. He turns to the camera eye, whispers "I love you," and walks away in the empty Piazza del Popolo square, alone. "The camera tilts up on a crane shot. When it stops, the words 'The End' appear on the screen."

The end came in late 1982, and it was not the one Petri had envisioned, although its final scene took place indeed in Piazza del Popolo.

In retrospect, the scene in *Buone notizie* where Giancarlo Giannini kneels down and starts screaming "I don't want to die!" sends shivers down the spine. Soon after finishing the film, Petri had been diagnosed with prostate cancer—"where temptation is stronger," as "M" would have had it—and had undergone surgery to the bladder. Something similar happened to Gian Maria Volonté, who was diagnosed with lung cancer and in March 1980 underwent an operation to remove his left lung, resulting in forced inactivity. However, the operation proved successful and Volonté resumed his acting career. He lived fourteen more years and had a fatal heart attack during the filming of Theo Anghelopoulos' *To vlemma tou Odyssea* (aka *Ulysses' Gaze*, 1995). He died on December 6, 1994.

The invasive surgery had left physical and psychological repercussions in Petri, and as a reaction he had plunged headlong into work. But cancer had spread all over his body. The illness manifested again at the end of 1981, and rapidly escalated. Giannini, who often visited him in Torvaianica during the scripting of *Chi illumina la grande notte* and then when the director got back to Rome, recalled:

> We would often see each other at night. He had become like a child, he would eat ice cream … and he would laugh, I remember he laughed. Until the day I stopped seeing him. I was told he was ill. I was working, I wouldn't ever go to see him. He would call me often. He would tell me not to come. He only wanted one thing, movies. I had a lot of tapes, many, many movies … and he would ask for movies. I remember it was hard to find Renoir's *La Grande Illusion*. Me, I had it. I made a copy for him, as well as of a few of De Sica's movies, *Sciuscià, Umberto D.* …[46]

Among Petri's last public appearances were those on May 6 and 12, 1982, when he attended a convention on "the audiovisual image of a political party, the PCI." His family surrounded him with a protective, impenetrable embrace.

In June 1982 newspapers still announced *Chi illumina la grande notte* as imminent.[47] But about a month before the scheduled start of shooting, Petri was hospitalized. The project was cancelled, and the director spent the last four months of his life in bed. It was a painful déjà-vu, for those who remembered the sight of Paolo Bonacelli bedridden in the clinic, passively surrendering to his wife's will, in *Buone notizie*. But an even more gripping memory came to mind: the days of Elio's childhood when his mother would put him in bed for the whole day, grounded. "To me, staying in bed during the day was a torture. It was the punishment I feared most," he had told journalist Dacia Maraini in a 1973 interview. "I'd rather be beaten up."[48]

Ugo Pirro's recollection of his friend's last months is heartbreaking, and not just because of the details of Petri's suffering, the pain that made him unable to leave his armchair and then his bed, and even use his typewriter. Unable to write, he dictated three long letters on tape recorder to "Peppe" De Santis, which overflowed with pessimism and anguish.

> I now find myself swallowed up in a dark side street, maybe even a blind alley. I'm going through a bad phase of my chipped, broken life, I feel only its oppressive, negative side. I have left home, I have literally left, I tried to leave everything behind me, but I feel I cannot. I have no desire to communicate with anyone except you … you have lived in hope, whereas I have lived in despair.[49]

When he was with his closest friends, Elio seemed not to be aware that his days were numbered, or at least he pretended to. Near the end, Pirro paid him a visit in the clinic. Marcello and Ruggero Mastroianni were there too. No one knew what to say. "We were all afraid of silence, of his questions, of our lies, because now the only thing we could do was deceive him."[50] So they started talking passionately about soccer, one of Elio's passions, like three old friends who have all the time in the world and no other thoughts.

"The illness was his masterpiece. He convinced everyone that he believed in his recovery, by lying to the others, not to himself," Pirro claimed.[51] According to Giuliana De Sio,

> He was too intelligent and too sensible to wholly deceive himself, and too many times we had talked about this illness which had affected many friends of ours. I think he lived on two parallel tracks: one knew, and one ignored it. He spoke competently about his arthrosis, for the doctors had told him that he was in pain because of that. They had been very good at pretending the cause of all his symptoms was bone decalcification. But a minute later he exclaimed, "To think I believed I would die of a heart attack!"[52]

Eraclio Petri left this Earth on November 10, 1982. The funeral took place in the Santa Maria di Montesanto church, in Piazza del Popolo, also known as "Chiesa degli Artisti" (Artists' Church). Petri was not a religious man, but his family had it otherwise. Even such a staunch atheist as Pirro showed up. To let those mortal remains of Elio Petri leave this world without one last salute from all those who had loved him and esteemed him would have been one last injustice, to a man who had already suffered too much.

It was De Santis who wrote the funeral eulogy, as a late response to his friend's oral letters. Franco Giraldi read it during the service. It was too painful for Peppe to attend.

> When we chose the profession that tormented us, but that also made us happy all our lives, we knew that we were committing a public act. We knew that we were choosing something that would lead us to civic and moral duties with a great amount of responsibility.... I want to tell you one last thing. I want to tell you how many times I was happy seeing one of your films that took a bite out of the "power behind the scenes," that accused and pointed the finger of civic zeal against them, that dug deep into our consciences. I was happy, dear Elio ... simply as an ordinary citizen ... really above all suspicion. A citizen who wanted—and still wants—rightly, and with all the rage that was turned loose in your films, change, transformation, the healing of our country from the worst evils that afflict it. A citizen like many others who felt represented by the strength of your stances.... My heart fills with pride at your films ... a pride that lives on today and will last forever, as I believe it will last in the hearts of those who ... loved and continue to love the truth and the courage of the truth.[53]

Looking on Darkness Which the Blind Do See

In remembering his late friend in a full-page article in the *Corriere della Sera*, a week after his death, Pirro talked about *Chi illumina la grande notte* in detail. "I have the script on my desk.... I received it in the afternoon and read it in one breath, with enthusiasm for a narration of exceptional intensity and the bewilderment of discovering that my friend had become so different, unbeknownst to me."[54]

The script was eventually published in a catalogue curated by Pirro and dedicated to the director for a retrospective hastily put together for the 1983 edition of the Venice Film Festival. It was accompanied by Petri's annotations and by Renzo Vespignani's illustrations. The director had mentioned it to his old friend while on his deathbed: "I'll let you read it, it's a weird thing, you'll see, it kind of looks like you...." The overall mood of the story was synthesized by Vespignani's words: "Together we breathed hope ... in the sultry air of post-war Rome, as well as the stench of what was dying, year after year, near and inside us."[55]

The original story devised by Petri and Ferrini started overseas. A 270-page "first draft" retained at the CSC (and still titled *Chi illumina la grande notte?*, with a final question mark) opens with a Shakespeare quote ("Looking on darkness which the blind do see") and with an extraordinary prologue set in Washington, D.C. The camera follows at ground level a male cat wandering outside the premises of a huge compound in the woods, lured by the meowing of a female cat on the other side of a high wall. The cat jumps over the wall but suddenly falls dead, electrocuted. Rising from its dead body in a zenithal shot, the camera discovers many other dead cats all around, all killed by the high voltage fence. The female cat, a beautiful Persian, walks away, her love calls once again unrequited. She passes by a man working in the garden, and we find out that the gardener is blind. Still following the Persian cat in an uninterrupted long take inside the compound and through its various ambients, we discover a whole array of blind men intent on various tasks. The place is a CIA hideout, and the blind are employed there for secrecy. In a room a secret film is about to be screened but the projectionist is missing. He has stolen the top-secret footage and fled to Rome, in an attempt to sell it to enemy spies. Petri and Ferrini's original opening was an extraordinary piece of visual filmmaking, possibly discarded because it would be too complex to shoot. Nevertheless, it showed how Petri was working at the top of his visual imagination, with the striking sight of the dead felines lured by a female one destined to remain alone working also as a metaphor for one of the story's central themes.

The final draft of *Chi illumina la grande notte* discards the prologue and starts in Rome, on the banks of the river Tiber. Marcello, the protagonist, an elegant man with big dark glasses which make him look like he is blind, is standing on a bridge, lost in his thoughts. He comes across another man who resembles him very much, but who is indeed blind. A brief conversation ensues, during which the blind man persuades Marcello to put on his glasses and gives him his cane as a joke. Suddenly, a car stops by and two men kidnap the blind man.

Marcello sees everything, but instinctively pretends he is blind to save his life. Soon he realizes he is being followed by the kidnappers and has to carry on his masquerade. He throws in the Tiber all the things he has in his pocket and which a blind man would never have on himself (his watch, his pen, his driving license, his wallet…). One of the kidnappers tests him to find out whether he can see or not and beats him severely. Alone and in pain, Marcello has to keep up his make-believe.

Things become weirder and weirder. Marcello is approached by strange characters—a threatening Arab, a beautiful young prostitute, two menacing blind men, an affable spy who meets a grisly ending. It turns out the kidnapped blind man, a certain Roberto Ferlinghetti, had been paid one million dollars in exchange for a mysterious film which has disappeared. Marcello finds some frames of a 35mm film negative which Ferlinghetti planted in his pocket before being kidnapped. He realizes that he has been caught in the middle of a spy intrigue.

Marcello starts hearing a female voice speaking to him as if she were in his head. Bewildered at first, he realizes there is an aural device hidden in Ferlinghetti's shades. He follows the voice and meets the person to whom it belongs, a beautiful sightless girl named Esther. She is keeping Ferlinghetti's guide dog, Homer. The dog leads Marcello to an underground secret base full of dead blind men, killed by some chemical weapon. The base is riddled with spies and Marcello pretends to be dead to escape them. He glimpses their boss, a man with an eyepatch named Rufus.

Back to the down-on-its luck cinema he owns, Marcello splices the frames of film negative into a reel of film. He finds out that Esther has followed him and she is the only spectator in the venue. Their brief idyll is interrupted by the arrival of some spies who torture Marcello to make him confess and temporarily make him blind. Another group of spies release him and take him to a villa where Ferlinghetti is being held prisoner. Marcello is tortured again and injected with truth serum, but he doesn't give away the hiding place of the 35mm frames. He wakes up again in his venue, tied to Ferlinghetti's dead body. He cuts the rope, recovers the film frames from the projectionist's room and flees just before the police show up.

Marcello ends up at the Istituto Omero (Homer Institute), a blind men's establishment which is actually another cover-up for the CIA. There he reunites with Esther, who has been kidnapped too and raped. It turns out Ferlinghetti, who loved the girl like a father, had stolen the top-secret material and asked for a one-million-dollar payback to collect the money to pay for an eye transplant that would allow Esther to recover her sight.

Marcello realizes that the film frames are encoded with Braille alphabet, and Esther deciphers the message: The money is inside Homer's bust. There is indeed a bust of the blind Greek poet in the institute library, but it turns out to be empty. Spies from different factions converge in the institute and a massacre ensues, with the blind men eventually overwhelming the secret agents and mercilessly dispatching them. Marcello and Esther flee on a boat full of blind men taking a sightseeing trip on the Tiber. There, they find out that the phrase "Homer's bust" actually referred to Ferlinghetti's guide dog, Homer, and the money is hidden in the dog's girdle (in Italian the word *busto* has both meanings).

The final confrontation with Rufus takes place on the boat. Rufus—who during the course of the story has eliminated all those about to kill Marcello, in order to find out the money's whereabouts and keep it all for himself—attempts to throw Marcello and Esther into the river, but they get the better of him. In the coda Esther and Marcello are watching the swans in Lake Geneva. The transplant has been successful, and it turns out it was Marcello (who now is wearing an eyepatch) who gave one of his eyes to the girl. The "long night" has been lit.

Underneath its labyrinthine spy plot, *Chi illumina la grande notte* is a deeply autobiographical film. Marcello is a patent stand-in for Petri, and his issues basically reprise those of the discarded main character for *Prima di morire*. He is a middle-aged, elegant man who "smells of cinema," as he himself puts it, and is undergoing an existential crisis. The script has several elements in common with *Buone notizie*, such as the encounter between the two men on the Lungotevere (with the idea of the protagonist meeting his double reprising also the starting point of Nabokov's *Despair*), a mysterious conspiracy plot, and a main character obsessed with impotence and sexual failure. In the 1979 film, the protagonist was fixated with sex and kept repeating the word "cazzo"; here Marcello confesses he suffers from premature ejaculation, a trait in common with Total in the original script for *La proprietà non è più un furto* and in the novelization.

Chi illumina la grande notte would have been a much more appealing project for the average audience than *Buone notizie*, at least plot-wise. It represented an ideal return to the cinema Petri loved as a kid, such as the spy intrigues helmed by Alfred Hitchcock and the suspense thrillers centered on an innocent man who finds himself at the center of a conspiracy, such as Fritz Lang's *Ministry of Fear* (1944). In a story stuffed with plot twists, characters and events, he took every opportunity to pay homage to the Golden Age of Hollywood: even the one-eyed villain, Rufus, is shaped to resemble legendary film director Raoul Walsh. But whereas the theme of the man pretending to be someone else in order to escape death has many notable antecedents, from Billy Wilder's *Five Graves to Cairo* (1943) to *North by Northwest* (repeatedly quoted in the script), in Petri's story it acquires symbolic and autobiographical nuances and so does the protagonist's own affection for old movies.

First and foremost, *Chi illumina la grande notte* is a disillusioned reflection on the state of contemporary cinema. An omnivorous cinephile, Petri was never dismissive of popular movies and was always adamant that cinema must be entertainment for the masses and not for an elite.

A communist critic can use the word "popular" from an artistic point of view, as if it were an insult. I, on the contrary, don't believe in that. I think that the insult that a communist should level against a writer or a filmmaker is the word "bourgeois" ... Why does a critic from a local communist newspaper not bother with the review of certain popular films? And even certain pornographic films? And why couldn't he talk about them seriously?[56]

Several years later his views were much more pessimistic. Cinema Reale (Real Cinema), the small venue owned by Marcello, runs a cycle titled "Cinema and nostalgia" which elicits little interest, whereas a nearby theater is running an imaginary film called *Pierino carabbiniere*, a sarcastic reference to the trashy sexy farces about the titular overgrown brat which did plenty of business at the box-office. (In the short story *Breve incontro* Petri mentioned an existing comedy, *I fichissimi*, as a symbol of the decadence of Italian cinema.) As the cashier tells Marcello, "Sell this cemetery, turn it into a supermarket, a three-story garage, a disco...." In a few years this is exactly what would happen to many second and third-run venues, forced to close down or be recycled into something else due to the constant loss of spectators.

In May 1982, Petri wrote a letter to *L'Unità*, commenting on an initiative from Christian Democrat MP Agostino Greggi, who had proposed to evaluate the morality of porn films by screening them in Parliament. The PCI had labeled the proposal as laughable and weird,[57] but Petri admonished:

In Italy there are several hundred venues that stopped screening mainstream movies and converted to the pornographic genre. The small group of films sent to the Cannes Film Festival constitute the majority of the so-called auteur production that is going to be distributed in our country in the next season. The disarray of the facilities and the degradation of Italian cinema, which is also technical, professional, and finally human, are under everyone's gaze ... and everybody knows it, but nobody says anything, especially in Parliament. In thousands of venues in the provinces and in the suburbs, moviegoers, especially young ones, have access to pornographic productions as their only cultural nourishment.[58]

Petri's disillusionment on the state of the dying Italian industry and his bleak view of contemporary cinema take a poetic and symbolic form in the script. Marcello becomes like one of the book-men in *Fahrenheit 451*, preserving the memory and soul of past cinema, while the foreign spies embody those who are polluting the market with bad and cheap products, destroying the magic of cinema for good. In a harrowing, scopolamine-induced monologue which forces him to tell *the absolute truth*, Marcello spits out:

I started as a projectionist.... I always saw Cary Grant films, I combed my hair like him, walked like him.... You know, back then working in a movie theater was so beautiful.... Everyone showed up, even for reasons that had nothing to do with the movies.... They came to make love, to sit in the dark and think.... But then, once inside, they all became part of the big screen.... They loved each other, hated each other, shot each other, cried, laughed.... Everything was a dream, everything was either good or bad. Everyone was beautiful, even the villains.... And we became beautiful too, for one hour and a half.... But now? ... Now you make bad B-movies with cheap plots, blood, massacres, guts spilled out live on camera.... We were better than you, our dead were not only fake but they died with class, with imagination, and it was clear why they died.... It's your fault if nobody loves cinema anymore...

For Petri, *Chi illumina la grande notte* was a vessel to escape from what Italian cinema had become. But it was also the last attempt to bring back the memories, the sense of wonder, the feeling of safety that the cinematic experience could give, and a final act of recognition of its shattering symbolic power.

In *Buone notizie*, Giancarlo Giannini's character could no longer find a meaning in the world surrounding him. Here, Marcello attempts to find the solution to the mystery by way of a moviola, reassembling the pieces of film Ferlinghetti gave him and splicing them into a reel of *North by Northwest*. Far from being a self-satisfied postmodernist cinephile game, it represents a tragic acceptance. Only cinema can give sense to a world which doesn't have it, through the simple gesture of putting together one frame after another. But cinema can also make you blind, as happens to Marcello, who is exposed to the blinding white light of a projector by his torturers: "The camera gets inside Marcello's eyes together with the projector's beam, and they pulsate as if cut open by a scalpel."

Petri's desperate view of the present takes on macabre traits. "I think life is rather macabre," the director told film historian Aldo Tassone in 1979, comparing the Los Angeles street traffic to "a huge funeral. I think our cities are now crowded with inordinate funerals. We are living every second in a nightmare and in the macabre. We continually bump into dead men, garbage bags, dead rats."[59]

The script's description of an ugly, indifferent world is as extreme as in *Buone notizie*. The Rome setting is no less apocalyptic as the one depicted in the 1979 film, a living hell of traffic jams and heartless people, trash and rats, and the surface world is doubled by a parallel, submerged universe (as in *Todo modo*) which rules over the former and pulls the strings of its inhabitants. In a way, *Chi illumina la grande notte* can be read as Petri's own answer to Argento's *Inferno*, or perhaps as a variation on Sartre's famous words, "Hell is other people."

But the script illuminates the story's darkness with bouts of humor. The depiction of the spy underworld is grimly satiric. "Here in Rome there are over forty secret service agencies, 2,000 agents and 18,000 part-time auxiliaries," Rufus explains. Even the "Strategy of Tension" has become a laughable spy game. To quote Marx, history repeats itself, first as tragedy and then as farce. At one point, a Maresciallo Panunzio shows up at Marcello's venue which the police have rented for a union meeting, in a nice in-joke referring to *Indagine*. At Istituto Omero, Marcello ends up at a radio station "made by the blind for the blind" which airs only music by blind artists (Ray Charles, Stevie Wonder, Art Tatum, George Shearing, José Feliciano…), an idea possibly coming from Donati.[60] The scene of the blind men's boat trip on the Tiber is another surreal gem: the river is dirty and polluted, but the guide (who is blind as well) describes it as a heavenly, idyllic landscape.

Even more biting is the final twist, with the discovery that the million-dollar payback serves to reward the donor who will give an eye to restore Esther's sight: "It's a girl from Genève with a pair of wonderful blue eyes … she wants a million to give one." The memory goes to *Il boom*, written by Zavattini, the story of an indebted entrepreneur who is offered a huge sum to give one eye to a rich man in need of corneal transplantation. In the end, it is Marcello who gives Esther one of his eyes—in the epilogue she has a blue eye and a brown one, while he is wearing an eyepatch just like Rufus did—and it is implied that they kept the million dollars for themselves. A love gesture, but also a very pragmatic one. As in De Sica's film, the punchline is a bitter take on the capitalist system: better be rich and one-eyed than poor and full-sighted. As the proverb says, in the land of the blind the one-eyed man is king…

Chi illumina la grande notte is packed full of plot twists and turns. No doubt this was the result of shaping the story as a homage to Hitchcock's films. Such an approach goes beyond the mere cinephile nods and becomes a stance against the violence and ugliness of contemporary cinema. In fact, violence is often explicit and nasty, with dozens of killings, torture scenes and grisly details, and Marcello's line of dialogue when he accuses the spies of setting up a bad second-rate film, with "blood, massacres, guts spill out live on camera" is telling.

Alfredo Rossi hypothesizes that the finished film would be as ambiguous as *La decima vittima* in its approach to the thriller genre.[61] Indeed, Petri keeps playing with stereotypes by subtly subverting the public's expectations. For instance, the script stages a chaotic battle among various groups of spies (their presence echoing the silent CIA killers at the end of *Todo modo*), featuring "silencer shots, deadly karate blows, silent stabbings," which takes place at the Istituto Omero, in a library full of blind people. The scene takes an unexpected turn after Marcello turns the lights off. In the dark, a small army of blind men show up and take revenge on the spies, savagely beating them to death with their canes, "mercilessly, in silence, with gestures that seem to release all their bitterness and pain." Even the use of the McGuffin—the 35mm frames whose visual content is actually useless, for it is the Braille signs engraved on them that give away the secret location of the money—allows for symbolic significance. Images are not important for what they show, Petri suggests, but for their deeper inner meaning.

As for the character of Esther, she is one of the most sensual in Petri's cinema, a mixture of innocence and disruptive sexual charge, and her feverish monologue during a passionate scene with Marcello allows the director to reflect on the concepts of beauty and desire:

> I don't know what "beautiful" means. Who is beautiful, to a blind person? Who is ugly? I am beautiful, but why? They tell me I have blonde hair. What does it mean? Are you handsome, are you ugly? I will never know. I made love so many times. *But I don't know with whom.* I don't know what a naked body is. I have never seen a mouth. It is only a hole to me.

It is Esther's words that give the film its title, as Marcello listens to her voice from a radio station calling him: "I have lost you in the long night but now everything is going to change. A light lights the long night."

Apparently, Petri was not fully satisfied with the script. The plot does have some holes, which, according to Ferrini, were the result of the director's refusal to prepare a proper story outline, so that all the pieces of the puzzle would fit in the end. "He said that in mysteries the question marks are much better than the answers that ensue."[62] Petri was also disappointed about the story having become excessively simplified and impoverished compared with its early drafts, after some notable changes that had resulted in subplots and bits of information being dropped, such as the Washington prologue. In the last draft, it is never fully clear what Ferlinghetti's role was, how he managed to steal the 35mm film frames, what is the real nature of the Istituto Omero, and so on.

The notes that accompany the third draft show Petri's doubts about the second half and specifically about the role of Esther's character in the plot. He was also considering a circular ending of sorts. Overall, however, he felt weary. "Even the ending seems already 'expired' and I couldn't say why," he annotated on the last page. "Maybe I'm just tired of the film. I'm done. Two years on this stuff is truly too much." But even though it is an unfinished, rough-around-the-edges work, *Chi illumina la grande notte* shines with ideas and possibilities. For someone who believed that cinema was dead, Petri was reinventing not only his own cinema, but he was also attempting to find a way for it to survive, even in spite of himself.

Perhaps what the director liked most about *Chi illumina la grande notte* was the parable of a man who finds the courage to change his life for good. Being caught in a spy intrigue is the chance Marcello was unconsciously waiting for to start anew. He throws away his ID card and becomes someone else by playing the part of a blind man. Once again, the theme of performance is central in the story, and even more than in *Indagine* or *La proprietà*, it becomes the only way to escape neurosis. To Marcello, pretending to be blind means to close his eyes on a world he no longer recognizes, a world where all illusions have died, a degraded, ugly world full of ugly people. A world full of blind men. When one of them says, "There are many of us, even I could not imagine how many. But we are hiding, we are ashamed…" one cannot help thinking of the ongoing cultural backflow. Paradoxically, his fake blindness gives Marcello a new look at the present, which no Hollywood film could soothe.

In the end Marcello takes advantage of his own apparent death to escape abroad with Esther and start a new life together in Genève. A middle-aged man, a beautiful young woman, their dog playing happily nearby. The End. It is a happy ending which delicately spoofs Hollywood movies, but at the same time it gives form to an impossible escapist wish, an ideal image of peace and love with subtle psychoanalytic touches (such as Marcello's eyepatch: a hint at his self-declared impotence, perhaps?). But the ending can also be read as a metaphysical landing, not too dissimilar from Lulù's dream of heaven in *La classe operaia*, or the appearance of the sunset on a squalid shoreline in *Buone notizie*.

As the director told Ferzan Özpetek, who volunteered to be his assistant on the film, "everything we do in life, we do it to shake off the idea of death."[63] After the loss of his beloved dog, Snoopy, Petri had shared with Alfredo Rossi a brief and stunning meditation on the mystery of passing.

> You see, Alfredo, even the riddle that a small and unaware animal brings in itself is not solved by death, which leaves everything pending and makes everything—also retrospectively—aleatory and unfinished for everyone, mute and talking animals alike. On the other hand, human language, our instrument to communicate, doesn't solve the riddles either; on the contrary, it complicates them. In this sense, an animal's mutism is a perfect symbol.[64]

Religion offers a promise of an afterlife, for everyone needs to hope for a happy ending. Petri was not a religious man and did not believe in the afterlife. The reflection on mortality accompanied him throughout his existence, in his work and in his privacy, and the happy ending of *Chi illumina la grande notte* was the only answer he realized his investigation would lead to, for himself and others.

In his last months, Petri co-wrote another treatment with Paola Pascolini, *Andamento stagionale* (Seasonal Trend). A tender intimate story between an elderly couple which Pirro compared to Nathaniel Hawthorne's short story, *Wakefield*, it marks a definite change from *Chi illumina la grande notte*, but in some parts it conveys the same need for soothing and solace.

Christmas time. After a futile argument, Aldo leaves his wife Margherita and goes to live in Torvaianica, in winter. Soon he gets bored and finds out that the "freedom" he craved for doesn't really mean anything to him now. He spends the day playing poker with friends, dreams of starting a snail farm, and becomes fond of a young maid, Lauretta, who becomes pregnant. Even though he is not the father, Aldo wants her to keep the baby.

Soon Margherita finds out she too cannot give up her marriage, and seeks comfort with her son Franco, a doctor who unwillingly becomes her confidant. Franco's life becomes affected by his parents' separation, as does that of Esther, their younger daughter, who has a drug problem.

The snail farm is a failure. Margherita attempts suicide. Aldo pays her a visit and announces that the heating in the house in Torvaianica has broken…. Next Christmas, Aldo has returned home. He and Margherita take care of Esther's little daughter while she is in a detox clinic. Franco and his wife pay them a visit: she is pregnant. Aldo and Margherita exchange their Christmas gifts. "There is a moment of tenderness … almost like old times … but then both have to run, because the baby is crying in the next room…."

The premise bears some resemblance with *I giorni contati*, for once again a man suddenly decides to start a new life, only to find out that he misses his old one. Here, though, it was not the alienation of a worker that interested Petri, but the meditation on a marriage worn off by the years. This leads to a separation, and finally to a reconciliation. Is the man returning under the family roof a defeated soul, someone who finally found peace with his inner self, or has he simply realized that all the suffering in life is too much for an individual to bear alone? Is *Andamento stagionale* something akin to the delusional vision of heaven for the working class evoked by Lulù in *La classe operaia*, or to the final image of *Chi illumina la grande notte*?

Perhaps in his final work, which he knew he would never turn into a film, Petri chose to put what little hope he had left in life and people. And leave behind a little gift of love and tenderness as a farewell gift, before facing the long night about to fall.

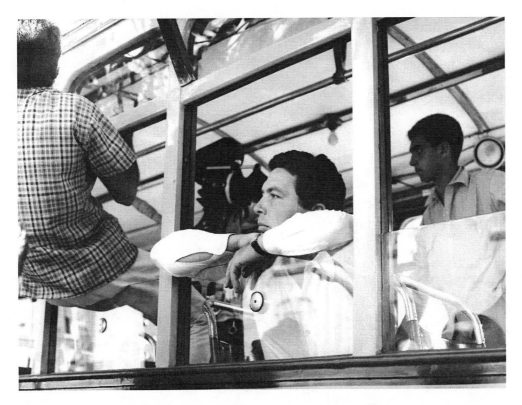

Elio Petri filming *I giorni contati* in the tramway where the opening and closing scenes take place.

Filmography

Titles are listed chronologically according to the Italian release date.

Abbreviations

AD: Assistant director; ArtD: Art director; C: Camera; CO: Costumes; CON: Continuity; DOP: Director of photography; D: directed by; E: Editor; GM: General manager; M: Music; MU: Makeup; PD: Production designer; PM: Production manager; PROD: Produced by; S: Story; SC: Screenplay; SD: Set decoration/set dresser.

As Scriptwriter

1952

Roma ore 11 (D: Giuseppe De Santis) (S, uncredited)

1953

Un marito per Anna Zaccheo (D: Giuseppe De Santis) (SC)

1954

Donne proibite (D: Giuseppe Amato) (SC)
Giorni d'amore (D: Giuseppe De Santis) (S, SC)

1956

Quando tramonta il sole (D: Guido Brignone) (S, SC)

1957

Uomini e lupi (D: Giuseppe De Santis) (S, SC)

1958

Un ettaro di cielo (D: Glauco Casadio) (SC)
La strada lunga un anno (D: Giuseppe De Santis) (SC)

1959

Vlak bez voznog reda (D: Veljko Bulajic) (SC)
Le notti dei teddy boys (D: Leopoldo Savona) (SC)

1960

L'impiegato (D: Gianni Puccini) (S, SC)
Vento del sud (D: Enzo Provenzale) (SC)
Il carro armato dell'8 settembre (D: Gianni Puccini) (S)
La garçonnière (D: Giuseppe De Santis) (SC)
Il gobbo (D: Carlo Lizzani) (S)

1962

Sodoma e Gomorra (D: Robert Aldrich) (S, uncredited)

1963

I mostri (D: Dino Risi) (S, SC)

As Director

1953

Nasce un campione

SC: Antonio [Tonino] Guerra, Elio Petri; M: Carlo Innocenzi; DOP: Angelo Baistrocchi (Ferraniacolor); E: Alberto Carosotti; Narrator: Corrado Mantoni. PROD: So.Du.It (Società Documentari Italiani); GM: Gianni Fucci. *Country*: Italy. Filmed on location in Santarcangelo di Romagna. *Running time*: 11 minutes. Visa n. 15215 (10.17.1953).

Note: Existing copies are in black-and-white.

1958

I sette contadini

SC: Cesare Zavattini, Luigi Chiarini, Renato Nicolai; M: Claudia Nizza; DOP: Roberto Gerardi (Ferraniacolor); E: Gabriele Varriale. *Cast*: Alcide Cervi; Narrator: Renato Cominetti. PROD: A.B. Cinematografica; GM: Quirino Papi. *Running time*: 10 minutes. Visa n. 27224 (06.25.1958).

1961

L'assassino

(aka *The Lady Killer of Rome*)
S: Antonio [Tonino] Guerra, Elio Petri; SC: Antonio Guerra, Elio Petri, Pasquale Festa Campanile, Massimo Franciosa; M: Piero Piccioni; DOP: Carlo Di Palma (b&w); E: Ruggero Mastroianni; PD: Giovanni Checchi, Renzo Vespignani; CO: Graziella Urbinati; AD: Adolfo Cagnacci, Giuliano Montaldo, Fabio Rinaudo, Giorgio Trentin; C: Carlo Di Palma; MU: Franco Freda. *Cast*: Marcello Mastroianni (Alfredo Martelli), Micheline Presle (Adalgisa De Matteis), Cristina Gaioni (Nicoletta Nogaro), Salvo Randone (Commissioner Palumbo), Andrea Checchi (Morello), Paolo Panelli (Paolo), Toni Ucci (Toni), Francesco Grandjacquet (Elderly man), Mac Ronay [Germain Sauvard] (Suicidal man), Franco Ressel (Dr. Francesconi), Giovanna Gagliardo (Rosetta), Eugenio Maggi (Cop with hat), Marco Mariani (Margiotta), Max Cartier (Bruno), Bruno Scipioni, Lucia Raggi, Liana Ferri, Carlo Egidi (Nello's friend), Ubaldo Micacchi, Silvio Bastianelli, Franco Freda (Tramp). PROD: Franco Cristaldi for Titanus—Vides (Rome), Société Générale de Cinématographie (Paris); PM: Gino Millozza. *Country*: Italy. Filmed on location in Rome and at Titanus Appia Studios (Rome). *Running time*: 106 minutes; Visa n: 34287 (03.27.1961). *Rating*: V.M.16. *Release date*: 04.01.1961. *Distribution*: Titanus (Italy), Pan World (U.S.A).

1962

I giorni contati

(aka *Days Are Numbered*)
S: Tonino Guerra, Elio Petri; SC: Tonino Guerra, Elio Petri, Carlo Romano; M: Ivan Vandor; DOP: Ennio Guarnieri (b&w); E: Ruggero Mastroianni; CO: Graziella Urbinati; AD: Berto Pelosso; C: Luigi Bernardini; Opening design: Renzo Vespignani. *Cast*: Salvo Randone (Cesare), Franco Sportelli (Amilcare), Regina Bianchi (Giulia), Lando Buzzanca (Cesare's son), Paolo Ferrari (Vinicio), Vittorio Caprioli (Art merchant), Vincenzo Falanga ("Mazzolatore"), Piero Guccione (Painter). PROD: Anna Maria Campanile for Titanus—Metro (Rome). *Country*: Italy. Filmed on location in Rome. *Running time*: 106 minutes; Visa n: 36648 (02.06.1962). *Rating*: V.M.16. *Release date*: 03.25.1962 (Mar del Plata Film Festival). *Distribution*: Titanus.

1963

Il maestro di Vigevano

S: based on Lucio Mastronardi's novel; SC: Age & Scarpelli [Agenore Incrocci, Furio Scarpelli], Elio Petri; M: Nino Rota, conducted by Franco Ferrara; DOP: Otello Martelli (b&w); E: Ruggero Mastroianni; PD: Gastone Carsetti; CO: Lucilla Mussini; AD: Vana Caruso, Berto Pelosso; C: Arturo Zavattini. *Cast*: Alberto Sordi (Antonio Mombelli), Claire Bloom (Ada Mombelli), Vito De Taranto (Headmaster Pereghi), Piero Mazzarella (Bugatti), Guido Spadea (Nanini), Anna Carena (Drivaldi), Egidio Casolari (Filippi), Agniello Costabile (Zarzalli), Gustavo D'Arpe (Amiconi), Eva Magni (Giuseppina), Bruno De Cerce (Cipolloni), Nando Angelini (Journalist), Lilla Ferrante (Miss Cuore), Gaetano Fusari (Doctor), Ignazio Gibilisco (Varaldi), Ezio Sancrotti (Carlo Badalassi), Tullio Scavazzi (Rino Mombelli). PROD: Dino De Laurentiis. EP: Alfredo De Laurentiis. *Country*: Italy. Filmed on location in Vigevano. *Running time*: 105 minutes; Visa n: 41887 (12.18.1963). *Rating*: All audiences. *Release date*: 12.24.1963. *Distribution*: De Laurentiis.

1964

Peccato nel pomeriggio

S, SC: Age & Scarpelli [Agenore Incrocci, Furio Scarpelli]; M: Armando Trovajoli, conducted by the author; DOP: Ennio Guarnieri (b&w); E: Giorgio Serrallonga; PD: Gianni Polidori; CO: Piero Gherardi. *Cast*: Charles Aznavour (Giulio), Claire Bloom (Laura). PROD: Gianni Hecht Lucari for Documento Film (Rome), S.P.C.E. (Paris). *Country*: Italy/France. Filmed on location in Rome. *Running time*: 90 minutes; Visa n: 42132 (01.22.1964; 02.21.1964). *Rating*: V.M.18. *Release date*: 01.22.1964. *Distribution*: De Laurentiis.

Note: Episode of the film *Alta infedeltà* (aka *High Infidelity*).

Nudi per vivere

D: Elio Montesti [Elio Petri, Giuliano Montaldo, Giulio Questi]. S, SC: Elio Montesti (commentary: Gian Carlo Fusco); M: Ivan Vandor; DOP: Giuseppe De Mitri, Ennio Guarnieri (color). PROD: Lorenzo Pegoraro for P3 G2 Cinematografica (Rome). *Country*: Italy. Filmed on location in Paris, Nice, and at Istituto Luce (Rome). *Running time*: 105 minutes; Visa n: 41657 (11.27.1963; 12.13.1963). *Rating*: V.M.18. *Release date*: 03.04.1964. *Distribution*: Dear Film (Italy).

L'Italia con Togliatti

Co-D: Giovanni Amico, Libero Bizzari, Carlo Lizzani, Francesco Maselli, Lino Micciché, Glauco Pellegrini, Elio Petri, Sergio Tau, Paolo Taviani, Vittorio Taviani, Marco Zavattini, Valerio Zurlini. DOP: Mario Bernardo, Vittorio Bernini, Mario Carbone, Tonino Delli Colli, Carlo Di Palma, Umberto Galeassi, Amerigo Gengarelli, Aldo Giordani, Blasco Giurato, Giovanni Mercuri, Claudio Racca, Ganni Raffaldi, Luiz Carlos Saldaña, Franco Vitrotti, Fausto Zuccoli (b&w). E: Mario Serandrei. Narrator: Enrico Maria Salerno. PROD: Unitelefilm. PM: Marcello Bollero, Riccardo Napolitano, Giuseppe Rispoli. *Running time*: 38 minutes; Visa n: 43969 (10.08.1964). *Rating*: All audiences. *Release date*: 10.11.1964. *Distribution*: Unitelefilm.

1965

La decima vittima

(aka *The 10th Victim*)

S: based on Robert Sheckley's short story *Seventh Victim*; SC: Tonino Guerra, Giorgio Salvioni, Ennio Flaiano, Elio Petri; M: Piero Piccioni, conducted by the author ("Spiral Waltz" by Sergio Bardotti and Piero Piccioni is sung by Mina); DOP: Gianni Di Venanzo (Technicolor); E: Ruggero Mastroianni; PD: Piero Poletto; CO: Giulio Coltellacci, Sorelle Fontana; AD: Berto Pelosso; C: Pasqualino De Santis. *Cast*: Marcello Mastroianni (Marcello Poletti), Ursula Andress (Caroline Meredith), Elsa Martinelli (Olga), Salvo Randone (Professor), Massimo Serato (Lawyer Rossi), Milo Quesada (Rudi), Luce Bonifassy (Lidia Poletti), George Wang (Chinese hunter), Evi Rigano (Victim), Walter Williams (Martin Tibbett), Richard Armstrong (Cole), Antonio Ciani, Jacques Herlin (Masoch Club manager), Wolfgang Hillinger (Baron von Rauschenberg), Mickey Knox (Chet), Anita Sanders (Relaxatorium girl), Giovanni Ivan Scratuglia (Priest in aeroplane). PROD: Carlo Ponti for Compagnia Cinematografica Champion (Rome), Les Films Concordia (Paris). EP: Joseph E. Levine. GM: Jone Tuzi. Country: Italy/France. Filmed on location in Rome, New York and at Titanus Appia Studios (Rome). *Running time*: 92 minutes; Visa n: 46068 (11.26.1965; 12.22.1965). *Rating*: V.M.18. *Release date*: 12.03.1965. *Distribution*: Interfilm (Italy); Embassy (U.S.A.)

1967

A ciascuno il suo

(aka *We Still Kill the Old Way*)

S: loosely based on Leonardo Sciascia's novel; SC: Elio Petri, Ugo Pirro; M: Luis Enrique Bacalov; DOP: Luigi Kuveiller (Technicolor); E: Ruggero Mastroianni; PD: Sergio Canevari; CO: Luciana Marinucci; AD: Marcello Crescenzi; C: Danilo Desideri; MU: Pierantonio Mecacci. *Cast*: Gian Maria Volonté (Prof. Paolo Laurana), Irene Papas (Luisa Roscio), Gabriele Ferzetti (Adv. Rosello), Salvo Randone (Prof. Roscio), Laura Nucci (Laurana's mother), Mario Scaccia (Curate of Sant'Arno), Luigi Pistilli (Arturo Manno), Leopoldo Trieste (Communist MP), Giovanni Pallavicino (Raganà), Tanina Zappalà, Luciana Scalise (Rosina), Orio Cannarozzo (Police inspector La Marca), Anna Rivero (Manno's wife), Michele Jannucci, Franco Tranchina (Dr. Antonio Roscio), Carlo Ferro, Carmelo Olivero (Arch-priest), Valentino Macchi, Aldo Cascino (Commissioner). PROD: Giuseppe Zaccariello for Cemofilm. GM: Luigi Millozza. Country: Italy. Filmed on location in Cefalù and Palermo, Sicily. *Running time*: 93 minutes; Visa n: 48625 (02.11.1967; 03.11.1967). *Rating*: V.M.18. *Release date*: 02.24.1967. *Distribution*: Panta Cinematografica.

1968

Un tranquillo posto di campagna

(aka *A Quiet Place in the Country*)

S: Elio Petri, Tonino Guerra, loosely based on Oliver Onions' short story *The Beckoning Fair One*; SC: Elio Petri, Luciano Vincenzoni; M: Ennio Morricone, executed by Gruppo di Improvvisazione Nuova Consonanza; DOP:

Luigi Kuveiller (Technicolor); E: Ruggero Mastroianni; PD: Sergio Canevari; APD: Amedeo Fago; CO: Franco Carretti, Giulio Coltellacci; AD: Mario Chiari; C: Ubaldo Terzano; MU: Pierantonio Mecacci; Paintings: Jim Dine. *Cast*: Franco Nero (Leonardo Ferri), Vanessa Redgrave (Flavia), Georges Géret (Attilio), Gabriella Grimaldi [Gabriella Boccardo] (Wanda), Madeleine Damien (Wanda's mother), Rita Calderoni (Egle), Renato Menegatti (Egle's friend), David Maunsell (The psychic), John Francis Lane (Male nurse at asylum), Valerio Ruggeri, Arnaldo Momo (Villager), Costantino De Luca (Villager), Marino Biagiola (Villager), Piero De Franceschi (Villager), Camillo Besenzon (Villager), Renato Lupi, Umberto Di Grazia, Giuseppe Bello, Bruna Simionato, Onofrio Folli, Elena Vicini, Sara Momo (Villager), Otello Cazzola (Villager), Mirta Simionato (Villager), Graziella Simionato (Villager), Giulia Menin (Villager). PROD: Alberto Grimaldi for P.E.A. (Rome), Produzioni Associate Delphos, Les Productions Artistes Associés (Paris); PM: Gino Millozza. *Country*: Italy/France. Filmed at Cinecittà Studios. *Running time*: 106 minutes; Visa n: 52702 (11.13.1968). *Rating*: V.M.18. *Release date*: 11.14.1968. *Distribution*: P.E.A.-United Artists.

Cinegiornale libero di Roma n. xyz

No credits available. *Running time*: 20 minutes.

Note: Petri interviews Daniel Cohn-Bendit near the Vatican.

1970

Indagine su un cittadino al di sopra di ogni sospetto

(aka *Investigation of a Citizen Above Suspicion*)
S, SC: Elio Petri, Ugo Pirro; M: Ennio Morricone, conducted by Bruno Nicolai; DOP: Luigi Kuveiller (Technicolor); E: Ruggero Mastroianni; PD: Romano Cardarelli; ArtD: Carlo Egidi; CO: Angela Sammaciccia; MU: Franco Corridoni; C: Ubaldo Terzano; AD: Antonio Gabrielli; 2ndAD: Lorenzo Magnolia; Continuity: Armenia Balducci. *Cast*: Gian Maria Volonté ("Doctor"), Florinda Bolkan (Augusta Terzi), Gianni Santuccio (Chief of Police), Orazio Orlando (Brigadier Biglia), Sergio Tramonti (Antonio Pace), Arturo Dominici

(Mangani), Aldo Rendine (Nicola Panunzio), Massimo Foschi (Terzi), Salvo Randone (Plumber), Aleka Paizi (Maid), Vittorio Duse (Canes), Pino Patti (Head of wire-tapping office), Fulvio Grimaldi (Patané the journalist), Filippo De Gara (Police official), Giuseppe Licastro, Ugo Adinolfi (Policeman), Franco Marletta (Policeman), Giacomo Bellini, Giuseppe Terranova, Vincenzo Falanga (Pallottella), Roberto Bonanni (Proietti), Guido Buzzelli, Gino Usai; *uncredited*: Gianfranco Barra (Policeman), Aristide Caporale (Man at police h.q.), Alfonso Giganti (Policeman); Ettore Geri, Franco Magno, Enrico Marciani, Enzo Mondino, Mario Silvestri (Officers attending final confession); Elio Petri (Man sleeping during speech), Alessandro Tedeschi (Man listening to speech). PROD: Daniele Senatore for Vera Films, Marina Cicogna for Euro International Films. PM: Romano Cardarelli. *Country*: Italy. Filmed in Novara and at Cinecittà (Rome). *Running time*: 115 minutes. Visa No: 55475 (02.05.1970) *Rating*: V.M.14. *Release date*: 02.09.1970. *Distribution*: Euro.

Materiale n. 2—Ipotesi sulla morte di G. Pinelli

S, SC: Elio Petri, Ugo Pirro; DOP: Luigi Kuveiller (b&w); E: Raimondo Crociani. *Cast*: Gian Maria Volonté, Renzo Montagnani, Luigi Diberti, Giancarlo Dettori. *Running time*: 11 minutes.

1971

La classe operaia va in paradiso

(aka *Lulu the Tool*)
S, SC: Elio Petri, Ugo Pirro; M: Ennio Morricone, conducted by Bruno Nicolai; DOP: Luigi Kuveiller; E: Ruggero Mastroianni; PD: Dante Ferretti; SD: Carlo Gervasi; CO: Franco Carretti; MU: Pierantonio Mecacci; C: Ubaldo Terzano; AD: Antonio Gabrielli, Franco Longo; 2nd AD: Lorenzo Magnolia; CON: Armenia Balducci. *Cast*: Gian Maria Volonté (Lulù Massa), Mariangela Melato (Lidia), Gino Pernice (Sindacalist), Luigi Diberti (Bassi), Salvo Randone (Militina), Mietta Albertini (Adalgisa), Renata Zamengo (Maria), Donato Castellaneta ("Carlo Marx"), Giuseppe Fortis (Valli), Corrado Solari (Mena), Flavio Bucci (Factory worker), Luigi Uzzo, Giovanni Bignamini, Ezio Marano (Timekeeper),

Adriano Amidei Migliano (Technician), Antonio Mangano, Lorenzo Magnolia (Magnolia), Federico Scrobogna (Arturo), Guerrino Crivello (Timekeeper), Alberto Fogliani (Factory worker), Carla Mancini (Factory worker), Orazio Stracuzzi, Marisa Rossi, Renzo Varallo, Eugenio Fatti, Massimo Patrone (Crazy man). PROD: Ugo Tucci for Euro International Films; PM: Claudio Mancini; UM: Stefano Pegoraro. *Country*: Italy. Filmed in Novara and at Cinecittà (Rome). *Running time*: 126 minutes. Visa No: 58881 (09.15.1971; 09.30.1971) *Rating*: V.M.18; V.M.14. *Release date*: 09.17.1971. *Distribution*: Euro.

1973

La proprietà non è più un furto

(aka *Property Is No Longer a Theft*)

S, SC: Elio Petri, Ugo Pirro; M: Ennio Morricone, conducted by Bruno Nicolai; DOP: Luigi Kuveiller (Technospes); E: Ruggero Mastroianni; PD, CO: Gianni Polidori; SD: Massimo Tavazzi; C: Ubaldo Terzano; AD: Rinaldo Ricci; Painting—Opening titles: Renzo Vespignani. *Cast*: Ugo Tognazzi (Butcher), Flavio Bucci (Total), Daria Nicolodi (Anita), Mario Scaccia (Alessandro Marzo "Albertone"), Orazio Orlando (Brigadier Pirelli), Luigi Proietti (Paco), Salvo Randone (Total's Father), Julien Guiomar (Bank Director), Cecilia Polizzi (Mafalda), Jacques Herlin (Bank Employee), Ada Pometti (Maid), Gino Milli (Zagané), Luigi Antonio Guerra (Protester), Pierluigi D'Orazio, Elena Fabrizi (Customer), Ettore Garofalo (Bocio), Alfonso Giganti (Policeman), Claudio Mancini (Bank Robber). PROD: Claudio Mancini for Quasars Film Company (Rome), Labrador Films (Paris). *Country*: Italy/France. Filmed on location in Rome and at Cinecittà (Rome). *Running time*: 125 minutes. Visa No: 62682 (06.28.1973) *Rating*: V.M.18. *Release date*: 07.01.1973. *Distribution*: Titanus.

1976

Todo modo

S: loosely based on Leonardo Sciascia's novel; SC: Elio Petri, with the collaboration of Berto Pelosso; consultant: Marco Ferronato; M: Ennio Morricone; DOP: Luigi Kuveiller (Eastmancolor); E: Ruggero Mastroianni; PD: Dante Ferretti; SD: Osvaldo Desideri; CO: Franco Carretti; C: Ubaldo Terzano; AD:

Umberto Angelucci. *Cast*: Gian Maria Volonté ("M"), Marcello Mastroianni (Don Gaetano), Mariangela Melato (Giacinta), Ciccio Ingrassia (Voltrano), Franco Citti (Driver), Renato Salvatori (Dr. Scalambri), Michel Piccoli (Him), Cesare Gelli (Arras), Tino Scotti (Cook), Adriano Amidei Migliano (Capra Porfiri), Giancarlo Badessi (Ventre), Mario Bartoli (Lombo's son), Nito Costa (Young priest), Guerrino Crivello (TV Speaker), Marcello Di Falco (Saccà), Giulio Donnini (Bastante), Aldo Farina (Restrero), Giuseppe Leone (Martellini), Renato Malavasi (Michelozzi), Riccardo Mangano (Cardinal Beccarisi), Piero Mazzinghi (Caprarozza), Lino Murolo (Mozio), Piero Nuti (Schiavò), Loris Pereira Lopez (Lombo Sr.), Riccardo Satta (Lomazzo), Luigi Uzzo (Aldo Lombo), Luigi Zerbinati (Caudo). PROD: Daniele Senatore for Cinevera S.p.A.; AssPROD: Francesco Genesi, Giorgio Cardelli. *Country*: Italy. Filmed at Cinecittà (Rome). *Running time*: 130 minutes. Visa No: 68416 (04.28.1976) *Rating*: V.M.14. *Release date*: 04.30.1976. *Distribution*: PIC.

1978

Le mani sporche

S: based on Jean-Paul Sartre's play *Les mains sales*; SC: Elio Petri; M: Ennio Morricone; DOP: Alberto Savi; SC: Filippo Corradi Cervi; CO: Barbara Mastroianni; SD: Letizia Amadei; Artistic Consultant: Lorenzo Vespignani; E: Gianni Lari. *Cast*: Marcello Mastroianni (Hoederer), Giovanni Visentin (Hugo), Anna Maria Gherardi (Olga), Giuliana De Sio (Jessica), Pietro Biondi (Louis), Omero Antonutti (Karsky), Massimo Foschi (Prince Paul), Bruno Pagni (Georges), Giorgio Trestini (Slick), Umberto Verdoni (Ivan), Ferruccio Cainero (Charles), Giovanni De Lucia (Frantz), Ezio Sancrotti (Léon), Elio Petri (Party Member). PROD: Nazareno Marinoni for Rai-Radio Televisione Italiana. *Running time*: 234 minutes. Aired in three parts on 11.14.1978, 11.15.1978, and 11.19.1978 (Rete 1).

1979

Buone notizie

S, SC: Elio Petri; M: Ennio Morricone; DOP: Tonino Nardi (Eastmancolor); E: Ruggero Mastroianni; PD: Amedeo Fago, Franco Pellecchia; CO: Barbara Mastroianni; MU: Michele Trimarchi; AD: Gianni Arduini, Fabio

Ferzetti. *Cast*: Giancarlo Giannini (Uomo), Ángela Molina (Fedora), Aurore Clément (Ada Milano), Paolo Bonacelli (Gualtiero Milano), Ombretta Colli (Tignetti), Ritza Brown (Benedetta), Franco Javarone (Commissioner), Ninetto Davoli (Colleague), Filippo De Gara (Sindacalist), Giovanni Baghino, Angelo Boscariol. PROD: Elio Petri, Giancarlo Giannini for Medusa Distribuzione. UM: Stefano Pegoraro; AUM: Pietro Buzzi, Ezio Busso. *Country*: Italy. Filmed at Incir De Paolis Studios and on location in Rome. *Running time*: 106 minutes. Visa No: 74275 (10.27.1979) *Rating*: V.M.14. *Release date*: 11.23.1979. *Distribution*: Medusa.

Chapter Notes

Introduction

1. Vittorio Spinazzola. *Inchieste: I registi degli anni '60. Elio Petri*, in Vittorio Spinazzola (ed.), *Film 1962* (Milan: Feltrinelli, 1962), 172.

2. Jean A. Gili (ed.). *Elio Petri* (Rome: Cinecittà Holding, 2000), 10.

3. Lietta Tornabuoni, "Incontri: La parola del giorno," *Corriere della Sera*, 11 June 1977.

4. Aldo Tassone, *Parla il cinema italiano. Volume secondo* (Milan: Il Formichiere, 1980), 278.

5. Jean A. Gili (ed.). *Elio Petri* (Nice: Faculté des Lettres et Sciences Humaines, 1974), 93.

6. *Ibid.*, 8.

7. Joan Mellen, "Cinema Is Not For an Elite But For the Masses': An Interview with Elio Petri," *Cinéaste*, Vol. 6, No. 1, 1973, 11–12.

8. Gili (2000), 17.

9. Lino Micciché, "Un regista serio, molto dialettico e dissacratore," *Avanti!*, 12 November 1982.

10. Tassone, 279–280.

11. In 2013 the Cineteca di Bologna and the Museo Nazionale del Cinema restored *La proprietà non è più un furto* (which won the prize for Best restored film at the 70th Venice Film Festival); the following year it was the turn of *Todo modo*.

12. Franca Faldini and Goffredo Fofi. *Il cinema italiano d'oggi 1970–1984 raccontato dai suoi protagonisti* (Milan: Mondadori, 1984), 60.

13. Tonino Guerra, in the documentary *Elio Petri. Appunti su un autore* (2005, Federico Bacci, Nicola Guarneri, Stefano Leone).

14. Federico Caddeo, *Journey Into Madness* interview with Franco Nero, extra featurette in the Scream Factory BD *A Quiet Place in the Country*.

15. Alessandro De Rosa, *Ennio Morricone: In His Own Words* (Oxford: Oxford University Press, 2019), 65.

Chapter One

1. "Après Budapest Sartre parle," *L'Express*, 9 November 1956.

2. Pietro Nenni, "L'insegnamento di una tragedia," *Avanti!*, 28 October 1956.

3. Dacia Maraini, *E tu chi eri? 26 interviste sull'infanzia* (Milan: Rizzoli, 1998), 277.

4. *Ibid.*, 279.

5. Elio Petri, *"Perché non ci vediamo mai?"*— *Tre lettere a Giuseppe De Santis*, 2–4 October 1982. In Elio Petri and Jean A. Gili (ed.), *Scritti di cinema e di vita* (Rome: Bulzoni, 2007), 218.

6. *Ibid.*, 221.

7. Maraini, 275.

8. Founded in 1926, Opera Nazionale Balilla was the name of the Italian Fascist youth organization. It took its name from an 18th century patriot, Giovan Battista Perasso, nicknamed Balilla. Children aged 6 to 8 were called *Figli della Lupa* (Children of the She-Wolf, alluding to the founding myth of Romulus and Remus). Boys aged 8 to 14 were called *Balilla*, whereas girls of the same ages were *Piccole italiane* (Little Italian girls). Those from 14 to 18 were called respectively *Avanguardisti* (Vanguardists) and *Giovani Italiane* (Young Italian girls). Conceived as a cultural institution with the aim of injecting the fascist ideology into young minds, ONB served also as a paramilitary group. Moreover, it took charge of all activities initiated by schools, including summer camps. Boys wore a uniform which recalled that of the Blackshirts (black shirt, fez, grey-green trousers, azure handkerchiefs), and were trained to perform military exercises as well. In 1937 ONB was absorbed into the Gioventù del Littorio (GIL), a youth section of the Fascist Party.

9. Maraini, 279.

10. *Ibid.*, 281.

11. *Ibid.*, 282.

12. Tassone, 238.

13. Maraini, *E tu chi eri?*, 283.

14. Lietta Tornabuoni, "Brevi Incontri. Così ricordano i primi anni," *La Stampa*, 7 June 1973.

15. Gili (1974), 22.

16. Enzo Siciliano, "Le due anime di Elio Petri," *La Stampa*, 24 June 1972.

17. Petri, *"Perché non ci vediamo mai?,"* 216.

18. *Ibid.*, 222.

19. *Ibid.*, 226.

20. *Ibid.*

21. *Ona zashchishchaet rodinu* (1943, Fridrikh Ermler).

22. *Ibid.*, 227.

23. "I remember him as a great man, even though we had many arguments when we were writing together our early stuff with Carlo Romano,"

Fulci said about Petri. See Michele Romagnoli, *L'occhio del testimone* (Bologna: Granata Press, 1992), 25. According to some sources, in the late 1940s Fulci and Petri wrote two scripts together, *Isolato 1962* and *Il settimo si riposa*, but this is unconfirmed. See As Chianese, Gordiano Lupi, *Filmare la morte: il cinema horror e thriller di Lucio Fulci* (Rome: Il Foglio, 2006), 18.

24. Mellen, "'Cinema Is Not for an Elite but for the Masses,'" 9–10.

25. Leo Canullo, "Elio Petri, un comunista "ribelle" che non ha mai abbandonato il partito," *L'Unità*, 10 December 1982.

26. Paola Pegoraro Petri, "Una non-presentazione," in Paola Pegoraro Petri and Roberta Basano (eds.), *Lucidità inquieta. Il cinema di Elio Petri* (Turin: Museo Nazionale del Cinema, 2007), 9.

27. *Ibid.*

28. Mellen, 10.

29. Tassone, 238.

30. "È morta una delle ragazze ferite nel crollo in v. Savoia," *L'Unità*, 16 January 1951.

31. Giuseppe De Santis, *Prefazione*, in Elio Petri, *Roma ore 11* (Palermo: Sellerio, 2004), 12.

32. Petri, *"Perché non ci vediamo mai?,"* 225–226.

33. Mellen, 10.

34. De Santis, *Prefazione*, 18.

35. Petri, *Roma ore 11*, 58.

36. Cesare Zavattini, *Prefazione*, in Elio Petri, *Roma ore 11* (Rome: Edizioni Avanti!, 1956), 14. Zavattini's foreword is not included in the 2004 edition.

37. Riccardo Costantini, Luciano De Giusti, and Federico Zecca, "Conversazione con Franco Giraldi," in Luciano De Giusti (ed.), *Franco Giraldi, lungo viaggio attraverso il cinema* (Turin: Kaplan, 2006), 185.

38. Carlo Lizzani interviewed, in Diego Mondella (ed.), *L'ultima trovata. Trent'anni di cinema senza Elio Petri* (Bologna: Pendragon, 2013), 194.

39. Tassone, 239.

40. Jean A. Gili, *Elio Petri. Artist & Intellectual*, in Elio Petri and Jean A. Gili (ed.), *Elio Petri. Writings on Cinema & Life* (New York: Contra Mundum Press, 2013), 17.

41. Lina Sotis, "Marcello Mastroianni: farò la televisione ma il cinema è un'altra cosa," *Corriere d'Informazione*, 6 March 1978.

42. Ugo Pirro, *Il cinema della nostra vita* (Turin: Lindau, 2001), 11.

43. The name (Portonaccio Gang) came from art gallerist Gasparo Del Corso and referred to a Roman neighborhood. See Pierpaolo De Sanctis, *Pop, Op e altre correnti. Arte, design e visual culture nel cinema anni '60 di Elio Petri*, in Gabriele Rigola (ed.), *Elio Petri, uomo di cinema* (Acireale: Bonanno, 2015), 74.

44. R. [Roderigo di Castiglia], "Segnalazioni," *Rinascita* #11, 1948.

45. Pirro (2001), 13.

46. Ugo Pirro, *Soltanto un nome nei titoli di testa* (Turin: Einaudi, 1998), 48.

47. "Il film *Uomini e lupi* proiettato in Pretura," *Corriere d'Informazione*, 7–8 February 1957.

48. "I cineasti italiani si schierano per la grazia ai Rosenberg," *L'Unità*, 14 June 1953.

49. "Da ogni parte d'Italia si chiedono concordemente misure energiche contro i mandanti del teppismo," *L'Unità*, 12 March 1955.

50. "Il dibattito sull'Ungheria all'interno del partito," *L'Unità*, 30 October 1956.

51. Nello Ajello, *Intellettuali e PCI. 1944–1958* (Bari: Laterza, 1979), 440.

52. Enzo Siciliano, "Falce e pennello," *Corriere della Sera*, 21 February 1993.

53. Franca Faldini and Goffredo Fofi, *L'avventurosa storia del cinema italiano raccontata dai suoi protagonisti: 1935–1959* (Milan: Feltrinelli, 1979), 371.

54. Gianfranco Miro Gori, *E' circal de giudéizi. Santarcangelo di Romagna nell'esperienza culturale del dopoguerra* (Bologna: CLUEB, 2000), 3.

55. Claudio Bertieri, "Fuori programma," *Cinema* #138, 25 July 1954, 438.

56. Gianni Rondolino, *Corale e intimistico*, in Lino Micciché (ed.), *Studi su dodici sguardi d'autore in cortometraggio* (Turin: Lindau/Associazione Philip Morris Progetto Cinema, 1995), 181.

57. Gili (1974), 28.

58. Oreste del Buono, *Addio alla semplicità della chiarezza*, in Micciché (ed.), *Studi su dodici sguardi d'autore in cortometraggio*, 196.

59. It is uncertain whether the chosen novel was *Pesma* (aka *Poetry*, 1952), *Beton i svici* (aka *Concrete and Fireflies*, 1955) or *Radni naslov beskraja* (aka *Working Title of the Eternity*, 1958).

60. Pirro (2001), 23.

61. As per the contract retained in the Elio Petri fund: AMNC, ELPE0144.

62. Roberto Amoroso, letter to Franco Giraldi, Tonino Guerra and Eraclio Petri, Rome, 28 September 1960 (AMNC, ELPE0147).

63. Tonino Guerra quoted in Marie-Christine Questerbert, *Les Scénaristes italiens* (Paris: Haltier, 1988).

64. See Tommaso Mozzati, *L'estate calda dei teddy boys* (Rome: Carocci, 2019).

65. Franca Faldini and Goffredo Fofi, *L'avventurosa storia del cinema italiano raccontata dai suoi protagonisti: 1960–1969* (Milan: Feltrinelli, 1981), 69.

Chapter Two

1. Elio Petri, letter to [Ennio] Della Nesta, presumably 1964 (AMNC, ELPE0258).

2. Tonino Valerii attempted to adapt Rossi's book in the early 1970s, but to no avail. In 1976 it became a TV mini-series, *Una spia del regime*, directed by Alberto Negrin and starring Vittorio Mezzogiorno. See Roberto Curti, *Tonino Valerii: The Films* (Jefferson NC: McFarland, 2016), 65, 217.

3. AMNC, ELPE0008.

4. Andrea Pergolari, *La fabbrica del riso* (Rome: Un mondo a parte, 2004), 24.

5. The crew featured another French member, assistant director Maurice Hartwig, whose presence

was nominal only. His main task was to take care of the French adaptation of the dialogue.

6. Giuseppe Sansonna, *Hollywood sul Tevere. Storie scellerate* (Rome: Minimum Fax, 2016), 32.

7. AMNC, ELPE0149; ELPE0150.

8. "Marcello Mastroianni 'giallo' fra due donne," *Corriere d'Informazione*, 3–4 February 1961.

9. "Un carcere nuovo di zecca per la famiglia dell'*Assassino*," *Corriere d'Informazione*, 2–3 January 1961.

10. "Un Panelli per Salerno," *Corriere d'Informazione*, 23–24 January 1961.

11. Excerpt from the original documentation retained at Rome's Archive of State.

12. Tommaso Chiaretti, "Storia tragicomica di un film tra i labirinti della censura," *Il Paese*, 5 April 1961.

13. Gili (1974), 31.

14. The rating was eventually changed to "all audiences allowed" in 1970 (Visa #56900, 7 October 1970).

15. Filippo Sacchi, "L'assassino," *Epoca*, 16 April 1961.

16. Mino Argentieri, "Le tentazioni letterarie dei giovani registi," *Cinema 60* #8–9, 1961, 8.

17. "L'assassino," *Corriere d'Informazione*, 3–4 April 1961.

18. l.p. [Lorenzo Pellizzari], "L'assassino," *Cinema nuovo* #151, May-June 1961, 243.

19. Elio Petri, letter to Morando Morandini, Rome, 11 April 1961 (AMNC, ELPE0153)

20. Tullio Kezich and Sergio Toffetti (ed.), *'Ndemo in cine. Tullio Kezich tra pagina e set* (Turin: Lindau, 1998), 154.

21. Faldini and Fofi (1981), 69.

22. *Ibid.*, 70.

23. Cynthia Grenier, "Berlin," *Film Quarterly*, Vol. 15, No. 2, Winter 1961–1962, 39.

24. Ian Wright, "New films in London," *The Guardian*, 4 October 1963. Another favorable review appeared a few months later, calling it "an effective film," noting its affinities with Fellini and Antonioni's cinema, and praising Mastroianni's "extraordinarily effortless" performance." "A Roman grilling," *The Guardian*, 10 February 1964.

25. "'Lady Killer of Rome' in Neighborhoods," *The New York Times*, June 9, 1966.

26. Gili (1974), 29.

27. Tassone, 247.

28. Sacchi, "L'assassino."

29. Camilla Zamboni, *Bad cops, dubious killers, and alienated citizens: Elio Petri's "The Assassin,"* essay included in the Arrow Blu-ray DVD release.

30. Faldini and Fofi (1981), 153.

31. "L'assassino," *Il nuovo spettatore* #22–23, 1961.

32. Alberto Farassino and Ugo De Berti, *Le invenzioni: dalla tecnica allo stile*, in Giorgio De Vincenti (ed.), *Storia del cinema italiano. Vol. X, 1960–1964* (Venice-Rome: Marsilio, Edizioni di Bianco & Nero, 2001), 376.

33. Giuliano Montaldo interviewed, in Mondella, 202.

34. Faldini and Fofi (1981), 152.

35. Gili (1974), 35.

36. *Ibid.*, 30.

37. Alfredo Rossi, *Elio Petri* (Milan: Il Castoro Cinema, 1979), 37.

38. Faldini and Fofi (1981), 153.

Chapter Three

1. "Rubrica: Da oggi in prima visione." *Stampa Sera*, 15 June 1962.

2. Petri, *"Perché non ci vediamo mai?,"* 220–221.

3. AMNC, ELPE0148.

4. Faldini and Fofi (1981), 153.

5. Sansonna, *Hollywood sul Tevere*, 34.

6. "Claudia Cardinale si darà al teatro?" *Corriere d'Informazione*, 12–13 February 1962, 7.

7. Yvonne Baby, *La vie retrouvée* (Éditions de l'Olivier, Paris 1992), 160.

8. Pegoraro Petri, "Una non-presentazione," 9.

9. *Ibid.*, 10.

10. "Il primo premio a Elio Petri per il film *I giorni contati*," *Corriere della Sera*, 2 April 1962.

11. l.q. [Lorenzo Quaglietti], "I giorni contati," *Cinema 60* #21–22, March-April 1962, 58.

12. "Tre nuovi film: tre nuove prospettive," *Cinema Domani* #2, March-April 1962, 17.

13. Elio Petri, "Note sulla sceneggiatura: Un gesto narrativo," *Cinema Domani* #2, March-April 1962, 19.

14. u.f. [Ugo Finetti], "I giorni contati," *Cinema nuovo* #157, May-June 1962, 222.

15. *I giorni contati* was released in Argentina in November 1962 and the following year in Finland (8 March 1963) and Sweden (22 April 1963). It came out in Portugal on June 17, 1965 and in Denmark on March 29, 1966. It surfaced in France only in 2012, in home video.

16. Callisto Cosulich, L' *"operazione Titanus"* in De Vincenti (ed.), *Storia del cinema italiano. Vol. X, 1960–1964*, 145.

17. Gili (1974), 26.

18. *Ibid.*

19. Tassone, 240.

20. *Ibid.*, 245.

21. Ugo Casiraghi, "*I giorni contati* di Petri: poemetto sull'alienazione," *L'Unità*, 7 April 1962.

22. Farassino and De Berti, *Le invenzioni: dalla tecnica allo stile*, 378.

23. "Elio Petri vorrebbe rifare il suo film *I giorni contati*," *L'Unità*, 10 April 1962.

24. *Ibid.*

25. In the original outline Cesare first meets Giulia at the doctor's office.

26. An international chain of "daytime hotels" for cleaning, steaming and grooming, the Cobianchi public baths had been the subject of one of Federico Fellini's early short stories for the *Marc'Aurelio* magazine, "Ma tu mi stai sentire ragazza dei bagni pubblici Cobianchi?" (Why, are you listening to me, girl at the Cobianchi public baths?).

27. Tassone, 241.

28. Cesare Zavattini, "Appello per un film sulla pace," *Rinascita*, 9 June 1962.

29. *Il cinegiornale della pace* was directed by Luigi Di Gianni, Giuseppe Ferrara, Ansano Giannarelli, Jean Lodz, Luciano Malaspina, Massimo Mida and Luciano Viazzi.

30. Spinazzola. *Inchieste: I registi degli anni '60. Elio Petri*, 175.

31. "Mastroianni produttore (con Elio Petri)," *Corriere d'Informazione*, 19–20 January 1962, 7.

32. Ugo Naldi, "Mastroianni tranquillo in un posto di campagna," *Corriere d'Informazione*, 15–16 October 1962, 15.

33. Elio Petri, letter to [Ennio] Della Nesta, presumably 1964 (AMNC, ELPE0258).

34. Rossi (1979), 58.

35. AMNC, ELPE0018.

36. Rossi (1979), 43.

37. Marcello Mastroianni and Francesca Tatò (ed.), *Mi ricordo, sì, io mi ricordo* (Milan: Baldini & Castoldi, 1997), 57.

38. *Ibid.*

39. Matilde Hochkofler, *Marcello Mastroianni. Il gioco del cinema* (Rome: Gremese, 2001), 134–135.

40. The fake Spanish title is a wordplay on the word "ruspante" (free-range).

41. Hochkofler, 135.

42. Alberto Crespi, *Dal Polo all'Equatore. I film e le avventure di Giuliano Montaldo* (Venice: Marsilio, 2005), 98.

43. *Ibid.*

44. For an in-depth view of Questi's career, see Roberto Curti, *Mavericks of Italian Cinema. Eight Unorthodox Filmmakers, 1940s-2000s* (Jefferson NC: McFarland & Co., 2018), 83–111.

45. Giulio Questi, *Se non ricordo male* (Bari: Rubbettino, 2014), 67.

46. *Ibid.*, 68.

47. The share capital of 900,000 lire was divided as follows: Montaldo put in 135,000; Pegoraro 270,000; Petri 180,000; Luigi Piredda 135,000; Questi 135,000; Aldo Sanchini 90,000.

48. Crespi, 99.

49. Questi, 68.

50. *Ibid.*, 69.

51. Crespi, 99.

52. *Ibid.*, 73.

53. Questi, 71–72.

54. Giuliano Montaldo interviewed, in Mondella, 201–202.

55. "Censurato il film *Nudi per vivere*," *Corriere della Sera*, 27 November 1963.

56. The film was first seized in Palermo on March 6, then in Rome, on March 8. "*Nudi per vivere* sequestrato a Roma," *Corriere della Sera*, 10 March 1964. On March 12 the police seized its reels at Dear Film's head office in Florence. "Sequestrato a Firenze Nudi per vivere," *La Stampa*, 13 March 1964.

57. Alberico Sala, "La brutta spina della censura," *Corriere d'Informazione*, 13–14 March 1964.

58. Crespi, 99.

59. "Aggiornata la causa per *Nudi per vivere*," *Corriere della Sera*, April 22, 1964.

60. "Assolto il produttore Pegoraro," *Corriere della Sera*, May 19, 1964.

61. ag.sa. [Aggeo Savioli], "Nudi per vivere," *L'Unità*, 10 March 1964.

62. "Nudi per vivere," *Il Messaggero*, 29 August 1964.

63. Vice, "Nudi per vivere," *Il Tempo*, 8 March 1964. The same line is almost literally reprised in the anonymous—and, unlike *Il Tempo*'s, quite positive—review in *Il Globo*. "Nudi per vivere," *Il Globo*, 8 March 1964.

64. It was Claudio Mancini, who was initially to work on the film (which he called "a weird operation"), who revealed the true identity of "Elio Montesti," in the first volume of *L'avventurosa storia del cinema italiano raccontata dai suoi protagonisti*. However, Questi is misspelled in print as *Testi*. Faldini and Fofi (1979), 384.

65. Crespi, 100.

Chapter Four

1. Claudio Risé, "I documentari sexy," in Vittorio Spinazzola (ed.), *Film 1964* (Milan: Feltrinelli, 1964), 87.

2. Tommaso Chiaretti, "Cinema per i pigri?" *L'Eco del Cinema*, 15 May 1954.

3. Gili (1974), 43.

4. Tullio Kezich and Alessandra Levantesi, *Dino. De Laurentiis, la vita e i film* (Milan: Feltrinelli, 2001), 151.

5. Gili (1974), 43–45.

6. Faldini and Fofi (1981), 146.

7. *Ibid.*, 145.

8. Giorgio Bocca, "Mille fabbriche, nessuna libreria," *Il Giorno*, 10 January 1962.

9. *Ibid.*

10. Piersandro Pallavicini, "Maestro di vite disperate," Ilsole24ore.com, 17 June 2012.

11. Pietro Radius, "Da oggi Sordi fa il maestro," *Corriere d'Informazione*, 11–12 September 1963.

12. Enzo Passanisi, "Mastronardi internato per due anni in clinica," *Corriere d'Informazione*, 15–16 October 1962.

13. Howard Thompson, "Claire in Bloom," *The New York Times*, 31 May 1964.

14. Gili (1974), 48. A news article mentioning that Vitti would be playing alongside Charles Aznavour confirms Petri's version. See "L'alta infedeltà di Monica Vitti," *Corriere d'Informazione*, 1 August 1963.

15. Furio Scarpelli, *A proposito di* Peccato nel pomeriggio, in Pirro (ed.), *Elio Petri* (Venice: La Biennale—XL Mostra Internazionale del Cinema, 1983), 52.

16. Manlio Cancogni, "Capitale corrotta, nazione infetta," *L'Espresso*, 11 December 1955.

17. Elio Petri, *For Whom Do We Write? For Whom Do We Shoot?*, in Petri and Gili (2013), 131.

18. Alberto Arbasino, *Fratelli d'Italia* (Milan: Adelphi 2015), 138.

19. Dino De Laurentiis, registered letter to Elio Petri, Rome, 22 July 1963 (AMNC, ELPE0199).

20. Marcel Pagnol (1895–1974) was a French novelist, playwright, and filmmaker. Among his most famous films are the two versions of his play *Topaze*, which he directed in 1936 and 1952, respectively, the latter starring the popular comedian Fernandel.

21. Georges Courteline (born Georges Victor Marcel Moinaux, 1858–1929) was a French dramatist and novelist whose work conveys a sharp and cynical humor.

22. "Sordi presto maestro a Vigevano," *Corriere d'Informazione*, 30–31 August 1963.

23. Sauro Borelli, "A Vigevano si attende il maestro "numero due,"" *L'Unità*, 14 September 1963.

24. "Sordi inizia *Il maestro di Vigevano* mentre muore il padre di Mastronardi," *Corriere d'Informazione*, 17–18 September 1963.

25. Radius, "Da oggi Sordi fa il maestro."

26. Borelli, "A Vigevano si attende il maestro "numero due.""

27. *Ibid.*

28. Dino De Laurentiis, telegram to Elio Petri, 4 October 1963 (AMNC, ELPE0203).

29. Giovanni Tesio, *Introduzione*, in Lucio Mastronardi, *Il maestro di Vigevano, Il calzolaio di Vigevano. Il meridionale di Vigevano* (Milan: Einaudi 2015), V.

30. L.C., "Senza scuola a Vigevano il "maestro" Alberto Sordi," *Corriere della Sera*, 20 September 1963.

31. Giovanni Grazzini, "Il maestro di Vigevano stasera al consiglio comunale," *Corriere della Sera*, 25 September 1963.

32. Alberico Sala, "Il romano di Vigevano," *Corriere d'Informazione*, 25–26 September 1963.

33. Grazzini, "Il maestro di Vigevano stasera al consiglio comunale."

34. Sala, "Il romano di Vigevano."

35. "La troupe di Sordi ha lasciato Vigevano" *Corriere della Sera*, 25 October 1963.

36. Publicity ad for *Il maestro di Vigevano* in *L'Unità*, 23 December 1963.

37. Alberto Moravia, "I contrattempi del dialetto," *L'Espresso*, 29 December 1963.

38. *Ibid.*

39. Mario Soldati, "Il maestro di Vigevano," *L'Europeo*, 24 April 1964. Collected in Mario Soldati, *Da spettatore. Un regista al cinema* (Milan: Mondadori, 1973)

40. Hawk, "Alta infedeltà," *Variety*, 26 February 1964.

41. "High Infidelity," *Morning Telegraph*, 2 July 1965.

42. Clifford Terry, "Italian Film Bright, Full of Nuances," *Chicago Tribune*, 17 January 1966.

43. Philip K. Scheuer, "Italian Sex Film Is Triumph of Genre," *The Los Angeles Times*, 9 April 1966.

44. Eugene Archer, "High Infidelity," 2d 4-Part Film From Italy This Week, Opens," *The New York Times*, 2 July 1965.

45. Richard L. Coe, "Four Incidents of Sly Amore," *The Washington Post, Times Herald*, 23 February 1966.

46. Terry, "Italian Film Bright, Full of Nuances."

47. Scheuer, "Italian Sex Film Is Triumph of Genre."

48. Faldini and Fofi (1981), 147.

49. *Ibid.*

50. "Already on *Il maestro di Vigevano* we understood that the exclusive deal could not last." Kezich and Levantesi, 156.

51. Gili (1974), 45.

52. Faldini and Fofi (1981), 147–148.

53. Goffredo Fofi, *Alberto Sordi. L'Italia in bianco e nero* (Milan: Mondadori, 2004), 152–153.

54. Deborah Toschi, *Il maestro di Vigevano, in bilico tra comico e grottesco*, in Rigola (ed.), *Elio Petri, uomo di cinema*, 164.

55. Gili (1974), 45.

56. Borelli, "A Vigevano si attende il maestro "numero due.""

57. Fernaldo Di Giammatteo, *Il maestro di Vigevano*, in Pirro (1983), 50.

58. *Ibid.*, 49.

59. Soldati, "Il maestro di Vigevano."

Chapter Five

1. "Cinema e fantascienza," *Cinema Domani* #4–5, July-October 1962, 16.

2. *Ibid.*

3. Paolo Milano, *Il lettore di professione* (Milan: Feltrinelli, 1960), 289.

4. "Cinema e fantascienza," 16.

5. *Ibid.*

6. *Ibid.* Mention of Petri and Mastroianni working on a sci-fi project turned up in newspapers in early 1962, although the plot as mentioned by the news article sounds puzzling and may refer to another unspecified project: "The actor … got it into his head to emulate Gagarin, Titov, Glenn, and even to overcome them. Devoting himself to space challenges, he will reach the satellite and land on the moon, but once there he will be turned into a mouse. This is, approximately, the story for a film project currently under consideration in Rome. Mastroianni will make his debut not only as astronaut but as film producer as well … in association with Pietro Notarianni. It will be a science fiction story, of course in a parodistic key. The direction would be entrusted to Elio Petri, a young filmmaker who has already directed Mastroianni in *L'assassino* and is now enjoying success with *I giorni contati*, starring Salvo Randone." Ugo Naldi, "Mastroianni astronauta," *Corriere d'Informazione*, 19–20 March 1962, 7.

7. Giovanni Grazzini, "Mastroianni: 'L'Oscar? Non ci ho mai capito niente,'" *Corriere della Sera*, 10 March 1963.

8. AMNC, ELPE0016.

9. Elio Petri, letter to Nate Monaster, Rome, 9 May 1963 (AMNC, ELPE0192). The letter is in English. The original text has been preserved with a few adjustments due to typos and errors.

10. Nate Monaster, letter to Elio Petri, 13 June 1963 (AMNC, ELPE0195).

11. Alberico Sala, "Fantascienza vera varata a Trieste," *Corriere d'Informazione*, 8–9 July 1963.

12. Elio Petri, letter to Nate Monaster, Rome, 22 July 1963 (AMNC, ELPE0201).

13. "Si dice che," *Corriere della Sera*, 3 March 1964.

14. Faldini and Fofi (1981), 374–375.

15. "Un film di Elio Petri sulle elezioni presidenziali," *L'Unità*, 20 December 1964.

16. Faldini and Fofi (1981), 374.

17. Saul Kahn, "The Tenth Victim," *Films and Filming* vol. 12 #7, April 1966, 57. A very similar article by Kahn on the film, but with some interesting differences (see text), had appeared several months earlier in the Beverly Hills-based magazine *Cinema*.

18. Kahn, *Films and Filming*, 58.

19. Gili (1974), 49.

20. Faldini and Fofi (1981), 374.

21. *Ibid.*, 375.

22. Ernesto Gastaldi, *Voglio entrare nel cinema. Storia di uno che ce l'ha fatta* (Milan: Mondadori 1991), 197.

23. *Ibid.*, 198.

24. *Ibid.*

25. *Ibid.*, 199.

26. "Attrice americana con licenza di uccidere Mastroianni," *Corriere d'Informazione*, 23–24 April 1965.

27. Gili (1974), 49.

28. "Attrice americana con licenza di uccidere Mastroianni."

29. Actually, the total cost, including an additional 33 million for postproduction and interests, amounted to over 665 million *lire*.

30. "Ursula ferita sul set," *Corriere d'Informazione*, 13–14 September 1965.

31. Robert Hawkins, "Will Marcello Become 'The Tenth Victim?,'" *The New York Times*, 15 August 1965.

32. Jeanne Molli, "'Tenth Victim' loaded with Gimmicks and Mastroianni," *Los Angeles Times*, 20 August 1965.

33. "Cinema e fantascienza," 17.

34. See Roberto Curti, *Riccardo Freda. The Life and Works of a Born Filmmaker* (Jefferson NC: McFarland, 2017), 114.

35. "The result of an exploding banana," according to Saul Kahn. But the bit of information is not in the film, hinting at some cuts in the scene. Saul Kahn, "The Tenth Victim," *Cinema* vol. 3 #1, December 1965.

36. Kahn, *Films and Filming*, 58.

37. De Sanctis, *Pop, Op e altre correnti*, 76–77. Fellini's declaration is taken from an installment in Luciano Emmer's 14-part TV series *Io e...* (1972), namely *Io e l'EUR*.

38. *Ibid.*, 77.

39. "Suspense e ironia dell'ultimo Petri," *Carlino Sera*, 30 May 1968.

40. Kahn, *Films and Filming*, 60.

41. De Sanctis, *Pop, Op e altre correnti*, 78.

42. Kahn, *Films and Filming*, 59.

43. Lucia Cardone, *Elio Petri impolitico* (Pisa: Edizioni ETS, 2005), 53.

44. "Ursula uccide Mastroianni," *Corriere d'Informazione*, 6–7 May 1965.

45. Kahn, *Films and Filming*, 59.

46. Israel Shenker, "The Man Who Made Apathy Irresistible," *The New York Times*, 12 December 1965.

47. Tassone, *Parla il cinema italiano*, 242.

48. Kahn, *Cinema*.

49. Kahn, *Films and Filming*, 59.

50. *Ibid.*

51. In 1993 the film was submitted again to the rating board (with minimal cuts) to revise the rating in prevision of TV airing. It was rated "all audiences."

52. Jean A. Gili and Aldo Tassone (eds.), *Parigi-Roma. 50 anni di coproduzioni italo-francesi* (Milan: Il Castoro, 1995), 130.

53. Incidentally, the slogan is a reworking of a punchline from famous Italian commercials for Brillantina Linetti, a popular hair pomade brand. Aired from 1957 to 1971, they were conceived as mini-mysteries and starred actor Cesare Polacco as the "infallible Inspector Rock." After solving the case, the inspector was congratulated by his aide, who marveled that he never made mistakes. To which, Inspector Rock replied, while taking off his hat and showing his bald head: "I made a mistake too. I didn't use Brillantina Linetti!" The punchline became proverbial in Italy, so much so that Petri had included a scene in *L'impiegato*, where Nino Manfredi's character dreams he is arrested by Inspector Rock.

54. Petri's answer to a questionnaire by Jean A. Gili. Quoted in Rossi, *Elio Petri e il cinema politico italiano*, 84.

55. Adele Gallotti, "Petri difende l'ultimo film e ne annuncia altri due esplosivi," *Stampa Sera*, 27 February 1967.

56. a.a. [Alberto Abruzzese], "La decima vittima," *Cinema 60* #57, March 1966, 57.

57. A.F. [Adelio Ferrero], "La decima vittima," *Cinema nuovo* #179, January-February 1966.

58. G.B. Cavallaro, "La decima vittima," *Cineforum* #50, December 1965, 876.

59. Giovanni Grazzini, letter to Elio Petri, 18 December 1965 (AMNC, ELPE0214).

60. Lino Micciché, *Cinema italiano: gli anni 60 e oltre* (Venice: Marsilio, 1975–2002), 175.

61. Cardone, 95–96.

62. Richard L. Coe, "'Tenth Victim' at the Embassy," *The Washington Post and Times-Herald*, 22 December 1965.

63. "The Big Hunt," *Newsweek*, 1 March 1966, 55.

64. Frank Morriss, "Satire of the Future Misses Its Target," *The Globe and Mail*, 29 December 1965.

65. Elio Petri, letter to Peter Witt, late 1967/early 1968 (AMNC, ELPE0257).

66. Elio Petri, answers to a questionnaire, circa 1970 (AMNC, ELPE0084).

67. Elio Petri, letter to Anatole Dauman, uncertain dating (AMNC, ELPE0298).

68. Gili (1974), 26.

69. *Ibid.*, 50.

Chapter Six

1. Gili (1974), 52.
2. Michael J. Hamilburg, letter to Elio Petri, 14 February 1966 (AMNC, ELPE0218).
3. Faldini and Fofi (1981), 214–215.
4. *Ibid.*, 215.
5. Pirro (2001), 49.
6. "Due pellicole in Italia," *Corriere della Sera*, 28 June 1966; Al. Cer. [Alberto Ceretto], "Per Ingrid Thulin nuovo film a Roma," *Corriere della Sera*, 22 July 1966. The other film Thulin was to do in Italy was Mauro Bolognini's *Delitto al circolo del tennis*, based on Alberto Moravia's short story. This too was shelved, and Moravia's tale was adapted for the screen by Franco Rossetti in 1969, without Thulin in the cast.
7. a.g. [Adele Gallotti], "La Taylor con le dive più famose approda alla rassegna di Taormina," *Stampa Sera*, 2–3 August 1966.
8. Faldini and Fofi (1981), 402–403.
9. Leonardo Sciascia. *La Sicilia come metafora. Intervista di Marcelle Padovani* (Milan: Mondadori, 1979), 69–70.
10. Pirro (2001), 27.
11. Gili (1974), 108.
12. A film adaptation of *Il giorno della civetta* had been announced as early as 1962, scripted by Ennio De Concini and to be shot on location with a cast of non-professionals. *Cinema nuovo #155*, January-February 1962, 55.
13. Elio Petri, "Gioco di squadra e specialità individuali," *Cinema 60 #44*, August 1964, 42.
14. Pirro (2001), 27–28.
15. Gili (1974), 108.
16. Pirro (2001), 33.
17. Gili (1974), 57–58.
18. *Ibid.*, 54.
19. Federico Caddeo, *The Best Man*, interview with Pierantonio Mecacci, extra featurette in the Arrow BD/DVD *Property Is No Longer a Theft*. Mecacci had worked on the Shell TV ads. He and Petri would work together again on *Un tranquillo posto di campagna*, *La classe operaia va in paradiso* and *La proprietà non è più un furto*. Petri and Sergio Donati were Mecacci's best men at the latter's wedding.
20. Mirko Capozzoli, *Gian Maria Volonté* (Turin: Add, 2018), 116.
21. Faldini and Fofi (1981), 403.
22. *Ibid.*
23. Alberto Ceretto, "In un film 'che scotta' Petri racconta la crisi di un intellettuale," *Corriere d'Informazione*, 31 October-1 November 1966.
24. *Ibid.*
25. Mario Foglietti, "Un intellettuale nuovo," *Il Popolo*, 29 August 1966.
26. Pirro (1998), 185.
27. Elio Petri, letter to Aldo Marcovecchio, 31 August 1966 (AMNC, ELPE0222).
28. The letters are retained in the Elio Petri fund. See also Gabriele Rigola, "Riderai, se ti dico che io mi sento un poco come Laurana?" in *Todomodo #5* (Florence: Leo S. Olschki Editore, 2015), 253–265. The underscores are in the originals.
29. *Ibid.*, 254.
30. Pirro (2001), 36.
31. *Ibid.*, 35.
32. Emiliano Morreale, *La vedova e il professore. A ciascuno il suo alle origini del "mafiamovie,"* in Rigola, 135.
33. Vittorio Albano, *La mafia nel cinema siciliano* (Manduria TA: Barbieri, 2003).
34. Elio Petri, *A ciascuno il suo: Sciascia's Sensuality*, in Petri and Gili (2013), 254. I adjusted the original translation ("sexually impotent") which didn't catch Petri's reference to a line of dialogue in *Indagine*, when Augusta Terzi calls the Doctor *"sessualmente incompetente"* (sexually incompetent).
35. *Ibid.*, 251.
36. *Ibid.*, 251–252.
37. Tassone, 246–247.
38. Faldini and Fofi (1981), 403.
39. Gili (1974), 54.
40. Petri, *A ciascuno il suo: Sciascia's Sensuality*, 253.
41. Leonardo Sciascia, letter to Elio Petri, Caltanissetta, 10 March 1967 (AMNC, ELPE0235).
42. Rigola, "Riderai, se ti dico che io mi sento un poco come Laurana?," 257.
43. Faldini and Fofi (1981), 403.
44. Morreale, *La vedova e il professore*, 140. See, in particular, *Il giorno della civetta* and *Gente di rispetto* (1975, Luigi Zampa).
45. "Nuova York: a febbraio in scena Macbird feroce satira dei Johnson e dei Kennedy," *Corriere d'Informazione*, 7–8 January 1967.
46. "Manifesto sequestrato: interpellanze," *Corriere della Sera*, 18 February 1967.
47. *Ibid.*
48. Federico Fellini, telegram to Elio Petri, Rome, 20 March 1967 (AMNC, ELPE0236).
49. Maurizio Ponzi, "A ciascuno il suo," *Cinema & Film #2*, Spring 1967, 245.
50. Faldini and Fofi (1981), 403.
51. Jacques Rivette, "De l'abjection," *Cahiers du Cinéma #120*, June 1961.
52. Jean Domarchi, Jacques Doniol-Valcroze, Jean-Luc Godard, Pierre Kast, Jacques Rivette, Eric Rohmer, "Hiroshima, notre amour," *Cahiers du Cinéma #97*, July 1959, 5.
53. Ponzi, "A ciascuno il suo," 246.
54. Leonardo Sciascia, letter to Elio Petri, Caltanissetta, 10 March 1967 (AMNC, ELPE0235).
55. Leonardo Sciascia, letter to Elio Petri, Caltanissetta, 11 June 1967 (AMNC, ELPE0241).
56. Elio Petri, letter to Leonardo Sciascia, late 1967/early 1968 (AMNC, ELPE0253).
57. In 1989 *Gioco di società* was adapted into a made-for-TV movie by Nanni Loy.
58. Elio Petri, telegram to Ugo Santalucia, 16 February 1967 (AMNC, ELPE0232).
59. "Ecco i "Nastri d'Argento,"" *Corriere della Sera*, 23 March 1968.
60. L.J. [Luciana Jorio], "A Petri il S. Fedele," *Corriere d'Informazione*, 28–29 May 1968.

61. M.Ba., "Tolto dal cartellone film di Petri a Zurigo," *Corriere della Sera*, 24 March 1968.

62. Pirro (2001), 43.

63. Mario Soldati, telex to *L'Espresso*'s editorial staff during the Cannes Film Festival, 29 April 1967 (AMNC, ELPE0238).

64. Angelo Maccario, "Petri farà un film sui rapporti familiari," *Corriere d'Informazione*, 29–30 April 1967.

65. Mellen, 9.

66. Here is the chronological list of foreign releases for *A ciascuno il suo*: West Germany (22 September 1967), Sweden (15 January 1968), U.S.A. (28 February), East Germany (12 April), Spain (Barcelona, May 17; Madrid, August 26), Denmark (May 22), Norway (May 30), France (May 31), Japan (June 16), Finland (August 16). It was even released in Colombia, in May 1969.

67. Faldini and Fofi (1981), 403.

68. Carlo Lizzani, *Attraverso il Novecento* (Turin: Lindau, 1998), 226.

Chapter Seven

1. "Elio Petri a Milano parla dei film che farà," *Corriere della Sera*, 22 February 1967.

2. The 23-page file titled "Appunti per *L'italiana*" is retained in the Elio Petri fund (AMNC, ELPE0049).

3. A.F. [Angelo Falvo], "Nostra signora metedrina [sic]," *Corriere d'Informazione*, 22–23 February 1967.

4. "Mastroianni: nuovo contratto," *Corriere della Sera*, 11 April 1967.

5. Maccario, "Petri farà un film sui rapporti familiari."

6. "Elio Petri a Milano parla dei film che farà."

7. AMNC, ELPE0058.

8. A few years later Lucio Fulci would direct *All'onorevole piacciono le donne* (1972), a satire on the DC starring Lando Buzzanca which underwent many troubles with the rating board due to its allusions to Christian Democrat politicians.

9. Elio Petri, letter to Ilya Lopert; letter to Alberto Grimaldi, 4 October 1968 (AMNC, ELPE0240; ELPE0283).

10. Gili (1974), 28.

11. Retained in the Elio Petri fund (ELPE0052; ELPE0053; ELPE0055).

12. *Ibid.*

13. A two-page sketch exists, dated Torvaianica, 4 September 1967 (AMNC, ELPE0054).

14. Elio Petri, letter to Erich Linder, April/May 1967 (AMNC, ELPE0239).

15. "Carroll Baker in Italia farà "La luna di miele," *Corriere d'Informazione*, 22–23 August 1967.

16. Elio Petri, letter to Leonardo Sciascia, Torvaianica, 4 September 1967 (AMNC, ELPE0245).

17. Luigi Lanzillotta, letter to Elio Petri, 2 May 1968 (AMNC, ELPE0274).

18. Sarah Khan, "Films For Friends. An interview with German director Christian Petzold," www.frieze.com. 27 August 2014.

19. Faldini and Fofi (1981), 404.

20. Caddeo, *Journey Into Madness*.

21. Gili (1974), 63.

22. "Storia di fantasmi per Vanessa Redgrave," *Corriere della Sera*, 28 March 1968.

23. l.m., "Vanessa, stringendosi a Franco Nero, si proclama "impegnata" e pacifista," *La Stampa*, 2 April 1968.

24. AMNC, ELPE0019; ELPE0020.

25. Elio Petri, letter to Anatole Dauman, uncertain dating (AMNC, ELPE0298).

26. Tassone, 249.

27. Scene 32, page 24 of the outline of the 1962 version (AMNC, ELPE0018)

28. Gili (1974), 59.

29. *Ibid.*, 62.

30. Petri actually shot a scene depicting the happening Flavia mentions early in the film, on July 8. In a telegram sent the next day to Grimaldi, he pointed out that he did it only to oblige to the producer's economic interests, despite his own professional disgust for the "sinister faces ... gathered for the occasion." He added that after watching the footage he would decide whether to keep the scene or not. Elio Petri, telegram to Alberto Grimaldi, Rome, 9 July 1968 (AMNC, ELPE0277). The happening is not in the film.

31. Tassone, 249.

32. The bi-weekly *Supersex* revolved around the adventures of the eponymous intergalactic pilot whose starship crashes on our planet. In order to survive, Supersex has to move from one human body to the next. Also, in order to discharge his exceeding vital energy, he has to have sexual intercourse. First published in June 1967, *Supersex* lasted only until mid-1968. Eight years later it reappeared in a hardcore version starring French porn actor Gabriel Pontello.

33. Valerio Mattioli, "Roma 60. Viaggio alle radici dell'underground italiano. Parte seconda," *Blow Up* #188, January 2014, 66.

34. De Rosa, 205.

35. Pegoraro Petri, "Una non-presentazione," 10.

36. Alberto Grimaldi, telegram to Elio Petri, Rome, 11 November 1968; Elio Petri, telegram to Alberto Grimaldi, Rome, 12 November 1968 (AMNC, ELPE0287; ELPE0288).

37. Alberico Sala "Pittore degli spiriti," *Corriere d'Informazione*, 23–24 November 1968.

38. Giovanni Grazzini, "Un tranquillo posto di campagna," *Corriere della Sera*, 23 November 1968.

39. *Ibid.*

40. l.p. [Leo Pestelli], "La follia del pittore informale," *La Stampa*, 6 December 1968.

41. r.a. [Roberto Alemanno], "Un tranquillo posto di campagna," *Cinema 60* #70, 1968, 45–47: 46.

42. E.B. [Edoardo Bruno], *Filmcritica* 193, December 1968, 551.

43. The other films awarded the Silver Bear were *Brasil año 2000* (Walter Lima, Jr.), *Greetings* (Brian De Palma), *Made in Sweden* (John Bergenstraahle) and *Ich bin ein Elephant, Madame* (Peter Zadek).

44. "Volatile Vanessa," *Playboy* vol. 16 #4, April 1969, 101–103.

45. Richard Gertner, "A Quiet Place in the Country," *Motion Picture Daily*, 31 August 1970.

46. Gordon Cow, "A Quiet Place in the Country," *Films and Filming*, vol. 17 no. 10, July 1971, 57.

47. Gili (1974), 60.

Chapter Eight

1. The short film is retained at the AAMOD (Archivio Audiovisivo del Movimento Operaio e Democratico) and can be watched online at http://patrimonio.aamod.it/.

2. Michel Tournier, letter to Elio Petri, Choisel, 11 March 1969 (AMNC, ELPE0303).

3. Michel Tournier, letter to Elio Petri, Choisel, 9 December 1969 (AMNC, ELPE0314).

4. Pirro (2001), 51–52.

5. *Ibid.*, 52.

6. Luca Pallanch, "Il prezzo della gloria. Conversazione con Federico Pantanella," in Domenico Monetti and Luca Pallanch (eds.), *Il caso Tretti* (Bari: Rubbettino, 2015), 110. Pantanella's quotes come from this interview.

7. Vincenzo Buonassisi, "Assegnate le "Grolle d'oro" alla Vitti, a Ferzetti e Nelo Risi," *Corriere della Sera*, 6 July 1969.

8. Pirro (2001), 60.

9. Buonassisi, "Assegnate le "Grolle d'oro" alla Vitti, a Ferzetti e Nelo Risi."

10. Guido Guidi, "Scirè, l'ex capo della Mobile di Roma arrestato per lo scandalo delle bische," *Stampa Sera*, 2 June 1969.

11. Gili (1974), 109.

12. "Volontè torna al cinema," *Corriere d'Informazione*, 22–23 August 1969.

13. Pirro (2001), 62.

14. Capozzoli, 156–157.

15. Marina Cicogna interviewed, in Mondella, 183.

16. Guy Braucourt, "Entretien avec Gian Maria Volonté," *Ecran 72*, #6, June 1972, 22.

17. Paolo Biondani, "Freda e Ventura erano colpevoli," *Corriere della Sera*, 11 June 2005.

18. Fioravanti (b. 1958) had been a popular child actor, his most notable appearance being in TV series such as *La famiglia Benvenuti* (1968). He also starred alongside Edwige Fenech in the cult erotic comedy *Grazie... nonna* (1975, Marino Girolami).

19. Gili (1974), 65.

20. Faldini and Fofi (1984), 60.

21. Tassone, 275.

22. Capozzoli, 158.

23. "Tutto incerto," *Corriere della Sera*, 8 February 1970.

24. "Inchiesta giudiziaria sull'ultimo film di Petri," *Corriere della Sera*, 17 February 1970.

25. "Il magistrato dice: 'Mi piace il film di Petri,'" *Corriere d'Informazione*, 17–18 February 1970.

26. "Perché il film di Petri non è denigratorio," *L'Unità*, 21 March 1970.

27. Pirro (2001), 69–70.

28. Adelio Ferrero, "Indagine su un film al di sotto di ogni sospetto," *Cinema nuovo* #204, March-April 1970.

29. Goffredo Fofi, "Due film "politici": Petri e Pontecorvo," *Quaderni Piacentini* #40, April 1970, 193–195.

30. C.Qu. [Claudio Quarantotto], "Indagine su un cittadino al di sopra di ogni sospetto," *Il Giornale d'Italia*, 21 February 1970.

31. Mino Argentieri, "Indagine su un cittadino al di sopra di ogni sospetto," *Rinascita*, 27 February 1970.

32. Giovanni Grazzini, "Indagine su un cittadino al di sopra di ogni sospetto," *Corriere della Sera*, 13 February 1970.

33. Gian Piero Brunetta, *Storia del cinema italiano. Dal miracolo economico agli anni novanta* (Rome: Editori Riuniti (1982) 2001), 272.

34. Gili, 65.

35. Alberto Tovaglieri, *La dirompente illusione. Il cinema italiano e il Sessantotto, 1965–1980* (Catanzaro: Rubbettino, 2014), 99.

36. *Ibid.*, 103.

37. Mino Argentieri, *I "grotteschi" di Elio Petri*, in Lino Micciché (ed.), *Il cinema del riflusso. Film e cineasti italiani degli anni '70* (Venice: Marsilio, 1997), 174.

38. Faldini and Fofi (1984), 60.

39. Gili (1974), 68.

40. Millicent Marcus, *Italian Film in the Light of Neorealism* (Princeton NJ: Princeton University Press, 1986), 279.

41. Capozzoli, 157–158.

42. Tovaglieri, 115.

43. *Ibid.*, 116. Petri explicitly distanced himself from the anarchist student: "I am for ... the systematic denunciation against every injustice, I'm not for the "so much, so worse" politics." Faldini and Fofi (1981), 61.

44. Lino Micciché, *Il cinema italiano degli anni '70. Cronache 1969–1979* (Venice: Marsilio, 1989), 56–57.

45. Adele Gallotti, "Un film sull'autunno caldo esce dalla "fabbrica" di Petri," *Stampa Sera*, 14 March 1970.

46. Paul Robinson, *The Freudian Left* (Ithaca, London: Cornell University Press, 1990), 233–234.

47. Mellen, 12.

48. Tassone, 250.

49. Angelo Maccario, "Mondanità in ribasso," *Corriere d'Informazione*, 4–5 May 1970.

50. Mellen, 11.

51. Braucourt, "Entretien avec Gian Maria Volonté," 22.

52. Micciché, *Il cinema italiano degli anni '70*, 58.

53. Capozzoli, 157.

54. Mellen, 11.

55. See Maurizio Grande, *Eros e politica: sul cinema di Bellocchio, Ferreri, Petri, Bertolucci, Taviani* (Siena: Protagon, 1995).

56. Giacomo Gambetti, "Petri: politico senza enigmi," *Cineforum* # 92/93, May-August 1970, 108.

57. Marcus, 269.

58. Gili (1974), 69.

59. *Ibid.*, 109.

60. De Rosa, 65.

61. *Ibid.*

62. *Ibid.*, 65–66.

63. Gili (1974), 73.

64. In 1968 several authors split from ANAC and created AACI (Associazione Autori Cinematografici), closer to the themes raised by the students' movement and more attentive to the strictly professional issues.

65. Luigi Diberti interviewed, in Mondella, 187.

66. The list goes as follows: "Signed: Age, Sergio Amidei, Alfredo Angeli, Nicola Badalucco, Mario Benocci, Bernardo Bertolucci, Mauro Bolognini, Tinto Brass, Franco Brusati, Alberto Caldana, Mario Carbone, Fabio Carpi, Liliana Cavani, Giuseppe Chiari, Luigi Comencini, Sergio Corbucci, Damiano Damiani, Giuseppe De Santis, Marco Ferreri, Pasquale Festa Campanile, Alberto Filippi, Marcello Fondato, Andrea Frezza, Ansano Giannarelli, Franco Giraldi, Ugo Gregoretti, Antonio Guerra, Luigi Kuiviller [Kuveiller], Aldo Lado, Carlo Lizzani, Franco Longo, Nanni Loy, Ruggero Maccari, Luigi Magni, Lorenzo Magnolia, Luigi Malerba, Ruggero Mastroianni, Enrico Medioli, Lino Micciché, Massimo Mida, Gianfranco Mingozzi, Mario Monicelli, Giuliano Montaldo, Valentino Orsini, Pier Paolo Pasolini, Elio Petri, Ugo Pirro, Gillo Pontecorvo, Maurizio Ponzi, Giulio Questi, Nelo Risi, Michele Romano, Francesco Rosi, Salvatore Samperi, Furio Scarpelli, Ettore Scola, Franco Solinas, Elda Tattoli, Paolo Taviani, Vittorio Taviani, Renato Tomasino, Florestano Vancini, Eriprando Visconti, Luchino Visconti, Piero Vivarelli, Gian Maria Volonté, Cesare Zavattini, Valerio Zurlini."

67. Gili (1974), 75.

68. "Il film di Petri non gradito a Cannes?" *Corriere della Sera*, 11 April 1970.

69. Giovanni Grazzini, "Cannes: gelato misto," *Corriere della Sera*, 4 May 1970.

70. Pirro (2001), 73.

71. *Ibid.*, 75.

72. *L'Avant Scène Cinéma* #111, February 1971.

73. Goffredo Fofi, "Conversation avec Elio Petri," *Positif* #126, April 1971, 39–50.

74. Robert Chazal, "*Enquete sur un citoyen au-dessus de tout soupçon*," *France Soir*, 19 October 1970.

75. Elio Petri interviewed, in the documentary *Elio Petri. Appunti su un autore*.

76. A.S. [Alberico Sala], "Colpo rovente," *Corriere della Sera*, 4 April 1970.

77. Alberto Pezzotta, *Regia Damiano Damiani* (Udine: Centro Espressioni Cinematografiche—Cinemazero, 2004), 226.

78. Alfonso Madeo, "Il cinema cerca un filone," *Corriere della Sera*, 14 November 1971.

79. Giovanni Grazzini, "Il braccio violento della legge," *Corriere della Sera*, 18 March 1972.

80. Argentieri, *I "grotteschi" di Elio Petri*, 174.

81. Steve Pond, "Dateline Hollywood," *The Washington Post*, 3 April 1986.

82. John J. Michalczyk, *The Italian Political Filmmakers* (London and Toronto: Associated University Presses, 1986), 222.

Chapter Nine

1. Guido Crainz, *Il paese mancato* (Rome: Donzelli, 2003), 323.

2. Sandro Bianchi (ed.) *Pio Galli. Da una parte sola. Autobiografia di un metalmeccanico* (Rome: manifestolibri, 1997), 147–148.

3. Law 20 May 1970, n. 300.

4. Ottaviano Del Turco, *La classe operaia va in paradiso*, in Pirro (1983), 72.

5. Gambetti, "Petri: politico senza enigmi," 106–107.

6. Danton J. Rissner, letter to Elio Petri, London, 8 June 1970 (AMNC, ELPE0346).

7. Si Litvinoff, letter to Paola Petri, London, 29 July 1970 (AMNC, ELPE0348).

8. Raphael Etkes, letter to Paola Petri, London, 3 September 1970 (AMNC, ELPE0353).

9. L.A. [Leonardo Autera] "Petri ha fiducia nel cinema d'oggi," *Corriere della Sera*, 12 February 1970.

10. A.F. [Angelo Falvo] "Petri: 'Il premio della bontà,'" *Corriere d'Informazione*, 12–13 February 1970.

11. Autera, "Petri ha fiducia nel cinema d'oggi."

12. *Ibid.*

13. Gambetti, "Petri: politico senza enigmi," 111.

14. L.Bo. [Lorenzo Bocchi] "Petri contestato a Parigi," *Corriere della Sera*, 3 June 1972.

15. Elio Petri, letter to Vladimir Kasaj, Rome, 27 May 1970 (AMNC, ELPE0343).

16. Pirro (2001), 83.

17. Gili (1974), 109.

18. *Ibid.*

19. Faldini and Fofi (1984), 83.

20. The shooting of Petri's film in Novara is the subject of a 2006 documentary, *La classe operaia va in paradiso. Retroscena di un film novarese*, by Serena Checcucci and Enrico Omodeo Salè.

21. Gili (1974), 82.

22. Pirro (2001), 89.

23. Michele Sancisi, *Tutto su Mariangela* (Milan: Bompiani, 2014), 112.

24. *Ibid.*, 113.

25. Mariangela Melato interviewed, in Mondella, 198.

26. Sansonna, 110.

27. "Veglia di protesta di operai e attori," *Corriere della Sera*, 31 December 1970.

28. Gian Vallini, "Volonté in provincia: ma è un divo?" *Corriere d'Informazione*, 9–10 February 1971.

29. Capozzoli, 167.

30. Braucourt, "Entretien avec Gian Maria Volonté," 22.

31. Ugo Pirro, *Ritratto privato*, in Pirro (1983), 17.

32. Pirro (2001), 83. The episode was confirmed by Claudio Mancini: Federico Caddeo, *The Middle-Class Communist*, interview with Claudio Mancini, extra featurette in the Arrow BD/DVD *Property Is No Longer a Theft*.

33. Marina Cicogna interviewed, in Mondella, 182.

34. "Tutti al lavoro," *Corriere d'Informazione*, 3–4 February 1971.

35. Gian Vallini, "Volonté in provincia: ma è un divo?"

36. Pirro (2001), 83–84.

37. A.P. "Il film 'segreto' di Elio Petri," *Corriere della Sera*, 26 March 1971.

38. Judith Crist, "The Year the Village Idiots Took Over," *New York*, 4 January 1971, 55.

39. "Investigation of a Citizen Above Suspicion," *Show*, July 1971, 58.

40. Stanley Kauffmann, "Investigation of a Citizen Above Suspicion," *The New Republic*, 23 January 1971.

41. "Investigation of a Citizen Above Suspicion," *Films in Review*, February 1971, 103.

42. Daniel Taradash, telegram to Elio Petri, Los Angeles, 6 March 1971 (AMNC, ELPE0368).

43. "Petri: 'La mia denuncia vale anche in America'" *Corriere d'Informazione*, 16–17 April 1971.

44. Caddeo, *The Middle-Class Communist*.

45. Del Turco, *La classe operaia va in paradiso*, in Pirro (1983), 73.

46. "Contestata la Biennale," *Corriere della Sera*, 10 February 1970.

47. "Polemica sui festival tra Petri e Visconti," *Corriere della Sera*, 10 October 1971.

48. *Ibid.*

49. Giovanni Grazzini, "Antonioni nella "spirale,"" *Corriere della Sera*, 12 December 1971.

50. Elio Petri, letter to Marco Ferronato, Rome, 13 September 1971 (AMNC, ELPE0388).

51. Tassone, 275. Some reported a slightly different version. According to *Cinema 60*, "in Porretta Terme, a young man with no brains proposed, a year ago, that *La classe operaia va in paradiso* be burned." "Contestazioni di comodo," *Cinema 60* #93, September-October 1973, 8. Still, film critic Alfredo Rossi, who was among the audience on that evening, confirmed it was Straub himself who took the microphone on that occasion, adding: "I, who was there, was hysterically on his side, that of the fire." Alfredo Rossi, *Ricordo di Elio*, in Mondella, 114.

52. Elio Petri, letter to Alfredo Rossi, 21 March 1978, in Pegoraro Petri and Basano, 38.

53. Micciché, *Il cinema italiano degli anni '70*, 101.

54. Gili (1974), 24.

55. Mellen, 10.

56. In Cavallone's film, a woman (Dirce Funari) is kept locked in a cage. She fills up Marlboro packets and Coca-Cola cans with her excrements and receives vacuum canned junk food and cigarettes in exchange. See Curti, *Mavericks of Italian Cinema*, 61.

57. Faldini and Fofi (1984), 82.

58. Gili (1974), 81.

59. Jean A. Gili, *Elio Petri & le cinéma italien* (Annecy: Rencontres du Cinéma Italien d'Annecy, 1996), 110.

60. Mellen, 10.

61. *Ibid.*, 12.

62. Sancisi, 116.

63. Gili (1974), 33.

64. Mino Monicelli, *Cinema italiano: ma cos'è questa crisi?* (Bari: Laterza, 1979), 153.

65. Caddeo, *The Middle-Class Communist*.

66. Gili (1974), 79.

67. *Ibid.*

68. *Ibid.*

69. Petri, *"Perché non ci vediamo mai?,"* 221.

70. Mellen, 10.

71. De Rosa, 67–68.

72. Lietta Tornabuoni, "Elio Petri: 'Le mie sequenze non sono oscene, né sensuali,'" *La Stampa*, 21 October 1973.

73. Giovanni Grazzini, "La classe operaia va in paradiso," *Corriere della Sera*, 18 September 1971.

74. Lino Micciché, "Cinéma italien 1971," *Ecran 72* #6, June 1972, 6.

75. "Lulù Massa e Superman. Un pezzo un film ... (su Petri)," *Ombre Rosse* #2, 1971, 76.

76. Goffredo Fofi, "La classe operaia va in paradiso," *Quaderni Piacentini* #44/45, October 1971, 261.

77. Braucourt, "Entretien avec Gian Maria Volonté," 22.

78. r.a. [Roberto Alonge], r.r. [Roberta Rivero], "La classe operaia va in paradiso," *Cinema nuovo* #213, September-October 1971, 373.

79. Sandro Zambetti, "L'operaio a una dimensione," *Cineforum* #112, March 1972, 36.

80. Claudio Bisoni, *La de-autenticazione di uno stile: un caso di rimozione e occultamento delle questioni stilistiche nella cultura cinematografica italiana tra anni Sessanta e Settanta*, in Enrico Biasin, Giulio Bursi, Leonardo Quaresima (eds.), *Lo stile cinematografico/Film Style* (Udine: XIII Convegno internazionale di studi sul cinema, Forum, 2007), 327.

81. "Veglia per Valpreda davanti a Regina Coeli," *Corriere della Sera*, 6 January 1972.

82. "Il 'Puccini' di Visconti avrà il volto di Mastroianni," *Corriere della Sera*, 19 January 1972.

83. Angelo Maccario, "Scontri e polemiche nell'incontro con Petri," *Corriere della Sera*, 17 May 1972.

84. A.M. [Angelo Maccario] "La classe operaia fa discutere Cannes," *Corriere d'Informazione*, 17–18 May 1972.

85. Tassone, 273.

86. Michel Ciment, "Cannes 1972," *Positif* #140, July–August 1972, 32.

87. Gili (2000), 13.

88. Michalczyk, 226.

89. Mellen, 10.

90. Lietta Tornabuoni, "Tutti gli applausi per Petri ed i pronostici per Volonté," La Stampa, 17 May 1972.

91. Mellen, 10.

Chapter Ten

1. Angelo Maccario, "Scontri e polemiche nell'incontro con Petri," *Corriere della Sera*, 17 May 1972.

2. Tassone, 260.

3. Ennio Flaiano, "Epigrammi veneziani," *Corriere della Sera*, 3 September 1972.

4. Tassone, 260.

5. "Intrigo padronale ai danni della 'Cagna' di Ferreri," *L'Unità*, 18 August 1973.

6. Lietta Tornabuoni, "'Tutto va bene' ma c'è o non c'è?," *La Stampa*, 2 September 1972.

7. Alfonso Madeo, "Avventuroso viaggio di Volonté (aereo e yacht) per portare il film di Godard all'antifestival," *Corriere della Sera*, 1 September 1972.

8. Flaiano, "Epigrammi veneziani."

9. Alfonso Madeo, "La lunga notte polemica di Godard," *Corriere della Sera*, 3 September 1972.

10. Mellen, 13.

11. Pirro (2001), 99.

12. Mellen, 10.

13. Carlo Galimberti "Petri va a Berlino con un film "bomba." Vincerà di nuovo?" *Corriere della Sera*, 17 June 1973.

14. Pirro (2001), 100.

15. The script is entirely told from Total's point of view. After resigning from his job, he performs a few thefts (at a pharmacy, at a supermarket, where he finds himself surrounded by thieves) before setting his eyes on Anita, "an object owned by her proprietor, who purchased her from someone else, subtracting her from collective use." He "steals" Anita from the butcher (called Modesti in the script), but she demands commodities such as a TV. The butcher replaces Anita with another girl who looks just like her (called Anita II) and who turns out to be her sister. Gradually Total "becomes" the butcher. He and Anita move into the same building, in the apartment on the upper floor. So there are two similar couples: Total and Anita, and Modesti and Anita II. In the end the butcher manages to have Total framed and trapped by the police. The script ends with Total claiming that he has "three options": get killed, kill himself, or surrender to the police. "I think I'll choose the first one" is the punchline.

16. Gili (1974), 110.

17. Pirro (2001), 101.

18. Caddeo, *The Middle-Class Communist*.

19. Dino De Laurentiis, telegram to Elio Petri, Rome, 22 February 1972 (AMNC, ELPE0410). The telegram has two postmarks, one dating "22-2-1972" and the other "1973 feb 21/22" but the second seems less likely, for by then Petri was busy shooting *La proprietà*.

20. Pirro (2001), 102.

21. Elio Petri, letter to Claudio Mancini, Rome, 6 September 1972 (AMNC, ELPE0435).

22. Caddeo, *The Middle-Class Communist*.

23. Lietta Tornabuoni, "Brevi Incontri: Un ritratto italiano," *La Stampa*, 17 May 1973.

24. For the butcher's hairstyle, Petri took inspiration from plastic surgeon Lionello Ponti, a well-known public figure at the time. "Ponti had this gorgeous, wavy hair," recalls Pierantonio Mecacci, "it was like a grey hair sculpture. We got a photographer, took some pictures, and went to see Rocchetti to get the wig done." Caddeo, *The Best Man*.

25. Chiara Berie, "Nudi è meglio," *Panorama* #394. 8 November 1973.

26. A.M. [Alfonso Madeo], "Bevilacqua dirige Manfredi," *Corriere della Sera*, 7 April 1974.

27. Monicelli, 149.

28. Caddeo, *The Middle-Class Communist*.

29. Galimberti "Petri va a Berlino con un film 'bomba.' Vincerà di nuovo?"

30. Leonardo Autera, "Berlino scossa dal film di Petri," *Corriere della Sera*, 3 July 1973.

31. Leonardo Autera, "L'Orso di Berlino sceglie l'India," *Corriere della Sera*, 4 July 1973.

32. Francesco Savio, "Tre giorni a Berlino," *Il Mondo*, 19 July 1973.

33. Tassone, 259.

34. "Gian Luigi Rondi lascia la mostra," *Corriere della Sera*, 28 February 1973.

35. Pirro (2001), 107.

36. Alfonso Madeo, "Clima rovente alle 'Giornate di Venezia,'" *Corriere della Sera*, 5 September 1973.

37. Alfonso Madeo, "Sono un uomo indignato e nauseato. La provocazione l'ho voluta io!," *Corriere della Sera*, 5 September 1973.

38. Tassone, 260.

39. A.F. [Angelo Falvo] "L'ultimo film di Elio Petri messo sotto sequestro a Genova," *Corriere della Sera*, 19 October 1973.

40. Giuseppe Marzolla, "Il film di Elio Petri sequestrato a Genova," *L'Unità*, 19 October 1973.

41. Tornabuoni, "Elio Petri: "'Le mie sequenze non sono oscene, né sensuali."

42. "Non è osceno il film di Petri per il giudice veneziano," *Corriere d'Informazione*, 22–23 October 1973.

43. "Film di Elio Petri e di Sergio Citti ancora nei guai," *Corriere della Sera*, 24 October 1973.

44. "I critici contro il sequestro del film di Petri," *Corriere della Sera*, 20 October 1973.

45. Arrigo Benedetti "Provocazione e cinema," *Corriere della Sera*, 4 November 1973.

46. Berie, "Nudi è meglio."

47. Caddeo, *The Middle-Class Communist*.

48. The series featured other novelizations, such as Rafael Azcona's *La grande abbuffata* and Robert Weverka's *La stangata* (*The Sting*).

49. "Troppi spettatori bloccato Petri," *Corriere d'Informazione*, 27–28 November 1973.

50. Ag.Sa. [Aggeo Savioli], "Duello tra ladro e ricco nella giungla della città," *L'Unità*, 5 October 1973.

51. Lietta Tornabuoni, "Brevi incontri. Criticando la critica," *La Stampa*, 6 September 1973.

52. Natalia Aspesi, "Dopo avere diretto nove film potrei fare il falegname," *Il Giorno*, 6 September 1973.

53. Francesco Savio, "Caro Petri," *Il Mondo*, 18 October 1973.

54. UP [Ugo Pirro], "Quando il critico imita Lo Bello," *il manifesto*, 26 October 1973.

55. "Contestazioni di comodo," 8. Another lengthy article, signed by Gian Piero Dell'Acqua, returned to the debate in the following issue, before turning into an in-depth (and negative) review of the film, "all the more conventional whenever it tries not to be, covering itself with second and third-hand intellectualism. Repetitive and monotonous ... it is also difficult to read ... inside there is nothing or, if one must really take it for good, only real confusion

and real dismay..." Gian Piero Dell'Acqua, "Il puzzle di Petri," *Cinema 60* #94, November-December 1973, 1–3, 31–32.

56. Oreste Del Buono, "Come criticare chi critica i critici?," *L'Europeo*, 9 November 1973.

57. Giovanni Grazzini "Gli ingegneri delle anime servono a qualcosa," *Corriere della Sera*, 4 November 1973.

58. Leonardo Autera and Maurizio Porro, "Armistizio a Ferrara tra critici e registi," *Corriere della Sera*, 12 November 1974. The proceedings of the conference were published in 1976: Francesco Bolzoni (ed.), *Critici e autori: complici e/o avversari?* (Venice: Marsilio, 1976)

59. Tassone, 259.

60. Savioli, "Duello tra ladro e ricco nella giungla della città."

61. Gili (1974), 83.

62. *Ibid.*, 84.

63. Gili and Tassone, 164.

64. Faldini and Fofi (1984), 85.

65. Jean A. Gili, *La proprietà non è più un furto*, in Pirro (1983), 77.

66. Gili (1974), 87.

67. Pirro (2001), 102.

68. Louis-Ferdinand Céline, *Journey to the End of the Night*, translated by Ralph Manheim (New York:, New Directions Publishing, 2006), 166.

69. Caddeo, *The Middle-Class Communist.*

70. Tassone, 244.

71. Caddeo, *The Middle-Class Communist.*

72. Roberto Chiesi, *Oggetti crudeli. Appunti su "La proprietà non è più un furto"* in Mondella, 90.

73. Dario Giugliano, *Immagini del denaro: scambio, temporalità e dispendio nel cinema*, in *Rivista di Estetica* #46 (Turin: University of Turin, 2011), 67.

74. Elio Petri and Ugo Pirro, *La proprietà non è più un furto* (Milan: Bompiani, 1973), 30.

75. Total's uncontrollable itch evokes *Il prurito, ovverosia la vita è mistero*, the short film directed by Carlo Levi for the ill-fated *Documento mensile*. See Curti, *Mavericks of Italian Cinema*, 68.

76. Gili (1974), 95.

77. Chiesi, *Oggetti crudeli*, 91–92.

78. Giugliano, *Immagini del denaro: scambio, temporalità e dispendio nel cinema*, 72.

79. Gili (1974), 88.

80. Petri and Pirro, 164.

81. Pirro, *Ritratto privato*, 15.

82. Tornabuoni, "Elio Petri: 'Le mie sequenze non sono oscene, né sensuali.'"

83. Gili (1974), 110.

84. Berie, "Nudi è meglio."

85. Gili (1974), 90.

86. Pirro (2001), 103.

87. Valerio Riva, "Fra un super 8 e un super P 38," *L'Espresso* #19, 14 May 1978, 92.

88. Chiesi, *Oggetti crudeli*, 94.

89. Gili, *La proprietà non è più un furto*, 75.

90. See Paul van den Hoven, *Gold Mining. The Art of Rhetorical Discourse Analysis* (Xiamen: Xiamen University Press, 2016).

91. Gili (1974), 95.

92. Madeo, "Sono un uomo indignato e nauseato. La provocazione l'ho voluta io!"

Chapter Eleven

1. Madeo, "Sono un uomo indignato e nauseato la provocazione l'ho voluta io!."

2. *Ibid.*

3. AMNC, ELPE0072.

4. Elio Petri, letter to Mickey Knox, Aglientu, 21 July 1973 (AMNC, ELPE0439).

5. Gili and Tassone, 163–164.

6. Riva, "Fra un super 8 e un super P 38," 91. A copy of Vidal's outline is also retained in the Francesco Rosi fund at the AMNC (AMNC, ROSI0746). One of Rosi's unmade projects was a story about the killing of a Pope, *L'uomo che ha venduto il Papa*, dated 1984 (AMNC, ROSI0745). Rosi and Vidal collaborated on the script of *Dimenticare Palermo* (1990).

7. Angelo Dallagiacoma, letter to Elio Petri, Parma, 20 April 1974 (AMNC, ELPE0457).

8. Alfredo Rossi, *Elio Petri e il cinema politico italiano. La piazza carnevalizzata* (Milan-Udine: Mimesis, 2015), 127.

9. AMNC, ELPE0050.

10. The 81-page treatment for *Identification* (in French and not dated) is retained at the Elio Petri fund (AMNC, ELPE0071).

11. AMNC, ELPE0051; ELPE0059.

12. Manuel Scorza, letters to Elio Petri, Paris, 7 December 1973; 22 April 1974 (AMNC, ELPE0448; ELPE0458).

13. Dmitri Nabokov, letter to Elio Petri, Monza, 7 December 1974 (AMNC, ELPE0471).

14. Angelo Falvo, "Non è morto e ha detto che delusione," *Corriere d'Informazione*, 4–5 November 1974.

15. Angelo Mastronardi, note to Elio Petri, 6 August 1974 (AMNC, ELPE0465).

16. "Moro con gli allievi alla seduta della Corte Costituzionale," *Corriere d'Informazione*, 22–23 January 1975.

17. See Leonardo Sciascia, *Nero su nero* (Milan: Adelphi, 1991), 64–65.

18. Giovanni Giuga, "Non obbedisco a niente e a nessuno," *La Fiera Letteraria* #28, 14 July 1974, 14.

19. Italo Calvino, *Lettere 1940–1985* (Milan: Mondadori, 2000), 1252–1253.

20. Antonio Maria Di Fresco, "Un romanzo sui democristiani," *L'Europeo*, 16 January 1975, 53.

21. Carlo Galimberti, "Rosi e Sciascia in tandem contro il marcio del potere," *Corriere della Sera*, 8 April 1975.

22. Paolo Squillacioti, *Note ai testi*, in Leonardo Sciascia, *Opere. Vol. I* (edited by Paolo Squillacioti) (Milan: Adelphi, 2012), 1897.

23. Leonardo Sciascia, "il mio *Todo modo* e quello del film," *L'Ora*, 5–6 May 1976.

24. Crainz, *Il paese mancato*, 526.

25. "Desiderio di novità," *Corriere della Sera*, 17 June 1975.

26. "Una vittoria troppo grande," *Corriere della Sera*, 18 June 1975.

27. Sandro Magister, "Storia di un leader," *L'Espresso* #19 (year 24), 14 May 1978, 15.

28. Memorandum of conversation dated August 1, 1975 at the Finlandia Hall in Helsinki, between the U.S. President Ford, Secretary Henry Kissinger, Assistant Secretary Hartman, Counselor Sonnenfeldt, Italian Prime Minister Moro, Foreign Minister Mariano Rumor, Secretary General Manzini and Diplomatic Adviser, Francesco Vallauri.

29. See the cover tagline of *L'Espresso*, "Fra bombe, incendi, inflazione si va alle elezioni più drammatiche della nostra storia," *L'Espresso*, 18 April 1976.

30. Elio Petri, letter to Jean A. Gili, Rome, 16 December 1974 (AMNC, ELPE0472).

31. Elio Petri, *Todo modo: Une comptabilité obsessionnelle*, in Petri and Gili (2013), 255.

32. Tassone, 252.

33. Jean A. Gili, *A Meeting with Elio Petri*, in Gili (2000), 49.

34. Petri, *Todo modo: Une comptabilité obsessionnelle*, 256.

35. Tassone, 252.

36. Petri, *Todo modo: Une comptabilité obsessionnelle*, 257.

37. Elio Petri, notes on *Todo modo*, 27 May 1975 (AMNC, ELPE0039).

38. Rossi (1979), 98.

39. Lina Coletti, "L'inferno usato come ricatto," *L'Europeo*, 5 December 1975, 96.

40. Caddeo, *The Middle-Class Communist*.

41. Pirro (2001), 118.

42. Quoted in Rossi (2015), 131.

43. Elio Petri, letter to Daniele Senatore, Rome, 12 August 1975 (AMNC, ELPE0487).

44. Caddeo, *Journey Into Madness*.

45. *Ibid.*

46. *Ibid.*

47. See also Fulvio Fulvi, "La mia vita? Un'avventura da Padre Pio a Hollywood, *Avvenire*, 21 August 2010; and Marina Paglieri, "Franco Nero film a Torino," *Repubblica*, 2 February 2019.

48. "Ursula proibita," *Corriere d'Informazione*, 9–10 August 1975.

49. Carlo Galimberti "Volonté operaio ribelle in Cile," *Corriere della Sera*, 20 July 1975.

50. Giovanna Grassi "Faccio politica ma col cinema," *Corriere d'Informazione*, 13 December 1975.

51. *Ibid.*

52. Gili and Tassone, *Parigi-Roma. 50 anni di coproduzioni italo-francesi*, 161.

53. "Volontè e Mastroianni nelle catacombe," *Corriere della Sera*, 12 December 1975.

54. Gili, *A Meeting with Elio Petri*, 52.

55. "Ferme le troupes cinematografiche," *Corriere della Sera*, 28 January 1976.

56. "Festival di Cannes gioca al rilancio," *Corriere della Sera*, 18 February 1976.

57. G. Gs. [Giovanna Grassi] "Per Cannes un'orgia di celluloide," *Corriere della Sera*, 5 March 1976.

58. Mario Luzzi, *Charlie Mingus* (Milan: Lato Side, 1983), 99.

59. Susan Graham and Charles Mingus, letter to Elio Petri, New York, 15 January 1976 (AMNC, ELPE0490).

60. *Ibid.*, 100.

61. d.g. [David Grieco], "Le prime: Charlie Mingus," *L'Unità*, 25 March 1976.

62. Bianchi judged Mixon "absolutely unfit" for the band during the Rome gigs (Luzzi, *Charlie Mingus*, 99) and according to reviews of the show even Mingus was uncomfortable with him. See Marcello Piras, "Concerti," *Musica Jazz*, May 1976.

63. Filippo Bianchi, "Mingus e *Todo modo*: storia di un fallimento," *Musica Jazz* #10 (year 60), October 2004, 68.

64. As Stefano Zenni argued, the choice was first rate: Del Bono and Sabatelli were first oboe and first bassoon at Opera Theatre Orchestra of Rome, Maltoni and Piana came from RAI National Radio Orchestra. Piana, a great jazz soloist, was a master of Italian jazz since the Fifties and one of the unsung heroes of valve trombone.

65. "It was Mingus' rebirth, because before that he lived like a homeless person in the streets of New York. Anyway, after a couple of lessons he practically antagonized everyone, I was the only one who stayed. I can't say it was a real composition course, because, well... for about 40 minutes he didn't speak, if he felt like it he sat on the piano and played something. In the end he gave you homework." Federico Sardo, "Al centro del suono: intervista a Roberto Laneri," www.noisey.vice.com, 22 September 2016.

66. *Ibid.*

67. Luzzi, 101.

68. *Ibid.*

69. The episode is recollected by Stefano Zenni, who intervened as guest during the same program. Mingus' appearance in Arbore's popular Sunday afternoon TV show *L'altra Domenica* during his stay in Italy seems to confirm Arbore's version that on the contrary he supported the musician. During the show Gianni Minà interviewed Mingus and asked him how his jazz music could be a good match for *Todo modo*. He replied jokingly: "Because I'm Italian! My music is Italian ... it's very emotional music."

70. In an interview dating a couple of years later, Mingus recalled the experience, still unaware that Petri hadn't used his music in the film. He claimed that it had been *Revelations* that had convinced the Italians to hire him to write the score, and that they were enthusiastic about the result. Arnold Jay Smith, "Charles Mingus: Developmental Changes," *Down Beat*, 12 January 1978, 22.

71. Krin Gabbard, *Better Git It in Your Soul: An Interpretive Biography of Charles Mingus* (Berkeley, CA: University of California Press, 2016), 98. Unfortunately, when working on the liner notes of the album, Filippo Bianchi forgot to add Maurino's name to the personnel list. So his name doesn't appear in the LP issue nor in the CD reissue, nor in any discographic source.

72. Sue Mingus, personal email to Stefano Zenni.

73. Lietta Tornabuoni, "Incontri: Il "dibattito,"" *Corriere della Sera*, 6 March 1976.

74. *Ibid.*

75. Lietta Tornabuoni, "Questo film non piace al partito. Rimandiamolo a dopo le elezioni," *Corriere della Sera*, 26 April 1976.

76. *Ibid.*

77. *Ibid.*

78. "Dicono i produttori: il film *Todo modo* non sarà ritirato," *Corriere della Sera*, 27 April 1976.

79. Franco Occhiuzzi, "De Laurentiis smentisce Petri," *Corriere della Sera*, 29 April 1976.

80. Lietta Tornabuoni, "Incontri: La calma," *Corriere della Sera*, 1 May 1976.

81. *Ibid.*

82. "Per *Todo modo* denunciato il regista Petri," *Corriere della Sera*, 25 June 1976. *Cadaveri eccellenti* had underwent a similar charge a month earlier. "Denunciato per vilipendio *Cadaveri eccellenti*," *Cinema d'Oggi* #18, 3 May 1976, 3.

83. Giovanni Conso, "Nel film di Elio Petri vilipendio a Moro?," *La Stampa*, 27 June 1976.

84. Crainz, *Il paese mancato*, 542.

85. Elio Petri, letter to Jean A. Gili, Rome, 26 July 1976 (AMNC, ELPE0500).

86. "Lettere al Corriere," *Corriere della Sera*, 21 May 1976.

87. "Cattivo, peggiore, pessimo: democristiano!" *L'Espresso* #20, 16 May 1976.

88. Lino Miccichè, "Todo modo," *Avanti!*, 1 May 1976.

89. Ottavio Rossani, "Per *Todo modo* Sciascia a suo modo," *Corriere d'Informazione*, 28 April 1976.

90. Francesco Savio, "Lettera di commiato a Elio Petri," *Il Mondo*, 20 May 1976.

91. V. [Vanna] Barenghi, "Intervista a Bartolo Ciccardini," *La Repubblica*, 8 May 1976.

92. Carlo Benedetti, "Il cinema di oggi in un convegno italo-sovietico," *L'Unità*, 20 October 1976.

93. Ernesto Baldo, "Hanno lodato il mio film ma poi lo sequestreranno," *La Stampa*, 30 April 1976.

94. "Volontè e Mastroianni nelle catacombe."

95. Rossi (2015), 127.

96. "Cattivo, peggiore, pessimo: democristiano!"

97. Robert Coles, "A Bullitt to Wilson," *The New Republic*, 28 January 1967.

98. Petri, *Todo modo: Une comptabilité obsessionnelle*, 256.

99. Lina Coletti, "L'inferno usato come ricatto," *L'Europeo*, 5 December 1975, 94.

100. Gili, *A Meeting with Elio Petri*, 52. Speaking of *Salò*'s critical reception with Gili, Petri was trenchant against the critics: "Pasolini died and they hurried to see the film…. They hurried to write. And so they simultaneously dissected the film and the man Pasolini. They confused the life of Pasolini with the film by doing revolting, truly revolting things." *Ibid.*, 51.

101. Pier Paolo Pasolini, "Cos'è questo golpe? Io so," *Corriere della Sera*, 14 November 1974.

102. Tornabuoni, "Questo film non piace al partito. Rimandiamolo a dopo le elezioni."

103. Alberto Stabile, "Bravo Petri, il tuo è un film pasoliniano," *La Repubblica*, 5 May 1976.

104. Alberto Moravia, "Appello per salvare il *Salò* di Pasolini," *Corriere della Sera*, 22 January 1977.

105. Umberto Rossi, "Ci rimproverate ma non ci avete mai difeso," *Cinemasessanta* #144, March–April 1982, 38.

106. Faldini and Fofi (1984), 278.

107. Elio Petri, *Todo modo. Interview with Simon Mizrahi*, in Petri and Gili (2013), 282.

108. Tassone, 278.

109. Frederic William Hawkins, *Annals of the French Stage from its Origin to the Death of Racine. Vol I* (London: Chapman and Hall, 1884), 15.

110. Tornabuoni, "Questo film non piace al partito. Rimandiamolo a dopo le elezioni."

111. Coletti, "L'inferno usato come ricatto," 94.

112. *Ibid.*, 95.

113. Tassone, 270.

114. Hochkofler, 117.

115. Malcom Pagani, "Marcello (Mastroianni) amore mio," *Vanity Fair* #25, 19 June 2018.

116. Petri, *Todo modo: Une comptabilité obsessionnelle*, 257.

117. *Ibid.* I adjusted the original, less faithful translation, "Are they right-wing demons?"

118. Coletti, "L'inferno usato come ricatto," 94.

Chapter Twelve

1. Enrico Berlinguer, *Austerità. Occasione per trasformare l'Italia* (Rome: Editori Riuniti, 1977), 18.

2. "Missiroli chiama Elio Petri a Torino," *Corriere della Sera*, 24 September 1976.

3. Jack Nicholson, letter to Elio Petri and Daniele Senatore, Beverly Hills, 9 November 1976 (AMNC, ELPE0501).

4. See Curti, *Mavericks of Italian Cinema*, 105.

5. "Jack Nicholson nel nuovo film di Petri," *Corriere della Sera*, 9 February 1977.

6. AMNC, ELPE0063.

7. Maurizio Berté, "Dopo 7 anni ripeto la mia denuncia contro il potere," *Corriere d'Informazione*, 13 December 1977.

8. AMNC, ELPE0528.

9. Rossi (2015), 143.

10. Tassone, 276.

11. "Tre donne per Altman," *Corriere d'Informazione*, 12 May 1977.

12. Luigi Irdi, "Campo de' Fiori: l'assassino è Claudio Volonté," *Corriere della Sera*, 28 July 1977.

13. "Claudio Volonté s'è ucciso in prigione," *Corriere della Sera*, 17 September 1977.

14. "Funerali solo civili per Claudio Volonté" *Corriere della Sera*, 21 September 1977.

15. Quoted in *Cineforum* #80, December 1968.

16. Franco Scaglia, "Il regista: ecco chi ha le mani sporche," *Radiocorriere TV* #46, 12–18 November 1978, 31.

17. Carlo Galimberti, "Marco Polo, Caruso e il Duce in TV," *Corriere della Sera*, 10 April 1978.

18. The project is discussed in a letter to a non-specified "Jean-Pierre," dating before August 1977 (AMNC, ELPE0512). The story of Dr. Petiot had inspired the British film *Seven Thunders* (1957, Hugo Fregonese).

19. *Ibid.*

20. Elio Petri, letter to Massimo Fichera, Milan, 15 March 1978 (AMNC, ELPE0526).

21. Lietta Tornabuoni, "Sartre sul video con *Le mani sporche,*" *Corriere della Sera,* 30 December 1977.

22. Jean-Paul Sartre, *Morti senza tomba / Le mani sporche* (Milan: Mondadori, 1966), 149.

23. Tassone, 267.

24. Ronald Aronson, *Camus and Sartre: The Story of a Friendship and the Quarrel that Ended It* (Chicago: University of Chicago Press, 2004), 167.

25. Tornabuoni, "Sartre sul video con *Le mani sporche.*"

26. Faldini and Fofi (1984), 405.

27. Paolo Valmarana, *Le mani sporche,* in Pirro (1983), 83.

28. Elio Petri, letter to Alfredo Rossi, 21 March 1978, in Rossi (2015), 185.

29. Tassone, 266.

30. Jean de Baroncelli, "*Todo modo* de Petri: Un film de combat," *Le Monde,* 23–24 January 1977.

31. "Mastroianni si butta nel groviglio di Sartre," *Corriere della Sera,* 14 November 1978.

32. Leonardo Autera, "Giornate particolari di Mastroianni," *Corriere della Sera,* 1 April 1978.

33. Elio Petri, letter to Alfredo Rossi, 21 March 1978, Rossi (2015), 185.

34. Daniele Senatore, letter to Elio Petri, New York, 9 April 1978 (ANMC, ELPE0527).

35. Fernaldo Di Giammatteo, "Elio Petri, furore e inquietudine," *Radiocorriere TV #5,* 29 January-4 February 1978, 32.

36. Mastroianni and Tatò, *Mi ricordo, sì, io mi ricordo,* 56.

37. Ernesto Baldo, "Mastroianni-Petri coppia inedita in TV," *Radiocorriere TV #3,* 15–21 January 1978, 5.

38. Faldini and Fofi (1984), 404.

39. Ignazio Senatore, *Io, Giuliana De Sio* (Naples: Guida Editore, 2017), 13.

40. Faldini and Fofi (1984), 404.

41. Carlo Brusati, "Noschese: quasi 3 milioni per 5 minuti di trasmissione," *Corriere d'Informazione,* 18 April 1978.

42. Elio Petri, letter to Alfredo Rossi, 21 March 1978, Rossi (2015), 185.

43. Giuseppe Tornatore and Ennio Morricone, *Ennio. Un maestro* (Milan: HarperCollins Italia, 2018).

44. Autera, "Giornate particolari di Mastroianni."

45. *Ibid.*

46. Valmarana, *Le mani sporche,* 84.

47. Mastroianni and Tatò, *Mi ricordo, sì, io mi ricordo,* 56.

48. Lietta Tornabuoni, "Moro, terribile fantasma," *La Stampa,* 28 March 1982.

49. Pierre Billard, "Un cinema au-dessus de tout soupcon," *Le Point #293,* 1 May 1978, 97.

50. Riva, "Fra un super 8 e un super P 38," 84.

51. Francesco Rosi, "Ma questo Billard va a caccia di streghe," *L'Espresso #19,* 14 May 1978, 87.

52. Riva, "Fra un super 8 e un super P 38," 89.

53. *Ibid.,* 92.

54. *Ibid.,* 97.

55. Valmarana, *Le mani sporche,* 83.

56. Tassone, 266.

57. "La storia dal buco della serratura," *L'Unità,* 21 November 1978.

58. Tassone, 266.

59. Lucio Colletti, *Un dramma, la politica e l'etica,* in AA.VV., *Le mani sporche,* RAI-Radio Televisione Italiana, Appunti dell'ufficio stampa #90, August-September 1978.

60. Alberto Bevilacqua, "Due giovani nella morsa," *Corriere della Sera,* 15 November 1978.

61. Elio Petri, letter to Alfredo Rossi, late October 1978, in Rossi (2015), 192–193.

Chapter Thirteen

1. Tassone, 262.

2. *Ibid.,* 264.

3. Tommaso Di Ciaula, letter to Elio Petri, Rome, 6 November 1978 (AMNC, ELPE0532).

4. Werner Zeindler, letter to Elio Petri, Zurich, 15 January 1979 (AMNC, ELPE0539).

5. Elio Petri, letter to Jean A. Gili, 10 September 1978, in Gili (1996), 131.

6. The film was made in 1980 by Gianni Barcelloni Corte, starring Lara Wendel, Stefania Sandrelli and Vittorio Mezzogiorno, and released as *Desideria: la vita interiore,* to negative reviews.

7. Rossi (2015), 58.

8. Senatore, *Io, Giuliana De Sio,* 12.

9. Gianni Amelio interviewed, in Mondella, 177.

10. Tassone, 261.

11. *Ibid.,* 281.

12. Petri's declarations to Alfredo Rossi, April 1979, in Rossi (2015), 151–152.

13. *Ibid.,* 153.

14. Giancarlo Giannini, interview with Jean A. Gili, October 1987, in Gili (2000), 109.

15. *Ibid.*

16. Giancarlo Giannini interviewed, in *Da non aprire,* extra featurette in the Italian DVD of *Buone notizie.*

17. Tassone, 282.

18. M.Po. [Maurizio Porro], "Dottoressa Ombretta Colli, occhio a Giannini," *Corriere della Sera,* 6 April 1979.

19. Tassone, 282.

20. "Non c'è che da scegliere nel 'mucchio selvaggio,'" *L'Unità,* 22 August 1979.

21. Paola Pegoraro Petri interviewed, in *Da non aprire.*

22. Gianni Amelio interviewed, in Mondella, 178.

23. "Roma città chiusa per Petri e Giannini?," *Corriere d'Informazione,* 28 June 1979, 13. Throughout the interview, the film's title is misspelled as *La buona notizia.*

24. Victor Ciuffa, "Metti, sul viale del tramonto e senza pensione," *Corriere della Sera,* 4 September 1979.

25. Leonardo Autera "Il cinema è in crisi? Ma i

giovani sono bravi," *Corriere della Sera*, 12 October 1979.

26. Tassone, 282.

27. Giannini, interview with Jean A. Gili, 110.

28. *Ibid.*, 111.

29. Giovanni Grazzini, "Con Petri e Giannini black-out della ragione," *Corriere della Sera*, 23 December 1979.

30. Giannini, interview with Jean A. Gili, 111.

31. f.p. [Franco Prono], "Buone notizie," *Cinema nuovo #264*, April 1980, 57.

32. Lorenzo Pellizzari, "Buone notizie," *Cineforum #191*, January-February 1980, 69–71.

33. Alberto Moravia, "Un apriscatole per la vita," *L'Espresso*, 16 December 1979.

34. Alberto Pezzotta, "Il vaso di Pandora. *Buone notizie* di Elio Petri e la rappresentazione della sessualità nel cinema italiano degli anni '70," *L'Avventura* #2/2017, July-December 2017, 266.

35. Tassone, 282.

36. Andrée Tournès, "La propriété selon Elio Petri," *Jeune Cinéma #74*, November 1973, 23.

37. Tassone, 282.

38. *Ibid.*, 283.

39. Rossi (2015), 153.

40. l.t. [Lietta Tornabuoni], "Petri, la TV ci trasforma in monaci di clausura," *La Stampa*, 26 October 1979.

41. Pezzotta, *Il vaso di Pandora*, 269.

42. AMNC, ELPE0055.

43. Tornabuoni, "Petri, la TV ci trasforma in monaci di clausura."

44. Callisto Cosulich, *I sei della crisi*, in Vito Zagarrio (ed.), *Storia del cinema italiano. Vol. XIII, 1977–1986* (Venice-Rome: Marsilio, Edizioni di Bianco & Nero, 2005)

45. Elio Petri, *Todo Modo. Interview with Simon Mizrahi*, 283.

46. Giancarlo Giannini interviewed, in *Da non aprire*.

47. Incidentally, the man with the dog scaring the two friends in the Lungotevere is *not* Petri, despite what some have claimed.

48. Amelio interviewed, 178.

49. Maria Serena Palieri, "Con l'orologio di Miller non si arriva mai tardi," *L'Unità*, 9 October 1980.

50. Pezzotta, *Il vaso di Pandora*, 266–267.

51. *Ibid.*

52. Pezzotta, *Il vaso di Pandora*, 272.

53. Tassone, 248.

54. ANMC, ELPE0069.

55. Roberto Curti, *Tonino Valerii: The Films* (McFarland, Jefferson NC 2016), 49.

56. Riva, "Fra un super 8 e un super P 38," 97.

57. This is actually an existing book, Irwin M. Marcus and Francis John's *La masturbazione* (*Masturbation: From Infancy to Senescence*, 1975), published in Italy by Feltrinelli in 1979.

58. Giannini interviewed in *Da non aprire*.

59. Prono, "Buone notizie," 57.

60. Pezzotta, *Il vaso di Pandora*, 276.

61. For an in-depth discourse on the fear of castration in Italian cinema of the period, see Pezzotta, *Il vaso di Pandora*, 275.

62. AMNC, ELPE0050.

63. Faldini and Fofi (1984), 84.

Chapter Fourteen

1. Tassone, 279.

2. "Stavolta Elio Petri "indaga" sull'amore," *Corriere della Sera*, 7 December 1979.

3. Rossi (2015), 173.

4. Tassone, 268.

5. Such was the convention "Dopo il cinema, quale cinema" (After Cinema, What Cinema) at the Mostra Internazionale del Cinema Libero (International Festival of Free Cinema) in Porretta Terme. "Elio Petri difende la mostra di Porretta," *Corriere della Sera*, 17 December 1979.

6. The outline for *Autobus* was published posthumously in 1992 in *L'Unità*, with the subtitle *Il sogno di un autista* (A Driver's Dream) and then in *Un amore lungo. Tre inediti di Elio Petri* (Milan: Feltrinelli, 2006), an anthology collecting a trio of Petri's unfilmed projects—*Autobus*, *Ninni* and *Andamento stagionale*—sold with the documentary DVD *Elio Petri, Appunti su un autore*.

7. b.g., "Presentato il cartellone del Teatro Metastasio," *L'Unità*, 4 August 1979.

8. Gianni Migliorino, "Elio Petri debutta in teatro per Miller," *Corriere della Sera*, 18 September 1980.

9. Leslie Bennets, "Miller Revives 'American Clock' Amid Resonances of '30s," *The New York Times*, 14 July 1988.

10. Franco Occhiuzzi "Stop all'orologio di Miller," *Corriere della Sera*, 3 December 1980.

11. Palieri, "Con l'orologio di Miller non si arriva mai tardi."

12. Paolo Cervone, "Petri: 'Farò un giallo sul caso De Broglie,'" *Corriere della Sera*, 24 March 1982.

13. Aggeo Savioli, "L'orologio della storia si è fermato al 1929?," *L'Unità*, 25 January 1981.

14. Roberto De Monticelli "L'America odio-amore di Miller," *Corriere della Sera*, 24 January 1981.

15. "la Rete 2 "ruba" registi al cinema," *Corriere d'Informazione*, 3 August 1981.

16. The outline of the project (not dated) is retained in the Elio Petri fund (AMNC, ELPE0070).

17. Pirro, *Ritratto privato*, 17.

18. Vito Faenza, "Un delitto d'onore su commissione?," *L'Unità*, 10 October 1979.

19. The term (literally: small middle-class man) refers to Mario Monicelli's film *Un borghese piccolo piccolo*, about an average middle-class father (Alberto Sordi) whose son is shot before his eyes by a young bank robber. The elderly man pursues a nasty private revenge: he kidnaps the murderer and sadistically tortures him to death. Monicelli's film caused a fuss for its grim, hopeless depiction of a humanity devoid of any redeeming value.

20. e.b., "C'è anche una criminalità sommersa," *L'Unità*, 10 October 1979.

21. The full script is included in Elio Petri, *Un amore lungo. Tre inediti di Elio Petri*, 25–164.

22. "Fare un film per averne tre," *L'Unità*, 24 July 1979.

23. Franco Ferrini, *Sul mio lavoro con Elio*, in Rossi (2015), 210.

24. Palieri, "Con l'orologio di Miller non si arriva mai tardi."

25. *Screen International* #299, 4 July 1981, 9.

26. Ferrini, *Sul mio lavoro con Elio*, 211.

27. Sergio Donati, *C'era una volta il West (ma c'ero anch'io)* (Rome: Omero, 2007), 78–79.

28. Paolo Cervone, "C'è un intrigo internazionale con Tognazzi 'cieco' per Petri," *Corriere della Sera*, 12 October 1981.

29. "La notte di Petri," *Radiocorriere TV* #47, 22–28 November 1978, 219.

30. Elio Petri, letter to France Degand, Rome, 21 October 1981 (AMNC, ELPE0573).

31. "La notte di Petri."

32. Elio Petri, letter to France Degand, Rome, 21 October 1981.

33. Elio Petri, letter to Jean A. Gili, December 1981, in Gili (1996), 134.

34. "Wertmuller, Rosi, Damiani, Petri e altri nei progetti della Gaumont," *L'Unità*, 2 April 1982.

35. Cervone, "Petri: 'Farò un giallo sul caso De Broglie.'"

36. Elio Petri, letter to Jean A. Gili, December 1981, 134.

37. Cervone, "Petri: 'Farò un giallo sul caso De Broglie.'"

38. *Ibid.*

39. Elio Petri, letter to Jean A. Gili, December 1981, 133.

40. Goffredo Fofi, *Su Elio Petri, un ricordo*, in Rossi (2015), 207.

41. Faldini and Fofi (1984), 291.

42. Rossi, "Ci rimproverate ma non ci avete mai difeso," 40.

43. *Ibid.*

44. m.a. [Mino Argentieri], "Postilla," *Cinemasessanta* #144, March-April 1982, 40.

45. Elio Petri, "Indifferente la sinistra verso il nostro cinema," *Cinemasessanta* #146, July-August 1982, 8.

46. Giancarlo Giannini, interview with Jean A. Gili, October 1987, in Gili (2000), 110.

47. "Petri torna sul set," *Corriere della Sera*, 17 June 1982.

48. Maraini, 280.

49. Petri, *"Perché non ci vediamo mai?,"* 213–214.

50. Pirro (2001), 130.

51. Pirro, *Ritratto privato*, 18.

52. Faldini and Fofi (1984), 290.

53. Giuseppe De Santis, memorial letter, pronounced at the funeral of Elio Petri, 12 November 1982. In Gili (2000), 87.

54. Ugo Pirro, "Delitti misteriosi, spie e ciechi nel film di Petri rimasto nel cassetto," *Corriere della Sera*, 20 November 1982.

55. Renzo Vespignani, *Chi illumina la grande notte*, in Pirro (1983), 106.

56. Jean A. Gili, *A Meeting with Elio Petri*, in Gili (2000), 54.

57. Giovanni Berlinguer, "L'On. Agostino delle luci rosse," *L'Unità*, 25 May 1982.

58. ANMC, ELPE0559.

59. Tassone, 242.

60. Donati, 79.

61. Rossi (2015), 164.

62. Ferrini, *Sul mio lavoro con Elio*, 210–211.

63. Ferzan Ozpetek interviewed, in Mondella, 205.

64. Elio Petri, letter to Alfredo Rossi, 21 March 1978. In Rossi (2015), 185.

Bibliography

Books by Elio Petri

Petri, Elio. *Roma ore 11*. Rome: Edizioni Avanti!, 1956; Palermo: Sellerio, 2004.

Petri, Elio. *L'assassino*. Milan: Zibetti, 1961.

Petri, Elio. *Un amore lungo. Tre inediti di Elio Petri*. Milan: Feltrinelli, 2006 (Book + DVD).

Petri, Elio, and Ugo Pirro. *Indagine su un cittadino al di sopra di ogni sospetto*. Rome: Tindalo, 1970.

Petri, Elio, and Ugo Pirro. *La proprietà non è più un furto*. Milan: Bompiani, 1973.

Petri, Elio, and Jean A. Gili (ed.) *Scritti di cinema e di vita*. Rome: Bulzoni, 2007.

Petri, Elio, and Jean A. Gili (ed.), *Writings on Cinema & Life*. New York: Contra Mundum Press, 2013. [Note: English language version of *Scritti di cinema e di vita*, lacking the final correspondence between Petri and De Santis]

Interviews with Elio Petri

In Books

Faldini, Franca, and Goffredo Fofi. *L'avventurosa storia del cinema italiano raccontata dai suoi protagonisti: 1935-1959*. Milan: Feltrinelli, 1979.

Faldini, Franca, and Goffredo Fofi. *L'avventurosa storia del cinema italiano raccontata dai suoi protagonisti: 1960-1969*. Milan: Feltrinelli, 1981.

Faldini, Franca, and Goffredo Fofi. *Il cinema italiano d'oggi 1970-1984 raccontato dai suoi protagonisti*. Milan: Mondadori, 1984.

Maraini, Dacia. *E tu chi eri? 26 interviste sull'infanzia*. Milan: Rizzoli, 1998.

Tassone, Aldo. *Parla il cinema italiano. Volume secondo*. Milan: Il Formichiere, 1980.

In Film Magazines

Braucourt, Guy. "Entretien avec Elio Petri," *Cinéma* #150, November 1970.

Fofi, Goffredo. "Conversation avec Elio Petri." *Positif* #126, April 1971.

Gambetti, Giacomo. "Petri: politico senza enigmi." *Cineforum* # 92/93, May-August 1970

Gili, Jean A. "Entretien avec Elio Petri," *Ecran* #31, December 1974.

Gili, Jean A. "Entretien avec Elio Petri," *Ecran* #54, January 1977.

Gili, Jean A., and Christian Viviani, "Entretien avec Elio Petri," *Ecran* #6, June 1972.

Haustrate, Gaston. "Le cinema italien des années soixante," *Cinéma* #190-191, September-October 1974.

Haustrate, Gaston. "Entretien avec Elio Petri," *Cinéma* #168, July 1972.

Jego, Claude Pierre-André. "Entretien avec Elio Petri," *Cinématographe* #11, January 1975.

Manceaux, Michèle. "Entretien avec Elio Petri," *Cinéma* #151, December 1970.

Martin, Marcel. "Entretien avec Elio Petri," *Cinéma* #71, December 1962.

Mellen, Joan. "Cinema Is Not For an Elite But For the Masses': An Interview with Elio Petri." *Cinéaste*, Vol. 6, No. 1, 1973.

Rossi, Umberto. "Elio Petri: ci rimproverate, ma non ci avete mai difeso." *Cinema 60* #144, March/April 1982.

Tassone, Aldo, and Andrée Tournès. "L'enfer selon Petri: Bonnes nouvelles," *Jeune Cinéma* #129, September-October 1980.

Tournès, Andrée. "Entretien avec Elio Petri," *Jeune Cinéma* #74, November 1973.

Tournès, Andrée. "Entretien avec Elio Petri," *Jeune Cinéma* #98, October 1976.

Zalaffi, Nicoletta. "Entretien avec Elio Petri," *Image et Son—La Revue du Cinéma* # 292, January 1975.

Books on Elio Petri

Bisoni, Claudio. *Indagine su un cittadino al di sopra di ogni sospetto*. Turin: Lindau, 2011.

Cardone, Lucia. *Elio Petri, impolitico: La decima vittima*. Pisa: Edizioni ETS, 2005.

Di Martino, Anna, and Andrea Morini (eds.). *Elio Petri*. Bologna: I Quaderni del Lumière #11, February 1995.

Gili, Jean A. (ed.). *Elio Petri*. Nice: Faculté des Lettres et Sciences Humaines, 1974.

Gili, Jean A. *Elio Petri & le cinéma italien*. Annecy: Rencontres du Cinéma Italien d'Annecy, 1996.

Gili, Jean A. (ed.). *Elio Petri*. Rome: Cinecittà Holding, 2000.

Mondella, Diego (ed.). *L'ultima trovata. Trent'anni di cinema senza Elio Petri*. Bologna: Pendragon, 2013.

Pegoraro Petri, Paola, and Roberta Basano (eds.). *Lucidità inquieta. Il cinema di Elio Petri*, Turin: Museo Nazionale del Cinema, 2007.

Pirro, Ugo (ed.). *Elio Petri*. Venice: La Biennale—XL Mostra Internazionale del Cinema, 1983.

Pirro, Ugo. *Il cinema della nostra vita*. Turin: Lindau, 2001.

Rigola, Gabriele (ed.). *Elio Petri, uomo di cinema*. Acireale: Bonanno, 2015.

Rossi, Alfredo. *Elio Petri*. Milan: Il Castoro Cinema, 1979.

Rossi, Alfredo. *Elio Petri e il cinema politico italiano. La piazza carnevalizzata*. Milan-Udine: Mimesis, 2015.

Articles, Books and Essays with Significant Mention of Petri's Work

Alemanno, Roberto. *Itinerari della violenza: il film negli anni della restaurazione (1970–1980)*. Bari: Edizioni Dedalo, 1980.

Argentieri, Mino. *La censura nel cinema italiano*. Rome: Editori Riuniti, 1974.

Bisoni, Claudio. *Gli anni affollati. La cultura cinematografica italiana (1970–1979)*. Rome: Carocci, 2009.

Bondanella, Peter. *Italian Cinema from Neorealism to the Present*. New York: Continuum, 2008.

Capozzoli, Mirko. *Gian Maria Volonté*. Turin: add editore, 2018.

Crespi, Alberto. *Dal Polo all'Equatore. I film e le avventure di Giuliano Montaldo*. Venice: Marsilio, 2005.

De Gaetano, Roberto. *Il corpo e la maschera: il grottesco nel cinema italiano*. Rome: Bulzoni, 1999.

De Rosa, Alessandro. *Ennio Morricone: In His Own Words*. Oxford: Oxford University Press, 2019.

Deriu, Fabrizio. *Gian Maria Volonté il lavoro d'attore*. Rome: Bulzoni, 1997.

Drake, Richard. "The Aldo Moro Case in Retrospect," *Journal of Cold War Studies*, Vol. 8, No. 2, Spring 2006.

Fofi, Goffredo. *Alberto Sordi. L'Italia in bianco e nero*. Milan: Mondadori, 2004.

Fofi, Goffredo. *Cinema italiano: servi e padroni*. Milan: Feltrinelli, 1971.

Gili, Jean A., and Aldo Tassone (eds.). *Parigi-Roma. 50 anni di coproduzioni italo-francesi*. Milan: Il Castoro, 1995.

Glynn, Ruth, Giancarlo Lombardi, and Alan O'Leary (eds.). *Terrorism, Italian Style: Representations of Political Violence in Contemporary Italian Cinema*. London: IGRS Books, 2012.

Grande, Maurizio. *Eros e politica: sul cinema di Bellocchio, Ferreri, Petri, Bertolucci, Taviani*. Siena: Protagon, 1995.

Hochkofler, Matilde. *Marcello Mastroianni: il gioco del cinema*. Rome: Gremese, 2006.

Liehm, Mira. *Passion and Defiance: Film in Italy from 1942 to the Present*. Berkeley: University of California Press, 1984.

MacBean, James Roy, "The Working Class Goes Directly to Heaven, without Passing Go: Or, the Name of the Game Is Still Monopoly," *Film Quarterly* #26.3, 1973.

Marcus, Millicent. *Italian Film in the Light of Neorealism*. Princeton NJ: Princeton University Press, 1986.

Micciché, Lino. *Il cinema italiano degli anni '60*. Venice: Marsilio, 1975.

Micciché, Lino. *Il cinema italiano degli anni '70. Cronache 1969–1979*. Venice: Marsilio, 1989.

Micciché, Lino (ed.). *Il cinema del riflusso. Film e cineasti italiani degli anni '70*. Venice: Marsilio, 1997.

Micciché, Lino (ed.). *Studi su dodici sguardi d'autore in cortometraggio*. Turin: Lindau/Associazione Philip Morris Progetto Cinema, 1995.

Michalczyk, John J. *The Italian Political Filmmakers*. London and Toronto: Associated University Presses, 1986.

Monicelli, Mino. *Cinema italiano: ma cos'è questa crisi?* Bari: Laterza, 1979.

O'Leary, Alan. *Tragedia all'italiana: Italian Cinema and Italian Terrorism*. New York: Peter Lang, 2011.

Pezzotta, Alberto. "Il vaso di Pandora. *Buone notizie* di Elio Petri e la rappresentazione della sessualità nel cinema italiano degli anni '70." *L'Avventura* #2/2017, July-December 2017.

Pirro, Ugo. *Soltanto un nome nei titoli di testa*. Turin: Einaudi, 1998.

Portis, Larry. "The Director Who Must (Not?) Be Forgotten: Elio Petri and the Legacy of Italian Political Cinema," *Film International* #4, Vol. 8 no. 2, 2010.

Quaglietti, Lorenzo. *Storia economico-politica del cinema italiano 1945–1980*. Rome: Editori Riuniti, 1980.

Questi, Giulio. *Se non ricordo male*. Bari: Rubbettino, 2014.

Renga, Dana (ed.). *Mafia Movies: A Reader*. Toronto: University of Toronto Press, 2011.

Rigola, Gabriele. "Riderai, se ti dico che io mi sento un poco come Laurana?" *Todomodo* #5, 2015.

Sancisi, Michele. *Tutto su Mariangela*. Milan: Bompiani, 2014.

Sansonna, Giuseppe. *Hollywood sul Tevere*. Rome: Minimum Fax, 2016.

Tinazzi, Giorgio. *Il cinema italiano degli anni '50*. Venice: Marsilio, 1979.

Tovaglieri, Alberto. *La dirompente illusione. Il cinema italiano e il Sessantotto, 1965–1980*. Catanzaro: Rubbettino, 2014.

Uva, Christian (ed.). *Strane storie: il cinema e i misteri d'Italia*. Bari: Rubbettino, 2011.

Vitti, Antonio. *Giuseppe De Santis and Postwar Italian Cinema*. Toronto: University of Toronto Press, 1996.

Index